CONTENTS

DUN & BRADSTREET
GUIDE TO
$YOUR INVESTMENTS$™: 1990

NANCY DUNNAN

1817

HARPER & ROW, PUBLISHERS
New York
Grand Rapids
Philadelphia
St. Louis
San Francisco
London
Singapore
Sydney
Tokyo
Toronto

For Lucille Snow, Iowa librarian, who devoted her life to the pursuit of knowledge and dissemination of accurate information.

Grateful acknowledgment is made for permission to reprint:

"Calculating Growth Rates" table from *Security Analysis,* Fourth Edition, by Benjamin Graham et al. Copyright © 1962 by McGraw-Hill, Inc. Reprinted by permission of McGraw-Hill, Inc.

List appearing in Chapter 20, "Betting on the Dollar," from the March 1985 issue of *The Market Letter.* Reprinted by permission of Shearman Ralston, Inc.

"How Bond Interest Compounds" table from *The Complete Book of Bonds* by Robert Holt. Copyright © 1980, 1981, 1985 by Robert Lawrence Holt. (1981: Harper & Row, Publishers, Inc.) Reprinted by permission of Waterside Productions, Inc.

Material from *Donoghue's Moneyletter, Donoghue's Money Fund Report*, and *The Treasury Manager* reprinted by permission of The Donoghue Organization, Inc., Holliston, MA 01746.

"Top Performers" table reprinted by permission of *The Hulbert Financial Digest*, 643 South Carolina Avenue SE, Washington, DC 20003.

"Dun & Bradstreet" is a registered trademark of The Dun & Bradstreet Corporation and is used under license. The title *$Your Investments$* is a registered trademark of Harper & Row, Publishers, Inc.

Designer: Gayle Jaeger

ISSN   73-18050
ISBN   0-06-055184-4
ISBN   0-06-096435-9 (pbk.)

ACKNOWLEDGMENTS

The Bond Buyer, New York, N.Y.: Robert Taylor
Brean Murray, Foster Securities, New York, N.Y.: John Schultz
Dow Theory Forecasts, Hammond, Ind.: Richard L. Evans
Dow Theory Letters, San Diego, Calif.: Richard Russell
Federal Reserve Bank, New York, N.Y.: Barton R. Sotnick
Investment Company Institute, Washington, D.C.: Betty Hart
Investment Quality Trends, La Jolla, Calif.: Geraldine Weiss
KPMG Peat Marwick, Houston, Tex.: William J. Goldberg, Nancy Haskins
Lewco Securities, Inc., New York, N.Y.: Robert Kramer
Merrill Lynch Capital Securities, New York, N.Y.: Robert L. Friedlander
National Association of Investment Clubs, Royal Oak, Mich.: Ken Janke
New York Stock Exchange, New York, N.Y.: Judy Poole
Noddings, Calamos & Associates, Inc., Oak Brook, Ill.: Thomas C. Noddings
Shearman Ralston, Inc., New York, N.Y.: Thomas B. Shearman
Silberberg Rosenthal & Co., New York, N.Y.: Jay J. Pack
Standard & Poor's Corp., New York, N.Y.: Carl Ratner, Daniel E. Mayper
Swiss Bank, New York, N.Y.: Ed Auden

Special thanks to:
  Helen Moore, Harper & Row, Publishers, Inc.
  Kathy Hom

PART ONE

STARTING OFF

- Investment advice for 1990
- Building your personal investment pyramid
- Safe, sure places for your money: banks, money market funds, and CDs
- The safety factor

INTRODUCTION

YOUR NEW GAME PLAN

Although Americans have had several years in which to recover from October 19, 1987, the day the Dow Jones Industrial Average plunged 508 points within a matter of hours, the long-term effects of this black debacle are still being felt by all sorts of investors. Those who were too young to experience the depression or too distant to listen to their parents' or grandparents' tales of economic hardship have suddenly come to realize that the old New England saying has some truth to it: that what goes up must come down. The so-called me generation and the young professionals on the fast track have joined, at least philosophically, those who knew, but were perhaps lulled into complacency by rising paper profits, that the most bullish of markets can turn bearish instantly.

All of this means it is no longer a viable plan, if indeed it ever was, to build a portfolio consisting solely of stocks or bonds. Thus, the 1990 edition of the *Dun & Bradstreet Guide to $Your Investments$* focuses on sound techniques for setting up a truly balanced portfolio and on the components of that portfolio—common stocks, corporate bonds, Treasury issues, mutual funds, tax-free investments, commodities, and that all-important yet frequently overlooked investment, *cash.*

The last component has become most critical in the postcrash era. Once viewed as the province of the frightened investor, a solution for the timid, or a fallback position for the uninformed, cash has taken on a new status and gained greater respectability than it has had at any other time since the Great Crash of 1929. It must be a major building block in every portfolio.

And you no longer need to apologize for income investing, for setting up a steady cash flow. After all, the Wall Street pros and the savvy individuals who positioned themselves for the market correction by moving assets into cash were the true winners when the bull returned to the barn. The best ways to get continual high returns on your cash are explained in Parts One and Two.

We have also included additional material on retirement planning, since the graying of the country's population means more and more of us are closer to the day when we leave our place of work for the very last time. The fact that we are living longer, working longer, leading healthier and active lives after ages 55, 65, or 75 necessitates more retirement savings and sound investing. Social Security and pension income may be quite inadequate to see you through. Smart retirement planning, starting today, is critical.

WHAT YOU CAN DO

It is a fact that a stock market crash, a recession, high unemployment, or generally hard times can return. Therefore, to put your trust in time or your spouse or parents, or even the corporation you work for, to take care of your present and future financial needs is childlike and unrealistic. Although many regulatory agencies, as well as the Securities and Exchange Commission, the stock exchanges, and the Federal Reserve Board, make every effort toward maintaining an orderly market and stable economy, you too should take certain steps to protect yourself in this new, fully globalized investing world. To choose to remain uninvolved or ignorant about the stock market, the direction of the economy, and the workings of the entire financial world is not only to court disaster but to invite financial loss.

Be informed. The two best defenses you have against trouble are relatively simple: The first is *information,* and the second is *diversification.* After taking time to learn how the economy, individual companies, the banks, interest rates, the dollar, and inflation affect your investments, you may still lose money some of the time, but you will win far more often if you are both diversified and informed.

Begin by reading at least one intelligent financial publication each week. Select one that matches your level of sophistication. Carry it with you (see the box). Watch the market news on CNN, FNN, or PBS television or listen to broadcasts on public radio. Know what's happening in this country and abroad.

YOUR FINANCIAL LIBRARY

Read one of these publications each week. They are arranged by approximate level of sophistication, beginning with the most elementary. Subscriptions are available for each one.
- *USA Today*
- Your local newspaper
- *Bottom Line Personal*
- *U.S. News & World Report*
- *Better Investing* (National Association of Investment Clubs)
- *Consumer Reports*
- *Money*
- Standard & Poor's *The Outlook*
- *New York Times*
- *Investors Daily*
- *Wall Street Journal*
- *Barron's*
- *Value Line*

Then, diversify—among types of investments and risk levels. Check your holdings against the investment pyramid on page 13. Make certain you have dollars invested in several levels.

HOW TO PICK WINNERS

There was a time when all an investor had to do was pick attractive stocks or bonds. Now you're faced with a bewildering variety of choices, often involving hefty commissions. It's important to determine if they are speculations or investments. To boost your success ratio:

- **Don't become involved with special "opportunities"** until you've developed a balanced portfolio. Stay away from futures, indexes, most new issues, and other complicated investments. These are dominated by the professionals, who have more skill, knowledge, and money than most individuals—and even they can get hurt.
- **Don't follow the crowd.** The majority opinion is often wrong. Every major market advance has begun when pessimism was loudest and prices lowest.
- **Don't dash in and out of the market.** You'll find your profits are eaten up by commissions.
- **Don't be in a hurry to invest your money.** If you miss one opportunity, there will be another just as good and possibly better along soon.
- **Don't fall in love with your investments.** There is always a time to be in a stock, a bond, a money market account, and a CD and a time to be out. Remember, with few exceptions most investments become overpriced, and no tree ever grows to the sky.

ADVICE FOR 1990

As we go to press in October 1989, two items are capturing the financial headlines: 1) the weakening of the junk bond market and 2) the possibility

HOW TO CALCULATE THE EFFECT OF INFLATION

YEARS FROM NOW	4%	5%	6%	7%	8%
5	1.22	1.28	1.34	1.40	1.47
10	1.48	1.63	1.79	1.97	2.16
15	1.80	2.08	2.40	2.76	3.17
20	2.19	2.65	3.21	3.87	4.66
25	2.67	3.39	4.29	5.43	6.85
30	3.24	4.32	5.74	7.61	10.06

SOURCE: Reprinted with permission from *Encyclopedia of Banking and Financial Tables,* copyright © 1980, 1986, Warren, Gorham & Lamont, Inc., Boston, Mass. All rights reserved.

that capital gains will be taxed at a new rate. If you are enticed by the extraordinarily high yields offered by junk bonds, think again and read Chapter 11 carefully. The better-quality junks are still performing extraordinarily well, so don't panic and sell, but do avoid all poorer-quality issues. And remember that even a junk bond mutual fund cannot offer adequate protection if all rush in to redeem their shares at once. When this happens, portfolio managers are forced to sell to meet the public's demand for cash. And a fund's phone lines will be busy to everyone, for those holding 100, 1,000, or 10,000 shares.

Be alert to the pending change in the tax law, under congressional review at this very moment. As you read each section of this book, factor in the new rate, if indeed there is one. If you are in doubt as to how any new law will impact on your financial situation and investments, check with your accountant or stockbroker. Don't plead ignorance and then make unwise decisions, particularly when selling assets that have appreciated in value.

You may also want to consider the impending changes that will take place in 1992 when the European Economic Community is united and a barrier-free market will begin. At that time, the European Economic Community will remove restrictive trade regulations, turning Europe into one consumer market with 320 million customers. Many American corporations, from the huge multinationals to small manufacturers, are making aggressive inroads into European markets in order to take advantage of this enormous new arena. The Coca-Cola Company, for example, has begun

---

STOCKS I CAN LIVE WITH IN 1990

John W. Schultz, managing director of Brean Murray, Foster Securities, of New York, was willing to go out on a limb, at least partway, and select stocks he can live with in 1990. Prices were as of September 29, 1989.

STOCK	SYMBOL	PRICE
American Business Products	ABP	24⅝
Dun & Bradstreet	DNB	54¾
Fireman's Fund Corp.	FFC	38¼
Healthco International	HLCO	18
Household International	HI	58⅛
Int'l Flavors & Fragrance	IFF	65½
ITT Corp.	ITT	60½
New York Times (Class A)	NYTA	31½
South Carolina National Corp.	SCNC	26¾

SOURCE: John W. Schultz, Brean Murray, Foster Securities, 67 Wall Street, New York, NY 10005; 212-422-2300.

construction on one of the world's largest plants in Dunkirk. Whirlpool has entered into a $2 billion joint venture to become a leader in the appliance field. American companies that already have a presence in Europe will probably lead the pack.

THE MAGIC OF COMPOUNDING

In view of our renewed emphasis on safe investing, one point that's worth repeating is the positive impact of compounding, or earning income on income, by prompt reinvestment of all interest, dividends, and realized capital gains. As shown in the accompanying tables, savings can mount at an astonishing rate over the years.

➤ THE RULE OF 72 For a quick calculation on how long it takes to double your money, use *the rule of 72:* divide 72 by the yield. Thus, at 9%, it will take 8 years; at 10% about 7 years; at 12%, 6 years to double your money.

LISTENING TO THE PROS

John Kenneth Galbraith, in his book *The Great Crash,* reminds us that John D. Rockefeller told the press after the crash of October 29, 1929, "Believing that fundamental conditions of the country are sound, my son and I have for some days been purchasing sound common stocks." To this Eddie Cantor replied, "Sure, who else had any money left?"

After reading the *Dun & Bradstreet Guide to $Your Investments$* and becoming an informed investor, you too will be able to decide if you wish

THE POWER OF COMPOUND INTEREST

A REGULAR INVESTMENT OF $100 PER YEAR, INVESTED AT:	WILL, COMPOUNDED ANNUALLY AT THE END OF EACH YEAR, GROW TO THIS SUM AFTER THIS NUMBER OF YEARS:							
	5	10	15	20	25	30	35	40
6%	$564	$1,318	$2,328	$3,679	$5,486	$7,906	$11,143	$15,476
8	587	1,449	2,715	4,576	7,311	11,328	17,232	25,906
10	611	1,594	3,177	5,727	9,835	16,449	27,102	44,259
12	635	1,755	3,728	7,205	13,333	24,133	43,166	76,709
14	661	1,934	4,384	9,102	18,187	35,679	69,357	134,202
16	688	2,132	5,166	11,538	24,921	53,031	112,071	236,076

To get the corresponding total for any other annually invested amount (A), multiply the dollar total given above for the yield and the number of years by $\frac{A}{100}$. Example: you plan to invest $75 per month, $900 a year. What capital sum will that provide after 35 years, at 12% compounded annually? Check where the lines cross for 12% and 35 years: $43,166 × $\frac{900}{100}$ = $388,494. Note: The totals will be greater if: (1) the deposits are made at the beginning of the year; (2) compounding is more frequent.

SOURCE: Reprinted with permission from *Encyclopedia of Banking and Financial Tables,* copyright © 1980, 1986, Warren, Gorham & Lamont, Inc., Boston, Mass. All rights reserved.

ANOTHER VIEW OF COMPOUNDING

	AVERAGE ANNUAL RETURN ON ORIGINAL INVESTMENT				
RATE OF RETURN	5 YEARS	10 YEARS	15 YEARS	20 YEARS	25 YEARS
6%	6.8%	7.9%	9.3%	11.0%	13.2%
7	8.1	9.7	11.7	14.3	17.7
8	9.4	11.6	14.5	18.3	23.4
9	10.8	13.7	17.6	23.0	30.5
10	12.2	15.9	21.1	28.6	39.3
11	13.7	18.4	25.2	35.3	50.3
12	15.2	21.0	29.8	43.2	64.0

to follow Rockefeller's notion or side with Mark Twain, who said, "October. This is one of the peculiarly dangerous months to speculate in stocks. The others are July, January, September, April, November, May, March, June, December, August, and February."

If not all your investment decisions turn out to be spectacular, and no one's ever are, and if at the same time you have adequately diversified, the worst scenario will still leave you upright and in good shape. But then, cut your losses. As Warren Buffett, the chairman of Berkshire Hathaway, Inc., said in one of his annual reports, "Should you find yourself in a chronically leaking boat, energy devoted to changing vessels is likely to be more productive than energy devoted to patching leaks."

Personally, I like Mae West's attitude best: "Too much of a good thing can be wonderful." May 1990 be a wonderful year for you and your investments.

2 BUILDING YOUR OWN INVESTMENT PYRAMID

A few years ago, the world of investing was a far simpler one than it is today: investment choices were pleasantly limited, and only a few basic concepts governed the ways in which you could make (or lose) money. If you were terribly conservative, you put your hard-won earnings in the local bank where you earned 5%; or perhaps your family broker bought some stock in AT&T or a carefully selected public utility company. If you were willing to assume a little more risk, you might have moved out of the blue chip arena into more speculative growth stocks. If you wanted a steady stream of income, you merely purchased high-quality corporate or government bonds and waited for the interest to roll in. But the only choices available for the general investor were basically stocks, bonds, and the bank.

But it's 1990 and no longer quite so easy. Several years of deregulation in the financial industry have brought about sweeping changes; the rules that governed this business for at least half a decade have given way to a very competitive atmosphere. Not only must you decide what to invest in when, but you are also competing with the highly sophisticated institutions. In addition, inflation, disinflation, and fluctuating interest rates have multiplied investment opportunities and risks. Once relegated to the three basic choices, today you face a bewildering array of products and institutions: certificates of deposit (CDs), money market funds, interest-bearing bank accounts, options, and index futures, as well as the traditional stocks, bonds, and savings account. And the number of people vying to sell you one of these "products" is growing rapidly. Your local bank and stockbroker are no longer the only two games in town. They are, in fact, becoming more and more closely intertwined, especially as the central asset account grows in popularity. Banks are steadily moving into the world of stocks, money market accounts, and other "nonbank" services, while brokers are now selling CDs and offering discount brokerage services. ATMs are located in supermarkets and gas stations. Shearson, American Express, and E. F. Hutton have joined hands, Sears and Dean Witter are coupled, and Prudential Insurance and Bache now work in tandem.

The proliferation of investment choices has made wise decision making far more complicated, and now more than ever before, information and knowledge are absolutely essential. In fact, the world of finance is changing so rapidly that unless you are up to date and well informed, you'll be left in the dust. That is why *$Your Investments$* can make the difference between a well-informed decision and pure guesswork. It helps you determine if you're better off buying a bank CD or a Treasury bond, making a play in commodity futures or looking for takeover targets, using your broker's research or following the charts.

Whether you're a new investor or a sophisticated money manager who has weathered numerous bull and bear cycles, this vital reference brings you more data on the more familiar vehicles, introduces you to new products, and, finally, offers you the best in smart money-making strategies as followed by the professional investment community.

If you are relatively new to the world of investing, or if you're somewhat rusty, we suggest that you read Part One carefully. Those of you who have been buying stocks and bonds for some time and know the basics can proceed directly to Part Two.

BECOMING A SAVVY INVESTOR

Before you plunge into your pocket and buy 100 shares of a reportedly "hot stock" or set up a personally tailored investment program with a stockbroker or financial planner, it's wise to take a few moments to decide your answers to three key questions:

1   What do I want to derive from such a move or investment?
2   How much can I sensibly afford to invest?
3   What are my major financial goals?

Random purchases of stocks, bonds, and limited partnerships may initially seem rewarding but are unlikely to fulfill your long-range goals. To get the most out of your investment dollar, the answers to these three questions and some background preparation are essential. The four homework assignments below can produce large benefits in the long run, enabling you to make better investment decisions whether you make them on your own or with professional guidance.

KNOW THY WORTH

Before making any type of investment expenditure, whether it's buying a stock, a bond, or a house, you must know your net worth. This is one of the first questions most stockbrokers, money managers, and bank mortgage officers ask. If, like most people, you're uncertain of the precise answer, don't panic. Figuring out your net worth is easy. All you need is a free evening, a calculator, your checkbook, bills, and a record of your income. Then follow these two easy steps:

1   Add up the value of everything you own (your assets).
2   Subtract the total of all you owe (your liabilities).

The amount left over is your net worth. You can use the worksheet on the following page as a guide for arriving at the correct amount. When figuring your assets, list the amount they will bring in today's market, which could be more or less than you paid for them originally. Assets include cash on hand, your checking and savings account balances, the cash value of any insurance policies, personal property (car, boat, jewelry, real estate, investments), and any vested interest in a pension or retirement plan. Your liabilities include money you owe, charge account debts, mortgages, auto payments, education or other loans, and any taxes due.

FINDING YOUR NET WORTH

Date _____
ASSETS

Cash on hand	$ _____
Cash in checking accounts	_____
Savings accounts, money market fund	_____
Life insurance, cash value	_____
Annuities	_____
Retirement funds	
IRA or Keogh	_____
401(k) plan	_____
Vested interest in pension or	
profit-sharing plan	_____
U.S. savings bonds, current value	_____
Investments	
Market value of stocks, bonds,	
mutual fund shares, etc.	_____
Real estate, market value of real	
property minus mortgage	_____
Property	
Automobile	_____
Furniture	_____
Jewelry, furs	_____
Sports and hobby equipment	_____
Equity interest in your business	_____
Total assets	$ _____

Date _____
LIABILITIES

Unpaid bills	
Charge accounts	$ _____
Taxes, property taxes, and quarterly	
income taxes	_____
Insurance premiums	_____
Rent or monthly mortgage payment	_____
Utilities	_____
Balance due on:	
Mortgage	
Automobile loans	_____
Personal loans	_____
Installment loans	_____
Total liabilities	$ _____

Assets	$ _____
Minus liabilities	_____
Your net worth	$ _____

KNOW WHERE THY WORTH IS GOING: BUDGETING

A budget, like braces on the teeth, is universally unappealing. It's a very rare person who likes either one, yet each has its place. Some form of budgeting should be part of your overall investment plan. It's not only a good way of knowing how much you're spending and on what, but it is also a sensible means of setting aside money for investing, our primary concern in this book. If you need help in establishing a budget for investing, use the worksheet on page 12. In order to budget dollars for investing, try setting aside a certain dollar amount on a regular basis, even if it's not an impressively large number. Mark it immediately for "savings/investing." Ideally you should try to save 5% to 10% of your annual income; if you make more than $60,000 a year, aim for 15%. Don't talk yourself out of budgeting for investing simply because it is a nuisance to keep track of what you spend. You'll be convinced of the wisdom of saving and the advantages of compound interest if you take a look at the table on the next page, which shows what happens to $1,000 over 20 years when you put it in an investment yielding 5¼% and the income earned is reinvested or compounded.

WHAT HAPPENS TO A $1,000 INVESTMENT AT 5¼%

FREQUENCY OF COMPOUNDING	1 YEAR	5 YEARS	10 YEARS	20 YEARS
Continuous	$1,054.67	$1,304.93	$1,702.83	$2,899.63
Daily	1,054.67	1,304.90	1,702.76	2,899.41
Quarterly	1,053.54	1,297.96	1,684.70	2,838.20
Semiannually	1,053.19	1,295.78	1,679.05	2,819.21
Annually	1,052.50	1,291.55	1,668.10	2,782.54

KNOW THY GOALS AND PRIORITIES

After you've accumulated money to invest, your next homework assignment is to decide what you want to accomplish by investing. If you were to take a trip to Europe or travel by car across the country, you would bring along a good road map. This should also be the case with investing, only the road map would consist of financial, not geographic, destinations. When you travel through France, you decide what towns, cathedrals, or vineyards you want most to visit, how long it will take you to get from one to the next, and approximately what it will cost. The same procedure should be applied to your financial journey through life. Your highlights or destination points may include some of these:

- Building a nest egg for emergencies
- Establishing an investment portfolio
- Reducing taxes
- Preparing for retirement
- Paying for a college education
- Buying a house, car, or boat
- Traveling or taking a cruise
- Investing in art or antiques
- Adding on a room or installing a swimming pool
- Setting up your own business

Goal-setting, you will discover, enables you to take firm control of your financial life, especially if you actually write your goals down. The process of listing goals on paper, perhaps awkward at first, forces you to focus on how you handle money and how you feel about risk versus safety. Divide your goals into two sections: immediate goals (those that can be accomplished in a year or less) and long-range goals.

If you're unmarried, your immediate goals could be:

- Obtain a graduate degree
- Join a health club
- Save for summer vacation

Longer-term ones:

- Buy a car
- Set up a brokerage account or buy shares in a mutual fund
- Purchase a co-op or condo with a friend

If you're married and raising a family, the goals might shift to include:

- Buying a house
- Setting up educational funds for children
- Building a growth portfolio

Singles and marrieds closer to retirement tend to seek other goals:

- Shift bulk of portfolio to safe income-producing vehicles
- Increase contribution to retirement plan
- Find appropriate short-term tax shelters
- Set up a consulting business; incorporate

Regardless of your age or income, individual goals make it easier and more meaningful to stick to a budget and to save for investing. Putting aside that 5% to 15% every month for an investment program suddenly has a very tangible purpose—one that you personally decided on.

YOUR CASH FLOW

WHERE IT COMES FROM		WHERE IT GOES	
INCOME	ANNUAL AMOUNT	EXPENSES	ANNUAL AMOUNT
Take-home pay	$_____	Income taxes	$_____
Bonus and commissions	_____	Mortgage or rent	_____
Interest	_____	Property taxes	_____
Dividends	_____	Utilities	_____
Rent	_____	Automobile maintenance	_____
Pensions	_____	Commuting or other transportation	_____
Social Security	_____	Insurance	
Annuities	_____	Homeowner's or renter's	_____
Tax refunds	_____	Life	_____
Other	_____	Disability	_____
Total	$_____	Child care	_____
		Education	_____
		Food	_____
		Clothing	_____
		Household miscellaneous	_____
		Home improvements	_____
		Entertainment	_____
		Vacations, travel	_____
		Books, magazines, club dues	_____
		Contributions to charities or organizations	_____
		Total	$_____
		Surplus or deficit	$_____

BUILDING YOUR INVESTMENT PYRAMID

Once you know why you want to invest, you are ready to think about your investments as part of a pyramid in which each level builds on the earlier ones. This approach to investing offers a carefully designed, diversified system that provides for financial growth and protection regardless of your age, marital status, income, or level of financial sophistication. As you can see by looking at the illustration, you begin your financial program on the pyramid at Level 1. It is the lowest in terms of risk and the highest in safety. As your net worth grows, you automatically move up to the next level, increasing both the amount of risk involved and the potential for financial gain.

Level 1 covers life's basic financial requirements and includes:

- An emergency nest egg consisting of cash or cash equivalents such as savings account, CDs, money market funds
- Health, life, and disability insurance
- A solid retirement plan, including an IRA, Keogh, or 401(K)

Before leaving this level, you will have saved enough cash or cash equivalents to cover a minimum of 3 to 6 months' worth of living expenses. This minimum is your emergency reserve, and when you've achieved this goal, you're financially solid enough to advance to Level 2.

Level 2 is devoted entirely to safe income-producing investments such as corporate, government, or municipal bonds; Treasury securities; longer-

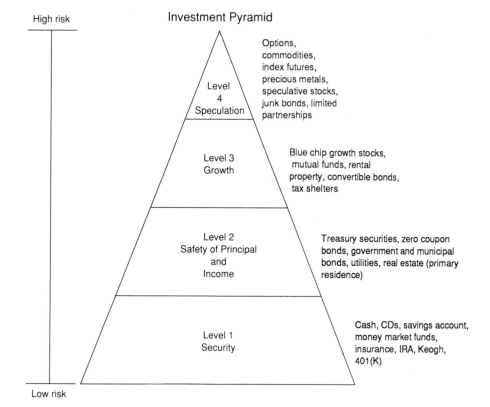

High risk

Investment Pyramid

Level 4
Speculation

Options, commodities, index futures, precious metals, speculative stocks, junk bonds, limited partnerships

Level 3
Growth

Blue chip growth stocks, mutual funds, rental property, convertible bonds, tax shelters

Level 2
Safety of Principal
and
Income

Treasury securities, zero coupon bonds, government and municipal bonds, utilities, real estate (primary residence)

Level 1
Security

Cash, CDs, savings account, money market funds, insurance, IRA, Keogh, 401(K)

Low risk

HINTS FOR THE BEGINNING INVESTOR

- Don't think you're going to get rich immediately. It takes time and wisdom to become a winning investor.
- Start by investing only in stocks or bonds of leading companies. They have proven track records, a lot of research on them is available, and there will always be a buyer if you should wish to sell.
- Buy a stock *only* if you can state a reason why it will appreciate in price or pay high dividends; merely feeling good about an issue is not a solid enough reason to justify purchase.
- Don't churn your own account so that commissions eat up any profits. Even if the average commission is only 5%, your stock will have to move up at least 10% to be even.
- Spread out your risks. Every company has the potential to be a loser some of the time.
- Decide on the maximum amount that you're willing to lose and stick to it.
- When you lose, if you do, try to determine why your security went down.
- Read about investing and investments regularly.

---

term CDs; zero coupon bonds; and real estate (your primary residence)—all of which are described in this book.

Although safety is key at this step, the liquidity factor emphasized in Level 1 is now traded off for a higher return or yield. And because some of these items, notably zero coupon bonds and CDs, are timed to mature at a definite date, they provide ideal means to meet staggering college tuition bills and retirement costs.

FINANCIAL RESOLUTIONS FOR 1990

I resolve to:
- Pay myself first every month—to make savings the first paid bill
- Live within my income
- Organize my financial papers
- Review or write my will
- Subscribe to a financial publication . . . and read it
- Be an informed investor, not a speculator
- Spend half an hour each day listening to or reading about financial matters
- Invest only in things I understand and learn about those I don't
- Read most of this book

Money to buy real estate is also included, not only because it gives you a place to live but also because historically real estate has appreciated significantly in value. At the same time, it offers tax benefits in the form of deductions for mortgage interest payments and real estate taxes.

Level 3 involves investing for growth. At this point you can afford to be more adventuresome, more risk-oriented, and less conservative; and this book shows you how to turn away from liquidity and assured income and toward growth and blue chip stocks, conservative mutual funds, convertible bonds, rentable property, and, depending on your tax bracket, tax shelters. If you find you're interested in the stock market, this is the ideal time to join an investment club and learn by doing so.

Level 4, the pinnacle of the pyramid, is given over to the riskiest investments, which may or may not yield spectacular returns. These include speculative stocks, stocks in new companies, takeover candidates, options, commodities, index futures, gold and precious metals, junk bonds, and limited partnerships, all vehicles discussed in detail in the following chapters.

3

SAFE PLACES FOR YOUR MONEY:
Banks, Money Market Funds, and CDs

Throughout your investment life there will be many times when varying portions of your assets should be kept liquid; that is, readily available. The traditional savings account simply won't do anymore; the interest rate is far too low. Fortunately, you have an abundance of other options.

Interest-bearing accounts are best for the portion of your money that calls for sure income and preservation of capital, as illustrated on Level 1 of your investment pyramid. Reserves for unexpected emergencies, safe places while you're looking for more rewarding opportunities, call them what you will—interest-bearing accounts are available through banks, savings and loans, credit unions, brokerage firms, and even mutual funds. Yields are high right now, and most are insured by the federal government. Banks may offer toasters, blenders, electric coffeepots, and other free gifts in order to attract your savings dollars.

Regardless of the giveaways, the premise is the same: whether you invest in savings accounts, certificates of deposit, or money market funds, you will always get back the same number of dollars you put in plus interest, unless, of course, you make an early withdrawal, in which case you may be penalized. The income earned is taxable along with your salary, wages, and other earnings, which means that if inflation advances more rapidly than interest rates, the purchasing power of both the principal and the interest will decrease every year.

FLIGHT TO SAFETY

Since the October 19, 1987, market crash, even the highest of the high rollers has been forced to consider what was once a wallflower concept: safety. During the bull market, which roared from 1982 until Black Monday, safe investments were largely overshadowed by stocks, real estate, and other more glamorous investments. But now the old standbys have assumed a more prominent position in the portfolios of all investors. Their secure and impressive yields make them alluring at this time. And even though the market has largely recovered from the crash, individual investors are still proceeding with caution, as well they should.

The key players in the flight to safety are money market mutual funds, bank money market accounts, certificates of deposit, Treasury bills and notes, EE savings bonds, and select mutual funds. The table on page 17 shows their current yields as we went to press as well as their average minimum requirements for investment. We don't by any means suggest that you put all your money in these safe havens, but you should certainly earmark one-fourth to one-third of your assets for this category. Investors—

amateur and pro—have come to realize that the stock market is indeed unpredictable, and diversification is not just mumbo jumbo from the mouths of conservative financial advisers and writers; it is the basis of protecting one's investments in economic climates of all kinds.

The best way to decide which safe haven is for you is to determine how long you would like to invest this portion of your money. Suggested designations are given in the table.

AT YOUR BANK

Banks now offer a wide variety of accounts with varying interest rates, so it pays to check several in your area before making a decision. Although it's time-consuming, it can mean as much as 1% to 2% difference in the interest earned on your account. Select an institution that will tell you about a bounced check ahead of time and that offers an automatic credit line, which will help eliminate the expense of bounced checks.

PASSBOOK SAVINGS

Fewer and fewer banks are offering the old-fashioned passbook savings account to their new customers. Most have replaced it with a *statement account,* which provides a monthly or

SAFE HAVENS

INVESTMENT	YIELD	AVERAGE MINIMUM INVESTMENT
1 to 3 Months		
Money market mutual funds	8.96%	$1,000
Bank money market accounts	6.36	1,000
NOW or SuperNOW bank accounts	5.50	2,500
Short-term CDs	8.61	500
3-month Treasury bills	8.00	10,000 initial; 5,000 thereafter
Passbook savings account	5.25	50
Credit union sharedraft	5.50	50
3 Months or Longer		
12-month CD	8.61	500
1-year Treasury bills	8.53	10,000 initial; 5,000 thereafter
5-year Treasury notes	8.37	5,000 (1-to-4-year maturities) 1,000 (4-to-10-year maturities)
10-year Treasury bonds	8.34	1,000
Short-term government bond funds	7.20	500
EE savings bonds	7.81	25

SOURCE: *Barron's,* July 3, 1989, and *New York Times,* July 2, 1989.

quarterly computerized update of your savings transactions. A statement account typically has a higher minimum deposit requirement than the $1 to $100 required to open a passbook account. Most passbook savings accounts still pay 5¼% at commercial banks but often 5½% at a savings and loan. Most statement accounts pay 5¼%. However, banks can pay whatever they like. The total yields will be based on (1) the starting date set by the bank, sometimes the day of deposit but more often the first of the succeeding month, and (2) the method of compounding. Faster reinvestment makes a difference: at 12%, $1,000 savings earns $175 more in a year when compounded daily than when compounded annually.

Unless you have a very small amount to save or are opening an account for a child, avoid savings accounts; better interest rates and returns are available through the other accounts described below.

NOW ACCOUNTS

A NOW (negotiable order of withdrawal) account is an interest-bearing checking account in which the rate of return is the same as with passbook accounts. Most require a minimum balance and may involve a monthly service charge and a computerized printout of transactions rather than a return of canceled checks.

By selecting the right NOW account, you can earn interest on idle money, but only if you select the right bank and understand the rules and the fee structure. To earn interest on your NOW account, you are required to maintain the minimum balance set by the bank. If you fall below this amount, you will lose interest and in some cases be subject to additional charges. Fees range from $5 per month and 15¢ per check to $12 to $20 and 25¢. Rates also vary, with the average 4.6% at banks and 5¼% at most savings and loans.

Geography may determine whether or not you should have a NOW account. In smaller cities and towns, required balances tend to be lower: $250 to $1,000. Major city banks often require $2,500. If you are a member

---

FINDING YOUR TRUE YIELD

To find out which NOW account offers the best deal, use this simple formula:

1 Take the minimum deposit and multiply it by the interest rate:

$$\$2,500 \times 6\% = \$150$$

2 Then multiply the monthly service fee by 12 and subtract the total from your annual interest income:

$$\$4 \times 12 = \$48$$

$$\$150 - \$48 = \$102$$

3 $102 ÷ $2,500 = 4.1%. This is your true yield.

of a credit union or can join one easily, open a sharedraft account: over 75% of credit unions offering this type of account do not have service fees. Dividends (the credit union equivalent of interest) on sharedrafts vary, too, but tend to be higher than interest on NOW accounts (see page 17).

$ HINT: "Daily" interest does not mean that the bank compounds interest daily. It means that the interest is compounded quarterly or semiannually based on the average of your daily balance. Select a bank that *compounds* interest daily.

SUPERNOW ACCOUNTS

A variation of the NOW account is the SuperNOW account, which pays a higher yield and requires a bigger balance, usually $2,500, with a return to the low passbook rate if this is not maintained. Monthly service fees run from $5 to $20, and there are often extra charges for each check written or deposited and for the use of the automatic teller. Shop around, because there may be bargains for depositors over 65 or when a new branch is opened. SuperNOWs pay whatever interest rate the bank wishes to offer. In many cases, SuperNOW accounts are regarded as NOWs: when the minimum is not maintained, the SuperNOW is automatically turned into a NOW. This is a great convenience for the depositor.

$ HINT: Once you have more than $2,500 in your NOW or SuperNOW account, move the excess into a money market deposit account or a money market mutual fund where rates and terms are better.

☐ CAUTION: The Consumer Federation of America has discovered that a number of banks overstate the rates they are paying on interest-bearing checking accounts. They may advertise, for instance, that they are paying 5% on NOWs, yet not all your money is actually earning that amount—only the so-called investable balance is. The bank may pay no interest on, say, 12% of the money in your account, thus effectively reducing the rate from 5.0% to 4.4%.

The basis for the term "investable balance" is that government regulations require banks to keep 3% to 12% of their assets in reserve at all times. However, that does not mean they are prohibited from paying interest on all of your deposit. Read the fine print before opening any interest-bearing checking account.

Example: If you kept a $3,000 balance all year in a SuperNOW account that paid 5% interest, you'd earn $150 before compounding. But if that bank deducted a 12% reserve, meaning that interest was calculated on a balance of $2,640, you'd earn only $132 in interest before compounding, for a 4.4% yield.

BANK MONEY MARKET DEPOSIT ACCOUNT

The counterpart of a money market mutual fund at a bank is a money market deposit account. Offered by most of the nation's banks, such accounts provide competitive interest rates as well as liquidity and, like all bank accounts, including the NOW and SuperNOW, are insured up to

$100,000 by the FDIC or, at a savings and loan, by the FSLIC. They tend to pay slightly lower yields than money market mutual funds and Treasury bills (T-bills). One reason for the lower yields is that banks are required to keep on deposit in the Federal Reserve Bank up to 12% of the balance of these accounts, which means that banks cannot make money on that portion of their deposits. The rates change daily or weekly along with changes in short-term interest rates. There's no guarantee that the rate quoted one day will be the same the next.

Yields and penalties for falling below the required minimum vary from bank to bank.

Find out if your bank avoids paying interest on a money market deposit account if the balance drops below a certain minimum, often $2,500 or $5,000.

$ HINT: Interest rates for money market deposit accounts vary as much as 3% between banks. Take time to call several to find the best deal.

As holder of a money market account, you are allowed to write only three checks per month to a third party and to make three preauthorized transactions (as might occur when you arrange in advance to pay a specific bill such as a mortgage payment). You may withdraw cash in person generally as often as you like. Some banks also allow use of ATMs for transfer of money, but money market deposit accounts are not intended to

---

METHODS OF COMPUTING INTEREST

This affects earnings as much as the frequency of compounding. The methods are listed in order of preference.

- *Day of deposit to day of withdrawal.* Money earns interest as soon as it is deposited. It keeps earning interest until, but not including, the day it is withdrawn.
- *Daily collected balance or investable balance.* Cash and checks from your bank begin to earn interest as soon as deposited; checks from other banks do not earn interest until officially cleared, 1 to 3 business days later, generally.
- *Low balance.* Interest is paid only on the lowest balance during the time period covered.
- *Last in, first out.* Withdrawals are deducted from the last deposit. For example, you deposit $3,000 on the 10th and then withdraw $2,000 on the 30th. The $2,000 withdrawal is deducted from the $3,000. No interest is earned on the $2,000 that was in your account from the 10th to the 30th.
- *First in, first out.* Withdrawals are deducted first from your initial deposit and then from subsequent deposits. For example, you have a balance of $5,000. You then make a $3,000 deposit on the 10th and a $1,000 withdrawal on the 20th. You earn interest on $4,000 from the 1st to the 10th and on $7,000 the rest of the month.

replace checking accounts. If you try to do that, you'll encounter extremely high fees.

CERTIFICATES OF DEPOSIT (CDs)

CDs, also officially known as time certificates of deposit, are safe, reliable saving instruments available at every local bank. The certificate indicates that you have deposited a sum of money for a specified period of time at a specified rate of

---

BANK CDs VS. T-BILLS

If you can afford to invest $10,000, compare the 6-month money market certificates with Treasury bills. In most cases (especially in states where income is taxed), the T-bills will be a better deal. Here's the calculation:

1 Since T-bills are sold at a discount, use this formula:

$$D = \frac{L}{360} \times SY$$

D = discount per $100 face value
L = life span of security
360 = number of days in financial year
SY = stated yield

With a 180-day T-bill and a 9% yield:

$$D = \frac{180}{360} = 5 \qquad .5 \times 9 = 4.5$$

Subtract the 4.50 ($450) from $10,000 to get $9,550 cost.

2 The true yield of the T-bill is more, because T-bill trading uses a 360-day year, but your money works 365 days and the stated yield is based on the cost.

$$TY = \frac{D}{C} \times \frac{365}{L}$$

TY = true yield
D = discount
C = cost
L = life span of security

With that 180-day T-bill, a yield of 9%, and a cost of $9,550 the true yield is 9.56%.

$$TY = \frac{450}{9550} \times \frac{365}{180}$$

$$4.71 \times 2.03 = 9.56\%$$

3 Interest on T-bills is exempt from state and local income taxes. Interest on the certificate is fully taxable.

4 If the certificate is cashed in early, there's a penalty. With T-bills, there's an active aftermarket, so you will get more than you invested since the sales price includes accumulated interest—unless there's a sharp rise in interest rates.

interest. Their low risk level, the fact that they're insured up to $100,000, and their current high yields make them especially appealing.

Although CD rates, terms, and size vary from bank to bank, the following varieties are generally available:

- 7- to 31-day CD with the yield tied to that of a 13-week T-bill
- 91-day CD with interest rate tied to that of a 13-week T-bill
- 6-month CD to yield about ¼% above the average T-bill rate for the most recent 4-week period
- 30-month CD with a fixed rate, typically 1% higher than that of shorter-maturity accounts

In most cases, the big type in the ads shows the compounded yield, which will, of course, be paid only when the CD is held to maturity. There are penalties for early withdrawal, but these are usually waived in two instances:

- If the owner dies or is found to be mentally incompetent
- If the time deposit is in a Keogh or IRA retirement plan and the depositor is over 59½ years old

Many banks offer adjustable-rate CDs, in which case the interest rate fluctuates weekly along with the average T-bill rate. For CDs of 32 days or more, issued after October 1983, there is no federally imposed ceiling on either the interest rate or the minimum size of the deposit. Banks are free to set their own numbers. CD minimums range from $500 to $5,000 and more. Those that are $100,000 or over are called "jumbo CDs." A number of banks will let you buy a "designer CD," one in which you set your own maturity date, so that you can time it to come due when your child goes off to college, when you retire, or when you will need a lump sum.

$ HINT: Before you buy a long-term CD, check out the Treasury note interest rate. T-note interest is exempt from state and local taxes, but you must pay taxes on CD interest.

When buying any CD, take the time to find out how frequently the bank compounds the interest and ask what the effective annual yield is. It can make an important difference.

To maximize your return, buy a CD in which interest is not actually paid out until maturity. This gives you the benefit of compounded interest.

HOW COMPOUNDING AFFECTS RETURNS ON A $1,000 CD OVER A 1-YEAR PERIOD

RATE	DAILY	MONTHLY	QUARTERLY	ANNUALLY
5%	$1,051.27	$1,051.16	$1,050.95	$1,050.00
6	1,061.83	1,061.69	1,061.37	1,060.00
7	1,072.50	1,072.28	1,071.86	1,070.00
8	1,083.28	1,083.00	1,082.44	1,080.00

SOURCE: Carteret Savings Bank, Morristown, N.J.

Caution: Interest is taxable in the year it is available for withdrawal without penalty.

NEW AGE CDs

To remain competitive with money market funds and each other, banks are marketing new-style CDs that feature an added element of speculation. These new CDs have yields tied to the S&P 500 index, to the price of gold, even to the cost of college tuition. But before rushing out to buy one of these new age CDs, find out precisely how the yield is calculated, whether it is tiered (the larger your deposit, the greater the interest rate), if it is automatically renewed upon maturity, and if so, whether at the same rate or a new one. You should also ask if your principal is in jeopardy, if your interest rate could fall to zero, if there's a minimum interest rate floor, if there are up-front costs. If you cannot do the necessary calculations yourself (and they can be complex), ask your accountant to help out. You should be familiar with two terms:

➤ BUMP-UP Bump-up CDs give you one or two opportunities to get higher returns if the bank raises its CD rates after you purchase yours.

➤ STEP-UP The rates on step-up CDs, also called "rate builders," move up at a set pace at a predetermined time, say, every 3, 6, or 12 months. Check the initial rate. Many step-up CDs start off about 1% lower than the going rate.

💲 HINT: If you have $50,000 to $100,000 or more to invest, negotiate your rate. Many banks will pay between ¼% and 1% more on large deposits.

CDs FOR THE ADVENTURESOME

BANK	SPECIAL FEATURE
Chase Manhattan Bank, New York, N.Y. (1-800-245-1032)	"Chase Market Index"
College Savings Bank, Princeton, N.J. (1-800-888-2723)	Rises with college tuition
Crossland Savings, Florida, Brooklyn, N.Y. (1-800-237-4256)	Bump-up rates
Dominion Federal S & L, McLean, Va. (1-800-368-2150)	Continual deposits; variable yields
First City National, Houston, Tex. (1-800-231-7531)	Penalty-free withdrawals; "Advantage"
Fleet National Bank, Providence, R.I. (1-800-325-5576)	Sports CD
Landmark Banks, St. Louis, Mo. (1-314-889-9500)	Prime-rate CDs; "Extender"
Northeast Savings Bank, Hartford, Conn. (1-800-637-2255)	Penalty-free withdrawals; "Take Ten"
Wells Fargo Bank, San Francisco, Calif. (1-800-458-2583)	Continual deposits

ZERO CDs

Some brokerage firms offer zero coupon CDs in a variety of maturities. This type of CD does not pay interest on a regular basis. Instead it is sold at a discount from face value. The interest accrues annually until the CD matures. You must report the income for tax purposes each year as it accrues.

$ HINT: Zero CDs are more volatile in price than regular CDs, so plan to hold them until maturity.

OUT-OF-STATE CDs

If you're seduced by ads for the higher yields available at out-of-state banks, remember that the grass isn't always greener. Proceed with caution and steer clear of troubled savings and loans. Even though your money is insured up to $100,000, if the institution is closed, there may be delays in getting your money out, and there have been cases where high yields have been reduced.

$ HINT: Know the difference between interest rate and yield. Interest rate is the annual return without compounding. The effective yield reflects compounding—daily, monthly, quarterly, annually. Compare bank *yields* if you plan to leave your earned interest in the bank. Compare bank *rates* if you are taking out your earned interest.

$ HINT: Robert Heady, publisher of *100 Highest Yields*, suggests purchasing CDs only from banks and savings and loans with a net worth–to–loan asset ratio of 3:1 for an S&L and 5:1 for a bank. (*100 Highest Yields*, P.O. Box 088888, North Palm Beach, FL 33408; 1-800-327-7717; 8 issues, $29; 52 issues, $395).

The Friday issue of the *Wall Street Journal* lists the top-yielding CDs in the country for 1-, 2-, 3-, and 6-month and for 1-, 2-, and 5-year maturities.

JUNK CDs

During recent months, banks have been pushing a new type of investment popularly known as junk CDs. Beware: They're actually subordinated notes and are *not* insured by the FDIC or FSLIC. Although they have high yields, 3 percentage points above Treasuries, they are not high enough to compensate for the fact that they are uninsured and that there's almost no secondary market. In addition, banks can call many of these notes prior to maturity. Denominations are as little as $1,000

☐ CAUTION: Heed the words of Arthur Micheletti, research director at Bailard, Biehr & Kaisen, San Mateo, Calif., investment advisers: "I'm sure a lot of people will be fooled into thinking they are insured; I wouldn't touch them unless it's a well-known S&L where you're absolutely sure you'll get your money back."

WHAT IS THE TRUE RATE?

Bank CD ads are often very confusing, with two rates given: fixed rate and yield. The yield figure is always higher, but to earn it, you must have your CD at the bank for one full year at the same annual rate. For example, if your bank advertises a fixed rate of 8.5% and a yield of 8.75%, and you buy a 6-month CD and take it out at maturity, you will earn only the 8.5% fixed rate.

$ HINT: Roll over your 6-month CD so that it is on deposit the full year in order to earn the effective annual yield. In most institutions, the original yield is applicable even if the yield falls.

BROKERED CDs

Buying a CD through your stockbroker is often a better deal than buying it through a bank, because yields tend to be higher. That's because brokers have access to CDs from banks across the nation and are not limited to just one institution. Merrill Lynch, for example, can tap 160 banks, which gives investors more choices in terms of maturity, yield, and risk factor. And since brokered CDs are still bank CDs, they are insured up to $100,000.

Brokered CDs are also more liquid than their bank counterparts, because they can be sold by your broker in a "secondary market." And there's no penalty for selling prior to maturity as there is with a bank CD.

☐ CAUTION: The value of CDs, just like bonds, rises and falls in direct relationship to interest rates: if interest rates rise, the price of your CD will fall and you'll receive less than face value if you sell. If interest rates fall, you may be able to sell your CD at a premium because it's worth more, since its rate is higher than that being paid on newly issued certificates.

FOUR WAYS TO MAKE MORE MONEY AT YOUR BANK

- *Stagger your maturities.* Mix your CD maturity dates, say, for 6 months, 12 months, and 15 months. If interest rates rise, you can reinvest CDs that mature at the new rate. If rates fall, your longer-term CDs will be earning the old, higher rate.
- *Invest your CD interest.* Ask your bank to invest your CD interest automatically in a money market deposit account. You'll earn interest on your interest yet have access to the money without incurring a withdrawal penalty.
- *Snowball a CD.* If your bank offers higher rates on larger CDs, it may pay to roll over several small CDs into one big one. Select a target date, say 1 month after your longest-term CD matures. When you renew your smaller CDs, have them mature on that date. Then all your CDs will mature on the same day and you can reinvest in one large CD with a high rate.
- *Establish your own interest-bearing checking account.* Instead of depositing your paycheck into your checking account, put it in your money market deposit account. Several times during the month, transfer money to cover your checks. You will earn money market rates and be less tempted to spend without thinking about it first.

BROKERED CDs

FIRM	MINIMUM	6-MONTH	1-YEAR	2-YEAR	5-YEAR
A. G. Edwards (1-314-289-3000)	$1,000	—	8.50%	8.40%	8.35%
Fidelity (1-800-544-6666)	5,000	8.80%	8.85	8.40	8.35
Edward D. Jones (1-314-851-2000)	5,000	8.65	8.50	8.20	8.10
Merrill Lynch* (any local office)	1,000	8.75	8.75	8.35	8.35
Piper Jaffray & Hopwood (1-612-342-6000)	1,000	8.70	8.65	8.30	8.30
Prudential-Bache (1-212-977-8500)	1,000	8.90	8.75	8.40	8.45
T. Rowe Price (1-800-638-5660)	10,000	8.80	8.85	8.25	—
Thompson McKinnon (1-212-804-8674)	1,000	8.65	8.50	8.35	8.35

* Merrill Lynch's CDs are rated by Standard & Poor's.
Data current on July 7, 1989.

$ HINT: Some brokers sell CDs of troubled S&Ls in order to get higher
yields. Make sure the CD you're buying is from a federally insured
institution. The broker must tell you the name of the bank.

◻ CAUTION: Your interest may not compound with a brokered CD as it
does with a bank CD. Check with your broker. Some brokered CDs pay
out on maturity, especially if they come due in 1 year or less; others
pay interest quarterly or annually. Many brokerage firms will
automatically "sweep" these interest payments into a money market
account if you so request.

Brokers usually do not charge fees for CDs, because they receive
their commission from the issuing bank. Most have a minimum of at
least $1,000.

$ HINT: The best indicator of trends in CDs and money accounts is the
federal funds rate—the rate banks charge each other for overnight

---

TAKE ADVANTAGE OF INTEREST RATE CHANGES

1 When rates are low: buy short-term CDs.

2 When rates begin to rise: put more money into your money market
account so you can ride up with the rates.

3 When rates are high: lock in yields with long-term CDs. Move
money out of money market accounts into higher-yielding CDs.

4 When rates are falling: immediately lock in with a CD before they
fall further.

5 When rates are low: invest over the short term and add to your
money market account so that your cash will be available for
reinvesting when rates begin to rise.

loans. If a bank has to pay more itself for money, it will try to raise money by offering higher yields to depositors.

MONEY MARKET MUTUAL FUNDS

Money market funds are pooled investments offered by mutual funds, insurance companies, and brokerage firms. Basically, they invest your money in high-yielding short-term financial instruments—Treasury bills, CDs, commercial paper, repurchase agreements, bankers' acceptances, etc.

THE PLUSES OF MONEY MARKET FUNDS

- *Daily income.* Dividends are credited to your account each day, which means that your money is always working for you.
- *Liquidity.* There is no minimum investment period, and there are no early withdrawal penalties. Money can be withdrawn quickly by telephone, mail, wire, or check.
- *Stability of principal.* Most money market funds have a constant share price of $1. This makes it easy to determine the value of your investment at any time. Earnings are also paid in shares, so the value of a share never increases above $1. For example, if your interest in a money market mutual fund averaged 8% and you invested $1,000, at the end of 1 year you would have 1,080 shares worth $1,080.
- *No fees or commissions.* When you open your account, all your money goes to work immediately.
- *Small minimum investment.* Some funds require as little as $500 to open; most minimums are between $1,000 and $2,000. In general, funds do not require shareholders to maintain the minimum investment as an average balance.
- *Safety.* Your money is used to buy prime debt of well-rated corporations or the U.S. government and its agencies. If you choose a fund that invests only in U.S. government securities, your yield will be ½% or so lower, but you can count on Uncle Sam's guarantee. Money market funds bought through your stockbroker are protected by the SIPC. This is because shares of money market funds are in fact securities (not cash). When held by an SIPC member in a customer's securities account, they are protected by the SIPC against the brokerage firm's failure but *not* against declines in the value of the securities (or shares) themselves.
- *Checkwriting.* Most funds offer this service free, although some require that checks written be for at least $250 or $500.
- *Continual high yields.* If rates drop, you will receive the higher interest rate for about a month afterward until the high-yielding securities are redeemed. With a bank, the yield changes more frequently, usually on a weekly basis.

Money market mutual funds have three objectives: (1) preservation of capital, (2) liquidity, and (3) highest possible yields.

Yields on money market funds fluctuate daily. Your interest is compounded by immediate reinvestment. Yields recently ranged from about 8% to 9½%.

$ HINT: Money market funds are best as parking places while deciding on more rewarding holdings. They are not a true investment except in an inflationary environment.

The simple virtues of safety, liquidity, and competitive rates make funds extremely popular with investors. Assets in money market funds are over 6%, up to more than $260 billion. It's not surprising: fund yields are higher than most bank accounts, there's no price volatility to be concerned with since shares are kept at a constant $1, and there are no sales charges. You can invest for as little as $250 or $500.

There are three types of money market funds: general, government-only, and tax-free. They are listed in the financial pages of most newspapers.

THE TRUTH ABOUT YIELDS

The yield of a money market fund changes on a daily basis and is never fixed or guaranteed, because it reflects the current money market rates earned by the underlying securities that make up the fund's portfolio. The yield that you receive as an investor in the fund is net of the expenses of the fund; in other words, the costs of running the fund (management fees and administrative expenses) are subtracted from the daily gross.

Money market funds price their shares at $1 each—or $10 occasionally. The stated yield, as reported regularly in the financial press, reflects the interest earned on investments. The base is the net asset value (NAV) per share. This is determined by subtracting all liabilities from the market value of the fund's shares and dividing the result by the number of shares outstanding.

Money market mutual funds lend your money for short periods of time, and the fund collects interest on these loans, paying it out to you, the shareholder. The money you deposit in a bank money market account, by

---

MAJOR USES OF MONEY MARKET FUNDS

- As a place to accumulate cash for a large expenditure, such as a house, a car, taxes, or a vacation
- As a place to deposit temporarily large amounts of cash received from the sale of a stock or a property, an inheritance, an IRA rollover, etc.
- As a parking place until you find a desirable stock, bond, or other investment
- As a resting place for funds when switching from one mutual fund to another within a family of funds

contrast, is not invested in any one area; it becomes part of the bank's general assets. Money market mutual funds are required to pay out all their earnings after expenses to shareholders and tend to pay higher rates than banks. Banks are required to pay only the rate that they decide on and advertise. The more competitive the banking atmosphere, of course, the higher the interest rate will be.

THE MONEY MARKET: WHAT IT IS

Contrary to popular belief, the money market does not exist in the heart of Wall Street, or in London, Brussels, or even Washington, D.C. Nor is it housed in an impressive Greek revival building. The money market runs throughout the country and is made up of large corporations, banks, the federal government, and even local governments.

When any of these institutions need cash for a short period of time, they borrow it from this seemingly elusive money market by issuing money market instruments. For example, the U.S. government borrows through Treasury bills, large corporations through commercial paper, and banks via jumbo CDs.

These instruments are purchased by other large corporations, banks, and extremely wealthy investors. The instruments pay high interest rates because the dollar amounts involved are so large, the maturity lengths are so short (1 year or less), and the borrowers are well known and considered

---

WHAT THE MONEY MARKET MUTUAL FUNDS BUY

- *Bankers acceptances:* drafts issued and sold by banks with a promise to pay upon maturity, generally within no more than 180 days
- *Certificates of deposit:* large-denomination CDs sold by banks for money deposited for a minimum time period (14 days, 91 days, etc.)
- *Commercial paper:* unsecured IOUs issued by large institutions and corporations to the public to finance day-to-day operations, usually in amounts of $100,000 for up to 91 days
- *Eurodollar CDs:* dollar-denominated certificates of deposit sold by foreign branches of U.S. banks or by foreign banks; payable outside the United States, the minimum is generally $1 million, with maturities of 14 days or more
- *Government-agency obligations:* short-term securities issued by U.S. government agencies
- *Repurchase agreements ("repos"):* short-term buy/sell deals involving any money market instrument (but usually Treasury bills, notes, and bonds) in which there is an agreement that the security will be resold to the seller on an agreed-on date, often the next day. The money market fund holds the security as collateral and charges interest for the loan. Repos are usually issued as a means for commercial banks and U.S. government securities dealers to raise temporary funds.

excellent risks. These money market instruments, not stocks and bonds, constitute a money market mutual fund's portfolio.

THE ISSUE OF SAFETY

All investors want to know how safe their money market fund or account is. It's very safe. But every investment has some degree of risk. Money market funds have an excellent safety record, primarily because they invest in short-term securities of the government, large institutions, and corporations.

The basic principle to keep in mind is: the shorter the maturity of an investment, the lower the risk. Money market mutual funds invest in short-term securities.

Short portfolio maturities keep a fund's risk level to a minimum, because a bank or corporation whose securities are sold in the money markets is not very likely to default in such a short time. In addition, securities that mature so quickly seldom fluctuate in value. (In 1979 a fund that was yielding 7% let its maturities run out to nearly 2 years. Then interest rates rose, and the 7% rate was no longer competitive.) Today, a money market mutual fund's securities must mature in 1 year or less, and no one individual security may make up more than 5% of a fund's assets.

$ HINT: The average maturity is about 40 days. You can check maturities in the financial section of your newspaper.

For the ultimate in safety, select a fund that invests only in Treasury issues. Such as Vanguard U.S. Treasury Money Market Portfolio. These are backed by the full faith and credit of the U.S. government. They are called ''government'' or ''Treasury-only'' funds. The yields are about 1% lower than nongovernment money market funds. Next in the safety lineup are funds that specialize in government agency paper issued by the Federal National Mortgage Association (''Fannie Mae'') and the Federal Home Loan Mortgage Corporation (''Freddie Mac'').

The next safest investments are funds that deal in commercial paper. Commercial paper is rated according to the solvency of the issuer. Moody's top ratings are P-1 and P-2; Standard & Poor's, A-1 and A-2.

Funds that have the highest yields are often those with fewest expenses deducted from the portfolio's earnings. According to *Donoghue's Money Fund Report*, expense charges generate nearly two-thirds of the discrepancy in yields. You can actually boost your returns by switching to a fund with lower expenses. Among the funds whose expenses have been low for a number of years are Vanguard and Kemper.

$ HINT: The average money fund's expense ratio as a percentage of assets is about 0.75%. Therefore, a fund earning 10% gives a yield to investors of 9.25%.

Two other factors contribute to the superior safety of money funds. (1) Money fund managers continually analyze and compile ratings of the strength of the issuers of money market instruments. Whenever an issuer's credit rating declines, the name is deleted from the acceptable list. (2) The SEC regulates the funds, requiring annual independent audits, detailed data in the fund's prospectus, and making other disclosure requirements.

MONEY MARKET FUNDS WITH CONTINUALLY HIGH YIELDS

Alger Fund	1-800-992-3863
Dreyfus Liquid Assets	1-800-645-6561
Dreyfus Worldwide Dollar Fund	1-800-645-6561
Evergreen Fund	1-800-235-0064
Fidelity Spartan	1-800-544-6666
Flex Fund	1-800-325-FLEX
Vanguard Prime Portfolio	1-800-662-7447

SOURCE: *Barron's*, July 3, 1989.

If your account is with a bank that has FDIC or a savings and loan that has FSLIC, it is insured up to $100,000 per account name. Money market mutual funds with your stockbroker are protected by SIPC. Money market mutual funds purchased directly from the fund are not insured unless the fund itself indicates that they are. Be sure to ask.

SELECTING THE RIGHT MONEY MARKET FUND

Although there are several hundred money market mutual funds, they fall into four basic categories. Knowing which one is best for meeting your investment goals will help narrow the search.

- *General funds.* Available from your stockbroker or directly from the fund itself, general funds invest in nongovernment money market securities.
- *Government-only funds.* Also available directly or from a broker, government-only funds limit their investments to U.S. government or federal agency securities. Because their portfolios are backed by the "full faith and credit" of the U.S. government, they are regarded as less risky; consequently, they have lower yields than general funds.
- *Tax-free funds.* Available directly or from a broker, tax-free funds restrict their portfolios to short-term tax-exempt municipal bonds. Their income is free from federal tax but not necessarily from state and local taxes. These are generally advisable only for investors in the 28% tax bracket. Their yields are, of course, much lower, sometimes about half those of a regular money market fund.

  Even though their yields are lower, tax-free money market funds are more appealing now that other ways of sheltering income are limited by the 1986 Tax Reform Act.
- *Triple tax-exempt money funds.* Designed for residents of high-income-tax states, such as New York, California, Massachusetts, and Connecticut, these invest in short-term tax-exempt municipals and are free from federal, state, and local taxes for residents of the states and localities that issue them.

By shopping around you will find that some funds have higher yields than others (see the table on page 31). At various times the yield discrepancy has been as much as 3% to 3½% on taxable funds. But the current yield is not the only factor to consider; look also at the 12-month yield and the character of the fund's holdings.

➤ MATURITY The risk factor—even though it's quite minimal with money market funds—rises with the portfolio's maturity. By law, any money market fund that says it keeps its net asset value at $1 per share is required to limit its average portfolio maturity to 120 days. If you're a conservative investor, select a fund with maturities of 90 days or less. If you're willing to assume more risk, you may get a slightly higher yield.

➤ QUALITY Lower-quality portfolios lead to higher yields but also higher risk.

➤ EXPENSES Money market funds take an annual management charge, called the *expense ratio,* from the investor's assets. These fees range from about 0.48% to 0.80%. Select a fund with a low fee or expense ratio.

SYSTEMATIC WITHDRAWAL PLANS (SWPs)

SWPs, long a favorite with retired people, are also ideal for making mortgage payments, paying insurance premiums, or other regular commitments. SWPs are an alternative to traditional written or telephone requests for withdrawal of your money from a mutual fund. Under an SWP, the fund periodically redeems the dollar value or percentage you request. Payment is made by check to you, to a third party, or to your bank account.

The amount required to maintain an SWP varies with each fund, but typical SWPs require a $5,000 or $10,000 minimum opening balance and a minimum $50 per month withdrawal. You can withdraw money monthly, bimonthly, or quarterly. Some funds permit you to withdraw only on the same day each month; others permit withdrawals on any day.

SWPs offer several advantages:

- Steady stream of controlled income prevents overspending.
- Paperwork is reduced.
- Plan eliminates telephoned withdrawal requests.

And some disadvantages:

- You may draw out more money than you need or than you earn on the principal.
- May lead to apathetic attitude about saving.

Funds offer one or more of four types of withdrawals: (1) straight dollar amounts, (2) a fixed number of shares, (3) a fixed percentage, and (4) a declining balance based on your life expectancy.

$ HINT: If you don't wish to tap your principal, remove your money at a lower rate than the fund's increase in net asset value.

Keep in mind that withdrawing a regular dollar amount is in effect reverse dollar cost averaging. In dollar cost averaging (see pages 70–71), you invest an equal dollar amount every month and in this way buy more fund shares for the same amount when the market is down and fewer shares when it's up. In a fixed-amount withdrawal plan, you are forced to

ULTRASAFE MONEY MARKET FUNDS

	YIELD (APRIL 1989)
Mutual Funds Specializing in U.S. Treasury Securities	
Capital Preservation Fund (1-800-472-3389; 1-800-321-7321)	8.92%
Capital Preservation Treasury Note Trust (1-800-227-8380)	9.12
Fidelity Government Reserves (1-800-544-6666)	9.00
Fidelity U.S. Treasury Money Market (1-800-544-6666)	8.40
GT Government Obligations Fund (1-800-824-1580)	11.13
Vanguard U.S. Treasury Money Market Portfolio (1-800-662-7447; 1-800-362-0530 in Pa.)	9.02
Tax-free Money Market Funds	
Calvert Tax-free Reserves (1-800-368-2748)	6.71
Dreyfus Tax-exempt Money Market (1-800-645-6561; 1-718-895-1206 in N.Y.)	6.31
Franklin Tax-exempt Money Fund (1-800-342-5236)	5.97
Lexington Tax-free Daily Income (1-800-526-0056; 1-800-632-2301 in Calif.)	6.01
USAA Tax-exempt Money Market (1-800-531-8000)	6.41
High-Income States: Triple Tax-exempt	
Fidelity Massachusetts Tax-free MM Portfolio* (1-800-544-6666)	6.49
Prudential-Bache New York Money Market Fund (1-800-223-2750; 1-212-983-8000 in N.Y.)	5.94
Seligman California Money Market Fund (1-212-488-0200)	5.61

* Double-exempt.

redeem more shares when the market is down to meet the set dollar amount and to sell fewer shares when the market is up.

If you use a percentage plan, the number of shares you need to sell in a down market will tend to be less.

$ HINT: Another way to withdraw money regularly is to keep your dividends and capital gains distributions from stock and bond funds instead of reinvesting them. This way, you won't need to sell shares. If your dividends and capital gains distributions add up to more money than you need, reinvest the excess in a money market fund.

Remember, too, that the day you pick to redeem your shares is not the day you'll receive your check. Ask the fund how soon checks are mailed out, and ask your bank how long it will take for checks to clear.

☐ CAUTION: Each withdrawal of funds is a taxable event, usually because of capital gains. Keep records of your withdrawals to simplify year-end tax calculations.

USES FOR SWPs

- To pay your mortgage
- As a monthly living allowance for college students
- As income while on maternity leave
- For retirement
- To provide care for someone in a nursing home
- To meet insurance premiums
- As income while on sabbatical
- For alimony or child support payments

BANK DEPOSIT ACCOUNTS VS. MONEY MARKET FUNDS

Competition between money market funds and bank deposit accounts is reflected in the extra services they advertise, such as free checking, discounts on brokerage services, no-fee credit cards and debit cards, extended lines of credit, and direct deposit of pension and dividend checks. Both institutions are vying for your dollars.

The key benefits of a bank account are these:

- Easy access at a number of local offices.
- Instant interest, as new deposits are credited immediately. With money market mutual funds, it takes a couple of days for the mail to get through and up to 5 days or more for the check to clear.
- Instant credit, as local merchants will accept checks drawn against your bank account but may balk at cashing one from a mutual fund's bank, especially if it is an out-of-state bank.

CREDIT UNIONS

A credit union is a cooperative, not-for-profit financial institution organized to promote savings among its members. Membership is limited to those having a common bond—occupation, association, etc.—and to groups within a community or neighborhood. Many credit unions allow members to remain members even if they move away or change jobs.

Credit unions are member owned and controlled, with each member having an equal vote and the opportunity to serve on the board of directors. The board, elected by the membership, sets dividend and interest rates. Board members are volunteers, except for the treasurer, and they may not receive payment for their services.

Credit unions are either state or federally chartered. State-chartered unions are supervised by a state regulatory agency. Federally charted ones are supervised by the National Credit Union Administration, an independent agency in the executive branch of the federal government. Member share accounts are insured up to $100,000 per account by the National Credit Union Share Insurance Fund.

There are approximately 15,900 credit unions representing more than $195 billion in assets and over 58 million individual member-owners.

Credit union CDs, sharedraft accounts (interest-bearing checking accounts), and money market deposit accounts pay extremely competitive rates, often 0.5% to 1% higher than banks. Loans may be 0.75% lower. Credit unions can afford to undercut their competitors because they are nonprofit corporations, don't pay taxes, and are essentially volunteer-run.

4

HOW TO PROTECT ALL YOUR INVESTMENTS

The ongoing wave of complex failures of financial institutions has caused even the most trusting investors and savers to question how safe their securities and cash are in the nation's banks, savings and loans, mutual funds, and brokerage firms—and rightly so.

AT YOUR BANK

Over the past several years, more banks and savings and loan associations have been liquidated or merged than at any time since the Great Depression. The number of commercial and savings banks on the FDIC's trouble list is now in excess of 1,000.

THE FACTS

Most of the country's commercial banks are insured by the Federal Deposit Insurance Corporation (FDIC), an independent government agency. To be eligible for membership in the FDIC, a bank must meet certain standards and be regularly examined by both federal and state agencies. Member banks pay insurance fees, which are in turn invested in federal government securities. This constitutes the FDIC's insurance fund. In addition, the FDIC may borrow several billion dollars from the U.S. Treasury, even though it has never had to do so in the more than 50 years since it was established.

Most savings and loan associations (also known as thrifts) which prior to August 9, 1989, were insured by the Federal Savings & Loan Insurance Corporation (FSLIC) are now insured by a new government entity, the Savings Association Insurance Fund (SAIF), which is administered by the FDIC. Some S&Ls are insured by state insurance, and a very few are privately insured. A handful of savings and loan associations have absolutely no insurance at all.

Most credit unions (84%) are insured by the National Credit Union Administration (NCUA); others, by state agencies.

The FDIC and NCUA are backed by the federal government, and money insured by them is considered safe since the government would presumably come to their rescue. Banks that are insured by a state or privately, however, do *not* have the backing of the federal government. The FDIC has sufficient reserves—$18.2 billion—but the FSLIC was in such sorry shape that it was declared insolvent by the General Accounting Office. The parent of FSLIC, the Federal Home Loan Bank Board, was abolished in the summer of 1989 under the Financial Institutions Reform Recovery & Enforcement Act. This act created the Office of Thrift Supervision as a bureau of the

---

GOVERNMENT PROTECTION

FEDERAL DEPOSIT INSURANCE CORPORATION
- Guarantees depositors for up to $100,000
- Consumer hotline: 1-800-424-4334
- Address for more information on evaluating your bank: 550 17th Street NW, Washington, DC 20429

SAVINGS ASSOCIATION INSURANCE FUND
- Guarantees depositors for up to $100,000
- Telephone: 1-202-906-6600
- Address for more information on evaluating your S&L: 550 17th Street NW, Washington, DC 20429

NATIONAL CREDIT UNION SHARE INSURANCE FUND
- Guarantees depositors for up to $100,000
- Telephone: 1-202-682-9650
- Address for more information on your credit union: 1776 G Street NW, Washington, DC 20456

Treasury Department, and the Resolution Trust Corporation (RTC) to deal with the crisis of failing S&Ls.

The solution is not to tuck your money under the mattress but to get information about your bank.

- Bank only at federally insured institutions.
- Keep in mind that individual depositors, not accounts, are insured up to $100,000, including interest and principal. That means that if you have four accounts in the same name in one institution, you are insured only for a total of $100,000, not $400,000.
- Cut back each account to under $100,000 to leave room for earned interest.
- If you are married, you and your spouse can insure up to $500,000 at one bank by establishing several types of accounts: two individual accounts, one for each of you; a joint account; and two testamentary revocable trusts, one set up for each of you (this type of account pays the balance to the beneficiary upon the death of the trustee).

$ HINT: Five types of accounts are insured separately from other accounts that you may have in one institution. Each is insured individually for $100,000: money market accounts, IRAs, Keoghs, testamentary accounts, and irrevocable trusts.

Note: In the first twelve months following the creation of SAIF it is expected that the insurance standards of both FSLIC and FDIC will remain in effect. Since the standards are different, however (for instance, the FSLIC insured IRAs and Keoghs each to the $100,000 limit, while the FDIC standard is to insure both to a combined total of $100,000), they are under review and may change in the future.

If a federally insured institution fails, regulators will liquidate the assets, and insured depositors will be paid in 7 to 10 business days. If you have money in excess of the $100,000 insured limit, however, you will have a pro rata stake for that portion in excess of $100,000, along with other creditors, and you may or may not get that portion of your money back.

BANK CHECKUP

You can protect your money by taking these steps:

1   Get a copy of your bank's annual report and financial statements.
2   Request and read the "Report of Condition" on your bank (not available for branches, only main banks). It will tell how much the bank is making, what its loan portfolio is made up of, and what percentage of loans is nonperforming. The FDIC will bill you $2.40. Do not send cash. Order from:

FDIC
C.S.B. Disclosure Group
Room F-518
550 17th Street NW
Washington, DC 20429
1-202-393-8400

HELP FROM REGULATORS

If you're having a problem with your bank, call one of the regulatory authorities listed below. They are surprisingly accessible, often more so than your local bank official. If you need to file a written complaint, include a brief statement describing the problem and a list of the steps you've taken to try to resolve it. Include your bank account number and copies of all documents.

Ask the customer service department which regulator oversees your bank—they are legally obligated to tell you

FDIC
Office of Consumer Affairs
550 17th Street NW
Washington, DC 20429
1-202-898-3356 or
1-800-424-5488

Federal Reserve Board
Division of Consumer Affairs
20th and C Streets NW
Washington, DC 20551
1-202-452-3946

Office of Thrift Supervision
Office of Community Investment
Division of Consumer Rights
1700 G Street NW
Washington, DC 20552
1-202-906-6237

U.S. Comptroller of the Currency
Consumer Activities Division
490 L'Enfant Plaza SW
Washington, DC 20219
1-202-447-1600

3 Request and read "Uniform Bank Performance Reports," which compare banks within a certain state or county. They cost $30 each. Order from:

Federal Financial Institutions Examination Council
U.B.P.R.
1776 6th Street NW
Washington, DC 20006
1-202-357-0177

4 Evaluate the safety of your bank. David C. Cates, president of Cates (Bank) Consulting Analysts, Inc., in New York, gives these guidelines for determining a bank's safety:

- Excessively rapid growth of commercial loans indicates a bank that hasn't enough expert people to check credit ratings and make loan assessments.
- Unusually high loan portfolio yields indicates that the bank may be making risky loans.
- Increased reliance on funds outside the bank's natural market suggests lack of client support and a pulling out of outsiders at the first sign of trouble.
- How solid is the bank's loan portfolio? Determine by comparing nonperforming assets (loans that are 90+ days overdue or are no longer accruing interest) to total loans, the FDIC bank standard being 1%.
- Could the bank handle a run? Look for a loan-deposit ratio of no more than 70% and a minimum of 5% in cash or short-term investments.

5 Keep all your bank records; many failed institutions have been guilty of sloppy record keeping.

IF YOUR S&L FAILS

Should the unthinkable happen and a federally insured S&L fail, the Savings Association Insurance Fund (SAIF) will liquidate the institution's assets to pay off depositors. You may have to wait, perhaps 48 hours, but you will receive your principal and interest.

In most situations, however, SAIF or FDIC does not liquidate; instead, through the RTC arrangements are made for a solvent institution to take over the S&L's assets and liabilities. Then your account is simply transferred to the new bank or S&L and you have access to your money the next day. The new institution is required to honor the interest rate you were receiving until that investment matures—even if that rate is much higher than what the healthy institution has been paying. If you have a loan, the loan cannot be called in by the new bank, under any conditions not spelled out by the original loan agreement.

IN A MUTUAL FUND

Since the 1987 stock market crash, questions that were once unthinkable—Could a mutual fund close down? Could it cancel the investor's right to redeem shares? Could it run out of cash to meet shareholders' demand?—are unthinkable no longer.

The mutual fund industry is governed by the Investment Company Act of 1940—but that doesn't guarantee total protection. Here are the facts:

➤ BANKRUPTCY The assets of a mutual fund belong to the shareholders, and all securities are held in trust by a third party. A fund's directors can theoretically ask shareholders to allow the fund to close down if assets have dwindled away and it is no longer profitable to operate, for example, but to date this has not happened.

It's far more likely that a troubled fund will merge into a larger, healthier one; this often happens when a bank, S&L, or brokerage firm goes bankrupt. However, a very small fund that is poorly managed might be unable to attract a merger candidate.

If a fund were to liquidate, the shareholders' fortunes would depend on market conditions and the quality of the fund's holdings. The SEC would oversee the sale and subsequent distribution of assets. A small fund with large holdings of thinly traded securities or little cash on hand could be in for losses if the market were down.

➤ SUSPENSION OF TRADING Trading can be suspended only in national emergencies—closing of the New York Stock Exchange, presidential assassination, war, etc. However, even under these circumstances, you still have the right to place a redemption order—and such an order would lock in the price at the end of the day.

➤ CASH RESERVES The fund managers hold cash and Treasury securities in their reserves, plus proceeds from security sales. Funds also have bank credit available to them: they can borrow $1 for every $3 of assets. Yet a heavily invested fund, when faced with a barrage of redemption requests, might have to sell stocks even when it would prefer not to.

$ HINT: Invest only in a fund that has 10% or more in cash reserves.

When the market crashed on October 19, 1987, previously strong equity funds that had only small cash positions were forced to dump their stocks at low prices because investors were selling their shares. Among these was the well-regarded Fidelity Magellan Fund, which had only 1.4% of its investments in cash on hand. According to Peter Lynch, the fund's portfolio manager, the cash reserve had been at that level or up to 2% for 10 years. During that time period it also grew to be the number-one stock fund in the country, in both size ($11.6 billion) and performance. After the crash, Lynch increased the fund's cash to about 4%, stating publicly that he's willing to go to 6% to 7% if the market so demands.

By contrast, two other popular stock funds, Templeton World Fund and Vanguard Windsor Fund, had high cash reserves before the crash: 22% and 14%, respectively. Consequently, they survived better than most funds.

➤ PROTECTING YOURSELF IN THE FUTURE (1) Find out if your fund has an office locally; if so, keep some of your money there, so you can have access to it in person. (2) Prepare the fund's official redemption form or letter, and be prepared to send it by Express Mail if the telephone systems are overloaded during some future crash.

$ HINT: It doesn't matter what time of day you put in your mutual fund buy or sell order; as long as it's in before 4 P.M., you're guaranteed the closing share price that day. Phones are busiest in the morning.

AT A BROKERAGE FIRM

The Securities Investor Protection Corporation is a $500 million fund supported by nearly 12,000 member brokerage firms. It also has a $1 billion credit line with the government. The SIPC is not a government agency, nor is it a regulatory agency. Rather, it is funded through assessment of dealer members. If a member brokerage firm fails, the SIPC appoints a trustee to liquidate the firm and perhaps transfer customer accounts to another broker. (If the firm is small, the SIPC may decide to cover losses from its funds immediately.)

If it has the securities on hand, the liquidating firm will send the securities registered in customers' names directly to them. If it does not have enough securities to meet all customer claims, the customers will receive them on a pro rata basis, and any remaining claims will be settled in cash. However, this ties up your money for several months.

If the brokerage house in liquidation does not have enough securities or funds to settle all claims, the rest will be met by the SIPC—up to $500,000 per customer, including $100,000 for any cash held in the brokerage account.

The SIPC covers only cash and securities, that is, stocks, bonds, CDs, notes, and warrants on securities. Commodities and commodity options are *not* covered. Shares in money market mutual funds *are* covered by the SIPC.

$ HINT: Extend your coverage by opening a second account as a joint account with your spouse, as a trustee for a child, or as a business account. Each account receives full protection—$500,000.

Keep in mind that the SIPC covers losses due to the failure of the firm, not losses because investments turned out to be of poor quality or because securities fell in price. And many brokerage firms carry additional insurance. Ask your broker.

Burned by the poor performance of the stock market in 1987 and the American investors' subsequent flight to safety, brokerage firms and sponsors of various investment products have added a new enticing feature to their advertisements, touting them as "guaranteed" or "insured." The idea, of course, is to make high-risk investments appear safe. Many of these guarantees have questionable value and are being investigated by the SEC. Ask your broker or financial planner these questions when you're faced with what appears to be a come-on:

- How much of my money is being invested in the primary product? Where will the rest be invested?
- How long is the guarantee or insurance good for?
- Am I protected against market loss?
- If the project or investment fails, who is responsible for covering the losses?
- Who backs the insurance or guarantee?

FOR FURTHER INFORMATION

For information about the SIPC and what it covers:

SIPC
900 17th Street NW
Washington, DC 20006
1-202-371-8300

For a copy of *How Safe Is Your Money?* send $2.50 to:

Bank Rate Monitor
P.O. Box 0888
North Palm Beach, FL 33408
1-800-327-7717

If you have a complaint or a question about your bank, write to the Consumer Services Division of your State Banking Commission or Department in your state capitol. If you live in New York, write to:

Consumer Services Division
New York State Banking Department
2 Rector Street
New York, NY 10006
1-212-618-6642

An overview of the financial condition of many commercial banks, savings and loans, and credit unions is available for a modest fee from:

Veribanc, Inc.
P.O. Box 2963
Woburn, MA 01888
1-617-245-8370

Cates Consulting Analysts
40 Broad Street
New York, NY 10004
1-212-968-9200

For information about a brokerage firm and its insurance:

Office of Consumer Affairs
Securities & Exchange Commission
450 Fifth Street NW
Washington, DC 20549
1-202-272-7440

5

MOVING FROM SAVER TO INVESTOR

TRUE GRIT

Now that you have accumulated/set aside money in several safe places where it is earning well above the savings account rate, you are ready to stretch your wings and move into the arena of the true investor. Incidentally, before you leap from saver to investor you should have a minimum of three and preferably six months[1] worth of living expenses in one of the safe havens discussed in the previous chapters. That means if you need $4,000 per month to operate comfortably, set aside $12,000 to $24,000 in a combination of CDs, Treasuries, and money funds. Then if you are hit with a financial emergency, such as losing your job or getting a serious illness, you will have immediate liquid resources to draw upon.

Moving from saver to investor is a step many people, especially those with a conservative bent, find difficult to take. Some, in fact, never manage to make the move at all. Although there's nothing inherently wrong with leaving your money in a safe haven, during inflationary periods you may actually lose money, and during a bull market, even a moderate one, you'll be on the sidelines. And, for those facing high taxes, these safe investments are not truly safe at all, for instead of reducing your federal income tax bite, they add to it.

Of course, no investment is for all seasons. Review the table on page 53 to help you determine what vehicles are best during various economic periods. Keep in mind that the greater the risk you take, the greater the potential return.

MUTUAL FUNDS VS. INDIVIDUAL SECURITIES

One of the first key decisions you will have to make as you move from saver to investor is whether to select your own stocks and bonds or to buy shares in a mutual fund. Mutual funds, in which professional portfolio managers make all the buy and sell decisions, are described in Chapter 6. There are more mutual funds than stocks trading on the New York Stock Exchange. By reading the chapters on mutual funds, stocks, and bonds, you can arrive at portfolio conclusions that suit your investing temperament and income level.

If you are interested in stocks, a good place to begin is in your own backyard. Investigate your local utility company or a corporation headquartered in your area. Call for the annual report and ask a local broker for additional research information. Another easy way to dip into the market is by purchasing shares in the company you work for or one whose products or services you use and like. If you are wedded to your IBM or Apple computer or if you love Kellogg cereals, you might like to start down the investor's path by purchasing stocks in those companies.

HOW TO SET UP A MONEY-MAKING PORTFOLIO

The world of finance is complex, competitive, subject to economic and political pressures, and dominated by shrewd, powerful people who control billions of dollars. For most Americans who can save only a few thousand dollars a year, making money in such an arena sounds difficult, if not impossible.

Yet everyone can be a successful investor if he or she takes time to set specific objectives, to learn the facts, to adhere to proven profitable rules, to be patient, and, most important, to use common sense. Sometimes success comes quickly, but over the long term, making money requires careful planning and conscientious management.

Since Black Monday you may have felt powerless about managing your own portfolio, convinced that the index arbitrageurs, institutional managers, huge fund managers, and program traders control the game. To a large extent they do—yet the market crash took them down too, in many cases more than the smaller individual investors who didn't panic and didn't sell out at overwhelming losses.

If you proceed with caution and gather sound information, you have one major advantage over the big guns: you care more about your money than any stockbroker, fund manager, or financial adviser ever will.

PREVENTIVE PORTFOLIO MANAGE-MENT

The market crash and the subsequent volatility of the stock and bond markets call for a new and more cautious approach to portfolio management than was the case while the bull was roaring. If you are adverse to risk or want to reduce your risk quotient, here are seven easy preventive techniques that will enable you to maintain a healthy portfolio and weather any future declines in the market.

- *Diversify.* To some extent you can protect yourself from market swings by owning a mixture of stocks, bonds, precious metals, real estate, and other investments, because seldom does everything decline at the same time.
- *Buy for the long haul.* If you plan in general to hold your stocks 1 to 3 years, day-to-day and month-to-month fluctuations can largely be ignored.
- *Select investments on the basis of quality.* Take advantage of low-priced high-quality stocks. Ignore rumors and study the fundamentals.
- *Include high-yield investments.* Common stocks with high dividends, preferred stock, high-yielding bonds, and CDs all help cushion dips in the market.

- *Investigate convertibles.* Their yields are higher than the underlying stock of the same company, and should the stock fall in price, the convertible (CV) will fall less.
- *Use dollar cost averaging.* With both mutual funds and stocks, this approach enables you to buy more shares at lower prices and fewer shares at higher prices, as well as to ignore short-term market gyrations. (See page 70 for more on dollar cost averaging.)
- *Don't buy on margin.* You will be able to hold your stock through all kinds of weather if you buy for cash. With a margin account, you are subject to margin calls from your broker. (See Chapter 31, on margin accounts.)

How you manage your money is largely determined by your personality, your specific financial goals, and your tolerance for risk. In the broad sense, your choices are (1) between sleeping well and lying awake worrying, (2) between managing your money and letting someone else do it, and (3) between income and growth. For most people, the first choice is the most important: don't make investments that keep you awake at night—money by itself is never as important as peace of mind. It's absolutely impossible to be a successful investor when you're fearful!

WHAT TYPE ARE YOU?

Investors fall into three broad categories: *conservative, aggressive,* and *speculative.* By and large, your portfolio should reflect some of each, the emphasis shifting with market conditions, how much money you have, your age, and family responsibilities.

➤ CONSERVATIVE The conservative investor seeks safety and income and aims to preserve capital. In most cases, conservative investors look at an investment's yield and pay little heed to the impact of taxes and inflation on their money.

Investment choices are (1) fixed assets such as CDs and short-term Treasury bills, notes, or bonds and (2) solid, income-producing stocks such as utilities and real estate investment trusts.

☐ CAUTION: Avoid taking the path of least resistance—that of being an ultraconservative investor who stashes large amounts of money in savings accounts or money market funds or, even worse, buys stocks and holds them until forced to sell because of the need for cash or money to live on.

The conservative approach provides peace of mind, but it's very poor protection against inflation and low interest rates. If, for instance, the cost of living rises 4% a year, and your conservative investments don't keep pace, you will actually lose. With a 4% rise, the real purchasing power of every $1,000 is cut to $822 in 5 years and to $703 in 10 years.

Conservative investments should, of course, constitute a portion of everyone's portfolio, but they are most appropriate for people who are retired or soon to be, are on fixed incomes, or earn low to modest salaries.

➤ AGGRESSIVE The aggressive investor is more comfortable moving money about and is interested in total return; that is, income plus price appreciation. Such an investor does not hesitate to sell in order to take profits.

Although some of this investor's money is in conservative holdings, the bulk is spread between quality growth stocks, corporate and municipal bonds, convertibles, and real estate.

The aggressive investor is likely to have substantial income, be at least a decade away from retirement, and not need investment income for day-to-day living.

➤ SPECULATIVE Speculative investors may not always be gambling Las Vegas style, but they often try to outwit the market and the pros. As long as speculators research their choices carefully and use only money they can afford to lose, they may very well make money—lots of it. However, they are just as likely to lose everything unless they force themselves to sell when their investments attain specific levels.

Speculative investors favor takeover candidates, junk bonds, precious metals, and leveraged real estate. Such investors should be well off, with steadily increasing sources of income.

For additional suggestions on equating your appetite for risk with your investment choices, see the pyramid on page 13.

FINDING MONEY TO INVEST

Saving is essential for achieving your personal economic goals, security, and a carefree life when it comes to money. But it is not enough to set aside money sporadically. You must save regularly.

$HINT: Make your first monthly check out to yourself; earmark it for investments or your IRA, Keogh, or money market account. Then begin paying your bills!

Other painless sources of money to invest:

- Dividend checks
- Gifts
- Bonuses
- A raise
- Tips
- Automatic payroll deduction plan
- Inheritance
- Free-lance activities
- Company savings plans
- Tax refunds

Much of the information you need to analyze the wide range of investments and develop your own personal strategy is readily available from annual reports, investment services, and financial newspapers and magazines. Investment newsletters are also helpful. See Appendix A.

Most portfolios consist of stocks, bonds, U.S. Treasury obligations, real estate, precious metals, and limited partnerships. No one portfolio should consist of only one type of investment—diversification is one of the best lines of defense against losses. We will introduce the various types of stocks, bonds, and other securities in the following chapters.

SPOTTING ECONOMIC TRENDS

To build and maintain a profitable portfolio, you must develop a sense of the country's economic strength or weakness. By following these six key short-term indicators, all of which are reported in the media, you can take the pulse of the nation.

- *New car sales.* Consumer buying trends are reflected in this purchase pattern, reported every 10 days. Keep track over a minimum of 2 months.
- *Retail sales.* Compare monthly sales with those of the previous month, 6 months, and 1 year.
- *Department store sales.* These reflect both regional and seasonal trends but can be an accurate indicator if they confirm other trends.
- *Housing starts.* Any improvement indicates optimistic consumer attitudes and, quite often, lower interest rates.
- *Unemployment.* This statistic reflects the overall status of the country's economy. Watch it regularly.
- *Federal funds rate.* This figure, which fluctuates daily, tracks the interest rate banks charge each other.
- *Prime rate.* Interest rate banks charge their most creditworthy customers. Follow at least 3 months.
- *Broker loan rate.* Interest rate for brokers borrowing money from banks.

DOS FOR SUCCESSFUL INVESTING

DO investigate BEFORE you invest. Do not buy on impulse, hunch, or rumor. Make all investments according to your goals for income and/or growth. Take nothing for granted. Get the facts lest the lack of facts get you.

DO limit your purchases until your forecast is confirmed. When you feel you have latched onto a winner, buy half the amount of shares you have money for even if it means buying less than a round lot. You may lose a few points' profit by waiting, but you will also minimize your losses. Watch the action in the marketplace, and when your judgment appears accurate, buy the other half of your position.

DO focus on the downside risk. The most important aspect of buying stocks is not how much you can make but how much you can lose. If a stock's dividend, asset value, or price history clearly indicates a limited downside risk, it's probably a good investment.

DO calculate the reward-to-risk ratio. This is the basis for all successful speculations. With stocks and bonds, you can develop your own ratios, but don't hesitate to rely on professional advisory reports and recommendations. With commodities, currency trading, and indexes, expert assistance is imperative, at least until you become knowledgeable and are able to devote time to research and analysis that can project reward-to-risk ratios.

Here's how to project reward-to-risk ratios. You feel that a stock (or any other type of easily traded property) now at 40 has the potential of moving up to 60. Or there's a risk of a decline to 35. The reward-to-risk ratio is 20 points up vs. 5 points down: a healthy 4:1 ratio.

You buy and the stock goes to 55. The potential gain is now only 5 points, but the risk is still 20 points down. That's a dangerous 1:4 ratio and a signal to sell or, possibly, to enter a stop order.

Be careful not to sell too soon when the ratio shifts from, say, 5:1 to 4:2.5. You will limit your profit potential and end up with relatively small gains.

DO buy only stocks quoted regularly in the *Wall Street Journal*, the *New York Times*, or *Barron's*. You want a ready market that will attract other investors when you sell.

DO investigate AFTER you invest. There is no such thing as a permanent investment. (Even IBM has bounced up and down over the years.) This caveat applies especially to small companies that show great promise at the outset but all too soon fall by the wayside.

DO watch trends: of the economy, of the stock market, of industry groups, and of the stocks in which you are interested. Stock market leaders change almost monthly, so what was favorable in January may be sliding in June.

DO set realistic goals and target prices when you make the original commitment. Roughly, these should be 35% to 50% higher than your cost, and the time frame should be 24 to 36 months. Once in a while, a stock will zoom up fast, but investments usually move up slowly and steadily, with interim dips, to new highs.

DO diversify, but carefully. As a rule of thumb, a $100,000 portfolio, should have no more than 10 securities, with no more than 20% in any one company or industry. However, you can put as little as 5% of your assets in special high-risk situations. Above $100,000, add one new security for each additional $10,000.

DO stay flexible. This will let you make the most profitable use of your money during any specific period. When yields on bonds, CDs, money market funds, and Treasuries are 8% or more, move part of your savings into these areas. When the yield drops, take your profits and invest the proceeds in quality common stocks where the chances of appreciation are greater.

DO keep a list of 10 "future" investments. Review them periodically to determine whether any offer greater prospects for faster rewards than the holdings you now have. This list should include stocks, convertibles, bonds, and, when appropriate, limited partnerships. Don't switch as long as your original investments are profitable and appear to have reasonable prospects of reaching your goals.

DO watch market timing, and never be in a hurry to spend your money. If you miss one opportunity, there will be another soon.

- *When trading is active,* buy at the market price. If you're dealing with a stock that is beginning to attract attention, you may save a point or two by waiting for a temporary dip. But if you are convinced that this is a wise investment, make your move, even if there is a decline later.

- *When trading is slow,* place your order at a set price and be willing to wait a while.

DO be patient. Never flit from one stock to another. This will make your broker rich, but it will cut your potential profits and, unless you are very wise and very lucky, will not increase your capital. Four trades a year, at an average cost of 1% of stock value, equals 4% of income. (You may save a few dollars by using a discount broker.)

In normal markets, it takes a quality stock 2 to 3 years to move from undervaluation to overvaluation. Always remember that by definition, investments are long-term commitments and rarely create millionaires overnight.

One of the major faults of amateurs is that they try too hard to make too much money too fast. As with most business decisions, take your time. Once in a great while, a stock will take off and rush up, but in most cases appreciation is slow and often erratic. It is possible to project long-term trends but only rarely short-term action.

DO upgrade your portfolio periodically. Review all holdings quarterly and plan to sell at least one security every 6 months. Replace the weakest securities with those on your "futures" list. Be slow to sell winners, because this will leave you with less profitable holdings. On the average, a successful portfolio will be turned over every 5 years, about 20% annually.

DO average up when you choose well. Buy more shares as the price of the stock rises.

DO set selling prices, preferably stop-loss orders at 15% to 20% below your cost or the recent high. This is discussed in greater detail in Chapter 30, but it is a key factor in successful investing. It is just as important to keep losses low as to keep profits high. At times, this can be a tough decision, so action should be taken only after you have learned the real reason for the price decline. If the company runs into temporary difficulties, don't panic. But if research concludes that profits will be below projections, it's usually smart to sell now. You can always buy back later.

DO stand by your investment rules. Once in a while, it will pay to make exceptions, but in successful investing, rules should seldom be broken.

DON'TS FOR SUCCESSFUL INVESTING

DON'T invest in a vacuum. You must have a systematic, sensible, long-range plan for your personal, business, and retirement savings. Wise planning is easy, enjoyable, and rewarding. Lack of planning leads to mistakes that can be more costly than spending the time to understand the fundamentals of investing.

DON'T be overly conservative. This means limiting the portion of your savings allocated to fixed asset or income investments, such as money market accounts, CDs, preferred stocks, and Treasuries. These are safe, but they rarely grow in value. Most of these holdings should be viewed as temporary parking places while you wait for more rewarding opportunities, or as a segment of your total portfolio.

DON'T be overly optimistic or pessimistic about the market or the securities that you own. Even the best corporations falter now and then: their growth slows or their markets change. Smart professionals recognize when this occurs and also when the stock price soars to an unrealistic level. When any stock becomes clearly overvalued by your standards, sell or set stop-loss orders.

DON'T be lured by the ''greater fool theory'': that the price will keep rising because someone else will be foolish enough to pay far more than the stock is worth. When you have a pleasant profit, cash in.

DON'T rush to buy bargains, regardless of the pressure from your adviser or broker. When a stock is at a low price, there is usually a reason. It may not appear to be logical, but major investors are either skeptical or uncomfortable. They will not start buying until their peers do so. Once you spot a bargain, wait until the price and volume start to rise, and then proceed cautiously, buying in small lots even if it costs more money.

DON'T average down. A stock that appears to be a good buy at 20 is seldom more attractive at 15. When there's a decline in your current favorite, either your research is inaccurate or your access to the latest information is inadequate. Ask your broker to check with the research

---

REVIEW YOUR PORTFOLIO WHEN . . .

- There's a significant move up or down in the stock market.
- Prime and other bank interest rates change.
- A new tax law is passed.
- The dollar becomes substantially stronger or weaker in the international market.
- There's been a major scientific breakthrough.
- Regulatory agencies adopt a new policy.
- The inflation rate changes.
- There's a change in political leadership.
- Foreign-trade restrictions are put into effect.
- A new international trade agreement is reached.
- New rules are passed on margin accounts.
- War begins or ends.
- The economy changes from boom times to recessionary times, or vice versa.
- Bond interest rates change.
- The level of government spending changes.

department. If you are wrong and keep buying as the price declines, you'll only compound your mistake.

DON'T assume that a quality rating will continue. With cost squeezes, foreign competition, governmental regulations and edicts, and fast-changing financial and market conditions, even stable corporations can become less attractive in a few months.

DON'T heed rumors. Wall Street is a center of gossip, hopes, and fears, but a rumor is *never* a sound reason for investment decisions. By the time you hear or read it, the professionals have made their move.

DON'T forget that a stock does not care who owns it. The price per volume of the trading of its shares is the result of forces far stronger and wealthier than you are or probably ever will be.

DON'T look back. There's no way that you can reverse your decision. If your judgment was wrong, there's nothing that you can do about it except learn from it.

REDUCING FEES: A PAINLESS WAY TO BOOST YOUR RETURNS

By reducing your investing costs, you can painlessly raise the returns you make on stocks, bonds, mutual funds, and other investments. The impact of these fees and other charges on your profits can be impressive.

There are three basic types of investing costs: (1) sales commissions, which you pay when you buy stocks, bonds, and load mutual funds; (2) mutual fund expenses; and (3) the spread: the difference between the ask price at which dealers sell a security to the public and the bid price at which they buy it back. Spreads are particularly heavy in purchasing zero coupon bonds, municipals, and over-the-counter stocks.

DISCOUNTERS

You can cut sales commissions by buying through discount brokerage firms, although you have to give up the research and personal feeding and care you get from a full service firm. Yet you'll save as much as 50% to 80%. (See Chapter 30 for more on discount firms.)

Discounters also relieve you of another, fairly new expense: annual fees for customers who do not actively trade their account. The leader of this charge, Merrill Lynch, charges $30 a year for accounts that generate less than $100 a year in commissions. Other firms are beginning to follow this trend.

U.S. TREASURIES

Banks and brokerage firms charge sales commissions for buying and selling Treasury securities, which range from $25 to $50+ for up to $10,000 worth of securities. Ask before you buy.

$HINT: Avoid commissions by purchasing direct from the Treasury through its Treasury Direct system. For a free brochure call your Federal Reserve Bank. (See Chapter 8.)

MONEY MARKET FUNDS

These mutual funds are sold without any sales charge or commission; however, their management expenses can take a bite out of your yield. (See Chapter 3 for a list of money funds with low expense ratios.)

$HINT: Call several funds or read their prospectuses to find a fund with an expense ratio below 0.6%. But remember, an extremely low expense ratio often means that management is absorbing some of the costs to push up the fund's yield and attract customers. This is often the case with new funds. Once the fund has new investors, it may raise expense charges.

MUTUAL FUNDS

Funds sold by brokers, called load funds, charge front-end loads or fees of as much as 8.5%. Many funds have back-end loads of up to 1.5%, which go into effect when you sell your shares. Still others have 12b-1 fees—an annual fee of up to 1.25% to cover marketing costs to bring in new shareholders. These 12b-1 fees are on top of annual management fees, which range from 0.3% to 1.5%. (Management fees are highest for international stock funds, which must be actively managed.)

The SEC passed a ruling in the spring of 1988 that all sales charges and fees must be listed in the fund's prospectus accompanied by a table showing their precise effect on a $1,000 investment after 1, 3, 5, and 10 years.

HINT: Select no-load funds; check the fund's expenses for the year.

STOCKS

The lower the number of stocks you buy and sell, the wider the spread. With actively traded stocks, which includes most blue chips, the spread is typically narrow—say 12¢ per share. Yet a thinly traded stock that sells over the counter could have an ask price of $5 and a bid price of just $4.50. Another point to keep in mind with OTC stocks: if you buy from the market maker (a broker/dealer firm that keeps the stock in its inventory), then you pay only the spread. On the other hand, if you buy through a broker who must in turn get the shares from a market maker, you wind up paying the spread plus the broker's commission.

If you buy less than 100 shares of any stock (100 shares being a round lot), you pay an odd lot charge, typically 12½¢ per share.

$HINT: Buy in round lots; buy OTC stocks from the market maker, listed in the "pink sheets" directory available from most brokers. (See page 149 for more on pink sheet listings.)

MUNICIPAL BONDS

Spreads, which are built into the bond's price, are higher for odd lot purchases. With munis, an odd lot is less than $25,000. If you buy a municipal bond in the secondary or aftermarket from a broker who does not have it in inventory, your yield is further reduced by about an eighth of a percentage point to cover the broker's costs in getting the bonds from another dealer.

$ HINT: Buy actively traded bonds, and new issues in particular. Spreads are typically 0.75%, compared to as much as 4% to 5% for odd lots. Try to pick bonds from your broker's inventory.

ZERO COUPON BONDS

The pricing of zeros tends to be confusing, and hefty spreads are not uncommon. Some brokers have been known to charge as much as 5%.

$ HINT: Shop among several brokers, asking how much you must invest per $1,000 face value for the particular zero you want. Then ask what the effective yield to maturity is. Buy from the broker with the lowest price and the highest yield.

KNOWING WHEN TO GO LONG

During the first six months of 1989 short-term interest rates were at their highest levels in about 4 years. Although they've dropped some Treasury bills and notes, money market funds, and CDs are still extremely attractive, especially for conservative investors.

Yet at some point rates peak and start to head back down; high yields are suddenly history. When that happens, you want to be locked in, not only to profit from the high rates but also to benefit from rising bond prices that always accompany falling rates.

WHEN INVESTMENTS PERFORM BEST

INVESTMENT	ADD TO YOUR PORTFOLIO	RISK LEVEL
Growth stocks	When economy is growing at above average rate. When interest rates are stable	Medium to high
Blue chip stocks	During slow to moderate growth periods. When interest rates are falling	Medium
Utility stocks	When interest rates are falling. When energy costs are falling	Low to medium
Long-term bonds	When interest rates are falling	Low to medium
Short-term notes and bills	When interest rates are stable or falling	Low
Money market funds and CDs	When interest rates are rising	Low

There's no magic formula for knowing when to go long (for knowing when interest rates have topped out), but these four common indicators provide an accurate view of interest rate trends:

- *Money market maturities.* The average maturity on money market funds reveals the direction the fund managers think rates will take. This figure, available from the funds and also reported in many newspapers, tells the maturity of Treasury bills, CDs, and other short-term securities in a fund's portfolio. Short maturities allow fund managers to capture high rates more immediately and also indicate that they think rates will climb even higher. Rates tend to turn downward when maturities reach 39 or 40 days.

- *Gold prices.* The price of gold is traditionally an indication of the direction of inflation. Rising metal prices mean rising inflation, which in turns signals rising interest rates.

- *Prime rate.* A drop in prime usually occurs after other short-term rates have fallen, indicating that banks anticipate the downward spiral to continue. When prime drops, investors should lock in high yields.

- *Yield curve.* This illustrates the relationship between short- and long-term interest rates (see page 101). Usually long-term rates are higher than short-term rates to reward investors for tying up their money for many years. When short-term rates are higher, the yield curve is "inverted." An inverted yield curve generally indicates that interest rates have not peaked.

JOIN AN INVESTMENT CLUB

If you'd like to start building a portfolio of stocks but feel uncertain about making your own selections, join an investment club in your area. By pooling your money with that of 15 to 20 other people and sharing research, you can comfortably begin to develop investment savvy.

Kenneth S. Janke, president of the National Association of Investors Corporation, says the following three guiding principles followed by clubs enable them to frequently outperform the S&P 500:

1 Invest a fixed amount regularly to eliminate the guesswork of trying to time the market.
2 Reinvest earnings to take advantage of the magic of compounding.
3 Invest in stocks growing faster than the economy.
   For details on joining a club, contact:

National Association of Investment Clubs
1515 East Eleven Mile Road
Royal Oak, MI 48067
1-313-543-0612

17 WAYS TO CASH IN ON HIGH YIELDS

With many rates at their highest levels in years, your money should be put to work earning money. Here are 17 ways to do just that. (Data as of October 1989.)

INVESTMENT	RISK LEVEL	YIELD
Money market funds	Low	8.16%
Treasury bills	Low	7.57%
Certificates of deposit (6 month)	Low	8.20%
Savings bonds (minimum, 5 year)	Low	6%
Treasury bonds	Low	7.87%
Treasury zeros	Low to moderate	7–8%
Ginnie Mae certificates	Low to moderate	8.13%
CMOs	Moderate	8%
Utility stocks	Moderate to medium	8–10%
Utility bonds	Moderate to medium	9.10%
Closed-end bond funds	Moderate to medium	9–11%
Municipals	Medium	7.31%
Municipal zeros	Medium	7.31%
REITs	Medium to high	7.5%
Convertible bonds	Medium to high	8%
Junk bonds	High	12%
Master limited partnerships	High	9%

FOR FURTHER INFORMATION

NEWSLETTERS

Call or write for sample issues if you are interested in receiving continual data on the funds.

Income & Safety
Institute for Econometric Research
3471 North Federal Highway
Fort Lauderdale, FL 33306
1-800-327-6720; 1-305-563-9000
Monthly; $49 per year

Covers money market funds, Ginnie Maes, and tax-free bonds.

100 Highest Yields
P.O. Box 088888
North Palm Beach, FL 33408
1-800-327-7717
Monthly; 8 issues for $29; 52 issues for $89

PAMPHLETS

Savings Makes Sense
Public Services Dept.
Federal Reserve Bank of Richmond
P.O. Box 27522
Richmond, VA 23261

Free; explains strategies for smart savings.

Money Market Mutual Funds
Investment Company Institute
1600 M Street NW
Washington, DC 20036

Free; explains how money market funds are regulated.

Why Save and Invest at Your Credit Union
National Credit Union Association, Inc.
P.O. Box 431
Madison, WI 53701

Free; explains benefits of using a credit union.

New York Stock Exchange Investors Information Kit. Contains:
- *NYSE: The Capital Market*
- *Understanding Stocks and Bonds*
- *Understanding Financial Statements*
- *Getting Help When You Invest*
- *Glossary*
- *Margin Trading Guide*

$10; prepay by check or money order. Send to:

New York Stock Exchange
P.O. Box 3499
Syosset, NY 11791

6 MUTUAL FUNDS

Although there's no one ideal investment for everyone, mutual funds come closest for many of us. Their popularity is unrivaled: every day millions of dollars move into funds. Why? Because for a relatively low cost you receive professional management, diversification, compounding of income, and liquidity. So unless you have full time to devote to managing your investments, you'll find funds an easy solution. Since there are more funds than companies on the New York Stock Exchange, read this chapter carefully to make certain you select the ones best suited to your personal goals.

ADVANTAGES OF MUTUAL FUNDS

➤ DIVERSIFICATION Unless you have $40,000, it is almost impossible to have a properly diversified portfolio. It's costly to buy in odd lots, and if you buy round-lot shares of quality corporations, your average per share cost will be about $40, so you can own only about 10 stocks—the minimum for a cross section of securities. Mutual fund portfolios, on the other hand, provide excellent diversification.

➤ SYSTEMATIC SUPERVISION Mutual funds handle all details of stock transactions efficiently, mail dividend checks promptly, provide accurate year-end summaries for income tax purposes, and are always ready to answer questions on their toll-free phone lines.

➤ PROFESSIONAL MANAGEMENT The records of some fund managers leave much to be desired, but the performances of the best ones have been superior to those of stock market averages. They have time, experience, and access to information needed for profitable investments and, on occasion, for rewarding speculations.

➤ SWITCHING PRIVILEGES When a management company sponsors more than one type of fund (and most do), shareholders may switch from one fund to another as the market changes. Some funds offer free switching; others impose nominal fees.

$ HINT: Select a fund that permits the portfolio manager to shift out of stocks and into U.S. Treasury bills, jumbo CDs, and other higher-yielding cash instruments when the stock market declines. This gives you added protection when the market or interst rates change.

HOW THEY WORK

All mutual funds operate along the same lines. They sell shares to the public at net asset value (NAV) price. (NAV per share equals the total assets of the fund divided by the outstanding shares minus liabilities.) The money received is then pooled and used to buy various types of securities. So when you buy into a fund, you are really buying shares in an investment company, but the assets of this company consist not of a plant or equipment but of stocks, bonds, and cash instruments. The price of your shares rises and falls every day with the total value of the securities in the fund's portfolio.

As the owner of mutual fund shares, you receive periodic payments, provided your fund does well. Of course, if the fund has a poor year, you stand to lose money; that is, your NAV will fall. Most funds pay dividends every quarter and capital gains distributions annually. Capital gains distributions result when a fund sells some of its securities at a profit. You may elect to have your earnings reinvested automatically in additional fund shares, usually at no cost.

➤ OPEN VS. CLOSED   Funds are either open- or closed-ended. In an *open-end fund*, shares are continually available to the public at NAV. The fund's shares are always increasing or decreasing in number depending on sales to the public.

A *closed-end fund* has fixed capitalization and makes one initial issue of shares. After that it trades as a stock on the major stock exchanges or over the counter. In other words, it closes its doors to new investors, and shares can be purchased only by buying the stock. Prices are determined by supply and demand: when buyers are plentiful, the price of the stock rises, and vice versa. Depending on market conditions, the price will be above NAV or below NAV. When a closed-end fund is selling at a discount from NAV, the investor has an opportunity to see profits from price appreciation. See page 66 for more on closed-end funds.

➤ LOAD VS. NO-LOAD   Mutual funds can also be categorized as load or no-load. *No-load funds* are sold directly by the fund and not by stockbrokers. Since no broker is involved, there is no commission, which is known as a "load" (or burden). Money market mutual funds are virtually all no-load. However, all other funds charge a management fee of about 0.5% of the fund's total assets per year. This covers the fund's administration. These expenses are paid from the fund's assets and are reflected in the price of fund shares.

Load funds are sold by stockbrokers or financial planners, who charge a commission every time you buy new shares. The highest load allowed by the National Association of Security Dealers is 8.5%. This amount is deducted from the amount of your initial investment. Thus, on a $10,000 purchase, the dollars that go to work for you are reduced by the 8.5% load to $9,150 ($10,000 − $850).

$ HINT: The formula for determining the load: subtract the net asset value from the offering price and divide the difference by the offering price. There are also *low-load funds*, which charge only 2% to 3%.

$ HINT: There is no evidence that load funds perform better than no-loads, so if you don't need help in selecting a fund, go with a no-load and save the fee. And if you plan to invest for 1 year or less, always select a no-load. One year is seldom long enough to make up an 8.5% commission.

➤ OTHER FEES   Until relatively recently the choices were simple: load or no-load. But today new fees keep coming out from under the rug. Not only are there the usual fees for management and operating expenses, but there are other charges—for redeeming shares, for example. These *redemption fees*, also called back-end loads or contingent deferred sales charges, may be a flat percentage of the share price or may be based on a sliding scale, usually 6% the first year, moving down to 0% in year 6. Sometimes a redemption fee applies only to your initial investment.

Worst of all are the so-called hidden fees, which aren't even called fees. They're called *12b-1 plans,* after the SEC regulation that authorized them in 1980. Under this ruling, funds that do not have their own salespeople can deduct up to 1.25% of their assets to pay for advertising and marketing expenses. Unlike front- and back-end loads, which come directly out of your investment, 12b-1 fees are generally subtracted from the fund's assets. The only way to find out about a 12b-1 plan is in the fund's prospectus under "Distribution Charges." According to Norman Fosback, editor of the newsletter *Mutual Fund Forecaster,* any such fee over 1% is "abusive to the investor."

$ HINT: A redemption fee is slightly better from an investor's viewpoint than a sales charge, because you can earn income on that amount until you sell your shares.

Reloading charges are levied by a few funds on reinvestment of capital gains distributions and are described in the prospectus. The maximum is 7.25% of the total investment. For example, if you receive a capital gains distribution of $100 and you automatically reinvest these gains, the fund can retain $7.25 as a selling fee and reinvest only $92.75 in new fund shares.

➤ HOW TO READ FUND QUOTES   You will find a listing of mutual funds in the financial pages of the newspaper (see the accompanying example). Funds

---

HOW MUTUAL FUND SHARES ARE QUOTED

	NAV	OFFER PRICE	NAV CHANGE
Eaton Vance Funds			
Gov Obli	11.95	12.55+	0.02
Growth	8.43	8.55+	0.10
Hi Inc r	10.04	N.L.	. . .
Hi Mun r	9.78	N.L.	. . .

r—redemption charge may apply.
NAV—net asset value.
N.L.—no initial load.

SOURCE: Wall Street Journal, May 1, 1987.

are listed under the sponsor's name, such as Vanguard or Fidelity. The first column is the name of the fund, then the NAV, or "Bid" as it may be called. (The NAV is the price at which fund shareholders sold their shares the previous day.) The next column, "Offer Price," is the price paid by new investors the previous day. Where the offer price is higher than the NAV there is a load: the difference between the NAV and the offer price is the sales commission. Funds with "N.L." in the offer column are no-loads. A small "r" next to a fund's name indicates that a redemption charge may apply. Funds do not always have an "r" when they should, according to a study done recently by the American Association of Individual Investors. (Redemption fees are also called back-end loads.)

$ HINT: When a distribution is made to shareholders, the NAV is reduced by the amount of the distribution per share. So, buy shares just after a distribution to save paying tax on the distributed amount. Call the fund to get exact dates.

Keep in mind that the NAV column states the price the fund will pay to buy back its shares; but from your viewpoint, it's the price at which your shares can be sold. The offer price is the price you will have to pay to buy shares in the fund.

$ HINT: Don't panic if a fund's quoted price doesn't change much over the year. You may buy shares at $10 per share and find them the same a year later. That's because 90% of income and capital gains have been distributed to shareholders. Instead, judge the fund's total performance (capital appreciation plus dividend income) as a percentage gain or loss. This figure is available by calling the fund.

FUND SERVICES

Not all funds offer all services, but here are some of the extras frequently available:

A VERY CONTRARIAN STRATEGY

$ IF YOU DARE: In timing purchases of shares of mutual funds, most investors look for the funds with the best records over the long term and then check recent performances and make their choices.

Says *Indicator Digest:* "This is wrong. The opposite strategy is more rewarding. Buy the funds that have performed worse, particularly after a substantial market move in either direction."

Their reasoning:

- The top-performing funds grow too big to be efficient. They can no longer make meaningful investments in small companies.
- Their managers move to better jobs or are too busy being interviewed by the media.
- Success may be due to fads and fashions. Favorites tend to fade when long-neglected securities start to become popular.

➤ AUTOMATIC REINVESTMENT This means that all dividend and capital gains disbursements will be automatically reinvested to compound your earnings. With a total average annual return of 10%, for example, your money will double in a little over 7 years. Automatic reinvestment is also a form of dollar cost averaging. By investing the same dollar amount on a regular basis, regardless of the stock's price, you buy more shares when the price is down and fewer shares when the market rises. To determine the average per-share price, add up all the prices and divide by the number of shares. Dollar cost averaging tends to reduce the average per-share price.

$ HINT: Automatic reinvestment may be a form of dollar cost averaging, but it may not always be in your best interests. Mutual funds pay their largest distributions when the stock market is relatively high. Instead of reinvesting at the high level, you may do better to take the cash and wait for the market to decline, when your cash will buy more shares.

➤ BENEFICIARY DESIGNATION You can name your beneficiary by means of a trust agreement so that your investment goes directly to your designated

HOW TO ANALYZE A MUTUAL FUND

	MARCH 31	JUNE 30	SEPTEMBER 30	DECEMBER 31
Investment Position				
Cash				
Common stocks				
Bonds and preferreds				
Income				
High dividends				
Modest dividends				
Growth or low dividends				
Quality				
NYSE blue chips				
NYSE average				
AMEX				
OTC established				
OTC new issues or high-tech				
Vulnerability				
Percentage of total in largest holding				
Percentage of total in 5 largest holdings				
Percentage of total in 10 largest holdings				

heir when you die, with none of the delays and expenses of probate. Consult your lawyer, because some states prohibit this transfer.

➤ REGULAR INCOME CHECKS Set up monthly or quarterly income in several ways: (1) by buying shares in several funds, each with different dividend months; (2) by arranging for regular quarterly dividends to be paid out; (3) by arranging to redeem automatically the dollar value of the number of shares you specify (there's usually a $50 minimum per month). The fund will mail a check to you monthly, quarterly, or annually.

➤ INFORMATION AND SERVICE Almost all investment companies provide toll-free numbers. You can call to learn about prices, minimum investments, charges, and types of other funds available for switching. You can also ask for forms for setting up automatic withdrawals and switching into other funds.

DISTRIBUTION OF INCOME

Mutual funds distribute money to investors in two ways: income dividends and capital gains distributions. *Income dividends* represent the interest and/or dividends earned by the fund's portfolio, minus the fund's expenses. *Capital gains distributions* represent a fund's net realized capital gains— when there are profits in excess of losses on the sale of the portfolio securities. Both income dividends and capital gains distributions can be reinvested in the fund automatically, usually at no cost.

Most funds operate as "regulated investment companies" so they can qualify for an exemption from corporate income taxes. A fund must meet these tests:

- Distribute at least 90% of its investment company taxable income to its shareholders each year. Thus, a shareholder receives dividends and capital gains distributions from a qualifying fund without any tax being levied on the fund. Instead, shareholders report these payments on their own tax returns.
- Distribute 97% of its income from dividends and interest and 98% of its net realized capital gains with respect to the calendar year in which they are earned or realized.

A summary of the distributions made to each shareholder annually, called a Form 1099, is sent to the shareholder and to the IRS.

TYPES OF FUNDS

Mutual funds come in all sizes, shapes, and combinations. It is extremely important that you match your personal investment objectives with those of the fund. The accompanying list summarizes the broad objectives and should be read carefully in order to familiarize yourself with the various terms or bits of jargon the funds use to describe what they do with your money.

TYPES OF MUTUAL FUNDS

FUND	OBJECTIVE
Aggressive growth funds	Seek maximum capital gains, not current income. May invest in new companies, troubled firms. Use techniques such as option writing to boost returns. Highly risky.
Balanced funds	Aim to conserve principal, generate current income, and provide long-term growth. Have portfolio mix of bonds, preferred stocks, and common stocks.
Corporate bond funds	Seek high level of income. Buy corporate bonds, some U.S. Treasury bonds or bonds issued by federal agencies.
Flexible portfolio funds	May be 100% in stocks or bonds or money market instruments. Have the greatest portfolio flexibility of all funds.
Ginnie Mae funds (GNMAs)	Invest in mortgage-backed securities. Must keep majority of portfolio in these securities.
Global bond funds	Invest in debt of companies and countries throughout the world, including the United States.
Global equity funds	Invest in securities traded worldwide, including the United States.
Growth funds	Invest in common stock of well-established companies. Capital gains, not income, is primary objective.
Growth and income funds	Invest in common stock of dividend-paying companies. Combine long-term capital gains and steady stream of income.
High-yield bond funds	Keep two-thirds of portfolio in lower-rated corporate bonds (junk bonds) to ensure high income.
Income bond funds	Invest at all times in corporate and government bonds for income.
Income equity funds	Invest in companies with good dividend-paying records.

BLUE SKY LAWS

Laws have been passed in various states to protect individual investors against securities fraud. The law requires sellers of new stocks or mutual funds to register and provide financial data, usually with the state attorney general's office. The term ''blue sky law'' originated when a judge reportedly said that a new stock issue was about as valuable as a patch of blue sky.

Most funds register in all states, but occasionally one will not because of excessive paperwork or delays. Always buy into a fund that is registered in the state of your legal residence.

FUND	OBJECTIVE
Income mixed funds	Seek high current income by investing in equities and debt instruments.
International funds	Invest in equity securities of companies located outside the United States.
Long-term municipal bond funds	Invest in bonds issued by states and municipalities. In most cases, income earned is not taxed by the federal government.
Money market mutual funds	Invest in short-term securities sold in the money market. Safe, relatively high yields.
Option/income funds	Seek high current return by investing in dividend-paying stocks on which call options are traded.
Precious metals/gold funds	Keep two-thirds of portfolio in securities associated with gold, silver, platinum, and other precious metals.
Sector funds	Concentrate holdings in a single industry or country.
Short-term municipal bonds	Invest in municipals with short maturities; also known as tax-exempt money market funds.
Single-state municipal bond funds	Portfolios contain issues of only one state so that income is free of both federal and state taxes.
Socially conscious funds	Avoid investments in corporations known to pollute, to have poor records in hiring minorities, and to be involved in the military, tobacco, and liquor industries.
U.S. government income funds	Invest in a variety of government securities, including U.S. Treasury bonds, mortgage-backed securities, and government notes.

Keep in mind that there are scores of other mutual funds, many of which are described in chapters relating to specific types of securities. Before you commit any money to a fund, do your homework and make certain you understand exactly what you are investing in.

SOCIALLY CONSCIOUS MUTUAL FUNDS

	APPRECIATION (1/1/89 TO 3/31/89)
Dreyfus Third Century (1-800-645-6561)	3.78%
Calvert Managed Growth (1-800-368-2748)	2.79
Pax World (1-603-431-8022)	6.10

HOW TO SELECT MUTUAL FUNDS

As with all types of investments, the number one factor is the competency of management, as measured by its ability to meet or surpass stated goals fairly consistently over a fairly long period of time: at least 5 and preferably 10 years.

Be wary of highly publicized, aggressively promoted funds, especially those with a "gimmick." You can judge a fund's future performance by checking the stocks shown in the last quarterly report. Watch to see if they rise or fall in price.

Study the performance in both up and down markets. Several major funds have never been first in any one year, but they do better than the market in good periods and lose less in bear markets. One of the best guides is the annual *Forbes* magazine report in the late August issue. This rates funds on the basis of performance in both rising and falling markets. To get a high score, the fund must perform consistently, in relation to other funds, in both up and down periods. Adjustments are made to prevent exceptional performance (good or bad) in any one period from having undue influence on the fund's average performance—calculated separately for both up and down markets. Popular periodicals such as *Money* and *Forbes* also track fund performance.

➤ YIELD VS. TOTAL RETURN It is important to know the difference between yield and total return when evaluating a fund. Yield is the income per share paid to the shareholder. It is derived from dividends and interest and is expressed as a percentage of the current offering price per share.

Total return measures the per-share change in the total value of a fund, from the beginning of the year to any given date. Total return is derived from dividend and interest income, capital gains distributions, and any unrealized capital gains or losses.

➤ SIZE The larger the assets of a mutual fund, the smaller the amount each investor pays for administration.

Stay away from funds whose assets have been under $50 million for over 10 years. If a fund hasn't grown, its performance must have been so poor that new shares could not be widely sold.

Conversely, when a fund becomes huge (over $500 million), there's a tendency for the managers to confine their investments to a relatively few major corporations that have millions of shares outstanding. In order not to upset the market, large commitments must be purchased or sold over a period of time and so may not always be traded at the most advantageous prices.

This lack of agility makes it difficult for major funds to beat the averages. In a sense, they are the market. By contrast, smaller funds can score welcome gains if they pick three or four winners. But large funds are likely to be more consistent in their returns.

➤ TURNOVER This shows the dollar amount of stocks sold in relation to

CLOSED-END FUNDS

FUND	NET ASSET VALUE	PRICE	ABOVE/BELOW NAV
Stock Funds			
Adams Express	$17.76	$14⅞	−16.24%
Gen. American	19.41	15⅞	−18.21
Source Capital	40.69	38⅜	−5.69
Zweig Fund	10.92	10⅝	−2.70
Convertible Funds			
Amer. Capital CV	22.98	21	−8.62
Bancroft CV	21.24	18⅜	−13.49
Castle CV	21.41	18⅜	−14.18
Special Equity Funds			
Duff & Phelps Utilities	7.72	7⅞	+2.01
Thai Fund	12.93	16⅞	+30.51
Korea Fund	17.43	33	+92.20

SOURCE: Barron's, May 8, 1989.

total assets. Thus if a fund had assets of $100 million and sold $75 million in stocks in one year, the turnover would be 75%. This is high and may indicate that the fund managers are speculating for short-term profits or are not making successful choices.

$ HINT: Set a stop-loss figure, say, 10%, 15%, or 20% below current NAV. That way you'll keep your losses small, even if you misjudge market trends.

LOW-COST FUNDS

Some funds, like some people, are more frugal than others. According to a study by Financial Planning Information of Cambridge, Mass., seven fund families have lower than average expenses. Although frugality should not be more important than performance in selecting a fund, begin your search by reading the box below.

LOW-COST FUND FAMILIES

FUND	EXPENSE RATIO
Vanguard	0.45%
Dreyfus	0.71
Federated	0.73
Merrill Lynch	0.74
USAA	0.78
T. Rowe Price	0.92

Other findings: international and precious metals funds usually have the highest expense ratios and fixed income funds the lowest.

$ HINT: To determine any fund's expense ratio: divide operating expenses (management's fees, etc.) by the average net assets.

TAX-FREE FUNDS

Should you be in a tax-free mutual fund? To compute how much you need to earn on a taxable investment to equal a tax-free one, use the following formula:

$$\frac{\text{tax-exempt yield}}{1 \text{ minus your tax bracket}} = \text{equivalent yield of a taxable investment}$$

For example, if you're in the 28% tax bracket and a tax-exempt bond is yielding 10%, you would have to receive a yield of 13.8% on a taxable investment to be equivalent:

$$\frac{.10}{1 - .28} = .138$$

$ HINT: In some states, dividends from U.S. Treasury money funds or bond funds are also tax-free, even though you have to pay federal tax on them. And you may be eligible for a foreign tax credit if you own a mutual fund that invests in stocks or securities of foreign corporations. Watch for an indication on your 1099-DIV form of foreign tax paid on your behalf.

MUNICIPAL BOND FUNDS AND TAXES

Not all bond fund income remains tax-free. There are three taxable situations:

A FUND IS NOT FOREVER

You revise your stock and bond portfolios; you should do the same with mutual funds. They should be evaluated periodically and weeded out. No fund is perfect for your needs forever. Switch out of a fund when:

- The market shifts dramatically. Equity funds generally suffer during bear markets. Bond funds tend to be hurt when interest rates rise. You can't hope to avoid short-term corrections, but plan to miss the longer-term ones.
  1. Switch from stocks to money market funds at the beginning of a bear market.
  2. As a bull market begins, move into conservative blue chip funds.
  3. As the bull begins to roar, put more dollars into aggressive growth funds.
  4. When interest rates rise, put cash into money market funds.
- Your fund lags the market averages, such as the S&P 500.
- Your fund consistently underperforms other similar funds.

THE PROSPECTUS

You must read the prospectus before investing in a fund. Although it may appear formidable at first glance, a half-hour with this step-by-step guide will crystallize the entire process and enlighten you about the fund. Here's what to look for:

- What the fund's investment objectives are. These will be spelled out at the beginning.
- A risk factor statement.
- What strategies will be used to meet the fund's stated goals.
- The degree of diversification. How many issues does it hold?
- What is the portfolio turnover? A low rate, below 75%, reflects a long-term holding philosophy, whereas a high rate indicates an aggressive strategy.
- Fees and expenses. Check in particular the cost of redeeming shares, which should not exceed 1% per year.
- Rules for switching within a family of funds and fees, if any.
- Restrictions. Will the fund sell securities short, act as an underwriter, engage in selling commodities or real estate? What percentage of total assets is invested in any one security? Be wary of a fund that is not adequately diversified.
- How much the fund has gained or lost over 1, 5, and 10 years.

- The 1986 Tax Reform Act designated the interest on certain so-called private activity bonds (bonds for nonessential municipal projects) issued after August 7, 1986, as a preference item when computing the alternative minimum tax. If a mutual fund invests in one of these bonds, there could be taxable income to shareholders if they have significant amounts of preference income.
- Many municipal bond funds reserve the right to invest (usually up to 20% of the portfolio) temporarily in U.S. government obligations or other taxable securities for protection when the market drops. These investment policies are described in the fund's prospectus.
- Although most or all of the income you earn in a municipal bond fund is not taxable, capital gains distributions are taxable. They represent part of any profit the fund makes when bonds are sold at a gain.
Remember, you must list all tax-exempt income on your 1040 tax form.

TAXES AND MUTUAL FUNDS

Each time you touch your mutual fund shares there are tax implications that must be reported to the IRS, including these:
- When you switch from one fund to another within a family, the IRS

considers this a sale in one fund and a purchase in another. You must report your profit or loss.

- When your fund earns dividends and taxable interest and passes them on to you, you must pay taxes on this distribution.
- When your dividends are automatically reinvested in more shares, you must report this as dividend income.
- When there are capital gains distributions, these must also be reported.

For further information, read IRS booklet No. 564, "Mutual Fund Distributions."

$ HINT: If you buy shares in a fund just prior to its annual earnings distribution, you will be taxed on this distribution even though the value of your new shares drops to reflect this distribution. Buy just after distribution.

MARKET TIMERS

The continuing popularity of mutual funds has given birth to an interesting side industry—market timers. The majority are publishers of newsletters who also offer, at additional cost, hotline telephone services that update their published recommendations. Subscribers are given a special number.

There are two basic systems: (1) timers who actually designate specific mutual funds and (2) timers who let you do the fund selection. Timers focus primarily on the stock market, although some deal with bonds, gold, international funds, and commodities.

EVALUATING THE TIMERS

In deciding whether or not to use a timer, take a long-term position. Hulbert says that since 1980, when he began following timers, about 50% of the time they have beaten the various averages. Too much short-term switching runs up transaction costs, and even if you use no-load funds, you may run into an obstacle: many have imposed limits on the number of switches you can make each year.

BUYING ON MARGIN

If you're an aggressive trader, you can buy mutual funds on margin. You must pay 50% of the total cost of your transaction up front. The rest you borrow from your broker. Before doing so, read Chapter 31 on how a margin account works, and beware of the pitfalls.

Among the brokerage firms offering mutual fund shares on margin are these:

- Charles Schwab & Co. (1-415-398-1000)
- Muriel Seibert (1-800-872-0711)
- Jack White (1-619-587-2000)

LEADING FUND TIMERS

	ANNUAL FEE
Fund Exchange Report (1-206-285-8877)	$125
Investors Intelligence (1-914-632-0422)	124
Lynn Elgert Report (1-308-381-2121)	225
Dow Theory Letters (1-619-454-0481)	225
Elliot Wave Theorist (1-404-536-0309)	233
Investech Mutual Fund Advisor (1-406-862-7777)	165

TIMERS VS. THE MARKET

A study done recently by Babson concluded that during the past 40 years, stocks went up in 26, were even in 3, and fell in 11. Translated into action that suggests two rules of thumb: (1) ride out the bear markets, and (2) stick to the time-honored buy-and-hold theory. That doesn't mean you should ignore your investments, but it does indicate that in certain cycles, timers have to be very good to beat the market. And you must select as good a timer as you do a stockbroker or even individual funds. In the final analysis, there is no magical, surefire, winning system.

EASY ALTERNATIVE: DOLLAR COST AVERAGING

A simple and widely used alternative to following a professional timer is dollar cost averaging. This involves regularly investing a set dollar amount in a fund—say, $150 to $500 per month. This system provides a steady way to save, and it also means you must buy when the market is down, thereby pushing down your average cost per share. You buy more shares

---

CLONES AND LOOK-ALIKE FUNDS

When a popular fund becomes unwieldy in size, it may close its doors to new investors even though it is an open-end fund. Then a new clone fund is established with the same or a similar name and investment goals. It may or may not have the same portfolio manager. There's no such thing as a perfect clone; if there were, it would be managed by computer. If you are interested in a clone, read the prospectus first and don't invest until the fund has been in existence at least 1 year.

FUND (1/1/89 TO 4/1/89)	RETURN	CLONE FUND (1/1/89 TO 4/1/89)	RETURN
Vanguard Explorer (1-800-662-7447)	4.34%	Vanguard Explorer II	3.68%
Nicholas (1-414-272-6133)	9.50	Nicholas Fund II	6.70
Pioneer Fund (1-800-225-6292)	7.59	Pioneer Fund II	9.13
20th Century Ultra (1-800-345-2021)	20.68	20th Century Vista	17.58
Vanguard Windsor (1-800-662-7447)	6.43	Vanguard Windsor II	9.91

HOW DOLLAR COST AVERAGING PAYS OFF

	REGULAR INVESTMENT	SHARE PRICE	SHARES ACQUIRED
	$100	$10	10
	100	5	20
	100	10	10
TOTAL	$500	$25	40

Average share cost: $7.50 ($300 − 40)
Average share price: $8.33 ($25 − 3)

for each dollar invested. Many funds will automatically transfer money from your bank account to the fund every month. Let's say you put $100 into a mutual fund every 3 months. The shares sell at $10 per share. You invest $100 and receive 10 shares. Then the market drops. You invest your $100 the next quarter, and at $5 per share you receive 20 shares. The next quarter the market returns and your fund is again selling at $10 per share, so you now receive 10 shares for your $100. *The bottom line:* you own 40 shares after a total investment of $300. However, with an ending market price of $10 per share, your shares are actually worth more than you paid for them.

The average price per share over three quarters was $8.33 ($25 divided by 3 = $8.33), but the average cost to you was less: $300 divided by 40 shares is $7.50.

SECTOR FUNDS

If you're confident about what industry or industries will do well during 1990 and 1991, consider a sector fund, one that invests in a single industry. Keep in mind, however, that although such funds offer greater profit potential than broader-based funds, they're also far riskier. This risk factor is reflected in their great price volatility.

☐ CAUTION:

- Stocks in a given group tend to fall in unison.
- Most sector funds stay fully invested or nearly so even when their industry has a slide. They are less likely to switch portfolios into Treasuries or cash equivalents. Select a fund that's part of a family of funds so you can switch out when your industry turns sour.
- It's difficult to use past performance to predict future performance in this group.
- Read one or two of the newsletters listed at the end of this chapter, plus *Value Line Investment Survey* and Standard & Poor's *Outlook* to keep up to date on industry developments.

TYPES OF SECTOR FUNDS

Agriculture	International
Chemicals	Leisure
Computers	Precious metals/gold
Defense/aerospace	Real estate
Energy	Service
Financial services	Technology
Foreign countries	Transportation
Health care	Utilities

$ HINT: Limit your investment in sector funds to 10%. Since they focus on one economic area, you'll reduce your chances for loss if that particular sector experiences a downturn.

INDEX FUNDS

It's not easy to beat the various market indexes year after year, but if you want to bet on the averages, you can do so with an index fund. These funds buy the same securities that make up an index, and therefore their performance mirrors that of the index, such as the S&P 500, the S&P 100, the NASDAQ 100, or the Wilshire 4500. One fund even buys the Morgan Stanley's Europe, Australia, Far East Index. Many institutional investors subscribe to the efficient market theory that trying to surpass the averages is not possible in the long run. These funds, on the other hand, at least keep pace with the market.

□ CAUTION: If the market declines, so will the value of your shares.

These funds provide excellent diversification and, of course, you know exactly what stocks you're invested in at all times.

According to SEI Corp., which measures the performance of institutional money managers, in 11 out of the last 18 years, stock index funds have outperformed the typical money manager.

CLOSED-END MUTUAL FUNDS

Closed-end funds, also called publicly traded funds, offer investors a way to buy securities, often at a discount. Because their shares are bought and sold on the stock exchanges or over the counter, these funds fluctuate in price with demand for shares. Unlike open-end funds, which continually sell new shares to the public, closed-end funds sell only a set number of shares once, and then the fund is closed. After that you can buy and sell the fund on the NYSE, AMEX, or OTC, while the portfolio manager buys and sells securities just as in an open-end fund.

INDEX MUTUAL FUNDS

FUND	TELEPHONE
Colonial Funds (Load)	1-800-248-2828
International Equity Index (4.75%) (Morgan Stanley's Europe, Australia, Far East Index)	
Small Stock Index Trust (4.75%) (smallest companies on the NYSE)	
U.S. Equity Index (4.75%) (S&P 500 Index)	
Gateway Option Index (no-load) (S&P 100 Index)	1-800-354-6339
Principal Preservation S&P 100+ (4.5%) (S&P 100 Index)	1-800-826-4600
Rushmore Funds	1-800-343-3355
OTC Index Plus (no-load) (NASDAQ 100 Index)	
Stock Market Index Fund (no-load) (S&P 100 Index)	
Vanguard Funds	1-800-662-7447
Bond Market Fund (no-load) (Salomon Bros. Broad Investment-Grade Bond Index)	
S&P Index-500 (no-load) (S&P 500 Index)	
Extended Market Portfolio (no-load) (Wilshire 4500 Index)	

Shares are purchased from stockbrokers. You pay their standard commission plus a management fee of 0.5% to 1% of your invesment. The funds are extremely liquid. Prices as well as whether a fund is selling above or below NAV are listed on Mondays in the *Wall Street Journal*. Similar data are also given in other major newspapers, including *Barron's* and the *New York Times*.

COMMON TYPES OF CLOSED-END FUNDS

➤ CONCENTRATED These invest in portfolios of stocks, bonds, convertible bonds, and foreign investments. That means some are income-oriented,

---

READING MUTUAL FUND QUOTES

(1) FUND NAME	(2) STOCK EXCHANGE	(3) NET ASSET VALUE	(4) STOCK PRICE	(5) PERCENT DIFFERENCE
ABC Fund	NYSE	8.26	6⅜	−22.8
DEF Fund	AMEX	17.18	19½	+13.5

Column 1: The name of the closed-end fund
Column 2: The exchange on which it trades
Column 3: The net asset value (NAV) per share, or the market worth, at the end of the prior week's trading, of the fund's total assets (securities, cash, and any accrued income), after deducting liabilities, then dividing by the number of shares outstanding
Column 4: The market price of the stock at the final transaction of the previous week
Column 5: The percentage premium (+) or discount (−) above or below the net asset value per share at which the shares are selling

---

others growth-oriented. For example, General American and Bancroft hold CVs. The Thai Fund invests in securities of Thailand-based companies.

➤ DUAL-PURPOSE   A special type of closed-end fund, this hybrid has two classes of stocks. Preferred shareholders receive all the interest and dividend income from the portfolio holdings, while common shareholders receive all capital gains that result from the sale of securities in the portfolio. Dual-purpose funds have a set expiration date, at which time preferred shares are redeemed at a predetermined price, and common shareholders receive the remaining assets. They vote at that time to either liquidate or continue the fund on an open-end basis. There are very few dual-purpose funds that trade.

PROS AND CONS

➤ ADVANTAGES   There are two key advantages to closed-end funds: (1) Since the portfolio managers are not involved in buying and selling in order to accommodate new investors or old investors selling shares, they can trade at times they deem best and not upon investor demand. (2) Shares can often be purchased at a price that is below NAV, apparently because the public mistakenly feels that fixed capitalization limits management's ability to take advantage of profitable market opportunities. If you buy at a discount and the NAV rises, you'll have a profit. For example, if a fund has a net asset value per share of $15, but based on the current value of its portfolio, it is priced at $12, it is selling at a 20% discount. To look at it another way, when a fund is selling at a 20% discount, every $12 invested puts $15 in assets to work for you.

With income funds, the yield is determined by dividing the annual dividend by the price of the stock. Thus if the dividend is $1 and shares with a $10 NAV are selling at $9, that $1 dividend yields 11.1%.

☐CAUTION: Keep in mind that the value of closed-end fund shares often moves quite independently of the value of the securities in the portfolio. This may lead to shares trading at a discount to NAV, a distinct disadvantage if you are selling.

FOR FURTHER INFORMATION

GENERAL DIRECTORIES

Individual Investor's Guide to No-Load Mutual Funds
American Association of Individual Investors
625 North Michigan Avenue
Chicago, IL 60611
1-312-280-0170

An annual guide with evaluative data on 300 funds; $19.95.

Donoghue's Mutual Fund Almanac
Donoghue Organization
P.O. Box 6640
Holliston, MA 01746
1-508-429-5930

Annual with data on more than 1,800 funds; $23 plus $3 shipping and handling.

The Handbook for No-Load Fund Investors
P.O. Box 283
Hastings-on-Hudson, NY 10706
1-914-693-7420

An annual directory with useful ideas on how to pick a no-load fund; $38.

Wiesenberger's Investment Companies
Wiesenberger Investment Companies Service
1 Penn Plaza (41st floor)
New York, NY 10119
1-212-971-5000; 1-800-950-1217
$3.95

Mutual Fund Fact Book
Investment Company Institute
1600 M Street NW
Washington, DC 20036
1-202-955-3543
$5

BOOKS AND PAMPHLETS

Warren Boroson, *Keys to Investing in Mutual Funds* (Hauppauge, N.Y.: Barron's Educational Publishing, Inc., 1989), $4.95.

The pamphlets below are free from:

> Publications Division
> Investment Company Institute
> 1600 M Street NW, Suite 600
> Washington, DC 20036
> 1-202-955-3543

A Close Look at Closed-End Funds
What Is a Mutual Fund?
Discipline: Dollar Cost Averaging
How to Explain Tax Consequences of Mutual Fund Transactions

NEWSLETTERS

> *The No-Load Fund Investor*
> P.O. Box 283
> Hastings-on-Hudson, NY 10706
> 1-914-693-7420

A monthly analysis of the no-load funds; $82.

> *NoLoad Fund X*
> 235 Montgomery Street, Suite 662
> San Francisco, CA 94104
> 1-415-986-7979

Monthly; lists top performers by investment goals; $100.

> *Mutual Fund Forecaster*
> 3471 North Federal Highway
> Fort Lauderdale, FL 33306
> 1-305-563-9000

Monthly; ranks funds by risk and profit potential; $49.

> *Telephone Switch Newsletter*
> P.O. Box 2538
> Huntington Beach, CA 92647
> 1-714-898-2588

Monthly; gives timing and switching advice; $117.

> *United Mutual Fund Selector*
> United Business Service Co.
> 210 Newbury Street
> Boston, MA 02116
> 1-617-267-8855

Twice a month; tracks major funds; $110.

Sector Fund Newsletter
P.O. Box 1210
Escondido, CA 92025
1-619-748-0805

Bimonthly; tracks the sector funds; $157.

For sampling of newsletters:

Select Information Exchange
2135 Broadway
New York, NY 10024
1-212-874-6408

SIE is a financial publications subscription agency providing a group of trial subscriptions to various investment newsletters. One trial group comprises 25 different mutual fund services for $18. SIE also monitors performance of advisory publications.

THE INVESTOR'S ALMANAC

Do you love to rummage through flea markets and antique shops and visit auctions? Or perhaps you're looking for an exciting, less traditional way to spend your bonus, small inheritance, or profit from sale of a stock.

There are endless numbers of "offbeat" investment choices if you are willing to be experimental. The Investor's Almanac highlights three of the most timely such choices. These do not come with a guarantee that you'll make a huge killing, but you certainly will have fun learning about a new field, and, of course, you may see a solid return on your investment over the long term.

Before you invest in any one of the three Investor's Almanac selections, spend some time doing background preparation. A suggested reading list is provided. If you know experts in these areas, ask them for advice and additional suggestions. In terms of collectibles in general:

- **Buy only what you like.** If later on the value should fall or if you decide to sell only part of your collection and keep this particular item, you should be left with something you love.
- **Focus on something.** Random collecting tends to be less valuable over the years. Decide on an art form or category. Then try to specialize in an artist, period, craftsman, or country. Unrelated individual pieces have less marketability than a cohesive collection.
- **Set aside a limited dollar amount.** You can revise this amount annually. Don't take all your money out of your money market fund or sell your IBM stock to move into exotic investments. If you should suddenly need cash when everything you have is tied up in baseball cards, farmland, or estate jewelry, you will be forced to sell, and if at the time

prices are low, you will have made a poor investment decision. It's always best to diversify.

- **Buy in your price range.** If your resources are modest to start with, begin small. As circumstances and finances improve, you can always go after more elaborate and expensive items. It is unwise to take a second mortgage to make your first purchase.

ANTIQUE WATCHES

If you're looking for a timely investment for the 1990s, this one is hard to beat. Wristwatches and other pocket timepieces, especially American-made ones, are a collectible whose time has come. But look now; prices are on the way up. At the high end of the market, potential price appreciation is particularly impressive. For example, Elgin Presentation watches (1929–1930) sold for only $650 in 1986 and in late 1989 were hitting the $4,000 mark. A Hamilton Spur of the same art deco era escalated from about $1,000 in the mid-1980s to nearly $5,000.

GETTING STARTED

Don't despair. You can move into the field for less. Look for "character pieces," those with faces of the famous and infamous. They are popular and far less pricey. A good-quality Mickey Mouse wristwatch dating from the 1930s can be purchased for less than $500; an FDR white metal, 12-inch high, standing clock for about $200.

Among the "character" names to look for:
Mickey Mouse
Donald Duck
Cinderella
Snow White
James Bond

Buck Rogers
Tom Mix
GI Joe
The Flintstones

The wristwatch is thought to have made its debut in the 18th century when women wore them as part of a bracelet. We also know that soldiers in the Swiss Army were issued wristwatches before the turn of the century. They became well known only during World War I when American soldiers began wearing them. Until then most men thought wearing a wristwatch was effeminate. When soldiers returned home, companies such as Waltham capitalized on the new market. Other names of the early era are Elgin, Illinois, Hamilton, Bulova, and Gruen.

With the advent of the quartz watch, which led to standardized design and production, older, handmade pieces started to become collector's items. Today those in great demand are pieces with the names listed above, Patek Philippe, Audemars Piguet, Vacheron & Constantin, and Rolexes of the 1930s and 1940s.

Among the most interesting styles to look for are the Rolex "doctor's" watch, with its separate dial for the second hand so the physician could take the patient's pulse; the German-made bombardier watch, worn on the soldier's forearm; the Hamilton Reverso, a 1930s watch whose case can be flipped over; the Curvex, which has a raised, curved case over its face; and the Moon phase, whose dial shows the waxing and waning of the moon.

Collectors new to the field should concentrate on American pieces, which are notably less expensive than European watches. Plan on $1,000 to start. American watches are gaining recognition among European and Japanese collectors, so this is a good time to buy.

WHERE TO BUY

You can find interesting watches and pocket pieces at flea markets, from dealers, and at the auction houses.

For information on sales and an auction catalog, contact:

Hake's Americana & Collectibles
P.O. Box 1444
York, PA 17405
1-717-848-1333

THE PROS AND CONS OF COLLECTING WATCHES

PROS
↑ Hedge against inflation
↑ Potential price appreciation
↑ Joy of collecting
CONS
↓ Fakes and overpricing exist
↓ No income unless you sell
↓ Fair liquidity

GUIDELINES FOR BUYING

1   Buy only pieces that you would enjoy wearing.
2   Look for those with original dials.
3   Make certain that the movement works. Pull out the stem; it should turn easily.
4   Ideally, the dial, case, and movement should be signed by the original manufacturer.
5   Verify the age and condition with an expert.
6   Comparison shop for prices.
7   Always get a 1-year warranty plus a statement of authenticity.

$ HINT: When buying at a flea market or from someone you don't know, get the dealer's name and business license number. Insist on some type of guarantee. If it's in a group setting, such as a large flea market, pay another dealer a flat amount to examine the piece and evaluate it for you.

FOR FURTHER INFORMATION

National Association of Watch and Clock
    Collectors
514 Poplar Street
Columbia, PA 17512
1-717-684-8261

For information on membership, publications, and use of the library.

79

Edward Faber and Stewart Unger, *American Wristwatches: Five Decades of Style and Design* (Westchester, Pa.: Schiffer, 1988), $79.95.

AUTOGRAPHS

What's in a name? Money if it's of someone important. Certain signatures, in fact, are worth a small fortune, like those of Abe Lincoln or Greta Garbo.

Autographs are a collectible that can be enjoyed by young and old, rich and not so rich, urbanites and country dwellers. They are readily available throughout the country, and prices for the signatures of many luminaries are still extremely affordable—but they're trending up, so start your collection now.

The discharge papers that George Washington signed for his soldiers at the end of the Revolutionary War, for instance, sold for about $1,000 to $1,350 in the early 1970s. Now they are fetching a minimum of $3,500. During that same 10-year period, a letter signed by Abraham Lincoln moved from $3,000 to $7,500. But the autographs that have appreciated most since 1970 are those from the movies, proving once again that Hollywood holds its mystique.

GETTING STARTED

You can begin building an interesting autograph collection with just several hundred dollars. It doesn't require a fortune to get started. In fact (according to Christopher C. Jaeckel, vice president of Walter R. Benjamin Autographs in Hunter, N.Y.), even $50 will launch your collection. His catalog regularly includes signatures in the $10 to $75 range. Other dealers report autographs at affordable prices: $5 for a Red Buttons, $25 to $35 for a Jimmy Stewart or Marlene Dietrich. But if you love Clark Gable you'll have to reach deeper into your pocket and come up with at least $350.

TIPS FOR BUILDING A TOP COLLECTION

- *Specialize.* As with most collections, one that is focused is more valuable than a hodgepodge gathering. Zero in on one particular type: movie stars, sports figures, astronauts, scientists, presidents, authors, painters, famous children, etc.
- *Recognize trends.* Not every group is continually popular. Religious figures, as collectibles, have been out of grace, so to speak, for some time. But baseball players, signers of the Declaration of Independence, Napoleon and his generals, and our own presidents seem to pass the test of time.
- *Get a letter.* A signed letter is worth considerably more than just a signature. And a handwritten letter is more valuable than one typed or produced by computer.

WHERE TO BUY

Autographs are sold at auction (see list of houses below), by dealers, and by other collectors. To find a reliable dealer, ask knowledgeable collectors and friends or contact the Universal Autograph Collectors Club for the name of a member dealer in your area.

$ HINT: Write an intelligent letter about a pertinent topic to a celebrity, enclosing a self-addressed, stamped envelope. If you have discussed a subject of interest, you're likely to get back a personally signed letter.

THE PROS AND CONS OF COLLECTING AUTOGRAPHS

PROS

↑ Prices are often low, beginning at $10 to $25.

↑ Autographs are easy to house; you can frame them, hang them up, and watch them escalate in price.

↑ They're an ideal gift.

↑ They are fairly easy to sell.

CONS

↓ Forgeries exist and are difficult for the novice to detect.

↓ A growing number of busy celebrities sign their letters with an automatic pen. Too even an appearance may alert you to this type of signature, but even the pros can be fooled at times.

FOR MORE INFORMATION

Join an association:

The Manuscript Society
David R. Smith, Executive Director
350 North Niagara Street
Burbank, CA 91505

Universal Autograph Collectors Club
P.O. Box 6181
Washington, DC 20044

Order catalogs from leading dealers:

Walter R. Benjamin Autographs
P.O. Box 255
Hunter, NY 12442

Hake's Americana & Collectibles
P.O. Box 1444
York, PA 17405

Abraham Lincoln Book Shop
18 East Chestnut Street
Chicago, IL 60611

RARE BOOKS

Like the stock market, the world of rare books has its ups and downs, its bull and bear cycles. In the late 1970s, much to everyone's surprise, even the experts', it became an overbought field as investors dumped their poorly performing stocks and turned instead to various hot tangibles, including books. The prices of many rare volumes quickly fell. Since 1978, however, the field has been making a steady recovery. That year, Bernard Breslauer, a New York dealer, bought the first complete Gutenberg Bible to come to auction since World War II. The price: $2.2 million! Suddenly rare book collecting was back in the news. The field made headlines again in 1982 when John F. Fleming paid $313,500 at a Christie's auction for a copy of the Declaration of Independence that is now in the Morgan Library in Manhattan.

Although you may not have such deep pockets, you can begin collecting with as little as several hundred dollars. And, as with any investment, the more knowledge you have, the finer the collection you can build, and at the right price.

SUBJECT AREAS TO CONSIDER

- Mystery books
- Cookbooks
- Romance
- Children's books
- Medical books
- Flower/garden books
- Biographies
- Art/architecture
- Books about political figures
- Books from small presses

BUILD A FOCUSED COLLECTION

From the very beginning, *specialize.* A focused collection is always worth far more than the sum of its individual parts. Among the areas to concentrate on are books on a particular subject, preferably one you know something about or love; books by a single author; books by a well-known illustrator; books by a particular printer; books from a certain geographical area or a certain period; and books about a famous person.

$ HINT: When you collect by subject matter, condition is slightly less important than when you buy only rare editions. If there's a chip off the spine it still reduces the value, but less so because the key factors in its value are the subject matter and the facts of publication.

WHAT TO LOOK FOR

There are six key ingredients in building a first-rate rare book collection.

- *Edition.* First editions are always more valuable than subsequent editions.
- *Condition.* The better the condition, the more valuable the book. Aim for the best.
- *Scarcity.* The more difficult the book is to find, generally the more valuable it's likely to be.
- *Completeness.* The book should be complete, with all pages and illustrations.
- *Dust jacket.* A dust jacket adds to any book's value. In fact, it can make the difference between a book being worth several hundred or several thousand dollars.

For example, a first edition of *The Maltese Falcon* by Dashiell Hammett commands $100 to $200, but with the original dust jacket the price leaps to $5,000. A mint copy of Raymond Chandler's *The Big Sleep* with the dust jacket recently sold for $2,500; but without the jacket it's worth only around $500.

- *The author's name.* This, too, can affect price and value. A copy of Ross Macdonald's first book, *The Dark Tunnel*, written under his real name, Kenneth Millar, is worth some $3,000.

WHAT TO AVOID

- Book club editions.
- Incomplete books made complete with pages or illustrations taken from another book.
- Facsimiles of the original.

ABOUT PRICES

It is not easy to determine the correct value of a rare book. Among the determining factors are scarcity, condition, col-lector's interest, the binding, provenance, and the significance of any inscriptions. And since there can be several copies of the same book, prices for individual volumes are set by individual dealers and at auctions. You can get a general overview of prices by consulting *Warman's Antiques and Their Prices*.

Because of the wide range of prices, it is crucial to use a reliable dealer. Before you buy your first book, read about collecting, go to at least one book fair, and attend two or three auctions. Then decide on your area of specialization and write to dealers who carry that type of book. Ask to be placed on their mailing list for catalogs. If possible, visit dealers in your area and join a collectors' club. Learn as much as you can.

FOR FURTHER INFORMATION

▶ BOOKS

Warman's Antiques and Their Prices, edited by Harry L. Rinkler (Willow Grove, Pa.: Warman Publishing Co., 1989).

To find a reliable dealer, send a #10 envelope with 56 cents postage to:

> Antiquarian Book Sellers Association
> 50 Rockefeller Plaza
> New York, NY 10020
> 1-212-757-9395

In addition to its directory, which lists dealers by geographic area as well as by speciality, the Association publishes a calendar of antiquarian book fairs.

> *The Armchair Detective*
> Mysterious Bookshop
> 129 West 56th Street
> New York, NY 10019
> 1-212-765-0900
> Quarterly; $20 per year

Otto Penzler's regular column focuses on one mystery author in each issue and tells where to find his or her books, the price range, how to judge condition, etc.

SELECTED RARE BOOK DEALERS

NEW YORK

Argosy Book Store
116 East 59th Street
New York, NY 10022

Martin Breslauer, Inc.
P.O. Box 607
New York, NY 10028

H. P. Kraus
16 East 46th Street
New York, NY 10017

John F. Fleming, Inc.
322 East 57th Street
New York, NY 10022

CHICAGO

Hamill & Barker
400 North Michigan Avenue
Chicago, IL 60611

Kenneth Nebenzahl, Inc.
333 North Michigan Avenue
Chicago, IL 60601

ENGLAND

A. Rosenthal Ltd.
9 Broad Street
Oxford OI1 3AP
England

Maggs Bros. Ltd.
50 Berkeley Square
London W1X 6EL
England

Bernard Quaritch Ltd.
5-8 Lower John Street
Golden Square
London 1R 4AU
England

For information on small presses that publish special, well-make books, usually in editions of fewer than 500 volumes:

> *Fine Print*
> P.O. Box 3394
> San Francisco, CA 94110
> $49 per year

For information on forthcoming rare book auctions and prices, read:

> *Auction Forum U.S.A.*
> 341 West 12th Street
> New York, NY 10014
> Monthly; $90 per year

BONDS AND FIXED-INCOME SECURITIES

Most people initially feel more at ease with bonds than stocks, perhaps because they know bonds provide fixed income. Yet bonds in recent years have become almost as volatile as stocks. So, even if you have always looked upon bonds as your safe investment, take time to read Part Two and update your position. You'll learn about the safest bonds (those issued by the government) as well as the riskiest (junk or high-yield bonds). In between there is information on how to evaluate bonds, use the rating services, read the quotes in the newspaper, and get call protection.

Part Two covers these broad categories:

- Bond mutual funds
- U.S. Treasury issues
- Savings bonds
- Convertibles
- Municipal bonds
- Junk bonds
- Ginnie Maes and Ginnie Mae funds
- Zero coupon bonds

7

BOND BASICS:
How Corporate Bonds Work

If you want to protect your principal and set up a steady stream of income, corporate bonds, rather than stocks, are the answer. Income is traditionally the most important reason people own bonds, which generally generate greater returns than CDs, money market funds, and stocks. They also offer greater security than most common stocks, since an issuer of a bond will do everything possible to meet its bond obligation. Interest on a corporate bond must be paid before dividends on common or preferred stocks of the same corporation, and it's payable before federal, state, and city taxes. This senior position helps make your investment safer. By contrast, a corporation can and often does decide to cut back or eliminate the dividend on its common stock.

HOW BONDS WORK

Bonds, unlike stock, are debt. They can best be described as IOUs, or as contracts to pay money. When you buy a bond, you loan money to the issuer and in return receive a certificate stating that the issuer will pay a stated interest rate on your money annually until the bond matures. The date of maturity is predetermined and ranges from 1 to 40 years. The interest rate received is called the *coupon rate* and is usually paid twice a year. At the date of maturity you get back the full purchase price, or face value, which is also called *par* and is usually $1,000.

Many investors think of bonds as being stable in price, almost stodgy. Not true. When they are first issued, they are sold at face value, but afterward they move up and down in price, trading in the secondary market either above par at a premium or below par at a discount in response to changes in interest rate markets. Rates and price move in opposite directions: when rates move down, prices move up. You

can therefore make money with bonds in two ways: (1) by earning a fixed rate of interest or (2) by selling at a higher price than you paid.

Note: Although bonds are issued at par ($1,000), in the financial pages of newspapers they're quoted on the basis of $100, so always add a zero to the price; for example, a bond quoted at $108 is really selling at $1,080.

Bonds are issued by corporations, by the U.S. government and its agencies, and by states and municipalities. The latter, also called "munis," are discussed in Chapter 10, high-yield or junk bonds appear in Chapter 11, and treasuries in Chapter 8.

In the last few years, the proliferation of new bond products has kept investors and brokers on their toes. New products such as zero coupon bonds, zero convertibles, and delayed payment bonds (which pay no interest for the first 5 or 6 years), among others, have all been used to raise capital in innovative ways.

Adding to the excitement, the introduction of bond futures, and options on these futures, has turned the traditionally conservative bond markets into areas of intense speculation. For the average investor, this host of new and fascinating products provides endless opportunities, and as long as you exercise caution and investigate carefully, you can make money. The increased action in bonds also opens the door to trading these securities for appreciation, as well as investing for income.

BOND YIELDS

Like stocks, bonds fluctuate in price, their market value changing any number of times a day in reaction to interest rate movements. This is because the only way the bond market can accommodate the changes in interest rates is by changing the price of bonds. If you buy a bond at par ($1,000) and its coupon rate (the annual interest rate bondholders receive) is 10%, you will receive $100 each year in interest payments. If interest rates move up, the same corporation will issue new bonds yielding a higher rate, say 10.5%. The older bonds then fall in price, perhaps to $960, in order to keep the yield competitive. (The yield is the equivalent of 10.5% on the new bond because of the $40 saved when buying it at $960.) If new bonds pay less interest, older bonds rise in price, because they immediately become more desirable due to their higher coupon rates.

Yield is a matter of definition and objective.

➤ COUPON YIELD This is the interest rate stated on the bond: 8.75%, 9%, etc. It is determined by the issuing corporation and depends on the prevailing cost of money at the time the bond is issued.

➤ CURRENT YIELD ON THE PURCHASE PRICE This is the rate of return per year that the coupon interest rate provides on the *net* price (without accumulated interest) at which the bond is purchased. It is *higher* than the coupon yield if you buy the bond below par and *lower* if you buy the bond above par.

➤ YIELD TO MATURITY Since maturities vary and the current yield only measures today's return, the bond market relies on the yield to maturity (YTM). This is the total return, comprising both interest and gain in price. Put another way, it is the rate of return on a bond when held to maturity. It includes the appreciation to par from the current market price when bought at a discount or depreciation when bought at a premium. To approximate the YTM for a discount bond:

1 Subtract the current bond price from its face value.
2 Divide the resulting figure by the number of years to maturity.
3 Add the total annual interest payments.
4 Add the current price to the face amount and divide by 2.
5 Divide the result of step 3 by the result of step 4.

Example: A $1,000 9% coupon bond due in 10 years is selling at 72 ($720). The current yield is 12.5% ($90 ÷ $720). The YTM is about 13.7%.

$$1,000 - 720 = 280$$
$$280 \div 10 = 28$$
$$28 + 90 = 118$$
$$720 + 1,000 = 1,720 \div 2 = 860$$
$$118 \div 860 = 13.7\%$$

The YTM is the yardstick used by professionals, because it sets the market value of the debt security. But to amateurs, the spread—between the current and redemption prices—is what counts, because this appreciation will be added to your income. You get a competitive return while you wait—usually over 8 years because with shorter lives, the current yield is modest: for example, AT&T 3⅞, '94 at 94. That's a current yield of 4.1%, but each year there will be an additional $60 price appreciation per $1,000 bond *if* the bond is held to maturity in 1994.

➤ DISCOUNT YIELD This is the percentage from par or face value, adjusted to an annual basis, at which a discount bond sells. It is used for short-term obligations maturing in less than 1 year, primarily Treasury bills.

It is roughly the opposite of YTM. If a 1-year T-bill sells at a 12% yield, its cost is 88 ($880). The discount yield is 12 divided by 88, or 13.64%.

WHY BUY BONDS

➤ CURRENT RETURN Annual interest payments must be made to bondholders at the stated fixed rate unless the company files for bankruptcy or undergoes a restructuring of its debt. In the latter case, the corporation will issue new securities in exchange for existing bonds. In other words, you are guaranteed an annual income.

➤ SENIORITY Interest on a corporate bond must be paid before dividends on common and preferred stocks.

➤ CAPITAL GAINS If you buy a bond at discount (below $1,000 face value) and you either sell or redeem it at a profit, this gain is taxed.

➤ SAFETY Ratings are available on corporate bonds that help determine how safe they are as an investment. Both Moody's and Standard & Poor's rate bonds on a continuing basis, as explained below.

UNDERSTANDING RISKS

As with all securities, there are some disadvantages to bonds, especially when purchased at par, which is the usual price when a bond is first sold to investors.

➤ LIMITED APPRECIATION Bond values move in the opposite direction to interest rates: up when interest rates fall and down when rates rise. The recent rises and falls in interest rates have sent bond prices moving like yo-yos, so the bond market is no longer the safe harbor it once was. If you buy a bond today and interest rates fall, you'll make a profit if you sell. However, if rates climb back up, you'll lose if you have to sell your bond before maturity.

➤ EROSION BY INFLATION Since bonds have set interest rates and pay back the principal at a future date, they do not offer a hedge against inflation.

➤ CORPORATE REVERSES Corporate financial woes can hurt bonds. Two prime examples: Chrysler and Navistar. Stick with high-rated companies, A or above (see table to right for bond ratings).

➤ FIXED RATE OF RETURN Stockholders have an opportunity to enjoy increased dividends, but bondholders do not receive interest rate increases unless they hold special floating-interest notes.

➤ CALLS Most corporate bonds are sold with a "call" feature that allows the issuer to redeem the bond before maturity. The conditions of a call are set when the bonds are first sold to the public. Bonds are not usually called in if the current rate of interest is the same as the bond's coupon rate or higher.

However, if interest rates fall below the bond's coupon rate, it is likely to be called in, because the issuer can now borrow the money elsewhere at a lower rate. When this happens, you lose your steady stream of income. You can protect yourself from early calls by purchasing bonds with "call protection," a feature that guarantees the issue will not be called in for a specific number of years, often 10. The call protection date is listed in the prospectus and in both Moody's and Standard & Poor's bond guides, available at your library or any brokerage firm.

➤ DIFFICULTY REINVESTING INTEREST Unless you buy zero coupon bonds or shares in a bond mutual fund, automatic reinvestment of interest is seldom available, as with stock dividend reinvestment plans. Therefore, you must find ways to reinvest your coupon payments as you receive them. One partial solution is, instead of

HOW BONDS ARE RATED

GENERAL DESCRIPTION	MOODY'S	STANDARD & POOR'S
Best quality	Aaa	AAA
High quality	Aa	AA
Upper medium	A	A
Medium	Baa	BBB
Speculative	Ba	BB
Low grade	B	B
Poor to default	Caa	CCC
Highly speculative default	Ca	CC
Lowest grade	C	C

Ratings may also have + or − sign to show relative standings in class.

depositing interest checks in a low-yielding savings or NOW account, to add to your shares of your money market fund. As long as the return is close to that of the bonds, you'll be OK. But if the fund pays 7% vs. 11% for the bonds, accumulate enough money to buy zeros or other high-yielding bonds.

➤ LIMITED MARKETABILITY With taxable bonds, there are two major markets: (1) the New York Stock Exchange, where a relatively small number of debt issues of major corporations are traded with daily quotations, and (2) the over-the-counter market, dominated by bond dealers who handle U.S. government bills, notes, and bonds; debt of smaller companies; and special offerings and packages via bid and asked prices.

With small lots (under 25 bonds), the prices can fluctuate widely from day to day or even during a given trading day. The spreads between the offers by the buyer and seller normally run from ⅜% to ½% in strong markets, up to 3% in weak markets, and even more with little-known issues.

$ HINT: Unless you have special knowledge, buy only bonds or debt issues whose trading is reported in the financial press.

WHAT TO LOOK FOR

Determining a corporate bond's value depends on two factors: the credit quality of the bond and the rate of interest. Bonds of a solid, successful corporation are certainly a better investment than bonds of a weaker firm. The interest rate factor must also be considered: if you buy a bond with a fixed rate of interest, say 8%, and rates rise to 10% or 11%, the bond will decline in value. There are three areas to consider when selecting bonds:

➤ QUALITY RATINGS Examining ratings is essential in choosing bonds for investments. Most investors should stick to A-rated bonds or better. True, you can get extra interest each year with lower-quality bonds, but your risks are greater. (See Chapter 11 on junk bonds.)

The ratings are made by independent research services that analyze the financial strength of the corporation, project future prospects, and determine how well the corporation is prepared to cover both interest and principal payments. By and large, the two top services, Moody's Investors Service and Standard & Poor's, reach the same conclusions about each bond.

Watch for changes in bond ratings. When a bond is upgraded, its market price will probably rise (and the yield dip) a bit; downgrading signals possible trouble, so the value will decline. Slight shifts are not too important so long as the rating is A or better.

➤ TERMS Most bonds issued by the federal government and corporations carry a fixed coupon as well as a fixed date of maturity. But there are occasionally serial bonds in which a portion of the issue will be paid off periodically. Usually, the earlier the redemption date, the lower the interest rate, by ¼% to ½% or so. These can be useful if you have a target date for need of money. Serial bonds are widely used with tax-exempt issues, CMOs, and REMICs, which are discussed in Chapter 11.

HOW TO MEASURE BOND QUALITY

A handy formula for determining investment-grade bonds is the number of times total annual interest charges are covered by pretax earnings for a period of 5 years

	BEFORE FEDERAL INCOME TAXES	AFTER FEDERAL INCOME TAXES
Industrial bonds	5×	3×
Public utility	3×	2×

➤ TYPE OF COLLATERAL This is the property behind each bond. There are two basic types: secured bonds and debentures, or unsecured bonds. Secured bonds are backed either by the company's real estate—these are mortgage bonds—or by equipment—called equipment certificates. Unsecured bonds are backed only by the promise of the issuer to pay interest and principal. The seniority ranking becomes most important when default or insolvency occurs. Secured, or senior obligation–backed bonds, receive preferential treatment.

Unsecured bonds or debentures are backed only by the general credit standing of the issuing company. The investor should assess the company's ability to pay annual interest plus the principal sum when due. The projection should consider recent historical ratios and trends and should apply to the *total* debt.

In practice, the ability of the corporation to pay is much more important than theoretical security, because legal obstacles to investors' collecting a bond's security in the event of insolvency are often formidable and time-consuming and can require litigation.

HOW TO READ BOND QUOTES

Unlike most stocks, many bonds have thin markets, trading only now and then. That means that quotes for these issues may not be listed in the newspaper. The trading transactions of bonds that you should consider owning are listed in financial publications: daily in

CHANGES IN BOND RATINGS

UP:	Phillips Petroleum	from Baa3 to Baa2
	Chicago Pacific	from B1 to A3
DOWN:	Quantum Chemical	from Baa3 to Ba2
	Health-Chem	from B2 to Caa

SOURCE: Moody's, May 1989.

major newspapers, weekly in *Barron's* and other specialized publications.

The table on page 91 shows a listing for AAA-rated AT&T with a coupon of 3⅞% and a 1990 maturity date. The last quotation was 93¾ ($937.50), and during the day, the high price was 93¾ and the low 93½, with the last sale at 93¾, unchanged from the price of the last sale on the previous day. Altogether, one hundred $1,000 bonds changed hands.

Each bond paid $37.85 annual interest, so the current yield was 4.1%. Investors were willing to accept this modest return because they knew that in about 2 years, each bond would be redeemed at 100 ($1,000) for a gain of 6¾ ($67.50). The yield to maturity was competitive with that of new issues.

BOOSTING YOUR SAFETY

The key point to keep in mind about investing in bonds is that the longer the maturity, the greater the susceptibility to price advances or declines. If long-term interest rates rise substantially (2 points or more), existing long-term bonds (10–30 years) will drop in price to a point where their yields are comparable to those on bonds issued at the new higher rates. The same process can work in reverse if interest rates drop.

- In general, the shorter the term of a bond, the lower the yield but the smaller the price swings.
- You can protect yourself against price declines to some extent by purchasing high-grade bonds at discount; that is, below face value. This is especially true if their maturity is not far away.
- Rather than having all bonds come due at the same time, own a spread of bonds to come due every year or so. That way you'll periodically receive cash, which you can reinvest to keep the cycle going. Spreading out maturities also tends to average out the effects of price changes.
- Diversify through a bond mutual fund or unit investment trust, which will also help reduce risk.
- **$** IF YOU DARE: To get the highest yields, invest for the shortest time possible while rates are rising. When rates have peaked, sell and buy longer-term bonds to lock in those higher yields.

THE BOND PROSPECTUS

In addition to using the S&P and Moody ratings and your stockbroker's research, you can evaluate bonds on your own by looking at the bond's prospectus. This document details the issue's financial features, the means of payment, what the money raised will be used for, and what analysts think about the issuer's creditworthiness.

The two key points to look for are:

- *The amount of debt the company has already issued.* Heavy debt means that much of the money raised by this issue could go toward interest payments on the company's debt.
- *The bondholder's claim on the company's cash flow.* Is it a first claim or subordinated? You want one with first claim. Often the employee pension plan has a higher claim on revenues than bondholders should there be a default. Note, too, whether the pension plan is funded or unfunded; if a large part is unfunded, discuss the appropriateness of the investment with your broker.

LBOs HIT CORPORATE BONDS

During 1989, the blue chip corporate bond market was severely shaken, and for the most part it has yet to fully recover. Here are the facts, beginning with the RJR Nabisco leveraged buyout (LBO).

The record $25 billion buyout of RJR Nabisco, Inc., by Kohlberg, Kravis Roberts & Co. created chaos in the bond market for both institutional and individual investors. Prices of RJR bonds and those of other big corporations immediately tumbled in price, with some falling as much as 20%. Bondholders suddenly faced a new fear—that other large corporations would saddle themselves with debt to finance leveraged buyouts and restructurings, thereby threatening the value of their existing bonds. The corporations' debt burden would mean that any new bonds they issued would tend to be junk bonds with high yields and low credit ratings. The previously existing bonds, which investors owned prior to the announcement of the LBO, would fall severely in price as soon as the LBO announcement was made. That's what happened to RJR.

Prior to the RJR announcement, the average weekly trading volume in new, investment-grade corporates was about $555 million. Since then it's dropped to $255 to $300 million.

POISON PUTS

As investors began to shun new blue chip bond offerings, issuers devised tough protections to guard against takeover trauma—it was just about the only way they could sell new issues. These new convenants or safeguards, nicknamed "poison puts," permit holders to return their bonds to the issuer at par in the event of a hostile takeover. However, most LBOs and other types of takeovers have the approval of the target company's board and therefore are in effect friendly.

Another version of the poison put allows investors to sell their bonds back to the issuer if the bond's credit rating is downgraded.

An increasing number of companies needing cash have taken to issuing commercial paper and short-term notes instead of long-term bonds. Consequently, there are fewer traditional corporate bonds coming to the market. The feeling on Wall Street since the RJR affair is that no company is too big to be restructured.

☐ CAUTION: Check with your broker to see if any new corporate bonds you may buy are protected by a poison put.

WHAT TO BUY

It is probably safe to purchase bonds of our largest corporations, such as IBM, Exxon, and DuPont. Bonds of most utilities are also considered safe from LBOs. Look into the so-called supranational issuers, such as the World Bank and the issues of Yankee bonds (dollar-denominated bonds sold in the United States by foreign governments. The safest bonds of all, of course, are U.S. Treasury issues.

§ HINT: If you own bonds of an LBO company and you have no appetite for risk, take your losses. Up to $3,000 in losses can be used to reduce your taxable income. If you can bear to wait it out, continue to hold for the high yields.

SPECIAL TYPES OF BONDS

The variety of bonds is almost endless, far too great to cover in a general investment guide such as this. Some of the more interesting ones are described below; foreign bonds are discussed in the chapter on junk bonds. The leading sources for in-depth bond research are given under "For Further Information" at the end of this chapter.

➤ DEEP-DISCOUNT BONDS This type of bond sells at a price substantially below par ($1,000), which means that the bond buyer receives not only the coupon rate but also the dollar appreciation to par at maturity. Some deep-discount bonds are initially offered at discounts; others drop in price because of credit uncertainties or changes in interest rates. These bonds can be extremely profitable, but those selling at a discount in the secondary market because their credit rating has deteriorated are highly speculative.

Example: Cleveland Electric, 8⅜%, due 2012, 80½, for a yield to maturity of 10.4%

➤ EQUIPMENT CERTIFICATES This classical type of bond is issued by airlines, railroads, and shipping companies to finance the purchase of new equipment. The certificate gives bondholders

---

HOW CORPORATE BONDS ARE QUOTED

STANDARD & POOR'S RATING*	ISSUE	CURRENT YIELD	SALES ($1,000s)	HIGH	LOW	CLOSE	CHANGE
AAA	AT&T 3⅞, '90	4.1%	23	94⅜	94	94	−¼

* The rating is not shown in the press.

SOURCE: Barron's, April 1989.

first right to the airplane, railroad car, etc., in the event that the interest and principal are not paid, thereby providing the investor with an added element of security.

Example: U.S. Air Equipment Trust Certificate, 10.3%, due 2009, 100.

➤ FLOATING-RATE NOTES These are notes on which the interest rate changes periodically, often as frequently as every 6 months. The rate is tied to a money market index such as T-bills. This variable interest rate enables investors to participate in rising interest rates, but it is far less appealing when rates are falling. Floating-rate notes, which usually have a 5-year maturity, tend to pay lower yields than fixed-rate notes with the same maturity.

Example: Citicorp Floating Rate Notes, 8.60%, due 1992, 99.8.

➤ FLOWER BONDS Flower bonds, issued between 1953 and 1963 at rates that today are no longer competitive, now are available *only* in the secondary market. They were designed to pay estate taxes after the death of the bondholder. The bonds today sell at a deep discount. You'll have to ask your broker for quotes.

The appeal of flower bonds is that they are valued at full face value at any time even prior to maturity provided they are used to pay estate taxes. To qualify, the bonds must have been purchased by the deceased; they cannot be purchased by the estate and used retroactively. If the portfolio of the deceased, for instance, contains $50,000 worth of par face value flower bonds, they will pay $50,000 worth of estate taxes, *even* if the market price at the time of death is only $25,000.

Note: Consult your accountant prior to purchasing flower bonds in the secondary market.

➤ OPTIONAL MATURITY These bonds can be redeemed by the investor at a variety of specified times, frequently after the first 5 years.

➤ USABLE BONDS These are special types of debentures that are sold with a detachable warrant to buy the common stock by using the bond instead of cash. The maturities for the bonds run from 5 to 20 years; those of the warrant, 5 years. With higher interest rates, most bonds sell at a discount, so the warrant can be exercised at savings of 15% to 25%. As the warrants expire, the demand for the debentures forces up their prices. To speculate, buy the warrants; to invest, buy the usable bonds.

Example: Carolco Pictures
Exercise price: $11.25
Expiration date: 6/1/93
Price of common: $9.60
Price of warrant: $2.00

Selling 1 share of common and buying 1 warrant generates $7.60 ($9.60 − $2.00) in cash.

➤ YANKEE BONDS These dollar-denominated bonds are issued in the United States by foreign governments, banks, and institutions. When market conditions are better here than abroad, these bonds tend to pay higher interest than other bonds of comparable credit quality.

Example: Kingdom of Sweden, 12.75%, due 1997, AAA-rated, NYSE, selling at 117¼.

INTEREST

This is the interest a bond earns between one coupon date and the next. When a bond changes hands between coupon dates, the buyer pays the seller all interest the

---

HOW BOND INTEREST COMPOUNDS FOR $10,000 AT 12% ANNUALLY

TIME	SEMIANNUAL INTEREST	CUMULATIVE GROWTH
6 months	$600	$10,600
1 year	636	11,236
1½ years	674	11,910
2 years	715	12,625
2½ years	758	13,383
3 years	803	14,186
3½ years	851	15,037
4 years	902	15,939
4½ years	956	16,895
5 years	1,014	17,909
5½ years	1,075	18,984
6 years	1,139	20,123
6½ years	1,207	21,330
7 years	1,280	22,610
7½ years	1,357	23,967
8 years	1,438	25,405
8½ years	1,534	26,929
9 years	1,616	28,545
9½ years	1,713	30,528

SOURCE: Robert Lawrence Holt, *The Complete Book of Bonds* (New York: Barnes & Noble Books, 1985).

PICKING THE RIGHT BOND OR NOTE

If you want to invest $10,000 in bonds for 10 years, you have these choices:
- A 6-month T-bill that will be rolled over at each maturity.
- A 2- to 3-year Treasury note that at maturity will be turned into a 7- to 8-year note at a somewhat more rewarding yield *if* interest rates go up.
- A 10-year bond to be held to redemption. This would be best if you expect interest rates to decline or stay about the same.
- A 15- to 20-year bond to be sold at the end of 10 years, best if you expect rates to fall, but the longer the maturity, the greater the risk if rates climb.

---

bond has earned from the last coupon date up to the time of ownership transfer. *Example:* 10 corporate bonds are sold at 79¾. The seller receives $8,046.67: the $7,975 price plus $71.67 interest (not counting commissions).

Alternatives:

1   Schedule your savings so that you will have enough extra money to add to the interest to buy additional bonds or stocks.
2   Buy shares of a bond mutual fund that provides automatic reinvestment of interest earned.

As shown by the table above, compounding makes an enormous difference.

GET CALL PROTECTION

To attract investors for long-term commitments, corporations usually include call protection when they issue new bonds.

When a bond is called, the issuer exercises a right (which will appear in the prospectus) to retire the bond, or call it in, before the date of maturity. This right to call gives the issuing corporation the ability to respond to changing interest rates. If, for example, a corporation issued bonds with an 11½% rate when rates were high and then rates dropped to 7%, it would be to the issuer's advantage to call in the old bonds and issue new ones at the lower prevailing rate. In fact, it is often so advanta-

geous that a corporation is willing to pay a premium over par to call its bonds.

There are three types of call provisions you should know about:
- *Freely callable:* issuer can retire the bond at any time; therefore, it has no call protection.
- *Noncallable:* bond cannot be called until date of maturity.
- *Deferred call:* bond cannot be called until after a stated number of years, usually 5 to 10.

The call price is the price the issuer must pay to retire the bond. It's based on the par value plus a premium, which in theory often works out to be equal to 1 year's interest at the earliest call date. For example, an 8% bond would theoretically have an initial call of $1,080—the $80 being the premium. However, there are many variations. For example, the call price can be specified, or it can be based on a declining scale, with greater premiums given for calling in during the earlier years.

REFUNDING PROVISIONS

This tricky feature permits a company to *replace* an old debt with a new one, usually to reduce its interest expenses. Some bonds offer refunding protection. The new bonds will pay a lower interest rate, a negative for the investor.

A call on a bond is nearly always bad news for the investor. That's because issuers seldom call a bond when interest rates are rising and when getting your money out would enable you to reinvest at the higher rates. On the contrary, bonds are generally called when rates are declining and you would prefer to lock in your higher yield by keeping the bond. So try to purchase bonds with call protection. Check the prospectus or ask your broker.

In effect, call protection guarantees a minimum period of investment income at the stated coupon rate. *Example:* Occidental Petroleum 11¾% debentures, due 2011, are noncallable until March 1996. This means that an investor who buys these bonds in 1989 can look forward to 7 years of receiving an 11¾% coupon.

If you pay any premium above par in buying these bonds, you must understand that this premium reduces your overall yield to the call date (see "Yield to Maturity," page 87).

CALL ALERT

Your broker should advise you about the call status of any bond; otherwise, be certain to ask. Calls are also listed in the bond's prospectus and in Standard & Poor's and Moody's bond guides, available from your broker or at your library. Here's how it looks in the bond dealer's guides or on quote sheets:

Corporate bond: "NCL" means noncallable for life.
"NC97" means not callable until 1997.

Government bond: "8½ May 1994–99" means the bond matures in May 1999 but is callable in 1994.

THE SINKING FUND

A sinking fund specifies how certain bonds will be paid off over time. If a bond has a sinking fund, the company must redeem a certain number of bonds annually before maturity to reduce its debt.

- *Advantage:* Bondholders get their principal back earlier than the maturity date.
- *Disadvantage:* If the coupon rate is high, bondholders will not want to retire the bond early.

If your bond is called in, you will be notified by mail and in the newspaper. You *must* take your money, because interest will cease at the specified time.

SINKING FUND PROVISIONS

Often a corporation borrows millions of dollars in any one bond issue, so quite obviously that amount of money must be available when the bond matures and the bondholders are paid back the full face value. In order to retire a portion of that enormous debt, some issuers buy back part of it, leaving less to be paid off at one time in a lump sum. In the process they shrink the debt. The money used to do this repurchasing is called a sinking fund. When a corporation sets up a sinking fund, it means that it must make periodic predetermined cash payments to the custodial account set up for this purpose.

With a sinking fund, the corporation pays less total interest. With a 25-year issue set up to buy back 3.75% of the debt annually, for example, 75% of the bonds will be retired before maturity. This means that the average life of the bonds will be about 17 years, not the 25 years anticipated by the investor.

A sinking fund adds a margin of safety for investors: the periodic purchases provide price support and enhance the probability of repayment when the bond matures. But it also narrows the time span of the bond, so that there will be less total income for the long-term investor. Sinking funds benefit the corporation more than the bondholder.

CAUTION: Watch out for call provisions on high-coupon utility bonds. An example is the case of Niagara Power 9% of 1997. These are callable from July 1, 1992, at a price of 102.70. Ask your broker to check the prospectus or call the company's investor relations division to inquire about

SELECTED HIGH-GRADE CORPORATE BOND FUNDS

	TOTAL RETURN (MARCH 1, 1989)	CURRENT YIELD (MARCH 31, 1989)
Axe-Houghton Income (1-800-431-1030; 1-914-631-8131)	.20%	8.55%
Bond Fund of America (1-800-421-9900; 1-213-486-9651)	1.30	9.10
Sigma Income Shares (1-800-441-9490; 1-302-652-3091)	1.20	8.20

possible call dates before buying any utility bond.

SWAPPING BONDS

To the serious (and affluent) investor, swapping bonds can be profitable: a loss can reduce taxes; a higher yield can boost income; a wise switch can raise quality and extend the maturity of the debt.

Example: Investor X owns 25 Telex Bonds, 9%, due in 1996—at par ($25,000). They drop in price to 85: (25M × $850 = $21,250). He gets an annual income of $2,250 with a 10.6% annual yield (9 ÷ 85 = 10.6).

Seeking a tax loss, he sells them, for a $3,750 loss ($25,000 − $21,250 = $3,750). This loss can be used against any capital gains he may have. If he has no capital gains, he is limited to a $3,000 capital loss against ordinary income (see Chapter 32).

He then buys 25 Sears 10¾s, due 2013, at 82 and thus replaces his bonds with a better-quality investment while establishing a tax loss.

If you have a sizable loss in bonds, consider swapping if the results are beneficial and help you to meet your investment objectives.

BOND MUTUAL FUNDS

Many of the negatives of bonds can be eased, if not eliminated, by buying shares of bond funds. (See Chapter 6 for details on mutual funds.)

Shares can be purchased for as little as $250 to $1,000, with smaller increments thereafter. Most funds encourage automatic reinvestment of interest for compounding—something that individuals rarely do on their own.

The yields may be a bit less than those available from direct investments, but you get diversification, convenience, and the opportunity to switch to other funds (bond, stock, or money market) under the same sponsor.

- *Evaluate the portfolio.* For safety, choose funds with the most A- or better-rated holdings. For good income, look for those with lower-quality issues (but not too low). For high returns, use junk bond funds (as explained in Chapter 11). A couple of big winners will offset the inevitable losers.
- *Check the performance.* Follow performance over at least 5 years, long enough to include both bad and good years for debt securities.
- *Look for frequent distributions.* A mutual fund that pays monthly ensures a steady cash flow. If this is reinvested, compounding will be at a more rewarding rate. Buy right before the distribution declaration date.

Open-end bond funds commonly called mutual funds, continually issue new shares to sell

CLOSED-END BOND FUNDS

FUND	YIELD	PRICE
High Yield Income	13.4%	$8
MFS Gov't. Markets	12.1	9
Putnam Master Inc. Trust	12.4	9
ACM Gov't. Income	11.0	9
First Boston Income	10.9	8
John Hancock Inc. Sec.	10.4	19
Ft. Dearborn Inc.	9.9	14

SOURCE: Standard and Poor's, *Stock Guide,* May 1989.

to investors. They are available directly from the fund or through your stockbroker.

Closed-end bond funds do not issue new shares or units after their initial offering. Instead they trade on one of the exchanges or over the counter. The capitalization of this type of fund is fixed at the outset, and investors must buy shares either at the initial offering or later in the secondary market or aftermarket. This means that the price of a closed-end fund is determined by two variables: (1) the public's demand for its shares and (2) the value of its portfolio. Therefore, such funds sell either at a premium or at a discount from the portfolio's net asset value. Like their open-end cousins,

---

THREE WAYS TO MAKE MONEY IN BONDS

- *Recognize a bull market in bonds.* It usually takes place before a recession when interest rates begin to drop because the demand for credit is easing up.
- *Recognize when to sell.* Sell just before an inflationary spell when interest rates climb because the demand for money is up.
- *Understand event risk.* Bonds tend to lose their value if their issuer is taken over or if the company is restructured. Buy only those new bonds that have protective provisions.

---

closed-end funds are professionally managed, contain a wide variety of bonds, and make monthly distributions. (See Chapter 6 for more on closed-end bond funds.)

$ HINT: New funds often have high sales fees, as much as 7%—which is part of the offering price. So wait and buy in the secondary market, where you'll pay only your broker's commission. Select a fund selling at a discount.

Closed-end bond funds are listed each Wednesday in the *Wall Street Journal.*

FOR FURTHER INFORMATION

BOOKS AND PAMPHLETS

Marcia Stigum and Frank J. Fabozzi, *The Dow Jones-Irwin Guide to Bond and Money Market Investments* (Homewood, Ill.: Dow Jones–Irwin, 1987).

"How the Bond Market Works"
Standard & Poor's Corp.
25 Broadway
New York, NY 10005
1-212-208-8000

"The Investor's Guide to Bonds"
Robert B. Taylor
KCI Communications, Inc.
1101 King Street
Alexandria, VA 22314
1-703-684-0807

NEWSLETTERS AND NEWSPAPERS

The Bond Buyer
One State Street Plaza
New York, NY 10004
1-212-943-8200
Published daily; $1,480 per year; $7.75 per copy

Investor's Guide to Closed End Funds
Thomas J. Herzfeld, Editor
P.O. Box 161465
Miami, FL 33116
1-305-271-1900
Monthly; $50 for 2-month trial, $275 per year

8

U.S. GOVERNMENT ISSUES

There are no safer securities than U.S. Treasury obligations, which are backed by the full faith and credit of the U.S. government. So if you're looking for a risk-free investment, invest in the federal government. Uncle Sam is continually borrowing money—more than $200 billion every year—and he has an excellent reputation for paying back his debts.

The four most popular government securities for individual investors, in order of maturity, are *EE savings bonds, Treasury bills, Treasury notes,* and *U.S. government bonds.* All four can be bought from any of the Federal Reserve banks or branches or from the Bureau of Public Debt in Washington, D.C., to avoid a broker or bank commission.

THE TREASURY DIRECT PROGRAM

In 1986 the Treasury ended its practice of issuing engraved certificates to purchasers of T-notes and bonds. In its place it began the new Treasury Direct System whereby your securities are recorded by computer. One year later, in 1987, it also included sale of Treasury bills by this method. You receive periodic statements of your account in lieu of a certificate. With this program you are required to supply your checking or savings account number and your bank's routing number (the nine digits that precede your account number), including hyphens. The refund due you after purchasing Treasuries, any interest payments, and money received upon maturity of a security are all deposited directly into your bank account.

When you buy a Treasury, you automatically establish a Treasury Direct account, or you can open one prior to making a purchase by submitting New Account Request Form PH 5182. If you are already holding Treasuries in your bank or brokerage account and wish to transfer them to Treasury Direct, use the same form.

HOW TO READ THE QUOTES

After a Treasury issue is first sold, it then trades in the secondary or aftermarket—not on the major exchanges but over-the-counter. The issues are quoted in dollars plus units of $1/32$ of a dollar (0.03125), with bid and asked prices daily. (*Barron's* lists the high, low, and last price; volume; and yield.) The quotations are per $1,000 face value. The first line in the table at the top of page 98 shows notes due in 1994 with a coupon of 9%, a bid price of 104–21 ($1,046.56), and an asked price of 104–27 ($1,048.44) with a yield of 7.73%. An investor who holds these notes until maturity will get about $419.40 per bond, less the premium of $48.44, for a net of $370.96, when redeemed in February of 1994.

The 12% bond due to mature in 2008–2013 has what is known as a double maturity, sometimes referred to as a call date. Its yield is calculated on the earlier maturity, 2008; however, at the Treasury's choice, the maturity may be extended to 2013. Notification appears in the newspaper, and in some cases by letter. All Treasury issues with this modified call feature can be identified in the paper by the hyphenated listing. A small "n" indicates that the issue is a note rather than a bond.

TREASURY BILLS

Treasury bills mature in 3 months, 6 months, or 1 year and are sold in book entry form, which means that you receive a statement of account rather than an engraved certificate as evidence of your purchase. T-bills, as they are often called, are issued in minimum denominations of $10,000, with $5,000 increments. They are sold at a discount from face value and are redeemed at full face value upon maturity. Because they are guaranteed by the full faith and credit of the U.S. government, investors have no risk of default. In fact, if the federal government goes into bankruptcy, it won't matter what types of investments you have!

T-bills constitute the largest part of the government's financing. They are sold by the Treasury at regular auctions where competitive bidding by major institutions and bond dealers takes place. Auctions are held weekly for 3- and 6-month maturities, monthly for 1-year bills. (Occasionally the government issues a 9-month T-bill.) The yields at these auctions are watched very carefully as indications of interest rate trends. Floating-rate loans, variable-rate mortgages, and numerous other investments tie their rates to T-bills.

➤ FIGURING YIELDS Because T-bills are sold at auction at a discount from face value, there is no stated interest rate. You can determine their yield by using the formula in this box:

HOW GOVERNMENT NOTES AND BONDS ARE QUOTED

ISSUE	BID	ASKED	CHANGE	YIELD
Feb. 94, 9	104–21	104–27	+07	7.73
Aug. 08–13, 12	135–22	135–28	+23	8.24
May 16, 7¼	90–31	91–03	+21	8.06
May 18, 9⅛	111–24	111–28	+24	8.06

SOURCE: *New York Times,* July 8, 1989.

---

advantage if you expect your income to be lower in 1990.

Example: You buy a $10,000 1-year bill in February 1990 for $9,380. Your real yield is 6.6% ($10,000 − $9,380 ÷ $9,380). When you cash in the bill in February 1991, you will receive $620 on a cash investment of only $9,380.

HINT: Use T-bills as a short-term parking place for money received in a lump sum, say from the sale of a house or yacht, as a bonus, or from a royalty check. Think of them as interest-bearing cash.

TREASURY NOTES

These intermediate-term securities mature in 2 to 10 years. They are issued in $1,000 and $5,000 denominations. The $1,000 minimum is usually available only on notes of 4 to 10 years. The interest rate is fixed and determined by the coupon rate as specified on the note. It is calculated on the basis of a 365-day year. Interest earned is paid semiannually and is exempt from state and local taxes.

T-notes are growing in popularity with investors, primarily because they are more affordable than T-bills (which have hefty $10,000 minimums), but also because their longer maturities usually give investors a higher yield. Another plus is the fact that they are not callable, so you are guaranteed a steady stream of income until maturity.

TREASURY BONDS

These long-term debt obligations are also issued in $1,000 minimums, with $5,000, $10,000,

---

DETERMINING THE YIELD ON A 1-YEAR T-BILL

$$\frac{\text{Face value} - \text{price}}{\text{price}} = \text{``annual interest rate''}$$

$$\frac{10,000 - 9,100}{9,100} = \frac{900}{9,100} = 9.9\%$$

Thus a 1-year 9.9% bill will be purchased for $9,100 and redeemed 12 months later at full face value, or $10,000. This gain of $900 is interest and subject to federal income tax but is exempt from state and local taxes.

➤ TO DEFER INCOME WITH T-BILLS Since Treasury bills are sold at a discount price—that is, at less than face value—and are redeemed at maturity or full face value, they do not pay an annual interest. Therefore, in the following example, you would not have to pay taxes until your T-bill matured in 1990. This is to your

$50,000, $100,000, and $1 million denominations also available. They range in maturity from 10 to 30 years. A fixed rate of interest is paid semiannually. The interest earned is exempt from state and local taxes. Unlike T-notes, these bonds are sometimes subject to a special type of call. If a specific bond is callable, its maturity date and call date are both listed in hyphenated form in the newspaper. In the example described on page 98, the 12% bond due to mature in 2013 could be called in at any time starting in 2008.

$ HINT: Because government bonds come in so many maturities, stagger your portfolio to meet future needs and to take advantage of any rise in interest rates.

SAVINGS BONDS

Savings bonds are a safe and extremely easy way to save, and thanks to the upgrading of interest rate formulas, they are a better investment than they were a decade ago. They are backed by the full faith and credit of the U.S. government, are inexpensive, entail no commis-

---

WHERE TO BUY U.S. TREASURIES

U.S. T-BILLS

NEW ISSUES (PRIMARY MARKET)

- Through a commercial bank or brokerage firm. Commissions range from $10 to $45 per T-bill; bank fees are usually in the neighborhood of $15 to $25.
- Through a "noncompetitive" bid in the Treasury's weekly auction at any of the Federal Reserve banks. There are no fees.
- Through the Bureau of Public Debt Securities Transaction Branch, Washington, DC 20026. Call: 1-202-287-4113.

EXISTING T-BILLS (SECONDARY MARKET)

- Through a brokerage firm. Minimum purchase is $10,000 with multiples thereafter of $5,000.

U.S. TREASURY NOTES AND BONDS

- NEW ISSUES: Directly from Federal Reserve banks as described above
- EXISTING ISSUES: From brokerage firms. Minimum purchase is $1,000, although $10,000 is regarded as a round lot. The secondary market for government issues is over the counter.

---

sions, and permit postponement of taxes. Their yields, compounded semiannually, are flexible. They can be bought at banks, at savings and loans, through payroll deduction plans, and through the Bureau of Public Debt.

From 1941 until 1979 the government issued Series E bonds. Starting in 1980 both Series EE and Series HH bonds were issued.

➤ SERIES EE SAVINGS BONDS These pay no coupon interest. Instead they sell for one-half their face value and are redeemed at full face value upon maturity. These are "accrual-type" bonds, which means that interest is paid when the bond is cashed in on or before maturity and not regularly over the life of the bond.

Denominations range from $50 to $10,000. A $50 bond costs $25; a $10,000 bond costs $5,000. The maximum annual investment in EE bonds is $30,000 face value per calendar year per person.

The interest on EE bonds purchased after November 1, 1986, is 4.16% for the first 6

A POTPOURRI OF RATES

INVESTMENT	YIELD/ RATE
6-month CD	8.59%
1-year CD	8.61
Money market mutual fund	8.96
Money market deposit account	6.36
1-year Treasury bill	8.53
5-year Treasury note	8.37
10-year U.S. government bond	8.34
30-year U.S. government bond	8.30
AA-rated 10-year corporate bond	9.20
A-rated 20-year corporate bond	9.35
High-yield (junk) corporate bond	12.00
Ginnie Mae certificate	10.00
Federal Home Loan Agency notes	8.95

SOURCE: *Barron's*, July 3, 1989, and *New York Times*, July 2, 1989.

months, 4.27% for the first year, and then moves up ¼% every 6 months until the fifth year, when it reaches 6%. (EE bonds purchased before November 1, 1986, retain the old 7.5% minimum.) After the fifth year, the interest rate is equal to 85% of the average yield paid on 5-year Treasury notes. On May 1, 1989, the rate was 7.81%. In addition, the government guarantees a minimum of 6% on bonds held 5 years or longer, which protects you against sharp drops in interest rates. You receive the accrued interest as the difference between the purchase price and the face value when you hold the bond to maturity. Interest is exempt from state and local taxes and deferred from federal tax until cashed in. Even then you can further delay paying federal taxes by swapping series EE bonds for series HH bonds.

$ HINT: Because their interest is credited only twice a year, redeem EE bonds right after their 6-month anniversary; if you redeem prior to that date, you will lose several months' interest.

If you still hold Series E and H savings bonds, cash them in or roll them over into EEs or HHs. On the old issues, no interest will be paid 40 years after the original date: before April 1952 for Es, before May 1959 for Hs.

$ HINT: To determine the average rate that applies to a bond, you must add up the different rates for all the periods you have held the bond and divide by the number of periods. Round that number off to the nearest quarter of a percentage point.

➤ SERIES HH BONDS These are available only through an exchange of at least $500 in Series E or EE bonds. They are issued in denominations from $500 to $10,000 and pay 6% over a 10-year period to maturity. Unlike EEs, they pay interest semiannually and are sold at full face value. You get the interest twice a year by Treasury check and, at redemption, receive only your original purchase price. There's a penalty for early redemption when bought for cash but not when exchanged for E or H bonds.

➤ AS A TAX SHELTER When you swap EEs for HHs, the interest—unlike that from savings accounts, money market funds, bonds, and many other investments—does not have to be reported to the IRS annually until you cash them in. By swapping, you can postpone the tax on the

accumulated interest for as long as 10 years. At that time, the amount of the accrued income is stamped on the face of the HH bonds, and from then on, you must pay taxes on the semiannual payments. Fill out form PD 3523 to make the transfer.

$ HINT: Buy bonds at the end of the month to gain more income, because the interest is credited from the first day of the month.

➤ LOCATING LOST SAVINGS BONDS If you've lost your savings bonds, get form PD 1048, an Application for Relief, from the U.S. Treasury. Write down as much information as you have: serial number; issuance date; name, address, and Social Security number of the original owner. Mail the form to Bureau of Public Debt, 200 Third Street, Parkersburg, WV 26106. Even with the partial data, the bureau may be able to locate or replace the bonds.

$ HINT: Use EE savings bonds to finance your child's education or other major expense. Target your bonds to come due in tandem with tuition bills. Until a child reaches 14, investment income earned from assets given by parents to the child is taxed at the parents' rate. (See Special Tips for Paying College Tuition, page 314.) However, there is no tax on income below $1,000 per year. After the child turns 14,

---

EE SAVINGS BONDS

PROS
↑ Safe; principal and interest guaranteed
↑ No fees or commissions
↑ If lost, replaced free of charge
↑ If held 5 years or more, get floating rate of interest with minimum of 6% guaranteed
↑ Federal taxes deferred
↑ No state or local taxes
↑ Market value does not drop when interest rates rise as with other bonds

CONS
↓ Floating rate minimum available only if bond held 5 years
↓ Cannot be used as collateral
↓ Limited purchase: $30,000 face value in 1 year per person
↓ Other vehicles may pay higher rates

HOW SAVINGS BONDS GROW

The more you can allot to savings bonds, the greater your total savings will be when you need them, and the faster you'll reach your savings goals.

SAVE EVERY 2 WEEKS	FOR 5 YEARS*	FOR 8 YEARS*	FOR 12 YEARS*
$7.50	$1,110.88	$1,962.68	$3,366.38
12.50	1,857.60	3,279.12	5,624.72
25.00	3,719.74	6,565.98	11,263.18
50.00	7,439.48	13,131.96	22,526.36
100.00	14,878.96	26,263.92	45,052.72

* Assumes an annual interest rate of 6% (current minimum rate). Rate could be higher.

the income is taxed at the child's lower rate. Consult an accountant about your personal situation.

ISSUES OF FEDERAL AGENCIES

Numerous other federal agencies also issue securities—notes, bonds, and certificates—in order to finance their activities. The agencies most popular with investors are those that promote home building and farming, such as the Federal Home Loan Bank System, the Government National Mortgage Association (Ginnie Mae), the Banks for Cooperatives, and the Federal Farm Credit Bank.

Some are guaranteed by the U.S. government, but most are considered only obligations of the government. Even so, they are regarded as akin to U.S. Treasury bills, notes, and bonds, the highest-quality securities available.

Yields on agency issues are generally slightly higher than Treasuries (because they are not considered quite as safe) but lower than most Aaa- or Aa-rated corporate bonds.

THE YIELD CURVE

A yield curve is a diagram that illustrates the relation between bond yields and maturities. Use it to decide which type of bond to buy at a certain period. It is published daily in the *Wall Street Journal*.

To draw a yield curve, professionals set out the maturities on graph paper on a horizontal line, from left to right, starting with the shortest maturities (30 days) and continuing over days or years to the longest (30 years). Then they plot the yields on the vertical axis and connect the dots with a line that becomes the yield curve.

$ HINT: When short-term rates are more than a percentage point above long-term rates, the yield curve is inverted. A recession typically follows, usually within 9 months.

The curve is used to tell if short-term rates are higher or lower than long-term rates. When short-term rates are lower it is called a "positive yield curve." When short-term rates are higher, it's a "negative" or "inverted yield curve." If there is only a modest difference between the two, it's known as a "flat yield curve."

Generally the yield curve is positive, and investors who are willing to tie up their money long term are rewarded for their risk by getting a higher yield.

Although any fixed-income securities can be plotted on a yield curve, the most common one illustrates Treasuries, from a 3-month T-bill to a 30-year bond.

YIELD CURVES OF TREASURY SECURITIES

This illustration shows the yield curves for 30-year bonds and 3-month Treasury bills for June 29 and July 3, 1989. The curves are very flat because T-bills of varying maturities yielded roughly the same at those times.

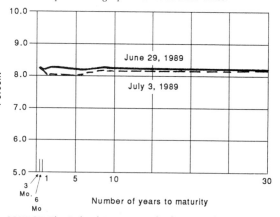

SOURCE: The Federal Reserve Bank of New York, 1989.

FOR FURTHER INFORMATION

Free pamphlets, "The Savings Bonds Question and Answer Book" and "Building Security: U.S. Savings Bonds Buyer's Guide" are available from:

> Department of the Treasury
> U.S. Savings Bond Division
> 1111 20th Street NW
> Washington, DC 20226
> 1-202-447-1775

Basic Information on Treasury Bills is free from your nearest Federal Reserve Bank or:

> Federal Reserve Bank of New York
> 33 Liberty Street
> New York, NY 10045
> 1-212-720-6130

For material on the Treasury Direct Program, call or write your area Federal Reserve Bank or write:

> Bureau of Public Debt
> Division of Customer Service
> 300 13th Street SW
> Washington, DC 20239-0001

Purchase yield curves from:

> United Business Service
> 208 Newbury Street
> Boston, MA 02116
> 1-617-267-8855

> William O'Neil & Co.
> P.O. Box 24933
> Los Angeles, CA 90024
> 1-213-820-2583

9

CONVERTIBLES:
Income Plus Appreciation

These bonds and preferred stocks can be exchanged for a specified number of common shares—almost always those of the issuing company. So investors can have their cake and eat it too. Generally, convertibles trade at prices that are 5% to 20% or even 25% above that of the common stock into which they can be converted. The reason behind this premium over the conversion price is that CVs tend to yield 3% to 5% more than common stock dividends. Thus these hybrids combine the safety and fixed income of bonds or preferred stocks with the potential price appreciation of common stock. They pay higher income than common stock and have greater appreciation than regular bonds. CVs pay a fixed rate of interest or a preset dividend and can be exchanged for shares of common stock of the same company, at a specific price.

There are two types of CVs:

Bonds, secured by the overall credit of the corporation, or *debentures,* a corporate bond that is not secured by specific property, are generally sold at $1,000 each and redeemable at par. They pay a fixed rate of interest, which as a rule is less than the interest on straight or nonconvertible bonds of equivalent quality and maturity.

Preferred stocks are junior to bonds in a corporate liquidation, and their dividends must be paid before any dividends on the common stock are paid. They pay a fixed dividend.

What makes CVs unique is that you can redeem them for the company's underlying stock at a fixed price. This means that CVs offer appreciation possibilities linked to the growth of the company, because as the common stock rises in price, the price of the CV also increases. More often than not, however, the issuing company calls the convertible bonds, forcing a conversion—but never below their conversion value. Bonds are generally called when interest rates fall so the corporation can save money by issuing new bonds at a lower rate.

💲 HINT: If the CV is called when the market value of the stock is greater than the conversion value of the bond, you should opt to convert.

HOW CONVERTIBLES WORK

Company ABC needs to raise capital for expansion but does not want to dilute the value of its common stock by issuing new shares at this time. It also rejects selling a straight bond since it would be forced to pay the going interest rate, which for this example is 12%. Instead, management offers a bond that can be "converted" into its own common stock. Because of this desirable conversion feature, investors are willing to buy the CV bond at a lower rate of only 10%. Bonds are quoted as a percentage of par, or face value, which is $1,000, so this bond is listed as 100. This is the *market price,* the price at which the CV can be bought and sold to investors.

When Company ABC issues the CV bonds, its common stock is selling at $32 per share. Management decides its offering will be attractive to the public if each $1,000 bond can be converted into 25 shares of common. This is the *conversion ratio*—the number of shares of common stock you receive by converting one bond. The *conversion price* of the ABC bond is $40 (divide 25 into $1,000). The current value of the total shares of ABC Corp. to which a bond can be converted is the *conversion value.* With ABC stock trading at $32 and a CV ratio of 25, the conversion value is $800.

On the day of issue, the difference between $40 (the conversion price) and $32 (the current market price) is $8. To determine the *conversion*

CONVERTIBLE BONDS

COMPANY/BOND	CV PRICE OF BOND*	PRICE OF COMMON	PRICE OF BOND	S&P RATING
Automatic Data Processing 6½s, 2011	$41.73	$40	$107	A+
Bank of Boston 7¾s, 2011	23.42	25	114	A+
Browning Ferris 6¼s, 2012	41.00	29	97	A
Hechinger 5½s, 2012	27.84	19	86	BBB+
Humana 8½s, 2009	37.80	26	97	BBB+
Reynolds Metals 6s, 2012	38.25	61	157	BB+
Tele-Communications 7s, 2012	34.00	28	103	B

* CV price of the bond is equal to the price at which you can convert the bond into stock.

SOURCE: Silberberg, Rosenthal & Co., May 1989.

premium, $8 is divided by $32 to yield 0.25, or a 25% CV premium. Another way to figure the conversion premium is to take the price of the bond ($1,000), subtract the CV value ($800), and divide the remainder ($200) by the CV value.

The *investment value* of ABC's CV is an estimated price, usually set by an investment advisory service, at which the bond would be selling if there were no conversion feature. For ABC it is 75.

The *premium-over-investment value* is the percentage difference between the estimated investment value and the market price of the bond. Here the investment value is 75 and the market price is 100, so the difference is 25, or 33% of 75. The premium-over-investment value is therefore 33.

HOW TO MAKE A PROFIT

IF THE STOCK GOES UP

In general, a CV's price will accompany the rise in price of the company's common stock, although it never rises as much. For example, let's say the underlying stock rises by 50%, from $32 to $48. To find the value of the CV bond, multiply the higher price by the conversion ratio: $48 × 25 = $1,200 (or 120, as bond prices are expressed). During the time in which this rise has taken place, the investor has received 10% interest on the bond and has participated in the appreciation of the common stock by seeing the value of the CV bond appreciate by 20%, from $100 to $120.

IF THE STOCK GOES DOWN

If the underlying stock falls in price, the CV may also fall in price, but less so. Let us assume that the

---

TIPS FOR INVESTING IN CVs

■ Buy a CV only if you like the common stock.

■ Avoid CVs of potential takeover companies; you may be forced to convert early.

■ Buy only high-rated issues—BB or above as rated by Standard & Poor's or Ba by Moody's

■ Know the call provisions; if a CV is called too early, you may not recover your premium.

price of ABC, instead of appreciating by 50% to $48, drops by 50% to $16 per share. Its conversion value is now only $400 ($16 × the CV ratio of 25). What happens to the price of the CV? The senior position of the bond as well as the 10% interest rate payable to bondholders serves as a brake on its decline in price. Somewhere between $100 and $40 the safety features inherent in a CV bond become operative, usually at the investment value, which in this case is 75. At 75 the bond's yield will rise to 13.33%.

$ HINT: When you want to make an investment but you fear that the company's common stock is too volatile and therefore risky, check to see if there are any convertible bonds or preferreds outstanding.

TO CONVERT OR NOT TO CONVERT

By and large, holders of CVs should stay with the security of the CV and not convert. Stock markets are uncertain, and prices of individual stocks have been known to fall 50% or even more. Therefore, the holder of a CV, which is senior to the common stock, should surrender or convert only under certain circumstances such as these:

- The company, in a restructuring, makes a tender offer for a large percentage of its

outstanding common stock at a price well above the market price. The CV bondholder must convert to common stock in order to participate in this tender offer.
- In another type of restructuring, the company pays stockholders a special dividend equal to most of the price of the common stock. Here again, the CV bondholder must convert in order to receive this special dividend. In July 1988, USG Corp. paid for each common share outstanding $37 in cash, plus other securities, in a corporate restructuring.
- Corporations in cyclical businesses pay oversized year-end dividends. General Motors, for instance, did this for many years. To receive a special dividend, CV bondholders must convert prior to the ex-dividend date.

CV MUTUAL FUNDS

If you have limited capital or prefer to let someone else make the selections, there are mutual funds that use a substantial portion of their assets to buy CVs and, in some cases, to write options.

When considering CV mutual funds, keep these tips in mind:

- Usual minimum investment is $1,000.
- Shares can be purchased directly from the fund or from a stockbroker.
- Read the fund's prospectus before investing.
- Check the quality of the fund's underlying stocks.
- Convertibles offer a hedge against volatile changes in the stock market.
- Automatic reinvestment of distribution into additional fund shares is available.
- If you invest in a family of funds and your yield declines, you can switch to higher-yielding funds within the family.

HEDGING WITH CVs

For experienced investors, CVs offer excellent vehicles for hedging—buying one security and simultaneously selling short its related security. The hedge is set up so that if the market goes up, one can make more money on the purchase than one can lose on the sale, or vice versa if

---

CONVERTIBLES

PROS

↑ When the stock market falls, CVs do not fall as much as the underlying stock.

↑ You can keep collecting regular income no matter what happens to the stock.

CONS

↓ You do not receive the full price gain when the stock goes up.

↓ You do not earn as much interest as you would had you bought the bond.

↓ When a takeover bid is made, the common stock usually soars in price.

↓ A proposed new takeover deal may eliminate CV holders' rights to exchange their bonds for stock.

↓ CVs are often issued by companies with poor ratings.

LEADING CONVERTIBLE
BOND MUTUAL FUNDS

FUND	APPRECIATION, JANUARY 1 TO MARCH 31, 1989
Dreyfus Convertible Securities (1-800-645-6561)	6.04%
American Capital Harbor Fund (1-800-421-5666)	6.29
Putman Convertible Income Growth (1-800-354-5487)	6.81
Aim Convertible Securities (1-800-231-0803)	5.73
Calamos Convertible Income Fund (1-800-323-9943)	4.28
Value Line Convertible Fund (1-800-223-0818)	4.96
Noddings Convertible Strategies Fund (1-800-544-7785)	4.49
Phoenix Convertible Fund Series (1-800-243-1574)	3.22

the market goes down. Such trading is best in volatile markets (of which there have been plenty in recent years).

Here's an example cited by expert Thomas C. Noddings: The CV debenture carries a 10% coupon and is convertible into 40 shares of common stock. The CV trades at 90; the common at 20. *Buy* 10 CVs at 90 at a cost of $9,000; sell short 150 common at 20—$3,000. Since the short sale requires no investment, the cost is $9,000 (not counting commissions).

- *If the price of the stock falls to 10,* the CV's estimated price will be 72, so there will be a loss of $1,800 ($9,000 − $7,200). But 150 shares of stock can be acquired for $1,500, for a profit of $1,500. Add $500 interest (10% for 6 months), and the net profit is $200.
- *If the price of the stock dips to 15,* the CV will sell at 80 for a $1,000 loss, but this will be offset by the $750 profit on the stock plus $500 interest, for a return of $250.

- *If the price of the stock holds at 20,* the CV will stay at 90. There will be no profit on either, but the $500 interest will represent an annualized rate of return of 11%.
- *If the stock rises to 25,* the CV will be worth 104, for a $1,400 profit, but there will be a $750 loss on the shorted stock. With the $500 interest, there'll still be a $1,150 profit.
- *And if the stock soars to 40,* the CV will trade at 160, for a whopping $7,000 gain, which will be offset by a $3,000 loss on the stock but enhanced by the $500 income for a total of $4,500 on that $9,000 investment—all in 6 months!

Says Noddings: "Selling short stock against undervalued CVs can eliminate risk while offering unlimited gains if the stock advances."

Best bet with hedges of CVs: Try out the "if projections" on paper until you are sure that you understand what can happen. By and large, the actual transactions will follow these patterns. At worst, the losses will be small; at best, the profits will be welcome.

WRITING CALLS WITH CVs

Noddings also shows how to write calls with CVs. This is a conservative way to boost income and, when properly executed, involves minimal risks and fair-to-good gains. Since the CVs represent a call on the stock, they provide a viable base. Let's say that a $1,000 par value CV debenture can be swapped for 40 shares of common; the CV is at 90, the stock at 20; the calls, exercisable at 20, are due in 6 months and carry a premium of 2 ($200) each.

Buy 10 CVs for $9,000 and sell 3 calls. (Since the CVs represent 400 shares of stock, this is no problem.) The $600 premium will reduce the net investment to $8,400. *If the stock jumps to 40,* the CV will sell at 160, for a $7,000 gain. Add $500 interest to get $7,500 income. But there will be a $5,400 loss because the calls will have to be repurchased with a (tax-advantageous) deficit of $1,800 each. The net profit will thus be $2,100.

Warning: Writing calls on CVs is *not* for amateurs. To be worthwhile, this technique should (1) involve a substantial number of shares (at least 300), (2) be done with the aid of a knowledgeable broker who watches for sudden aberrations in price spreads, (3) be initiated with adequate cash or margin reserves that may be needed to buy back calls early, and (4) be undertaken only by individuals in a high enough tax bracket to benefit from the short-term losses.

FOR FURTHER INFORMATION

BOOKS

Thomas C. Noddings, *Low Risk Strategies for the High Performance Investor* (Chicago: Probus Publishing Co., 1985).

Thomas C. Noddings, *Superhedging* (Chicago: Probus Publishing Co., 1986).

NEWSLETTERS

Value Line Convertibles
711 Third Avenue
New York, NY 10017
1-212-687-3965
48 times per year; $445

RHM Convertible Survey
172 Forest Avenue
Glen Cove, NY 11542
1-516-759-2904
50 times per year; $235

10

MUNICIPAL BONDS:
Last of the Tax Shelters

Tax-exempt bonds (also called municipals) are debt issues of states, local governments, and certain public authorities. Their interest is free of federal income taxes; if issued in the investor's state of residence, they are also exempt from local and state income levies. Debt issues of Puerto Rico, Guam, and the Virgin Islands are tax-exempt in all 50 states.

Because of their tax-exempt status, munis pay a lower interest rate than taxable bonds. They are issued in units of $5,000 or $10,000. Most brokers are reluctant to sell just one bond, and many have $20,000+ minimums.

Tax-free income has always been appealing, and municipal bonds are one of the few ways left to achieve this goal since the 1986 tax reform.

SINCE TAX REFORM

For some time, the federal government has sought to reduce the number of local government bonds issued, maintaining that because the interest on these bonds is exempt from federal income tax, the government loses billions in revenues. In 1980 some $47 billion of municipals were issued, but by 1983 the dollar amount had soared to $83 billion, and by 1985 it topped $161 billion. The Fed viewed the mushrooming of munis as providing unfair tax loopholes for the wealthy investor as well as preventing Washington from collecting its fair share of taxes. Consequently, the restrictions written into the Tax Reform Act of 1986 have continued to reduce the number of municipals issued each year.

The 1986 Tax Reform Act made the municipal bond market one of the few legitimate shelters left in town. But it also dramatically reduced the volume and types of bonds that state and local governments can issue. So unless you do your homework, you could be in for some surprises.

CATEGORIES OF MUNICIPAL BONDS

In broad terms, the Act divides municipals into four categories.

▶ GENERAL OBLIGATION BONDS (GOs) Also known as public-purpose bonds, these have not been touched much by reform. The bill maintains the historic tax-exempt status for these bonds, which are sold to finance roads, schools, and government buildings. However, these issues, which are the most conservative of the municipals, are now tax-exempt only when no more than 10% of their proceeds is used by a private entity. Under the old rules, GOs were tax-exempt unless more than 25% of the proceeds benefited a private entity.

General obligation bonds are the most common and generally the safest municipals. They are backed by the full taxing power of the issuer. The payment of their interest and redemption is a primary obligation, so they usually have the highest safety ratings but often the lowest yields.

▶ INDUSTRIAL DEVELOPMENT BONDS (IDBs) As soon as more than 10% of the dollars raised by the sale of a muni is used by a private entity, the bond is classified as an industrial development bond. IDBs are issued by states or authorities to finance construction of plants, buildings, and facilities that are then leased to private firms such as Exxon, K mart, or McDonald's. Because of the backing by major firms, many of these issues carry top ratings.

To permit small investors to participate, brokerage firms offer packaged industrial development bonds in limited partnerships at $5,000 per unit. The income increases with the gross revenues from the tenant. The aftermarket is limited, there's little diversification, and costs and fees tend to be high. Investigate carefully before purchasing.

☐ CAUTION: If you buy an IDB issued after August 7, 1986, beware: the interest earned is treated as a "preference" item and must be added to your taxable income *if* you are required to calculate the alternative minimum tax (AMT). This means that IDBs are suitable for people not likely to be subject to the AMT. The one exception: bonds issued by private, nonprofit hospitals and universities; these so-called 501(c) bonds are not taxable.

$ HINT: As compensation for the fact that the interest income, by its nature as a "tax preference," may be subject to the 21% alternative minimum tax, industrial development bonds pay a slightly higher yield than general obligation or public-purpose bonds.

➤ TAXABLE MUNICIPALS The new law eliminates issuance of tax-exempt bonds for what Congress deems nonessential purposes, such as pollution control facilities, sports stadiums, convention and trade shows, industrial parks, and parking facilities. For the most part, these bonds continue to be exempt from state and local taxes where issued, even though they are now subject to federal taxes.

To win over investors who traditionally purchased Treasury and corporate bonds, the new taxable municipals, or "private-activity bonds" as they're also called, are being conservatively designed to assure top rankings from Moody's and Standard & Poor's. Yields so far are generally 2 to 3 percentage points higher than fully tax-exempt municipals.

➤ PRE–AUGUST 7, 1986, BONDS You can avoid the problems that accompany newly issued municipals by purchasing in the secondary market bonds issued prior to August 7, 1986. These are generally not taxable. A number of firms packaged pre–August 7 bonds, but the supply of older bonds is dwindling now because of aggressive purchases by both bond mutual funds and trusts. As is always the case, the demand is boosting prices and lowering yields.

ZERO COUPON MUNIS

Thanks to the 1986 Tax Reform Act, there's a new twist to municipal bonds that enables smaller investors to participate for a relatively low dollar amount.

"Stripped munis," as the new product is called, remove or strip off the semiannual coupons from a municipal bond and then sell both parts separately—the principal and the series of coupon interest payments. By dividing the bond into two pieces, maturities are created that never existed before in the municipal bond market. Before, bondholders had to wait 20 to 40 years for a muni to mature; zeros mature in less than half that time.

When you buy a stripped muni, you are in essence buying a couponless bond with zero interest, hence the name "zero coupon." You will never receive interest on this bond, but to offset this disadvantage, the zero coupon muni sells at a discount (below par). You receive the full face value ($1,000) at maturity.

And there are tax advantages: if, for example, you buy a zero at $800, when it matures you'll receive $1,000, but there will be no federal tax due on the $200—the profit made during the holding period.

Alternatively, you can buy one or a whole series of coupons. The coupon, of course, costs far less than the bond. And again there will be no federal tax on the earned interest.

$ HINT: Use zero munis to pay for college or plan for retirement or other distant obligation. Place them in your child's

---

PRE–AUGUST 7, 1986, BONDS

PROS
↑ Virtually the only tax shelter available
↑ Higher yields than Treasury bonds in many cases
↑ Excellent ratings
↑ Especially valuable in states with high local taxes

CONS
↓ Dominated by institutional investors
↓ Limited market if selling bonds before maturity
↓ Lower tax rates reduce attractiveness

STRIPPED MUNIS

PROS
↑ Can time your balloon payment
↑ No problem of where to reinvest income
↑ Noncallable
↑ Know exactly what you will receive
↑ Shorter maturity dates than regular munis

CONS
↓ Interest is locked in; yield could rise
↓ Should be held to maturity
↓ Slim secondary market at present

---

name. There is no federal tax on zero munis.

Bonds used for stripping are noncallable, so you are assured of your position. But to reap full benefits, you should plan to hold these securities until maturity. Talk to your accountant or broker first—the details vary from issue to issue. Strips are sold by Salomon Brothers as M-Cats, by Goldman Sachs as Municipal Receipts, and by Morgan Stanley as MBears.

CORPORATE-BACKED MUNICIPALS

The recent upheaval in the corporate bond market (because of the rash of takeovers and buy-backs) has begun to impact on the muni market—in particular on industrial development and pollution control bonds, also known as IDBs. These bonds were marketed until 1986, when Congress curbed their sale through the Tax Reform Act. The bonds were issued by municipalities but backed by corporations, not by governments.

According to Van Kampen Merritt, Inc., the Naperville, Ill., muni bond specialists, Philip Morris, Dow Chemical, Pillsbury, Exxon, Bethlehem Steel, and International Paper are among the many companies that have backed municipals. Proceeds of these tax-exempt bonds have gone to finance pollution control projects and other endeavors believed to be good for the local economy.

When these corporations become involved in buy-outs and are burdened with debt, their bond ratings are frequently suspended or dropped below investment grade. Kroger bonds, for ex-

ample, were downgraded by both Moody's and S&P as a result of that company's restructuring. Included were $125 million in Kroger-backed tax-exempts, among them some Hilliard, Ohio, municipals.

$ HINT: Many times investors are unaware that they own IDBs. Make certain you know the tax status of your bonds.

CONVERTIBLE MUNICIPALS

You're now familiar with zero coupon Treasuries—STRIPS—yet there is another variation on the theme—zero coupon convertible municipal bonds. Like other zeros (see Chapter 11), they sell at a deep discount to face value. Their unique feature, however, is that at a certain time they convert into regular interest bonds.

For example, a 25-year zero muni bond pays out no interest during the first 10 years. Then in the 10th year it converts into a regular bond. At that point the investor starts to receive 10% interest (in cash) and continues to receive it for the remaining 15 years. At maturity, the bond returns the full face value of $1,000. Both appreciation and income are free of federal income tax.

There are two major drawbacks, however: states may impose tax on the imputed interest, and a zero muni can be called in early.

$ HINT: Buy only zero munis that are issued in your own state, so that interest is tax-free, and that are noncallable or can be called only *after* they start paying out cash interest. This way you'll capture the most interest.

PREREFUNDED BONDS

These high-coupon bonds are quasi-tax-free Treasuries. They come into existence when municipalities issue new bonds at lower rates and invest this money in Treasury bonds. The money from the sale of the second bond is used to pay off the old bonds, usually at the first call date. The first bonds, then, are prerefunded. They have AAA ratings and higher yields than many other munis.

Their only negative is that they will be called within a matter of years.

Example: New York State Urban Development 8⅞s, yield 7.3%, due to be called in 1996.

LEADING SINGLE-STATE MUNICIPAL BOND FUNDS

STATE	TAX RATE	MUTUAL FUND	YIELD (APRIL 1989)	TOTAL RETURN (APRIL 1989)
Minnesota	14%	Franklin Minnesota Insured (1-800-632-2180)	6.79%	8.83%
New York	13	Putnam New York (1-800-225-1581)	7.04	−0.08
West Virginia	13	MFS Managed West Virginia (1-800-225-2606)	6.78	0.80
California	11	MFS Managed California (1-800-225-2606)	6.17	0.40
Oregon	10	Oregon Municipal Bond Fund (1-503-295-0919)	5.48	0.62

SINGLE-STATE BONDS

If you live in a high-tax state, look for munis issued by your own state and local governments. You can add as much as 1½ percentage points to your yield. Among the highest-taxed states are California, Connecticut, Massachusetts, Minnesota, and New York. Single-state unit trusts and mutual funds are listed in the box above.

Funds that specialize in single-state bonds must purchase bonds from a smaller pool than regular bond funds and consequently have less choice when it comes to bond grade, type, and maturity. This adds an element of risk to these bonds.

$ HINT: If you pay high state and/or local income taxes, look into single-state bond funds that invest only in your state. Whether you select a bond mutual fund or a unit trust, read the prospectus first and determine the minimum rating set by management. Beware of any fund with a large portion of its holdings in issues with a B rating. (See Chapter 11, on junk bonds.)

YOUR TAXES AND MUNICIPALS

One of the unfortunate fallouts of tax reform that affects a great many investors stems from the provisions covering the alternative minimum tax (AMT). According to the terms of the 1986 Tax Reform Act, interest earned on all newly issued IDBs, with the sole exception of those issued by private, nonprofit hospitals and universities, called 501(c) bonds, is subject to a 21% AMT for individuals and a 20% AMT for corporations, if, of course, they are subject to the AMT. Check with your accountant.

$ HINT: Municipal bond income is taxable under certain circumstances for some retirees. Up to half of a retiree's benefits can be taxed if municipal bond interest income plus adjusted gross income plus half of Social Security payments is more than $32,000 for couples or $25,000 for singles. Ask your accountant.

- In a state that has local or state income taxes, the interest on municipal bonds issued in that state is exempt from these taxes as well as the federal income tax. Thus if you live in New Jersey, buy bonds issued there.

BUYING MUNICIPAL BONDS

- If, after calculating your tax rate, you find that municipals turn out to be advantageous, start with general obligation bonds. These bonds typically yield less

FEDERAL EQUIVALENT YIELDS FOR 1989

This table compares taxable and tax-free yields. You can use it to see the effect of tax-free investing in your tax bracket. This table is based on 1988 federal and state tax-rate bracket amounts and personal exemption amounts. New brackets reflecting inflation adjustments will be available in late 1989. Income tax brackets assume two exemptions for joint income and one exemption for single income.

TAXABLE INCOME, SINGLE RETURN	$0–17,850	$17,851–43,150 or over $100,760*	$43,151–$100,760
TAXABLE INCOME, JOINT RETURN	$0–29,750	$29,751–71,900 or over $171,650*	$71,901–$171,650
TAX BRACKET	15%	28%	33%

Tax-free Yields (%)	Taxable Yield Equivalents (%)		
3.5	4.12	4.86	5.22
4.0	4.71	5.56	5.97
4.5	5.29	6.25	6.72
5.0	5.88	6.94	7.46
5.5	6.47	7.64	8.21
6.0	7.06	8.33	8.96
6.5	7.65	9.03	9.70
7.0	8.24	9.72	10.45
7.5	8.82	10.42	11.19
8.0	9.41	11.11	11.94
8.5	10.00	11.81	12.69
9.0	10.59	12.50	13.43
9.5	11.18	13.19	14.18
10.0	11.76	13.89	14.93
10.5	12.35	14.58	15.67
11.0	12.94	15.28	16.42
11.5	13.53	15.97	17.16

* Taxpayers with taxable income over this amount will lose the benefit of any additional personal exemption by the imposition of a 5% surcharge. The range over which this surcharge applies extends $11,200 for each exemption.

SOURCE: Benham Capital Management Group, July 1989.

---

than riskier municipals because they are the most conservative.

- All municipals are sold with legal opinions attached to their offering circulars. These will tell you if the issue is tax-free or not.
- As with all investments, the number one checkpoint is *quality,* best indicated by the ratings set by Moody's and S&P.

For investments, buy only bonds with A ratings. They are safe, and in most cases their yields will be only slightly lower than those of poor-quality bonds.

For speculations, a Baa rating involves as much risk as anyone seeking income should take. If you want to gamble, do not buy tax-exempt bonds unless you are very experienced and very rich. (For lower-rated bonds, see Chapter 11, on junk bonds.)

Once in a while, you may be asked to buy unrated issues: those from municipalities that are so small or have such modest debt that they have never been rated. If you personally know the

10 TAX-EXEMPT BOND FUNDS	
FUND	YIELD (APRIL, 1989)
Calvert Tax-free Long Term (1-800-368-2748)	6.85%
Dreyfus Intermediate Tax-exempt (1-800-645-6561)	7.03
Fidelity Municipal Bond (1-800-544-6666)	7.09
Financial Tax-free Income (1-800-525-8085)	7.21
New York Muni Fund (1-212-608-6864)	7.12
T. Rowe Price Tax-free Intermediate (1-800-638-5660)	5.81
Scudder Managed Municipal (1-800-225-2470)	7.00
Stein Roe Intermediate Municipal (1-800-621-0320)	6.54
Value Line Tax-exempt Fund (1-800-223-0818)	7.29
Vanguard Long-Term Municipal (1-800-662-7447)	7.36

community and its officials, these can be viable investments, but keep the maturities short, because you will have difficulty selling in a hurry.

CHECKPOINTS FOR TAX-EXEMPTS

➤ MATURITY DATE   For bonds with the same rating, the shorter the maturity, the lower the yield and the greater the price stability. Unless you plan to buy municipals regularly, it is usually prudent to stick to those with maturities of less than 10 years. In many cases, these will be older bonds selling at a discount. Select maturities according to your financial needs and time schedule. If you plan to retire 8 years from now, pick a discount bond that will mature at that time. Munis range from 1 month (notes) to 30 years.

➤ MARKETABILITY   The most readily salable municipals are general obligation bonds of state governments and revenue bonds of large, well-known authorities. Smaller issues have few price quotations, and the cost of selling, especially in odd lots, can be high.

➤ CALL PROVISION   Larger issues usually permit the bonds to be called—redeemed before maturity—at a price above par. With older low-coupon issues, there's no problem, because they will be selling below par. But with high-coupon issues, when interest rates decline, watch out.

If a bond is trading at 115, it will be callable at 105, and it will pay the issuer to retire the bonds and refinance at a lower interest rate.

➤ YIELD DISPARITIES   If you buy more than 10 bonds, shop around. It's best to buy from your broker's inventory; but even if you do, you will find wide differences between munis of comparable ratings.

➤ TYPES OF BONDS   Prior to 1983 there were two types of tax-free bonds: *bearer, or nonregistered, bonds* whose holders detached coupons and sent them in or went through a bank to receive the interest, and *registered bonds* with the name and owner identified on the face of the certificate or, more likely, in a central filing

BONDS SUBJECT TO PERSONAL ALTERNATIVE MINIMUM TAX

- General obligation issues in which more than 10% of the proceeds is used by a private entity
- Single- and multifamily housing bonds
- Student loan bonds
- Bonds financing small industrial development projects
- Bonds for airports and other ports not owned by local governments

system of the issuer. Today, all munis are issued in registered form. They therefore cost less to handle and usually eliminate printed certificates. A registered bond can be transferred to another owner *only* when endorsed by the registered owner. Bearer bonds are actually nonnegotiable instruments and payable only to the bearer or holder. They do not require a legal endorsement.

➤ BROKER'S REPUTATION If you get a hard sell on tax-exempts, especially by phone, be *very* cautious. Do business only with your regular broker, or one you trust.

➤ SERIAL MATURITIES Unlike most corporate bonds, which usually have the same redemption date, municipals often mature serially: a portion of the debt comes due each year until the final redemption. Select maturities to fit future needs: college tuition, retirement, etc.

HINT: If you're in the 28% tax bracket, an 8% tax-free municipal is equal to an 11% federally taxed bond.

MUNICIPAL BOND MUTUAL FUNDS

For small investors, one of the best ways to buy municipals is through a mutual fund. Mutual funds provide diversification (by type, grade, coupon, and maturity), continuous professional management, the opportunity to add to your portfolio with relatively small dollar amounts, the ability to switch to other funds under the same sponsorship, and, most important, prompt reinvestment of interest to buy new shares and benefit from compounding.

Unless you have over $10,000 and can watch the market, a fund is the best way to invest in munis. The yields may be lower than you could obtain with individual bonds, but you won't be tempted to spend the income if you have the fund automatically reinvest it. Minimum investments are generally $1,000. (See Chapter 6 for details on selecting mutual funds.)

In a fund that is open-ended the portfolio contains bonds with varying maturities. The manager continually buys and sells bonds in order to improve returns, switching from short to long-term maturities when yields are high and doing the opposite when yields decline. When interest rates shift quickly, some funds do extremely well; some do not. Keep in mind that your income from the fund will fluctuate, unlike that from an individual bond or a unit trust (explained next), where the yield is locked in.

MUNICIPAL BOND UNIT TRUSTS

These are closed-end funds with fixed portfolios of municipal bonds that remain in the trust until maturity, unless they are called. The trust aims to lock in the highest yield possible with good-quality issues at the time of the initial offering. Each trust has a limited number of shares for sale, but new trusts are continually being brought to the market. Sponsors also buy back existing units from investors who want to sell before the trust matures. The units are registered in the name of the investor, and monthly, quarterly, or semiannual checks are mailed out to the holder. A handful of unit investment trusts have reinvestment privileges.

INSURED MUNICIPAL BOND MUTUAL FUNDS	
FUND	YIELD (APRIL 1989)
Vanguard Muni Bond Insured Long Term (1-800-662-7447)	7.38%
Merrill Lynch Muni Insured Portfolio (1-609-282-2800)	7.25
American Capital Tax-exempt Insured (1-800-847-5636)	6.61
Dreyfus Insured Tax-exempt Bond Fund (1-800-645-6561)	6.84
Van Kampen Merritt Insured Tax-free Income (1-800-225-2222)	6.47

MUTUAL FUND VS. UNIT TRUST

- A managed mutual fund is generally a better investment for people who expect to sell in less than 10 years. The shares react quickly to fluctuating interest rates. Check the 1-, 5-, and 10-year performance records of several before investing.
- Unit trusts are best for long-term holdings, especially when the initial yield is high enough that you want to lock it in.

Most provide income for a limited period—3, 5, 10, 20, or 30 years.

When the bonds mature, are sold (rarely), or are called, the principal is returned to the unit holders as a return of capital. If the sponsor feels a bond is endangering the trust's interest, it can be sold and proceeds paid out. Unit trusts, of course, are vulnerable to the risks of rising interest and early call on bonds in the portfolio.

Units can be sold in the secondary market, but doing so entails a commission. If interest rates have fallen, you could make a profit, but if they've gone up, you may not get back your original investment. Unit trust prices are based on the price of the securities in the portfolio and are determined either by the sponsor or by an independent evaluator. Nuveen, for instance, which has a number of trusts, sets the price on a daily basis. Although unit prices are not given in the newspaper, you can call the sponsor for up-to-date quotes.

There are two kinds of trusts: general and state. General trusts include bonds from various states and territories, while state trusts have bonds only from a single state, hence the name "single-state unit trusts." Income is generally free from state and local taxes in the issuing state as well as from federal taxes.

Unit trusts are usually sold in $1,000 units and have a one-time sales charge that typically ranges from 2% to 5% plus annual fees in the neighborhood of 0.15%. Both these costs are factored into the yield. Mutual funds, by contrast, may be subject to a sales charge ("load") or not ("no load").

MUNICIPAL BOND INSURANCE

Years ago, investors never doubted that a municipal bond issuer would pay the annual interest and pay back the principal. Then along came the default of the Washington Public Power System. Now an increasing number of tax-free issues, as well as mutual funds and trusts, offer insurance for additional peace of mind. According to the Chicago-based bond counsel firm of Chapman & Cutler, fewer than 1% of the municipals issued since the Great Depression have defaulted. Of those defaults, approximately 77% occurred with bonds issued to finance revenue-producing facilities such as utilities, bridges, and nuclear power plants.

To insure its bonds, the issuer pays an insurance premium ranging between 0.1% and 2% of total principal and interest. In return, the insurance company will pay the principal and interest to the bondholders should the issuer default. Generally, policies for new issues cannot be canceled, and the insurance remains active over the lifetime of the bond. With a bond fund or unit trust, the insurance is generally purchased for the entire portfolio. The oldest insurers are the American Municipal Bond Assurance Corp. (AMBAC) and the Municipal Bond Insurance Association (MBIA). Both are rated Aaa by Moody's and AAA by Standard & Poor's.

Once a bond is insured, it is given an AAA rating by S&P *even if the bond originally had a BBB rating.* So remember that if you are

INTEREST RATE RISK

Interest rate risk is a greater problem than defaults for municipal bonds. According to the Value Line Investment Service, a 20-year bond with an interest coupon of 9% that is trading at par declines in value by 8.6% when interest rates rise 1 percentage point; it rises in value by 9.9% when rates decline 1 percentage point. This volatility increases as the bond's maturity lengthens and its coupon rate declines.

purchasing an AAA insured bond, it may really be a BBB bond with insurance.

Insured municipal bonds pay lower yields, usually 0.1 to 0.5 percentage points less than comparable uninsured bonds. If the insurer's rating drops, so do the ratings of all the issues that the company has insured. This happened to the $6 million of tax-exempts insured by the Industrial Indemnity Co. after S&P dropped its rating of the parent company, Crum & Forster (a division of Xerox Corp.), from AAA to AA.

$ HINT: Insurance does not protect you against market risks: if interest rates go up, the value of bonds still goes down.

FOR FURTHER INFORMATION

''Muni Week''
1 State Street Plaza
New York, NY 10004
1-212-943-8200
Weekly; $525 per year; $14 per copy

11 THE WORLD OF BONDS: Maes, Junk, and Zeros

THE MAE FAMILY

High yields, safety, and convenience, that's what the various mortgage-backed securities in the Mae family offer. These securities, which are shares in pools of secured mortgages, are often called *pass-throughs* because the sponsor who packages the loans passes through the income (minus a modest fee) directly to investors. Payments are monthly, and yields tend to be 1.5+ points higher than those on comparable Treasury bonds, largely because the monthly payments include principal as well as interest. In this respect the Mae family does not behave like regular bonds, which provide a return of principal upon maturity. Instead you receive monthly checks that reflect both interest *and* principal. It is important to understand this distinction. Many investors mistakenly believe that these monthly checks are interest only. They are both interest *and* part payment of principal.

The pass-through technique allows individual investors to share the income derived from monthly mortgage payments and prepayments. They are similar to mutual funds in that investors do not own one particular mortgage but pieces of many mortgages.

Ginnie Maes are the only securities, other than U.S. Treasury issues, that carry the direct full faith and credit guarantee of the U.S. government. Others in the Mae group, to be described shortly, carry an indirect guarantee.

GINNIE MAEs

"Ginnie Mae" stands for the Government National Mortgage Association (GNMA), a wholly owned corporation of the U.S. government that functions as part of the Department of Housing and Urban Development. The objective of Ginnie Mae is to stimulate housing by attracting capital and guaranteeing mortgages. A GNMA certificate represents a portion of a pool of 30-year FHA- or VA-insured mortgages. The GNMA provides payment of interest and principal on a monthly basis.

When a homebuyer takes out a mortgage, the house is pledged as collateral. The bank or savings and loan pools this loan with others of similar terms and rates, thus creating a package of mortgages worth $1 million or more. Ginnie Mae reviews the mortgages to make certain they meet certain standards and then assigns a pool number. Stockbrokers and others sell pieces of this pool, called certificates, to the public.

Homebuyers then make their payments (interest and principal) to the bank, which deducts a handling fee as well as a Ginnie Mae insurance fee. The rest of the money is "passed on" to the investors from the mortgage bankers.

Because GNMA certificates carry the guarantee of the U.S. government, they have made mortgage investments especially safe. And since certificates can be traded in the secondary market, they also offer liquidity.

The minimum investment for a GNMA is $25,000, with $5,000 increments thereafter. Monthly interest is considered ordinary income and is taxed, whereas monthly principal payments are considered a return of capital and are exempt from taxes. Monthly payments are *not* uniform—they are based on the remaining principal in the pool. As homeowners make their mortgage payments, the mortgage pool gets paid down, and although you receive the stated coupon interest, it is on a declining amount of debt. In other words, each month the proportion of interest received is slightly less and the proportion of principal slightly more. Over the long term, GNMAs are therefore self-liquidating. When the pool of mortgages is paid in full by homeowners, that's it. You don't receive a lump payment or a return of face value as you do

117

with a zero or straight bond. *Note:* When interest rates fall, homeowners pay off their mortgages and refinance at lower rates. This means your Ginnie Mae is "called in" quickly.

You can purchase Ginnie Maes for less than $25,000 through mutual funds (discussion follows), or you can buy older Ginnie Maes in the secondary market. Older Ginnie Maes have been partially paid down and are usually bid down in value to compensate for the declining stream of income.

☐CAUTION: Ads for Ginnie Maes and their mutual funds often claim they are totally safe and 100% government guaranteed. This is not true. Ginnie Maes are *not* completely risk-free.

- The government does *not* guarantee the yield.
- The government does *not* protect investors against declines in either the value of the fund's shares or the yield.
- The government, however, *does* indeed protect investors against late mortgage payments as well as foreclosures. If homeowners default, you will still receive payments on time.

$ HINT: If you're considering Ginnie Maes, bear in mind that the average 30-year Ginnie Mae is repaid in about 12 years.

GINNIE MAE MUTUAL FUNDS

For investors who don't want to invest $25,000, Ginnie Maes are available through unit investment trusts and mutual funds for as little as $1,000. In a unit trust, once the trust's portfolio is assembled, it's set. The portfolio manager cannot make adjustments, so if interest rates drop, you face exactly the same dilemma you do in owning a GNMA certificate. Unit investment trusts are explained in greater detail in Chapter 10.

A Ginnie Mae mutual fund is not a pass-through security like the certificates. The fund itself receives interest and principal payments from the certificates in its portfolio. You then own shares in the fund, which in turn pays you dividends. The market value of your shares fluctuates daily.

☐CAUTION: The fund's yield is not fixed, nor is it guaranteed. If interest rates fall, as mortgages are paid off, principal payments

GNMA ISSUES

RATE	BID	ASKED	YIELD
8.00%	$87-11	$87-15	10.02%
8.50	90-01	90-05	10.12
9.00	92-25	92-29	10.21
9.50	95-08	95-12	10.35
10.00	97-28	98	10.46
10.50	100-12	100-16	10.59
11.00	102-18	102-22	10.76
11.50	104-11	104-15	10.99
12.00	105-28	106	11.26
12.50	107-15	107-21	11.50
13.00	108-24	108-30	11.79
13.50	109-23	109-29	12.13
14.00	110-12	110-16	12.53
15.00	111	111-04	12.02

SOURCE: Wall Street Journal, May 2, 1989.

are received by the mutual fund. The manager then must reinvest this money. If interest rates are declining, your yield will fall also.

One advantage of a fund over a unit trust is that portfolio managers can shift the maturities of the certificates in the fund to reflect changing economic conditions. For example, if it appears that inflation is returning, they will move to shorter maturities to protect the return. And in certain types of funds, part of the portfolio can be shifted into other types of investments. The Kemper U.S. Government Securities Fund, for instance, also invests in intermediate Treasury bonds.

An advantage the funds have over straight

HIDDEN RISKS IN GINNIE MAEs FOR RETIREES

- If you spend each monthly check, you are using up both interest and principal.
- You may want to reinvest your monthly payments. Finding a better rate with equal safety is often difficult.
- Monthly checks are not all the same, which is worrisome if you need a set dollar amount to live on.

Ginnie Mae certificates is that they will reinvest the principal payments received from homeowners in more fund shares if you so request.

Funds are best for investors who want high current income rather than capital appreciation. Plan on a long-term play, since these funds are volatile and subject to market risks.

⬜ CAUTION: In seeking high yields, many GNMA funds use almost speculative strategies, investing in put and call options, interest rate futures contracts, etc. Others invest in mortgage-related securities that do not carry the full government guarantee. Check the prospectus, and remember that a fund's shares may go down in value as well as its yield.

Ginnie Mae funds are offered by many of the large family funds, including Vanguard, Lexington, Franklin, Kemper, Fidelity, and Shearson. Their yields ranged from 7.96% to 9.57% as of July 10, 1989.

For every 1% change in interest rates, the value of the average Ginnie Mae fund will move in the opposite direction almost 6%. Therefore, Ginnie Maes are well suited to tax-deferred portfolios, where regular contributions over a period of time cushion the negative effect of price swings.

FREDDIE MACs

The Federal Home Loan Mortgage Corp., known as Freddie Mac, issues its own mortgage-backed securities, which are called participation certificates, or PCs. Freddie deals primarily in conventional single-family mortgages, which are backed by the Veterans Administration, but it also resells non-government-backed mortgages. If homeowners do not make their mortgage payments on time, you will receive your monthly payment on time, but you may have to wait several months to a year to receive your share of the principal. A key difference between Freddie and Ginnie is that Ginnie Maes are backed by the U.S. government; Freddies are guaranteed by private mortgage insurance. Even though they're not quite as secure as GNMAs, they are considered very safe. Because of the discrepancy in safety, Freddie often pays slightly higher yields.

Freddie Mac PCs are sold for $25,000. Since the market is dominated by institutional investors, there are fewer mutual funds: Vanguard and Federated Investors are two. The US AA Income Fund divides its assets between Ginnie and Freddie.

FANNIE MAEs

The Federal National Mortgage Association (FNMA, or "Fannie Mae") is a private shareholder-owned corporation that buys conventional mortgages, pools them in $1 million lots, and sells them in $25,000 units. Although not backed by the full faith and credit of the U.S. government, Fannies are AAA-rated by both S&P and Moody's. Fannie Mae shares also trade on the NYSE.

Both Freddie Mac and Fannie Mae are corporations chartered by Congress and are *not* officially part of the federal government. Therefore, they do not carry the unconditional guarantee of Ginnie Mae. One advantage this discrepancy in safety brings is a slightly higher yield. Another is that the mortgage pools are larger than the Ginnie Mae pools. The more

---

ESTIMATING A FANNIE MAE'S YIELD TO MATURITY

A Fannie Mae with: 10% coupon
price of 85 (85% of par)
11.76% current yield
25 years to maturity

1 Divide the amount of the discount by the number of years to maturity.

$$\frac{100 - 85 = 15}{25} = 0.60$$

2 Divide the result by 2 to factor in discounting.

$$0.60 \div 2 = 0.30$$

3 Add this number to the current yield.

$$0.30 + 11.76 = 12.06$$

4 This is your approximate current yield: 12.06%.

SOURCE: Fact magazine, February 1985.

mortgages, the more accurately you can predict how fast the principal will be returned.

After their initial offering, both Freddie and Fannie PCs trade in the secondary market.

CMOs

Collateralized mortgage obligations (CMOs) were introduced in 1983 by the Federal Home Loan Mortgage Corp. Their advantage is a more predictable payout of interest and principal than with Ginnie Maes. Instead of buying mortgage securities directly, you buy a AAA-rated bond. These bonds are sold against mortgage collateral comprised of GNMA- and FNMA-guaranteed mortgages. Each bond is divided into four classes, or tranches, having different dates of maturity ranging from 3 to 20 years. Investors receive semiannual interest payments, *but*, and here's the difference, principal payments are initially passed through only to investors in the shortest maturity class, class A. Once that group has been paid in full, principal payments go to the next class. In the fourth and final class, investors get all interest and all principal in one lump sum.

These certificates generally have slightly lower yields than the regular pass-throughs, because the size and length of payments can be more accurately determined and you have some protection against prepayments. CMOs are available from larger brokerage firms in $5,000 units.

SONNY MAEs

These bonds are backed by fixed-rate single-family home mortgages. Proceeds are used to subsidize below-market-rate mortgages for first-time homebuyers. These are regular bonds, not pass-throughs, and therefore pay interest only until they mature. They are all rated Aa by Moody's and are exempt from federal taxes for everyone and from state and local taxes for residents of New York State.

SALLIE MAEs

Created in Congress in 1972 to provide a nationwide secondary market for government guaranteed student loans, Sallie Mae (the Student Loan Marketing Association) is to students what Ginnie Mae is to homeowners. It issues bonds, rather than certificates, based on a pool of loans. Each bond is backed by Sallie Mae, and since its assets are made up of loans that have a government guarantee, these bonds are regarded as almost as safe as Treasuries. However, and this is key, this federal backing is only implied, not explicit. They yield about ¼% more than equivalent Treasury bonds.

Sallie Mae is a publicly owned company chartered by the government. Its stock trades on the New York Stock Exchange. Originally issued at $20 per share, it recently was trading at more than $75. It also issues floating rate notes and convertible bonds. The need for student loans is expected to continue into the 1990s.

JUNK BONDS

If you're looking for very high yields, a solution is the so-called high-yield or junk bond, which yields substantially more than higher-quality bonds. These extra 3 to 5 points, however, march in tandem with extra risk. Over $180 billion has been invested in junk bonds over the last 15 years. They now represent about one-quarter of all corporate debt.

Junk bonds are those rated BB or lower by Standard & Poor's and Ba or lower by Moody's. Some have no ratings at all. The world of junk bonds comprises new or old companies with uncertain earnings coverage of their fixed obligations (bond interest payments) along with blue chip companies that have been forced into heavy debt in order to fend off a takeover or to finance an acquisition or a buy-back of their own stock. For example, Holiday Corp., in an effort to avoid a takeover attempt by Donald Trump, paid its shareholders a special distribution of $65 per share and financed it by issuing close to $2 billion worth of junk bonds.

When these situations occur in a blue chip company, a new set of circumstances comes into being:

- Low-earning or unprofitable assets are sold off.
- Costs are cut, reflecting corporate efforts to become "lean and mean."

The credit rating gradually improves as these changes are implemented. Thus a good junk bond is always one in which the coverage of fixed charges increases with time.

$ IF YOU DARE: An astute investor can find the amount of projected cash flow and future asset sales for a corporation and thus identify bonds with substantial prospects for improvement.

However, default is not out of the question, which is why, unless you have sufficient money with which to speculate, you should invest in junk bonds only through a mutual fund, where the element of risk is diversified.

JUNK BOND DEFAULTS

Junk bonds offer top interest rates, but in turn you give up a large degree of safety. Many experts feel they will depreciate or even default if the U.S. economy goes into a recession. So proceed with caution and information.

According to a study published in 1989 by Harvard University professor Paul Asquith, prior junk bond studies were biased and the risks of this investment are far greater than acknowledged by Wall Streeters.

The Harvard group found that a portfolio consisting of all junk bonds issued in 1977 and 1978 would have had a 34% default rate by November 1, 1988. This is in sharp contrast with the most widely quoted study—that done by New York University professor Edward I. Altman, which reports that the average default rate for junks from 1970 to 1985 was never more than 2.1%.

Regardless of which study you choose to believe, this is obviously an area in which to proceed with caution.

JUNK BOND MUTUAL FUNDS

High-yield junk bond mutual funds offer professional management plus portfolio supervision. As with other mutual funds, track records vary, so care must be exercised. The publicity attached to the Ivan Boesky insider trading scandals sent shock waves through the junk bond markets, but junk bonds have fared well despite the adverse publicity provoked by these and other notorious cases (see table above).

The sponsors of junk bond funds, or course, are quite apt to play up the diversification point and de-emphasize the risks involved. They make much of the fact that their portfolios are diversified and continually monitored so that issues in trouble can be jettisoned. This is, of course, absolutely true *if* the portfolio manager is astute. But there's another risk involved—the risk of changing interest rates. Like any fixed-income security, junk bond funds are vulnerable to broad changes in interest rates, and as those rates rise, the value of the fund falls.

According to Lipper Analytical Services, junk bond funds posted a 69.1% total return from January 1, 1984, through December 31, 1988, and as we go to press, yields on long-term bonds have risen to above 9%, prompted in part by the resurgence of inflation.

HOW JUNK BONDS FARED IN 1989

COMPANY	S&P RATING	1986 HIGH	PRICE (SPRING 1989)
Coastal Corp. 11¾%; 2006	B+	$104	$97
GATX Corp. 11½%; 1996	BB+	105½	100½
Holiday Corp. 11%; 1999	B−	N.A.	94
Nat'l. Medical Enterp. 12%; 2000	BBB+	107⅞	100
Occidental Petrol. 11¾%; 2011	BBB	105	103
Showboat 13%; 2004	B	N.A.	99

SOURCE: Standard & Poor's.

HIGH-YIELDING JUNK BOND MUTUAL FUNDS

FUND	YIELD (APRIL 1989)
Oppenheimer High Yield (1-800-525-7048)	11.57%
T. Rowe Price High Yield (1-800-638-5660)	12.76
Bull & Bear High Yield (1-800-847-4200)	12.55
American Capital High Yield (1-800-847-5636)	13.39
Prudential-Bache High Yield Corp. Fund (1-800-872-7787)	12.61

Some of the top-yielding junk bond funds in the first five months of 1989 are listed in the table. If one bond in a fund defaults, it means a decrease in the overall fund yield, certainly less of an impact than if you owned the bond directly. However, if several bonds default, the fund share price will suffer.

MUNICIPAL JUNK BONDS

High-yield municipal bond funds are another matter altogether, since tax revisions have made some municipals taxable. Check each fund's prospectus for its policy on taxable munis. Some of the best performers among the high-yield municipal funds for the first quarter of 1989 are listed in the table on the lower left side of this page.

Junk bond munis are regarded as riskier than corporates. Corporates are frequently issued by new companies without a past history of earnings. Theoretically, these companies are on their way up. Munis that are low rated are more often than not the result of a fundamentally risky situation that is unlikely to improve.

Fund managers try to cut risks primarily by diversifying their portfolios according to both bond type and bond rating. A number of them limit their holdings of any one issue to 5% of the fund's total assets. Others offset risk by adding a mixture of investment-grade bonds. More frequent review of the portfolio—monthly or quarterly—is another risk-cutting technique. In selecting a junk bond fund, if you're concerned with risk, call the fund and inquire about the portfolio mix and management's position. Don't shy away solely because there are nonrated

HIGH-YIELDING MUNICIPAL BOND FUNDS

FUND	YIELD (APRIL 1989)
Franklin High Yield Tax-free Income (1-800-342-5236)	8.24%
Fidelity Aggressive Tax-free Portfolio (1-800-544-6666)	8.08
Stein Roe High Yield Muni (1-800-338-2550)	7.53
T. Rowe Price Tax-free High Yield (1-800-638-5660)	7.59

issues: some smaller municipalities have local appeal although they do not request a rating from S&P or Moody's.

JUNK BOND UNIT INVESTMENT TRUSTS

Unit investment trusts are closed-end investment companies. Because they have fixed portfolios, their yields are more predictable than those of a mutual fund. However, they have far less flexibility in terms of adjusting the portfolio and getting rid of poor bonds. Since they are not actively managed, *investors are at risk* should there be a default. "The unit investment trust is fine for quality bonds but should be avoided for junk issues," warns Peter Hegel, bond expert at Van Kampen Merritt.

CRAMDOWN SECURITIES

The acquisition of a company by an outsider or by the company's own management (as in the case of a leveraged buyout) usually occurs in two steps. In the first step, a substantial amount of common stock, often as much as 50%, is bought for cash. This sets the stage for the second step—the exchange of the remaining shares of common for either debentures or preferred stock. These second-stage securities are called "cramdown" securities because they are figuratively crammed down the shareholder's throat. The shareholder has no option but to accept them or sell any remaining common shares that were not tendered.

These cramdown securities (debentures or preferred stock) are speculative in nature because such transactions force the issuer to assume a great deal of debt. In many cases they start out as zero coupon issues and then pay cash interest after a specified time period. Some cramdowns, on the other hand, pay interest or dividends not in cash but in additional debentures or preferred stock. This system is known as "payment in kind," or PIK.

Because of the speculative nature of cramdowns and their rather unorthodox payment methods, original shareholders often decide to sell this paper when they receive it as part of a merger or acquisition. But investors willing to gamble may find it attractive because of the potentially high compound returns that will be paid *if* the company thrives and succeeds financially.

If you are interested in cramdown securities, do your homework first. Examine carefully the coupon rate, the yield to when cash payments will be made (YTC), and the yield to maturity (YTM). Focus in particular on the YTC because it is likely that the company will try to refinance this debt at lower rates before cash interest or dividends are due.

Ed Auden, arbitrageur at Swiss Bank in New York, suggests that investors ask their brokers these 11 questions before purchasing cramdowns:

- Is the company's cash flow sufficient on a current basis to pay interest and principal requirements? If so, by what margin?
- Would the cash flow be sufficient if zero coupon and PIK securities were obliged to pay their obligations on a current cash basis?
- If not, how will the company increase its cash flow stream to meet payments when they are due? (Sales growth, price hikes, increased operating efficiencies, and sale of assets are acceptable answers.)
- Will the company's ability to meet its obligations be adversely affected in a recession?
- How has the company done (relative to its original projections) in meeting cash requirements and growth?
- How long does the PIK or zero coupon provision last? (The sooner the transition to a cash position the better. A 3- to 5-year YTC should be sufficient time for healthy restructuring.)

- How much control does the company have over pricing of its product line?
- What are the call provisions?
- Is the company in an industry that is stable or declining?
- What rights do owners of preferred cramdowns have in the event of default?
- What are the S&P or Moody ratings for the senior securities (i.e., the original bonds) and for the new cramdowns?

ADVICE FOR 1990

Junk bonds can be a mine field for the unsophisticated investor. Yet it's hard to say no to a 12% yield. Here are nine ways to protect yourself if you decide to take the risk.

- Put no more than 10% to 15% of your portfolio in junk bonds.
- If you want to buy individual bonds, use a broker who knows the area well.
- Watch the market closely and be prepared to sell quickly.
- If you buy individual bonds, diversify among types: fallen angels (companies facing difficulties), emerging growth (companies that have yet to achieve quality ratings), and LBO bonds (companies going through restructuring and/or a leveraged buyout). LBO bonds are the riskiest, since they involve massive debt.
- Only buy publicly listed bonds—they are quoted daily and somewhat easier to sell.
- Avoid bond issues under $75 million; they tend to be illiquid.
- Buy bonds with a protective covenant so that if a hostile takeover occurs,

POPULAR CRAMDOWNS
Ask your broker for current prices and particulars regarding payout dates.

ISSUER	TYPE	EST. YTC
RJR Holdings Group	Floating rate PIK preferred stock	20%
RJR Holdings Group	Senior convertible debentures	20
GAF Corp.	Floating rate merger debentures	16¼
Hospital Corp. America	Cummulative exchangable preferred stock	27
Hospital Corp. America	Discount debenture; zero	19

SOURCE: Ed Auden, Swiss Bank Corp., Investment Banking, 222 Broadway, New York, NY 10038, Spring 1989.

bondholders can sell the bonds back to the corporation at par. This is called a "put feature"—you put the bonds to the issuer.

- Use a mutual fund for diversification unless you can afford to buy 10 to 15 bonds.
- If you buy a mutual fund, select it based upon total return, not just yield. A solid fund should generate capital gains along with income. Also, pick a well-diversified fund with no more than 2% to 3% of its assets in any one company's bonds. This broad base enables the fund to weather any adverse situations.

ZERO COUPON BONDS

Zero coupon bonds ("zeros"), are an excellent choice if you know you will be needing a lump sum of money at a certain date in the future. These bonds, offered by both corporations and the U.S. government, are sold at a deep discount from face value ($1,000) and pay no interest. Worthwhile? Yes, as long as you understand the facts. These bonds are "stripped" of their interest coupons and, instead of being paid out, this interest is added to the principal every 6 months. So when zeros mature, you get this interest back in a balloon payment. In this respect they are much like EE savings bonds. In other words, they are fully redeemed at par or face value. The difference between the fractional price paid initially and the value at maturity is the return on your investment, that is, the yield to maturity. For example, a zero coupon Treasury recently selling for $121 will be worth $1,000 at maturity in 2004. That is a yield to maturity of 11.25%.

➤ TAXATION The annual appreciation (or undistributed interest) is subject to tax. *You must pay taxes* annually all along the way, just as if you had actually received the interest payments. Zeros tend to be volatile in price because of this compounding effect; in fact, since there are no interest payments to cushion market swings, zeros can fall dramatically in price when interest rates rise. Therefore, if you buy zeros, plan to hold them to maturity.

➤ WAYS TO USE ZEROS Zeros are tailor-made for retirement accounts, such as IRAs and Keoghs, so you can avoid paying taxes every year on interest you don't actually receive. Recently, for example, a BankAmerica zero due

1993 sold at 62½ ($625 per bond) with a yield of 9.86%. In 1993 bondholders will receive $1,000 per bond.

Zeros are also ideal for saving for a specific goal, such as college tuition payments or a vacation home. If you use zeros to finance a child's college education, have your broker select ones that come due in the years your child will be in school. Better yet, put them in your child's name; when they mature, they'll be taxed at the child's lower rate after age 14.

➤ AVOIDING THE NEGATIVES Locking in your yield can turn out to be a disadvantage if interest rates rise over the life of your zero so that other investments are offering higher yields. To tackle the dual problem of rising interest rates and increasing inflation:

- Select zeros with medium-term maturities—3 to 7 years, possibly 10—and avoid being committed to an interest rate over the long term.
- Purchase zeros continually—say every year—as part of your IRA, to take advantage of changing rates.
- Purchase zeros with varying maturities to cover yourself in case interest rates decline.

$ HINT: Zero coupon Treasuries are backed by the full faith and credit of the U.S. government and are one of the safest and simplest ways to invest for your retirement. You lock in a fixed rate of return, thus eliminating unpredictability.

TYPES OF ZEROS

➤ GOVERNMENT ZEROS In 1982 Merrill Lynch devised the idea of Treasury zeros by purchasing long-term government bonds, placing them in an irrevocable trust, and issuing receipts against the coupon payments. This created a series of zero coupon Treasuries, one for every coupon date. In other words, Merrill "stripped" the interest coupons from the principal of the Treasury bond and sold each portion separately. Merrill called these TIGRs (Treasury Investment Growth Receipts). Then along came Salomon Brothers with their version—CATS (Certificates of Accrual on Treasury Securities). All are certificates held in irrevocable trust in a custodial bank.

➤ CORPORATE ZEROS These are not generally suggested for individual investors because of their potential credit risk: if the issuer defaults after you've owned the bond for some time, you've more to lose than with a straight bond since you've received no interest along the way.

➤ DINTS Deferred Interest Securities, also known as DINTS, are unique corporate zero coupon bonds that were issued by Exxon Shipping Company and General Motors Acceptance Corporation before the IRS ruled in 1983 that corporate zero interest was taxable. Their yields range between 8% and 9% with maturities in 2012 and 2015.

➤ TREASURY STRIPS In 1985 the government entered the act, introducing its own coupon-stripping program called STRIPS (Separate Trading of Registered Interest and Principal Securities). Because they are issued directly by the Treasury, they are safer than all other types of zeros. Yields are slightly less than those of TIGRs, LIONs, and CATS, because of the greater degree of safety. Treasury STRIPS must be purchased from a stockbroker.

Example: A 20-year bond with a face value of $20,000 and a 10% interest rate could be stripped into 41 zero coupon instruments: the 40 semiannual interest coupons plus the principal. The body upon maturity is worth the $20,000 face value. The other coupon zeros would be worth $1,000 each, or half the annual interest of $2,000 (10% of $20,000) on the payment date.

☐ CAUTION: Brokers and others may fail to emphasize that the price volatility of long-term Treasury zeros is above average. In fact, zero coupon Treasuries run a greater interest rate risk than straight Treasury coupon bonds of the same maturity.

➤ MUNICIPAL ZEROS Issued by state and local governments, these are exempt from federal taxes and generally also from state taxes in the state where issued. They are suggested for investors in high tax brackets. An AA-rated muni zero issued by Northern Minnesota Power Agency, due 2007 with a yield of 7.45%, recently sold for $1,350 for a $5,000 unit. That means that in the year 2007 you would receive $10,000 for a $2,700 investment.

☐ CAUTION: Zeros issued with call features should be shunned (see Chapter 7 for additional details).

➤ MORTGAGE-BACKED ZEROS These are backed by securities issued by Ginnie Mae, Fannie Mae, and Freddie Mac (see pages 117–20). The securities are secured by AAA-rated mortgages. You'll see some of them referred to as ABCs (agency-backed compounders).

☐ CAUTION: You may not get to hold your mortgage-backed security until maturity if mortgages are paid off early.

➤ ZERO COUPON CONVERTIBLES This hybrid vehicle allows you to convert the bond into stock of the issuing company. Merrill Lynch, the leading marketer of zero CVs, calls them LYONs (Liquid Yield Option Notes). Conversion premiums on LYONs are generally lower than on traditional coupon issues; therefore, they offer potential appreciation if the underlying stock moves up in price. LYONs are sold at a substantial discount from par. They give the holder the right, after a certain date, to sell the

THE POWER OF COMPOUNDING:
How Much $1,000 in Zeros Will Grow, Before Taxes, at Various Compounding Rates

| MATURITY | SEMIANNUAL COMPOUNDING RATE | | | | | |
	8%	9%	10%	11%	12%	13%
5 years	$1,480	$1,552	$1,629	$1,708	$1,791	$1,877
10 years	2,191	2,411	2,653	2,918	3,207	3,523
15 years	3,243	3,745	4,322	4,984	5,744	6,614
20 years	4,801	5,816	7,040	8,513	10,286	12,416

SOURCE: Merrill Lynch, 1986.

THE POWER OF COMPOUNDING:
How Much $1,000 in TIGRs Will Grow at Various Compounding Rates

	SEMIANNUAL COMPOUNDING RATE				
MATURITY	10%	11%	12%	13%	14%
5 years	$1,629	$1,708	$1,791	$1,877	$1,967
10 years	2,653	2,918	3,207	3,524	3,870
15 years	4,322	4,984	5,744	6,614	7,612
20 years	7,040	8,513	10,286	12,416	14,975

SOURCE: Merrill Lynch, 1986.

issue back to the issuer at the original issue price plus accrued interest. This so-called "put" feature can reduce some of the market risk that accompanies convertibles. (See Chapter 9 on convertibles.) For example, a recent Merrill Lynch LYON sold for $226.25 for a yield of 9.5%. It converts into 5.31 shares of common at $42.61 or can be redeemed at $238.81.

➤ ZERO COUPON CERTIFICATES OF DEPOSIT These are really CDs but sell at discount and do not pay current interest. They are sold by banks and stockbrokers.

ZERO COUPON TREASURY BONDS

PROS
↑ Lock in fixed yield
↑ Maturity dates can be tailored to meet future needs
↑ Call protection available
↑ Predictable cash payment
↑ Guaranteed by U.S. government
↑ Tax-deferred in retirement accounts
↑ No reinvestment decisions
↑ Less expensive than most bonds
CONS
↓ If interest rates rise, you're locked in at a lower yield
↓ Inflation erodes purchasing power of the bond's face value
↓ Commissions and/or sales markups not always made clear
↓ Many zeros have call provisions permitting issuer to redeem them prior to maturity

---

$ HINT: Buy zeros that are the last callable issues in a particular series to partially protect yourself against call provisions.

ZERO COUPON FICO STRIPS

These zero coupon obligations derived from bonds issued by the federally sponsored agency FICO, the Financing Corp., first appeared on the scene in May 1988. They were the first zeros created from the bonds of a federally sponsored agency.

FICO was created by Congress to raise money for the ailing Federal Savings & Loan Insurance Corp. (FSLIC). FICO was authorized to raise about $11 billion over a 3-year period. The lead underwriter, Salomon Brothers, purchased $750 million of 10% bonds maturing in 30 years. It then stripped all 60 interest coupons from the bonds, creating 61 separate entities. Investors can purchase either the coupon strip or the principal strip.

The principal of these bonds is secured by U.S. Treasury securities that match the maturities on FICO bonds. Interest on the bonds is paid from assessments made on the S&L industry.

FICO zeros have higher yields than Treasury bonds. The longest-maturing FICOs pay the highest returns.

Although S&P does not assign credit ratings to FICOs, it has stated that it believes these bonds are "very high quality, the equivalent of AAA issues, based on a commitment of Congress to both FICO and FSLIC."

FICO strips trade over the counter and can be purchased from a stockbroker. Like other bonds, when interest rates rise, their value

ZERO COUPON BOND MUTUAL FUNDS

Zeros, like straight bonds, rise in price when interest rates fall and fall when rates rise. And since they are even more sensitive to interest rates, they should be held until maturity. If this is not your plan, use a mutual fund. You'll avoid both being forced to sell early and paying a broker's commission.

Benham Target Fund (1-800-227-8380; 1-800-982-6150 in Calif.)

Scudder U.S. Government Zero Coupon Target Portfolio (1-800-225-2470)

drops, and vice versa. The minimum face value of a FICO coupon strip is $1,000; of a principal strip, $20,000.

FOR FURTHER INFORMATION

THE MAE FAMILY

To determine the yield on your GNMA investment at any time, consult *Financial Pass-through Yield and Value Tables for GNMA Mortgage–backed Securities,* Publication 715, available for $42.00 plus shipping and handling from:

Financial Publishing Co.
82 Brookline Avenue
Boston, MA 02115
1-617-262-4040

Call for details on other tables.

Investor Relations Department
Federal Home Loan Mortgage Corp.
1759 Business Center Drive
P.O. Box 4112
Reston, VA 22090
1-800-424-5401

Investor Relations
Student Loan Marketing Association
1050 Thomas Jefferson Street NW
Washington, DC 20007
1-202-333-8000

JUNK BONDS

Edward I. Altman and Scott A. Nammacher, *Investing in Junk Bonds* (New York: John Wiley & Sons, 1987).

STOCKS

At the heart of every portfolio are, of course, stocks. Whether you have only dreamed about owning a stock or whether you and your money manager are trading hundreds of shares every morning and afternoon, we suggest you read this entire section. The basic information is essential to the beginner and the lists of suggested stocks and the tips on trading options, getting in on new issues, and ways to make money with rights and warrants can help even the most wizened investor.

In Part Three you will learn about:

- Common and preferred stocks
- How to pick winners
- When to buy and when to sell
- Over-the-counter stocks
- Electric utilities and water companies
- New issues
- Options
- Stock rights and warrants

STOCKS: COMMON AND PREFERRED

WHY STOCKS?

The two basic tools of investing are stocks and bonds, or equity and debt, to use a little Wall Streetese. Bonds have been discussed. The first part of this chapter is devoted to common stocks; then we describe preferred stocks. There are several truly compelling reasons for investing in stocks, and one or two reasons why you shouldn't—at least at certain times, in certain stocks. Sorting out the who, what, where, when, and how of making money in stocks hinges on two simple concepts that are frequently ignored in the excessively technical discussions of financial wizards and pundits.

- *Over the long run, stocks outperform bonds*—although sometimes it may indeed be a very long run. Both trade in the marketplace, which historically rewards risk rather than caution. There are, of course, periods when you're better off in T-bills or corporate bonds, but the fact that stocks are better profit-makers remains a truism of investing.
- *Stocks tend to keep pace with inflation.* With stocks, at least you have a fighting chance of staying even. Not so with bonds: once you buy a bond, the interest rate is locked in. If, for example, oil prices go up, it doesn't matter—your bond will pay exactly the same whether crude is at $18 or $35 a barrel. (Bonds do compensate for this factor by moving up or down in price, however.) If you own shares in Exxon or Occidental Petroleum, however, you'll participate in the increase in oil prices through higher dividends *and* a rising price for your shares. Stocks, in fact, respond directly to inflation: if the buying power of your dollar is reduced to 50¢ by rampant inflation, you and everyone else

buying Exxon will have to pay more for the company's shares. At the same time, inflation will eat away at interest earned on fixed-income securities.

TYPES OF STOCKS

There is no such thing as a stock that's always an excellent holding. It's a mistake to expect all things from any stock. A great number of investors are unaware of the fact that stocks are *not* all designed to do the same thing. In fact there are two distinct types of stocks: those that generate income and those that appreciate in price. Income-oriented stock, such as utility stocks, real estate investment trusts (REITs), and closed-end funds that trade on the exchanges, should be held primarily for income; you should not also expect appreciation from these issues, or at least not very much.

Stocks selected for appreciation are an entirely different matter. Within this growth category you must narrow your selection even further: to low-risk growth stocks or speculative stocks. Throughout this book you will find various lists of stocks suggested for growth, income, or total return.

- *Blue chip stocks* represent ownership in a major company that has a history of profitability and continual or increasing dividends with sufficient financial strength to withstand economic or industrial downturns. Examples: IBM, General Electric, Exxon, Du Pont, Sears. (See list on page 131.)
- *Growth stocks* represent ownership in a company that has had relatively rapid growth in the past (when compared with the economy as a whole) and is expected to continue in this vein. These companies tend to reinvest a large part of their

STILL BLUE CHIP—EVEN AFTER THE CRASH
Standard & Poor's List: 1976 and 1989;
All ranked A or A+

Apparel
Angelica Corp.
Nordstrom, Inc.
V.F. Corp.

Beverages
Anheuser-Busch Co.
Coca-Cola

Chemicals
Betz Labs

Construction
Masco Corp.

Diversified
MMM
National Service
 Industries

Drugs, Cosmetics
Bard (C.R.) Inc.
Becton Dickinson
Gillette Co.
Pfizer, Inc.
SmithKline Beckman
Upjohn Co.

Electrical
Emerson Electric
General Electric

Electronics
IBM

Food
General Mills
Quaker Oats

Printing, Publishing
Dun & Bradstreet
Dow Jones & Co.
Knight-Ridder
Meredith Corp.

Retailers
Dayton Hudson
Maytag Co.
Melville Corp.
Winn Dixie Stores

Tobacco
American Brands

Utilities
Central & South West
Consolidated Edison
Rochester Telephone
Texas Utilities

Miscellaneous
Rubbermaid, Inc.

SOURCE: Standard & Poor's, May 1989.

earnings in order to finance their expansion and growth. Consequently, dividends are small in comparison with earnings. Examples: Barnett Banks Inc., Limited Inc.; and Wal-Mart Stores. (See list on page 137 for additional companies.)

- *Cyclical stocks* are common stocks of companies whose earnings move with the economy or business cycles. They frequently have lower earnings when the country is in a slump and higher earnings when the economy is in a recovery phase. Examples of cyclical industries: aluminum, steel, automobiles, machinery, housing, airlines, and travel and leisure. (See list on page 133.)

- *Income stocks* have continually stable earnings and high dividend yields in comparison with other stocks. Income stocks generally retain only a small portion of earnings for expansion and growth, which they are able to do because there is a relatively stable market for their products. Examples: public utility companies, international oil companies, closed-end bond funds, and REITs. (See list on page 143.)

Now you're ready to start selecting stocks for your own personal portfolio, keeping the following key consideration in mind: *every investment involves some degree of risk*. Stocks vary in their degree of risk, depending on the stability of their earnings or dividends and the way they are perceived in the marketplace.

§ HINT: The general rule is that return is correlated to risk: the greater the risk, the greater the expected return.

HOW STOCKS WORK

When you buy shares in a company, you become part owner of that company, and you can make money in one of two ways: through dividends or through price appreciation when you sell your shares at a profit.

Dividends, a distribution of earnings, are generally declared when the company is comfortably profitable. The dollar amount is decided by the board of directors and is traditionally paid to shareholders quarterly.

A stock may appreciate for a variety of reasons, not all of which are completely rational:
- The company is profitable.
- It has an exciting new product.
- It is part of an industry that is performing well.
- It is the subject of takeover rumors or actual attempts.
- Wall Street likes it.

If a corporation earns 15% on stockholders' equity (the money invested by shareholders), it ends the year with 15¢ per dollar more. After payment of a 5¢-per-share dividend, 10¢ is reinvested for future growth: research and development, new plants and equipment, new

UNDERVALUED BLUE CHIPS

STOCK	PRICE	P/E RATIO	YIELD	ACTIVITY
American Brands	$68	10	3.5%	Cigarettes, whiskey
Consolidated Edison	47	10	7.2	Electric utility
General Motors	41	5	7.2	Automaker
GTE	49	13	5.4	Independent telephone company
Raytheon	70	9.3	3.1	Defense and appliances

SOURCE: Quotron, May 2, 1989.

products and markets, etc. Thus the underlying value of the corporation doubles in about 7½ years. Eventually, these gains will be reflected in the price of the common stock. That's why the best investments are shares in companies that continue to make the most money!

As you might expect, it can fall in price for similar reasons and others: a poor earnings report, ineffective management, negative publicity, or even a mass dumping that feeds on itself, perhaps unrelated to the performance of the company.

Timing is an important factor in stock selection. In general there are times when you should move out of the market and times when you should be in high-yielding fixed-income securities. Just think about the world around you: industries change with the times, and so do common stocks. Utilities face nuclear problems; the electronics and computer field has become overbuilt and competition is tough; the Koreans now make cheaper steel; the Japanese and Germans, better cars. Woe to the investor who psychologically locks into a stock as though

it were a CD. To make a profit, always be prepared to sell your stock when the time is right.

$ HINT: The single most common mistake of investors is *inertia.* The market constantly changes, and no one stock (or any other investment) is right for all seasons. Do not buy a stock, even a solid blue chip, and then never look at it again. While your back is turned the company could be taken over, enter bankruptcy, or just have a bad year. In each case, you should be ready to take some form of action—buy more shares, sell all your shares, or sell some of your shares.

ADVANTAGES OF COMMON STOCKS

► GROWING VALUES Stocks are *live* investments. The market value of a common stock grows as the corporation prospers, whereas the face value of bonds remains the same, so that over the years, their real value, in terms of purchasing power, decreases.

The prices of bonds are almost completely controlled by interest rates and change almost immediately when rates do. When the cost of money rises, bond values drop to maintain competitive returns; when interest rates decline, bond prices rise. Bonds, therefore, are traded by yields; stocks, by what investors believe to be future corporate prospects.

► SAFETY Quality stocks are often as safe as corporate bonds. As long as the corporation meets quality standards—financial strength, growth, and profitability—your money is safe.

FOUR STOCKS WITH LONGEST RECORD OF DIVIDENDS

Bank of Boston	1784
Fleet/Norstar Financial	1791
Midlantic	1805
First Maryland Bancorp	1806

SOURCE: Standard & Poor's Corp.

CYCLICAL AND SPECULATIVE STOCKS

COMPANY	EARNINGS PER SHARE		1987–1989 PRICE RANGE	RECENT PRICE	P/E RATIO*	YIELD	REMARKS
	E1988	E1989					
American Express	$2.55	$3.10	$40^5/_8$–$20^3/_4$	28	9.0	3.0%	Earnings rebound anticipated; stock well below high.
Armstrong World	3.60	3.90	$47^3/_8$–$22^1/_2$	34	8.7	2.9	Shares modestly valued; takeover candidate.
COMPAQ Computer	5.60	6.55	$78^1/_2$–$19^1/_4$	64	9.8	Nil	Strong position in high-performance PC market.
Eastern Gas & Fuel	2.15	2.45	$33^1/_4$–19	24	9.8	5.4	Stock undervalued on improved earnings outlook.
Hasbro	1.25	1.90	$26^1/_2$–10	17	8.9	0.7	Toy maker poised for strong earnings growth.
Microsoft†	A2.22	3.10	$79^1/_4$–$23^3/_4$	53	17.1	Nil	Leading software company's earnings growth strong.
Norfolk Southern	3.35	3.40	$38^1/_4$–21	33	9.7	4.0	Well-managed transportation firm.
Nucor Corp.	3.00	2.90	$49^1/_2$–$29^1/_4$	46	15.9	0.9	Steel producer aided by R&D and expansion programs.
PAR Technology	0.15	0.65	$15^1/_2$–$4^3/_4$	7	10.8	Nil	Low-priced turnaround situation.
Westvaco‡	A3.10	3.60	$37^1/_2$–23	30	8.3	3.1	Strong specialty paper niches being developed.
Zurn Industries§	1.85	2.10	$30^3/_4$–15	28	13.3	2.4	Improving resource recovery business to increase profits.

E = Estimated.
A = Actual
* Based on latest shown estimated earnings.
† Year ending June.
‡ Year ending October.
§ Year ending March of following year.

SOURCE: Standard & Poor's for estimated earnings.

The company will continue to pay dividends, usually with periodic increases; and with higher earnings, the value of its shares will increase. If a well-known corporation pays dividends for more than 40 years, its stock is certainly as durable as its bonds.

➤ GROWING DIVIDENDS This is important for investors who want ever-higher income. Almost all quality companies keep boosting their payouts because of higher earnings.

➤ LIQUIDITY Common stocks traded on major stock exchanges can be quickly bought or sold at clearly stated prices, the ranges of which are quoted in the financial press. You can instruct

INCOME WITH INFLATION PROTECTION

COMPANY	EARNINGS PER SHARE			INDI-CATED DIVIDEND	1987–1989 PRICE RANGE	RECENT PRICE	P/E RATIO	YIELD	DIVIDEND HISTORY	
	1987	1988	E1989						NO. OF ANNUAL INCREASES 1983–1988	5-YEAR AVERAGE PAYOUT
Ameritech	4.24	4.68	4.55	$2.92	$51^1/_2$–37	51	11.2	5.7%	N.A.	58%
Bklyn. Un. Gas†	2.43	2.49	2.55	1.78	$28^1/_2$–$18^5/_8$	24	9.4	7.4	5	69
Consol. Edison	4.42	4.93	4.95	3.44	52–$37^1/_2$	47	9.5	7.3	5	52
Pacific Enterprises	3.69	E3.50	3.50	3.48	$61^1/_4$–$45^3/_4$	38	10.9	9.2	3	114
Pacific Telesis	2.21	2.81	3.05	1.76	$34^1/_2$–$22^1/_2$	33	10.8	5.3	N.A.	65
Potomac Elec. Pwr.	2.11	E2.20	2.30	1.46	$27^3/_8$–18	20	9.6	7.3	5	64
Southwestern Bell	3.48	3.53	3.70	2.48	$45^1/_4$–$27^1/_2$	43	11.6	5.8	N.A.	63
Wisconsin Energy	2.55	E3.10	3.15	1.54	$28^7/_8$–21	27	8.7	5.7	5	52

E = Estimated.

† Year ending September.

SOURCE: Standard & Poor's, *The Outlook*, Feb. 1, 1989.

your broker to buy or sell at a specific price or at "market," which will be the best price attainable at that time. The complete transaction will take 5 working days, but immediately after the transaction, you can get exact data from your broker.

RISKS OF COMMON STOCK OWNERSHIP

There are, of course, risks associated with ownership of common stocks. The risks are far less with quality corporations and, to a large degree, can be controlled by setting strict rules for selling and by using common sense. As long as the company continues to make more money, its stock price is likely to rise, but this may take time, often longer than you are prepared to accept financially or mentally.

➤ PERMANENT LOSS OF CAPITAL You may lose all your profits and some of your capital. When you speculate in high-flying stocks that are temporarily popular, the odds are against success. Only a few strong-minded people have the courage to sell such stocks when they become overpriced. When such equities start down, many

people hang on in hope of a comeback that seldom materializes.

$ HINT: *Speculation in stocks should be limited to half the money you can afford to lose.*

➤ STOCK MARKET RISK Regardless of whether you opt for income or appreciation, you certainly want all your stocks to be winners. This means avoiding ridiculous risks and instead incorporating *realistic risk* into your selections. A totally riskless portfolio is by its very nature doomed to mediocrity, since nothing exciting will happen to it. For risk-free investments, turn to EE savings bonds, bank CDs, or money market accounts.

You can, however, reduce your risk quotient and still make a profit with common stocks. Here are the best ways: (1) buy stocks with low betas (see page 136 for a full explanation of how beta works), (2) diversify by type of stock and industry, (3) spread out your risk over a number of stocks and industry groups, and (4) be defensive by moving in and out of the market when appropriate.

➤ INTEREST RATE RISK Certain stocks are "interest-sensitive," which means they are directly affected by changes in interest rates. These stocks include utilities, banks, financial and

DIVIDENDS EVERY MONTH

You can receive a dividend check every month of the year by purchasing a group of stocks with different dividend-payment dates. The following is a list of issues broken down by payout dates. By purchasing stocks from each of the groups, you will have a portfolio of stocks producing dividend checks every month of the year.

January, April, July, October
CIGNA
Dow Chemical
Eastman Kodak
General Electric
Greyhound
Kimberly-Clark
McKesson
Morgan (J.P.) & Co.
Northern States
    Power
Ogden
Philip Morris
    Companies
SCEcorp
Sears, Roebuck &
    Co.
USF&G
Xerox

February, May, August, November
Aetna Life &
    Casualty
American Tel. &
    Tel.
BellSouth
Bristol-Myers
Brooklyn Union Gas
Citicorp
Consolidated
    Natural Gas
Lincoln National
Marsh & McLennan
    Companies
Orange & Rockland
    Utilities
Penney (J.C.) Co.
Rochester
    Telephone
Southwestern Bell
TECO Energy
WPL Holdings

March, June, September, December
Allied-Signal
American Brands
American Home
    Products
Chevron
Dennison
    Manufacturing
Du Pont (E.I.) de
    Nemours & Co.
Exxon
General Motors
IBM
K mart
Norfolk Southern
Potomac Electric
    Power
South Jersey
    Industries
Southern Indiana
    Gas & Electric
Westinghouse
    Electric

SOURCE: Richard L. Evans, director of research, *Dow Theory Forecasts,* 7412 Calumet Avenue, Hammond, IN 46324; 1-219-931-6480.

brokerage companies, housing and construction, REITs, and closed-end bond funds. You can cut your risk in these stocks by moving to other investments when interest rates are high or on the way up. The reason why these industries suffer during high-interest-rate seasons is described by Jeffrey Weiss in his book *Beat the Market* (New York: Viking Penguin, 1985):

1 Utility companies have to pay more on monies borrowed for expansion or upgrading of facilities.
2 Banks and finance companies are forced to pay more on money deposited in their institutions as well as for money they borrow.
3 Building falls off because of higher interest rates.

WAYS TO SELECT STOCKS

Eight analytic tools are used most often in stock selection and appraisal.

➤ EARNINGS PER SHARE For the average investor, this figure distills the company's financial picture into one simple number. Earnings per share is the company's net income (after taxes and preferred stock dividends) divided by the number of common shares outstanding. When a company is described as growing at a certain rate, the growth is then usually stated in terms of earnings per share.

Look for a company whose earnings per share have increased over the past 5 years; 1 down year is acceptable if the other 4 have been up. You will find earnings per share in *Moody's, Value Line, Standard & Poor's,* or the company's annual report.

➤ PRICE-EARNINGS RATIO (P/E) This is one of the most common analytic tools of the trade and reflects investor enthusiasm about a stock in comparison with the market as a whole. Divide the current price of a stock by its earnings per share for the last 12 months: that's the P/E ratio, also sometimes called the "multiple."

You will also find the P/E listed in the daily stock quotations of the newspaper. A P/E of 12, for example, means that the buying public is willing to pay 12 times earnings for the stock, whereas there is much less interest and confidence in a stock with a P/E of 4 or 5. A company's P/E is of course constantly changing and must be compared with its own previous

P/Es and with the P/Es of others in its industry or category.

It is important to realize that the P/E listed in the paper is based on the last 12 months' earnings; however, Wall Street professionals refer to the earnings of the current year. So when considering a stock to buy or sell, remember to focus on its future, not its past.

Although brokers and analysts hold varying views on what constitutes the ideal P/E, a P/E under 10 is regarded as conservative. As the P/E moves above 10, you start to pay a premium. If the P/E moves below 5 or 6, it tends to signal uncertainty about the company's prospects and balance sheet.

Try to buy a strong company with favorable prospects and a conservative P/E *before* other investors become interested in it and run it up in price. Sometimes growth industries—for example, cellular telephones—fall into economic slumps and may provide this type of investment opportunity.

➤ BOOK VALUE This figure, also known as stockholders' equity, is the difference between a company's assets and its liabilities, in other words, what the stockholders own after all debts are paid. That number is then divided by the number of shares outstanding to arrive at book value per share. The book value becomes especially important in takeover situations, which are described in depth in Chapter 24. If book value is understated—that is, if the assets of the company are worth substantially more than the financial statements say they are—you may have found a real bargain that the marketplace has not yet recognized. (This is often true with in-the-ground assets such as oil, minerals, gas, and timber.)

➤ RETURN ON EQUITY (ROE) This number measures how much the company earns on the stockholders' equity. It is a company's total net income expressed as a percentage of total book value and is especially useful when comparing several companies within one industry or when studying a given company's profitability trends. To calculate a "simple" ROE, divide earnings per share by book value. A return under 10% is usually considered poor.

➤ DIVIDEND Check the current and projected dividend of a stock, especially if you are building an income portfolio. Study the payouts over the past 5 years as well as the current dividend.

There are times when a corporation reinvests most of its earnings to ensure its future growth, in which case the dividend will be small. Typically, the greater the current yield, the less likelihood there is of stock price appreciation. However, it's best if a company earns $5 for every $4 it pays out.

➤ VOLATILITY Some stocks go up and down in price like a yo-yo, while others trade within a relatively narrow range. Those that dance about obviously carry a greater degree of risk than their more pedestrian cousins.

The measurement tool for price volatility, called *beta*, tells how much a stock tends to move in relation to changes in the Standard & Poor's 500 stock index. The index is fixed at 1.00, so a stock with a beta of 1.5 moves up and down $1\frac{1}{2}$ times as much as the Standard & Poor's index, whereas a beta of 0.5 is less volatile than the index. To put it another way, a stock with a 1.5 beta is expected to rise in price by 15% if the Standard & Poor's index rises 10% or fall by 15% if the index falls by 10%. You will find the beta for stocks given by the investment services as well as by good stockbrokers.

➤ TOTAL RETURN Most investors in stocks tend to think about their gains and losses in terms of price changes, not dividends, whereas those who own bonds pay attention to interest yields and seldom focus on price changes. *Both approaches are mistakes.* Although dividend yields are obviously more important if you are seeking income, and changes in price play a greater role in growth stocks, the total return on a stock is extremely important. It makes it possible for you to compare your investment in stocks with a similar investment in corporate bonds, municipals, Treasuries, mutual funds, and unit investment trusts.

To calculate the total return, add (or subtract) the stock's price change and dividends for 12 months and then divide by the price at the beginning of the 12-month period. For example, suppose you buy a stock at $42.00 a share and receive $2.50 in dividends for the next 12-month period. At the end of the period, you sell the stock at $45.00. The total return is 13%.

Dividend	$2.50
Price appreciation	+ 3.00
	$5.50 ÷ $42 = 13%

SELECTED COMPANIES WITH SUPERIOR EARNINGS GROWTH

COMPANY	EARNINGS PER SHARE						
	5-YEAR GROWTH RATE	EPS 1987	EPS 1988	EPS E1989	P/E RATIO*	YIELD	RETURN ON EQUITY
Abbott Laboratories	18%	2.78	3.33	3.75	13.6	2.4%	33%
Albertson's, Inc.	16	[1]1.88	[1]E2.40	[1]2.90	13.8	1.4	20
Amer. Home Products	10	5.73	6.38	7.00	12.6	4.4	43
Anheuser-Busch Cos.	18	2.04	2.45	2.75	12.4	2.1	23
Automatic Data Proc.	18	[3]1.76	[3]2.20	[3]2.50	15.2	1.4	22
Barnett Banks	12	3.26	3.75	4.20	7.6	3.3	20
Becton, Dickinson	23	[5]3.42	[5]3.69	[5]4.50	11.8	1.9	20
Bemis Co.	27	1.18	1.48	1.65	15.2	2.4	15
Borden, Inc.	14	3.62	4.22	4.90	11.4	2.8	33
Bristol-Myers	13	2.47	2.88	3.30	13.6	4.4	25
Browning-Ferris	20	[5]1.15	[5]1.51	[5]1.80	15.6	2.0	25
Cincinnati Bell	14	2.01	2.63	3.10	13.2	2.7	17
COMPAQ Computer	110	3.59	6.30	7.50	9.1	Nil	39
Computer Associates Int'l	55	[2]1.29	[2]E1.90	[2]2.35	15.3	Nil	38
Ethyl Corp.	23	1.57	1.91	2.20	10.9	2.0	22
Harland (John H.)	19	1.26	1.41	1.75	12.0	3.2	25
Houghton Mifflin	10	1.66	1.70	2.05	24.4	1.3	15
Kellogg Co.	21	3.20	3.90	4.35	14.0	2.8	39
Kimberly-Clark	17	3.73	4.71	5.40	11.3	4.3	18
King World Prod.	86	[4]1.11	[4]2.28	[4]2.55	9.0	Nil	87
Lilly (Eli)	11	4.41	5.33	6.35	14.6	2.9	25
Masco Corp.	17	1.65	2.10	2.60	10.4	1.8	28
McDonald's Corp.	15	2.89	3.43	3.85	13.0	1.1	22
Merck & Co.	25	2.22	3.05	3.75	16.5	2.4	41
MNC Financial	20	5.19	5.86	6.90	6.7	4.1	16
Owens & Minor	11	0.95	1.00	1.20	10.8	2.0	12
Philip Morris	23	7.75	9.12	11.60	9.3	4.2	83
Rubbermaid	19	1.15	1.35	1.55	16.8	1.7	23
Russell Corp.	17	1.17	1.36	1.50	12.7	1.5	17
Upjohn Co.	18	1.63	1.90	2.30	13.0	2.9	19
UST Inc.	18	1.13	1.41	1.65	12.7	4.4	33

E = Estimate.
* Based on estimated 1988 earnings.
[1] Year ending January of following year.
[2] Year ending March of following year.
[3] Year ending June.
[4] Year ending August.
[5] Year ending September.

SOURCE: Standard & Poor's, *The Outlook*, March 1, 1989.

➤ NUMBER OF SHARES OUTSTANDING If you are a beginning investor or working with a small portfolio, look for companies with at least 5 million shares outstanding. You will then be ensured of both marketability and liquidity, because the major mutual funds, institutions, and the public will be trading in these stocks. You are unlikely to have trouble buying or selling when you want to. In a smaller company, your exposure to sharp price fluctuations is greater.

FINDING WINNERS

➤ CONTINUITY For investors who place safety first, the best common stocks are those of companies that have paid dividends for 20 years or more. Many have familiar names: Anheuser-Busch, Bristol-Myers, H. J. Heinz, Johnson & Johnson, Melville Corp., Philip Morris, Woolworth.

Always check a company's annual report to see if (1) the dividends have increased fairly consistently as the result of higher earnings and (2) the company has been profitable in recent years and appears likely to remain so in the near future. It's great to do business with an old store, but only if the merchandise is up to date and priced fairly.

➤ INSTITUTIONAL OWNERSHIP Pick stocks chosen by the "experts"—managers of mutual funds, pension plans, insurance portfolios, endowments, etc. With few exceptions, these are shares of major corporations listed on the New York Stock Exchange.

Institutional ownership is no guarantee of quality, but it does indicate that some professionals have reviewed the financial prospects and for some reason (not always clear) have recommended purchase or retention. Without such interest, stocks are slow to move up in price.

In most cases, these companies must meet strict standards of financial strength, investment acceptance, profitability, growth, and, to some extent, income. But institutions still buy name and fame and either move in after the rush has started or hold on after the selling has started. Use the list on page 144 for companies that appear attractive. If the stock is owned by more than 50 institutions, you'll be in good (but not always the most profitable) company.

Institutions are not always smart money managers, but since they account for nearly three-fourths of all NYSE transactions (and a high percentage of those on the AMEX and OTC), it's wise to check their portfolios when you consider a new commitment.

💲 HINT: Every investment portfolio should contain at least three stocks whose shares are owned by at least 250 institutions.

If you want to track portfolio changes, watch for reports on actions of investment companies in *Barron's*.

☐ CAUTION: Public information comes months after decisions have been made. By the time you get the word, prices may have risen so much that your benefits will be comparatively small. Or you may be buying just before the portfolio managers on Wall Street, realizing their mistake, start selling.

➤ MOST PROFITABLE COMPANIES An important standard of safety is high and consistent profitability. It can be determined by calculating the rate of return on shareholders' equity, a minimum annual average of 11%. By sticking to these real winners, you will always make a lot of money—in time.

The table on page 139 shows how one investment advisory firm projects winners in the next couple of years, listing companies that are expected to achieve high total returns because of higher profits and current undervaluation.

CALCULATING YOUR RETURN

To know when to sell a stock, you should monitor your rate of return on each investment. To make this calculation, divide the total end value by the starting value, subtract 1, and multiply by 100:

$$R = \left(\frac{EV}{BV} - 1\right) \times 100$$

where R = rate of return
    EV = value at end of period
    BV = value at beginning of period

For example, in early January you bought 100 shares of OPH stock at a cost of $3,315 (price plus commissions and fees). During the

WHERE BIG EARNINGS GAINS ARE EXPECTED FOR 1989

COMPANY	EARNS. $ PER SHARE		EST. 1989 GAIN	CURRENT PRICE
	1988	E1989		
American Cynamid	3.41	4.00	17%	51
American Express	2.31	3.00	30	30
Boeing Co.	4.02	6.50	61	68
Borden, Inc.	4.22	4.90	16	58
Coca-Cola	2.85	3.30	15	51
COMPAQ Computer	6.30	7.50	19	72
Deere & Co.	[5]4.06	[5]4.75	16	50
Disney (Walt)	[4]3.80	[4]4.55	19	76
Dow Chemical	12.82	15.00	17	90
Federal Paper Board	3.51	5.20	48	26
Foxboro Co.	0.80	2.00	150	31
Galoob (Lewis) Toys	0.72	1.50	108	8
General Instrument	[2]2.60	[2]3.20	23	28
Giant Foods CI 'A'	[2]1.60	[2]2.00	25	23
Halliburton Co.	0.81	1.20	48	30
Harland (John H.)	1.41	1.75	24	20
Hasbro Inc.	1.24	1.90	53	18
Hewlett-Packard	[5]3.36	[5]3.90	16	52
Lilly (Eli)	5.33	6.35	19	101
Mack Trucks	0.84	1.55	84	14
Mallard Coach	[5]1.15	[5]1.40	21	9
Olin Corp.	4.63	6.00	29	52
Potlatch Corp.	4.04	4.65	15	32
Schering-Plough	3.48	4.15	19	62
Shaw Industries	[3]2.13	[3]2.85	33	24
Union Carbide	4.88	6.00	22	30
Upjohn Co.	1.90	2.25	18	28
Warner-Lambert	5.00	5.80	16	83
Waste Management	2.05	2.45	19	43
Westvaco Corp.	[5]3.10	[5]3.60	16	29

SOURCE: Standard & Poor's, *The Outlook*, April 5, 1989.

year, OPH pays dividends of $3 per share. In December, the stock is at 45. For that year, the rate of return is 45%.

$$R = \frac{4,500 + 300}{3,315} = \frac{4,800}{3,315} = 1.45$$

The gain is 1.45 − 1 = 0.45 = 45%.

If you had held the stock for 2 years and the dividends rose in the second year to $3.50 per share but the stock price stayed at 45, the rate of return would be 55% over 2 years, or 27.5% per annum.

$$\frac{4,500 + 300 + 350}{3,315} = 1.55$$

The gain is 1.55 − 1 = 55% ÷ 2 = 27.5%.

To make similar calculations with a time-weighted rate of return (where the rates of return vary and there are additional investments over a period of time), use the same gen-

---

SELECTED LOW-RISK STOCKS

COMPANY	INDUSTRY GROUP
Abbott Laboratories	Medical supplies
American Home Products	Drugs
Boeing	Aircraft
Bristol-Myers	Drugs
Campbell Soup	Food processing
Coca-Cola	Beverages
Consolidated Edison	Electric utility
Dun & Bradstreet	Publishing
Exxon Corp.	Petroleum
Genuine Parts	Manufacturing
IBM	Computers
Johnson & Johnson	Drugs
Maytag Corp.	Home appliances
Pfizer, Inc.	Drugs
Procter & Gamble	Drugs
Ralston Purina	Food processing
Royal Dutch Petroleum	Petroleum
Weis Markets	Grocery
Winn-Dixie Stores	Grocery
Wisconsin Energy	Electric utility

SOURCE: Value Line, April 28, 1989.

---

eral formula but calculate each time frame separately.

For example, you started the year with a portfolio worth $10,000 and reinvested all income. At the end of March, your portfolio was worth $10,900; on June 30, it was up a bit to $11,100. On July 1, you added $1,000. At the end of the third quarter, the value was $13,500, and $15,000 at year-end. Here's how to determine the return.

$$\text{March 30:} \quad \frac{10,900}{10,000} = 1.09, \text{ or } 9\%$$

$$\text{June 30:} \quad \frac{11,100}{10,900} = 1.01, \text{ or } 1\%$$

$$\text{September 30:} \quad \frac{13,500}{12,100} = 1.12, \text{ or } 12\%$$

$$\text{December 31:} \quad \frac{15,000}{13,500} = 1.11, \text{ or } 11\%$$

Now use the quarterly figures according to the formula:

$$1.09 \times 1.01 \times 1.12 \times 1.11 = 1.37$$

The gain is $1.37 - 1 = 0.37 = 37\%$.

Thus 37% is the time-weighted rate of return, but the average rate of return is much lower.

WHEN TO SELL A STOCK

Financial whiz kids and Wall Street gurus are always weaving complex theories about when to buy a stock. That's the easy part. They shy away from explaining when to sell, which is a much trickier business.

Although there's no foolproof system for making certain you always buy low and sell high, you can make an educated decision.

- You should consider selling when you think the market is headed for a serious setback. But, of course, not all stocks react to a declining market to the same degree. So to judge how much an individual stock fluctuates against broad market drops, check its beta in *Value Line Investment Survey*. The higher the beta, the more it moves and the faster you should sell.
- You should also consider selling if you think the company is in serious trouble and its earnings prospects are poor and not likely to recover quickly.
- If your stock suddenly drops in price by 20% or more within a short period—a month or less—you need to find out why and then consider selling.
- If your stock has become overvalued—you can tell if its P/E suddenly moves up and is way above the average P/E of the S&P 500—find out if it's soared because of good news, in which case hold, or because it's out of line, in which case sell and take your profit.

These four indicators, all reported in the *Wall Street Journal* as well as most major newspapers, should be your signposts for selling.

- *Stock prices are inflated.* This is indicated by a high P/E ratio for the S&P 500. In August 1987, just before the crash, it hit 23. Check the ratio regularly. In July 1989, it was 11.

- *There's a rise in interest rates.* Escalating interest rates hurt stocks as money moves to CDs and bonds. Watch the 3-month T-bill rate and the Federal Reserve discount rate. The market tends to fall when the Fed has raised the discount rate three or four consecutive times. It also falls if the T-bill rate is double the S&P 500 dividend yield. On September 27, 1989, the T-bill rate was 7.89% and the dividend yield on the S&P 500 was 3.3%.

- *A recession is in the wings.* The market tends to decline 6 to 9 months before an economic slump. Watch the Department of Commerce's leading economic indicators, which are reported monthly. If they are down for three consecutive months, the market may soon follow.

- *The market breadth is narrowing.* Often a group of stocks pushes the Dow Jones Industrial Average (or some other indicator) higher even though most other stocks are declining. This is called a narrowing of the market's breadth. You can spot this trend by following the advance/decline line that is reported in *Investor's Daily* and *Barron's.* It reflects

the difference between the number of stocks that gain and lose each day. In August 1987 the market was moving up but the advance/decline line was moving down. In fact, the Dow reached its all-time high of 2722 during that period.

HOW HIGH DIVIDENDS PAY

Dividend-paying stocks are not just for retirees and ultraconservative investors. They are important to everyone because they both boost the value of a stock and generally indicate that the company is a mature one, no longer in the throes of expensive expansion. A company that can afford to pay high dividends is no longer reinvesting all its profits in the company.

Another reason why high-dividend stocks are looked upon with such favor is that the dividend is likely to increase if the company's earnings grow—unlike a bond, whose coupon rate remains the same throughout its life.

$ HINT: Dividend-paying stocks fall less in price when the market falls. A study by Avner Arbel, professor of finance at Cornell University, shows that high-dividend stocks fell only 21% in the 1987 crash while nondividend payers dropped 32%.

To determine if a company is likely to continue making dividend payouts:

- Check the dividend-payout history for the past 10 years in *Standard & Poor's Stock Guide* or *Value Line Investment Survey.* Those with uninterrupted payouts are your best bet.

- Check the company's payout ratio: total dividends paid divided by net operating income. If the payout ratio is less than 50% the company will probably continue to pay dividends.

- Check the company's cash flow per share. If cash flow is three times the dividend payout, dividends will probably continue to be paid.

- Avoid or invest very carefully in stocks that have extraordinarily high yields for the industry group. Extremely high yields can signal trouble.

- Don't buy a high-yield stock near the ex-dividend date. That is the beginning of the time period during which purchasers of the stock cannot receive the next quarterly

---

CONSIDER INCREASING OR DECREASING YOUR POSITION IN AN INDIVIDUAL STOCK WHEN . . .

- The price changes substantially.
- New management takes over.
- Earnings increases or decreases are announced.
- A new product comes on line.
- A merger or acquisition takes place.
- The company is listed on or unlisted from one of the exchanges.
- Substantial legal action is brought against the company.
- Dividends are increased, cut, or canceled.
- The P/E multiple changes dramatically.
- The stock is purchased or sold by the institutions.
- The company spins off unprofitable divisions or subsidiaries.

A SAMPLING OF COMPANIES RATED A THAT HAVE INCREASED DIVIDENDS FOR 10 CONSECUTIVE YEARS

Abbott Laboratories*
Albertson's, Inc.
American Brands*
American Home Products*
American Water Works
Anheuser-Busch*

Bard (C.R.)
Barnett Banks
Borden, Inc.*

Clorox Co.
Coca-Cola*
Consolidated Natural Gas

Deluxe Corp.*
Dow Jones & Co.*
Dun & Bradstreet*

Emerson Electric
First Alabama Bancshares
Flowers Industries

Gannett Co.*
General Electric*

Heinz (H. J.)*
Hershey Foods*
Hillenbrand Industries

Kellogg Co.*
Knight-Ridder Inc.

Lilly (Eli)*

Melville Corp.*

Pfizer, Inc.*
Philip Morris Cos.*

Quaker Oats*

Ralston Purina*
Rubbermaid, Inc.

Service Master L. P.
Sunwest Financial SV*

Texas Utilities*
Tucson Electric Power*

V. F. Corp.

Walgreen Co.*
Winn-Dixie Stores*

* Has paid dividends for 50 consecutive years

SOURCE: Standard & Poor's, May 1989.

---

dividend, generally paid 3 to 4 weeks later. Usually stock prices are inflated just before the ex-dividend date, and on that date they tend to fall. If you buy the stock at an inflated price in order to receive the dividend, you may not break even since you'll be paying tax on the dividend income.

$ HINT: Sign up for a company's dividend reinvestment plan so your dividends will automatically be reinvested in additional shares of stock. Most companies do not charge a brokerage fee for these purchases, and some companies offer a 5% discount off market price for shares purchased through dividend reinvestment. Approximately 1,000 companies have dividend reinvestment plans.

$ HINT: Call the investors relations division of any company you own shares in to see if they have a dividend reinvestment plan, or obtain a list by sending $2 to:
Standard & Poor's Corp.
Public Relations
25 Broadway
New York, NY 10004

HEDGING GAINS

Of course the most obvious way to keep your gains is simply to sell your investment when you've made a profit. This approach has several drawbacks—you have to pay taxes on the gain, and if the market goes up you won't benefit. Here are four ways to protect your position on the downside and profit on the upswings.

- *Enter stop orders.* Have your broker sell your stock if it drops to a particular price. This protects you against major declines.
- *Sell into strength.* Each time the market makes a major move on the up side, sell a portion of your holdings. For example, if you own 500 shares of Xerox and you have big gains, sell 100 shares each time it appreciates 10%. You reduce your risk, and at the same time you're selling your stock at higher prices.
- *Buy put options.* This gives you the right to sell 100 shares of a stock at a particular price within a certain time period, up to 9 months. These options set a selling floor. For example, if you own a $50 stock, you

CANDIDATES FOR DIVIDEND INCREASES

	CURRENT ANN. DIVID. RATE	PROBABLE NEW ANN. RATE	APPROX. STOCK PRICE	YIELD (%) ON CURRENT RATE	YIELD (%) ON PROB. NEW RATE
Aluminum Co. of America	2.72	3.02	64	4.3	4.7
Bank of New York	1.92	2.04	39	4.9	5.2
Bristol-Myers	2.00	2.20	47	4.3	4.7
British Petroleum	3.28	3.50	57	5.8	6.1
Citicorp	1.48	1.60	28	5.3	5.7
Clorox Co.	1.04	1.12	33	3.2	3.4
Crane Co.	1.00	1.16	26	3.8	4.5
Dun & Bradstreet	1.74	2.00	56	3.1	3.6
Emerson Electric	1.12	1.20	32	3.5	3.8
Emhart Corp.	0.88	1.00	28	3.1	3.6
Exxon	2.20	2.40	45	4.9	5.3
Fieldcrest Cannon	0.68	0.80	22	3.1	3.6
Foote, Cone & Belding	1.20	1.30	24	5.0	5.4
General Electric	1.64	1.80	48	3.4	3.8
Goodrich (B.F.)	1.72	1.88	55	3.1	3.4
Humana Inc.	0.92	1.00	27	3.4	3.7
K mart	1.32	1.44	39	3.4	3.7
May Dept. Stores	1.28	1.44	38	3.4	3.8
Mobil Corp.	2.40	2.55	48	5.0	5.3
Monsanto	3.00	3.20	91	3.3	3.5
Olin Corp.	1.80	2.00	52	3.5	3.8
Rockwell Int'l	0.72	0.80	22	3.3	3.6
Security Pacific	1.96	2.16	39	5.0	5.5
Syntex Corp.	1.30	1.44	42	3.1	3.4
Tambrands	2.04	2.16	55	3.7	3.9
TECO Energy	1.42	1.50	23	6.2	6.5
Thomas & Betts	1.84	2.00	53	3.5	3.8
Westinghouse Electric	2.00	2.10	56	3.6	3.8
Weyerhaeuser	1.20	1.32	27	4.4	4.9
Woolworth	1.64	2.00	53	3.1	3.8

SOURCE: Standard & Poor's, *The Outlook*, February 15, 1988.

buy a put allowing you to sell 100 shares for $45 at any time within the next 6 months. The put costs about 75¢ per share and it limits your loss to $5 per share.

- *Switch to convertibles.* Move out of common stock into convertibles to lower your risk and still profit from a rise in the market.

PREFERRED STOCK

Individual investors usually gravitate toward preferred stocks because of their high, secure dividends. Many are issued by utilities.

As their name implies, preferred stocks enjoy preferred status over common stocks. Preferred shareholders receive their dividend pay-

LOW- OR NO-DEBT COMPANIES

COMPANY	PRICE	YIELD	ACTIVITY
A. G. Edwards	$20⁵/₈	3.3%	Brokerage firm
Eldon Industries	18¹/₂	1.3	Office accessories
Int'l. Flavors & Fragrances	54³/₈	3.5	Food flavoring
Long's Drug Stores	36⁷/₈	2.3	Drugstore chain
Weis Markets	30³/₄	1.8	Supermarket
Wm. Wrigley Jr.	44³/₄	1.7	Chewing gum

SOURCE: Silberberg Rosenthal & Co., May 3, 1989.

ments after all bondholders are paid and before dividends are paid on common shares. Like bonds, preferreds have a fixed annual payment, but it's called a dividend. It is set at a fixed dollar amount and is secure for the life of the stock. If a payment is skipped because of corporate losses, it will be paid later when earnings recover. That's why preferreds are sometimes called *cumulative,* because the dividends accumulate and must be paid out before common. Most preferreds are cumulative and are indicated by the initials "cm" in the stock guides.

There are also *noncumulative preferreds:* if a dividend is skipped, it is not recovered. It's best to avoid this type of preferred.

➤ PROS   Although there have been a few incidents of corporations skipping preferred dividends, on the whole these securities have an excellent safety record. And if the yield is high, it remains permanently high.

➤ CONS   Inflation and high interest rates can have a large negative impact on preferreds. That's because the dividend is fixed, and when rates rise, holders are locked in at the old lower rate. Not only are they shut out of rising interest rates, but the opportunity for substantial price appreciation of their shares is limited.

Although preferreds trade like bonds on the basis of their yields, unlike bonds they have no maturity date. With a bond you know that at a specified time you will get back your initial investment, the face value. There is no such assurance with a preferred. Market conditions

INSTITUTIONAL FAVORITES

Owned by More Than 500 Institutions
American Express
American Home Products
Bristol-Myers
Coca-Cola
Du Pont (E. I.)
Exxon Corp.
General Electric
IBM
MMM
Philip Morris
Sears, Roebuck
Westinghouse Electric
Xerox Corp.

Owned by 400 to 500 Institutions
American Brands
Borden, Inc.
FPL Group
Sara Lee Corp.
Southern Co.
Time Inc.
Toys "R" Us
Union Carbide

Owned by 250 to 400 Institutions
Chase Manhattan
Clorox Co.
Dresser Industries
Federal Express
Grace (W.R.)
Humana Inc.
Knight-Ridder Inc.
Rubbermaid, Inc.
Snap-On Tools
Tribune Co.

SOURCE: Standard & Poor's, July 1989.

are the sole determinant of the price you will receive when you sell.

SELECTING PREFERREDS

The basic criteria for selecting preferreds are *quality* of the issuing corporation, as shown by financial strength and profitability; *value,* as indicated by the yield; and *timing,* taking into account the probable trend of interest rates. Then:

- **Deal with a brokerage firm that has a research department that follows this group of securities.** Not every broker is familiar with preferreds, and many will not be able to provide enough pertinent information.
- **Recognize the inherent volatility because of limited marketability.** Preferreds listed on a major stock exchange may drop (when you want to sell) or rise (when you plan to buy) 2 or 3 points the day after the last quoted sale. If you have to sell in a hurry, this can be expensive. Preferreds sold over the counter (OTC) may fluctuate even more because of their thin markets. As a rule, place your orders at a set price or within narrow limits.

$ HINT: Ask your broker about *adjustable-rate preferreds.* The quarterly dividend fluctuates with interest rates and is tied to a formula based on Treasury bills or other money market rates.

$ HINT: *Participating preferreds* entitle shareholders to a portion of the company's profits. In *nonparticipating preferreds,* shareholders are limited to the stipulated dividend.

➤ QUALITY Choose preferred stocks rated BBB or higher by Standard & Poor's or Baa or higher by Moody's if you are conservative. But if you are willing to take greater risks, you can boost your income by buying BB-rated preferreds,

such as Philadelphia Electric 7.80% cm pfd selling at 70 with a yield of 11.2%.

Usually, but not always, the higher rating will be given to companies with modest debt. Since bond interest must be paid before dividends, the lower the debt ratio, the safer the preferred stock. For example, look for utilities with balanced debt and then check the preferred stocks. Buy several differed preferreds so you can benefit from diversification.

➤ CALL PROVISION This provision allows the company to redeem or call in the shares, usually at a few points above par (face value). When the original issue carries a high yield, say over 10%, the company may find it worthwhile to retire some shares (1) when it can float new debt or issue preferred stock at a lower rate, say, 8% or (2) when corporate surplus becomes substantial. In both cases, such a prospect may boost the price of the preferred by a point or two.

⬜ CAUTION: Preferred stock, especially of small, struggling corporations often has special call or conversion provisions. And utilities sometimes take advantage of obscure provisions in their charters to use other assets to call in their preferreds. You may end up with a modest profit, but if the redemption price is less than that at which the stock was selling earlier, you will lose money. Always check a preferreds' call features.

➤ SINKING FUND Corporations use "sinking funds" to accumulate money on a regular basis in order to redeem the corporation's bonds or preferred stocks from time to time so that the entire issue is retired before the stated maturity date. For example, starting 5 years after the original sale, a company might buy back 5% of the stock annually for 20 years. The yields of such preferreds will usually be slightly less than those for which there is no such provision.

$ IF YOU DARE: Look for a company that has omitted dividend payouts for several years. It will probably be selling at a discount. Should earnings recover, it will pay off all accumulated dividends, and the price of the stock is likely to rise.

$ HINT: Buy participating preferreds to ensure receiving a percentage of any exceptional profit gain, as for example, if the corporation sells a subsidiary and has excess profits for the year.

CALCULATING BENEFITS OF PREFERRED STOCK INVESTMENTS

Assumptions: 12% preferred stock dividend rate; 70% corporate tax exclusion on dividends; 40% corporate tax rate.

1 What is the effective after-tax rate of the dividend?

12% dividend − 12% (1 − .70 [.40]) = 10.56% after-tax return

2 Should you borrow to invest?

Borrowing cost: 16% (1 − 40) = 9.6%

Effective yield − borrowing cost = 10.56% − 9.60% = 0.96%

SOURCE: © *The Treasury Manager* (P.O. Box 540, Holliston, MA 01746; $325 per year).

SELECTED PREFERRED STOCKS

COMPANY	DIVIDEND	STANDARD & POOR'S RATING	RECENT PRICE	RECENT YIELD
Alabama Power "F"	$9.00	A–	$89	10.0%
Chase Manhattan "B"	6.75	A	68	9.8
Du Pont (E.I.) "A"	3.50	AA	40	8.8
Georgia Power "A"	2.75	A	26	10.4
Pennsylvania Power & Light "J"	8.00	BBB+	81	9.9
Southern Calif. Edison "D"	1.08	AA	11	9.3
Transco Energy "A"	4.75	B+	50	9.4
Virginia Electric "H"	7.45	A	78	9.6

SOURCE: Standard & Poor's for ratings; prices, May 3, 1989.

PREFERRED STOCK

PROS

↑ Generally pays higher dividends than common

↑ Receive your dividend before common stockholders

↑ Dividends generally cumulative; if dividend skipped, made up in future

↑ Know what your dividend income is

↑ Possibility of capital gain in price of stock

CONS

↓ If company's earnings rise, you don't share in increases unless it is a participating preferred

↓ Dividend fixed, with few exceptions

↓ Call provisions allow company to redeem your stock at stated price

↓ No protection against inflation

CONTINUAL DIVIDENDS

Sharp investors may get as many as 12 dividends a year by rolling over preferred stocks. By buying shares just before the dividend date, they get the full payout. They sell the next day and buy another preferred with an upcoming dividend payment date. Because of the commission costs and need for constant checking, this technique is difficult for amateurs. Yet it can work well when it involves 500 shares or more and you work with a discount broker.

Timing is the key. After the payout date, the price of the preferred may drop almost as much as the value of the dividend. A 12% preferred might thus trade at 100 before the dividend date and drop back to just over 97 the next day. If you sell, you take a small loss. If you wait a week or so and are lucky in a strong market, you may be able to sell at 100. If you have the time, money, and a feel for this type of trading, you could make substantial profits.

FOR FURTHER INFORMATION

The Meaningful Interpretation of Financial Statements, by Donald E. Miller, $9.95. American Management Association, Inc. 135 West 50th Street New York, NY 10020 1-212-586-8100

Understanding Financial Statements New York Stock Exchange 11 Wall Street New York, NY 10005

Louis Engel & Brendon Boyd, *How to Buy Stocks* (Boston: Little, Brown & Co., 1953; Bantam paperback).

Lawrence J. Gitman and Michael D. Joehnk, *Investment Fundamentals* (New York: Harper & Row, 1988).

Benjamin Graham & David L. Dodd, *Security Analysis*, 4th ed. (New York: McGraw-Hill, 1962).

Charles J. Rolo, *Gaining on the Market* (Boston: Little, Brown & Co., 1982).

Richard J. Teweles and Edward S. Bradley, *The Stock Market* (New York: John Wiley & Sons, 1982).

Andrew Tobias, *The Only Investment Guide You'll Ever Need* (Orlando, Fla.: Harcourt Brace Jovanovich, 1978; Bantam paperback).

13 | OVER-THE-COUNTER STOCKS

A good investment is not always an obvious one, dancing in the limelight of the New York Stock Exchange. Even the venerable Benjamin Graham, father of security analysis, subscribed to this theory. He advised investors to consider making one out of three securities in their portfolios an over-the-counter (OTC) stock. (The term *over-the-counter* stems from the days when securities were sold over the counter in banks and stores, right along with money orders and dry goods.)

This is an area of the market traditionally dominated by individual investors rather than the institutions, and 11,000 to 12,000 securities trade OTC. Of these, approximately 5,400 are listed on NASDAQ (National Association of Securities Dealers Automated Quotation system), more than twice the number on the American and New York exchanges.

Since requirements for listing on NASDAQ are less stringent than for either the New York or American exchange (see box), the OTC companies tend to be smaller, newer, and less well known. This is reflected in their lower prices but higher risk level. And since fewer OTC stocks are owned by institutions or closely followed by analysts, research is not abundant on many of these issues, a fact that can work to your advantage, since it means neither Wall Street nor the public has run up the prices.

Although some OTC stocks have moved up in price, many are still undervalued by historical standards. Some OTCs have only recently emerged from their early stages of development; others have been trading and paying dividends for years. Because of their relatively small size, many grow faster than stocks trading on the major exchanges. As they grow, institutions often become interested, thus boosting price-

earnings ratios. This is also fertile ground occasionally for takeover candidates.

THE OTC MARKET

Unlike the New York and American stock exchanges, the OTC does not have a centralized trading floor. Instead, stocks are bought and sold through a centralized computer-telephone network linking dealers across the nation. There are two "divisions" of the OTC market: NASDAQ, a self-regulated trade group, which publishes daily quotes; and the National Quotation Bureau, a private company, which distributes daily data to brokers about small, thinly traded stocks, on what Wall Streeters call the "pink sheets" (because the data are printed on pink paper).

OTC trading is sometimes an expensive proposition. On the major and regional exchanges, specialists (who concentrate on particular stocks) match buy and sell orders received from brokerage firms. If no match is possible, the specialist usually fills the order from a personally held inventory. But when you trade OTC, your broker will fill your order from his or her inventory if there is one. Otherwise, your broker will buy the stock from another broker who makes a market in it and will then in turn sell it to you. The price is determined by a number of factors: the amount of stock the market maker has, the prices of recent trades, the markup, and the level of demand.

When you read the quotes in the paper, remember that the bid (or lower price) is what brokers or dealers are offering to pay for the stock. The higher (or asked figure) is what they will sell it for. The difference between these two numbers is the spread. On most exchanges, the spread is just a few pennies, but on the OTC the market makers actually negotiate the prices, and spreads are typically larger because of the greater risks involved.

$ HINT: The SEC requires all brokers who make a market in a stock to state their markup to clients. Be sure you ask.

GUIDELINES FOR SELECTING OTC STOCKS

- Start in your own backyard. Do research on companies in your region. Check with a local stockbroker for ideas. Read annual reports and visit the company personally.
- Buy only companies with established earnings growth and, if possible, low debt. Ideally, the assets-to-current liabilities ratio should be 2:1.
- Study wide economic and industrial trends and select companies that have a timely product or service.
- Find companies that have a market niche.
- Allow 2 to 10 months for price and/or earnings movement.
- Avoid penny stocks (stocks that sell for less than 50¢); the bid/asked price spread is often over 25%.

USING THE KEY INDICATORS

If and when you believe the big stocks are overpriced, it's time to move some of your portfolio into smaller issues. To help you time your move, watch these key indicators:

➤ NASDAQ COMPOSITE INDEX   Listed in the major newspapers, its direction and progress can be compared with those of other major indexes. If its trend is up, the environment is favorable.

➤ OTC VOLUME   Volume tends to verify the direction, up or down, of a market or individual issue. If the market rises on low volume, for example, generally the rise will be short.

➤ NEW HIGHS AND LOWS   A number of new highs over new lows is a positive buy sign.

➤ BLOCK TRADING   When trades of 10,000 shares or more take place, it probably signals institutional participation and future interest in the stock.

➤ S&P OTC 250 INDEX   Like the NASDAQ index, Standard & Poor's indicates the overall direction of secondary issues. It is especially valuable to

---

REQUIREMENTS FOR LISTING OF STOCKS ON EXCHANGES

NEW YORK STOCK EXCHANGE
- Pretax income: $2.5 million for most recent year and $2.0 million for each of 2 preceding years
- Number of shareholders: 2,000
- Number of shares: 1.1 million
- Value of shares outstanding: $18 million

AMERICAN STOCK EXCHANGE
- Pretax income: $750,000 for previous year or 2 out of the last 3 years
- Number of shareholders: 800 (if 500,000 shares outstanding) or 400 (if 1 million shares outstanding)
- Value of shares outstanding: $4 million

NATIONAL ASSOCIATION OF SECURITIES DEALERS AUTOMATED QUOTATION SYSTEM (OVER THE COUNTER)
- Total assets: $2 million
- Number of shareholders: 300
- Number of shares: 100,000
- Stockholders' equity: $1 million

---

compare it to the S&P 500. Since the beginning of 1988, many OTC stocks have recovered from their lows of October–November 1987.

➤ SHADOW STOCK INDEX   In January 1986 the American Association of Individual Investors, a nonprofit educational organization, introduced this index, which covers less well-known stocks. The market value of a company's outstanding stock must fall between $20 million and $100 million to qualify for inclusion. This means that all companies in the Shadow Stock Index have some sort of track record. Most trade OTC.

THE PINK SHEETS

This is also fertile territory for investors, but only for speculators, since these stocks are not listed on the NASDAQ electronic system, usually because of limited capitalization or the small number of shares outstanding. They are listed in *The Pink Sheets*, NASDAQ's daily publication, which gives bid and asked prices for more than 11,000 OTC stocks. *The Pink Sheets* tells your broker who makes a market in the stock, although the prices are negotiable. These small and thinly traded companies offer high growth potential, which of course means high risk. Occasionally you'll find a stock that's been delisted by one of the exchanges or is bankrupt. However, there are well-known companies among this group too, such as Doubleday & Co., Carvel, Lee Myles, and Lear Siegler.

$ HINT: Look for local companies or firms that make products you like; chances are they will be trading over the counter.

⌐CAUTION: According to a *Wall Street Journal* article on February 2, 1988, "flagrant fraud" exists in the pink sheet market.

The most common scam is "pump and dump"—promoters pump up the price with hype and false publicity and then dump the stock on unknowing investors for huge profits.

Pink sheet fraud was once confined to the penny stock centers of Denver and Salt Lake City, but today, says Gary Lynch, the former SEC enforcement director, it is a "national problem."

OTC MUTUAL FUNDS

FUND	APPRECIATION, JANUARY 1 TO APRIL 1, 1989
OTC Securities Fund (1-800-523-2578)	10.30%
Fidelity OTC Portfolio (1-800-544-6666)	11.37
T. Rowe Price New Horizon (1-800-638-5660)	6.89
Capital (CAP) Fund (1-800-638-5660)	6.81
American Capital OTC (1-800-421-5666)	6.50

In addition to scams, there are other problems with pink sheet stocks: (1) The spreads between the bid and asked prices can be huge on thinly traded stocks, and (2) illiquidity is common.

$ HINT: Don't buy a pink sheet stock unless you can find adequate information on the company from reliable sources. Even then, stick to the well-researched OTC stocks that trade frequently.

SMALL CAP STOCKS

Another area that is often overlooked by investors is small cap stocks, those with a limited number of shares outstanding and small capitalization. (Capitalization is determined by multiplying the number of shares by the current market value of one share.) These are discussed in Chapter 25.

USING MUTUAL FUNDS

If you want a professional to make the buying and selling decisions in the OTC market, you can invest in one of several mutual funds. These funds invest in stocks of small companies. During the first six months of 1988, the five major funds had growth rates between 6% and 11%, well above that of general growth funds. It remains to be seen whether or not their rally will be sustained, but in terms of diversification, investors may want to take a modest position

---

OTC STOCKS THAT MERIT FURTHER INVESTIGATION

- **Ashton-Tate** Microcomputer business strong
- **Baldwin Piano & Organ** Maker of pianos and electric organs
- **Cellular Communications** Cellular telephone system in Ohio
- **La Petite Academy** Day-care center operator
- **Lin Broadcasting** Expanding cellular telephone company
- **Mack Trucks** Solid gain expected this year
- **Noxell Corp. (B)** Beauty and health aids growing
- **Stokely USA** Markets canned goods
- **TRC Co.** Environmental engineering company
- **Wheelabrator Tech.** Refuse-to-energy plant manufacturing

SOURCE: Silberberg, Rosenthal & Co., May 1989.

OVER-THE-COUNTER STOCKS

PROS

↑ In an OTC mutual fund, professional management, diversification, liquidity, possibility of switching into other funds within
the same family

↑ Prices often low

↑ Potential capital appreciation

CONS

↓ May be thinly traded

↓ Can be difficult to sell when negative
news appears

↓ Research difficult to find, sometimes non-
existent

↓ Losses can be large

↓ Value of fund shares can decline

---

in one of these funds. But remember, higher
interest rates and inflation will hurt stocks.

Tips for selecting a fund:

■ Invest only in a fund that has $100
million or less in assets. A larger fund
may have to buy stocks of larger
companies, or its portfolio may become too
unwieldy to manage effectively.

■ Portfolio turnover should be 30% per year
or less.

■ Check the prospectus and quarterly reports
to make certain the fund is indeed
investing in small companies with
capitalization below $100 million.

FOR FURTHER INFORMATION

The 1989 NASDAQ Company Directory
NASD
Book Order Department
9513 Key West Avenue
Rockville, MD 20850
1-202-728-8000
$10

Lists all NASDAQ stocks with their symbols.

OTC Review (magazine)
37 East 28th Street, Suite 706
New York, NY 10016
1-212-685-6244
Monthly; $42 per year; $84 for 3 years

Contains studies of individual stocks.

Growth Stock Outlook (newsletter)
P.O. Box 15381
Chevy Chase, MD 20815
1-301-654-5205
Twice monthly; $175 per year

Published by Charles Allmon; covers stocks with
potential appreciation.

The OTC Handbook
Standard & Poor's
25 Broadway
New York, NY 10004
1-212-208-8000
$65 per year

Published every 6 months; lists historical data
and prices for the larger OTC companies. Check
your library.

OTC Insight (newsletter)
P.O. Box 127
Moraga, CA 94556
1-415-376-1223
Monthly; $195 per year

Scans data on 1,100 OTC stocks and provides
sample portfolios.

Value Line OTC Special Situation Service
711 Third Avenue
New York, NY 10017
1-212-687-3965
Bimonthly; $395 per year

Reliable coverage of OTC and small cap stocks.

UTILITIES AND NEW ISSUES

During the first part of 1987, public utility stocks underperformed the overall stock market, yet immediately after the October crash, thousands of investors flocked to them for safety and high yields. The result: the utilities outperformed the industrials for the next several months. As we go to press, the 100 utilities followed by Value Line had an average yield of 8.5%, well above those of most other common stocks.

AN ELECTRIC SHOCK

The utility industry, which consists of electric power, gas distribution, water, and telephone companies, has historically appealed to the conservative investor because of ever-higher dividends and slow yet steady growth in the value of the stocks. In the past, in fact, investors tended to think of utilities as being in the same safe category as bonds and Treasury issues, and together they were the cornerstone of many conservative portfolios. But investing in utilities isn't what it used to be.

CONTINUING RISK

What has always been true in other industries is now true for utilities. They, too, are subject to the basic premise that risks and rewards go hand in hand, which means that you will generally find the highest yields in what are regarded as the riskiest companies. The top-yielding utilities are not appropriate for the conservative investor, since they tend to be heavily involved with large nuclear power plant construction programs or regulatory difficulties.

In addition, a number of new developments are boosting the overall risk level of the group. You should know about these pitfalls before purchasing shares in any utility, including the ones that supply your home or office with gas, electricity, and water.

➤ NUCLEAR PROBLEMS Companies with nuclear generating plants under construction are under intense pressure from both consumer and political groups to abandon their units. Due to cost overruns and disallowance of construction costs at the Nine Mile Point project, four utility companies were forced to reduce their dividends: Central Hudson & Gas, New York State Electric & Gas, Niagara Mohawk Power, and Rochester Gas & Electric. Also in serious trouble due to construction problems are Long Island Lighting and Gulf State Utilities. The Public Service Company of New Hampshire actually entered bankruptcy proceedings under Chapter 11, making it the first major public utility to so distinguish itself since the Great Depression.

➤ DECOMMISSIONING A number of nuclear plants are approaching the end of their usefulness, and their nuclear reactors must be scrapped over the next 10 to 15 years. Some experts estimate that between 50 and 60 nuclear plants will cease operations by the year 2010, at a minimum cost of $100 million per plant. Stocks of these utilities should not be included in the average portfolio.

➤ OVERRUNS AND MISMANAGEMENT The industry's regulators have been taking closer looks at construction costs and in a number of cases are making shareholders pay for some of these expenses.

➤ LOSS OF MONOPOLY STATUS Utilities are gradually losing their so-called monopoly status as large customers begin constructing their own generating plans or alternative sources of energy.

➤ NEW ACCOUNTING RULES The Tax Reform Act of 1986 basically penalizes companies with construction programs by eliminating the investment tax credit. It also makes the allowance for funds used during construction (AFDC),

151

formerly a nontaxable credit, partially taxable. This credit goes to utilities to compensate for their capital costs.

GUIDELINES FOR SELECTION

In the past, utility stocks moved pretty much as a group, but today the difference between the best and the poorest has widened and skepticism should be your guiding principle. When making a utility selection you should ask:

- How good is management?
- Is the dividend safe?
- What is the nuclear situation?
- What is the regulatory environment?
- What is the reserve margin? (Reserve margin is power capacity above peak-load

---

UTILITIES WITH NUCLEAR PLANTS IN OPERATION

Most electric utility companies are involved in either construction or generation of nuclear power. The 1979 accident at Three Mile Island resulted in major construction revisions to all nuclear projects, pushing up costs and magnifying financial as well as political problems. But once a nuclear plant is completed, its operation is far less expensive than that of a comparable oil, gas, or coal facility. Nuclear fuel sells for only about 10% of the cost of fossil fuel.

COMPANY	PERCENT NUCLEAR	VALUE LINE SAFETY RATING	YIELD (MAY 1989)
Baltimore G&E	46%	1	7.0%
Commonwealth Ed	77	3	9.1
FPL Group	30	1	7.6
Iowa Ill. G&E	37	1	8.6
Iowa Resources	40	3	9.8
Northeast Util.	68	2	9.3
Wisconsin Energy	30	1	6.2
Wisconsin Public Ser.	19	1	7.8
WPL Holding Inc.	19	1	7.7

SOURCE: Shearman Ralston, Inc.

NO NUKES

COMPANY	VALUE LINE SAFETY RATING	YIELD (MAY 1989)
Allegheny Power	1	8.5%
Central Illinois Public Service	1	8.5
Hawaiian Electric Company	1	7.0
Idaho Power Company	2	7.8
Ipalco Enterprises	1	7.6
Kansas Power & Light	1	7.7
Louisville G&E	2	8.3
Oklahoma G&E	1	7.4
Orange & Rockland	1	8.2
Potomac Electric Power	1	7.4
Southwestern Public Service	1	8.6
Tucson Electric	2	8.7

SOURCE: Shearman Ralston, Inc.

---

usage; if it is especially high, the company may have unused plants and high costs. The industrywide average is around 25%.) Moreover,

- Don't select a utility stock solely on the basis of its yield. (A high return often reflects Wall Street uncertainty about the safety of the dividend.)
- Do select stocks that have expectations for higher earnings and growth rates.
- If all other things are equal, select a utility that has a dividend reinvestment plan. You will save on commissions.
- Diversify. Buy utilities from several states, to avoid any one state's unfavorable regulatory policies.

With stocks of quality utilities, the wise investor can look for total returns of about 11.5%: 7% to 9% from dividends and the balance from appreciation. At some point, most shares will become fully valued and should be sold, typically after 3 or 4 years.

To achieve such returns, you must be selective and be armed with plenty of information such as:

- **Bond rating,** as determined by Standard & Poor's or Moody's. This is a measure of the company's financial strength.
- **Regulatory climate.** The attitude of state authorities toward permitting the utility to earn an adequate rate of return is an important factor.
- **Return on equity.** This is that basic standard of quality—the ability of management to make money with your money. It is often a reflection of the state authorities, who may or may not permit an adequate rate of return.
- **AFDC (allowance for funds during construction).** Under this form of accounting, new construction and equipment expenses are shifted off the income statement (where they reduce earnings) onto the balance sheet (where they become part of the base used to ask for higher rates). This is legal, logical, and generally acceptable by regulatory authorities, but it's a yellow light for investors, because these are not *true* earnings.

AFDC is a noncash bookkeeping transaction that lowers the quality of corporate profits. This information is available from Moody's Investor Services or your broker.

- **Main fuel.** This is a key criterion for many analysts. Utilities that use water (hydroelectric plants) have no cost worries; those that use coal seldom have major problems with the supply or price of their fuel; those that rely on gas or oil are subject to conditions beyond their control; and those with nuclear plants are regarded as questionable to dangerous. This pessimism stems from huge overrun costs and standstills involving Public Service of New Hampshire and Long Island Lighting.
  Note: With utilities, state laws often prescribe actions that in other industries would be management's prerogative.

$ HINT: Look for utilities with strong internal cash flow that have completed or are facing diminishing construction programs.

BRIGHT LIGHTS

Despite these problems, there are a number of bright lights on the horizon.

- Construction programs are winding down, which means stronger balance sheets.
- Many utilities are diversifying into nonutility areas, such as TECO Energy's move into shipping and transportation.
- Cash flows are up, thus enabling a number of companies to boost dividends, reduce high-cost debt, repurchase shares, or diversify.
- The group remains recession-resistant, since electricity, water, and gas are necessities. That means that in a recession, these stocks should suffer far less than most.

THE SAFEST COMPANIES

High-quality utilities are listed in the table on page 152. These companies are well able to cover their dividend earnings, even in a recession. They are suggested for conservative portfolios— and, in fact, a number are likely to increase

---

THE BELL COMPANIES

As a result of the great AT&T breakup, there are eight different Bell companies. Shares of all are traded on the NYSE. Yields range from 5.7% to 3.4%.

Phone company stocks have held up well since the October crash, with most rising significantly in price.

COMPANY	PRICE (MAY 1989)	P/E RATIO	YIELD
AT&T	$34	15	3.4%
Ameritech	56	12	5.1
Bell Atlantic	82	12	5.3
Bell South	46	13	5.4
NYNEX	74	11	5.8
Pacific Tel	38	13	4.9
Southwest B	48	13	5.4
U.S. West	65	10	5.7

SOURCE: Silberberg Rosenthal & Co., May 4, 1989.

their dividends over the next few years. Despite their high safety rankings, you should monitor their activities on a regular basis, and at the first sign of a problem, ask your broker for an up-to-date research report or check Value Line or Standard & Poor's coverage of the company.

UTILITY MUTUAL FUNDS

If you prefer professional management of your money and a broadly diversified utility portfolio, turn to one of the utility funds listed on page 156. However, select with care. All funds are not created equal—Fidelity's Select Utilities, for example, does not pay out dividends to investors but instead reinvests them in the fund.

WATER COMPANIES

Telephone and electric companies have always been in the spotlight, hogging center stage in the utility industry. Yet stocks of public water companies also deserve a place in the limelight. This group, which has low institutional ownership, over the years has turned in a solid performance.

- It provides a commodity everyone needs.
- It has no competition; there is no alternative to water.
- It has no nuclear exposure.
- Many water companies are profitably diversified.

Although there are an estimated 65,000 water companies in the United States, about 85% are municipally owned and regulated by city governments. That leaves about 350 investor-owned operations, and of these, only 18 have above $15 million in total capital. American Water Works is the largest. It serves over 1.4 million customers in 500 communities in 20 states. Its largest customer is Monsanto.

☐ CAUTION: If you decide to invest in a water company, keep in mind that rate increases are determined by area regulatory bodies and that various local situations, including the weather, and the economy have a major effect on earnings. Residential customers dominate the industry, and companies therefore tend to benefit from hot weather spells when Americans use more water. Companies must continually meet the water standards set by the Environmental Protection Agency.

The larger, better-known water firms are listed in the table on page 156. You may also want to investigate your local water company—find out if it is publicly traded—but read the last two annual reports and the current quarterlies before purchasing shares.

UTILITY BONDS

When RJR Nabisco's CEO told the investment world last year that he planned to take his company private by floating new debt, the value of Nabisco's bonds immediately fell by nearly 20%. Suddenly investors in other high-grade corporate bonds were fearful, wondering if their bonds would do the same if a takeover or leveraged buyout came their way.

Certain bonds, however, are relatively free from takeover troubles: Treasury issues, for example, are not vulnerable to an LBO since it's unlikely anyone will try to take over the Treasury! Another fairly safe haven lies in high-rated utility bonds, whose yields tend to be slightly above those of Treasuries. Most utility bonds have high ratings because these corporations provide continually needed services and are relatively recession-resistant. Bondholders receive interest semiannually, and as we go to press their yields ranged from 8½% to 9½%.

☐ CAUTION: Buy only bonds rated A or above and check the call feature. Most utilities have only 5-year call protection, whereas Treasuries are essentially noncallable. Avoid bonds of companies with nuclear or regulatory problems.

Many high-yielding utility bonds have early redemption clauses built into their issues. These call provisions permit a utility to buy back its bonds at face value or even a bit higher, but more often than not at prices below the current market. Utility companies are allowed to use these special "calls" to cut expenses by retiring high-yield or high-coupon bonds.

NEW ISSUES

After the October 1987 crash, new issues, also known as initial public offerings (IPOs), plummeted. Not surprisingly, investors lost their enthusiasm for what was once one of the most

GETTING A STEADY STREAM OF INCOME

Use the utility stocks listed below to set up a consistent dividend stream. The 24 companies are grouped according to the dates on which they pay their quarterly dividends. If you buy 6 stocks, one in each of the 6 payment slots, you will receive 24 dividend checks each year, with your income spaced evenly on a semimonthly basis throughout the year.

	INDICATED QUARTERLY DIVIDEND	NUMBER OF SHARES	QUARTERLY DIVIDENDS RECEIVED	RECENT PRICE	DIV. YIELD	P/E RATIO*
Early Jan., Apr., July, Oct.						
Baltimore Gas & Electric	$0.50	100	$50	30	6.7	8.7
Potomac Electric	0.37	135	49	20	7.4	8.7
Public Service Enterprises	0.51	100	51	25	8.2	9.4
SCANA Corp.	0.62	80	49	30	8.3	10.0
Mid Jan., Apr., July, Oct.						
IPALCO Enterprises	0.43	115	49	23	7.5	8.5
National Fuel Gas	0.32	160	50	18	7.1	9.7
Northern States Power	0.53	95	50	32	6.6	9.7
Peoples Energy	0.40	125	50	22	7.3	9.4
Early Feb., May, Aug., Nov.						
Ameritech	0.73	70	51	54	5.4	11.5
Brooklyn Union Gas	0.45	110	49	25	7.2	9.8
Pacific Telesis	0.47	105	49	37	5.1	12.1
Southwestern Bell	0.65	75	49	46	5.7	12.4
Mid Feb., May, Aug., Nov.						
Eastern Utilities Assoc.	0.63	80	50	33	7.7	9.4
PacifiCorp	0.66	75	50	36	7.3	9.9
Pacific Enterprises	0.87	55	48	40	8.7	11.4
TECO Energy	0.38	140	50	24	6.3	10.7
Early Mar., June, Sep., Dec.						
Black Hills	0.38	130	49	26	5.8	10.6
Southwestern Public Service	0.55	90	50	26	8.5	10.4
Tenneco	0.76	65	49	52	5.8	12.2
Wisconsin Energy	0.39	130	50	26	6.0	8.5
Mid Mar., June, Sep., Dec.						
Consolidated Edison	0.86	60	52	47	7.3	9.5
Dominion Resources	0.80	65	52	42	7.6	9.3
Duke Power	0.74	65	48	45	6.6	9.6
FPL Group	0.55	90	50	30	7.3	9.0

* Based on estimated 1989 earnings.

SOURCE: Standard & Poor's, *The Outlook*, April 26, 1989.

UTILITY MUTUAL FUNDS

FUND	MINIMUM	TOTAL RETURN (1/1/89 TO 4/1/89)	CURRENT YIELD (APRIL 1, 1989)
ABT Utility Income (1-800-441-6580; 1-800-582-7396 in Ohio)	$1,000	6.22%	6.6%
Fidelity Select Utilities (1-800-544-6666; 1-617-523-1919 in Mass.)	1,000	5.83	DR*
Fidelity Utilities Income (1-800-544-6666; 1-617-523-1919 in Mass.)	2,500	.74	DR*
Financial Strategic Utilities (1-800-525-8085; 1-800-525-9769 in Colo.)	250	4.29	4.59
Franklin Utilities (1-800-632-2350; 1-800-247-1753)	100	−0.42	N.A.
Pru-Bache Utilities Fund (1-800-872-7787)	1,000	22.75†	N.A.
Stratton Monthly Dividend (1-215-941-0888)	2,000	4.9	8.71

* Dividends reinvested.
† 1/1/88 to 12/31/88.

exciting areas of the market. Nevertheless, some analysts and investors continue to be drawn to the new issues market, largely by the dream of huge profits, especially since new stock offerings outperformed the S&P 500 in 1988. If you're tempted, if you think you can double your money, learn the facts and follow our guidelines for selecting fledgling companies to back. It is possible to make money in IPOs, but it requires far more research than most investments, as well as an understanding of the market. Norman G. Fosback, editor of *New Issues*, favors com-panies that have reported profits for at least 5 years and whose earnings are trending up.

If you don't buy an IPO when it's first issued, you can buy shares in the aftermarket when they trade OTC. If it's a weak market, chances are you won't pay much more, if anything; but in a hot market, expect a 20% to 25% increase in the aftermarket. If you are enamored of the issue but cannot buy at a reasonable price, follow the stock's progress carefully. Wait for the first blush to fade, and move in when it takes a tumble. Often a new

WATER COMPANIES

COMPANY	EXCHANGE: SYMBOL	PRICE	YIELD
American Water Works	NYSE: AWK	$18	4.0%
Citizens Utilities (A)	OTC: CITU-A	44	Nil
Consumers Water	OTC: CONW	17	6.2
The Hydraulic Co.	NYSE: THC	27	5.7
Philadelphia Suburban	NYSE: PSC	13	7.0
Southern California Water	OTC: SWTR	25	8.0
United Water Resources	NYSE: UWR	17	5.2

SOURCE: Quotron, May 10, 1989.

PENNY STOCKS

Most penny stocks have been and still are offered in Denver. They are pure speculations. If you are lucky or related to one of the promoters, you may make a lot of money. But most of these "opportunities" are better for their sponsors than they are for outside speculators. The markets for these shares are more or less controlled; their initial price is "negotiated" by the company, the selling shareholders, and the underwriter and rarely have much relation to value. Most important, once the shares have been distributed, there's seldom any sustained interest.

Most penny stocks are brought out by underwriters on a "best efforts" basis, which puts such issues on shaky ground from the beginning. The promoters seldom pledge a nickel of their own funds to guarantee the selling out of the offering.

There is, however, one saving grace: full disclosure as required by the SEC. Few people bother to read the prospectus to discover that "the offering price . . . bears no relationship to assets, earnings, book value, or other criteria of value. . . . There is no trading market for the securities . . . no assurance that such a market will develop."

The lure is the low price and huge number of shares. For $1,000, speculators can own thousands of shares and profit from a slight price rise (usually initiated by the promoters). But over a period of time (as little as 3 months), the losses can be as sensational, because very few of the companies ever report significant earnings, and once the initial enthusiasm is withdrawn, no one is interested. With all penny stocks, you are shooting dice, and the house sets the odds—against you.

---

company will lose its initial luster or report lower earnings, thus pushing the price down temporarily.

Learning about new issues is less difficult than you might think. A number of the larger brokerage firms publish a list of them on a regular basis, but unless you're a major client, you won't hear about them. Your broker or library may subscribe to the bible in the field, *Investment Dealer's Digest*, which lists all IPOs as they are registered with the SEC.

THE UNDERWRITER

Your chances for success will be increased if you select IPOs from reputable investment bankers. First-class underwriters will not allow themselves to manage new issues that are of poor quality or highly speculative. Moreover, if a fledgling company runs into a need for additional financing, a first-rate banker will be ready to raise more capital. Thus the prime consideration is the reputation of the underwriters. However, this is not written in stone.

THE PROSPECTUS

Once you learn about a new issue, your first investigative step is to read a copy of the prospectus, generally available when an offering is registered with the SEC. (It's also called a "red herring" because of the red-inked warning that the contents of the report are not final.) Despite its many caveats, the prospectus will help you form a rough opinion about the company and what it may be worth. Look for:

➤ DETAILS ABOUT MANAGEMENT The success of a company is often determined by the quality of the management team. The officers and directors should have successful experience in the company and/or similar organizations; they should be fully involved in the firm and should not treat it as a part-time activity.

➤ TYPE OF BUSINESS New ventures have the best chance of success in growth areas, such as electronics, specialty retailing, and biotechnology. Manufacturing, specialty retail chains, and waste disposal are expected to do well in 1989–1990. The risks are greatest with companies in exciting but partially proven fields such as biotechnology, genetic engineering, and computer software. These companies are tempting but pay off only after heavy capital investments and successful R&D. Try to invest in an area you know something about or a business located near you. A good prospectus will also list some of the company's customers.

➤ FINANCIAL STRENGTH AND PROFITABILITY Apply the following criteria to the current balance sheet. Glance at the previous year's report to catch any major changes.

- Modest short-term debt and long-term obligations of less than 40% of total capital. With $40 million in assets, the debt should not be more than $16 million.
- Current ratio (of assets to liabilities) a minimum of 2:1 except under unusual, temporary conditions.

- Sales of at least $30 million to be sure that there's a market for products or services. Double-check if revenues exceed $50 million. That's the threshold for the big leagues, where competition is sure to heighten.
- High profitability: a return on equity of 20% annually for the past 3 years—with modest modifications if recent gains have been strong. This will assure similar progress in the future.

➤ EARNINGS The company should be able to service its debt. Look for the most recent P/E and compare it with P/Es of competitors, listed in the newspaper. If a P/E is significantly higher than the industry average of a similar-sized company, shares are overpriced. Robert S. Natale, editor of Standard & Poor's *Emerging & Special Situations* newsletter, states that a young company often hasn't had time to produce much in the way of earnings, so instead look for a ratio of total offering price to annual sales. On the whole, this market-capitalization-to-sales ratio should not be greater than 2:7.

➤ USE OF PROCEEDS Check out what the company plans to do with the newly raised capital. It should not be devoted to repaying the debt or bailing out the founders, management, or promoters. Most of it should be used to expand the business. If 25% or more is going toward nonproductive purposes, move on. Avoid firms whose management or a founding shareholder is selling a large percentage of the shares (30% or more).

$ HINT: Whenever the public is chasing after new issues and creating a shortage, unscrupulous operators and bucket shops tend to fill the void. Beware of telephone solicitations from brokerage firms with names that sound legitimate. These people will offer shares at $1 or $2 and guarantee that they'll be trading at double those prices when they go public. Careful: you're skating on thin ice.

MUTUAL FUNDS THAT INVEST IN SMALL, EMERGING COMPANIES

Access American
 Capital Co.
P.O. Box 256
Kansas City, MO 64141
1-800-231-3638

Alliance Technology
 Fund
500 Plaza Drive (3rd
 floor)
Secaucus, NJ 06094
1-800-247-4154

Fidelity Growth Fund
21 Congress Street
Boston, MA 02109
1-800-544-6666

Keystone S-4 Fund
1 Athenaeum Street
Cambridge, MA 02142
1-800-225-2618

The Nautilus Fund
24 Federal Street
Boston, MA 02110
1-800-225-6265

New Horizon Fund
T. Rowe Price Associates
100 East Pratt Street
Baltimore, MD 21202
1-800-638-5660
1-301-547-2308

The Nova Fund
260 Franklin Street
Boston, MA 02110
1-800-572-0006

Putnam Health Sciences
 Fund
P.O. Box 2701
Boston, MA 02208
1-800-225-2465

20th Century Ultra
 Investors OTC
P.O. Box 419200
Kansas City, MO 64141-
 6200
1-816-531-5575

Vanguard Explorer Fund
P.O. Box 2600
Valley Forge, PA 19482
1-800-662-7447

FOR FURTHER INFORMATION

To help you spot the winners and avoid the losers when firms go public, you may want to read one of the following advisory newsletters for background data:

Emerging and Special Situations
Standard & Poor's Corp.
25 Broadway
New York, NY 10005
1-212-208-8000
Monthly; $180 per year

New Issues
Institute for Econometric Research
3471 North Federal Highway
Ft. Lauderdale, FL 33306
1-305-563-9000
Monthly; $95 per year

Ground Floor
The Hirsch Organization
6 Deer Trail
Old Tappan, NJ 07675
1-201-664-3400
Monthly; $115 per year

Investment Dealers Digest
2 World Trade Center (18th floor)
New York, NY 10048
1-212-227-1200
Weekly; $295 per year

Everyone who owns securities should understand options and use them at times. They can produce quick profits with little capital, make possible protective hedges, and usually limit losses. But to make money with options, you must work hard, research thoroughly, review often, and adhere to strict rules. To be really successful, you should have ample capital and recognize that compared with stocks and bonds, the commissions as a percentage of the option prices are high.

Before you allocate savings to any type of options, discuss your plans with your broker, and test out your ideas on paper. If you are not willing to follow your hypothetical choices for several months, get quotations for the previous 13 weeks from newspaper files at your library.

With careful selections and constant monitoring, *selling* options can boost annual income by 15% or more; *buying* options can bring quick gains. With options, you have the power of leverage (a small sum can control a large investment), low costs, and a variety of choices (in types of underlying assets, strike prices, and time frames).

Options are a cross between trading in stocks and trading in commodities. They permit holders to control for a specified period of time a relatively large amount of stock with a relatively small amount of capital. An option represents the *right* to buy or sell a specific stock at a specific price (called the strike price) for a limited time. You do not need to own the stock to buy an option. If the stock rises, the option should rise too, giving you a profit if you sell. Of course, if the stock falls in price, so will the option, and you'll face a loss.

In effect, options have a limited life of 9 months. They pay no dividends and, by definition, are diminishing assets. The closer the expiration date, the less time there is for the value of the option to rise or fall as the buyer anticipates.

TERMS USED IN OPTION TRADING

➤ PUTS AND CALLS The most popular and widely used option is a *call*—the right to buy the underlying stock. A *put* is the opposite—the right to sell the stock. For sophisticated traders, there are complex combinations: spreads, strips, straps, and straddles.

➤ PREMIUM The cost of the option is called the *premium.* It varies with the duration of the contract, the type of stock, corporate prospects, and the general activity of the stock market. Premiums run as high as 15% of the value of the underlying stock; that is, for a volatile stock selling at 50 ($5,000 for 100 shares), the premium for a call to be exercised 9 months from now might be 7½ ($750) when the exercise price is also 50. Shorter-term options on more stable stocks carry smaller premiums: from 2% for those expiring in a month or so to 5% for those with longer maturities. Commissions will cut those returns.

➤ STRIKE PRICE This is the price per 100 shares at which the holder of the option may buy (with a call) or sell (with a put) the related stock.

For stocks selling under $100 per share, the quotations are at intervals of 5 points: 45, 50, 55, etc. For stocks trading at over $100 per share, the quotations are every 10 points: 110, 120, etc.

New listings are added when the stock reaches the high or low strike price; that is, at 40, when the stock hits 35 and at 25 when the stock falls to 30. When you see a long list of strike prices, the stock has moved over a wide range.

➤ EXPIRATION DATE The option expires the Saturday following the third Friday of the month in which it can be exercised. Maximum length is 9 months.

➤ DIVIDENDS AND RIGHTS As long as you own the stock, you continue to receive the dividends. That's why calls for stocks with high yields sell at lower premiums than those for companies with small payouts.

A stock dividend or stock split automatically increases the number of shares covered by the option in an exact proportion. If a right is involved (see Chapter 16), its value will be set by the first sale of rights on the day the stock sells ex-rights.

➤ COMMISSIONS These vary with the number of contracts traded: for a single call, the maximum is often $25; for 10 calls, about $4 each. As a guideline, make your calculations, in multiple units, at $14 per contract, less if you use a discount broker. Ask your broker his rates *prior* to trading.

You may be able to save on commissions when you write calls for a premium of less than 1 ($100). A call traded at $^{15}/_{16}$ ($93.75) will cost $8.39 compared with $25 for one priced at 1 or higher.

➤ RESTRICTED OPTION This may occur when the previous day's price closed at less than 50¢ per option and the underlying stock price closed at more than 5 points *below* its strike price for calls or more than 5 points *above* its strike price for puts. Opening transactions (buying or writing calls) are prohibited unless they are covered. Closing transactions (liquidations) are permitted. There are various exceptions, so check with your broker.

HOW PREMIUMS WORK

The cost of the option is quoted in multiples of $^{1}/_{16}$ for options priced below $3, $^{1}/_{8}$ for those priced higher. To determine the percentage of premium, divide the current value of the stock into the quoted price of the option. When there's a difference between the exercise price of the option and the quoted price of the stock, add or subtract the spread.

Here's how options were quoted in the financial pages when EFG stock was at 32⅜ (see the table on page 162):

The April 30 call prices ranged from a high

RELATIVE PREMIUMS
As Percent of Price of Underlying Common Stock When Common Is at Exercise Price

MONTHS TO EXPIRATION	LOW	AVERAGE	HIGH
1	1.8–2.6	3.5–4.4	5.2–6.1
2	2.6–3.9	5.2–6.6	7.8–9.2
3	3.3–5.0	6.7–8.3	10.0–11.7
4	3.9–5.9	7.9–9.8	11.8–13.8
5	4.5–6.8	9.0–11.2	13.5–15.8
6	5.0–7.5	10.0–12.5	15.0–17.5
7	5.5–8.2	10.9–13.7	16.4–19.2
8	5.9–8.9	11.8–14.8	17.7–20.6
9	6.4–9.5	12.7–15.9	19.0–22.2

of 4¾ ($475) to a low of 2¾ ($275) and a closing price of 3⅛ ($312.50) for a net change from the previous week of −⅛ ($12.50). There were 1,317 sales of contracts for 100 shares each.

The second line lists the action with April 30 puts: a high of $^{9}/_{16}$ ($56.25), a low of ¼ ($25), and a closing price of ⅜ ($37.50). For the week, the net change was −$^{1}/_{16}$ ($6.25). There were 996 contracts traded.

Traders looking for quick profits were pessimistic, as shown by the heavy volume in puts: 1,422 contracts for the April 35s and 2,219 for the April 40s. But there were fairly sharp differences of opinion, as the April 35 puts were up $^{5}/_{16}$ and the April 40s up ⅜.

Investors were more optimistic and appeared to believe that EFG stock was ready for an upswing: April 40 calls, due in a few weeks, were quoted at ⅛, whereas the farther-out October 40s were quoted at 1⅝. Much of the spread, of course, was due to the time factor.

The prices of the options reflect temporary hopes and fears, but over a month or two they will tend to move with the underlying stock. But do not rely solely on this type of projection: near the expiration date, the prices of options move sharply.

One key factor to keep in mind is that the premium at the outset reflects the time factor. This will fall rapidly as the expiration date nears. In the last 3 months of a call, the premium can be cut in half because of the dwindling time.

HOW OPTIONS ARE QUOTED

NAME, EXPIRATION DATE, AND PRICE	SALES	HIGH	WEEK'S LOW	LAST	NET CHG.
EFG Apr30	1,317	$4^3/_4$	$2^3/_4$	$3^1/_8$	$-^1/_8$
EFG Apr30 p	996	$^9/_{16}$	$^1/_4$	$^3/_8$	$-^1/_{16}$
EFG Apr35	3,872	$1^1/_4$	$^3/_8$	$^1/_2$	$-^3/_{16}$
EFG Apr35 p	1,422	$3^1/_8$	$1^5/_8$	$2^{15}/_{16}$	$+^5/_{16}$
EFG Apr40	1,526	$^3/_{16}$	$^1/_{16}$	$^1/_8$	$-^1/_{16}$
EFG Apr40 p	2,219	$7^7/_8$	$5^7/_8$	$7^7/_8$	$+^3/_8$
EFG Jul30	426	6	$4^1/_2$	$4^1/_2$	$-^1/_2$
EFG Jul30 p	805	$1^3/_8$	$^7/_8$	$1^3/_8$	$+^1/_8$
EFG Jul35	1,084	3	2	$2^1/_{16}$	$-^3/_{16}$
EFG Jul35 p	870	$3^7/_8$	$2^3/_4$	$3^7/_8$	$+^1/_4$
EFG Jul40	1,145	$1^1/_8$	$^3/_4$	$^3/_4$	$-^1/_8$
EFG Jul40 p	523	$7^3/_4$	$6^1/_8$	$7^3/_4$	$+^3/_8$
EFG Oct35	346	$4^3/_8$	$3^1/_8$	$3^1/_8$	$-^1/_4$
EFG Oct35 p	261	$4^3/_8$	$3^1/_2$	$4^3/_8$	$+^3/_8$
EFG Oct40	137	$2^1/_4$	$1^5/_8$	$1^5/_8$	$-^1/_4$
EFG Oct40 p	326	$7^7/_8$	$6^1/_2$	$7^3/_4$	$+^1/_4$

Stock price: 32⅜. Table does not show open interest because of space limitations.

WRITING CALLS

When you write or sell calls, you start off with an immediate, sure, limited profit rather than an uncertain, potentially greater gain, which is the case for puts. The *most* you can make is the premium you receive, even if the price of the stock soars. If you write calls on stock you own, any loss of the value of the stock will be reduced by the amount of the premium. Writing covered calls (on stock you own) is a conservative use of options. You have these choices.

➤ ON-THE-MONEY CALLS These are written at an exercise price that is at or close to the current price of the stock.

Example: In December, Investor One buys 100 shares of Company A at 40 and sells a July call, at the strike price of 40, for 3 ($300). He realizes that A's stock may move above 43 in the next 7 months but is willing to accept the $3 per share income.

Investor Two is the purchaser of the call. He acquires the right to buy the stock at 40 at any time before the expiration date at the end of July. He anticipates that A's stock will move up well above 43.

Investor One will not sustain a dollar loss until the price of A goes below 37. He will probably keep the stock until its price goes above 43. At this price, the profit meter starts ticking for Investor Two, so let's see what happens if company A's stock jumps to 50. At any time before late July, Investor Two can exercise his option and pay $4,000 for stock now worth $5,000. After deducting about $400 (the $300 premium plus commissions), he will have a net profit of about $600, thus doubling his risk capital.

Investor Two will sell the call at $2 and lose $1 per call. Investor One will end up with about $375: the $300 premium plus two dividends of $50 each minus the $25 commission for the sale of the call.

➤ IN-THE-MONEY CALLS In-the-money calls are those where the exercise price is below the price of the underlying stock. This is a more aggressive technique that requires close attention but can result in excellent profits.

Example: In January, Karen buys 300 shares of Glamor Electronics Co. (GEC) at 105 ($31,500) and sells three June 100 calls at 8 each ($2,400). If GEC stock drops below 100, she keeps the premiums and the stock. If it goes to 110, she can buy back the calls at, say, 11, $1,100 ($3,300 total), to set up a loss of $900.

➤ DEEP-IN-THE-MONEY CALLS These are calls that are sold at strike prices far *below* the current quotation of the stock—8 to 20 points below. Writing them is best when the investor is dealing in large blocks of stock because of the almost certain commissions that have to be paid when the underlying stock is called. With this approach, the best selection is a stable, high-dividend stock. Your returns may be limited, but they are likely to be sure.

The technique used by professionals is called *using leverage:* when the exercise price of the call is below that of the current value of the stock, both securities tend to move in unison. Since the options involve a smaller investment, there's a higher percentage of return and, in a down market, more protection against loss.

Example: Pistol Whip, Inc. (PWI), is selling at 97⅝. The call price at 70 two months hence is 28, so the equivalent price is 98. If PWI goes to 105, the call will keep pace and be worth 35.

If you bought 100 shares of the stock, the total cost would be about $9,800. Your ultimate profit would be about $700, close to a 7.1% return. If you bought one option, your cost would be $2,800 and you would have the same $700 profit. Your return would be about 25%.

Note: All too often, this is more theory than practice. When an option is popular, it may trade on its own and not move up or down with the price of the stock. This separate value will shift only when the expiration date is near.

When one volatile stock was at 41 in March, the November 45 call was trading at 2 1/16. Three weeks later, when the stock fell to 35½ (−16%), the call edged down to 2: a 3% decline. The professionals had moved in and set their own terms.

But remember that at times the price of the call may drop further percentagewise than that of the stock.

A variation of this use of deep-in-the-money calls is to create cost by basing the return on the total income received from premiums plus dividends.

Example: In January, one professional money manager seeking extra income for his fund bought 1,000 shares of Wellknown Chemical at 39½. He then sold April 35 options for 6⅞ each, thereby reducing the price per share to 32⅝. He could count on a 45¢-per-share dividend before the exercise date.

When the call is exercised, the total per-

share return will be $6.87 on a $32.62 investment: a 21% gross profit in 4 months. Even after commission, the annual rate of return will be excellent. The stock will have to drop below 33 before there's any loss.

➤ OUT-OF-THE-MONEY CALLS This is when the strike price is above the market price of the underlying stock for a call or the strike price is below the market price of the underlying stock of a put.

WRITING NAKED CALLS

Some calls are sold by speculators or investors who do not own the underlying stock. This is referred to as writing a naked call. The writer is betting that the stock will either remain at its current price or decline. He receives a premium, which he pockets if the stock does not rise above the call price. But if it does, he then *must* buy back his call at a loss.

$ HINT: Don't get involved unless you maintain a substantial margin account, have considerable experience, and feel confident that the price of a stock will stay flat or decline. It's risky, because if the stock hits the strike price before or at the exercise date, you are obligated to deliver the shares you do not own.

RULES FOR WRITING OPTIONS

- Define your goal.
- Work on a programmed basis.
- Concentrate on stocks that you would like to own.
- Set a target rate of return.
- Buy the stock first.
- Write long-term calls.
- Calculate your net return.
- Keep your capital fully employed.
- Be persistent.
- Watch the timing.
- Protect your capital.
- Use margin to boost profits.
- Watch the record date of high-dividend stocks.
- Keep a separate bookkeeping system.

You can, of course, cover your position by buying calls, but if the stock price soars, the loss can be substantial. At best, your premium income will be reduced.

One technique that works well is to write two out-of-the-money calls for every 100 shares you own. This gives you double premiums. Do not go too far out, because a lot can happen in a few months.

Example: You own 300 shares of Company XYZ at 32. The 35 call, due in 4 months, is 3, but you are not convinced that the market, or the stock, will rise soon. You sell six calls, pocket $1,800 (less commissions), and hope that the stock stays under 35. If it moves to 36, you can buy back three calls for, say, 1½ ($450) and let the stock go. But if the stock jumps to 40, you're in deep trouble.

BUYING CALLS

Investors buy calls in anticipation of an increase in the price of the underlying stock. If that happens, the call may also rise in price and you can sell at a profit. Buying calls means you can invest a fraction of the cost of the stock and obtain greater leverage. You also limit your risk since the most you can lose is the cost of the option.

$ HINT: The basic problem with buying options is that calls are wasting assets. At expiration date, their values can decline to zero if the stock price moves opposite to your expectations or stays fairly stable.

Example: On February 15, ABC's common is selling at $40 per share. An October 40 call can be purchased for $500 (100 shares at $5 per share). On April 15, ABC is selling at $46 per share and the October 40 call is trading at a value of $750. The investor, anticipating an increase in the value of ABC, had purchased the call for $500 and sold if for $750, realizing a $250 profit.

Here are the ways leverage works in this situation:

	STOCK	CALL
Bought—February 15	$4,000	$500
Sold—April 15	4,600	750
Profit	600	250
Return on investment	15%	50%

In this example, the call buyer can lose no more than the $500 he paid for the October 40 call, regardless of any decline in the stock, but he can lose the entire $500 if he is wrong. However, he may be able to resell his option in time to recover some of his cost. Keep in mind that if he had purchased the stock itself for $4,000 and it had gone down in price, he would have lost more than $500 if he had sold. If he decided to hold the stock and it appreciated, he would have another opportunity to make a profit.

A put buyer does not have to resell a profitable call but can instead exercise it and take delivery of the underlying stock. He can then sell the stock for a gain or hold it for long-term appreciation.

$ IF YOU DARE: *In an up market*, buy calls on up stocks on either of these terms:

- Long-term, out-of-the-money options at a low premium, typically 1 or less. By diversifying with four or five promising situations, you may be lucky enough to hit it big with one and make enough to offset the small losses on the others.

- Short- or intermediate-term in-the-money or close-to-the-money options of volatile stocks: 2 months to expiration date, a stock within 5% of the strike price, and a low time premium. If the price of the premium doubles, sell half your holdings. Advice from one expert: "Never pay a premium of more than 3 for a call on a stock selling under 50 or more than 5 for one trading over 60. Both prices should include commissions."

$ HINT: The strike price of the option and the market price of the stock should change by about half as many points as the change in the stock price: for example, if a 30 option is worth 5 when the stock is at 30, it should be worth 2½ when the stock falls to 25 and worth 8 when the stock moves up to 36.

PUTS FOR PROFIT AND PROTECTION

In a broad sense, a put is the opposite of a call: it is an option to *sell* a specified number of shares (usually 100) of a specified stock at a specified price before a specified date. Puts have the same expiration months and price intervals as listed calls. The put buyer profits when the price of the underlying stock declines significantly. Then he sells the put at a profit, with the holder buying the stock at the lower current market price and selling it at the higher exercise or striking price.

The value of a put moves counter to that of the related stock: *up* when the price of the stock falls, *down* when it rises. You buy a put when you are bearish and anticipate that the market or stock will decline. Vice versa with selling puts. As with all options, a put is a wasting asset, and its value will diminish with the approach of the expiration date.

Here again, the attraction of puts is *leverage*. A few hundred dollars can acquire temporary control of thousands of dollars' worth of stock. The premiums are generally smaller than those of calls on the same stock because of lower demand, reflecting the small number of people who are pessimistic. Sharp traders take advantage of this situation, because they realize that most people tend to be optimistic about the stock market.

➤ SELLING (WRITING) PUTS   This provides instant income but involves your responsibility to buy the stock if it sells, before the expiration date, at or below the exercise price.

Example: Ed owns Xanadu stock, now selling at 53, well above the purchase price. He's hopeful that the market will keep rising but decides to write a put at 50 for 2 ($200).

As long as the stock stays above 50, the put will not be exercised and Ed keeps the $200 per contract. But once the stock falls below 50, Ed must buy the shares or buy back the put, thus cutting or eliminating the opening profit.

➤ BUYING PUTS   These can be used to protect positions and, of course, to score a quick gain. The profits come when the price of the stock falls.

Example: In March, Ann becomes skittish about the stock now trading at 47. She buys a July put at the strike price of 50 for 4 ($400). This put has an intrinsic cash value of 3, because the stock is selling 3 points below the exercise price. In effect, she is paying 1 ($100) to protect her position against a sharp market or stock decline.

If Ann's prediction is right and the price of the stock drops, the value of the put will rise: to over 7 when the stock falls to 43.

In late July, the stock price is 45, so Ann sells the put for 5 for a $100 gross profit. If the price of the stock goes below 43, her profit will be greater.

As with calls, the important factor in profitable puts is the related stock. The best candidates for both writing and buying puts are stocks that:

- *Pay small or no dividends.* You are hoping that the value of the stock will decline. Dividends tend to set a floor because of their yields.

- *Sell at high price-earnings ratios.* These are more susceptible to sharp downswings than stocks with lower multiples. A stock with a P/E of 25 runs a greater risk of a quick decline than one with a P/E of 10.

- *Are historically volatile*—with patterns of sharp, wide swings in price. Stable stocks move slowly even in an active market.

- *Are unpopular with institutions.* At the outset, when selling starts, the price drops can be welcome. Later, however, when panic selling is over, there's likely to be minimal action, because there will be few buyers.

TECHNIQUES FOR HIGH ROLLERS

➤ SPREADS   A spread is the dollar difference between the buy and sell premiums. Spreads involve buying one option and selling another short, both on the same stock. If the cost of the option is greater than the proceeds of the option sold, it is a "debit." If the reverse is true, it's called a "credit." If the costs and proceeds are the same, the spread is "even money." *Your goal:* to capture at least the difference in premiums—at least ½ point between the cost of options exercisable at different dates and/or at different prices. *Make your calculations on paper first,* and make no commitments until you are sure you understand the possibilities or probabilities.

Here's an example involving POP stock priced at 50 in April. The premiums for 50 calls are 3½ for July, 4 for October.

If POP is below 50 in July, you keep $350 and still own an option worth $250 to $300.

If POP goes up by October, the option will

Sell July 50 for 3½	+$350
Buy October 50 for 4	− 400
Cash outlay	− 50
Commission	− 25
Total cost	−$ 75

be worth $500 or more, so you have a profit of $850.

If POP is at 60 at the end of July, that month's option will be worth 10, so you have to buy it back at a loss of about $650 plus in-and-out costs. But the October call might be at 14, so you could sell that for a gross profit of $1,000 to offset the July loss.

MAKING YOUR OWN PUT

Options are flexible and can be combined so that the stock purchases, sales, or short sales protect positions and make profits. Here's an example, by Max Ansbacher, of how to create your own put.

Assume that in late summer, your stock is at 69⅞ and the January 65 call is 9¼. You sell short 100 shares of the stock and buy the call. Here are the possibilities:

- If the stock falls to 55 by the end of January, the call will be worthless, so you lose $925. But your profit from the short sale is $1,487.50 ($6,987.50 sale; $5,500 buy-back cost) for a net profit of $562.50 (not counting commissions and fees).

- The option limits your risk of loss on the short sale even if the stock price should rise. Thus if the stock jumps to 100, an unprotected short sale would mean a loss of $3,012.50 ($10,000 purchase price minus $6,987.50 received from the short sale).

- But with a short sale of the stock and a purchase of a call, the loss will be only $437: the purchase price of 9¼ ($925) minus $488 (the spread between the stock price of 69⅞ and the exercise price of 65)—again not counting costs.

If the stock falls below 46½, you will lose money unless there's a recovery by October. But with such a stable stock in a rising market, this is not likely. The key factor is the small spread, which keeps the maximum loss low.

▶ PERPENDICULAR SPREAD   Also called a price or vertical spread, it is based on buying and selling options with the same exercise date but different strike prices.

Example: Easy Rider (ER) is at 101¾. The market is moving up and you are bullish. Sell 10 ER October 100s at 12¼ and buy October 90s at 16⅞. This requires an outlay of $4,625. Your maximum loss will occur if ER plunges below 90.

If it goes to 95, you will still make $375. At 100 or higher, your profit will be a welcome $5,375, a 120% return on your investment.

If the market is declining, set up a bearish spread. Psychologically, the risk is greater, so it is best to deal with lower-priced stocks, selling at, say, 24⅝.

Buy 10 October 25s at 2⅛ and sell 10 October 20s at 5⅜. This brings in $3,250 cash. Since the October 20 calls are naked, you'll need $5,000 margin (but the premiums cut this to $1,750) to control nearly $50,000 worth of stock.

If the stock goes to 22, you will make $1,250. At 20 or below, your profit is $3,250 for a 180% return. With perpendicular spreads, you know results at any one time. With horizontal spreads, there's the added risk of time.

▶ STRADDLE   A straddle is a double option, combining a call and a put on the same stock, both at the same price and for the same length of time. Either or both sides of a straddle may be exercised at any time during the life of the option—for a high premium. Straddles are profitable when you are convinced that a stock will make a dramatic move but are uncertain whether the trend will be up or down.

Traditionally, most speculators use straddles in a bull market against a long position. If the stock moves up, the call side will be exercised and the put will expire unexercised. This is more profitable than writing calls, because the straddle premiums are substantially higher than those of straight calls.

But this can be costly in a down market. If the underlying stock goes down, there's a double loss: in the call and in the put. Therefore, when a straddle is sold against a long position, the straddle premium received must, in effect, protect 200 shares.

In a bear market, it is often wise to sell straddles against a short position. The odds are better.

Here's how one self-styled trader did it:

"In January, QRS stock was at 100. This was close to the last year's high, and since the stock had bounced as low as 65, I felt the best straddle was short term, so I picked a February expiration date. Simultaneously, I bought a call and a put, both at 100: 5 ($500) for the call and 4 ($400) for the put. With commissions (for buying and selling) of about $100, my exposure was $1,000.

"To make money, QRS had to rise above 110 or fall below 90. I guessed right. The stock's uptrend continued to 112. I sold the call for $1,300 and was lucky to get rid of the put at $50: profit—$350 in one month!

"I would do OK if the stock fell to 88. Then the call would be worth ½ but the put would bring at least $1,200, so I end up with about $250.

"The risk was that the stock's price would hold around 100. This would mean an almost total loss. But from experience I know that I'll lose on about 25% of my straddles, so I have to shoot for a high return on the other deals."

➤ STRIP   A strip is a triple option: two puts and one call on the same stock with a single option period and striking price. A strip writer expects the stock to fall in the short term and rise over the long term. He offers to sell 100 shares that he owns above the market price or take 200 shares below the market. The premium is higher than for a straddle.

➤ STRAP   This is also a triple option: two calls and one put on the same stock. The writer gets top premium—bullish over the long term but more negative than the strip seller on short-term prospects.

➤ INSURANCE   To protect a profit, buy a put on stock you own. *Example:* your stock has soared from 30 to 60, so you expect a setback. You buy a short-term put, at 60, for $400. If the stock dips to 50, the put will be worth 10 ($1,000), so you sell for a profit of $600 and still own the stock. If the stock keeps moving up to 70, the put expires worthless. You lose $400, but you have a paper profit of $1,000 on the stock, so you are $600 ahead.

➤ LOCK IN CAPITAL GAINS   The same technique can be used to lock in a capital gain. By buying the put at 60 for $400, you reduce the stock value to 56. If it falls to 50, you sell the stock at the exercise price of 60 for $6,000. Deduct the $400 premium from the $3,000 profit (from cost of 30) and you still have $2,600. That's $600 more than if you had held the stock until its price fell to 50.

16 STOCK RIGHTS AND WARRANTS

STOCK RIGHTS

Stock rights are a special type of option that permits current shareholders to buy more corporate securities, usually common stock, ahead of the public, without commissions or fees, and typically at a discount of 5% to 10%.

Most rights allow shareholders to buy new shares on the basis of the number of shares of common already held; therefore, two or more rights are often required to buy one new share. The price, given in the prospectus, is called the exercise or subscription price. It is always below the current market price.

Rights are a convenient way for corporations to raise additional capital at a modest cost. In a sense, they are a reward to shareholders. They are often used by utilities eager to issue more common stock to balance their heavy debt obligations. The discount makes it possible for investors (who obviously have confidence in the company) to acquire additional shares at a bargain price or to pick up a few extra dollars by selling the rights in the open market. But rights are worthwhile only when the additional money raised by the company can be expected to generate extra profits and eventually lead to higher dividends on the additional shares. This is an important aspect of judging rights, because essentially they represent a dilution of your ownership in the company.

To be eligible for rights, you must own the common stock on a stated date. Most offerings must be exercised within a short time, usually less than 30 days, so watch your mail, and if the shares are held by your broker, be doubly alert. Failure to take advantage of this opportunity is foolish and can be costly—causing loss of the actual value of the rights.

Rights have an intrinsic value, but they are also speculative because of the high leverage

they offer: a 10% rise in the price of the stock can mean as much as a 30% jump in the value of the right. Or vice versa on the loss side.

Let's assume that the stock is trading at $28 per share, that shareholders get one right for every 5 shares, and that each right entitles the holder to buy 1 new share at $25 each.

$$VR = \frac{MP - EP}{NR + 1}$$

where VR = value of right
MP = stock's market price
EP = exercise price
NR = number of rights needed to buy one share

To calculate the value of one right *before* the ex-date, add 1 to the number of rights:

$$VR = \frac{28 - 25}{5 + 1} = \frac{3}{6} = 0.50$$

Thus each right is worth 50¢, and the stock at this time is worth that much more to investors who exercise their rights.

After the stock has gone ex-right, there'll be no built-in bonus for the stock, and the right will sell at its own value, or possibly higher, if the price of the stock advances, lower if it declines.

ADVANTAGES TO SHARE-HOLDERS

- **Maintenance of ownership position.** If you like a company well enough to continue as a shareholder, pick up the rights. Historically, 80% of stocks bought with rights have outperformed the market

168

HOW RIGHTS ARE QUOTED

52 WEEKS					WEEK'S	
HIGH	**LOW**	**STOCK**	**SALES 100s**	**YIELD**	**HIGH**	**LOW**
68	42	XYZ Corp.	132	3.7	64	62¼
1	⅜	XYZ Corp. rts	27		⅞	½

in the year following the issue. That's logical; management was optimistic.

- **Bargain price.** When Southwestern Public Service issued 29.2 million rights, the offer permitted shareholders to buy one additional common share at $10.95 for each 10 shares already held. At the time, the stock was trading at $11.50, so the new shares were available at a 4.8% discount. If you owned 1,000 shares, you could save about $55 on the deal, because there were no transaction costs.
- **Profits from rights themselves.** If you do not want to acquire more stock, you can sell the rights in the open market: through your broker or through a bank designated by the company. With Southwestern, each right was worth 4⅝¢ ($4.625 for each 100 rights).
- **Trading rights.** You can buy rights either to exercise or to speculate. Trading in rights starts as soon as the offer is announced. For a while, the prices of both the basic stock and the rights are quoted—the latter on a "when issued" (wi) basis, as shown with XYZ Corp. in the table. As a rule, it's best to buy rights soon after they are listed in the financial press; it's best to sell a day or two before the lapse date.

Note: Foreign rights (including those of Canadian corporations) may not be exercised by U.S. residents except in the rare cases in which the issuer has registered the related securities with the SEC. Best bet: sell the rights and avoid possible problems.

SPECIAL BENEFITS

There are two other invest-ment advantages with rights. These give you the opportunity to purchase:

1 The stock with a very low margin in a special subscription account (SSA). This is a margin account set up to use the rights to buy extra stock within 90 days after the rights issue. To open an SSA, deposit rights—your own or purchased—with your broker.

In addition to no commission for exercising that purchase, the *advantages* are a 25% margin, compared with 50% for stocks, and a year to pay if you come up with 25% of the balance each quarter.

Example: You have rights to buy Kwick Kick common, selling at 63, for 56 on the basis of 1 new share for 10 old shares. You acquire 100 rights, so you need $5,600 to complete the purchase. You can borrow up to 75% ($4,200), so you can make the deal with only $1,400 in cash or collateral. Every 3 months you must reduce the outstanding balance by 25%.

The *disadvantages* of SSA are that the price of the stock may decline, so you will have to come up with more margin, and you cannot draw cash dividends or use the securities for collateral as long as they are in this special account.

Neither the receipt nor the exercise of the right results in taxable income to the stockholder. But you will have to pay taxes on ultimate profits when the stock is sold.

2 Oversubscription privileges. Some shareholders will not exercise their rights, so after the expiration date, you can buy these rights, usually on the basis of your original allotment. You must indicate your wish to participate in the oversubscription early, preferably when you send in your check for the new shares.

⑤ HINT: Rights offerings often put
         downward pressure on the price of the
         stock and therefore represent a good
         investment opportunity.

WARRANTS

Warrants are pure speculations. Their prices are
usually low, so there can be high leverage if the
value of the related stock rises.

A warrant is an option to buy a stated
number of shares of a related security (usually
common stock) at a stipulated price during a
specified period (5, 10, 20 years, or, occasionally,
perpetually). The price at which the warrant
can be exercised is fixed above the current
market price of the stock at the time the warrant
is issued. Thus when the common stock is at
10, the warrant might entitle the holder to buy
1 share at 15. (This differs from a right, where
the subscription price is usually lower than the
current market value of the stock and the time
period is typically several weeks.)

Since the two securities tend to move somewhat in parallel, an advance in the price creates
a higher percentage gain for the warrant than
for the stock.

Example: Let's say that the warrant to buy
1 share at 15 sells at 1 when the stock is at 10.
If the stock soars to 20 (100% gain), the price
of the warrant will go up to at least 5 (400%
gain).

But the downside risk of the warrant can
be greater than that of the stock. If the stock
drops to 5, that's a 50% loss. The warrant,
depending on its life span, might fall to ⅛, an
88% decline.

A warrant is basically a call on a stock. It
has no voting rights, pays no dividends, and has
no claim on the assets of the corporation. Warrants trade on the exchanges and are usually
registered in the owner's name. Some warrants
are issued in certificate form although most
are not.

The value of a warrant reflects hope: that
the price of the stock will rise above the exercise
price. When the stock trades *below* that call
price, the warrant has only speculative value:
with the stock at 19 and the exercise price at
20, the warrant is theoretically worthless. But
it will actually trade at a price that reflects the
prospectus of the company and the life of the

warrant. When the price of the stock rises above
the specified exercise price, the warrant acquires
a tangible value, which is usually inflated by
speculation plus a premium, because it is a
lower-priced way of playing the common stock.
However, the closer a warrant gets to its expiration date, the smaller the premium it commands. Conversely, the longer the life of the
warrant, the higher the premium if there is real
hope that the price of the stock will rise. After
expiration, the warrant is worthless.

⑤ HINT: The main advantage warrants have
         over options is that they run for much
         longer. The longest an option lasts is 9
         months. Warrants, however, run for years
         and some in perpetuity, which gives the
         investor a chance to speculate on a
         company over the long term at a relatively
         low cost. This time frame makes warrants
         less risky than options.

CALCULATING THE VALUE OF A WARRANT

The speculative value of a
warrant is greatest when the
warrant price is below the
exercise price. If the stock moves up, the price
of the warrant can jump fast. The table below
shows guidelines set by warrant expert S. L.
Pendergast for the maximum premium to pay.
For example, when the stock price is at the
exercise price (100%), pay at most 41% of the
exercise price. Thus with a stock at the exercise
price of 30, the maximum price to pay for a
warrant (on a one-for-one basis) would be about
12. In most cases, better profits will come when
the warrant is bought at a lower price.

An actual example is Fannie Mae warrants
that expire February 25, 1991, trading on the
NYSE at $11, with an exercise price of $44.25.

MAXIMUM PREMIUM TO PAY

STOCK PRICE AS PERCENT OF EXERCISE PRICE	WARRANT PRICE AS PERCENT OF EXERCISE PRICE
80	28
90	34
100	41
110	46

The market price of the stock, as of May 1, 1987, was $43½.

$$43½ \div 44.25 = 98\%$$

$$11 \div 44.25 = 25\%$$

These percentages fall into the acceptable buying range using the table.

HOW TO SELECT PROFITABLE WARRANTS

Warrants are generally best in bull markets, especially during periods of great enthusiasm. Their low prices attract speculators who trade for quick gains. At all times, however, use these checkpoints:

➤ BUY ONLY WARRANTS OF A COMMON STOCK THAT YOU WOULD BUY ANYWAY If the common stock does not go up, there's little chance that the warrant's price will advance.

The best profits come from warrants associated with companies that have potential for strong upward swings due to sharp earnings improvement, a prospective takeover, newsmaking products or services, etc. It also helps if they are temporarily popular.

In most cases, the warrants for fast-riding stocks, even at a high premium, will outperform seemingly cheap warrants for issues that are falling.

At the outset, stick with warrants of fair-to-good corporations whose stocks are listed on major exchanges. They have broad markets.

When you feel more confident, seek out special situations, especially warrants of small, growing firms. Many of these "new" companies rely on warrants in their financing. Their actual or anticipated growth can boost the price of their warrants rapidly.

But be wary of warrants where the related stock is limited or closely controlled. If someone decides to dump a block of stock, the values can fall fast.

➤ BUY WARRANTS WHEN THEY ARE SELLING AT LOW PRICES The percentages are with you when there's an upward move, and with minimal costs the downside risks are small. But watch out for "superbargains," because commissions will eat up most of the gains.

Also watch their values and be cautious when their prices move to more than 20% of their exercise figure.

SOME POPULAR WARRANTS

COMPANY	EXERCISE PRICE TERMS	RECENT PRICE OF COMMON STOCK	RECENT PRICE OF WARRANT
Atlas Corp.	$31.25	$26.00	$9.00
Fannie Mae	44.25	70.00	30.00
Eli Lilly*	75.98	54.00	38.00
Global Marine	3.00	1.50	0.75
McDermott Int'l	25.00	18.00	0.62
Rymer	17.50	12.00	2.37

* Each warrant is exchangeable at $75.98 for 2 shares.

SOURCE: Silberberg Rosenthal & Co., May 1989.

➤ WATCH THE EXPIRATION OR CHANGE DATE After expiration, the warrant has no value. If you're conservative, stay away from warrants with a life span of less than 4 years. When you know what you are doing, short-life warrants can bring quick profits if you are smart and lucky. But be careful. You could end up with worthless paper.

➤ AVOID DILUTION If there's a stock split or stock dividend, the market price of the stock will drop but the conversion price of the warrant may not change. The same caveat goes for warrants subject to call. Warrants of listed companies will generally be protected against such changes, but take nothing for granted.

Once in a while, warrants will be reorganized out of their option value. This occurs with troubled corporations taken over by tough-minded operators who are unwilling to pay for past excesses or to provide profits for speculators.

➤ SPREAD YOUR RISKS If you have sufficient capital, buy warrants in five different companies. The odds are that you may hit big on one, break even on two, and lose on the others. Your total gains may be less than if you had gambled on one warrant that proved a winner, but your losses will probably be less if you're wrong.

➤ LOOK FOR SPECIAL OPPORTUNITIES SUCH AS "USABLE" BONDS WITH WARRANTS ATTACHED Some bonds are sold along with detachable warrants. In many cases the bonds can be used at par ($1,000) in paying the exercise price. In other words, they can be used in lieu of cash to pay for the stock at the specified warrant price.

Should the bond trade at 90, a discount to par, the discounted price of the bond also discounts the exercise price of the warrant.

Except in unusual situations, all warrants should be bought to trade or sell and not to exercise. With no income, usually a long wait for appreciation, and rapid price changes, warrants almost always yield quick gains to speculators who have adequate capital and time to watch the market.

10 POINTS FOR EVALUATING WARRANTS

1 *Underlying stock price.* The higher the stock price, all other things being equal, the higher the value of the warrant.
2 *Stock volatility.* The higher the volatility of the underlying stock, the higher the value of the warrant. Volatile stocks are more likely to appreciate or depreciate substantially. A warrant, too, will benefit from appreciation.
3 *Dividend.* The higher the dividend on the underlying stock, the lower the value of the warrant. Warrant holders are not entitled to receive dividends paid to stockholders.
4 *Strike price.* The lower the exercise price, all other things being equal, the higher the value of the warrant.
5 *Time to expiration.* The longer the warrant's life, the higher the value of the warrant.
6 *Interest rates.* Higher rates tend to increase the value of warrants.
7 *Call features.* Call features shorten the life of the warrant and detract from its value.
8 *Usable bonds.* A usable bond can be used at par to pay the exercise price of a warrant. This gives a warrant added value.
9 *Ability to borrow the underlying stock.* This tends to depress the warrant's value.
10 *Takeovers.* If the company is taken over at a high price, warrants will appreciate.

WHERE TO FIND WARRANTS

WARRANTS ARE ISSUED:
- With bonds as a sweetener to buy them
- As part of initial public offering packages consisting of shares of common plus warrants
- In conjunction with mergers and acquisitions

WHERE TO FIND WARRANTS:
- Brokerage firm research lists
- Newspaper securities listings, where they are identified by the letters "wt"

SELLING WARRANTS SHORT

Selling short means selling a security you do not own, borrowing it from your broker to make delivery. This is done in anticipation of a decline in price. Later you expect to buy it at a lower price and make the profit between that lower price and your original short sale.

But short selling is always tricky, and with warrants there can be other problems: (1) limited markets because of lack of speculator interest; (2) exchange regulations—e.g., the American Stock Exchange prohibits short selling of its listed warrants several months before expiration date; (3) the possibility of a "short squeeze"— the inability to buy warrants to cover your short sales as the expiration date approaches; (4) the possibility that the life of the warrants may be extended beyond the stated expiration date, advancing the date when the warrants become worthless, so a short seller may not be able to cover a position at as low a price as was anticipated.

FOR FURTHER INFORMATION

R.H.M. Survey of Warrants (newsletter)
R.H.M. Associates, Inc.
172 Forest Avenue
Glen Cove, NY 11542
1-516-759-2904
Weekly; $185 per year or $110 for 6 months

REAL ESTATE

The world of real estate investing is an endless one, stretching from home ownership, the most common form, to limited partnerships, the most unusual, with much in between. This section focuses on two uses of real estate, as a tax shelter and as an investment. Whether you own your home or would like to or are interested in investing in real estate through the stock market, you'll find useful information in Part Four.

The specific topics covered are:

- Your home as a tax shelter
- Rental income from vacation and second homes
- Time-shares
- Selecting the right mortgage
- Swapping property
- Farmland
- REITs and other stocks
- Limited partnerships

17

YOUR HEDGE AGAINST INFLATION

For generations, owning a piece of the American dream has meant buying a home: steady appreciation, tax benefits, shelter—all rolled into one. But the 1986 tax law and a changing economy make it necessary to think twice about real estate as a surefire investment. The 1986 Tax Reform Act touched upon one of America's most sacred cows, the home mortgage, by limiting its use for personal loans. Yet if you make the right decisions, you can still benefit handsomely from real estate investments. So before you leap, read this chapter and discuss the implications with your accountant.

A key to success in this area is choosing the right type of real estate. Your first choice is whether to invest directly or indirectly. If, for example, you don't want the bother and hassle of owning and caring for property, a real estate investment trust (REIT) or limited partnership (RELP) might be the answer. In any case, you should understand the impact of taxes before making a move.

USING YOUR HOME AS A TAX SHELTER

Unlike interest on consumer loans, your mortgage interest and property taxes are still fully tax-deductible. And you can continue to *postpone gains made on the sale of your principal residence,* as long as you buy another that costs at least as much as the one you sold within 2 years of the sale date. If your new home costs less, you must pay taxes on the lesser of either the house sale profits or the difference between the price of the old and the new home. Deferring these profits is particularly important, since any profit from a home sale is now taxed at your regular income tax rate and no longer at a favorable long-term capital gains rate. It is possible to keep deferring taxes by moving,

provided you do not move more frequently than once every two years, unless the move is job-related; and if you do so until you are age 55, you can then take advantage of a special break: a one-time $125,000 capital gains exemption from taxes on home sale profits for people age 55 and over.

YOUR HOME AS A FINANCING TOOL

Under the new rules, you can deduct interest on first and second mortgages, including loans for capital improvements and home equity lines of credit. There are no restrictions on the use of the money borrowed *if* the total does not exceed the purchase price plus the cost of improvements, within certain limits. To state it another way, the 1986 Act permits deduction of interest on home loans only up to the price the owner paid for the house plus the value of any improvements made, within certain limits. For example, if you paid $100,000 for your home and you added $15,000 worth of improvements, you can now deduct interest expense on a loan up to $115,000. Of course, the actual cash you can raise is reduced by the amount of any outstanding mortgage. The new law basically sanctions tax-deductible borrowing using your home as collateral. Be sure to keep careful records of your expenditures as well as detailed invoices from contractors and repair companies to document the cost of home improvements for the IRS.

☐ CAUTION: Be aware that the total amount of acquisition indebtedness may not exceed $100,000, nor may the total amount of home-equity indebtedness exceed $100,000.

$ HINT: If you have already borrowed against your house and have exceeded the limit under the new law, a grandfather clause permits interest deduction on loans outstanding *before* August 17, 1986, for "up to the fair market value" of the house, no matter what the money is used for. (See also Chapter 28 on retirement and housing.)

DEDUCTIONS YOU MAY TAKE ON RENTAL PROPERTY
■ Maintenance   ■ Utility bills
■ Depreciation   ■ Insurance
■ Repairs

GETTING RENTAL INCOME

Rental property, whether it's a condo in Florida, a ski house in Montana, or a center-hall colonial in the suburbs, if purchased after January 1, 1987, does not fare as well as before. It must be depreciated over a much longer period of time. The write-off period, formerly 19 years on residential property, has been stretched out to 27½ years (31½ years for commercial property). In the past, as a landlord, you could deduct the total value of your investment over 19 years, writing off greater amounts in the first years, but now you must take deductions in equal amounts each year over 27½ years.

If property produces rent, the income or losses generated are considered "passive," which means you cannot offset salary or investment income with these rental losses, with one exception: if your adjusted gross income is under $100,000, ($50,000 for married couples filing separately), the new tax law allows you to write off up to $25,000 a year in rental property tax losses against other income, including your salary—*provided you actively manage the property*. This special $25,000 allowance is phased out as you become wealthier; if your adjusted gross income exceeds $150,000 ($75,000 for married couples filing separately), there is no such break.

$ HINT: Recalculate the return you receive on any property. If your property generates a loss *and* your income is less than $150,000, make certain you satisfy the IRS requirement of being an "active" participant in order to get the loss allowance.

To be considered an active manager, you must own 10% of the property involved as well as make decisions on repairs, rents, and tenants. If you hire a manager but provide guidance, you will still be considered active provided you can document your involvement to the IRS.

In considering rental property, keep in mind that the new restrictions for deducting losses mean you must invest in property that produces a positive cash flow; that is, rents must be greater than costs.

If you make more than $150,000 annually, you can still reap some benefits, because the new changes pertain to tax reporting, not to your cash flow. This means that if your rental income covers mortgage payments, the only plus you've lost is the tax shelter aspect. In the meantime, keep a running account of your losses and apply them when you eventually sell the property or to offset passive income from limited partnerships or other rental income.

VACATION HOMES FOR PROFIT

If you do not rent out your vacation home, you can deduct interest on your mortgage up to the original purchase price plus the cost of improvements.

Your vacation home is considered a "residence" *if you use it personally for more than 14 days a year or more than 10% of the time you rent it out* (at a fair market rate), whichever is greater. Time that you spend on repairs and upkeep does not count toward personal or rental use. Deductions for rental expenses on a "residence" are for the most part limited to the income received. The IRS formula is precise; check with your accountant.

$ HINT: If you rent out for no more than 14 days a year, the income is tax-free and you are not even required to report it, but the expenses, other than property taxes and interest, are not deductible.

If you rent out more than 14 days or 10% of the time, the house is classified as rental (not

SEAFARING LOOPHOLE

Although tax reform eliminated interest deductions on most consumer credit loans, yacht owners and houseboat dwellers got a break. If your boat qualifies as a personal residence by having a head, galley, and sleeping facilities, you can probably deduct interest on any loan you take out to buy the floating home. Have your accountant check new code section 163(h) 5(A) (i) II, which governs interest deductions for qualified residences.

residential) property. If the property was placed in service prior to January 1, 1987, you can still use the 19-year accelerated depreciation schedule, which allows larger deductions in early years. Otherwise, you must use the new 27½-year depreciation schedule. Rental expenses cannot be used to offset regular income since they are considered passive losses. Under the 1986 law, these expenses can only be deducted from passive income from other rental properties or from limited partnerships and *not* from your wages, salary, or portfolio income. *Note:* There is an exception for those whose adjusted gross income is $150,000 or less, as explained earlier.

$ HINT: If your income is too high to benefit from the $25,000 active rental allowance, you may be better off converting a "rental" vacation home into a "residential" property and writing off the full amount of the mortgage interest.

TIME-SHARES

Time-sharing, which combines vacationing with a very small degree of investing, should be viewed cautiously if not with complete skepticism. When you buy a time-share, you purchase the right to use a studio, apartment, or house in a vacation complex year after year. Time-shares are usually 1- to 4-week periods. For example, you may purchase a 2-week time slot in Aspen for a fixed period, say the first 2 weeks in January, or for a floating period that changes from year to year.

The primary advantage is cost. It's an affordable way to vacation—1 week can range from $2,000 to $25,000+ depending on the location, season, and facilities. There is often an annual maintenance fee as well. You only pay for the days you use your space, and in most situations you can sublet if you are unable to occupy your time-share. The interest on your mortgage is tax-deductible.

Many time-share investors have been disappointed that their property did not escalate in value as much as traditional real estate. The resale potential of time-shares depends on their location, how well they're managed, and the market.

The concept of time-sharing is less popular today than when it first came to the public's attention more than 20 years ago. Since then it has suffered as a result of industry mismanagement and a period when dishonest operators were more common than they are now. Federal and state regulations now protect the investor, so it is possible that time-sharing will regain some popularity. However, with the widespread trend toward co-ops and condos, this remains a less than timely investment.

☐ CAUTION: Buy a time-share for vacationing, not primarily as an investment.

WHERE TO FIND BARGAINS IN RENTAL REAL ESTATE

- Someone desperate to sell—who has already moved, is being transferred, or has purchased another piece of property.
- An REO (real estate owned), also known as a foreclosure. Local bankers maintain listings. Prices are often well below market.
- Estate liquidations and family breakups.
- Distressed properties sold through sheriff's sales, IRS seizures for back taxes, and other forced sales.
- Discounted mortgages. These are existing loans sold by the lender for less than the balance owed. Check with real estate brokers, or place an ad in the newspaper. Review state foreclosure laws carefully.

TIPS ON MORTGAGES

While the purpose of this chapter is to discuss real estate as an investment, a key part of successful investing is leverage—that is, your mortgage. For current rates and information, keep up to date by reading the popular press and talking to bank loan officers. To help you make informed decisions, consult these sources.

➤ FINDING A MORTGAGE
HSH Associates
1200 Route 23
Butler, NJ 07405
1-800-UPDATES

This group operates a mortgage hotline (1-201-838-8197), which lists the national average rates on 15- and 30-year mortgages. For $18 HSH will send you a 2-week listing of mortgage rates in your area. HSH covers 50 metropolitan areas.

➤ REFINANCING For tables to determine if you should refinance or pay off your mortgage early, write:

Mortgage Bankers Association of America
1125 15th Street NW
Washington, DC 20005

➤ PREPAYMENT Design your own mortgage prepayment schedule with *A Banker's Secret.* The book ($9.95 plus $2.00 handling) or software package ($29.95) is available from:

Good Advice Press
Post Office Box 78
Elizaville, NY 12523
1-914-758-1400

➤ ADJUSTABLE RATE MORTGAGES For a copy of "Consumer Handbook on Adjustable Rate Mortgages," contact:

Publications Department
Federal Home Loan Bank Board
1700 G Street NW
Washington, DC 20552
1-202-377-6000

➤ VACANT LOTS Know your legal rights and avoid problems by reading the Department of Housing and Urban Development's brochure "Buying Lots from Developers."

Consumer Information Center
Department 128R
Pueblo, CO 81009
$2.50

☐ CAUTION: Make certain that any "points" you pay in connection with your mortgage are for interest (1 point equals 1% of the loan amount). As long as you pay points up front, with a separate check, they are tax-deductible in the year you buy the property. Points that are really origination fees are not deductible until you sell your property for a profit. Points paid for refinancing a mortgage are not deductible in full in the year they were paid. They must be deducted over the term of the mortgage.

SWAPPING PROPERTY

The 1986 tax law gave a boost to a rather obscure yet legal technique that allows real estate investors (in theory) to sell one piece of investment property and buy another while deferring capital gains taxes. In fact, you can swap any number of times and not pay taxes until you actually sell for cash. The exchange must be completed within 180 days.

💲HINT: Discipline yourself to invest the money that would have gone to pay the capital gains tax.

To qualify for this tax deferral you must:

■ Exchange like pieces of property
■ Use the property for business or hold it as an investment; your home does not qualify, nor does an interest in a real estate limited partnership.

If the two pieces of property involved in a swap are not of equal monetary value, cash or an additional piece of property is used to make up the difference. *Note:* The cash or extra property is a taxable transaction.

☐ CAUTION: As we go to press, Congress is considering eliminating or reducing this tax break. Check with your accountant for current status.

FOR FURTHER INFORMATION

National Timeshare Council
12201 L Street NW
Washington, DC 20005
1-202-371-6700

Federal Trade Commission
Sixth and Pennsylvania Avenue NW
Washington, DC 20580
1-202-326-2222

18

THE MANY WAYS TO INVEST IN REAL ESTATE

FARMLAND

If the roller coaster aspect of the stock market causes you concern, and it certainly should, then earmark part of your portfolio for tangible assets, such as gold, precious metals, and, in particular, farmland. Like all types of investments, land falls in and out of favor, moves up and down in price, and runs the gamut from high to low risk. But at this time, the outlook for the farm economy is brighter than it's been in years and farmland is beginning to "hot up" after a long and serious period of decline. If you filled in Levels 1 and 2 in your investment pyramid (see page 13), then this could be the right time to diversify into land with a portion of your disposable cash. Keep in mind that the 1988 summer drought temporarily reduced the price of land and boosted the prices of some agricultural crops at the same time.

PRICES

From 1981 to 1986, the cost of farmland fell throughout the country by as much as 60%. Prior to that, in the late 1970s, rich Iowa, Illinois, and Minnesota farmland commanded prices as high as $4,000 an acre; then it dropped dramatically to $1,800 and even lower. Today, however, with prices moving up, the signs of a recovery are on the horizon. As of mid-1989, prices for good land were up as much as 25%, with the best land in the Midwest going for $3,000 to $4,000 an acre.

$ HINT: For the current price of land in most areas of the United States, call Farmers National Co. in Omaha, Neb.; 1-402-496-3276.

You don't have to wear overalls and gloves and carry a pail to buy farmland—although it helps if you can or if you have the time to learn how. Nevertheless, at least one-quarter of all the farmland that changed hands recently was sold to investors who in turn rented it out to experienced farmers or to a professional management company. Savvy farmers who were not overextended during the hard times and who want to expand before prices rise any further are gobbling up the rest.

But don't rush out and buy just any piece of land. Two factors determine whether or not a farm is a successful investment: (1) raising hearty crops or livestock, and (2) knowing when to sell them. Neither is simple. In fact, farming has become increasingly technical and complex, with the need to understand soil conservation, chemicals, fertilizers, breeding techniques, disease control, etc. And to complicate matters even more, you no longer just load your corn or hogs in a wagon and haul them off to market. You must make educated guesses about future commodity prices, government support systems, and interest rates. Unless you have time to devote to a myriad of farm details, turn to a professional to help you both buy and operate your land.

HOW TO FIND A FARM

If you live in a rural area, you may hear about farms for sale by word of mouth. But if you're a city slicker, your approach must be altogether different. Follow these steps:

1 Begin by contacting local banks, the agricultural extension service, or the Farm Credit System in the county you're interested in. (The Farm Credit System, which lends money to farmers, and the Farmers Home Administration hold thousands of acres of acquired land that they sell from time to time when doing so will not depress prices. Their prices are generally fair, and low financing is often available.)

SELECTED FARM MANAGERS AND BROKERS

Farmers National Co.
Omaha, Nebr.
1-402-496-3276

Doane's Farm Management
Bettendorf, Iowa
1-319-355-1244

Agricultural Investment Associates
Evanston, Ill.
1-312-492-3440

Batterymarch, AgriVest. Co.
Glastonbury, Conn.
1-203-659-3711

Iowa Farm Associates
Fort Dodge, Iowa
1-515-576-1011

Westchester Group, Inc.
Champaign, Ill.
1-217-352-6000

American Agricultural Investment
  Management
Lombard, Ill.
1-312-810-0040

---

2 Contact Realtors Land Institute at 1-312-329-8440 for the name of a farm broker in your area.

3 Study newspapers for auction announcements.

4 Contact a farm management company that also operates as a broker for details on property for sale. These firms network throughout large areas and will scout out sales for you. Select only an accredited manager who is a member of the American Society of Farm Managers and Rural Appraisers, and check the firm's references. A professional farm consultant should provide you with the following information on a prospective farm purchase: soil condition, water and irrigation facilities, conservation regulations of the area, mineral rights, potential labor pool, transportation facilities, and nearby markets.

$ HINT: To locate the name of a certified land manager and/or broker in any section of the United States, call the American Society of Farm Managers and Rural Appraisers, Denver, Colo.; 1-303-758-3513.

5 Attend farm fairs. The Chicago Farmers Club, 2 North Riverside Plaza, Chicago, IL 60606 (1-312-454-0857) sponsors the largest annual farmland investors' fair, which brings farmers and realtors together to discuss farmland investment opportunities.

PLOWING AHEAD: RUNNING YOUR FARM

➤ RENTING The simplest way to operate a farm is to rent it to an experienced farmer who will plant and harvest crops and raise and sell livestock. He or she keeps all the proceeds, and your income is solely the rent, which is based on the value of the land and its productivity level, and your mortgage, taxes, insurance, and building upkeep.

➤ SHARECROPPING In this arrangement, the farmer pays a lower rent but then splits the profits with you 50-50. You pay the taxes and cover the repairs, but you and your tenant divide the cost of seed and fertilizer, with the tenant generally supplying the machinery. The profit potential and your risk level are both greater under this plan than any other.

➤ PROFESSIONAL MANAGEMENT If you hire someone else to oversee your farm, they will charge 5% to 10% of the farm's gross income. You generally bear all the expenses and risks, but you also get to pocket all the profits, minus the manager's fee. A good manager, either a solo operator or an organization, will offer the following:

- A 3- to 5-year improvement plan
- Negotiation of leases
- Payment of bills
- Quarterly cash flow projections

- Budgets
- Periodic soil tests and inspections
- Collection of rent and income
- Annual tax statement

IT'S RISKY BUSINESS

Unlike EE savings bonds, U.S. Treasuries, and cash under your mattress, farming is risky business. Among the negatives to keep in mind are:

- As an absentee owner, you are dependent upon others to manage the property.
- The prices for commodities and other products can drop at any time and at best are volatile.
- The government can elect to reduce or even withdraw price supports. It currently subsidizes corn, cotton, grains, peanuts, rice, soybeans, and some dairy products, but not fruits and vegetables.

INVEST WITH OTHERS

You may not want to be responsible for a 450-acre farm, a herd of dairy cattle, or thousands of clucking turkeys that must be to market by Thanksgiving. If so, a limited partnership is a viable solution. Here your money is pooled with that of other limited partners and used to purchase farms, orchards, or vineyards. The sponsor, generally a large farm management company, operates the property. As a limited partner, you share the income tax benefits, if any, and capital gains when the partnership is sold—usually in 5 to 10 years.

There are a handful of limited partnerships available in the field of agribusiness. Most are private placements requiring $10,000 to $20,000 minimum investment, although public partnerships, with minimums of only $5,000, are occasionally available.

Your broker will provide you with details about private offerings, or contact those in the box on page 179. Have your accountant review the prospectus with you before investing.

REAL ESTATE INVESTMENT TRUSTS (REITs)

One of the easiest and least expensive ways for investors to participate in commercial real estate is through real estate investment trusts. REITs trade on the major exchanges as well as OTC. Benefiting from lower interest rates and the fear of returning inflation, many were yielding 6% to 16% in May 1989.

REITs are corporations that operate basically like mutual funds but pool investors' money to invest in managed, diversified portfolios of real

LEADING REITs

	PRICE	YIELD
Mortgage REITs		
Lomas & Nettleton (LOM)	$14	16.6%
MONY Real Estate Inv. (MYM)	8	8.8
Mortgage & Realty Trust (MRT)	17	17.7
Strategic Mortgage Inv. (STM)	11	14.5
Equity REITs		
Federal Realty Inv. Trust (FRT)	23	6.0
HRE Properties (HRE)	24	7.2
Pennsylvania REIT (PEI)	21	7.7
Santa Anita REIT (SAR)	30	6.9
Washington REIT (WRE)	19	5.0
Weingarten REIT (WRI)	27	6.5
Hybrid REITs		
First Union Real Estate (FUR)	19	7.7
Property Capital Trust A:PCT	19	7.4

Data as of May 3, 1989

SOURCE: Silberberg Rosenthal & Co.

HEALTH CARE REITs

	PRICE	YIELD
Beverly Investment Properties	$12	12.6%
Health Care Property Investment	25	10.6
Health Care REIT	13	12.3
HealthVest	16	16.7
Meditrust	17	12.1
Universal Health Realty	13	10.5

SOURCE: Quotron, May 10, 1989.

estate properties and mortgages. These properties or mortgages generate cash flows; 95% of its REIT taxable income must be passed on to shareholders in the form of dividends during the calendar year in which they are earned.

TIPS FOR SELECTING REITs

- *Dividends* Should have been paid out every year for 8 to 10 years. Stay clear of any REIT that has recently cut its dividend.
- *Management* Select a REIT run by a team that's been in the field 8 to 10 years.
- *Debt* Should never be more than 30% of shareholder's equity.
- *Diversify* Select several REITs that invest in different sections of the country.
- *Cash flow* The REIT's profits should stem from ongoing operations, not from a one-time sale of properties.

REITs were little affected by the 1986 tax overhaul because they never really did center around tax benefits.

Although REIT shares can and do appreciate in price, they are primarily suggested for their high yields and as a way to participate in real estate. With lower individual tax rates, REIT investors can now keep more of these dividends.

There are three types of REITs. *Equity REITs,* which build and develop income-producing properties such as shopping malls, apartments, and office complexes, are less speculative than *mortgage REITs,* which lend money to developers and involve greater risk. *Hybrid REITs* combine both properties and mortgages.

Regardless of the type of REIT you purchase, it will be either self-liquidating or perpetual life. In a self-liquidating REIT the property is sold or the mortgages ended (say in 10 years), and profits are passed on to shareholders. These are also known as FREITs (finite real estate investment trusts).

Each REIT varies in risk level, depending on the makeup of its portfolio. In general:
- Equity REITs benefit from rent increases and growing property values.
- Equity REITs tend to be less volatile than mortgage REITs, which are more sensitive to interest rate swings.
- CAUTION: Avoid REITs made up of blind pools of unidentified properties.

REITs are interest-sensitive, which means that when rates rise, their price typically falls, and vice versa. They are also subject to changes in the commercial real estate market. In many areas of the country, this type of real estate is

REAL ESTATE MUTUAL FUND

	MINIMUM INVESTMENT	APPRECIATION (1/1/89 TO 3/31/89)	CURRENT YIELD
Fidelity Real Estate Fund (1-800-544-6666)	$2,500	2.01%	N.A.

flat due to overbuilding or poor local economics, which has sent some REIT prices tumbling.

$ HINT: If you're not averse to risk, buy shares in a REIT while prices are deflated.

Note: Until 1985 only one REIT invested in health care properties. Today there are about a dozen. Their earnings, dividends, and prices fluctuate continually. Always obtain up-to-date information before investing.

REAL ESTATE STOCKS

The stock market provides yet another way to invest in real estate indirectly. The industry is well covered by *Value Line Investment Survey.* You can select any number of stocks that are in the business of building, finishing, furnishing, or financing homes, shopping centers, and commercial real estate.

☐ CAUTION: When interest rates are high and mortgages are harder for people to afford, the real estate industry tends to turn sour.

REAL ESTATE LIMITED PARTNERSHIPS

Hardest hit by the new tax regulations were real estate limited partnerships (RELPs), which make up about 70% of all limited partnerships. These shelters traditionally generated large amounts of passive or phantom losses. Now these losses can be used *only* to offset other passive income and not salary or investment income. By 1991 passive losses are completely phased out, but 10% of losses in a RELP can be taken against other income in 1990. Most syndications now generate cash returns rather than tax benefits.

Public limited partnerships, registered with the SEC, are usually sold in $5,000 denominations ($2,000 for IRAs), and liability is limited to the amount invested. Private programs, not SEC-registered, have larger minimum investments ($10,000 to $100,000).

What to look for: partnerships purchasing real estate for cash (since borrowing now generates unusable write-offs) and generating rental income, which is now sheltered by depreciation. *Example:* miniwarehouses. (See Chapter 34 for more on real estate as a tax shelter.)

PIGs

Passive income generators, or PIGs, are being advertised as a solution for investors who can no longer use all the tax deductions generated from RELPs. PIGs pay cash returns that can be offset by losses from passive investments. *Caution:* It takes a lot to make a PIG bring home the bacon. If you have $10,000 in passive losses, you need to invest $100,000 in a partnership paying 10% in non-sheltered income to use your full $10,000 worth of losses.

For a thorough analysis of PIGs, read:

The Stanger Report: A Guide to Partnership Investing
1129 Broad Street
Shrewsbury, NJ 07702-4314
1-201-389-3600
Monthly; $345 per year

Stanger suggests buying old or "used" untraded real estate partnerships that are close to liquidation *if* their rental income is generating taxable income.

SHOPPING CENTERS

Shopping centers, from large malls to simple strips, have become attractive since tax reform because the well-run ones are earning steady streams of income from their tenants' rent. This in turn is passed on to the limited partners. Many shopping center deals are currently yielding 8% to 10%. For instance, Concord Assets' Milestone

Income Fund has been distributing 9%. Milestone II, which recently came to the market, is expected to equal that return. Summit Insured Equity II, sold by Prudential-Bache, has an interesting guarantee: a cash flow of 125% of the money put up over 10 years.

$ HINT: Another new area that is proving successful for RELPs is apartment houses. Higher interest rates are locking potential homebuyers out of the market, and demand for apartments is expected to boost rents by 6% to 8% over the next 2 to 4 years.

Look for deals in which the tenants pay their share of "CAM," common area maintenance, and have triple net leases in which they pay all operating expenses, insurance, and property taxes. These factors protect the partnership from rising costs. Another favorable arrangement is one in which the lease includes "overages" or "percentage rents"—once a tenant's corporate or business sales pass a certain level, a percentage of this excess goes directly to the partnership.

$ HINT: A shopping center partnership that has a popular anchor tenant, such as a Wal-Mart store, is more likely to attract other tenants and retail customers.

PUBLICLY TRADED PARTNERSHIPS (PTPs)

Trading on the exchanges just like stocks, PTPs offer hefty yields—but often in exchange for high risk. Many PTPs are former corporations that turned to the partnership format for tax advantages. (Partnership income is taxed just once to the shareholder. Corporate income can be taxed twice, once to the corporation and once to the shareholder when he or she receives dividends.) Current payouts are high—in the neighborhood of 10% to 12%—and some of these distributions are tax-free cash flows.

□ CAUTION: These corporations, like others, are vulnerable to industry and market risks. Your yield is not guaranteed, so before leaping automatically for the highest yield, find out if the partnership can cover its payouts.

A partnership that was publicly traded on December 17, 1987, will be treated as a corporation in tax years beginning after December

---

REAL ESTATE PTPs
American Income Properties
CRI Insured Mortgage
Emerald Homes
EQK Green Acres
Equitable Real Estate Shopping Center
Interstate General
Shopco Laurel Center
Standard Pacific
UDC-Universal Development
VMS Mortgage Investors

31, 1997. PTPs with passive investments and certain natural-resource activities are exceptions.

FOR FURTHER INFORMATION

FARMLAND

➤ PAMPHLETS The following materials, published by the U.S. Department of Agriculture, are available from the Superintendent of Documents, Government Printing Office, Washington, DC 20402:

"Living on a Few Acres" ($13)
"Getting Started in Farming on a Small Scale" ($3.25)
1-202-447-2791

➤ PERIODICALS
Landowner Newsletter
Professional Farmers of America
219 Parkade Avenue
Cedar Falls, IA 50613
1-319-277-1276
Every other week; $79 per year

Successful Farming
Meredith Corporation
1716 Locust Street
Des Moines, IA 50336
1-515-284-3000
Monthly; $12 per year

Agricultural Letter
Federal Reserve Bank of Chicago
Public Information Center

P.O. Box 834
Chicago, IL 60690
1-312-322-5322
Biweekly; free

Doane's Agricultural Report
Doane's Publications
11701 Borman Drive
St. Louis, MO 63146
1-314-569-2700
Weekly; $72 per year

Doane's Agricultural Executive
Same address as above
Monthly; $78 per year

REITs

Realty Stock Review
Audit Investments, Inc.
136 Summit Avenue, Suite 200
Montvale, NJ 07645
1-201-358-2735

Bimonthly newsletter; tracks the performance
of 100 REITs; $288 per year

National Association of REITs
1129 20th Street NW, Suite 705
Washington, DC 20036
1-202-785-8717

PART FIVE

LIFE IN THE FAST LANE

There are occasions when a portion of your savings can be used for speculations. Recognize the hazards and limit your commitments to 20% of your capital. If you are smart—and lucky—enough to score, put half your winnings into a money market fund or certificate of deposit to build assets for future risks.

Speculations are not investments. This statement sounds simple-minded, but most people fail to make the distinction. Investments are designed to preserve capital and to provide income. The decisions are made on the basis of fundamentals: the quality and the value of the investment.

Speculations involve risks and are profitable primarily because of market fluctuations. They should *never* be included in retirement portfolios. They should be entered into only when you understand what you are doing *and with money that you can afford to lose*. Before getting into details about speculations:

- Recognize that there is usually a sound reason why a security is selling at a low price or paying a very low yield. Investors are not interested, so you must be certain that there are facts to justify higher future values.
- Be realistic with new issues, because their market values depend largely on unsubstantiated optimism and hard selling by the sponsoring brokers.
- In making projections, cut in half the anticipated upward move and double the potential downswing.
- Speculate only in a rising market unless you are selling short. Worthwhile gains will come when more people buy more shares—not likely in a down market.
- Be willing to take quick, small losses, and never hold on in blind hope of a recovery.
- When you pick a winner, sell half your shares (or set a protective stop-loss order) when you have doubled your money.
- *Most important, buy a rabbit's foot.*

On the next few pages you will read about:
- Commodities
- Precious metals
- Financial futures and market indexes
- Takeovers
- Splits, Spin-offs, small caps, and stock buy-backs

19

FOREIGN STOCKS AND BONDS

The electronic age makes the flow of money and information almost instantaneous, so whatever happens on the Hong Kong stock exchange or to the price of gold in London impacts directly on investors in Des Moines, Duluth, and Davenport. As we draw closer and closer to one market, it is essential for investors also to widen their horizons. If you're not convinced, just consider this fact: the U.S. stock exchanges now account for less than 35% of the world's equity capitalization. Until 1986 that figure was always 50% or more.

At various times and in certain economic cycles, astute investors are able to make substantial profits by "going global" because of the international ripple effect: each country's economic cycle is a separate one, so when one nation is in the midst of a poor stock market, others are inevitably thriving. Wise investors realize the advisability of not locking themselves into a narrow geographical investment sphere.

MAKING PROFITS

An investment in a foreign stock offers at least two ways to make a profit or loss:

- The price of the stock can go up (or down) in its local currency.
- The value of the foreign country's currency can rise (or drop) relative to the U.S. dollar, thereby increasing or decreasing the value of your stock.

The best situation obviously exists when the price of the stock rises *and* the value of the country's currency likewise rises against the dollar. An important fact to keep in mind is that a rising currency can sometimes save you from the pitfalls associated with a poor or only mediocre foreign stock.

Despite these compelling reasons for inter-national investing, many otherwise clever investors still remain unschooled in the mechanics of successful investing in foreign stocks. The necessary guidelines, given here, can be mastered by anyone with the time and inclination to do so. But first let's examine the key pros and cons of international investing.

UNDER-STANDING THE RISKS

With all companies that have substantial foreign interests, there are extra risks resulting from gains or losses through foreign exchange. Since the company's earnings are in local currencies, they can lose a portion of their value when transferred back into dollars. The stronger the dollar, the lower the net earnings reported by the parent company. The impact can reduce profits by as much as 10%. Some international or foreign companies try to hedge against these currency swings by geographical or product diversification, but this can be expensive and is not always effective. (See the discussion of multinationals in Chapter 20.)

Currency fluctuations also affect the value of a company's nonmonetary assets (plant, equipment, inventories). When the dollar's value rises, that of the foreign currency declines. But the assets are shown at the exchange rates that were in effect when these items were purchased. That's why constant monitoring of the dollar's value is so important when going global. A good stockbroker or the international division of a large bank can keep you abreast of currency fluctuations and how they may affect your investments. (See sources of information at the end of this chapter.)

Although there are several methods for investing in foreign stocks, the three most popular are American Depository Receipts (ADRs), mutual

FOREIGN INVESTMENT

PROS

↑ Provides diversification

↑ Provides additional investment opportunities not available in U.S. markets

↑ Provides hedge against U.S. monetary or economic troubles such as inflation, dollar depreciation, slump in stock market

↑ As vitality shifts from one country to another, foreign firms may represent attractive alternatives

CONS

↓ Currency fluctuations

↓ Local political situations

↓ Less information available on foreign companies than on U.S. firms

↓ Foreign firms not required to provide the same detailed type of information as U.S. firms

↓ Different accounting procedures, which can make accurate evaluation complex

↓ Foreign brokers and foreign exchanges seldom bound by regulations as strict as those imposed by the SEC (every country has its own set of regulations)

↓ Quotes sometimes difficult to obtain

funds, and multinational companies, which are discussed in the next chapter.

AMERICAN DEPOSITORY RECEIPTS (ADRs)

ADRs are negotiable receipts representing ownership of shares of a foreign corporation that is traded in an American securities market. They are issued by an American bank, but the actual shares are held by the American bank's foreign depository bank or agent. This custodian bank is usually but not always an office of the American bank (if there is one in the country involved). If not, the bank selected to be custodian is generally a foreign bank with a close relationship to the foreign company for which the ADRs are being issued.

ADRs allow you to buy, sell, or hold the foreign stocks without actually taking physical possession of them. They are registered by the SEC and are sold by stockbrokers. Each ADR is a contract between the holder and the bank, certifying that a stated number of shares of the overseas-based company have been deposited with the American bank's foreign office or custodian and will be kept there as long as the ADR remains outstanding. The U.S. purchaser pays for the stock in dollars and receives dividends in dollars.

When the foreign corporation has a large capitalization, so that its shares sell for the equivalent of a few dollars, each ADR may represent more than 1 share: 10, 50, or even 100 shares in the case of some Japanese companies, where there are tens of millions of shares of common stock.

ADRs are generally initiated when an American bank learns that there is a great deal of interest in the shares of a foreign firm. Or a foreign corporation may initiate action if it wants to enter the American market. In either case, the bank then purchases a large block of shares and issues the ADRs, leaving the stock certificates overseas in its custodian bank.

The most important test in a foreign company's selection for an ADR is whether a market exists in the United States for the shares. In other words, the ADR process is not designed to make a market for the shares of a foreign company so much as it is to follow the market.

$ IF YOU DARE: For risk-oriented investors, ADRs offer excellent opportunities for

HOW ADRs ARE PURCHASED

1 Investors give a buy order to their broker.

2 Brokers place a buy order abroad.

3 Foreign brokers buy the stock.

4 The stock is deposited with the custodian banks in the foreign country.

5 Custodians instruct the American depository bank (Citicorp, Chemical, Irving Trust, Morgan Guaranty, for example) to issue an ADR.

6 The ADR is issued to the American investors.

SELECTED ADRs

COUNTRY	COMPANY	INDUSTRY	EXCHANGE: SYMBOL
Australia	The Broken Hill Proprietary Co., Ltd.	Mining and oil	OTC: BRKNY
Denmark	Novo Industries A/S	Industrial enzymes; drugs	NYSE: NVO
Great Britain	Courtaulds plc	Rayon yarn	AMEX: COU
	Glaxo Holdings plc	Drugs, foods	OTC: GLXOY
	The Plessey Company plc	Telecommunications	NYSE: PLY
	The Rank Organization plc	Electronic equipment	OTC: RANKY
Ireland	Elan Corp. plc	Drug research and technology	OTC: ELANY
Israel	Teva Pharmaceutical Industries, Ltd.	Veterinary products	OTC: TEVIY
Japan	Canon Inc.	Cameras	OTC: CANNY
	Fuji Photo Film Co., Ltd.	Photo products	OTC: FUJIY
	Hitachi, Ltd.	Electrical manufacturing	NYSE: HIT
	Honda Motor Co., Ltd.	Motorcycles and autos	NYSE: HMC
	Kubota, Ltd.	Agricultural machinery	NYSE: KUB
	Matsushita Electric Industrial Co.	Electronics equipment	NYSE: MC
	Pioneer Electronic Corp.	Audio equipment	NYSE: PIO
	Sony Corporation	Electronic products	NYSE: SNE
	TDK Corporation	Video and audio tapes	NYSE: TDK
	Tokio Marine-Fire	Insurance	OTC: TKIOY
Mexico	Tubos de Acero de Mexico, S.A.	Steel	AMEX: TAM
South Africa	Anglo-American	Gold, diamonds	OTC: ANGLY
	Blyvooruitzicht Gold Mining	Gold, uranium	OTC: BLYVY
	DeBeers Consolidated Mining	Diamond mining	OTC: DBRSY
	Free State Consolidated Gold	Gold producer	OTC: FREEY
	St. Helena Gold Mines	Gold mining	OTC: SGOLY
	Western Deep Levels	Gold mining	OTC: WDEPY
Sweden	Gambro, Inc.	Medical devices and systems	OTC: GAMBY
	Ericsson (L.M.) Telephone Co.	Telecommunications	OTC: ERICY
	Pharmacia A.B.	Medical science products	OTC: PHABY

arbitrage (the simultaneous purchase and sale of identical or equivalent investments in order to profit from the price difference). You can take advantage of the price differences between the stocks traded locally and the ADRs selling in New York. With gold shares, for example, there can be three different quotations: London, Johannesburg, and New York. A sharp trader, noting the wide spread, can buy shares in London and sell short ADRs in the United States.

$ IF YOU DON'T: Stick with mutual funds specializing in foreign stocks and let someone else do the decision making and trading for you.

MUTUAL FUNDS

Perhaps the easiest way to go global, especially if you do not have the time or inclination to do your own research, is to purchase shares in one of the mutual funds specializing in foreign investments. In this way, you can participate in a diversified portfolio and, as with domestic mutual funds (see Chapter 6), you reap the advantages of professional management—in this case with foreign expertise. Although many of these funds are American owned and operated, they have foreign consultants providing up-to-date material on specific stocks as well as on the country's political situation and outlook.

PROS AND CONS OF ADRs

PROS

↑ ADRs eliminate a lot of headaches that generally accompany direct investment in foreign stocks that are not sold as ADRs. An ADR enables you to make your purchase simply and quickly. If you do not buy an ADR, you must place an order with your local broker, who then forwards it to a New York broker or correspondent, who sends it overseas for execution. You can have the certificate left in the country of issue or it can be sent to you, which may take 2 to 3 months. Since you generally cannot sell your stock until you have possession of the certificate, you could lose money should you wish to sell before the certificate arrives. Even when the certificates are held abroad, transfers can take as long as 6 to 8 weeks. All this is eliminated when trading ADRs, because you are dealing with foreign companies in American markets.

↑ ADRs reduce language and accounting problems. Foreign companies registering with the SEC are required to publish their annual reports in English and also use standard accounting systems.

↑ ADRs are registered as regular stocks, with the owner's name printed on the ADR. Most foreign securities are issued in bearer form. If they are lost or stolen, they can be sold by anyone who presents them to a broker.

↑ ADRs are almost always more liquid than the underlying stock.

↑ Your dividends are paid in dollars. If you buy foreign shares directly, you will receive dividend payments in yen, francs, pounds, etc.; and if you are living outside a major metropolitan area, you may be forced to wait several weeks to receive your money.

↑ Immediate price quotes are available for ADRs.

↑ ADRs eliminate routine problems. In some countries there is a stamp tax, and when investors sell their securities abroad, they must send in the shares and wait for their money.

↑ The bank handles all the mechanical details of dividends, stockholder voting, etc.

↑ Although foreign investments have additional political and economic risks not part of U.S. stocks, most of the corporations that have ADRs are large international organizations not likely to be severely affected by shifts in their own country. For the average investor who does not have access to extensive research facilities, ADRs are a handy way to buy a position in the expanding world economy.

CONS

↓ Quotations can be misleading. Sometimes if the price of the underlying foreign stock is particularly low, its ADR may be issued in equivalents. Ask your broker to check; even he may be unaware of this factor.

↓ ADRs do not protect you against currency fluctuations. For example, if you buy an ADR worth 1,000 yen and a year later the yen has dropped against the dollar, even if your investment is still worth 1,000 yen, you will have a dollar loss if you sell.

↓ ADR owners may not exercise rights issued by foreign corporations unless the new stock is registered with the SEC (a rare situation). Such rights are automatically sold by the depository bank.

Some funds consist entirely of foreign stocks; others mix foreign and American stocks. Most are members of a larger family of funds and thus offer the advantage of free switching from one fund to another.

$ HINT: Before signing on with any of these mutual funds, write or call for a copy of the prospectus. Investment philosophies of the funds vary widely from conservative to very aggressive.

IN THE KNOW: 10 Terms to Impress
Your Broker

- **ADR**   American Depositary Receipt; document indicating you own shares in a foreign stock held by a U.S. bank. ADRs trade on the exchanges or over the counter.
- **Big Bang**   October 27, 1986, when the London Stock Exchange ended fixed brokerage commissions.
- **Bourse**   French word for stock exchange (from purse). Also used by exchanges in Switzerland and Belgium.
- **Denationalization**   When a government-owned corporation is turned over to private ownership.
- **ECU**   European currency unit; developed by nations of the European Common Market.
- **Eurobond**   Bond issued in one European country's currency but sold outside that country.
- **Gilts**   Government bonds and money market securities in Britain.
- **Out-sourcing**   Shopping the world for the least expensive suppliers of parts or products and services.
- **SDRs**   Special drawing rights; credits issued by the International Monetary Fund to its member countries; can be traded on the open market to stabilize the value of a currency in the foreign exchange market.
- **Supranationals**   Agencies formed by groups of countries to help their economies: International Monetary Fund, World Bank.

FOREIGN MARKETS TO WATCH

WEST GERMANY

Stocks have never played a crucial role in Germany's postwar expansion, but the situation is just beginning to change. During 1988, the German market rose by nearly a third, and the advance is expected to continue since long-term economic growth is strong. Adding to the appeal for U.S. investors, of course, is the weak dollar. The following ADRs are available from your broker:

BASF
Bayer
Bayerische Vereinsbank
Daimler-Benz
Deutsche Bank
Deutsche Lufthansa
Dresdner Bank
Hoechst
Rosenthal
Siemens
Thyssen
Volkswagen

You can also participate through a closed-end fund, Germany Fund, which trades on the New York Stock Exchange.

AUSTRALIA

Crocodile Dundee, along with Qantas Airline's koala bears, heightened America's interest in things Australian, and now the emphasis is on the country's stock and bond markets. This huge continent is rich in natural resources and offers many investment opportunities for the long term. Note that the Aussies have done what we're still attempting: turned their budget from an $8 billion (A) deficit to a $2+ billion surplus. Two Down Under funds to consider are The First Australia Fund and First Australia Prime Income Fund.

FOREIGN COUNTRY SECTOR FUNDS

These funds are an excellent way for investors to participate in foreign bull markets without having to select individual stocks. However, they are not risk-free and should not be confused with international mutual funds.

These funds for the most part are *closed-end,* which is part of the reason why they remained in relative obscurity until recently. They are still less popular than their close cousin, open-end mutual funds, and there are fewer to select from: 110 closed-end foreign country sector funds versus 1,600 open-end mutual funds.

LEADING INTERNATIONAL MUTUAL FUNDS

FUND	TELEPHONE	APPRECIATION (1/1/89 TO 4/1/89)
Dean Witter World Wide Investment Trust	1-212-392-2550	2.46%
Fidelity Overseas Fund	1-800-544-6666	2.96
Financial Group Portfolios	1-303-779-1233	6.20
First Investors International Security Fund	1-212-248-7900	6.26
G. T. Pacific Fund	1-800-824-1580;	13.30
	1-800-821-8361 in CA	
Kemper International Fund	1-800-621-1048	−17.99
Keystone International Fund	1-800-225-1587	−2.14
New Perspective Fund	1-800-421-0180	4.00
Paine Webber ATLAS Fund	1-201-902-3000	5.05
T. Rowe Price International Discovery Fund	1-800-638-5660	4.10
Prudential-Bache Global Fund	1-800-225-1852	0.40
Putnam International Equity Fund	1-800-225-1581	3.54
Scudder International	1-800-225-2470	5.00
Shearson Global Equity International Fund	1-212-528-2669	5.00
Templeton World Funds	1-800-237-0738	6.80
Transatlantic Fund	1-212-983-4000	3.62

Unlike open-end funds, which continually issue new shares to the public, closed-end funds sell their shares just once, when they begin operating. After that shares can only be bought or sold on stock exchanges or over the counter through a broker. Their prices then move up and down with investor demand just like any stock. Consequently, their price is often above or below net asset value (NAV), the value of the holdings in the portfolio divided by the number of shares. When the price of a fund is above NAV, it is being sold at a "premium"; when it falls below NAV, it's at a "discount."

MAKING PROFITS

These funds derive strength from two key forces: strong overseas stock markets and strong foreign currencies. Both forces are expected to continue during 1989.

The weak U.S. dollar adds to their appeal, for even if a foreign stock does not move up in price in its own currency, it will move up in U.S. dollar value *if* the foreign currency rises vis-à-vis the dollar. The dollar has been allowed to plummet, partly in an effort to reduce our huge trade deficit and stave off protectionism.

A weaker dollar makes our products more competitive abroad while boosting the cost of foreign imports for Americans.

The dollar is also held down by low inflation and interest rates. Back in 1983–1984, high rates were a leading factor in the dollar's impressive strength. Then as rates fell, foreign investors took their dollars out of high-yielding interest-bearing U.S. securities and reinvested elsewhere.

BUYING AT A DISCOUNT

Closed-end funds provide investors with the possibility of buying a dollar's worth of common stock for less than $1. This occurs if you buy shares at a discount and thereafter the shares move up to or above NAV.

§ HINT: This can work negatively in reverse: if you're forced to sell your shares at the same or a lower discount, you'll lose money.

Most closed-end shares trade at a premium to NAV for a spell just after their initial public offering. Then, if they continue to sell at premium, it's often because they've cornered the market. Generally, however, closed-end funds trade at a discount to NAV, partly because there are no salespeople keeping them in the public eye.

$ IF YOU DARE: Purchase closed-end shares at a discount and hold until they are selling at or above NAV. When funds reach NAV, they may become takeover targets or be converted into a regular mutual fund, at which point they are automatically repriced at 100¢ on the dollar.

$ HINT: To find out if a fund has an official antitakeover provision, get a copy of the prospectus and check the section under "Common Stock," or call and ask the fund's manager.

SPECIAL FOREIGN SECURITIES

There are also foreign debt securities that provide high yields, short maturities, and generally low risk. They include:

➤ YANKEE BONDS These are debt issues of foreign governments and corporations funded in U.S. dollars and registered with the SEC. Their yields have been as much as 1% higher than equivalent domestic debt; their maturities are relatively short (6 to 15 years); and many have mandatory requirements for redeeming the whole issue in equal annual amounts, usually after a grace period of 5 years. Thus a 15-year issue would be retired in 10 equal payments between the 6th and the 15th year.

FOUR WAYS TO MAKE A PROFIT IN OVERSEAS STOCKS

- When the price of a stock rises
- When a foreign currency rises against the U.S. dollar
- When you buy shares in a closed-end investment company at a discount to NAV and the discount narrows because of increased demand
- When both the stock and the foreign currency advance, creating a compounding effect

---

FOREIGN COUNTRY SECTOR FUNDS

PROS
↑ Professionally managed
↑ Offer diversification within a country, which reduces risk
↑ Provide a hedge against U.S. market
↑ Way to maintain position in overseas markets
↑ High liquidity
↑ May be able to buy shares at a discount

CONS
↓ If foreign currency declines, value of your investment drops
↓ Value of stocks in fund can fall
↓ May be special taxes for Americans
↓ Political uncertainty
↓ Price of funds subject to fluctuations, like any stock
↓ Foreign markets less well regulated than U.S. market

➤ COMMON MARKET DEBT These are bonds of government or industry groups such as the European Investment Bank and the European Community. The combine borrows in dollars and then lends the proceeds to individual companies for expansion and modernization. They are safe and carry yields 1% more than those of comparable U.S. issues but have limited marketability. They are best for major investors.

➤ CONVERTIBLE DEBT To raise capital, some foreign companies offer special convertible bonds. Inco, Ltd., the huge nickel company, shares foreign exchange risks with investors by means of a 25-year bond with a 15¾% coupon. The plus is that the payment at maturity can be either in dollars or in sterling at the set rate of $1.98 per pound.

CANADIAN SECURITIES

Canadian securities are so similar to those of U.S. companies that the same criteria for buying and selling apply. The stocks of most major Canadian corporations are listed on American exchanges, but there are many other securities that can be considered for diversification. Most of these are of relatively small local companies

FOREIGN STOCK EXCHANGES

Amsterdam Stock Exchange
Vereniging voor de Effectenhandel
Postbus 19163
NL-1000 GD Amsterdam
Netherlands

Frankfurt Stock Exchange
Frankfurter Wertpapierbörse
6000 Frankfurt a. Main 1
West Germany

Hong Kong Stock Exchange
Exchange Square
GPO Box 8888
Hong Kong

Johannesburg Stock Exchange
P.O. Box 1174
Diagonal Street
Johannesburg 2000
South Africa

London Stock Exchange
Old Broad Street
London EC2N 1HP
England

Bourse de Luxembourg
11, Avenue de la Porte-Neuve
L-2227 Luxembourg

Milan Stock Exchange
Borsa Valori di Milano
Piazza degli Affari, 6
I-20123 Milan
Italy

Paris Stock Exchange
Bourse de Paris
4, place de la Bourse
F-75080 Paris Cedex 02
France

Singapore Stock Exchange
16 Raffles Quay
Hong Leong Building
Singapore 0104

Sydney Stock Exchange
20 Bond Street
Sydney, N.S.W. 2000
Australia

Tel Aviv Stock Exchange
13 Allenby Road
Tel Aviv 65127
Israel

Tokyo Stock Exchange
6, Nihombashi-Kabuto-cho
I-chome, Chuo-ku
Tokyo 103
Japan

Toronto Stock Exchange
2 First Canadian Place
Toronto, Ontario M5X 1J2
Canada

Vienna Stock Exchange
Wiener Börsekammer
Wipplingerstrasse 34
A-1011 Wien 1
Austria

Zurich Stock Exchange
Bleicherwege 5
CH-8021 Zurich
Switzerland

---

that serve the limited north-of-the-border market. A few, primarily involved with natural resources, are large and active in international trade.

DO invest and not gamble. Look for companies that will benefit from the long-term growth of the country. Forget about "penny" oil, gas, or mining stocks. There is almost no way that you can be sure of the integrity of the promoter or the authenticity of the seller's claims.

DO deal with a broker with good research facilities. Information on many Canadian issues is limited in the United States. Look for a major

American brokerage firm with offices north of the border.

DO subscribe to a factual investment advisory service such as Canadian Business Service, 133 Richmond Street, West Toronto, M5H 3M8, Canada.

DON'T deal in shares of Canadian companies listed only on Canadian stock exchanges until you are familiar with the corporation. There are plenty of Canadian firms listed on American exchanges.

DON'T buy any security over the telephone. Despite attempts of authorities to control bucket shop operations, they still exist and continue to lure naïve speculators.

DO make all investments in U.S. currency to avoid exchange rate losses.

In January 1989, the United States and Canada signed a free trade pact that will eliminate the majority of tariffs between the two nations during the next 10 years. This is expected to benefit Canadian companies that supply the U.S. with basic goods and commodities.

You can play the Canadian connection through two mutual funds:

- Fidelity Canada: 1-800-544-6666
- Mackenzie Canada: 1-800-456-5111

FOREIGN BONDS

If you're income-oriented, you want to own nondollar assets, and the U.S. dollar remains weak, consider mutual funds that own foreign bonds. Your return is based on three factors: (1)

MUTUAL FUNDS THAT INVEST IN FOREIGN BONDS	
Fidelity Global Bond	1-800-544-6666
Paine Webber Master Global	1-800-762-1000
T. Rowe Price Int'l Bond	1-800-638-5660
Shearson Lehman Global Bond	1-800-451-2010
Templeton Income	1-800-237-0738
Transatlantic Income	1-212-983-4000

the bond yields, (2) the price changes due to interest rate changes abroad, and (3) currency fluctuations. Since most individuals cannot monitor all three areas, mutual funds are the logical way to invest.

☐ CAUTION: Although fund managers can move in and out of various countries, foreign bond funds are riskier than a U.S. one because of the myriad of economic and political variables. Therefore, put no more than 10% of your portfolio into one of these funds.

MORE ABOUT DIVERSIFICATION

As with any investment, diversification greatly reduces the level of risk involved. With foreign

LEADING SINGLE FOREIGN COUNTRY SECTOR FUNDS

FUND	EXCHANGE	NAV	PRICE PER SHARE	DISCOUNT (−) OR PREMIUM (+) FROM NAV
ASA Limited*	NYSE	$56.71	$41⅛	−27.48%
France Fund	NYSE	11.87	11	−7.33
Germany Fund	NYSE	8.36	7⅝	−8.79
Italy Fund	NYSE	10.04	8⅛	−19.07
Korea Fund	NYSE	17.43	33	+92.20
Malaysia Fund	NYSE	11.10	9⅞	−11.04
Mexico Fund	NYSE	9.44	7½	−20.55
Thai Fund	NYSE	12.93	16⅞	+30.51
United Kingdom Fund	NYSE	12.31	10⅛	−17.75

* Invests in South Africa.

SOURCE: Barron's, May 8, 1989.

stocks, it is especially important to avoid reliance on the performance of any one stock, one industry, or even one country. Risk reduction is best achieved by spreading out your investment dollars in at least one of the following ways:

- *By country.* When some foreign stock markets fall, it is inevitable that others will rise. Diversification by country offers a hedge against a poor economic climate in any one area. Keep in mind that the U.S. market tends to be an anticipatory one, reflecting what the American investor thinks will happen in the forthcoming months.

- *By type of industry.* Buying shares in more than one industry—high-tech, computers, oil, automobiles, etc.—likewise provides protection.

- *By company within the industry.* For example, an energy portfolio could include stocks from a number of companies located in the North Sea area, Southeast Asia, Canada, the Middle East, and the United States.

- *By region.* Diversify among the regions of the world. Never become too dependent on any one area. Use a currency-weighting system to balance your portfolio. The *U.S. dollar* bloc, which consists of U.S., Canadian, and occasionally Mexican stocks, should be about 45%. The *Pacific Rim* bloc, which includes Japanese stocks plus those of Hong Kong, Singapore, and Australia, should be 35%. The *European Community* (EC) is made up of 12 member countries. It should represent 20% of your portfolio. If the dollar declines, reduce the U.S. bloc to 35% and increase all others.

Buy stocks with P/E ratios that are lower than those of comparable U.S. companies. There should always be a compelling reason to purchase a foreign security, such as a low P/E or a unique industry position.

FOR FURTHER INFORMATION

FOREIGN STOCKS

➤ BOOKS You can add to your list of multinationals by studying one of the standard reference books such as Moody's *Handbook* and *Standard & Poor's Stock Market Guide* or *Value Line.* All three give the percentage of a company's earnings and sales derived from foreign operations. You should also read various company annual reports to learn what areas their sales come from. Earnings from Western Europe and Japan are currently more stable than those from Latin America.

> *Moody's International Manual & News Reports*
> Moody's Investors Service
> 99 Church Street
> New York, NY 10007
> 1-212-553-0300
> 2-volume annual; $1,395

Contains financial information on over 5,000 companies and institutions in 100 countries.

➤ PERIODICALS The following periodicals provide coverage of foreign markets as well as individual stocks:

> *Wall Street Journal*
>
> *Barron's National Business & Financial Weekly*
>
> *The Economist*
>
> *Investor's Chronicle* (London)
>
> *Far East Economic Review*
>
> *Japan Economic Journal*
>
> *The Financial Times* (London)
> Bracken House
> 10 Cannon Street
> London EC4P 4BY
> $420 per year
>
> *The Asian Wall Street Journal*
> Dow Jones & Company
> 200 Liberty Street
> New York, NY 10281
> $225 per year
>
> *Global Investor*
> Euromoney Publications
> Nestor House
> Playhouse Yard
> London EC4V 5EX
> England
> Monthly; $155 per year
>
> *Euromoney (London)*
> Reed Business Publications

205 East 42nd Street
New York, NY 10017
1-212-867-2080
Monthly; $226 per year

▶ NEWSLETTERS The following newsletters regularly cover foreign stocks. Also see Appendix A on evaluating newsletters.

Capital International Perspective
Capital International, S.A.
3, place des Bergues
CH-1201 Geneva, Switzerland
Monthly and quarterly; SF 1,850

Dessauer's Journal of Financial Markets
P.O. Box 1718
Orleans, MA 02653
1-508-225-1651
Semimonthly; $195 per year

The International Advisor
P.O. Box 2289
Winter Park, FL 32790
1-407-629-1400; 1-800-333-5697
Monthly; $78 per year

The International Harry Schultz Letter
c/o FERC
P.O. Box 141
CH-1815 Clarens-Montreux, Switzerland
Monthly; $125 per year

Tony Henrey's Gold Letter
P.O. Box 5577
Durban 4000
South Africa
$95 per year

International Bank Credit Analyst
BCA Publications Ltd.
3463 Peel Street
Montreal, Quebec H3A 1W7
1-514-398-0653
Monthly; $565 per year

International Fund Monitor
Research International Inc.
P.O. Box 5754

Washington, DC 20016
1-202-363-3097
Monthly; $72 per year

FOREIGN-BASED MUTUAL FUNDS OR UNIT TRUSTS

International Investment & Business
    Exchange
139A Sloane Street
London SW1, England

This service organization publishes a newsletter and *The World Wide Directory of Mutual Funds* ($39.95). Membership costs $99 a year plus a one-time entry fee, also $99.

Unit Trust Yearbook
Financial Times Business Publishing Ltd.
102 Clerkenwell Road
London EC1M 5SA, England
$35

CLOSED-END FOREIGN FUNDS

The *Wall Street Journal's* Monday issue lists closed-end funds under "Publicly Traded Companies." You'll find the NAV, share price, and discount or premium as of the preceding Friday.

Investor's Guide to Closed-End Funds
Box 161465
Miami, FL 33116
1-305-271-1900
Monthly; $275 per year

Directory of Closed-End Funds
Investment Company Institute
Research Dept.
1600 M Street NW, 6th floor
Washington, DC 20036
1-202-955-3584

20 BETTING ON THE DOLLAR

Between 1981 and the early months of 1985, the value of the U.S. dollar in relation to the major foreign currencies rose approximately 50%, reaching historic highs against the pound, lira, franc, and mark and prompting many to call it the "superdollar."

This strong dollar was sustained by a sharp decline in the rate of inflation, high interest rates (especially in relation to many other countries), and a continually improving American economy. The high interest rates in combination with the overall political stability of the United States were responsible for attracting a flood of overseas money into the United States as foreigners purchased dollar-denominated securities and U.S. property.

Starting in the spring of 1985, the dollar began to trend downward, eventually reaching new lows against the yen and other currencies, thus rekindling investor interest in speculating on the dollar. Since the market crash of 1987, the dollar has shown renewed strength now and then but essentially has never recovered. But the low dollar has a positive effect on several investments:

- Domestic manufacturing companies that have weathered stiff foreign competition are able to boost their domestic sales.
- Earnings of multinationals, when translated into dollars, are enhanced.
- Leading U.S. exporters become more competitive (see table on page 198).

Among the stocks that are doing well under the current situation are those in industries that can compete favorably against the cheaper foreign imports, such as aluminum, machine tools, chemicals, and paper.

However, investment decisions should not be made solely on the basis of the dollar's movement. Stock selection should always include the fundamentals emphasized throughout this book. In order to help you take advantage of the opportunities a lower dollar may provide, the top recommendations of several leading investment services are listed in the box. AMP, Inc., for instance, is the world's leading maker of electronic connection devices. Even if the dollar stabilizes, demand for its products is on the rise. Boeing has a huge backlog of orders from all over the world.

MULTINATIONAL CORPORATIONS

Multinational corporations—companies with substantial portions of earnings and profits derived from foreign business—stand to reap the greatest benefit from the decline in the dollar and offer sound long-term investment choices. Multinationals also provide another way to diversify your investment portfolio and to invest globally at the same time.

The key factor to keep in mind when investing in multinationals is that when foreign currencies rise relative to the dollar, earnings from an American company's foreign subsidiary or division are instantly worth more.

Who are the multinationals? A number of companies depend heavily on international sales for at least one-third of their earnings. They tend to manufacture either popular products or necessities. These companies for the most part fall into five basic categories: cosmetics and household products, drugs, food, industrials, and chemicals.

$ HINT: A strong dollar tends to hurt the multinational stocks: it makes U.S. products expensive for foreign buyers and foreign products cheap for American consumers. A strong dollar also creates an "exchange loss"; that is, if the money an American company earns abroad loses value against the dollar, the earnings for the company and its stockholders are

---

DOLLAR DROP SIDE EFFECTS

- Modest rise in inflation
- Healthier U.S. stock market
- Long-term rise in interest rates
- Possible rise in gold stocks
- Rise in prices of foreign stocks

BENEFICIARIES OF THE LOWER DOLLAR

AMP, Inc.	Kellogg Co.
Avery International	Kimberly-Clark
Boeing	MMM
Bristol-Myers	Merck
Burroughs	Protcer & Gamble
Coca-Cola	Sara Lee
Colgate Palmolive	Schering-Plough
Data General	Schlumberger Ltd.
Digital Equipment	Sealed Air
Gillette	Squibb
Heinz (H.J.)	Weyerhauser
IBM	

SOURCE: Silberberg, Rosenthal & Co.

---

reduced. The more a U.S. multinational depends on exports for sales, the more it will benefit from a weaker dollar. Thus multinationals are a good hedge against a declining dollar.

FOREIGN CDs

One of the more conservative ways to bet on the falling dollar is to buy foreign currency CDs—they're available at the large U.S. branches of overseas banks and the currency traders, such as Deak-Perera International. Most are sold in $5,000 units with maturities of 1, 3, 6, or 12 months. Although yields are set, if the dollar drops, your earnings when translated into U.S. currency will be higher.

Among the most popular foreign CDs are those denominated in Japanese yen, Swiss francs, and West German marks.

☐ CAUTION: Foreign CDs are a good investment *only* if the dollar is weak and/or the foreign interest rate is higher than you can get at home. If the dollar rises, you could suffer significant losses.

LEADING U.S. EXPORTERS

	EXPORT SALES (% OF TOTAL SALES)		
	1986	1987	1988
Boeing Co.	45%	45%	46%
Crown Cork & Seal	38	38	44
Exxon	76	61	61
Heinz (H.J.)	37	40	42
Polaroid Corp.	41	43	44
Squibb Corp.	43	43	43
Wrigley (Wm.)	33	33	36

SOURCE: Value Line.

Deak-Perera International Ltd. is assembling a term deposit that invests dollars in one of 14 currencies. The minimum investment is around $3,000, depending on the currency you select. Maturities are 1, 3, 6, 9, and 12 months. In some cases, interest rates are above those paid on U.S. bank CDs. If the dollar falls, your gain will be even greater. Details are available from any Deak-Perera office.

GLOBAL CASH PORTFOLIO

This multicurrency money market fund invests in high-quality, short-term debt of 12 different currencies, including the U.S. dollar. Its advantages:

- Portfolio diversification
- Liquidity
- Professional management

In 1987, Global Cash Portfolio posted over a 20% total return. For the current return, call Huntington Advisors (1-800-826-0188).

Huntington also offers individual portfolios for currencies from Australia, Canada, Great Britain, Japan, Switzerland, West Germany, and the United States. You can switch your investment among these various portfolios in response to currency movements.

TRAVELER'S CHECKS

A low-cost way to play the game is to purchase traveler's checks in the currency you feel will

MULTINATIONALS

INDUSTRY	PERCENTAGE OF FOREIGN BUSINESS
Chemical	
Dow Chemical	54%
Du Pont	33
Cosmetics or Household Products	
Colgate Palmolive	64
Gillette	51
International Flavors & Fragrances	68
Procter & Gamble	38
Drugs	
Abbott Laboratories	24
American Home Products	25
Bristol-Myers	26
Johnson & Johnson	48
Merck	50
Pfizer	46
Foods	
Coca-Cola	52
CPC International	59
Heinz (H. J.)	42
International Multifoods	38
McDonald's	30
Ralston-Purina	24
Industrials	
Caterpillar Tractor	48
IBM	54
Ingersoll-Rand	40
MMM	38

SOURCE: *Value Line,* May 1989.

rise against the dollar. Cash them in when that currency rises to pocket your gains.

The key disadvantage with traveler's checks is that you do not earn interest on your money.

CURRENCY OPTIONS

These operate like stock options (see Chapter 15). If you think a given currency will rise against the U.S. dollar, you buy a call. If you think it will fall, purchase a put.

Say you believe that the dollar will fall against the Japanese yen. By purchasing a call option on the yen, you gain the right to purchase a stated number of yen at a predetermined strike price in dollars. You have that right until the expiration date—usually at 3-month intervals.

☐CAUTION: If the option exercise date comes up and the yen is below your strike price, your entire investment is lost.

The Philadelphia Stock Exchange trades options in five currencies. You can also buy options on the New York Commodity Exchange's U.S. Dollar Index, which contains a basket of 10 currencies. Generally, options on the index are less volatile than options on individual currencies; nevertheless, this is an area *for speculative investors only*.

$HINT: Make certain you use a broker who specializes in foreign currency options—most do not.

HOW TO SPECULATE IN FOREIGN CURRENCIES

Trading in foreign currencies can be exciting and profitable.

Futures contracts of foreign currency are traded on the International Monetary Market Division (IMM) of the Chicago Mercantile Exchange. Basically, positions are taken by importers and exporters who want to protect their profits from sudden swings in the relation between the dollar and a specific foreign currency. A profit on the futures contract will be offset by a loss in the cash market, or vice versa. Either way, the businessperson or banker guarantees a set cost.

The speculation performs an essential function by taking opposite sides of contracts, but unlike other types of commodities trading, currency futures reflect reactions to what has already happened more than anticipation of what's ahead.

For small margins of 1.5% to 4.2%, roughly $1,500 to $2,500, you can control large sums of money: 100,000 Canadian dollars, 125,000 West German marks, 12.5 million Japanese yen, etc.

The attraction is leverage. You can speculate that at a fixed date in the future, the value of your contract will be greater (if you buy long) or less (if you sell short).

The daily fluctuations of each currency

futures contract are limited by IMM rules. A rise of $750 per day provides a 37.5% profit on a $2,000 investment. That's a net gain of $705 ($750 less $45 in commissions). If the value declines, you are faced with a wipeout or, if you set a stop order, the loss of part of your security deposit. Vice versa when you sell short.

One of the favorite deals is playing crosses, taking advantage of the spread between different currencies: buying francs and selling liras short, etc. For example, when the West German mark was falling faster than the Swiss franc relative to the U.S. dollar, an investor set up this spread:

April 15: He buys a June contract for 125,000 francs and sells short a June contract for 125,000 marks. The franc is valued at .6664¢, the mark at .5536¢. Cost, not including commissions, is the margin: $2,000.

May 27: The franc has fallen to .6461, the mark to .5120. He reverses his trades, selling the June contract for francs and buying the mark contract to cover his short position.

Result: The speculator loses 2.03¢ per franc, or $2,537.50, but he makes 4.16¢ per mark, or $5,200.00. The overall gain, before commissions, is $2,662.50, a return of 133% on the $2,000 investment—in about 6 weeks.

Warning: IMM is a thin market. Small speculators may not be able to get out when they want to at the price they expect. On a one-day trade, the value of a currency can swing sharply, so that the pressure can be intense.

▶ CURRENCY OPTIONS According to some traders, currency options can be the fastest game in town (or perhaps they should say "in the free world"). The premiums are small, so the leverage is high.

The options, traded on the Philadelphia Exchange, are for five currencies: Deutsche mark (DM), pound sterling, Canadian dollar, Japanese yen, and Swiss franc. The premiums run from $25 for a short-life out-of-the-money option to $2,000 for a long-term deep-in-the-money call or put.

The option represents the currency value against the dollar, so traders buy calls when they expect the foreign money to gain ground against the dollar and puts when they anticipate the reverse. The options expire at 3-month intervals.

The quotations are in U.S. cents per unit of the underlying currency (with the exception of the yen, where it's $1/100$¢): thus, the quote 1.00 DM means 1¢ per mark, and since the contract covers 62,500 DM, the total premium would be $625.

▶ OPTIONS ON FUTURES These are now available on the Chicago Mercantile Exchange, where the currency futures are already traded. They are similar to regular options except that they give the holder the right to buy or sell the currencies themselves, *not the futures.*

The CME rules permit the speculator to do the following:

- Generate extra income by writing calls or selling puts (but this can be very expensive if you guess wrong and the option is exercised).
- Exercise the option at any time. But once you do so, you may not liquidate your option position with an offsetting option as you can do in futures trading. So you have to sell to, or buy from, the other party the required number of currency units at the option exercise price.

These options on futures sound risky—but only for the speculator. Business firms use them to hedge the prices of foreign goods at a future delivery date.

FOREIGN CURRENCY WARRANTS

This is a relatively new investment item, one issued by corporations to raise money. Each warrant allows you to purchase $50 at a certain

---

ISSUERS OF FOREIGN CURRENCY WARRANTS

WARRANTS IN YEN
- AT&T Credit Corp.
- General Electric Credit Corp.
- Citicorp
- Xerox Credit Corp.
- Student Loan Marketing Association

WARRANTS IN MARKS
- Citicorp
- General Electric Credit Corp.
- Emerson Electric
- Student Loan Marketing Association

SPECIAL TERMS IN COMMODITIES TRADING

- **Arbitrage** Simultaneous purchase and sale of the same or an equivalent security in order to make a profit from the price discrepancy.
- **Basis** The difference between the cash price of a hedged money market instrument and a futures contract.
- **Contract month** Month in which a futures contract may be fulfilled by making or taking delivery.
- **Cross hedge** Hedging a cash market risk in one financial instrument by taking a position in a futures contract for a different but similar instrument.
- **Forward contract** An agreement to buy or sell goods at a set price and date, when those involved plan to take delivery of the instrument.
- **Hedge** Strategy used to offset an investment risk that involves buying and selling simultaneously in the futures market.
- **Index** Statistical composite that measures the ups and downs of stocks, bonds, and commodities; reflects market prices and the number of shares outstanding for the companies in the index.
- **Long position** Futures contract purchased to protect the investor against a rise in cost of a future commitment or against a drop in interest rates.
- **Mark to the market** Debits and credits in each account at the close of the trading day.
- **Open interest** Contracts that have not been offset by opposite transactions or by delivery.
- **Physical** The underlying physical commodity.
- **Selling short** A popular hedging technique involving sale of a futures contract that the seller does not own. A commodity sold short equals a promise to deliver at a future date.
- **Spot market** Also known as the actual or physical market in which commodities are sold for immediate delivery.
- **Spread** Holding opposite positions in two futures contracts with the intent of profit through changes in prices.

---

exchange rate. As the dollar moves up and down, so does the value of your warrant, or the right to buy the $50.

Most warrants have been issued against the Japanese yen and the German mark. They trade on the AMEX.

Warrants, which tend to be more volatile than the underlying issue, were selling for $2 to $4 as of May 1988. The AT&T Credit Corp. yen warrant, for instance, gives investors the right to buy $50 from AT&T at 158.25 yen per U.S. dollar by July 1992. If the dollar rises 10 yen above the conversion price (168.25), it will be worth nearly $3.

Most warrant holders, however, tend to sell when their warrants go up rather than hold until the expiration date.

FOR FURTHER INFORMATION

Stanley Knoll, *Knoll on Futures Trading Strategy* (Homewood, Ill.: Dow Jones–Irwin, 1987).

I. Dee Belveal, *Speculation in Commodity Contracts and Options* (Homewood, Ill.: Dow Jones–Irwin, 1988).

COMMODITIES

FUTURES TRADING

The concept of buying or selling agricultural goods at a price agreed on today but with actual delivery of the goods sometime in the future is a time-honored practice dating back to the early 19th century. Today futures are traded in many areas: grain, meat, poultry, lumber, metals, foreign currencies, interest-bearing securities such as Treasury bonds and notes, and even stock indexes.

A futures contract is an obligation to buy or sell a commodity at a given price sometime in the future. If you buy a contract, you are betting that prices will rise. If you sell a contract, you are betting that prices will fall.

The theory behind futures is twofold: (1) they are supposed to transfer risk from one party to another, and (2) they are designed to even out price fluctuations. Although the theory tends to be true in agricultural markets, the proliferation of financial and stock index futures has led to increased volatility and speculation.

Trading futures is *not* an area for the novice, the conservative, or the timid. Proceed with great caution.

Futures traders are of three types: the hedgers, the speculators, and the scalpers.

Hedgers own the commodity or financial instrument and use futures to protect themselves against potential losses due to changes in the price of the commodity. With a financial commodity, such as a T-bond or stock index, futures contracts provide protection against changes in interest rates.

Speculators do not own the underlying commodity. They aim to capture profits from the volatility of the contracts. By doing so they give the market its liquidity.

Scalpers, or exchange floor traders, buy and sell contracts, seeking small profits on a daily (or even hourly) basis.

Futures contracts are closed by offsetting transactions. This is when you sell the contract before its expiration date, the date when the commodity must be delivered. For instance, if you had purchased a May 1990 wheat contract and you wanted to get out of the market, you would sell a May 1990 contract, thus closing out the position. The two positions cancel each other out. If you don't offset, you are obliged to take physical delivery. It's cumbersome and costly to have wheat unloaded into your living room.

COMMODITIES

During uncertain times in the stock market, diversification into nonequity areas with a portion of one's portfolio is often advantageous. The top commodity funds in 1988 had returns ranging from 47% to 125%.

Commodities include a variety of bulk products such as grain, metals, and foods, which are traded on a commodities exchange. The exchange deals in futures trading, for delivery in future months, as well as spot trading, for delivery in the current or "spot" month.

Futures contracts are agreements to buy or sell a certain amount of a commodity at a particular price within a stated time period. The price is established on the floor of a commodities exchange.

Note: A futures contract obligates the buyer to buy and the seller to sell *unless* the contract is closed out by an offsetting sale or purchase to another investor before the so-called settlement or delivery date.

Commodities are one of the quickest ways to get rich, but they can also be a fast way to lose money. These futures contracts are almost always 100% speculation because you must try to guess, months in advance, what will happen to the prices of food products, natural resources, metals, and foreign currencies.

Trading in commodities involves active, volatile markets, high leverage, hedging, and short selling. It's a game that requires ample capital, emotional stability, frequent attention to trends, and experience. Although everyone should understand trading in commodities markets, you should get involved only with money you can afford to lose.

In addition to the normal hazards of speculations, there are special risks beyond the ken or control of most participants. With skill and luck, an individual can score high on occasion, but the odds are always against the amateur. According to a recent study, *75% of all commodities speculators lose money.*

The great appeal of trading commodities lies in the impressive amount of leverage they provide. Your broker will require you to meet certain net worth requirements and make a margin deposit. Nevertheless, there are low cash requirements: 7% to 10% per contract, depending on the commodity and the broker's standards. That means that $2,000 could buy, say, $29,000 worth of soybeans.

The lures of fast action, minimal capital, and high potential profits are enticing—but before you start trading contracts for corn, wheat, soybeans, or silver, heed these warnings from professionals:

- **Be emotionally stable.** You must be able to control your sense of fear and greed and train yourself to accept losses without too great a strain.
- **Be ready to risk at least $10,000:** $5,000 at once, the rest to back up margin calls.
- **Deal only with a knowledgeable commodities broker** who keeps you informed of new risks.
- **Recognize that you are always bucking professionals.** These experienced or big operators are hedging; you're only speculating.

HOW THE MARKET OPERATES

Commodity trading is different from investing in stocks. When you buy a common stock, you own a part of the corporation and share in its profits, if any. If you pick a profitable company, the price of your stock will eventually rise.

With commodities, there is no equity. You basically buy hope. Once the futures contract has expired, there's no tomorrow. If your trade turned out badly, you must take the full loss. And it's a zero sum game: for every $1 won, $1 is lost by someone else.

➤ HEDGING Let's say a hog farmer has animals that will be ready for market in 6 months. He wants to assure himself of today's market price for these hogs, which he does by selling a contract for future delivery. When the hogs are ready for market, if the price has dropped, he will be forced to take a lower price on the actual hogs, but he will have an offsetting gain, because the contract he sold 6 months ago was at a higher price. In other words, he closes that contract with a profit.

- *The advantage to the sellers:* They have themselves locked in a price, thereby protecting themselves from any future fall in the price of hogs. In effect, they have transferred this price risk to the buyers.
- *The advantage to the buyers:* They also have locked in a price, thereby protecting themselves from any future rise in the price of hogs. The buyer in this hypothetical case might be a speculator, a meat packer, or a meat processor.

➤ MARGIN Since payment is not received until the delivery date, a type of binder or good faith deposit is required. It is called "margin." The margin in the world of commodities is only a

---

AGRICULTURAL COMMODITIES CONTRACTS

COMMODITY	SYMBOL	ONE CONTRACT EQUALS
Soybeans	S	5,000 bushels
Soybean oil	BO	60,000 pounds
Soybean meal	SM	100 tons
Oats	O	5,000 bushels
Wheat	W	5,000 bushels
Corn	C	5,000 bushels
Silver	AG	1,000 troy ounces
Gold	K	1 kilogram

SOURCE: Chicago Board of Trade.

small percentage of the total amount due, but it serves as a guarantee for both buyer and seller. Unlike margin for stocks, which is an interest-bearing cost, margin for commodities is a security balance. You are not charged interest, but if the price of your futures drops by a certain percentage, more money must be deposited in the margin account or your position will be closed out by your broker.

In reality, most futures trading is not this simple. More often than not, the opposite side of each transaction is picked up by speculators who believe they can make money through favorable price changes during the months prior to delivery.

➤ TRADING LIMITATIONS The commodity exchanges set "day limits," based on the previous day's closing prices, specifying how widely a contract's trading price can move. The purpose of these limits is to prevent excessive short-term volatility and therefore also to keep margin requirements low. But trading limits can also lock traders into positions they cannot trade out of because the contract held is either up or down to the daily limit.

For example, an investor buys one gold contract (100 ounces) at $500 per ounce on June 30. On July 1 gold falls to $470 an ounce. The trading limit on gold is $20 per day, which means that on that day gold can be traded anywhere from $480 to $520 per ounce. Since the price has dropped below $480, trading is halted and the investor is locked into his position, unable to sell on that day. On the next day, July 2, the trading limits change to $460 to $500.

➤ PRICE QUOTATIONS Commodity prices are printed in the papers in various ways. In general you'll find the "high" (highest price of the day), the "low," and the "close." "Net change" refers to the change from the prior day's settlement price. The final column gives the high-low range for the year. Grain prices are given in cents per bushel; for example, wheat for December may be listed at a closing price of 3.71 per bushel.

STEPS TO TAKE

➤ GET CURRENT INFORMATION There is no inside information about commodities. All statistics are available in government reports, business and

---

COMMODITIES

PROS
↑ Large potential capital gains
↑ High amount of leverage available
↑ Small initial investment
↑ High liquidity
CONS
↓ Extremely risky
↓ Requires expertise
↓ Highly volatile
↓ Must continually monitor position
↓ Could lose total investment

---

agricultural publications, newsletters, and special service. Always check two or three for confirmation and then review your conclusions with your broker. It will help to become something of an expert in both the fundamental and technical aspects of a few major commodities. When you become experienced, you can move into other areas where information is not so widely available.

➤ CHOOSE AN EXPERIENCED BROKER Deal only with a reputable firm that (1) has extensive commodities trading services and (2) includes a broker who knows speculations and can guide you. Never buy or sell as the result of a phone recommendation until it has been confirmed in written or printed form.

➤ ZERO IN ON A FEW COMMODITIES Preferably those in the news. For instance, during the drought in the Midwest in spring 1988, soybeans and grains experienced wild price gyrations. Watch for such movements and remember that in commodities "the trend is your friend."

➤ AVOID THIN MARKETS You can score when such a commodity takes off, but the swings can be too fast and may send prices soaring or plummeting, and the amateur can get caught with no chance of closing a position.

➤ LOOK FOR A RATIO OF NET PROFIT TO NET LOSS OF 2:1 Since the percentage of losses will always be greater than that of profits, choose commodities where the potential gains (based on confirmed trends) can be more than double the possible losses.

➤ PREPARE AN OPERATIONAL PLAN Before you risk any money, test your hypothesis on paper until you feel confident that you understand what can happen. Do this for several weeks to get the feel of different types of contracts in different types of markets.

With an active commodity, "buy" contracts at several delivery dates and calculate the potential profits if the price rises moderately.

➤ NEVER MEET A MARGIN CALL When your original margin is impaired, your broker will call for more money. Except in most unusual circumstances, do not put in more money. Liquidate your position and accept your loss. This is a form of stop-loss safeguard. When a declining trend has been established, further losses can be expected.

➤ BE ALERT TO SPECIAL SITUATIONS Information is the key to profitable speculation. As you become more knowledgeable, you will pick up many points, such as these:

■ If there's heavy spring and summer rain in Maine, buy long on potatoes. They need ideal weather.

■ If there's a bad tornado over large portions of the Great Plains, buy wheat contracts. Chances are the wheat crop will be damaged, thus changing the supply and demand.

➤ TRADE WITH THE MAJOR TREND, AGAINST THE MINOR TREND With copper, for example, if you project a worldwide shortage of the metal and the market is in an uptrend, buy futures when the market suffers temporary weak spells. As long as prices keep moving up, you want to accumulate a meaningful position.

The corollary to this is never to average down. Adding to your loss position increases the number of contracts that are returning a loss. By buying more, you put yourself in a stance where you can lose on more contracts if the price continues to drop.

Generally, if the trend is down, either sell short or stay out of the market.

➤ WATCH THE SPREADS BETWEEN DIFFERENT DELIVERY DATES In the strong summer market, the premium for January soybeans is 8¢ per bushel above the November contract. Buy November and sell January.

If the bull market persists, the premium should disappear and you will have a pleasant limited profit. Carrying charges on soybeans run about 6½¢ per month, so it is not likely that the spread will widen to more than 13¢ per

bushel. Thus with that 8¢ spread, the real risk is not more than 5¢ per bushel.

➤ NEVER SPREAD A LOSS Turning a long or short position into a spread by buying or selling another contract month will seldom help you and in most cases will guarantee a locked-in loss. When you make a mistake, get out.

$ HINT: If you don't dare play the commodities game yourself, invest in one of the publicly traded commodity funds. They're diversified and professionally managed. You could, of course, lose money if the fund performs poorly, but you'll never be subject to margin calls.

➤ WATCH THE PRICE PEAKS AND LOWS Never sell at a price that is near the natural or government-imposed floor, and never buy at a price that is near its high.

Similarly, do not buy after the price of any commodity has passed its seasonal high or sell after it has dropped under its seasonal low.

➤ RISK NO MORE THAN 10% OF YOUR TRADING CAPITAL IN ANY ONE POSITION And risk no more than 30% of all capital in all positions at any one time—except when you have caught a strong upswing and can move with the trend. These limits will ease the effect of a bad decision. Few professionals count on being right more than half the time.

COMMODITY FUTURES OPTIONS

COMMODITY	SYMBOLS	ONE CONTRACT EQUALS
Options on T-bond futures	CG, PG	One T-bond futures contract
Options on soybean futures	CZ, PZ	One soybean futures contract
Options on corn futures	CY, PY	One corn futures contract
Options on silver futures	AC, AP	One 1,000-ounce silver futures contract
Options on 10-year Treasury futures	TC, TP	One 10-year Treasury futures contract

SOURCE: Chicago Board of Trade.

➤ BE SLOW TO LISTEN TO YOUR BROKER Unless the recommendations are backed by absolutely clear analyses. In most cases, by the time you get the word, smart traders have made their moves. To be successful, you must anticipate, not follow. The same caveat applies to professional newsletters.

➤ USE TECHNICAL ANALYSIS Especially charts, because timing is the key to speculative success, and with commodities, what has happened before is likely to be repeated.

COMMODITY FUNDS

Commodity funds offer an easier (but not risk-free) way to participate in the action. Professionals make the buy and sell decisions for you—and most guarantee that you won't lose more than half your investment. The typical minimum for a pool is $5,000.

These funds are a hybrid, a mix of mutual fund and limited partnership. Like mutual funds, they are professionally managed pooled investments. Most cover 20 to 30 different futures markets, so they offer wide diversification. For example, a loss in gold could be offset by a gain in corn. Their performance is best when there is a long steady direction in prices.

They are also similar to limited partnerships in that as an investor, you are part of a corporation, and your losses are limited to the dollar amount you invest.

$ HINT: Although most commodity funds permit investors to get out, either monthly or quarterly, do not invest unless you plan

---

TIPS ON INVESTING IN COMMODITY FUNDS

Read the prospectus to determine:
- The average annual performance
- Rules regarding redeeming shares
- Net worth and income requirements for investing
- Fees
- If the adviser is registered with the Commodities Futures Trading Commission; if not, do business elsewhere.

---

to stay in for at least a year. On a short-term basis, commodities are more volatile than stocks, fluctuating as much as 5% to 7% per month. Funds also have hefty fees: sales charges range from 5% to 8% of your initial investment plus an annual management fee.

The prospectus reports the month-by-month track record for traders for the last several years. Examine that record closely to help you determine how well the fund is run. Yet even with this data it's hard to pick winners. As with *all* investments, caveat emptor!

COMMODITY ADVISERS

One response investors have made to the trading scandal in Chicago is to hire professionals to do

---

LEADING COMMODITY FUNDS

FUND	TELEPHONE	1988 RETURN
Wilson	1-800-238-6044	125.3%
Memphis, Tenn.	1-901-683-5400	
Stotler's Heartland Futures Fund I	1-312-987-2700	49.5
Chicago Ill.		
Cornerstone Fund	1-212-392-2642	37.6
New York, N.Y.		
Tudor Select Futures Fund	1-212-608-0901	32.3
New York, N.Y.		
Western Futures Fund	1-800-621-0757	32.3
Chicago, Ill.		

FINDING A COMMODITY ADVISER

A. T. A. Research Inc. Dallas, Tex. 1-214-373-7606	Managed Account Reports Columbia, Md. 1-301-730-5365
Barclay Trading Group Fairfield, Iowa 1-515-472-3456	Trading Adviser, Inc. Denver, Colo. 1-303-572-6093

the trading for them. The advisers must be registered with the Commodity Futures Trading Commission. They charge in one of two ways: a percentage, usually 6%, of the funds turned over to them, or an incentive fee, typically 15% of any profits generated by the adviser.

$ HINT: Select an adviser who has an annual rate of return of at least 25% for a minimum of 3 years.

Several research firms monitor and recommend trading advisers.

FOR FURTHER INFORMATION

"Commodity Traders Consumer Report"
Advanced Trading Seminars, Inc.
1731 Howe Avenue
Sacramento, CA 95825
1-916-677-7562
Bimonthly; $195 per year

22 PRECIOUS METALS

Some say it's a hedge against inflation; doomsayers swear its our only protection against the inevitable downfall of our entire economic system. And in between are those who believe in diversification. Whatever the reason, precious metals have a place in every well-balanced portfolio *as long as one realizes they are a volatile long-term holding.*

There are a number of ways to participate in the precious metals markets:

- *Bullion.* You can buy the bullion itself through larger banks, brokerage firms, and major dealers.

$ HINT: Bullion coins should not be confused with rare coins. Bullion coins have very little value as a collectible; their price is based on their gold content. Rare coins purchased at auction from other collectors or dealers have numismatic value that is based upon their age, rarity, condition, and popularity.

- *Certificates.* Unless you want to take physical delivery and fill up your living room with bars or coins, certificates are an easy way to own precious metals. The minimum is usually $1,000. They are sold at roughly 3% over the price of the metal. You also pay an annual storage fee of about 1%.
- *Mutual funds.* Funds specializing in precious metals are undoubtedly the easiest way to build a portfolio in this area. However, this is not a "pure play"—you are of course buying partial shares of stocks of companies that mine metals, not the metal itself. Your profit will depend largely on how well the fund is managed.
- *Stocks.* Another route is to purchase the individual stocks of mining companies. Stocks offer potential price appreciation and dividend income, yet at the same time they leave you subject to market risks, political upheavals, labor unrest, and mining strikes.
- *Futures and options.* This is by far the riskiest way to invest in metals because it involves betting on the future direction of prices. With a gold, silver, or platinum futures contract, you agree to buy or sell a certain quantity at a specified future price. You are required to put up 5% to 10% of the value of the contract as "margin." Therefore, you control a large amount of metal for very few dollars, but at the same time, you can lose your entire investment if your bet is incorrect.

The true gold bug or fanatic shuns mutual funds and certificates, maintaining that if the world caves in, only the real tangible metals will be valuable. If you're less of a purist, then you may be content with a certificate or shares of stock or a fund.

☐ CAUTION: Put no more than 5% to 8% of your portfolio in precious metals.

GUIDELINES FOR BUYING

Here are the key facts to keep in mind about the big three: gold, silver, and platinum.

GOLD

To enhance your potential profits in gold, watch for changes in these leading indicators and then take appropriate action:

- Political situation in South Africa
- The trend of inflation and the Consumer Price Index

BEFORE BUYING A PRECIOUS METAL

Follow these guidelines and heed these warnings:

- Paper trade for at least 1 month. Make decisions, calculate margins, set stop-loss prices, and monitor how well you are doing in theory.
- Never commit more than half of your risk capital to metals. If you are trading contracts, keep the balance in a money market account to meet any margin calls.
- Read the commodity columns in the *Wall Street Journal* and *Barron's*. Ask several dealers to send you their research reports.
- Track the direction of interest rates, inflation, and the spot prices of the metals. (Spot price is the cash price for metals that are delivered at once.)
- Never give discretionary powers to anyone in the business.
- Never place an order over the phone with someone who has called you cold.

LEADING GOLD COINS

American Gold Eagle	Canadian Maple Leaf
Mexican 50 peso	Mexican onza
Austrian 100 Corona	Australian Nugget
Hungarian Corona	Chinese Panda

- Movement of interest rates
- Direction of the dollar
- Third World debt and related banking problems
- Any increase or decrease in gold production

Remember, gold vies with the dollar as the world's reserve currency (i.e., the world's safest currency). When the dollar is strong, gold tends to be low in price and vice versa.

SILVER

Silver is primarily an industrial metal; its price is directly related to supply and demand and less (as is the case with gold) to inflation, interest rates, and politics. Silver is used in coins, jewelry, and silverware, but its greatest demand is in the photographic, electronic, dental, and medical fields. Its industrial uses are so great, in fact, that the world consumes as much silver as is mined.

The American silver bullion coin is called the Silver Eagle.

PLATINUM

Although platinum has generally been considered more valuable than gold or silver because of its limited availability, it has never been as popular with investors. Its primary uses are in the electronics, chemical, and automobile industries. It is an essential ingredient in the production of catalytic converters for pollution control in cars. During the past decade, the world generally consumed more platinum than it produced.

Platinum coins include the Noble, Canadian Maple Leaf, and Australian Koala.

BUYING METALS BY PHONE

Although you should never succumb to a high-pressure salesman, you can indeed buy bullion bars and coins by phone from reliable dealers whom you know; however, check several for prices and fees first.

- *Citibank's Precious Metals Division* allows clients to use their Visa or Mastercard to buy precious metals. Call: 1-800-223-1080. Their 24-hour Quoteline gives the latest spot prices: 1-212-826-0500.
- *Merrill Lynch's "Blueprint"* program has a minimum purchase of only $100 with $50 thereafter. Call: 1-800-221-2856.
- *Benham Certified Metals* has a discount brokerage division. The minimum for silver is $1,000 and $2,000 for gold and platinum. Call: 1-800-447-4653.

■ *Rhode Island Hospital Trust National Bank* of Providence sells coins, bars, and certificates to individuals. It also has an accumulation account for only $100 per month. Call: 1-800-343-8419 or 1-401-278-7595.

FOR FURTHER INFORMATION

Jeffrey Nichols, *The Complete Book of Gold Investing.* (Homewood, Ill.: Dow Jones–Irwin, 1986), $30.

Dow Theory Letters
P.O. Box 1759
La Jolla, CA 92038
1-619-454-0481
$225 per year

"Your Introduction to Investing in Gold"
Gold Institute
1026 16th Street NW
Washington, DC 20036
$3

For a directory of recommended dealers, contact the Industry Council for Tangible Assets, 1-202-783-3500

23 FINANCIAL FUTURES AND MARKET INDEXES

FINANCIAL FUTURES

If trading corn and pork bellies is too tame, you can move along to another type of commodity: interest-bearing securities, such as Treasury bonds and notes, CDs, and Ginnie Maes. For amateurs, financial futures and stock indexes are just about the riskiest areas of Wall Street. Yet professional money managers use them as investment tools, as a way to hedge their portfolios. Just as agribusinesses rely on commodities futures, so money managers and others use financial futures to protect their profits.

Financial futures trading requires an ability to predict correctly the short-term or intermediate movements of interest rates, because futures involve debt issues whose values move with the cost of money; that is, with interest rates. With tiny margins (as small as $800 to control $1 million), a shift of ½% in the interest rate can double your money—or lose most of your capital.

The swings of financial futures are often dramatic, but the forecast of higher interest rates by only one financial guru can send these contracts down as fast as a punctured balloon.

If you are a modest investor, skip this chapter. If you have over $100,000 in a portfolio, read it rapidly. If you are a speculator who can afford to lose half your stake, study the explanations and then deal with an experienced broker.

HOW FINANCIAL FUTURES WORK

Basically, these are contracts that involve money. They are used by major investors, such as banks, insurance companies, and pension fund managers, to protect positions by hedging: what they gain (lose) in the cash market will be offset by the loss (profit) in the futures market.

The terms and rules of trading are set by the exchanges.

A financial futures contract is in essence a contract on an interest rate. The most popular are Treasury bills, bonds, and notes; Ginnie Maes; and CDs. They are sold through brokers or firms specializing in commodities. Contract sizes vary with the underlying security and the exchange, but they range from approximately $20,000 to $1 million. However, since margin requirements are low, sometimes only 5% to 10% of total value, your actual outlay is surprisingly little, relatively speaking.

The value of a financial futures contract is determined by interest rates:

- When rates rise, the price of fixed-income securities and the futures based on them *fall*.
- When rates decline, these investments *rise* in value.

§ HINT: Place stop orders with your broker. These provide instructions to close out your position when the price falls to a certain level, which will help limit any potential losses.

U.S. TREASURY BOND FUTURES

Since their introduction in 1977, U.S. T-bond futures have become the most actively traded futures contract worldwide. Although there are various other financial futures traded, we will illustrate the principle with T-bonds and T-notes. ("For Further Information" at the end of this chapter lists more in-depth studies of trading financial futures.)

Like all futures contracts, T-bond futures contracts are standardized (see box). Their only variable is the price, which is established on the floor of the Chicago Board of Trade. Bond prices, of course, move in inverse relationship to interest rates: when rates rise, bond prices fall. Speculators and others use T-bonds to take advantage of anticipated interest rate changes; hedgers focus more on reducing and managing risk for their portfolios.

➤ IF YOU EXPECT INTEREST RATES TO FALL Such an expectation implies that bond futures will rise. This means you'll want to take a long position in order to take advantage of the potentially rising bond market (to be long on a contract is to buy it; to short a contract is to sell). For example, if bond futures are now trading at 72% of par, you go long one $100,000-face-value bond contract. If bond prices then rise to 74% of par, you offset your original long position by going short for a profit of 2 points, or $2,000.

Long one contract @ 72 or $72,000
Short one contract @ 74 or $74,000
Profit: $2,000

➤ IF YOU EXPECT INTEREST RATES TO RISE You then take a short position. Then when bond prices fall to 69, you can offset your original position by going long for a $3,000 profit.

Short one contract @ 72 or $72,000
Long one contract @ 69 or $69,000
Profit: $3,000

➤ SPREADS Speculators usually trade financial futures by going long on one position and short on another with both contracts due in the same month. But you can also use spreads: buying one contract month and selling another. This technique is used when there's an abnormal relation between the yields and thus the prices of two contracts with different maturities. These situations don't come often, but when they do, they can be mighty rewarding, because the gains will come from a restoration of the normal spread.

Example: An investor notes that June T-bonds are selling at 80-11 (each $1/32$% equals $3.125 of a standard $100,000 contract) and that September's are at 81-05. The basis for

---

U.S. TREASURY BOND FUTURES

Trading unit: $100,000 face value of U.S. T-bonds

Deliverable: U.S. Treasury bonds with a nominal 8% coupon maturing at least 15 years from delivery date if not callable; if callable, not for at least 15 years from delivery date

Delivery method: Federal Reserve book entry wire transfer system

Par: $1,000

Price quote: Percentage of par in minimum increments of $1/32$ point, or $3.125 per "tick," e.g., 74-01 means $74 1/32$% of par

Daily price limit: $64/32$ or $2,000 per contract above or below the previous day's settlement price

Delivery months: March, June, September, or December

Ticker symbol: US—traded on Chicago Board of Trade

---

quotations is an 8% coupon and 15-year maturity.

Based on experience, he decides that this $26/32$ difference ($81 5/32 - 80 11/32 = 26/32$) is out of line with normal pricing. He *sells* the September contract and *buys* the June one. In a couple of weeks, prices begin to normalize: the September contract edges up to 81-08 and the June one surges to 80-24. Now he starts to cash in: he loses $3/32$ ($93.75) on the September contract but gains $13/32$ ($406.25) on the June one: $312.50 profit minus commission.

RULES TO FOLLOW

If you have money you can afford to lose, time enough to keep abreast of developments in the financial world, strong nerves, and a trustworthy, knowledgeable broker, trading in financial futures may be rewarding and surely will be exciting. Of course, if you're involved with substantial holdings, you probably are already familiar with hedging, so you can stick to protective contracts. Otherwise, follow these rules:

- *Make dry runs on paper for several months.* Interest rates change slowly. Pick different types of financial futures each week and keep practicing until you get a feel for the market and risks and, over at least a week, chalk up more winners than losers.
- *Buy long when you look for a drop in interest rates.* With lower yields, the prices of all contracts will rise.
- *Sell short when you expect a higher cost of money.* This will force down the value of the contracts, and you can cover your position at a profit.
- *Set a strategy and stick to it.* Don't try to mix contracts until you are comfortable and making money.

$ HINT: Set stop and limit orders, not market orders. A market order is executed immediately at the best possible price. A stop order, to buy or to sell at a given price, becomes a market order when that price is touched. A limit order is the maximum price at which to buy and the minimum at which to sell.

OPTIONS ON FUTURES

Another way to participate in the futures market is through options (see Chapter 15). A futures option is a contract that gives you the right to buy (call) or sell (put) a certain futures contract within a specified period of time for a specified price (called the premium).

➤ OPTIONS ON COMMODITIES Options are traded on futures for agricultural commodities, oil, livestock, metals, etc. Quotes are listed in the newspaper under "Futures Options." These involve far less money than contracts do: roughly, $100 for an option compared to $1,800 for a futures contract. There are no margin calls, and the risk is limited to the premium. But these are for professionals and gamblers. If you ride a strong market trend, you can make a lot of money with a small outlay and rapid fluctuations, or you can make a modest profit by successful hedging. *Be cautious and limit your commitment.* It's easy to con yourself into thinking you're a genius when you hit a couple of big winners fast, but unless you bank half of those profits, you will lose money over a period of time if only because of the commissions.

➤ OPTIONS ON FINANCIAL FUTURES Options are also traded on some interest-bearing securities, such as Treasury bills and notes. T-bond options, for example, are traded on the Chicago Board of Trade. The T-bond futures contract underlying the option is for $100,000 of Treasury bonds, bearing an 8% or equivalent coupon, which do not mature and are noncallable for at least 15 years. When long-term interest rates fall, the value of the futures contract and the call option increases while the value of a put option decreases. The opposite is true when long-term rates rise.

CONTRACT SPECIFICATIONS OF FUTURES

	U.S. TREASURY BONDS	10-YEAR U.S. TREASURY NOTES	GNMA-CDR	GNMA II
Basic trading unit	$100,000 face value	$100,000 face value	$100,000 principal balance	$100,000 principal balance
Price quotation	Full points (one point equals $1,000) and 32nds of a full point			
Minimum price fluctuation	$1/32$ of a full point ($3.125 per contract)			
Daily price limit	$64/32$ (2 points or $2,000) above or below the previous day's settlement price			
Date introduced	Aug. 22, 1977	May 3, 1982	Oct. 20, 1975	1984
Ticker symbol	US	TY	M	GT

SOURCE: Chicago Board of Trade.

Premiums for T-bond futures options are quoted in $1/64$ths of 1% (1 point). Thus $1/64$ point equals $15.63 ($100,000 $\times$ 0.01 $\times$ $1/64$). A premium quote of 2–16 means $2^{16}/64$, or [(2 $\times$ 64) + 16] $\times$ $15.63, or $2,250.72 per option.

The profit is the premium you receive when the option is sold minus the premium paid when you purchased the option.

➤ SETTING UP HEDGES Options provide excellent opportunities to set up hedges if you plan your strategy and understand the risks and rewards. Here's an example cited by Stanley Angrist in *Forbes.*

In March, the June T-bond contract is selling at 52–05 (72⅝). Calls at 72, 74, and 76 are quoted at premiums of 2–06, 1–20, and 0–46, respectively; puts at 68, 70, and 72 are available at 0–30, 0–61, and 1–54. You think that the market will remain stable, so you make these paper projections of hedges with a margin of $3,000:

Sell June 72 call	$2,093.75
Sell June 72 put	1,843.75
Total income	$3,937.50

If the T-bond is still worth 72 on the June strike date, both options will expire worthless,

so you have an extra $3,937.50 minus commissions.

Sell June 74 call	$1,312.50
Sell June 70 put	953.13
Total income	$2,265.63

This is less risky, and less profitable, because both options will expire worthless if the last-day price is between 70 and 74.

Sell June 76 call	$ 718.75
Sell June 68 call	468.75
Total income	$1,187.50

If the final price is between 68 and 76, you will do OK. You swap a lower income for a broader price range.

STOCK INDEXES

You can also trade options on stock index futures. Both index options and index futures options are available.

These are the fastest-growing area of speculations and make it possible to play the market without owning a single share of stock. They combine the growth potential of equities with the speculative hopes of commodities.

With a stock index, you are betting on the future price of the composite of a group of stocks: *buying* if you anticipate a rise soon, *selling* if you look for a decline. You put up cash or collateral equal to about 7% of the contract value vs. 50% for stocks. All you need is a little capital and a lot of nerve. A minor jiggle can produce sizable losses or gains. And there are also options that require even less money.

To emphasize the speculative nature of indexes, some brokerage firms advise their brokers to limit trading to individuals with a net worth of $100,000 (exclusive of home and life insurance).

These stock indexes currently have futures contracts and/or options on futures available:

- **Standard & Poor's 500 (SPX):** stocks of 500 industrials, financial companies, utilities, and transportation issues, all listed on the NYSE. They are weighted by market value. This means each stock is weighted so that changes in the stock's price influence the index in proportion to

GOVERNMENT INSTRUMENT FUTURES CONTRACTS

COMMODITY	SYMBOL	ONE CONTRACT EQUALS
U.S. Treasury bonds	US	Face value at maturity: $100,000
10-year T-notes	TY	Face value at maturity: $100,000
GNMA	M	$100,000 principal balance
30-day Treasury repo	—	$2.5 million face value
90-day Treasury repo	—	$1 million face value
Zero coupon T-bonds	—	Discounted
Zero coupon T-notes	—	Discounted

SOURCE: Chicago Board of Trade.

the stock's representative market value. Contracts are valued at 500 times the index. They are traded on the Chicago Mercantile Exchange. Generally, this is the index favored by big hitters, as contracts are extremely liquid and it's widely used to measure institutional performance. *Options* on the SPX trade only on the Chicago Board of Options Exchange (CBOE).

- **Standard & Poor's 100:** a condensed version of the S&P 500 index (known as OEX). It is weighted by capitalization of the component corporations, all of which have options traded on the CBOE. The value is 100 times the worth of the stocks.
- **Value Line Composite (XVL):** an equally weighted geometric index of about 1,700 stocks actively traded on the NYSE, AMEX, and OTC. Contracts are quoted at 500 times the index. This tends to be difficult to trade because of a thin market on the small Kansas City Board of Trade. Options trade on the Philadelphia exchange.
- **AMEX Market Value Index (XAM):** measures the changes in the aggregate market of over 800 AMEX issues. The weighting is by industry groups: 32% natural resources, 19% high technology, 13% service, 11% consumer goods. No one company accounts for more than 7% of the total.
- **Major Market Index (XMI):** based on 20 blue chip NYSE stocks and price-weighted so that higher-priced shares have a greater effect on the average than lower-priced ones. Options trade on the American exchange.
- **AMEX Oil & Gas Index (XOI):** made up of the stocks of 30 oil and gas companies with Exxon representing about 17%. Options trade on the AMEX.
- **Computer Technology Index (XCI):** stocks of 30 major computer companies, with IBM accounting for about half and Hewlett-Packard, Digital Equipment, and Motorola another 16%. Options trade on the American.
- **NYSE Composite Index (NYA):** a capitalization-weighted average of about 1,500 Big Board stocks. Options trade on the New York Stock Exchange.

- **Standard & Poor's Computer & Business Equipment Index (OBR):** a capitalization-weighted average of a dozen major office and business equipment companies, with IBM about 75%, Digital Equipment, Wang, and NCR about 18%.
- **Technology Index (PTI):** a price-weighted index of 100 stocks of which 45 are traded OTC. Very volatile. Options trade on the Philadelphia Stock Exchange.
- **Gold & Silver Index (XAU):** options trade on the Philadelphia Stock Exchange.
- **National OTC Index (NCMP):** options trade on the Philadelphia Stock Exchange.
- **NYSE Beta Index (NHB):** options trade on the New York Stock Exchange.

GUIDELINES FOR SUCCESS

- *Follow the trend.* If the price of the index is higher than it was the day before, which in turn is higher than it was the previous day, go long. If the reverse, sell short.
- *Set stop-loss prices at 3 points below cost.* If they are too close, one erratic move can stop you out at a loss even though the market may resume its uptrend soon.
- *Recognize the role of the professionals.* To date, most contracts have been traded by brokerage houses active in arbitrage and spreads and in hedging large block positions. Only a handful of institutional managers have done more than experiment. So the amateur is competing with top professionals who have plenty of capital and no commissions to pay and who are in positions to get the latest information and make quick decisions.
- *Study the price spreads.* Contracts for distant months are more volatile. In a strong market, buy far-out contracts and short nearby months; in a weak market, buy the closer months and short the distant ones.
- *Be mindful that dividends can distort prices.* In heavy payout months, these discrepancies can be significant.
- *Use a hedge only when your portfolio approximates that of the index:* roughly a minimum of $250,000 (very rarely does a

major investor buy only 100 shares of a stock). In most cases, any single portfolio has little resemblance to that of the index.

OPTIONS ON STOCK INDEXES

These are the ultimate in speculations. For a few hundred dollars, you can control a cross section of stocks worth $75,000 or so. The action is fast and exciting. The options, both calls and puts, have expiration dates every 3 months, they are quoted at intervals of 5 points, and their premiums reflect hopes and fears, the time premiums declining with the approach of the strike date. There are no margin calls, and the risks are limited.

Example: An investor has $60,000 worth of quality stocks and anticipates a drop in the overall stock market. The Standard & Poor's 500 index is at 151.50. She sells short one September contract. By mid-September the index is up to 153, so she didn't need the protection. She paid $150 for insurance, but the value of her holdings was up about $600.

With volatile stocks, options on the special indexes can be useful. You're bullish (but hesitant) on high-tech stocks. Here's what to do, according to *Indicator Digest:*

- In January the XCO options index is at 100.79. You buy a March 100 call at 4⅜ and sell a March 105 call at $1^{13}/_{16}$: a net cost of $2^9/_{16}$ points, or $256.25 (not counting commissions).
- If the XCO trades at 105 or above at expiration (about +4%), you make 2¼ points ($225)—more than an 80% gain. The maximum loss will be the cost of the spread if the index trades at 100 or less at expiration.

With all options on indexes, settlements are made in cash. When the option is exercised, the holder receives the difference between the exercise price and the closing index price on the date the option is exercised.

☐ CAUTION: This can be far from the price the day the assignment notice is received. A hedge can lose on both the long and short side!

FOR FURTHER INFORMATION

Mark J. Powers, *Inside the Financial Futures Markets* (New York: John Wiley & Sons, 1984).

Edward W. Schwartz, *Financial Futures* (Homewood, Ill.: Dow Jones–Irwin, 1988).

Contact the following exchanges for pamphlets on futures trading:

The Options Exchange
LaSalle at Van Buren
Chicago, IL 60604
1-312-786-5600

Chicago Board of Trade
Marketing Department
La Salle at Jackson
Chicago, IL 60604
1-312-435-3500

Chicago Mercantile Exchange
30 South Wacker Drive
Chicago, IL 60606
1-312-930-1000

Chicago Mercantile Exchange
67 Wall Street
New York, NY 10005
1-212-363-7000

24 TAKEOVERS

HOW TO WIN THE GAME

Despite the October 1987 crash, mergers and acquisitions are still very much with us. During the first quarter of 1988, $50 billion worth of tender offers were made on 55 public corporations. Many were surprise announcements, and shareholders were forced into making quick decisions. Selling was sometimes better than tendering, but not always. Holding was also profitable, depending on the situation.

The dollar's decline since 1985 has created an interesting takeover situation: American companies are bargains to overseas investors. In 1988, foreigners accounted for about 15% of all U.S. mergers and acquisitions.

Among the areas of current interest are capital equipment manufacturers, small electric utilities, the food business, and industries in which at least one deal has already taken place, such as banks, publishing, and retailers.

TAKEOVER MANIA

American public corporations are owned by their stockholders, yet for decades a large percentage of corporate managements have been more interested in keeping their jobs and "perks" than in rewarding their stockholders. Dividend increases have been deemed less important than executive salaries, and many managements have ignored the prices at which their stocks were trading. Wall Street analysts have described these managements as "not very stock-minded." In fact, stockholders were held in disdain by many managements.

During the past few years, this neglect of stockholder interests has come to a screeching halt. The catalyst for this great change has been the plethora of corporate raids and takeovers. One after another, complacent and neglectful managements have found themselves under attack from corporate raiders, leveraged buyout (LBO) specialists, and aroused stockholder groups.

Before you play the takeover game, let us review what we mean by cash flow per share and net asset value per share, since these two factors are instrumental in understanding the takeover phenomenon.

CASH FLOW PER SHARE

Every corporation needs income from operations to pay for:

- Dividends
- Expansion
- Working capital
- Interest on and repayment of debt

These financial needs are met by both income and depreciation. Depreciation is a noncash charge made against earnings to replace assets as they wear out. Income after taxes and interest charges (but before dividends) is then added to depreciation and is called "cash flow."

Cash flow per share is calculated by dividing the cash flow by the number of common shares outstanding.

NET ASSET VALUE PER SHARE

NAV per share, or book value per share, is derived by subtracting all liabilities from total assets (after depreciation) and dividing by the number of shares outstanding.

However, the real net asset value of a company can be determined only by learning what the assets would sell for in today's market. Here we depart from stated book value and look for:

- Real estate—land and buildings with a substantial current market value
- Lumber and forest reserves

```
┌─────────────────────────────────────────┐
│                                           │
│   POTENTIAL TAKEOVER TARGETS              │
│   ▄▄▄▄▄▄▄▄                                │
│                                           │
│   Avon Prod. Preferred                    │
│   Champion International                   │
│   Clark Equipment                         │
│   Federal Paper Board                     │
│   Gibson Greetings                        │
│   Greyhound                               │
│   Ingersoll-Rand                          │
│   International Paper                      │
│   McGraw-Hill                             │
│   Mead                                    │
│   Nevada Power                            │
│   Owens Corning                           │
│   Scott Paper                             │
│   Sierra Pacific Resources                │
│   Stone Container                         │
│   Sundstrand                              │
│                                           │
└─────────────────────────────────────────┘
```

- Oil and gas reserves that are proven and commercial
- Radio and TV stations
- Mineral resources
- Trucks, trailers, railway cars, with substantial resale value
- Retail chains, fast-food facilities, textile, metal, and manufacturing facilities—anything with a profitable "going concern" value

When we have corrected our assets and arrived at a true picture of net asset value, we can then divide by the number of shares to find the real net asset value, or breakup value, per share:

$$\frac{\text{Total assets adjusted} - \text{all liabilities}}{\text{Number of common shares}}$$

FINDING A TAKEOVER TARGET

Companies with substantial cash flow per share and/or real net asset value per share have been takeover targets in the past, and they continue to attract attention from a wide range of potential acquirers. The accompanying Standard & Poor's stock report illustrates what skillful readers of this guide might look for to discover a takeover target. Indeed, professional money managers and security analysts do this sort of cash flow and asset study all the time.

Since takeovers and mergers are rampant, you need to determine what to do if one of your stocks becomes involved. Here are the facts.

$ HINT: If you own stock in a takeover target, you must be prepared to act quickly in order to get the best deal. Your broker will explain your options, and the management of the company will tell you if it approves or disapproves of the proposal—in other words, if it's a friendly or unfriendly takeover.

The acquirer, or firm trying to buy shares in another company, solicits the target company's shareholders through a tender offer. The information that must appear in this offer includes:

- The price to be paid
- The number of shares that will be accepted
- The method of payment—cash, securities, or both
- The date when the offer opens
- The date when the offer expires
- Whether shareholders have a right to withdraw shares that have been tendered
- Who is making the tender offer
- Where one gets further information

A tender offer is not written in stone: it can be amended or even canceled if not enough shareholders offer their shares or if another acquirer makes a better bid.

If you hold a stock that is the subject of a takeover, you'll find that it's not easy to sort out the value of the offer and decide what to do. Even the professional arbitrageurs have trouble in the most intricate deals; after all, the takeover game is rife with fast plays and unpredictable maneuvers. Its uncertainties and complications are so intricate that even the most skillful can lose. Clues are given along the way, but you must first understand the type of offer that you're dealing with.

FRIENDLY TAKEOVERS

A friendly tender offer, as opposed to the unfriendly version, is often unopposed. The terms are outlined in the initial announcement and are seldom changed, with management of the company about to be taken over generally agreeing to them.

LEVERAGED BUYOUTS

A leveraged buyout is one in which management, along with investment bankers, buys out all the common stockholders and takes the company private. Over the past several years, this variation on the friendly takeover theme has become increasingly popular. A leveraged buyout is initiated by a company's management for three reasons:

- To avoid takeover by another corporation
- To keep control of the company
- To take the company private

In other words, in this type of deal, the company's assets and earning capacity are used to secure loans to finance the purchase. Debt is used in a highly leveraged way to buy out all the common shareholder equity.

If you own stock in a company that is offered a leveraged buyout, you have no choice but to sell your stock. Frequently the announcement creates additional interest in the stock, which may drive up the price. You will obtain the best price by waiting until the offer is closed.

Of course, there is risk in holding the stock, too. If the deal becomes unglued because of government regulations, licensing problems in transferring assets, or any other complication, your shares could fall in price.

BUY-BACKS

This type of tender offer is quite often successful. In a buy-back, the company offers to purchase some of its own stock back from its stockholders. In this way, a company can reduce its cash on hand—cash that might make it a likely candidate for a hostile bidder. It also increases its earnings per share.

Frequently, the price of a stock rises upon news of a buy-back. If you have faith in the company, you may not want to tender your shares. Your broker or a good financial service, such as Standard & Poor's or Value Line, can advise you further. (See Chapter 25 for more on buy-backs.)

UNFRIENDLY TAKEOVERS

Pursuing and purchasing a stock based purely on takeover rumors can often mean you're skating on thin ice. The classic example, the

---

HOW TO EVALUATE A TENDER OFFER

- Read the offer-to-purchase statement sent by the bidder to all shareholders.
- Is the offer friendly or hostile? Friendly deals are more likely to be accepted by management, but a hostile offer may attract other offers at higher prices. Consider tendering at any rate, but be alert to what professional arbitrageurs are doing. If they're not tendering, neither should you; if they are, you should consider doing so.
- Find out, if you do tender your shares, how long you have to take them back should you have a change of heart.
- Note if the bid price applies to all shares tendered or if it's only a partial tender. Tenders for all stock are generally more profitable than partial tenders. You'll also be faced with the prospect that not all the shares that you tender will be accepted if the offer is oversubscribed.
- Is the takeover for cash, securities, or some of each? Cash is more certain in value than securities, which tend to fluctuate in price. Any newly issued securities may weaken the credit rating of the company.
- Are there possible antitrust problems? It's more likely if the company is part of a regulated industry such as banking, communications, insurance, or utilities.
- Does the acquirer have a successful or poor record for completing mergers? Or has the bidder sold out for greenmail in the past?

Walt Disney deal, remains the best example even though it took place in 1984. Look at the bath you would have taken after Reliance's attempted takeover. Here's what happened.

In 1984 financier Saul P. Steinberg and a small group of investors, over a period of 10 weeks, bought about 11% of Disney shares. Then in the spring of that year, Steinberg bid $67.50 per share for an additional 37.7% of Disney. During the first 3 weeks of the offer, owners of Disney stock saw their holdings soar some 25%. As it turned out, the wisest course of action was to sell, for those who hesitated lost. Why? Because Disney management, in a surprise move, bought back Steinberg's 11% holdings for $77.50 per share. Steinberg and his company, Reliance Group Holdings, Inc., had a nifty profit of $31.7 million, and Disney agreed to pay Steinberg $28 million for legal and financing fees. The news for the shareholders was far less pleasant: in only 2 days, Disney stock temporarily fell from $60+ to a little above $45 per share.

The term "greenmail," a play on the word "blackmail," refers to money paid by a corporation to make a potential acquirer go away. It buys the greenmailer's stock at a higher price than the going market price and leaves the rest of the shareholders with stock that usually drops in price.

The corporation, to save itself, buys back its stock, and the only winner is the greenmailer. The stockholders in such a situation seldom make money, unless they move very quickly. The thousands of Disney shareholders, in fact, were furious not only because they were denied the greenmailer's premium price but also because their shares dropped in price. The incident forced changes in Disney management, which resulted in higher prices for the stock in the long run.

When an offer to buy is unwanted, the game obviously becomes intense, with the potential risks and rewards much greater than those in a friendly situation. The price of the stock can go sky high. Then again, the whole deal can be shattered.

Because tender offers work quickly (1 month vs. 3 to 6 months for a merger), they are popular with hostile bidders. Shareholders, however, must be told by the target company within a 10-day period whether the tender is hostile or friendly.

TO TENDER OR NOT TO TENDER?

After reading this material, you're still faced with the million-dollar question: Should you tender or not?

You have three choices:

1 Tender to the bidder
2 Wait to see if a higher bid is made by a rival company
3 Sell in the market

You must decide between selling your shares upon announcement of the tender offer or waiting until the final settlement—often 3 to 6 months. As the deal comes closer to completion, the price spread tends to narrow. The chances of the deal's being successful are greater if the terms are presented in a formal contract. An agreement in principle is still not a signed deal.

Professional arbitrageurs engage in the business of buying stock after a deal is announced, gambling that a bidding war or a merger will push up the price. They have huge financial resources and exhaustive research facilities, and they calculate every aspect of a deal, including the cost of their money and the possibility of the deal breaking up.

One way to handle the situation is to follow what the arbitrageurs are doing. If, for example, the stock is at 30 when the bid is announced for $40 per share, and the stock opens the next day at 42½, the "arbs" see the offer as solid. If it opens at 33, the arbs are uncertain. Another is to sell up to half your stock once the takeover intention has been announced, thus protecting your gain against the possibility of the deal's collapsing. Hang on to the rest of the shares until you're within 10% to 15% of the acquisition bid; then sell.

When you receive notice of a tender offer, talk to your broker immediately, and read the circular that is mailed to you. It gives the terms and tells you how to tender shares. Look to see if there is a proration deadline. This happens when only part of your company's shares are needed for a takeover. Your tender is then accepted on a prorated basis. The SEC has ruled that every investor who tenders within 10 days of the offer be given like treatment. This ensures that part of any shares you tender prior to the deadline will be accepted. But shares tendered after the deadline could be returned.

You should also follow news of your company in the *Wall Street Journal* each day.

If management is absolutely determined to thwart a takeover, it may (1) sell assets off to make it less appealing to the acquirer, (2) down a poison pill, giving shareholders rights to the company's stock at a huge discount, or (3) attempt to buy its own company and take it private.

Because the top managers must consider all offers, if they fight off predators, they generally offer a bonus or reward to existing shareholders—a boost in the dividend, a special dividend, a buy-back of shares—or they may find a white knight. But management today is generally forced to accept the highest offer to meet its fiduciary responsibility to shareholders.

If you decide to tender, you may receive cash, securities, or some of both.

$ HINT: If at least 50% of the acquired company's stock is tendered for the stock of the acquiring company, the transaction is tax-free. Check with your accountant, as this is being reviewed by the IRS.

THE CASE FOR SELLING

Begin by noticing how the price of the stock is reacting to the offer and whether or not the deal is likely to go forward. If the price soars, give very serious consideration to selling in the market, especially if the premium is 50% or better. Another occasion for selling: if you're nervous that the deal will collapse, it's better to take the money and run, putting aside any thoughts that you have about making a few extra points if the takeover is successful.

Sometimes, of course, holding on can involve risks. If the deal falls through, the stock may drop to the level it was trading at prior to the tender offer.

THE CASE FOR TENDERING

In many deals the initial offering is merely an opening gambit in what becomes an intense, fierce battle for control of the company. How can you tell if there is likely to be a better offer? *Value Line* suggests these guidelines:

- If management does not endorse the offer, a better deal or no deal at all is likely.
- If management has been holding discussions with the company making the initial offering, it's likely that the deal will be sweetened.
- If a major shareholder is dissatisfied with the initial terms of the offer, he or she will try to bring pressure to bear for better terms.
- If there are other overtures from serious contenders, a better deal is likely.

With the exception of 1978, about half the time an offer has been successful the deal was sweetened, points out *Value Line*.

With all takeovers, you must be ready to act quickly on the basis of answers to questions such as these:

- Is this a friendly or hostile takeover? If it's hostile, there's likely to be a battle and higher offers. This can be profitable but will be nerve-racking, and there's always a chance that the deal will be called off and you'll be left with little or no gain. Almost half of attempted takeovers fail.
- Is the offer for cash, securities, or both? For most people, cash is best, because it's sure.
- What is the *real* value of the offer—as calculated in the financial press or, better, by your broker's research department? If the stock price of the target company keeps moving up, insiders expect another bidder will move in.
- Who owns large blocks of stock? When the officers or directors of the acquiring company are major shareholders, they will probably stay the course. When a substantial portion of the shares of the target company is closely held, these insiders will call the shots.
- Does the tender offer apply to all or part of the shares? When Sunbeam was acquired by Allegheny International, the winning bid was $41 per share for 50% of the common stock. The rest was swapped for convertibles worth $29 each.

When you own shares of the acquiring company, it's usually wise to sell. Management is using your money for what it believes is a more profitable future, but let them prove it first! Du Pont spent billions to take over Conoco in 1981, near the top of the market for crude oil prices. Since then they have seen the price decline substantially, pressing (squeezing) profit margins.

When you own shares of the target company, the odds are in your favor but can be improved by watchful waiting. Once a tender offer has been announced:

- *Sit tight.* Wait until all offers are in before you make any decision. Most offers are originally viewed as unfavorable by management. There's an irate outcry that the price is too low and a scurry to find another potential partner (white knight) to boost the proposed purchase price. Usually these maneuvers will boost the bid.
- *If the deal involves exchanging securities,* consider whether you want to own shares of the acquiring company. Usually, as with Du Pont, the stock price will fall.
- *After the bidding has stopped and there's a firm offer,* sell on the open market rather than wait for full details. This eliminates risks that (1) the tender will be withdrawn (which can be done without legal penalties), (2) only part of your shares will be acquired and you will end up with a mix of securities you don't want, or (3) poor timing will cost you money.

IDENTIFYING TAKEOVER TARGETS

The current wave of corporate takeovers has certainly encouraged private investors as well as institutions to play the "guess who's coming to our company" game. Companies likely to become takeovers possess certain common characteristics (see box below, lower right).

If you're looking for takeover candidates, try thinking as an acquirer does and gather as much data as possible: annual reports, 10(k)s, proxy statements, research reports, etc. No one factor alone makes for a takeover, but in combination, you may find a winner. Yet never buy any company if it is not a good investment in and of itself. Select a stock with solid fundamentals—one that, should there never be a takeover, you'd be happy owning or one whose basic qualities fit your investment goals.

TAKEOVERS

In 1986 there were 3,336 U.S. mergers, acquisitions, takeovers, divestitures, and instances of companies going private. That's the highest number since 1974, when there were 4,040. The amount of money involved in 1986 was $173.1 billion. In 1987 there were 2,032 mergers, involving $163.7 billion. In 1988 there were 2,258 mergers, involving $246.9 billion.

SOURCE: W. T. Grimm & Co., Chicago (merger and acquisition consultants).

TAKEOVER INGREDIENTS

- A stock selling below book value per share. Purchase of this type of company provides the buyer with assets that can easily be sold, or it can result in the acquisition of assets far below the present cost of constructing them.
- Low debt when compared with equity. This gives a company untapped borrowing power for financing a leveraged buyout.
- Selling at less than 5 times cash flow.
- Selling below 10 times earnings. A low P/E ratio enables the acquirer to pay for the acquisition more readily.
- Large cash holdings. These help the purchaser pay for the acquisition.
- Hidden assets (assets carried on the balance sheet at less than their current value)
- Business value (worth of the business to an acquirer, based on historical earning power, product line, and market penetration)
- Small number of shares outstanding
- History of takeover interest and previous bids
- Owners who may be willing to sell
- Low debt
- Well-known brand names
- Valuable real estate
- Portion of company already owned by another company

Start by looking at a company's balance sheet, which is a matter of public record. The ingredients that make a firm appealing to an acquirer are readily identifiable. One item alone, such as plenty of cash, is unlikely to capture a suitor's fancy, but in combination with other ingredients, it may tempt a knight or two.

Other signs of a takeover:

➤ THE 5% SIGN Whenever a company or individual buys 5% or more of another company's stock, that could be an indication of takeover interest.

The company must report its 5%+ purchase to the SEC within 10 days in a 13D filing. You can read about it in the daily *SEC News Digest* and in the monthly *SEC Official Summary of Security Transactions and Holdings*. These can be purchased from the SEC or read in regional SEC offices.

Under SEC regulations, a company planning to seek control of another company must make its offer known within 5 days of filing the 13D. The company naturally does not want to tell the world of its intentions, so many times they

MAJOR INSIDER TRANSACTIONS

COMPANY	INSIDER, TITLE	DATE	SHARES TRADED	SHARES HELD‡	PRICE RANGE
Purchases					
Baker Hughes	J. F. Maher, Dir.	3/27/89	10,000	20,000	$16.88
Castle & Cooke	D. H. Murdock, Dir.†	3/22/89–3/23/89	40,900	13,203,982	$25.50–$26.00
GWC Corp.	A. Rosenberg, Chair.	3/7/89	7,000	10,000	$17.13
Kroger Co.	W. Sinkula, V.P.	3/1/89	17,003	78,202	$9.52
Masco Corp.	S. I. Valenti, Officer	3/21/89–3/27/89	16,500	80,000	$24.75–$25.13
Microsoft Corp.	S. A. Ballmer, V.P.	3/20/89–3/31/89	945,000	4,145,002	$46.00–$50.25
Omnicom Group	B. E. Crawford, Dir.	3/1/89–3/2/89	20,000	NA	$20.38–$20.75
Petrie Stores	M. J. Petrie, Chair†	3/1/89–3/2/89	147,000	28,303,874	$17.68–$18.30
SafeCard Services	S. J. Halmos, Dir.	3/1/89	50,000	1,457,260	$5.38
WMS Industries	S. Redstone†	3/3/89–3/31/89	47,000	2,175,100*	$6.75–$7.63
Sales					
Bemis Co.	H. J. Curler, Chair.	3/13/89–3/22/89	103,394	366,658	$26.25–$27.00
Charming Shoppes	S. Sidewater, Dir.	3/9/89	100,000	1,595,928*	$16.63
Citicorp	W. J. Heron, Officer	3/21/89–3/30/89	37,769	20,900	$28.13–$29.38
Dover Corp.	R. Ohrstrom, Dir.	3/6/89–3/30/89	86,000	854,974	$27.63–$29.25
Heinz (H.J.)	K. Vonderheyden, V.P.	3/20/89	31,800	NA	$48.00–$48.75
Lands' End	P. C. Kramer, V.P.	3/28/89	30,000	160,000	$33.28
MCA Inc.	I. Azoff, V.P.	3/2/89–3/6/89	32,500	372,553	$50.38–$52.25
MCI Communications	W. McGowan, Chair	3/7/89–3/16/89	95,000	4,186,334	$25.25–$27.63
Multimedia, Inc.	W. Bartlett, Pres.	3/9/89	30,000	57,220	$94.00
National Data Corp.	J. B. Elliot, Dir.	3/13/89–3/30/89	152,510	188,000	$25.38–$27.63
Philip Morris	G. Weissman	3/10/89	10,000	NA	$113.88
Tiffany & Co.	W. R. Chaney, Pres.	3/31/89	29,000	150,500	$42.00
Toro Co.	K. Melrose, Chair.	3/15/89–3/22/89	66,102	59,883	$20.00–$20.50
Waste Management	P. H. Huizenga, Dir.	3/3/89–3/31/89	66,900	566,129	$44.00–$45.00
Wellman Inc.	T. M. Duff, Pres.	3/7/89	30,000	397,000	$45.00

* Includes indirect ownership of common stock.
† Beneficial owner of more than 10% of common stock.
‡ Beneficial ownership at end of month in which transaction occurred.

SOURCE: *Value Line*, April 28, 1989.

ACQUISITION-SPEAK

A bewildering assortment of elaborate techniques and strategies has been developed by target companies to fend off corporate raiders. In the process, a brand new lexicon has blossomed.

- **Arbitrage**   Buying shares in a company that may be taken over and selling short the shares of the acquiring company.
- **Bear hug**   An offer that's so good the directors of the takeover target company can't refuse.
- **Crown jewel**   A takeover target company's most prized subsidiary, which it may sell to discourage the raider.
- **Front loading**   Quickly acquiring control of a company by making a high cash offer to insiders and then paying off other shareholders with securities or a combination of securities and cash that is worth less.
- **Gray knight**   A company that enters uninvited into the scene of a hostile merger and offers to buy the target company. It's regarded as gray until its terms are revealed.
- **Pac-man**   A maneuver in which the takeover target firm ''bites back'' at the raider by turning the tables and trying to take it over. A counterbid for control.
- **Poison pill**   Giving holders the right to buy additional shares or shares of a new issue at an enormous premium, often 50%. This boosts the cost to an acquiring company and is meant to discourage it.
- **Porcupine provisions**   Corporate bylaws designed to put obstacles in the way of an acquiring company; also known as shark repellent.
- **Risk arbitrage**   The purchase of shares of a takeover candidate at the market price in the hope that the merger or takeover will go through at a higher price.
- **Saturday night special**   A maneuver in which raiders elect their own candidates to a board of directors to help take control of the company.
- **Scorched-earth policy**   Means by which a company tries to turn itself into an ugly duckling and therefore appear unattractive to any buyer. *Example:* arranging for all debts to come due right after a merger.
- **Shark repellents**   Defensive methods used by companies to fend off takeovers; see also porcupine provisions.
- **Staggered boards**   A shark repellent in which companies adopt bylaws that permit only half the board of directors to come up for election each year. This prevents a Saturday night special.
- **Supermajority**   A very large majority of stockholders whose approval is required for a takeover. The corporation determines what constitutes a supermajority—it can be as much as 90% to 99%.
- **Tender**   A bid to buy shares of a corporation.
- **Two-tier bid**   A maneuver in which a combination of cash now and securities later is offered to pressure shareholders into surrendering their stock early on in the game and before another corporation makes a counteroffer. The SEC ruling gives stockholders a minimum of 20 business days to respond to this type of offer.
- **White knight**   A company that will block an unfriendly merger, often at the suggestion of the target company, by taking it over on more favorable terms.

will file the 13D but indicate that they're doing so for investment purposes only. Later on they change direction and make the tender offer.

➤ INSIDER TRADING   When corporate insiders trade in a stock, it must be reported to the SEC. Every week the commission compiles a list of stock purchases, sales, and exercises of options by corporate insiders. This is public information and also appears in the *SEC Official Summary of Security Transactions and Holdings.*

Insider movement may indicate that something is afoot, especially if the trading increases or decreases sharply. Insider buys are obviously a better indication of takeover possibilities than insider sales. Corporate insiders are much closer to their firm's activities than the brightest security analyst and you. Although they may not legally buy shares based on material nonpublic information that might have an impact on the stock's price, they can purchase stock because they believe in a new product, feel that the company is currently undervalued, or have faith in its future. Such legitimate trading is a matter of public record and may be useful to investors seeking news about a company. The data are recorded on a regular basis in *Value Line*, as shown on page 223, and in the *Wall Street Journal.* However, insider transactions are not necessarily a sign of takeover activity or impending troubles.

Standard & Poor's studied the insider trading activity of 294 OTC stocks over an 18-month period. They selected stocks in which three purchases and no sales were made by a minimum of two different insiders. Of the 294 companies, 6 were taken over before the end of 9 months, and in just 3 months' time, 56% of the remaining 288 stocks went up in price, 42% fell, and 2% remained unchanged.

Although this was a narrow study, it does indicate that following insider trading is one way to pick stocks that should outperform the market. However, it must be done in conjunction with other analysis of the company and not viewed merely as a surefire way to make money in the market.

➤ OPTION TRADING If rumor of a takeover is floating around Wall Street and option trading in the stock has increased, it *may* mean the story has substance.

➤ TRADING An unusual amount of stock-trading activity may signal takeover activity.

$ IF YOU DARE: Play the options as one way to guard against losing if a takeover deal falls apart.

$ IF YOU DON'T: Sell in the marketplace as soon as the stock hits your target goal.

FOR FURTHER INFORMATION

The 1989 Merger & Acquisition Sourcebook
Quality Services Company
5290 Overpass Road
Santa Barbara, CA 93111
1-805-964-7841
$249

A 675-page looseleaf directory that lists financial data on the buyers and sellers involved in the year's mergers as well as facts on the deals that fell through.

United and Babson's Report
210 Newbury Street
Boston, MA 02116
1-617-267-8855
$119 for 6 months, $215 per year

The section "Action Items—Our Advice" discusses tender offers now in progress and what to do about them. Newsletter is a weekly, but this column may or may not appear weekly.

Acquisition/Divestiture Weekly Report
Quality Services Company
5290 Overpass Road
Santa Barbara, CA 93111
1-805-964-7841
$495

A weekly newsletter that provides data on companies involved in mergers plus a list of companies looking to buy and looking to sell.

Special Situation Report
P.O. Box 167
Rochester, NY 14601
1-716-232-1240
$230

Issued every 3 weeks.

Business & Acquisition Newsletter
2600 South Gessner Road
Houston, TX 77063
1-713-783-0100
$300

A monthly newsletter reporting on companies
up for sale.

Mergers & Acquisitions
229 South 18th Street
Philadelphia, PA 19103
1-215-875-2638
$219

A bimonthly magazine devoted to professional
analysis of mergers.

The Outlook
Standard & Poor's Corp.
25 Broadway
New York, NY 10004
1-212-208-8000
$255 per year (48 issues)

"The Limelight" section gives current advice on
stocks in takeover situations.

Value Line OTC Special Situations
  Service
711 Third Avenue
New York, NY 10017
1-212-687-3965
$395

Bimonthly newsletter with facts on OTC mergers.

Consensus of Insiders
P.O. Box 24349
Fort Lauderdale, FL 33307
1-305-776-3994
$59

A hotline that reports on insider trading in
corporate stock options.

The Insiders
3471 North Federal Highway
Fort Lauderdale, FL 33306
1-305-563-9000
1-800-327-6720
$49

Semimonthly newsletter that ranks companies
and industries by insider trading activity.

Street Smart Investing
13-D Research
Southeast Executive Park
100 Executive Drive
Brewster, NY 10509
1-914-278-6500
$350

Biweekly newsletter that tracks the 13D filings
with the SEC made by any shareholder who
acquires 5% or more of a company's stock.

25

SPLITS, SPIN-OFFS, SMALL CAPS, AND STOCK BUY-BACKS

This is a catchall chapter for opportunities during 1990 that are at once both investments and speculations. The definition depends on the type of security, the quality of the corporation, and the trading techniques used.

- **Splits.** Companies that split their stocks can be excellent investments when these splits are justified by profitable growth. The techniques used in buying and selling, however, can be speculative: that is, when it appears that a company may split its stock, the price of its shares will usually rise rapidly and, after the split, fall sharply. The long-term investor who bought the shares when undervalued will probably benefit automatically. The speculative investor, however, buys as the prospects of a split catch Wall Street's fancy and sells at a quick profit right after the announcement.
- **Spin-offs.** When a company divests itself of a subsidiary, the investor in the parent company automatically owns stock in the new company as well. This provides possible price appreciation.
- **Small caps.** Companies with a small number of shares can be investments when you know, and have confidence in, the owners, but they are speculations when there are problems because of limited capital, poor management, or threats of acquisition.
- **Stock buy-backs.** Companies often buy back their own shares to maintain control. This procedure often boosts the stock's price.
- **Bankrupt companies.** Bankrupt stocks offer speculative investors an opportunity to make money if the company pulls itself together or restructures successfully.
- **Stubs.** Stubs are mini-stocks left over

after the company paid a special high dividend. They often rise quickly in price.

COMPANIES THAT SPLIT THEIR STOCKS FREQUENTLY

One of the most rewarding and exciting investments can be a corporation that increases the number of its shares of common stock: issuing 1, 2, 3, or more shares for each outstanding share. Such splits usually occur when:

- The price of such a stock moves to a historic high so that individual investors are unwilling or unable to buy shares. Psychologically, a stock trading at 50 will attract far more than double the number of investors who are willing to pay 100.
- A small, growing company, whose shares are traded OTC, wants to list its stock on an exchange where the rules for listing are far tougher. The NYSE, for example, requires a minimum of 1.1 million common shares and at least 2,000 shareholders with 100 shares or more. Such a listing broadens investment acceptance as many institutions prefer the liquidity of an established market, and more individuals can use the shares as collateral for margin loans.
- A corporation seeks to make an acquisition with minimal cash or debt.
- The price of the stock is about $75 per share. The most attractive range for most investors is $20 to $45 a share, so few splits are declared when the stock price is that low.
- Management becomes fearful of an unfriendly takeover. When the top officials hold only a small percentage of the outstanding shares, a stock split will make more shares available at a lower price and

thus, it is hoped, lessen the likelihood of a raid.

- Earnings are likely to continue to grow, which means that the price of the shares will keep rising. With more stock, the per-share profits will appear smaller—for a while.
- The company has a record of stock splits. This indicates that the directors recognize, and are familiar with, the advantages of adding shares to keep old stockholders and attract new ones.

SPIN-OFFS

These take place when the parent company divests itself of a division, which may be unrelated to the rest of the business or may not fit into the parent company's future plans. The new division becomes an independent company. The parent company then issues shares in this new corporation to shareholders of the parent company in proportion to their original investment. Now they hold shares in two companies instead of one.

The theory behind a spin-off is that the division will be better off operating independently and that the parent company will be better off without this particular division. A prime example: General Mills' spin-off of its fashion and toy divisions. Similarly, after Allied Corp. and Signal Corp. merged, the parent company selected a number of businesses in which it was less interested and spun these off as an entity called Henley Group. Thus shareholder value was maintained and the parent company's objectives were met.

If you have a good sense of timing, you may be able to cash in on spin-offs. Most follow a fairly similar pattern:

- After the new spin-off stock is issued, it falls in price.
- It then tends to move back up within several months.

The case of Singer Co. illustrates how nimble investors can sometimes capture profits in a rising spin-off. In 1986, in order to concentrate on electronics and military operations, Singer spun off its sewing machine division to shareholders. Shares in S.S.M.C. Corp., the new unit, quickly fell from about $16–$17 to $11–$12. However, a year later, due to improved earnings,

S.S.M.C. reached a high of $26.50. As of July 1988, the stock was trading at $24.50.

Not every spin-off is a winner. Often the motivation for spinning off a unit is that management wants to unload a low-margin or poor-performing business.

$ IF YOU DARE: Buy spin-off shares after they decline, if you have faith in the company, and hold for the long term or until they have rebounded close to their initial price.

SMALL CAP OR SECOND-TIER STOCKS

Small cap companies typically have a capitalization of $150 million or less. With blue chips up in price, small caps, like OTC issues, offer an excellent defensive position against a market correction, as well as an alternative to paying high premiums for quality stocks.

Second-tier stocks are also being pushed to the foreground because of the diminishing supply of moderately priced blue chips due to takeovers and leveraged buyouts, which remove common shares from the trading arena.

Small caps are not without their problems, however. So spend the time to research your selections carefully. Small caps are not heavily followed by Wall Street pros, which means little readily available research, but that also means they're often undiscovered and still low in price.

When corporations have a limited number of shares, their stock prices can move sharply: up when there's heavy buying, down when there's concerted selling. Theoretically, when a company has fewer than 500,000 shares, it should be an excellent speculation. Typically, the price-earnings ratios are low and the dividends sometimes relatively high. These firms are often targets for merger or acquisition and thus profitable speculations.

However, it pays to buy shares of small corporations only when you know, and are impressed by, the officers and directors and their ability to manage the business. The hopes of hefty profits are small, and the risks of losses, or at best small gains, are substantial.

If you prefer to have a professional select small cap stocks, then investigate one of the mutual funds that specialize in these companies. (see box below).

STUBS

This relatively new vehicle can be potentially profitable, provided you are in the right place at the right time.

Stubs, as their name implies, are small stocks, the result of a takeover attempt. Stubs are the company's leftover stock after it has issued a special, one-time, high dividend to shareholders in order to defend itself from an unwanted takeover.

A classic example is Holiday Corp. When the nationwide hotel chain was threatened with a takeover, management decided to take preventive measures. It issued a special $65 dividend to existing shareholders. The result: the stock soared in price.

Following the dividend payout, the regular shares of Holiday Corp. were still in existence, but now as stubs, and sold at about $17 per share. Approximately a year later, the stubs had recovered somewhat and had been as high as $38. In May 1989 the stubs were trading at $31.

How do stubs fend off corporate raiders? They reduce the stock's appeal because they are full of debt, which an acquirer does not want to assume. Take the case of Holiday Corp. It borrowed $1.5 billion to pay its special dividend to shareholders. Then to reduce its new debt, the corporation had to sell assets—in this case, a large number of its hotels and motels.

SMALL-COMPANY GROWTH MUTUAL FUNDS	
	TOTAL RETURN (1/1/89 TO 5/1/89)
Shearson Lehman Small Capital (1-617-573-1455)	6.46%
Colonial Small Stock Index (1-800-248-2828)	10.25
Ariel Growth (1-800-368-2748)	7.23
Naess & Thomas Special Fund (1-800-662-7447)	5.87
Quasar Associates (1-800-221-5672)	13.74

TIPS FOR BUYING STUBS

You can participate in stubs:
- Automatically, if you own stock in a company that is restructuring and if that company issues a cash dividend for your existing shares
- By purchasing existing stubs of corporations you feel offer substantial growth potential

Existing stubs: Harcourt Brace Jovanovich, Holiday Corp., Owens-Corning.

COMPANIES WITH LOW PRICE-EARNINGS RATIOS

Buy a stock when nobody else wants it and wait for the "inevitable" turnaround or return to fashion. That's the stock selection strategy of many fundamental investors. The degree of speculation depends on the quality and prospects of the company.

With stocks selling at low multiples, it's important to do your research. That low price may be a sign of real trouble that can continue longer than anticipated. When you start with stocks at low price-earnings ratios, take the next step and check the estimates of future profits (available from your broker or Standard & Poor's). If there are not strong prospects of a corporate comeback, the stock price will probably continue to decline.

The table on the next page shows typical speculations that could turn into investments. All the companies are well rated and have the potential of becoming quality corporations.

STOCKS SELLING BELOW BOOK VALUE

As explained on page 136, book value is the net worth per share of common stock: all assets minus all liabilities. When the stock price is below book value, it is at a bargain level in that (1) the corporation may be worth more dead than alive: if it were liquidated, shareholders would get more from the sale of assets than the current value of the stock; (2) the company may

STOCK DIVIDENDS

Stock dividends are extra shares issued to current shareholders, usually on a percentage basis: that is, a 5% stock dividend means that 5 new shares are issued for every 100 old shares. Such a policy can be habit-forming, and most companies continue the extra distributions year after year because it conserves cash, keeps shareholders happy, and provides an easy, inexpensive way to expand the number of publicly owned shares and, usually, stockholders.

It's pleasant to receive such a bonus, but be sure that the payout is justified. The actual dollar profits of the corporation should keep rising. If they stay about the same or decline, stock dividends may be more for show than growth. To evaluate a stock dividend in terms of a company's earning power and the stock's current price:

1 Find the future earnings yield on the current stock price. Use anticipated earnings per share for the current year. If the projected profits are $3 per share and the current price of the stock is 50, the earnings yield is 6%: $3 ÷ 50 = 0.06.

2 Add the stock dividend percentage declared for the current year to the annual cash dividend yield. If the stock dividend is 5% and the cash dividend is 2%, the figure is 7%—the total dividend yield.

If the second figure (7%) exceeds the first (6%), a shareholder faces earnings dilution and probable price weakness *unless* the corporate prospects are strong.

But if the profits are $5 per share, the earnings yield is 10%. Since this is more than the total dividend yield (7%), the stock dividend is not excessive.

be a candidate for a takeover: when Gulf Oil was acquired by Chevron, Gulf stock was selling at about 60% of its book value; (3) this may be a low base if corporate profits improve.

The usefulness of book value as a criterion

SELECTED STOCKS SELLING WELL BELOW BOOK VALUE

COMPANY	PRICE (MAY 1989)	% BOOK VALUE
Grubb & Ellis (GRIT)	6⅝	75
Advest Group (ADV)	6⅞	74
Travelers Corp. (TIC)	39	74
Mead Corp. (MEA)	38	75
McDonnell Douglas (MD)	83½	74
Chrysler (C)	23	75
Bank America Corp. (BAC)	25⅜	70
Munsingwear (MUN)	4	71
Coors (Adolph) "B" (ACCOB)	18	70
Farah Inc. (FRA)	11⅛	70
U.S. Home (UH)	1⅞	69
Long Island Lighting (LIL)	15½	65

SOURCE: Silberberg, Rosenthal & Co., May 1989.

depends on the type of corporation. Steel firms and manufacturers of heavy machinery have huge investments in plants and equipment, so they usually have a high book value. But they rarely make much money.

By contrast, a drug manufacturer or retailer will have a low book value but will often have excellent earnings. The trick in using book value effectively is to find a company whose stock is trading below that figure and is making a comeback that has not yet been recognized in the marketplace.

In such a situation, you will get a double plus: buying assets at a discount, and a higher stock price due to better profits. Just make sure that the assets are real and that the earnings are the result of management's skill, not accounting legerdemain.

BANKRUPT COMPANIES

These companies have gone through the wringer and so start off on a solid base. If new management is competent, the value of the stock will rise. It takes time for the improved performance to be recognized.

■ *Look for corporations that have resources and a strong position in their field.* The broader the customer base, the greater the chance of success.

- *Diversify with at least three holdings.* If you're lucky, one will prove to be a winner, the second will stay about even, and the loss on the third will be small. Hopefully, that right choice will pay off well enough to make all the risks worthwhile.
- *Buy soon after emergence from Chapter 11.* At that point, there's the greatest uncertainty and maximum risk but also a low base for future gains.

According to the National Institute of Business Management, investors can identify a company preparing for a strong comeback by looking for these traits:

- A large tax loss carryforward that can be written off against future earnings, thus sharply boosting after-tax profits
- Substantial salable assets relative to debt, indicating that the securities will appreciate even if the company is partially or completely liquidated
- A new management team, especially one with turnaround experience
- Selling off of unprofitable divisions or buying of profitable new ones
- Restructuring of debt to improve cash flow
- Reduced leverage

$ IF YOU DARE: Since many institutions shy away from stocks of troubled companies, individual investors willing to assume the high degree of risk involved can sometimes make large profits in turnaround situations. To be on the safe side of an unsafe situation, wait until the company has announced a reorganization plan, or buy secured debt of the company.

STOCK BUY-BACKS

A corporate action that has become more prevalent than in the past is the stock buy-back. Like spin-offs and stubs, the buy-back bears study because it reflects the shifting action on the part of companies to protect themselves. Many companies, in an effort to raise their earnings per share and the price of their stock, have been buying back their common shares, either by making public tender offers or by simply going into the open market.

The motives are often clear. Managements, fearing a hostile takeover, try to give their stockholders nearly the same benefits as a takeover by raising their own stock's price.

Here again, as in the case of takeovers, cash flow and high asset values provide the money for corporate buy-backs of stock. When cash flow per share is high, cash is obviously available for common stock buybacks.

Large understated assets may enable a corporation to raise cash from sales of those same assets and use the cash to buy back its own stock, thus closing some of the gap between market price and breakup value. (See the table for a list of companies with repurchase programs.)

Companies with high NAV and strong cash flows tend to benefit stockholders because they have the capability to buy back their own shares. The three main reasons behind a stock buy-back are (1) to fend off hostile takeovers, (2) to boost shareholder values, and (3) to increase earnings per share. Therefore, investors are well advised to search for companies already embarked on buy-back programs.

PART SIX

SMART RETIREMENT PLANNING

Retirement—it should be a time when the frenetic pace of the working years gives way to a much-deserved period of self-indulgence, fun, and new beginnings. But in order for that dream to come true, serious planning is required. And the earlier you begin, the more financially secure your "golden" years will be.

In this section we will look at the most important areas of financial planning as they relate to retirement:

- Social Security
- IRAs, Keoghs, SEPs, and 401(k) plans
- Your pension plan
- Insurance as an investment
- Housing alternatives
- GICs

26

SOCIAL SECURITY, IRAs, KEOGHs, 401(k) PLANS, SEPs, AND GICs

The time to start planning for a financially secure retirement is the day you receive your first paycheck, although few of us ever do. But don't agonize over the fact; just avoid further delays and start now. This chapter is not intended to be a complete retirement guide, but the information here will help you lay the financial groundwork that makes the difference between merely getting along and continuing life at full tilt.

SOCIAL SECURITY

In order to plan your retirement investments intelligently, start by taking a close look at your Social Security situation. Then build around this basic data. It may seem like a nuisance, but ignoring Social Security records could lead to lower benefits than you're legitimately entitled to, since benefits are based on the Social Security Administration's records of what you have earned. It's up to you, and not the Social Security Administration, to find out if your records are accurate. Serious errors could cost you thousands of dollars in benefits.

➤ STEP 1. REQUEST A WRITTEN STATEMENT OF EARNINGS Call, visit, or write your local Social Security office to get a copy of Form SSA 7004, Request for Social Security Statement of Earnings. Send it in and at the same time request an estimate of the monthly payment you will be entitled to at age 65. Do this every 3 years, beginning when you're age 40. You'll receive a computerized statement in 4 to 6 weeks showing all earnings credited to your account. The 7004 request will give you a year-by-year listing of your earnings from 1983 on, with a lump sum total for your working years. For a longer and more detailed report, use Form SSA 7050.

If you suspect errors on your statement, contact your Social Security office. Provide as much data as possible, including dates of employment, wages received, employer's name and address, copies of W-2 forms, and paycheck stubs.

➤ STEP 2. CALCULATE YOUR BENEFITS If you're near retirement, the Social Security estimate of your monthly benefits will be fairly accurate. If you're younger, make your own rough estimate.

➤ STEP 3. DETERMINE WHAT PERCENTAGE OF YOUR FINAL SALARY YOU'LL NEED TO LIVE ON Financial advisers suggest between 50% and 80%; obviously, Social Security alone will not be adequate. Gerald Richmond, associate pension actuary at New England Mutual Life Insurance Co., says that for the average wage earner, the 41% of earnings replaced by Social Security benefits should be supplemented by 20% to 25% from a pension plan and at least 10% from personal savings.

➤ POINTS TO REMEMBER ABOUT SOCIAL SECURITY

- Working spouses who pay Social Security taxes earn their own benefits.
- Nonworking spouses qualify for a retirement benefit that is equal to half what their retired spouses receive.
- You can supplement your retirement income by working, but any amount earned over $8,880 will reduce benefits for retirees aged 65 to 70; earnings above $6,480 reduce benefits for those under age 65. If you are 70, there is no limit. If your earnings go over these limits, Social Security withholds $1 in benefits for every $2 of earnings above the limits. As of 1990, $1 in benefits will be withheld for each $3 in earnings for people age 65 to 70.
- Social Security payments rise 3% for each year you delay collecting them. This credit escalates until it reaches 8% in 2008.

FOR ADDITIONAL HELP

Several hundred lawyers specialize in resolving Social Security problems, such as denial of disability benefits and errors in retirement benefits. They are members of the National Organization of Social Security Claimants' Representatives, which operates a nationwide referral service. Check your phone book for a member in your area. In New York State, call collect: 1-914-735-8812.

- Benefits may be taxed if your modified adjusted gross income exceeds the base amount: $32,000 for filers of joint returns, $0 for marrieds filing separately who lived with their spouse at any time during the year, and $25,000 for all other filers. The formula for determining how much is taxed is: the lesser of (1) one-half the net Social Security benefits or (2) one-half the amount by which modified adjusted gross income plus half the Social Security benefits exceeds the base amount.

Example: A married couple receives $10,000 in Social Security benefits, $30,000 in pensions, and $5,000 in tax-free municipal bond interest. Their modified adjusted gross income is $35,000 ($30,000 + $5,000). To that figure, add half their Social Security benefits, or $5,000, for a total of $40,000. Then subtract the base figure of $32,000 from $40,000 for $8,000. Half of $8,000 is $4,000 which is $1,000 less than half their Social Security benefits. Therefore, they must pay taxes on the $4,000.

- There is a new *Medicare surcharge* of 15%, rising to 28% by 1993, up to certain amounts. It is a levy on one's tax liability (see page 250).

Now that you know what you're likely to receive from Social Security, you're undoubtedly impressed with the fact that you will need a great deal more to continue a comfortable lifestyle after age 65!

HOW AN IRA CAN PAY OFF

The second column shows the results achieved by Investor A, who invests his $2,000 on January 1 every year. The third column shows the results realized by Investor B, who waits until the last minute, April 15, to make his contribution. The last column shows Investor C's position. He invests at the beginning of the year, but outside an IRA, and he invests only $1,000. There's no question about the winner—Investor A, who proves that the early bird gets the worm.

VALUE OF $2,000 ANNUAL INVESTMENT ASSUMING 10% ANNUAL YIELD

INVESTMENT PERIOD	IRA INVESTOR A MAKES ANNUAL INVESTMENT ON JAN. 1	IRA INVESTOR B MAKES ANNUAL INVESTMENT ON APRIL 15 OF FOLLOWING YEAR	NON-IRA INVESTOR C IN 50% TAX BRACKET MAKES ANNUAL $1,000 INVESTMENT ON JAN. 1
10 years	$35,062	$29,195	$13,207
20 years	126,005	109,989	34,719
30 years	361,886	319,548	69,761

SOURCE: Merrill Lynch.

INDIVIDUAL RETIREMENT ACCOUNTS (IRAs)

If you've been stashing away $2,000 a year since 1981, when IRAs were made available to all workers even if they had a pension plan, you have a sizable amount of money on hand. Your philosophy should be shifting too—away from thinking of your IRA as savings to be ignored or placed in a CD toward realizing that it's an investment requiring diversification and thoughtful management.

Where you should invest it depends on several factors: the current economic environment, your age, other sources of income, and your appetite for risk. The closer you are to retirement, of course, the less risk you should take. You must also decide if you are temperamentally suited to manage your account or if you need a professional. In general, high-yield conservative investments should form the basic core of most IRAs, but there are exceptions and variations. At a certain point, part of your IRA should go into other vehicles such as growth stocks, which protect your nest egg from reduced returns when interest rates are low and yet take advantage of a rising stock market.

Only a few investments are excluded by law from IRAs: collectibles (such as gems, stamps, art, antiques, and Oriental rugs), commodities, and leveraged investments (those made with borrowed cash). The 1986 Tax Reform Act permits inclusion of U.S. legal tender gold and silver coins acquired after December 31, 1986, but they must be held by a custodian, not the IRA owner. You may borrow money to put in your IRA, but margined stocks, commodity futures, and mortgaged real estate are out. Among the tax-advantaged investments that make no sense in an IRA are municipal bonds, tax shelters, and deferred annuities. (See "Investment Choices for Pension Plans," page 241.)

Originally, the $2,000 annual deduction was available to all who earned at least that much in salary form. That's no longer true:

- If your adjusted gross income (before IRA contribution) is over $50,000 ($35,000 for singles) *and* you or your spouse is an active participant in an employer's pension plan, you are no longer entitled to any IRA tax deduction, but you can make nondeductible contributions.

- If your gross adjusted income (before IRA contribution) is between $40,000 and $50,000 ($25,000 to $35,000 for singles) *and* you or your spouse is an active participant in an employer's pension plan, your IRA deduction is reduced.

- If you or your spouse is not an active participant in such a plan, you can still deduct the full $2,000 IRA contribution.

- Full $2,000 deduction is available to workers who are active participants in employer-maintained retirement plans only if their adjusted gross income is below $25,000 for singles and $40,000 for those filing jointly.

SHOULD YOU HAVE AN IRA?

If you no longer qualify for the $2,000 tax deduction, you may decide it's not worth contributing to your IRA anymore. This is a mistake for most investors. If you can afford to buy this book, then in all likelihood putting aside the $2,000 is not a hardship. Over the long run, your money will accumulate on a tax-deferred basis, more than offsetting the fact that it's not an immediate tax deduction. And, of course, it is a forced way of saving. In general, the higher the rate you earn on your IRA and the higher your tax bracket, the more valuable this shelter is. And there's no guarantee that Congress won't raise the tax brackets before you retire.

$ HINT: Contributions that do not qualify as a tax deduction should be paid into a separate IRA to avoid confusion.

Make your IRA contribution as early as possible in the new year—this will boost the value of your account in the long run. Most people delay until April 14 to fund their IRA because they either feel that they can't spare the $2,000 or they can't decide where to invest the money.

$ HINT: Use an automatic plan with a mutual fund or your stockbroker. Plan to deposit $167 each month, even if it's into a money market fund. You will have accumulated $2,000 within a year, painlessly.

The following retirement programs disqualify you from making a fully deductible IRA contribution: Keogh, SEP, money purchase pension plan, profit-sharing plan, defined benefit

---

STOCKS FOR YOUR IRA

Despite tax law changes, an IRA continues to hold plenty of appeal for building retirement funds. These stocks combine good capital gains potential with attractive yields, dividend growth prospects, and above-average safety.

STOCK	REASON
American Home Products	Top dividend record
Amoco	Strong total return potential
Bell South	Growing service region
Bristol-Myers	Attractive drug issue
Citizens Utilities ±B'	Provides utility growth
Consolidated Natural Gas	Energy play
Indiana Energy	Split enhances affordability
Kimberly-Clark	Record results expected
Morgan (J.P.) & Co.	Leader in banking field
Southwestern Bell	Appeal of cellular business
WPL Holdings	Expanding via acquisition

SOURCE: Dow Theory Forecasts, 7412 Calumet Avenue, Hammond, IN 46324; 1-219-931-6480; $198/year.

---

plan, 401(k), employee stock option plan, government employee retirement plan, 403(b) (teachers' annuity), 457s (municipal employee retirement plan), and Taft-Hartley plan (union employee retirement plan).

$HINT: If you can only make nondeductible IRA contributions, you may want to consider a deferred annuity contract. These, too, allow you to accumulate interest and dividend earnings tax-free. Two added pluses: there is no limitation on the amount you can invest, and the early withdrawal penalty is usually less than the 10% for an IRA.

SELF-DIRECTED IRAs

When your IRA contains $5,000 to $10,000, you're ready to benefit from diversification. Consider doing so through a self-directed account, which can be set up at a brokerage firm for $25 to $30 plus a yearly fee. Designed for those who want to guide their own accounts, it allows you to invest in stocks, bonds, limited partnerships, options, Treasuries, zeros, or mortgage-backed securities. If you want advice on managing the portfolio, use a full-service broker; otherwise, save on commissions with a discount broker. A self-directed account takes time and vigilance on your part, yet it offers the greatest degree of flexibility along with the greatest potential for appreciation. It also involves the most risk.

☐CAUTION: Avoid investments that are attractive largely for tax advantages, such as tax-exempt municipal bonds. Since IRAs are already sheltered from taxes, the exemption is wasted. In addition, all income, including tax-free yields, will be taxed when withdrawn.

$HINT: The Cleveland Electric Illuminating Co. was the first company to establish an IRA for those who buy the stock through its dividend reinvestment plan. There are no brokerage commissions, and dividends can be automatically reinvested. Check with the electric utility company in your area.

YOUR IRA AND YOUR HEIRS

If you're blessed with sufficient income from other sources, you may want to leave IRA funds to your heirs. Although the IRS views IRAs primarily as a retirement benefit, not a death benefit, the new mortality tables

IRA BASICS

- Annual contribution: $2,000 of earned income if under age 70½.
- You can wait until April 15 to make your contribution for the previous year.
- If you and your spouse both work, you may each have an IRA.
- You can contribute a total of $2,250 to a spousal account; this amount can be split between accounts as long as neither gets over $2,000.
- IRA money must be invested with an IRS-approved custodian, such as a bank, savings and loan, stockbroker, mutual fund, or insurance company.
- You can open as many IRA accounts as you like using a different custodian or investment each year and thus spreading out your risk.
- There is a 10% penalty for withdrawing money before you are 59½.
- Money withdrawn from IRAs funded by deductible contributions is taxed as ordinary income. (Only the earnings from IRAs funded by nondeductible contributions are taxed as ordinary income upon withdrawal). If you withdraw before age 59½, you pay both the tax *and* the 10% penalty.
- You must withdraw money starting at age 70½ or be penalized.

CALCULATING MINIMUM IRA WITHDRAWALS

AGE AT WITHDRAWAL		DIVIDE ACCOUNT
MEN	WOMEN	BALANCE BY:
65	70	15.0
70	75	12.1
75	80	9.6
80	85	7.5
85	90	5.7
90	95	4.2
95	100	3.1

Note: Other figures are used for joint life expectancy.

SOURCE: Internal Revenue Service..

help those who want to leave money behind by making it possible for them to withdraw less money from their IRAs. You must start withdrawing money by April 1 of the year after you turn 70½; otherwise, you face a stiff 50% excise tax on excess accumulations. Study the table above and check with your accountant or financial planner to determine your withdrawals.

$ HINT: If you contribute $2,000 annually to an IRA, assuming a 25-year growth period, accumulations at 10%, and a 28% tax bracket, your IRA will be worth $113,253 more than a similar taxable investment.

☐ CAUTION: An IRA left to a beneficiary is fully taxable to the heir. If it is left to an heir under age 14, it is taxed at the parents' rate. These funds cannot be rolled over, and thus another tax benefit is eliminated.

IRA ROLLOVER

If you receive a partial or lump sum distribution from a qualified retirement plan or tax-sheltered annuity, you may roll it over into an IRA. The amount you roll over may not include your after-tax contributions to the plan. But you may roll over all or only part (but at least 50%) of the distribution that would otherwise be taxable. Once in the IRA rollover, the savings continue to accumulate tax-free until payouts start— permissible after age 59½, mandatory at 70½. The transfers must be made within 60 days after the distribution. Be extremely careful when rolling over or transferring these funds, especially if the transfer is to yourself. The safest method is from trustee to trustee.

AVOID PENALTIES

If for any reason you have inadvertently put too much money into your IRA, take it out immediately. For each year the excess remains in the account, a 6% excise tax is levied on both it and earnings. Earnings on the excess must be reported as income in the year earned. The excess and earnings on the excess may also be subject to a 10% penalty when withdrawn.

MOVING YOUR IRA, SEP, OR KEOGH

As your account grows or as market conditions change, you may want to invest your dollars elsewhere. The IRS has strict rules to follow.

A TRANSFER

- If you arrange for a direct transfer of funds from one custodian to another, there is no limit on the number of switches you can make.
- Plan on transfers taking at least a month. Banks, brokerage firms, and even some mutual funds are often backlogged with paperwork.
- Get instructions early on, ideally in writing, from both the resigning and accepting sponsor. Pay fees and notarize necessary papers immediately. Keep track of details as well as deadlines; don't depend on the institution to do this for you.

A ROLLOVER

- You may take personal possession of your money once a year for 60 days.
- If you hold the money longer than 60 days, you'll be subject to the 10% penalty.

KEOGH PLANS

Designed for the self-employed and proprietors of small companies, Keoghs work much like IRAs but have several added advantages. You can put away as much as $30,000 a year and, as with an IRA, your Keogh contribution is deductible from income when calculating your taxes. Earnings are not taxed until withdrawn. If you have a Keogh, you may also have an IRA.

To get your annual deduction, however, you must have a Keogh in place by the end of that year, although contributions don't have to be completed until you file your tax return.

If you, as a self-employed person, establish a Keogh for yourself, you must extend its benefits to your employees. Employees must get comparable benefits on a percentage basis; for example, if you put in 15% of earned income for yourself, you must match that 15% for each employee.

There are two basic types of Keoghs: defined-contribution plans and defined-benefit plans.

➤ DEFINED-CONTRIBUTION PLAN The more common and simpler of the two is one in which you decide how much to put in. In other words, the annual contribution is predetermined and what you receive upon retirement is variable, depending on how well you've invested your deposits. Contributions are set forth in the plan's document by formula—usually it's a percentage of earned income up to a maximum of 25% of compensation (compensation is limited to $200,000), not to exceed $30,000 a year. Sometimes this figure is given as 20%, which is also accurate: it's 25% of compensation minus your Keogh contribution, which works out to 20% of net earnings. For example, if you make $100,000, you can contribute $20,000 ($100,000 − $20,000 contribution = $80,000 compensation (compensation is limited to $200,000), 25% of $80,000 = $20,000). This is known as a "money purchase" plan, and the percentage contribution initially established continues in the future. In a "profit-sharing" plan, you can set aside up to 13.0435% of your earned net income, up to $30,000 a year. Under this plan, the percentage contribution can vary. It may make sense to combine these two plans to avoid being locked into paying the same percentage each year. This is called a "paired plan."

➤ DEFINED-BENEFIT PLAN This is the equivalent of a corporate pension plan. Designed to pay a predetermined benefit each year after you retire, it allows you to put aside up to 100% of your self-employment income annually. A pension actuary determines how much you need to deposit each year to provide for your benefits, which can be up to $98,064 for 1989. The 1990 amount will be adjusted for inflation. This type of Keogh makes particularly good sense for the investor who is over 50 since there are fewer years left in which to put aside retirement funds.

SIMPLIFIED EMPLOYEE PENSION PLANS (SEPs)

There is another type of tax-saving retirement plan that has received far less publicity than either the IRA or Keogh, yet it permits employer contributions greater than $2,000 a year. Called a *Simplified Employee Pension Plan* (SEP), it is suitable for small businesses and sole proprietors. Designed to cut red tape, it's considerably easier to set up and administer than a Keogh. Although its initial purpose was to encourage small and new firms to establish retirement programs, self-employeds without Keoghs can use it too. The deadline for setting up a SEP is April 15, just as it is with a regular IRA. (With a Keogh, the date is December 31.)

When an employer—which can be you as a sole proprietor—establishes a SEP, the employee then opens an IRA at a bank, mutual fund, or other approved institution. The employer can put up to 15% of an employee's annual earnings in the SEP, to a maximum of $30,000. The contributions made on your behalf are not included in total wages on your W-2 and no deduction for the amount contributed in your behalf is allowed.

401(k) PLANs

This plan, also called a "salary-reduction" plan, was authorized by Congress in 1980, but due to an IRS delay in issuing rules for it, it got off to a slow start. By now, however, nearly four out of five major firms offer it as a fringe benefit. Employers like it because it reduces the firm's pension costs by encouraging employees to save more themselves. The main attraction is the plan's tax break along with the fact that employers often add dollars to it for their employees.

HOW THEY WORK

1   Your employer sets up the plan with a regulated investment company, a bank trust department, or an insurance company.

2   You set aside part of your salary into a special savings and investment account. You have several options, typically a guaranteed fixed-rate income fund, a portfolio of stocks or bonds, or short-term money market securities. The amount set aside is *not* counted as income when figuring your federal income tax. For example, if you earn $50,000 and put $5,000 into a 401(k), you report only $45,000 compensation. In addition,

earnings that accumulate in the 401(k) plan do so free of tax until withdrawn.

3   Many companies match employee savings, up to 5% or 6%. Most often a firm chips in 50¢ for each $1 the employee saves.

4   The maximum you can contribute for 1989 is $7,627, and there is a 10% penalty for withdrawing funds before age 59½. The maximum contribution for 1990 will be adjusted for inflation.

5   If you change jobs or take out the balance in a lump sum after age 59½, you can take advantage of 5-year averaging, another tax break. (You treat the total payout as though you received it in 5 annual installments.)

6   You can withdraw money without paying a penalty:
    - When you reach 59½
    - If you separate from service and you are age 55 when the distribution occurs
    - If you are disabled
    - If you need money for medical expenses that are greater than 7.5% of your adjusted gross income

7   If you borrow funds from the plan, assuming the plan permits borrowing, interest paid on loans taken out after December 31, 1986, is not taxable.

DIPPING INTO YOUR 401(k)

New regulations, which went into effect January 1, 1989, make it tougher to touch your 401(k) money. Even if you meet the so-called hardship qualifications, you must have no other sources of money reasonably available, and you will still have to pay the 10% early withdrawal penalty unless the money is going for medical expenses that exceed 7.5% of your adjusted gross income.

Hardship reasons for borrowing that will satisfy the IRS:
- Medical expenses for you, your spouse, or dependents
- Down payment on your principal home
- Post-secondary tuition for you, your spouse, or dependents
- Prevention of foreclosure on or eviction from principal residence
- Funeral costs for a member of the family

INVESTMENT CHOICES FOR PENSION PLANS: A SHOPPER'S BAZAAR

There are many places to invest your IRA, Keogh, or 401(k) dollars. This section explains the most popular and successful choices.

➤ CERTIFICATES OF DEPOSIT (CDs) If low risk is your goal, bank or savings and loan certificates of deposit offer that plus convenience, safety (they are insured up to $100,000), and low cost. CD rates are locked in. While interest rates are down, buy short-term CDs with 6-month to 1-year maturities.

§HINT: Most banks allow IRA customers over age 59½ to cash in their CDs early without incurring a penalty.

Check with your bank about its policy.

➤ ZERO COUPON BONDS Ideal for pension plans because there is no need to report the annual appreciation. When they are held in personal portfolios, the individual investor must pay taxes on the assumed interest.

The yields (currently from about 7% to 10%) are locked in, but there are risks that (1) interest rates will soar and thus reduce the value of the bonds, (2) the company may not be able to pay off at maturity, and (3) the true value of the paid-up loan will be reduced by inflation.

§HINT: Buy stripped U.S. government bonds. Their prices are a bit higher, so their yields will be lower, but you're sure of getting your money at maturity (see page 124).

➤ COMMON STOCKS Select only quality corporations that have made lots of money and have logical prospects of continuing to do so in the near future. You can choose income-oriented stocks (primarily utilities and banks) or stocks for total returns (modest dividends and substantial appreciation). Dividend income is not taxed until withdrawn.

§HINT: Convertibles qualify as common stocks and can be excellent long-term holdings for IRAs.

➤ MUTUAL FUNDS Invest according to your goal. Funds offer a wide range of choices, from high-risk stock funds to conservative money market funds. In most cases you can switch funds under the same management for little or no fee. A full explanation of mutual funds is found in Chapter 6.

➤ BONDS Select treasuries and corporate notes and bonds with interest that is taxable, because your pension plan is a tax shelter. Aim for issues that will mature when cash is needed for retirement.

For total returns, buy discount bonds that will ensure good income and steady appreciation. Insist on A-rated issues. Select your maturity date and work backward: for example, if you plan to retire in 1999, have your broker find a 10-year maturity. Remember, bonds preserve capital and lock in yields.

➤ REAL ESTATE Land is only for the more aggressive investor! Consider pooled projects, such as real estate investment trusts (REITs) and limited partnerships (RELPs). These are generally more suitable for personal holdings that can benefit from tax deductions.

Be cautious with all real estate. It is always easier to get in than to get out. A well-structured pension plan should be flexible and liquid enough to provide money quickly to pay for benefits due participants at severance, death, or retirement. Do not invest fiduciary money in real estate until total assets are $100,000, and then keep the percentage below 20%.

Whatever amount you borrow must be paid back within 5 years, although extensions are usually granted if the loan is helping you purchase your principal residence.

GUARANTEED INVESTMENT CONTRACTS (GICs)

Few people realize that the most popular investment in most 401(k) and company pension funds is a *guaranteed investment contract,* or GIC. GICs are fixed-rate, fixed-term debt instruments sold by insurance companies to corporate pension plans. They offer a stated, fixed rate of return for a specific period. They are the life insurance industry's equivalent of bank CDs.

HOW THEY WORK

GICs run as long as the retirement manager likes, generally 1 to 10 years. The insurance company invests the cash it raises in a number of conservative investments, such as long-term bonds, public utility bonds, real estate and mortgages, and, to some extent, stocks. The rate of return is guaranteed by the issuer, but no specific pool of funds backs a GIC. The assets of the insurance carrier back the principal contract, so any default of an underyling issue or drop in interest rates is absorbed by the insurance company.

Most employees who select where to invest their retirement funds select GICs but know little about them, since the contracts are sold to institutions, not individuals. Make sure you learn about them. (They may also go by other names, such as "guaranteed income" or "fixed income.")

If rates rise, as with any fixed-income vehicle, you are locked into a lower yield. If rates fall, you benefit.

CHECK THE QUALITY

A. M. Best Co. publishes ratings of insurance companies, including those that sell GICs. In addition, Standard & Poor's and Moody's rank the insurance companies. Check at your library and with your broker, accountant, or pension officer at work. Find out if the parent life insurance company or a pension subsidiary issues your GIC. If the subsidiary has any financial problems, will the parent company bail it out? Some states, including New York, have regulations requiring bailout of failed insurers. Call the state insurance commissioner in the state where the insurer is domiciled.

Distribute your retirement funds among several well-rated GIC issuers, heeding the age-old wisdom of never putting all your eggs in one basket.

☐ CAUTION: GICs guarantee only the interest rate; the ability to pay is not guaranteed and depends upon the creditworthiness of the insurance company.

YOUR PENSION PLAN

One of the first scheduled stops on your road map for an enjoyable retirement should be your company pension plan. The crash of '87 proved to all of us that the value of even the best-run pension plan can decrease, just as a personal portfolio can. So even if you have little or no control over where your plan is invested, you need the facts. Ask. Find out what you can expect to receive. The answer will help you determine what additional savings you will need to live comfortably in your later years.

Here are 12 questions you should gather the answers to during the course of 1990.

- Am I eligible to receive retirement benefits? If not now, when will I be?
- What type of retirement plan do I have, defined benefit or defined contribution? (A defined-contribution plan gives you some flexibility regarding where the money is invested, but it doesn't guarantee you any set amount when you retire. A defined-benefit plan is less flexible, but it guarantees you a certain amount when you retire.)
- What choices do I have about where my pension is invested? How many times a year can I move my money from one place (usually a mutual fund) to another?
- What are the penalties for early withdrawal?
- Can I borrow money from my plan? How much? At what rate?
- Can I make contributions to my plan to build up the dollar amount? How much? How often?
- How much is my plan worth today?
- How much do you estimate it will be worth when I retire?

- How will the benefits be paid out? What are the advantages and disadvantages of taking it in a lump sum?
- What happens if I become disabled? If I die?
- What happens to my pension if the firm is bought by another company or if the firm closes down?
- What is the estimated amount I will receive on a monthly basis when I retire?

$ HINT: If you have no pension plan, you're not alone. According to AARP, thousands of Americans are in this situation. The organization has two booklets that will help you: "Working Options" and "Planning Your Retirement." Order from: AARP Fulfillment Office, 1909 K Street NW, Washington, DC 20049.

TAKING YOUR PENSION IN A LUMP SUM

The new legislation makes taking lump sum pension dollars all at once upon retirement less appealing than in the past, especially for people covered by defined-benefit plans.

The lump sum choice causes cash flow problems for some companies. When an employee opts to take a pension in a lump sum, the plan considers the estimated life span of the retiree, using standard mortality tables. Then the plan estimates the interest rate the retiree could earn. The higher the rate, the less money the company has to turn over to the retiree up front.

The Retirement Equity Act of 1984 requires companies to use the rate stated monthly by the Pension Benefit Guarantee Corp., a federal agency.

The attractive tax features for lump sum distributions are not available for lump sum distributions from IRAs.

You may now roll over a partial distribution from a company retirement plan and defer taxes on this distribution if it is at least 50% of your total balance in that plan.

If you leave your job before age 59½, and you begin to take distributions from your company retirement plan, you will not have to pay the early withdrawal penalty on those distributions *if* you are at least 55 years old.

RETIREMENT TAX BITE

There is a new tax retirees should be aware of, called the 15% excise tax. It is levied on excess distributions from qualified retirement plans and IRAs on top of income tax. The excise tax will be applied to retirement distributions received in a given year that exceed $150,000. Or, if you withdraw all your money in a lump sum from a qualified plan (not an IRA), any amount above $750,000 will be taxed. Money accumulated prior to August 1, 1986, is protected by a grandfather clause, if the proper election was made.

⊙ CAUTION: The IRS formula is extremely complicated, so check with an accountant before you make any withdrawal decisions.

ANNUITIES AND YOUR PENSION

If you're close to retirement or changing jobs, you're faced with the issue of how to handle the balance in your pension account. There are three basic choices: (1) cashing it in for a lump sum distribution, (2) taking it in monthly payments, and (3) rolling it over into an IRA. Your accountant should be consulted prior to making a final decision.

- With a *lump sum payment*, you will have control over your investment choices and you may also be able to take advantage of the 5- or 10-year averaging tax formula.
- If you decide on *monthly payments*, your employer uses your pension dollars to buy an annuity. As discussed in Chapter 27, annuity returns vary widely. Find out. Of course, you can also buy your own individual annuity.
- With an *IRA rollover*, your money will grow tax-free until withdrawn, starting no later than age 70½.

If you elect an annuity, you can specify how your pension savings will be invested: for *fixed income*, where the holdings will be bonds and mortgages to provide a set sum each month, or *variable income*, where the investments are split between bonds and stocks and the returns will vary, depending on how well the portfolio performs.

FOR FURTHER INFORMATION

Retirement Income Guide
A. M. Best Company
A. M. Best Road
Oldwick, NJ 08858
1-201-439-2200
Twice a year; $50 per year

United Retirement Bulletin
United Business Service Inc.

210 Newbury Street
Boston, MA 02116
1-617-267-8855
Monthly; $25 per year

"Retirement Planning Guide"
(IRA Fact Kit)
Fidelity Investments
P.O. Box 193
Boston, MA 02191
1-800-544-6666
Free

27

INSURANCE AS AN INVESTMENT

It may never have occurred to you, but you can turn your life into a tax shelter. Certain types of life insurance double as an investment, a tax-deferred way to save, and as coverage on your life. That's because Congress preserved the tax-free buildup of savings (called "cash value") inside both insurance policies and annuities, making them one of the few ways left to defer taxes since the 1986 Tax Reform Act was passed.

There are other advantages to this type of tax shelter: in a crisis you can cash in your policy and get most of your money back. With some policies, you can withdraw part of your cash value or borrow against the policy at below market rates, save for future expenses, and of course, provide for your beneficiaries.

In this chapter we concentrate on *insurance as an investment*. However, do not overlook health and disability coverage, both of which should be part of your overall financial planning. Both annuities and life insurance are long-term investments, and many impose heavy sales charges and early surrender fees. If you decide to purchase either life insurance or an annuity, deal only with a financially stable company, one rated A or A+ by A. M. Best Co., the nationwide rating service. Most libraries and all insurance salespeople have the A. M. Best rating service.

TERM INSURANCE

There are two basic types of life insurance plans—*term* and *cash*. Term, which is not an investment, provides pure life insurance protection for a specified time, usually 1, 5, 10, or 20 years or up to age 65. It has absolutely no savings feature. When the policyowner dies, the beneficiary of a term policy receives the full face value of the policy.

Term insurance must be renewed every term, generally once a year. If you stop paying premiums, then the insurance coverage also stops. Premiums are relatively low when you are young but move up significantly with your age. Although there is no cash buildup inside a term policy, a "convertible" term policy can be converted, for a higher premium, into a cash value policy without requiring you to meet new medical standards. Term is initially cheaper than other types of policies for the same protection. It is best for those who need coverage for a certain time period—parents of young children, home buyers, etc.

$ HINT: Make certain any term policy you buy has a "renewable" provision. Then you do not have to prove you are insurable each time.

CASH VALUE OR WHOLE LIFE INSURANCE

Cash value policies, also called straight or permanent life, are part insurance and part investment since they have a savings feature. You pay a premium based on your age when you purchase the policy, and this amount remains fixed as long as the policy is in effect. Premiums are paid monthly, annually, or quarterly. During the early years, the premium exceeds the insurance company's estimated cost of insuring your life. Then after several years the surplus and interest are channeled into a cash or surplus fund. You do not select where your cash value is invested—the insurance company does—usually in conservative, fixed-rate, long-term bonds and mortgages and blue chip stocks. The insurance company uses part of this cash fund to pay administrative costs and any agent's commission. If you cancel your policy, you receive the cash value (or most of it) in a lump sum.

TYPES OF WHOLE LIFE INSURANCE

- *Modified life:* Premium is relatively low in the first several years but escalates in later years. Designed for those who want whole life but need to pay lower premiums when they are young.
- *Limited-payment whole life:* Provides protection for the life of the insured, but the premiums are payable over a shorter period of time. This makes the premiums higher than for traditional whole life.
- *Single premium whole life:* Provides protection for the insured's life, but the premium is paid in one lump sum when you take out the policy.
- *Combination plans:* Policies are available that combine term and whole life within one contract. Generally premiums for combination plans do not increase as you get older.
- *Universal life:* Can pay premiums at any time in virtually any amount subject to certain minimums.
- *Variable life:* The cash value fluctuates according to the yields earned by the fund in which the premiums are invested.

Because of the cash reserve feature, premiums for whole life insurance are generally higher than those for term.

☐ CAUTION: Keep in mind that sales charges are high, consuming 50% or more of the first year's premium.

When the policyowner dies, the beneficiary receives *only* the face value of the policy and not the cash reserve. This face value is a predetermined amount, selected when you buy the policy. The latter is used to pay off the claim. For example, if the face value of your policy is $200,000, but the cash value has built up to $175,000, the insurance company needs to put up only $25,000 to pay off the claim.

You can borrow from your cash reserve, typically at low rates, currently in the neighborhood of 5% to 8%, and still be insured. The loan is repaid either prior to death or is deducted from the death benefit.

Taxes on your cash reserve are deferred until it is withdrawn or surrendered, and then you pay only on the amount of cash that exceeds the total amount of premiums you paid in.

TERM VS. CASH

When purchasing life insurance, keep in mind that commissions are highest for whole life. Agents, aware of this fact, may try to steer you away from term, saying it is really only a temporary solution. However, term almost always provides the most insurance coverage for the price and is initially cheaper.

Yet term premiums become extremely expensive as you get older. If your family is adequately covered by your pension and other sources of income, you could conceivably drop term in your later years.

Term tends to be best for those who need large amounts of coverage for a given time span: parents of young children, for example, or homeowners.

$ HINT: Purchase a term policy that is convertible *and* renewable. Then switch to whole life as your age and family circumstances change.

UNIVERSAL LIFE

Universal life, a fairly new form of whole life, has grown in popularity because of its unique and flexible features:

1   The death benefit, i.e., the face value, can be increased or decreased.
2   The premium payments can vary, subject to a basic minimum. You can elect to pay annually, quarterly, or monthly.
3   You can use money from your cash buildup value to meet premium payments.
4   You can borrow against the cash value at low interest rates.
5   You can cash in the policy at any time and receive most of your savings.

With universal life, part of each premium is used to cover sales commission and administrative fees; this is called a load charge. The rest of your premium is invested in various low-risk vehicles. With some universal life policies you can designate how much you want to go for insurance and how much into savings. The company, however, determines the rate of return, which is often tied to an index, such as the Treasury bill rate. Rates generally are guaranteed for 1 year but when changed will not fall below the minimum stated in the policy—about 4% to 5%.

Some companies now offer a variable universal life plan that lets you switch your investments among several mutual funds sponsored by the insurance company.

At the present time, standard universal life policies are paying between 7½% and 9%, although the yield is actually less after fees and commissions are deducted.

❏ CAUTION: Sales fees and other costs can eat up as much as 55% of your first year's premium and between 2% and 5% annually thereafter. So plan to hold your policy at least 10 years.

No-load universal life is now being offered by some companies. The premiums are less because of course there are no commissions. However, you must buy your policy through a salesperson, such as a financial planner, who receives a fee. No load, however, does not mean no cost. There are still administrative costs and other fees. For a list of people handling no-load universal policies, contact The Council of Life Insurance Consultants, P.O. Box 803653, Chicago, IL 60680; 1-800-533-0777.

VARIABLE LIFE

Another relatively recent type of cash value insurance is variable life. Its premiums are fixed; however, the death benefits and the cash value vary based on how successfully your cash reserve is invested. Most companies offer a number of choices, including stocks, bonds, and money market funds, as well as the opportunity to switch from one to another.

With this type of insurance, you have the potential of a far greater return than with other types of cash value policies, but there is also substantially more risk.

❏ CAUTION: If your investment choices turn out to be poor, you could conceivably wind up with less cash value in a variable policy than with other types of insurance.

There are two types of variable: scheduled premium and flexible premium. Premiums in the scheduled premium plans are fixed, both in timing and dollar amount. With a flexible pre-

mium plan, you can change both the timing and the amount.

TIPS FOR INVESTING IN LIFE INSURANCE

A recent study by the Federal Trade Commission concluded that (1) life insurance is so complicated that the public is practically unable to evaluate the true costs of various policies; (2) the savings portions of cash value policies that do not pay dividends offer an extremely low rate of return; (3) prices for similar policies vary widely; and (4) the public loses large amounts of money when they surrender cash value policies within the first 10 years.

As a result of these FTC conclusions, the National Insurance Consumer Organization (NICO), an independent consumer advocacy group, devised these guidelines for selecting an insurance policy.

■ *Don't buy if you don't need it.* If you are without dependents you probably don't need life insurance, and don't buy a policy to cover your children's lives.

RATING THE INSURANCE COMPANIES

The insolvencies of several companies have highlighted the importance of dealing with an A-rated company. Check with these sources.

■ *Best's Insurance Reports*
A. M. Best Co.
Oldwick, NJ 08858

■ *Insurance Regulatory Information System Reports:* lists companies designated for regulatory attention by the National Association of Insurance Commissioners
Insurance Forum
P.O. Box 245
Ellettsville, IN 47249
$5

■ *Standard & Poor's Insurance*
Rating Service
25 Broadway
New York, NY 10004

- *Buy only annual renewable term insurance.* If you buy term, purchase only this type.
- *Don't buy credit life insurance.* This pays off your loan when you die and is way overpriced in most states, although New York is an exception.
- *Don't buy mail order life insurance* unless you compare its price to annual renewable term and find it less expensive.
- *Don't let an agent talk you into dropping an old policy.* If it still pays dividends you may be better off borrowing out any cash value and reinvesting it elsewhere at higher rates.

HOW MUCH INSURANCE DO YOU NEED?

When you decide to buy any kind of insurance, don't automatically rely on an agent's advice. They have an inherent desire to sell you as much coverage as possible. Instead, begin with these general guidelines and then adapt them to your particular situation. Keep in mind that the amount of life insurance you should have is related to other coverage.

➤ LIFE Depends upon how many people need your financial help. If you have several small children, you want enough coverage to support them until they are 18 or through college, but if you are single, put your money elsewhere. The rule of thumb is 65% to 75% of the breadwinner's income—but this does not all have to come from life insurance. Because insurance needs are so individual, even the old formula—which said your coverage should equal 5 times your total annual takehome pay—no longer holds. Instead, assess your assets, liabilities, and income requirements using the worksheet in "A Consumer's Guide to Life Insurance," available free from American Council of Life Insurance, 1-800-423-8000.

➤ HEALTH You need a major medical policy that covers at least 80% of doctor and hospital bills above your deductible. Avoid a policy that has exclusions for expensive diseases such as cancer.

➤ DISABILITY Get a policy that replaces 60% to 80% of your net income. Select one that will pay out when you cannot work at your *own*

INSURANCE TIPS

DO:
- Take the maximum deductible you can afford.
- Ask if you qualify for a discount.
- Get coverage through a group when possible; it's cheaper.

DON'T:
- Buy narrow policies; they frequently duplicate coverage you may have in other policies.
- Switch from one policy to another without studying the costs; fees and commissions are high.
- Use life insurance only for an investment; your first goal is coverage, then investment.

---

occupation, not when you cannot do any type of work.

➤ AUTO Meet these minimums: $100,000 for one injury; $300,000 total per accident, and $50,000 for property damage. If your car has lost at least one-third of its initial value, consider canceling collision. Your state may require you to be covered against uninsured motorists.

➤ HOMEOWNERS Be covered for at least 80% of the replacement cost of your home, not including land value, plus a minimum of $100,000 for liability.

➤ UMBRELLA POLICY If your assets are above $100,000, you have a swimming pool, throw lots of parties, race cars, or are exposed to lawsuits, take out an umbrella policy for $1 million.

BORROWING AGAINST LIFE INSURANCE

Although your agent may say you can borrow up to 95% of the cash value of your policy at below market rates, the true cost of the loan is not always clear. (The cash value is the sum by which the premiums and the dividends earn money above the insurer's estimated cost of coverage.) Read the fine print first, and watch in particular for dividend cuts. Some policies continue paying the same dividends on the entire cash value, but many cut earnings on that portion of cash equal to the loan amount. This is known as a "two-tier" dividend treatment.

☐ CAUTION: You do not have to pay back a policy loan, but generally all outstanding loans plus interest are deducted from the amount paid to the beneficiary.

Loans taken out against single-premium life policies are called "zero percent loans." Because you pay a large single premium up front ($5,000 to $100,000+), you begin earning large dividends immediately; consequently, the policy has a high cash value sooner than other types of life insurance. These loans are "wash loans," because the insurer charges the same rate for the loan as it pays on the policy—if you borrow against the earnings. Single-premium policies have many twists, so check the prospectus carefully for penalties and other restrictions.

To determine the actual cost of borrowing from your life insurance policy, subtract the after-loan rate from the rate you earned before the loan. Add to that figure the stated policy loan rate. This is the true cost of borrowing.

Preloan rate − Postloan rate

　12%　−　　6.5%

　　　　　+ Policy loan rate = Loan cost
　　　+　　　8%　　　= 13.5%

NO-LOAD UNIVERSAL LIFE POLICIES

The following companies have no-load universal policies. This list is not an endorsement but serves merely to start you on your search for information.

- American Life of New York (1-212-581-1200)
- Bankers Life of Nebraska (1-402-467-1122)
- Colonial Penn (1-800-356-9946)
- First Penn Pacific (1-312-495-3336)
- USAA Life (1-800-531-8000; 1-512-498-2211)

INSURANCE QUOTE FIRMS

Insurance quote firms provide four or five of the lowest-cost policies in their computer files. Most deal only with highly rated companies. Some operate in all states; others are licensed only in certain areas.

Insurance Information
41 Pleasant Street
Methuen, MA 01844
1-800-472-5800

Insurance Quote
3200 North Dobson Road, Building C
Chandler, AZ 85224
1-800-972-1104

LifeQuote
800 Douglas Road
Coral Gables, FL 33134
1-800-521-7873

SelectQuote
140 Second Avenue, 4th floor
San Francisco, CA 94105
1-800-343-1985

SWITCHING YOUR LIFE INSURANCE POLICY

Before changing your policy, take time to compare the death benefit, annual premium, initial rate of cash buildup, and, most importantly, the net yield—what your money earns after all charges and fees.

For help, write:

National Insurance Consumer Organization
121 North Payne Street
Alexandria, VA 22314

For $45 NICO will compute and compare the rate of return on your current cash value policy with the one you are considering.

MEDIGAP INSURANCE

This supplemental policy is designed to fill the gaps between your medical bills and what Medicare covers. Before you buy such a policy, be clear about what Medicare now covers:

- Unlimited hospital stays after annual deductible
- Up to 150 days in a skilled nursing facility
- Unlimited hospice-care benefits for the terminally ill
- 80% of limited prescription drugs; 50% of all prescription drugs by 1991
- Doctor's bills that exceed a cap of $1,370

However, it does not cover long-term nursing home care.

Whether or not you need a Medigap policy depends on what other coverage you already have. Review your existing policies carefully, and take full advantage of the "free look" provision required by the National Association of Insurance Commissioners (NAIC), which gives you 30 days to change your mind after purchasing a policy. And follow these guidelines:

- Buy one comprehensive policy, not several with possible overlapping coverage.
- Buy a policy that is renewable for life.
- Find out about exclusions for pre-existing conditions and waiting periods.
- Turn down any policy that says it is government sponsored or guaranteed; its not.
- Only write a check to the insurance company, not the agent. If your policy does not arrive in 30 days, call your state insurance office.

Heed the words of Robert Hunter, president of the National Insurance Consumer Organization in Alexandria, Va., "I wouldn't pay more than $500 a year for a Medigap policy."

MEDICARE TAX

Everyone eligible for Part A Medicare now owes a "supplemental premium" equal to 15% of their tax liability. That means that for every $150 in federal taxes you owe for 1989, the surtax will be $22.50, up to a maximum of $800 for singles and $1,600 for couples filing jointly if both spouses are eligible for Part A Medicare. This surtax will rise annually until it reaches 28% in 1993, with caps of $1,050 for singles and $2,100 for couples filing jointly.

According to the American Association of Retired Persons, 56.2% of those eligible for Medicare have taxable incomes that are too low

NURSING HOME INSURANCE PROVIDERS	
COMPANY	TELEPHONE
Aetna Life	1-516-358-3000
151 Farmington Avenue	
Hartford, CT 06156	
AIG Life	1-800-521-2773
One Alico Plaza	
P.O. Box 667	
Wilmington, DE 19899	
CNA	1-800-262-9568
CNA Plaza	1-312-822-5944
Chicago, IL 60685	
AMEX Life Assurance Co.	1-800-456-7766
1650 Los Gamos Drive	
San Rafael, CA 94903	
Prudential AARP	1-800-245-1212
P.O. Box 7000	
Allentown, PA 18175-0400	

to be affected. Those who are eligible should check the taxable vs. tax-free table on page 112 to see if they will benefit from tax-free income. Brokerage firms have been using this new situation to push tax-free municipal bonds. Do your calculations before buying lower-yielding tax-frees. You may still be better off with fully taxable high-yielding investments.

Starting this year, those who fail to pay the tax, through withholding or estimated tax payments, may face penalties.

Read IRS publication 934, "Supplemental Medicare Premium," which explains the rules and provides a worksheet.

NURSING HOME INSURANCE

As you (or members of your family) approach your late 60s or 70s, part of retirement planning should deal with long-term care. Depending on your financial situation, you may want to consider this new type of insurance. Nursing homes are expensive—the average cost of care is $75 to $85 a day, or over $25,000 a year. Many senior citizens incorrectly believe that Medicare will pick up the total bill. It does not.

Although an insurance policy may initially seem the logical solution, this particular field is complex and riddled with problems. A 1988 survey by the United Seniors Health Cooperative in Washington revealed that beneficiaries of many leading long-term care insurance policies had very little chance of getting money back from their claims, even though they had paid premiums ranging from $2,000 to $8,000 a year. The consumer group does say, however, that many of the new policies coming on the market are much improved.

More than 100 companies now sell long-term care coverage, according to the Health Insurance Association of America. And although the National Association of Insurance Commissioners has issued guidelines for policies, insurers are not legally forced to abide by them. This means you must do some serious research before purchasing a long-term care policy. The companies listed in the box may be a good place to begin gathering information, as are the sources listed at the end of this chapter. Before taking out a policy, discuss the matter with your insurance agent or financial planner and study at least two, preferably three, different plans before making a final decision.

TIPS FOR EVALUATING INSURANCE POLICIES

Select a policy that:

- Covers these three areas: skilled, intermediate, and custodial care.
- Does not require being hospitalized before receiving long-term care. Those with Alzheimer's, for instance, are not usually hospitalized before entering a home.
- Covers long-term care in the home.
- Guarantees renewability for life.
- Covers "organically-based mental conditions" (i.e., Alzheimer's).
- Has an inflation clause—you want to have your benefits ride up with the cost of living.
- Covers any type of health-care facility, not just a Medicare-certified nursing home.

ANNUITIES: A SAVINGS ALTERNATIVE

If you'd like to stockpile tax-deferred savings for your retirement years, then take a close look at an annuity—it's one of the few investment vehicles that survived the 1986 Tax Reform Act relatively unscathed. Annuities have all the benefits of an IRA, but no $2,000 cap on annual contributions, and with most you can continue to invest on an after-tax basis beyond age 70. The minimums are low, often only $1,000, and with most you can invest as much as you like. However, annuities are complicated, riddled with fees, charges, rules, and restrictions, so do your homework first.

THE BASICS

An annuity is simply a contract between you and an insurance company in which you pay a sum of money and in return receive regular payments, for life or for a stated period of time. The money grows on a tax-deferred basis until you begin receiving it, typically after age 59½. At that point you can postpone the tax bite by annuitizing; that is, converting your assets into a monthly stream of income. Then, only that portion of the payout representing growth or interest income is taxed.

Annuities are often confused with life insurance. They are not the same. An annuity provides a steady stream of income while you are alive, while a life insurance policy pays off upon your death and benefits your heirs.

There are two basic types of annuities: fixed and variable.

➤ FIXED ANNUITIES With a fixed annuity the premiums are invested in fixed rate instruments, usually bonds or mortgages. Your money earns a fixed rate of return that is guaranteed for a certain time period, anywhere from 1 to 5 years, occasionally longer. After the guarantee period is over, your assets are automatically rolled over for a new time period at a new rate. The new rate will have moved up or down, depending upon the general direction of interest rates.

Most fixed annuities have a "floor" or guaranteed rate below which your return will not drop. This floor, often tied to the T-bill rate or other index, lasts the life of the annuity.

☐CAUTION: Watch out for any plan that entices investors with an initially high teaser rate and then reduces it drastically when the guarantee period is up. And make certain when you roll over that the new rate is equal to that being paid to new customers.

➤ VARIABLE ANNUITIES A variable annuity, which works rather like a tax-deferred mutual fund, has more pizzazz as well as more risk. Your premiums are invested in stocks, bonds, real estate, money market instruments, and managed portfolios, thus offering the potential of a higher return than with a fixed annuity. You can direct your assets among portfolios (or have the insurance company do so for you). Your return varies, depending upon the portfolio's performance, hence the name variable annuity.

PAYING FOR AN ANNUITY

You can select either a single-premium annuity, in which case you make a one-time payment, or an installment or flexible premium, which you pay for in stages over time. You can also purchase an annuity long before you retire, which is known as a deferred annuity, or close to retirement, known as an immediate annuity. An immediate annuity, in which payments begin almost at once, is often used by those who receive a lump sum payment from a company pension plan. In a deferred payment annuity, no payments are made until at least a year or more after you've paid your premium.

GETTING YOUR MONEY BACK

When you reach 59½ your money is returned to you in one of several ways: in a lump sum, in regular monthly payments, or as lifetime income for you and your spouse. Payments vary depending on the amount you have contributed, your age, the length of time your money has been compounding, and the rate of return on the portfolios. Taxes must be paid on all payouts.

☐CAUTION: If you withdraw money before age 59½ there is a 10% IRS tax penalty.

SURRENDER CHARGES

Cashing in your annuity is expensive. As mentioned above, there's a 10% IRS penalty for money taken out before you reach 59½. In addition, most insurance companies only let you take out up to 10% of your assets before they impose a surrender charge. Go beyond that 10% and you'll be slapped with a fee, typically 6% of the withdrawal during the 1st year, going down to 0% by the 7th year. (One plan, The Specialty Manager from Western Capital Financial in Los Angeles, lets you cash out up to 15% with no fee. Another, Colonial Liberty/John Hancock Variable Annuity, has waived all surrender fees by reducing broker's commissions to 2% from 4%.)

The combination of surrender charges and a 10% penalty means an annuity *must* be viewed as a long-term investment.

☐CAUTION: Look for a plan that has a "bailout" clause so you can cash out with no surrender charge *if* the insurer lowers the renewal rate by more than 1% below the initial rate.

SELECTING AN ANNUITY

Annuities are not federally protected or guaranteed. If you need that type of security, you should purchase a bank CD, which is covered by FDIC or FSLIC insurance, or Treasury securities, which are backed by the full faith and credit of the U.S. government. With an annuity, you must depend on the financial strength of the insurance company. It should have an A or A+ A. M. Best rating. (Most large libraries carry this rating book, or ask the insurance company what its rating is.)

It's a good idea to check the ratings periodically, since insurance companies can be downgraded. Remember, Baldwin United, which filed for bankruptcy just over 5 years ago, once had an A+ rating! (The company had approximately $3.4 billion in annuities. The investors did not lose their principal, but a great many did not have access to it for several years.)

If your company's rating drops, you can make a tax-free exchange into another annuity. Called a 1035 exchange, it is similar to a tax-free IRA rollover.

Additional protection is provided in those states that have guarantee funds. If one insurer goes bankrupt, the state fund assesses charges against other insurance companies in the state to cover investor losses. Call your state insurance

SPONSORS OF LOW- OR NO-LOAD ANNUITIES

COMPANY	MINIMUM	CURRENT FIXED RATE
Essex Life Insurance Co. West Orange, NJ 1-201-325-3655	$2,000	9.5%
The Specialty Manager Western Capital Financial Group Los Angeles, CA 1-213-556-5499 1-800-423-4891	10,000	8.5% (also has variable)
USAA Annuity and Life Insurance Co. San Antonio, TX 1-800-531-8000	5,000	8.5
Lincoln Benefit Life Lincoln, NB 1-402-475-4061	1,000	tiered: 8.75 to 9.75

commission to determine if you live in one of these states.

The current rates for over 200 fixed annuities are tracked by Comparative Annuity Reports (P.O. Box 8488, Albuquerque, NM 87981). For $75 you can get current rates for fixed annuities sold in all states; a single state report is $45. Returns on variable annuities are tracked by Lipper Analytical Services of Summit, N.J. and reported weekly in *Barron's.*

The tax-deferred advantages of an annuity do not come cheap. Sales charges, surrender fees, management costs, and other expenses can eat away at your return. You can reduce some of these costs by purchasing a no- or low-load annuity.

QUESTIONS TO ASK YOUR INSURANCE COMPANY

Before purchasing an annuity, read the contract, have your accountant or financial adviser review it as well, and make certain you know the answers to these questions:
- What is the current interest rate?
- What were the rates for the last 3 to 5 years?
- How long is the rate guaranteed for?
- How is the rate determined?
- What are the bond ratings in the portfolio? (Select a policy with bonds rated A or above.)
- How long has the insurance company been selling this particular annuity?
- What is the company's A. M. Best rating? (Again, it should be A or above.)

FOR FURTHER INFORMATION

For a listing of over 100 companies that meet high insurance standards, send $3 for:

The Insurance Forum Newsletter
P.O. Box 245
Ellettsville, IN 47429
1-812-876-6502

David Kennedy, *Insurance: How Much Do You Need? How Much Is Enough?* (Los Angeles: Price, Stern, Sloan, 1987), $19.95.

LIFE
INSURANCE

For a copy of *A Consumer's Guide to Life Insurance* (c-346), a free pamphlet, contact:

> The American Council of Life Insurance
> Community and Consumer Relations
> 1001 Pennsylvania Avenue NW
> Washington, DC 20004-2599
> 1-202-624-2000

NICO will run a computer comparison of policies for $30, enabling you to compare prices and benefits. Also ask for the organization's list of publications, as well as "Rate of Return."

> NICO
> 121 Payne Street
> Alexandria, VA 22314
> 1-703-549-8050

For details and an evaluation of rates, bailout provisions, and suitability of over 30 insurance companies offering single-premium whole life, single-premium annuities, term, and universal life insurance, contact:

> Tax Planning Seminars
> Frank Miller
> 2 Echelon Plaza
> Voorhees, NJ 08043
> 1-800-445-6914

LONG-TERM
CARE
INSURANCE

> "Long Term Care: A Dollars and Sense Guide"
> United Seniors Health Cooperative
> 1334 G Street NW
> Washington, DC 20055
> $6.95

"How Do I Pay for My Long-Term Care?"
Berkeley Planning Associates
440 Grand Avenue
Oakland, CA 94610
$12.95

"Consumer's Guide to Long Term Care Insurance"
Health Insurance Association of America
1001 Pennsylvania Avenue NW
Washington, DC 20004
Free

The Association will also send you a list of private insurers offering long-term health care policies in your state.

MEDIGAP
INSURANCE

"Guide to Medigap Policies"
The Health Insurance Association of America
P.O. Box 41455
Washington, DC 20018

"Medicare Catastrophic Protection and Other Benefits"
Consumer Information Center
Dept. 65
Pueblo, CO 81009

"Catastrophic Coverage under Medicare: New Healthcare for Older Americans"
AARP Fulfillment
1909 K Street NW
Washington, DC 20049

Department of Health and Human Services:
1-800-888-1770

HOUSING AND RETIREMENT

As retirement draws near, most people begin to reevaluate their housing needs. So should you, if you haven't already done so. The house you bought 20, 30, or 40 years ago may indeed be your most valuable asset, one that you can put to active use to provide income and security as well as shelter.

TO MOVE OR NOT TO MOVE

Your rambling three-story Victorian was probably perfect for raising a family, but now it may be empty most of the time. Perhaps you'd like to sell and move to smaller quarters, all on one floor, maybe in a warmer climate. Or you may be so attached that you don't want to move but would like to make better use of the space. Either way, you can profit from the fact that you own a valuable piece of property.

Among the investment-related alternatives to consider are:

- Selling and moving to a less expensive, smaller house or apartment
- Renting out part of your house
- Sharing your house with a friend or relative, especially if you live alone
- Remodeling to create a separate, self-contained apartment, either to live in or to rent
- Selling and moving to a retirement or planned community

If you're thinking of this last possibility, be certain that you want to live with people all the same age. If so, select a place where you have friends or can easily make new ones, where you are near work if you would like to work part-time or as a consultant, and where you have the kinds of activities you enjoy close at hand—golf, swimming, schools, etc. Adequate transportation and health facilities are also important when relocating.

If you buy into a community, select one that is accredited by the American Association of Homes for the Aging, preferably one that has a waiting list. Both are indications of a well-run establishment. Among the other points to check out before making a financial commitment are:

- Management's experience and reputation
- The corporation's balance sheet
- Potential price increases
- Restrictions on use of the property (pets, children, car space, visitors)
- Any deed restrictions

$ HINT: If you are age 55 or older, $125,000 of the proceeds of the sale of a house that is your primary residence is tax-free. This is a once-in-a-lifetime tax break.

FREEING UP THE ASSETS IN YOUR HOUSE

Here is a thumbnail sketch of techniques that can turn your house into a source of income. For more on each one, check the source list at the end of this chapter. And regardless of which path you take, consult your accountant or tax lawyer well in advance. Laws change, and state regulations vary widely.

➤ SELLING TO THE CHILDREN You can sell your house to your children and then lease it back, paying them a fair market value. This gives them the tax advantages associated with real estate as well as your rental money with which to meet their costs. You can invest the money from the sale, perhaps in an annuity or other vehicle that provides you with a steady stream of income.

➤ MOVE TO A RENTAL THAT MAY GO CO-OP OR CONDO Check the local and state laws first. In many areas, when a rental building converts to co-op or condo, tenants over a certain age can stay on forever as renters. This is known as a noneviction plan. If the rent is modest, this could be to your financial advantage.

➤ TAKE OUT A MORTGAGE ON YOUR HOME   Then invest the proceeds. You can deduct the interest portion of your mortgage payments.

$ HINT: Be cautious about selling your home, especially to someone outside your family, and certainly if it is your only residence. Your house is immune from claims by the government, even if you or your spouse apply for Medicaid, particularly if one of you lives in it. Cash is not.

➤ GET A REVERSE MORTGAGE   This allows you to take the equity in your home and turn it into regular monthly income without giving up your property. If the house is free and clear, you then mortgage it based on its value, not on your income. "Short-term" reverse mortgages tend to run 3 to 10 years, which can be a problem if you outlive the loan—you must repay the loan in full, refinance, or sell. "Long-term" reverse mortgages establish payments until the owner dies or sells the house. The amount you receive monthly is based on the value of your home, your age, prevailing interest rates, and the percentage of future increases in the value of the house that you agree to share with the lender or bank. Called IRMAs (individual reverse mortgage accounts), they are not available in every state.

In a special program that began in the spring of 1989 and will run until 1991, the Federal Housing Administration will issue up to 2,500 reverse mortgages written by private lenders, banks, and thrifts. Borrowers generally must be over 62, and they are guaranteed the right to stay in their homes as long as they like.

Note: These new FHA-insured loans will not have to be repaid until the borrower dies or sells, even if the amount due is greater than the value of the house. When the mortgage comes due, the lender is repaid by the borrower or the heirs. The FHA makes up the difference if there is one.

The amount of monthly income one receives depends upon age, the loan amount, and the interest rate. If, for example, you own a $100,000 house and are 65, depending upon the type of reverse mortgage you take out, your monthly check could range from $207 to $496.

Always have a lawyer and an accountant review all terms before signing any papers.

FOR FURTHER INFORMATION

FHA: 1-800-245-2691, for a list of participating lenders.

For a list of available mortgages and a publications list, send a self-addressed, stamped envelope to:

National Center for Home Equity Conversion
110 East Main Street
Madison, WI 53703
1-608-256-2111

AARP Home Equity Information Center
1909 K Street NW
Washington, DC 20049

"HomeMade Money: Consumers' Guide to Home Equity Conversion"
AARP
Box 2240
Long Beach, CA 90801
1-213-496-2277

American Association of Homes for the Aging
1129 20th Street NW, Suite 400
Washington, DC 20036
1-202-296-5960

Free literature plus a directory of member homes for $75

"Consumer Info on Continuing Care"
American Association of Retired Persons Resource Center
1909 K Street NW, Suite 430
Washington, DC 20049
1-202-728-4880
Free

Discusses contacts, payment plans, and financial matters, plus how to evaluate communities

American Homestead Mortgage Corporation
305 Fellowship Road
Mt. Laurel, NJ 08054
1-609-866-0800

Offers IRMAs in certain states; free literature

National Center for Home Equity Conversion
110 East Main Street
Madison, WI 53703
1-608-256-2111

Literature on conversions and sale leasebacks.

PART SEVEN

YOU AND YOUR ACCOUNT: INVESTING LIKE A PRO

You might think you've done enough once you've learned what investments are best and when to buy and sell them. Yet surprisingly, your education will not be complete then. After you've set your financial goals, selected various securities, and worked out a balanced portfolio, you need to correctly implement your plan, to put it into action in the most effective way possible.

The financial planner or broker you select, the firm you use, and the type of account you have make the difference between success and failure, between being in charge of your money or merely letting someone else, often a stranger, pull the strings. So, before you start trading securities, read this section carefully, or if, unfortunately, you are in the midst of a situation you're displeased with, study the suggestions for changing brokers and arbitrating disputes.

In Part Seven you will learn:

- How to find, interview, and select the best professionals
- How to settle discord
- Whether to use a full-service broker or a discount broker
- The advantages of regional stockbrokers
- The type of account that's best for you
- What types of orders to use and when
- Easy ways to build your portfolio
- Whether or not to have a margin account

Many people who are willing to spend some time in research and analysis, to adhere to principles such as are outlined in this guide, and to use common sense can be successful investors. But there are times when professionals can be useful: for *direction* when you are starting out, for *confirmation* when you become more experienced, and for *management* when you have substantial assets.

Be slow to let anyone else manage your money without understanding your goals. It's yours; you worked hard to earn it, and in most cases, you know your risk tolerance and needs better than anyone else does.

There are three general categories of people whose job it is to help you with your investments. There are also various institutional planning departments.

STOCK-BROKERS

These are representatives or agents who act as an intermediary between a buyer and a seller of securities. Brokers, who receive commissions for their services, are sometimes partners in a brokerage firm, but if not, they are called registered representatives (reps) and are regular employees. Brokers and registered reps must first be employed by a member firm of the National Association of Security Dealers (NASD) and then pass a comprehensive exam. Only upon successful completion of the exam is the broker registered and allowed to buy and sell securities for customers.

INVESTMENT ADVISERS

This all-inclusive term covers pension fund managers, publishers of investment newsletters, and personal money advisers who provide investment advice for a fee. The SEC requires all investment advisers to register, although it does not impose any special training or qualifications to register. The SEC does ask, however, that advisers disclose all potential conflicts of interest with their recommendations, that is, if the adviser owns the security that he or she is recommending or selling to customers.

Investment advisers are individuals or groups; some operate independently, but most are associated with other financially oriented organizations. Roughly, their fees are 2% of portfolio value with a minimum of $500 a year. Above $1 million, the fees are scaled down. Small accounts, under $250,000, are usually handled through standard portfolios designed for various investment objectives. Larger holdings receive personal attention.

➤ ADVISERS' BIGGEST PLUS You have someone to talk to, someone who can keep you up to date on economic and financial developments, back up recommendations with research reports, and explain the pros and cons of various opportunities or options.

Investment advisers are worthwhile when (1) they provide factual, intelligible, useful information; (2) you have substantial assets that require more attention than you are willing or able to give; (3) you can afford the luxury of someone to hold your hand with respect to investment. In most cases, for most sophisticated people, the benefits of investment advice are more psychological than real.

➤ THE TEAM APPROACH It is essential to *use advisers in related areas:* a competent lawyer to set up a retirement plan or trust, a tax expert to make certain that you are taking advantage of legitimate ways to reduce taxes, and an experienced accountant to prepare complicated tax returns. A professional money manager can be valuable when you are involved with large sums in a fiduciary capacity, but for personal and pension savings, the primary role of the investment adviser should be to establish a system that will enable you to make your own decisions. Once you have a sound base, you can decide whether you want to handle your savings directly or with help, or to turn management over to someone else—for a fee.

Ask your lawyer, accountant, or stockbroker for names of reliable investment advisers. You can also get a list by writing to:

Investment Counsel Association of America
50 Broad Street
New York, NY 10004
1-212-344-0999

FINANCIAL PLANNERS

These generalists, who theoretically help you develop an overall financial plan and then implement it with you, are not licensed, or regulated by the government. Most work independently or in a small practice. They usually charge a fee for drawing up a written plan for what you should do, covering your budget, insurance, savings, investments, taxes, and overall goals. This is then reviewed periodically. Planners receive a fee for their services, which can range from $150 to several thousand dollars, depending on the size of your portfolio. Almost anyone can be a financial planner, although planners tend to be insurance salespeople, brokers, bankers, or lawyers. They may or may not have taken special courses. Unless a planner is a stockbroker, they do not advise on stocks and bonds. Instead, they favor mutual funds or refer you to a broker.

At least 250,000 people call themselves financial planners according to the Consumer Federation of America, but only 15% to 20% have ever completed a course in the field. With no federal regulations and no nationwide accreditation requirements, it's not easy to weed through the crop. Before you turn your money over to a planner, read this section carefully. There are three basic categories of financial planners—determined by what they charge clients.

➤ FEE-ONLY These planners charge either an annual fee, based on your assets and investment activity, or an hourly fee, ranging from $75 to $250+. Fee-only planners give advice but do not sell products; therefore they are not burdened

John C. Boland, writing in the *New York Times*, pointed out that when a stockbroker of a large firm offers investment ideas it may actually "have very little to do with the broker's own judgement." Boland's research discovered, not surprisingly, that brokers must "toe the line" and suggest only stocks from the firm's recommended list. A number of firms also put pressure on their brokers to sell packaged products, tax shelters, and commissionable mutual funds.

by potential conflict of interest in promoting a particular investment, such as stocks, insurance, or limited partnerships. However, you still have to pay for any securities you eventually purchase from someone else, and of course you are charged for the plan, whether you follow it or not.

➤ COMMISSION ONLY Some planners do not charge a fee but receive a commission on the investments they sell—for example, on a mutual fund or insurance product. With a commision-only planner, you benefit from one-stop shopping. Since any financial plan entails investments with a commission, you can do it all with the same person. However, the commission-only planner may have a vested interest in selling particular commission products. If you have a good relationship with your planner, this need not be a problem.

➤ FEE PLUS COMMISSION Many planners charge a fee for their overall plan and a commission on investments you purchase. In many cases the commission is lower than with a commission-only planner, simply because under this arrangement the adviser also receives a fee. In addition, the fee is almost always lower than with a fee-only planner.

$ HINT: Always get a written estimate of what services you can expect for what price before making a commitment to a planner.

SELECTING A PLANNER OR ADVISER

Don't use a financial planner, broker, or investment adviser who:

- Has a criminal record or a history of securities-related complaints. Check with your state Securities Agency, or write to The National Association of Securities Dealers, P.O. Box 9401, Gaithersburg, MD 20898, and ask for an information request form.
- Has no staff or operates from a post office box or telephone answering service. Insist on visiting the office, and then check out the person's ties with other professionals. No one planner can master the U.S. Tax Code, pension laws, stocks, bonds, real estate, and insurance!

Unless you know an exceptional financial planner personally, confine your search to those who have demonstrated their seriousness by obtaining one of the several degrees offered in the field. For example, those who have the designation CFP after their names have studied and been awarded this degree by the International Board of Standards & Practices for Certified Financial Planners, in Denver. Other degree programs and designations are listed here. Although meeting the requirements is not a guarantee of brilliance, it does represent dedication to the field. Contact each organization for names of planners in your area.

- **CFP** (Certified Financial Planner). Has 3 years' experience and has completed a six-part course (2 years) with a 3-hour exam for each of the six sections. Course covers financial planning, insurance investments, taxes, retirement, and employee benefits, and real estate. It is given at colleges accredited through:

  College for Financial Planners
  Institute of Certified Financial Planners
  2 Denver Highlands
  10065 East Harvard Avenue
  Denver, CO 80231
  1-303-751-7600

- **ChFC** (Chartered Financial Consultant). An outgrowth of the Chartered Life Underwriter course for insurance agents, this is a correspondence course of six parts, including four electives, with two 10-hour exams.

  American College
  270 Bryn Mawr Avenue
  Bryn Mawr, PA 19010
  1-215-526-1000

- **CLU** (Chartered Life Underwriter). An insurance agent who has completed course work at the American College (see above).
- **MSFS** (Master of Science in Financial Services). Granted by the American College to those who complete an advanced course in financial planning.
- **RFP** (Registered Financial Planner). Presented by International Association for Financial Planning to members who prove they have had 3 years full-time practice as a planner and have either a business degree plus a brokerage securities license or an insurance license. Only about 1,000 qualify as RFPs.

  International Association for Financial Planning
  2 Concourse Parkway
  Atlanta, GA 30328
  1-404-395-1605

- **RIA** (Registered Investment Advisor). Indicates registration with the SEC. Has provided written information about fees, types of clients, investment specialties, education, industry affiliation, and compensation. No formal training required.

For additional listings contact:

International Association for Financial Planning
2 Concourse Parkway
Atlanta, GA 30328
1-404-395-1605

International Association of Registered Financial Planners
4127 West Cypress Street
Tampa, FL 33607
1-813-875-7352

FINDING THE BEST

Select a financial adviser the same way you do your doctor: with great care and caution. Your financial well-being is second only to your physical health. Don't be tempted by tips you hear at cocktail parties or Little League baseball games. By following these steps you will find the person best suited to guide your financial future.

Step 1 Ask for names from friends and colleagues whose business judgment you respect.

Step 2 Ask your lawyer and accountant for referrals.

Step 3 If you have a contact at a particular firm, ask the manager or president for the names of two or three brokers.

The number one consideration in choosing any type of investment adviser is comfort: select someone you respect, whose advice you are willing to follow, who operates in a professional manner (with integrity, intelligence, and information), who answers your questions and eases your doubts and fears.

These criteria eliminate brokers hustling for commissions; salespeople who make quick recommendations without considering your assets, income obligations, and goals; and everyone who promises large, fast returns.

Look for the following:

➤ PERFORMANCE OVER THE LONG TERM Select someone with at least 10 years' experience in order to cover both bull and bear markets. Anyone can be lucky with a few stocks for a few years, but concentrate on an individual or firm whose recommendations have outpaced market averages by at least 2 percentage points: higher in *up* markets, lower in *down* periods. This applies to total returns—income plus appreciation or minus depreciation—and refers primarily to stocks but is a sound guideline for debt securities. A minimum expectation of return on investment from an investment adviser should range between 15% and 20% including income and appreciation. The cost of this advice, including commissions and fees, will be at least 2%, according to veteran money manager Harold C. (Bill) Mayer.

Superior performance should be a continuing criterion. Every 6 months, compare the returns on your investments with those of a standard indicator: for *bonds,* the Dow Jones Bond Average or, for tax-frees, the Dow Municipal Bond Average; for *stocks,* Standard & Poor's 500 (which is broader and more representative than the Dow Jones Industrial Average). Then subtract the commissions you paid to see whether you're getting your money's worth.

➤ REPUTATION Assess reputation on the basis of longevity of the organization and the judg-

ments of noncompeting professionals. Comments from old customers are most valuable for helping you learn how you are likely to be treated, including promptness and efficiency of service and reports. Is extra cash moved quickly into a money market fund? Are orders executed promptly and correctly? Are dividends posted immediately? Are monthly reports issued on time?

➤ COMPATIBILITY Choose an adviser whose overall investment philosophy matches your objectives of income or growth. If you're conservative, stay away from a swinger who constantly comes up with new issues, wants you to trade frequently, suggests speculative situations, and scoffs at interest and dividends.

If you're aggressive, look for someone who keeps up on growth opportunities and is smart enough to recognize that no one should always be fully invested in equities and not to recommend bonds or liquid assets under unfavorable stock market conditions.

➤ STRATEGIES AND TECHNIQUES Find out by asking questions such as these:

- **Where do you get investment ideas?** From in-house research or from brokerage firms?

- **What are your favorite stock-picking strategies?** Out-of-favor stocks with low price-earnings ratios? Small company growth stocks? Larger corporations whose shares are now undervalued according to predictable earnings expectations?

- **How diversified are the portfolios?** Do you shoot for big gains from a few stocks or seek modest profits from a broader list?

➤ WILLINGNESS TO SELL Successful investing relies on two factors: how much you make and how little you lose. Check the composition of all portfolios for the past 10 years. If they are still holding glamor stocks bought at peaks and now near lows, move on! Don't stick with professionals who ignore their losses.

➤ SAY NO After you've made a choice, **don't be afraid to say no** if you don't understand or if you lack confidence in the recommendations. Nothing is more important than trust when you are dealing with money. You can forgive a few mistakes, but if they mount up, cancel the agreement. Remember, it is your money and you have every right to call the shots.

INTERVIEWING POTENTIAL ADVISERS AND BROKERS

Whatever you do, don't select someone to help you with your investments by walking into a firm cold off the street. And never sign on with the first person you talk with. Set up interviews with several candidates. Go to the interview prepared with a series of questions and compare how each of your potential advisers answers them.

Jay J. Pack, a broker and author of *How to Talk to a Broker*, suggests the following six basic questions:

- What do you suggest that I do with my $25,000 (or whatever amount you have)? Beware of the person who suggests you put it all in one product.
- How long have you been in business? With this firm?
- Will you give me several references so that I may check on your record?
- What will it cost me to use your help? Get specifics about fees and commissions, in writing.
- What sort of return can I expect from my investment?
- What research materials do you rely on?

Any good planner, adviser, or broker should:

- Be willing to meet with you in person for a free consultation
- Provide you with references or sample portfolios
- Ask you about your net worth, financial goals, and tolerance for risk
- Offer you several alternatives and explain them
- Be able to refer you to other professionals for specific help
- Set up a schedule for reviewing your securities, assets, and overall financial picture
- Answer your phone calls promptly

SETTLING DISPUTES: ARBITRATION

As with all businesses, there are individuals who either deliberately or carelessly give poor advice. In the brokerage business, integrity is paramount—all the exchanges have strict

---

BEFORE YOU UNDERTAKE ARBITRATION . . .

Arbitration is a long and often unpleasant procedure and should never be entered into casually.

According to Jay J. Pack, author of *How to Talk to a Broker:*

- The odds for an arbitration settlement in your favor are typically 50-50.
- You will improve your chances if you are prepared ahead of time. Gather proper documentation and other evidence to support your case.
- In 1987 the SEC ruled that arbitration results are binding. Therefore, if you decide to go to arbitration and the case is not decided in your favor, you cannot turn around and sue your broker.
- Act immediately if you are planning to go to arbitration. Arbitrators won't look favorably upon your complaint if you wait to see whether the investment in question goes up in price.

For further information, see sources listed at the end of this chapter.

---

rules, and most firms have compliance officers whose responsibility it is to monitor trading, make sure that full information is provided to all clients, and act promptly when there are deviations.

The trouble comes when the customer does not understand an investment or when the broker is not clear about all the facts or has not made them clear to the client. When the price of the securities goes down, recriminations start. If you take a flier, you can't blame the broker for your mistake. But brokers may be at fault if they cross the line between optimism and misrepresentation.

If you have had a misunderstanding with your broker that cannot be resolved, you may wish to go to arbitration, which is a "uniform binding arbitration procedure." Your case will be reviewed by an impartial board for a nominal fee. Although the average case at the New York

HOW TO PROTECT YOURSELF

- Keep track of all your trades, including monthly statements.
- Note all important conversations with your broker in a diary.
- Contact your firm's manager if there's a problem—the company wants to keep, not lose customers.
- If you're not satisfied, contact an experienced lawyer; ask about fee structure.
- Figure out your brokerage losses plus the lawyer's fee. Is it worth taking the next step?

Stock Exchange takes 9 months to settle, about 40% of all cases are settled before they reach arbitration.

The areas in which problems most often arise are options, commodities, and margin accounts, or what are called "other, esoteric" investments. Every broker is required to know each customer and not put any customer in an inappropriate, high-risk investment. A client's net worth, income, investment objectives, and experience help determine what is suitable. (We introduced these topics in Chapter 2.)

If you have a problem with your broker, begin by trying to settle it informally. Talk to the broker first, then to the broker's supervisor or branch manager. Brokerage firms do not want to earn bad reputations with the public or have a number of vociferous, complaining clients. If the problem remains unresolved, write a letter of complaint to the broker and the firm's compliance officer, with a copy to the branch manager. Request a written response from the compliance officer. Also send a copy to the state securities administrator. The North American Securities Administrators Association is the national organization for all 50 state securities officials. Call NASAA for the person in your state: 1-202-737-0900. Then contact the SEC, Office of Consumer Affairs, 450 15th Street NW, Washington, DC 20549. If your problem involves a commodities or futures contract, a copy should go to the Commodities Futures Trading Commission, Office of Public Informa-

tion, 2033 K Street NW, Washington, DC 20581. Finally, send a copy to the exchange involved (see Appendix B for addresses).

If you cannot resolve your complaint on this level through phone calls and letters—and if it involves a great deal of money, you probably can't—the next step is arbitration.

When you opened your brokerage account, you signed a customer's agreement form of some sort. Many forms specify which arbitration body will hear a case if there is a dispute.

Arbitration panels sponsored by the industry's self-regulatory bodies are believed by lawyers representing investors to be somewhat pro-broker. There is no specific, hard evidence to support this contention other than the fact that sometimes retired brokers or employees are panel members. Nevertheless, the SEC recently asked the NASD and exchanges to tighten up their selection process for public arbitrators.

By contrast, the American Arbitration Association has absolutely no connection to the brokerage industry. Another impartial source for arbitration is the Council of Better Business Bureaus, 1515 Wilson Boulevard, Arlington, VA 22209; 1-703-276-0100. Among the brokers who permit arbitration with the AAA are Dean Witter Reynolds, Drexel Burnham Lambert, Fidelity, and Paine Webber. Check your agreement. Although it may be more impartial, filing with the AAA is also more costly—from $300 for a dispute involving $20,000 or less to $2,650 for disputes of $500,000 or more. At a regulatory organization, it is $15 for $1,000 or less and $1,000 for amounts over $500,000.

DISCOUNT STOCKBROKERS

If you like to make your own buy-and-sell decisions, do your own research, and can operate independently of a full service brokerage firm, it is possible to save between 30% and 80% on your commissions by using a discount broker.

These no-frills operations are able to offer lower rates because they do not provide research, they hire salaried order clerks and not commissioned brokers, and they maintain low overheads. Yet many have a surprisingly complete line of investment choices available: in addition to stocks and bonds, many handle Treasury issues, municipals, options, and mortgage-backed securities and will set up self-directed IRAs or

Keoghs. The country's largest discounter, Charles Schwab & Co., also offers to trade mutual fund shares. Shearman Ralston and Securities Research have distinguished themselves in the field by publishing a monthly market report news-

DISCOUNTERS

Baker & Co., Cleveland, Ohio
 (1-800-321-1640; 1-800-362-2008 in Ohio); $35 minimum

Fidelity, Boston, Mass. (1-800-225-1799; 1-800-882-1269 in Mass.); $36 minimum

Cary Grant & Co., Chicago, Ill.
 (1-800-621-1410; 1-800-572-1139 in Ill.); $30 minimum

Pacific Brokerage Services, Beverly Hills, Calif. (1-800-421-8395; 1-800-421-3214 in Calif.); $25 minimum

Quick & Reilly, New York, N.Y.
 (1-800-221-5220; 1-800-522-8712 in N.Y.); $35 minimum

Charles Schwab & Co., San Francisco, Calif. (1-800-648-5300; 1-800-792-0988 in Calif.; 1-800-431-3112 in N.Y.); $39 minimum

Shearman Ralston, Inc., New York, N.Y. (1-800-221-4242; 1-212-248-1160 in N.Y.); $40 minimum

Securities Research, Inc., Vero Beach, Fla. (1-800-327-3156); $30 minimum

Muriel Siebert & Co., New York, N.Y. (1-212-644-2400); $34 minimum

StockCross, Inc., Boston, Mass.
 (1-800-225-6196; 1-800-392-6104 in Mass.); $25 plus 8.5% per share minimum

Max Ule, New York, N.Y. (1-800-223-6642; 1-212-766-2610 in N.Y.); $35 minimum

Wilmington Brokerage Services, Wilmington, Del. (1-800-345-7550; 1-302-651-1011 in Del.); $39 minimum

SHOULD YOU USE A DISCOUNT BROKER?

YES, IF:
- You have investment savvy.
- You enjoy following the stock market and have time to do so.
- You have clear ideas about what to buy and sell, and when.
- You subscribe to an investment service or to serious professional periodicals.
- You follow technical indicators.
- You read market news on a regular basis.
- You trade often.
- You are not afraid to make mistakes.

NO, IF:
- You cannot decide what to buy and sell.
- You require investment advice.
- You are too busy to follow the market.
- You are nervous about things financial.
- You are inexperienced.

SOURCE: Jay J. Pack, *How to Talk to a Broker* (New York: Harper & Row, 1985).

letter and offering modest amounts of research free to customers.

Several discounters have also moved into the computer field: Max Ule and Fidelity Brokerage Services market software programs enabling customers to place trades from their home computers, to receive stock quotes, and even to evaluate their portfolios.

As a general rule, you will be able to save $25 to $75 when doing a 300-share trade. But discounters set up varying schedules, so it definitely pays to shop around when selecting a firm. With some—called value brokers—the rates escalate with both the number of shares and their price. With others—called share brokers—rates are tied solely to the number of shares traded. You will save more with lower-priced shares if you use a value broker and with higher-priced stocks if you use a share broker.

As guidelines, use a discount broker if you:
- Have a portfolio of $100,000
- Trade at least twice a month in units of 300 shares or more

COMMISSIONS: FULL-RATE FIRMS VS. DISCOUNT BROKERS

	100 SHARES @ 51	200 SHARES @ 28	300 SHARES @ 38	500 SHARES @ 60
Merrill Lynch	$92	$122	$204	$435
E.F. Hutton	90	120	201	430
Shearson-Amex	97	124	206	440
Paine Webber	90	121	205	435
Chas. Schwab	45	70	91	156
Fidelity Source	40	62	93	150
Quick & Reilly	48	63	89	189
Pace Securities	35	35	45	60

- Feel so confident of your stock market skill that you do not want someone else to monitor or question your decisions
- Are sure that the savings in commissions are worthwhile: at least 20% below rates negotiated with regular stock brokerage firms
- Are not involved with special securities such as convertibles, options, or warrants, where accurate information is difficult to obtain

If you are a heavy trader, play it both ways: get information from your regular broker, and handle large deals through the discount house.

Don't assume that all discount firms are alike. Always ask what services are offered in addition to buying and selling stocks at a discount. For example, Charles Schwab & Co., headquartered in San Francisco, makes it possible for clients to:

- Purchase any of 350 no-load mutual funds through any of their 110 branch offices
- Place buy and sell orders 24 hours a day
- Purchase all fixed-income securities: Treasuries, municipals, corporate bonds, etc.
- Use the Schwab Investors Library service for substantial discounts on investment newsletters, financial periodicals, and books
- Trade your account by modem and access stock market research through its Equalizer software package, available to those with an IBM-compatible computer.
- Get high rates (currently 9%) on a CMA-type account, called the Schwab One Account

REGIONAL STOCKBROKERS

Regional brokerage firms, those with home bases outside New York, are no longer second stringers to Wall Street and the big national houses.

Although they've always been recognized for their personal touch, local knowledge, and independent nature, recently they've added an item to their list of pluses: success in picking stocks. According to a study by Zacks Investment Research, Inc., of Chicago, A. G. Edwards's 1988 stock selections were the best of all the firms Zacks tracked—their value-oriented picks had a 27.5% estimated return for the year, topping the S&P 500 by 11 points.

Regional brokers are also in excellent positions to spot promising unnoticed stocks and bonds of local companies, ones Wall Street firms either ignore or do not follow closely. For investors, this means a chance to buy a stock before the rest of the investment world becomes bullish.

The regionals also pride themselves on better service. Brokers tend to stay longer at these firms, which lessens the chances of a rookie or

---

BEWARE OF THE PONZI SCHEME

Every year, intelligent people are taken in by seemingly attractive, smart embezzlers through the Ponzi scheme—a swindle in which the first few investors are paid interest out of the proceeds of later investors. The latter end up with zero when the balloon breaks and the swindler pockets the remaining money. Ponzi schemes masquerade as tax shelters, deals in precious metals, gold and diamonds, real estate, and collectibles.

A sure sign: a guarantee of far higher interest rates or returns than the prevailing market is paying.

REGIONAL BROKERAGE FIRMS

FIRM	NUMBER OF BRANCHES	TELEPHONE
Advest Inc. 280 Trumbull Street Hartford, CT 06103	75	1-205-525-1421
Blunt Ellis & Loewi 111 East Kilbourn Avenue Milwaukee, WI 53202	72	1-414-347-3400
J. C. Bradford & Co. 330 Commerce Street Nashville, TN 37201	60	1-615-748-9000
Alex Brown & Sons Co. 135 East Baltimore Street Baltimore, MD 21202	12	1-301-727-1700
Crowell, Weedon & Co. 624 South Grand Avenue Suite 2800 Los Angeles, CA 90017	8	1-213-620-1850
Dain Bosworth Inc. 100 Dain Tower Minneapolis, MN 55402	50	1-612-371-2711
D. A. Davidson & Co. P.O. Box 5015 Great Falls, MT 59403	10	1-406-727-4200
Edward D. Jones & Co. 201 Progress Parkway Maryland Heights, MO 63042	1,400	1-314-851-2000
A. G. Edwards & Sons, Inc. One North Jefferson Avenue St. Louis, MO 63103	435	1-314-289-3000
Interstate/Johnson Lane 2700 NCNB Plaza Charlotte, NC 28280	75	1-704-379-9000

broker-of-the-day handling your account. They also have the freedom to sell products of other firms—mutual funds, unit investment trusts, limited partnerships, and so forth.

$ HINT: To check out a regional firm, read the annual report to see if it's been profitable during bull and bear cycles.

THE BIG THREE

If you decide to do your own research or supplement that offered by your stockbroker or adviser, three publication services will be enormously helpful. They are expensive, so you may

FIRM	NUMBER OF BRANCHES	TELEPHONE
Janney Montgomery Scott Inc. 5 Penn Center Plaza Philadelphia, PA 19103	35	1-215-665-6000
Legg Mason Wood Walker 111 South Calvert Street Baltimore, MD 21202	74	1-301-539-3400
McDonald & Co. 2100 Society Building Cleveland, OH 44114	24	1-216-443-2300
Piper, Jaffray & Hopwood 222 South 9th Street Minneapolis, MN 55402	63	1-612-342-6000
Prescott, Ball & Turben 1331 Euclid Avenue Cleveland, OH 44115	40	1-216-574-7300
Raymond James & Associates 880 Carillon Parkway St. Petersburg, FL 33716	44	1-813-573-3800
Rauscher Pierce Refsnes, Inc. Plaza of the Americas 2500 RPR Tower Dallas, TX 75201	29	1-214-978-0111
Sutro & Co. 201 California Street San Francisco, CA 94111	12	1-415-445-8500
Van Kasper & Co. 50 California Street San Francisco, CA 94111	3	1-415-391-5600
Wheat First Securities 707 East Main Street Richmond, VA 23219	150	1-804-649-2311

want to use them at your library or broker's office before buying your own copies.

MOODY'S

Moody's Investors Service
99 Church Street
New York, NY 10007
1-212-553-0300

A leading research and information service aimed primarily at the business community, Moody's (a Dun & Bradstreet Corporation company) is known throughout the world for its bond ratings and factual publications. It is not an investment advisory service.

➤ MOODY'S MANUALS The company publishes eight manuals on an annual basis. Each is continually updated, some as often as twice a week. The manuals cover 20,000 U.S. and foreign corporations and 14,000 municipal and government entities. Each one gives financial and operating data, company histories, product descriptions, plant and property locations, and lists of officers. The eight are:

- *Banks and Finance.* Covers 12,500 financial institutions, including insurance companies, mutual funds, banks, and real estate trusts.
- *Industrial.* Covers every industrial corporation on the NYSE and AMEX plus 500+ on regional exchanges.
- *OTC Industrial.* Covers 3,300 industrial companies traded on NASDAQ or OTC.
- *OTC Unlisted.* Covers 2,000 hard-to-find companies not listed on major or regional exchanges or in NASDAQ's National Market System.
- *Public Utility.* Covers every publicly held U.S. gas and electric utility, gas transmission, telephone, and water company.
- *Transportation.* Covers airlines, railroads, oil pipelines, bridge and tunnel operators, bus and truck lines, and auto and truck rental and leasing firms.
- *International.* Covers 5,000+ international corporations in 100 countries.
- *Municipal and Government.* Covers 14,700 bond-issuing municipalities and government agencies; includes bond ratings.

➤ MOODY'S HANDBOOKS These soft-cover books, published quarterly, give concise overviews of 2,000 corporations. Useful for instant facts and financial summaries. They are called *Handbook of Common Stocks* and *Handbook of OTC Stocks.*

➤ OTHER PUBLICATIONS *Moody's Dividend Record.* Detailed reports on current dividend data of 14,700 stocks; updated twice weekly.

Moody's Industry Review. Ranks 4,000 leading companies in 145 industry groups.

Moody's Bond Record. Monthly guide to 40,700 fixed-income issues including ratings, yield to maturity, and prices.

Moody's Bond Survey. Weekly publication on new issues.

➤ A WORD ABOUT MOODY'S BOND RATINGS Their purpose is to grade the relative quality of investments by using nine symbols ranging from

Aaa (the highest) to C (the lowest). In addition, each classification from Aa to B (for corporate bonds) sometimes has a numerical modifier: the number 1 indicates that the security ranks at the highest end of the category; the number 2, in the middle; and the number 3, at the lower end.

STANDARD & POOR'S

Standard & Poor's Corp.
25 Broadway
New York, NY 10004
1-212-208-8000

For over 120 years Standard & Poor's has been providing financial information, stock and bond analysis, and bond rating and investment guidance. Its materials are used by investors as well as the professional and business community.

➤ MAJOR PUBLICATIONS

- *Corporation Records.* Seven volumes covering financial details, history, and products of 1,000 corporations. One volume, *Daily News*, provides continually updated information 5 days a week on 10,000 publicly held corporations.
- *Stock Reports.* Analytical data on 4,000 corporations. Includes every company traded on the NYSE and AMEX plus 2,000 over-the-counters. There are two-page reports on each company.
- *Industry Surveys.* This two-volume looseleaf is continually updated and covers 65 leading U.S. industries. Surveys cover all aspects of an industry including tax rulings.
- *Stock Guide.* A small paperback containing 44 columns of statistical material on 5,000 stocks. A broker's bible.
- *The Outlook.* A weekly advisory newsletter covering the economic climate, stock forecasts, industry predictions, buy-and-sell recommendations, etc. Presents a "master list of recommended stocks" with four separate portfolios: long-term growth, promising growth, cyclical and speculative stocks, and income stocks.

- *Trend-Line Publications.* Publishes marketing behavior charts providing investors with a visual look at a company's performance. Includes charts of indexes and indicators.

➤ OTHER PUBLICATIONS *Credit Week, Bond Guide, Commercial Paper Ratings Guide, Poor's Register of Corporations, Directors and Executives, Security Dealers Handbook and Statistical Service.*

➤ A WORD ABOUT STANDARD & POOR'S FIXED-INCOME RATINGS Standard & Poor's rates bonds from AAA (the highest) to D (bonds in default). Those with ratings between AAA and BBB are considered of investment quality. Those below BBB fall into the speculative category. Ratings between AA and B often have a + or − to indicate relative strength within the larger categories.

VALUE LINE

Value Line, Inc.
711 Third Avenue
New York, NY 10017
1-212-687-3965

An independent investment advisory, Value Line, Inc., publishes one of the country's leading investment advisory services, the *Value Line Investment Survey,* as well as several other publications and the Value Line index.

➤ MAJOR PUBLICATION *The Value Line Investment Survey,* begun in 1935, is a weekly advisory service published in a two-volume looseleaf binder. It covers reports on each of 1,700 common stocks divided into 92 industry groups.

➤ OTHER PUBLICATIONS *The Value Line OTC Special Situations Service.* Covers fast-growing smaller companies. Published 24 times a year.

Value Line Options. Evaluates and ranks nearly all options listed on the U.S. exchanges.

Value Line Convertibles. Evaluates and ranks for future market performance 580 companies and 75 warrants.

FOR FURTHER INFORMATION

ARBITRATION

Director of Arbitration
New York Stock Exchange

11 Wall Street
New York, NY 10005
1-212-656-2737

Director of Arbitration
National Association of Security Dealers
33 Whitehall Street
New York, NY 10004
1-212-858-4400

Office of Consumer Affairs
Securities & Exchange Commission
450 Fifth Street NW
Washington, DC 20549
1-202-272-7440

American Arbitration Association
140 West 51st Street
New York, NY 10020
1-212-484-4000

"Coping with the Crash: A Step-by-Step Guide to Investor Rights"
North American Securities Administrators Association
555 New Jersey Avenue NW
Washington, DC 20001
1-202-737-0900

Lists telephone numbers and addresses of state administrators and federal agencies.

BROKERS

Jay J. Pack, *How to Talk to a Broker* (New York: Harper & Row, 1985).

70% Off! The Investor's Guide to Discount Brokerage (New York: Facts on File, 1984).

"Tips on Selecting a Stockbroker"
Council of Better Business Bureaus, Inc.
4200 Wilson Boulevard, 8th floor
Arlington, VA 22203
1-703-276-0100
$1 plus SASE

FINANCIAL PLANNERS

"Comsumer's Guide to Financial Independence"
International Association of Financial Planning
2 Concourse Parkway
Atlanta, GA 30328
Free

"How to Select a Financial Planner"
Institute of Certified Financial Planners
10065 East Harvard Avenue, Suite 320
Denver, CO 80231
Free

"Tips on Financial Planners"
Council of Better Business Bureaus, Inc.
151 Wilson Boulevard
Arlington, VA 22209
Free

Directory
Registry of Financial Planning Practitioners
2 Concourse Parkway

Atlanta, GA 30328
$2.50

"Fee-only Planners"
National Association of Personal Financial
    Advisors
P.O. Box 2026
Arlington Heights, IL 60006
$1

"Before You Say Yes; 15 Questions to Turn
    Off an Investment Swindler"
National Futures Association
200 West Madison Street
Chicago, IL 60606
1-312-781-1300
Free

30 YOU AND YOUR BROKERAGE ACCOUNT

In the previous chapter you learned how to select a top-notch pro to help you buy and sell securities and manage your overall portfolio. Once you've lined up this adviser, you're not off the hook. You still have some decisions to make—such as what type of account to use, what types of orders to place, and the degree to which you want to be involved in running your account, all topics covered in this chapter.

YOUR ACCOUNT

First you must decide between a *margin account* and a *cash account*. Most investors should and do use a cash account. In a cash account you pay for your securities within 5 business days after the transaction.

A margin account is not only more risky, since it involves borrowing, but it can lead to actual dollar losses if you do not monitor your position on a regular basis. Margin accounts are discussed in detail in the next chapter.

➤ DISCRETIONARY OR NONDISCRETIONARY AC-COUNTS If you are just beginning to work with your broker, do not, repeat, *not* sign a discretionary account agreement. This type of account gives the broker the power to buy and sell securities without consulting you first. Discretionary accounts should be used only with brokers you have worked with for a number of years and you trust more than your own mother. Not surprisingly, discretionary accounts often cause problems—customers think the broker is churning their account (executing too many trades merely to rack up commissions) or not buying the right types of securities. The customer may or may not be right. Mismanagement of an account is hard to pinpoint, but it does happen. So don't let it become a possibility—stick with a cash account instead.

➤ IN STREET NAME Your broker will also ask you if you want your securities held in "street name"—that is, held with the firm—or if you want them registered in your own name with the certificates sent directly to you. If you decide to take physical possession of your securities, you will have to wait several weeks for them to arrive. If they are in street name, they become simply a computerized book entry at your firm, and your dividends and any stock splits are automatically collected and recorded for you.

$ HINT: If securities are in the broker's custody, transfer of shares when you sell them is easier than if the stock is registered in your name. Then you have to deliver the actual certificates to the broker's office.

➤ JOINT ACCOUNTS Before you open your account, check with your lawyer, especially if you are involved in estate planning. You may want to establish a joint account.

In a *joint tenancy with the rights of survivorship*, if one person dies, the other receives all the securities and cash in the account. The assets bypass probate and go directly to the survivor, although estate taxes may have to be paid.

In a *tenancy-in-common account*, the deceased's share of the account goes to the deceased's heirs, not to the joint account holder. The survivor must then open a new account.

If you have children, you may want to open a *Uniform Gifts to Minors account*. Whoever establishes the account names a "custodian" for the minor—very often they name themselves. All trading activity is then done by the custodian for the child's benefit. When the child reaches majority (age 18 or 21) he or she can legally take control of the account.

TYPES OF STOCK MARKET ORDERS

Once you have opened your account you're ready to trade. Although both dividend reinvestment plans and dollar cost averaging, discussed later on, are sensible ways to buy shares of stocks or mutual funds, they only work for securities you already own. When adding to your holdings or selling stocks, you need to know what type of order to place.

Most investors simply call their broker and place an order, called a market order, to buy or sell a security, leaving it up to the broker to get the best price possible. However, there are several other ways to go about it. Armed with a little more information, you can place a specific type of order and thereby protect your portfolio.

➤ MARKET ORDER This is the most common type of order. It tells your broker to buy or sell at the best price obtainable at the moment, or at the market. If the order is to buy, the broker must keep bidding at advancing prices until a willing seller is found. If the order is to sell, the broker bids at increasingly lower prices. With a market order, you can be certain that your order will be executed.

➤ LIMIT ORDER Usually a market order is sufficient, but when prices are fluctuating, it is wise to enter a limit order, which tells the broker the maximum price you're willing to pay, or if you're selling, the minimum you'll accept. For example, if you put in a limit order to buy a stock at 20 when the stock is trading at 22, your order will not go through unless the stock falls to 20.

➤ DAY ORDER This is an order to buy or sell that expires unless executed or canceled the same day it is placed. All orders are day orders unless you indicate otherwise. The key exception is a "good until canceled order."

➤ GOOD UNTIL CANCELED ORDER Also known as an open order, this is an order that remains in effect until executed or canceled. If it remains unfilled for long, the broker generally checks to see if the customer is still interested in the stock should it reach the designated or target price.

➤ SCALE ORDER An order to buy or sell specified amounts of a security at specified price increments. For example, you might want to buy 5,000 shares but in lots of 500 each in stages of ¼ points as the market falls. Not all brokers will accept scale orders since they involve so much work.

➤ STOP AND LIMIT ORDER Both full and discount brokers will execute stop and limit orders, but they may refuse to do so for odd lot orders— those of less than 100 shares. (Orders consisting of 100 shares are called round lots.) And, depending upon your broker, you may or may not be able to set stop and limit orders on OTC securities.

➤ STOP LOSS ORDERS An order that sets the sell price below the current market price. Stop loss orders protect profits already made or prevent further losses if the stock falls in price.

☐CAUTION: Both the New York and American stock exchanges have the power to halt stop orders in individual stocks to prohibit further sell-off in a declining stock. However, they very rarely use this power and in fact did not do so during the 1987 market crash.

HOW TO USE STOP ORDERS

Stop orders basically provide protection against the unexpected by forcing you to admit your mistakes and thus cut your losses. In effect, they say that you will not participate above or below a certain price. For example, if you bought a stock 6 months ago at $50 per share and it's now at $75, you can set a stop loss order to sell at $60. Then, should it fall in price, you know that your broker will sell you out at $60. Stop orders are useful for the following purposes.

➤ TO LIMIT LOSSES ON STOCKS YOU OWN You buy 100 shares of Allied Wingding at 50 in hopes of a quick gain. You are a bit queasy about the market, so at the same time you enter an order to sell the stock at 47⅜ stop. If AW drops to 47⅜, your stop order becomes a market order and you've limited your loss to 2⅝ points per share.

Traders generally set their loss target at 10% below cost or recent high. Those who are concerned with long-term investments are more cautious and prefer a loss figure of about 15%: say, 42⅜ for a stock bought at 50.

$HINT: For best results, set stop prices on the down side and have courage enough to back up your decisions. Once any stock starts to fall, there's no telling how far down it will go. Cut losses short and let your profits run.

➤ TO ENSURE A PROFIT A year ago you bought 100 shares of a stock at 42 and it is now at 55. You are planning a vacation trip and do not want to lose too much of your paper profit, so you give your broker an order to sell at 51 stop, good until canceled. If the market declines and the sale is made, you will protect most of your 9-point-per-share gain.

Similarly, the stop order can protect a profit on a short sale. This time, you sell short at 55. The price falls to 40, so you have a $15-per-share profit. You look for a further price decline but want protection while you're away. You enter a buy order at 45 stop. If the stock price does jump to 45, you will buy 100 shares, cover your short position, and have a $1,000 profit (assuming that the specialist is able to make the purchase on the nose).

➤ TO TOUCH OFF PREDETERMINED BUY, SELL, AND SELL-SHORT ORDERS If you rely on technical analysis and buy only when a stock breaks through a trend line on the up side and sell or sell short when it breaks out on the down side, you can place advance orders to "buy stop," "sell stop," or "sell short stop." These become market orders when the price of the securities hits the designated figure.

Example: Your stock is at 48¾ and appears likely to shoot up. But you want to be sure that the rise is genuine, because over the years there's been resistance at just about 50. You set a *buy stop order* at 51⅜. This becomes a *market order* if the stock hits the price 51⅜.

HOW TO SET STOP PRICES

Broadly speaking, there are two techniques to use:

➤ SET THE ORDER AT A PRICE THAT IS A FRACTION OF A POINT ABOVE THE ROUND FIGURE At 50⅛, for example. Your order will be executed before the stock drops to the round figure (50), which most investors will designate.

⬜CAUTION: There is no guarantee that your stock will be sold at the exact stop price. In a fast-moving market, the stock may drop rapidly and skip the stop price, and thus the sale will be at a lower figure than anticipated.

➤ RELATE THE STOP PRICE TO THE VOLATILITY OF THE STOCK This is the *beta*. In making calculations, the trader uses a base of 1, indicating that the stock has historically moved with the market. A stock with a beta of 1.1 would be 10% more volatile than the overall market; one with a beta of 0.8 would be 20% less volatile than the market. If your stop price is too close to the current price of a very volatile stock, your order may be executed prematurely.

Use these guidelines for relating your stop order to the volatility or beta of your stock:
- Under 0.8, the sell price is 8% below the purchase price.
- Between 0.8 and 1, the stop loss is set at 10% below the cost or recent high.
- 1.1 to 1.3: 12% below
- 1.4 to 1.6: 14% below
- Over 1.6: 16% below

Example: XYZ stock is acquired at 50. Its beta is 1.2, so the stop loss is set at 44: 12% below 50. If the market goes up, the stop is raised for every 20% gain in the stock price. At 60, the sell order would be 53: 12% below 60.

The lower the price of the stock, the greater the probable fluctuations; the higher the price of the stock, the smaller the swings are likely to be.

Thus Teledyne, at 150 with a 1.1 beta, would normally have a stop loss price of 132, but because of its high price, it would probably be about 139. (See Chapter 12 for more on how to use beta in investing.)

SELLING SHORT

Selling short is a technique that seeks to sell high and buy low—or reverse the order of what most investors seek to do. It's speculative but can be used as a protective device. You sell stock you do not own at the market price in anticipation of a drop in price. You borrow the stock from your broker, who either has it in inventory, has shares in the margin account of another client, or borrows the shares from another broker. If the stock drops to a lower price than the price at which you sold it short, you buy it, pocket the profit, and return the stock you borrowed to your broker.

Example: The stock of Nifty-Fifty, a high-technology company, has soared from 20 to 48 in a few months. A report from your broker questions whether NF can continue its ever-higher earnings. From your own research—of the company and the industry—you agree and decide that after the next quarter's report, the price of the stock will probably fall sharply. You arrange with your broker to borrow 500 shares and sell these shares at 48.

Two months later, the company announces lower profits, and the stock falls to 40. Now you buy 500 shares and pocket a $4,000 profit (less commissions). Or if you're convinced that the price will continue to go down, you hold out for a lower purchase price.

This technique seems easy, but short selling is one of the most misunderstood of all types of securities transactions and is often considered un-American and dangerous, as indicated by the Wall Street aphorism "He who sells what isn't his'n buys it back or goes to pris'n." Yet when properly executed, selling short can preserve capital, turn losses into gains, defer or minimize taxes, and be profitable.

$ HINT: With few exceptions, the only people who make money with stocks in a bear market are those who sell short.

Here's another example. Say that in anticipation of a bear market, you sell short 100 shares of AW at 50. To reduce your risk if you are wrong and the market rises, you enter an order to buy 100 shares of AW at 52⅞ stop. If the stock price advances that high, you'll limit your loss to $287.50 (plus commissions).

With a stop-limit price, you specify a price below which the order must *not* be executed. This is useful with a volatile stock in an erratic market. Then if the price of the stock slips past the stop price, you won't be sold out.

Say you enter an order to sell 100 AW at 50 stop, 50 limit. The price declines from 50½ to 50. At that point, your order becomes a *limit* order at 50; *not a market order.* Your stock will *not* be sold at 49⅞, as can happen with a stop order at 50.

Short selling is not for the faint of heart or for those who rely on tips instead of research. You may have some nervous moments if your timing is poor and the price of the stock jumps right after you sell short. But if your projections are correct, the price of that stock will fall—eventually. You must have the courage of your convictions and be willing to hang on.

RULES AND CONDITIONS FOR SELLING SHORT

Because it's a special technique, short selling of all securities is subject to strict operational rules:

➤ MARGIN   All short sales must be made in a margin account, usually with stock borrowed from another customer of the brokerage firm under an agreement signed when the margin account was established. If you own stock, you can sell "against the box," as will be explained. The minimum collateral must be the greater of $2,000 or 50% of the market value of the shorted stock.

$ HINT: For those who want to feel more comfortable with a short sale, it's best to maintain a margin balance equal to 90% of the short sale commitment. This will eliminate the necessity for coming up with more cash.

➤ INTEREST   There are no interest charges on margin accounts.

➤ PREMIUMS   Once in a while, if the shorted stock is in great demand, your broker may have to pay a premium for borrowing, usually $1 per 100 shares per business day.

➤ DIVIDENDS   All dividends on shorted stock must be paid to the owner. That's why it's best to concentrate on warrants and stocks that pay low or no dividends.

➤ RIGHTS AND STOCK DIVIDENDS   Because you are borrowing stock, you are not entitled to rights or stock dividends. You must return all stock rights and dividends to the owner.

If you know or suspect that a company is going to pass or decrease its payout, you can get an extra bonus by selling short. The price of the stock is almost sure to drop. *But be careful.* The decline may be too small to offset the commissions.

➤ SALES PRICE   Short sales must be made on the uptick or zero tick: that is, the last price of the stock must be higher than that of the previous sale. If the stock is at 70, you cannot sell short when it drops to 69⅞ but must wait for a higher price: 70⅛ or more.

Exception: The broker may sell at the same price, 70, provided that the previous change in the price was upward. There might have been three or four transactions at 70. A short sale can be made when the last different price was

69⅞ or lower. This is called selling on an even tick.

CANDIDATES FOR SHORT SALES

In choosing stocks for short sales, professionals use computers to analyze economic, industry, and corporate factors—plus guesswork based on experience. Amateurs must rely on simpler indicators such as these:

- **Insider transactions.** That is, if officers and directors of the corporation have sold stock in the previous few months. The assumption is that when the number of insiders selling exceeds the number buying, the stock is at a high level and these knowledgeable people believe a decline is ahead.
- **Volatility,** as measured by the beta of the stock. This is the historical relation between the price movement of the stock and the overall market. A stock that moves with the market has a beta of 1.0; a more volatile issue is rated 1.5 because it swings 50% more than the market.

    The more volatile the stock, the better it may be for short selling. You can hope to make your profit more quickly.

- **Relative strength,** or how the stock stacks up with other companies in the same or similar industries. This calculation takes into account the consistency and growth of earnings and whether the last quarter's profits were lower or higher than anticipated by Wall Street. These data are available from statistical services such as Value Line and Standard & Poor's Earnings Forecast.

    When corporate earnings are lower than the professional forecasts, the stock will almost always fall sharply. Helene Curtis Industries stock dropped over 11 points, even though its annual earnings rose to $1.96 from $1.40, simply because this was below expectations. Catching such a situation so that you can sell short early will depend on your own projections, which can be based on news stories or information that you have gleaned from your personal contacts.

WHAT TO SELL

As a rule of thumb, the best candidates for short selling are (1) stocks that have zoomed up in a relatively short period; (2) one-time glamor stocks that are losing popularity; after reaching a peak, these stocks will be sold rapidly by the institutions, and since these "professionals" follow the leader, the prices can drop far and fast; (3) stocks that have begun to decline more than the market averages; this may be an indication of fundamental weakness; (4) warrants of volatile stocks, which are selling at high prices.

WHAT NOT TO SELL

The least attractive stocks for short selling are (1) thin issues of only a few hundred thousand outstanding shares; a little buying can boost their prices, and you can get caught in a squeeze and have to pay to borrow, or buy back, shares; (2) stocks with a large short interest: more than the volume of 3 days' normal trading; they have already been pressured downward, and when the shorts are covered, this extra demand will force prices up.

GUIDELINES FOR SUCCESSFUL SHORT SELLING

DON'T buck the trend. Do not sell short unless both the major and intermediate trends of the market—or, on occasion, those of an industry—are down. Make the market work for you. You may be convinced that an individual stock is overpriced, but do not take risks until there is clear, confirmed evidence of a fall in the market and in your target stock.

DON'T sell short at the market when the stock price is heading down. Place a limit order at the lowest price at which you are willing to sell short.

DO set protective prices. *On the up side,* 10% to 15% above the sale price, depending on the volatility of the stock. In most cases, a quick small loss will be wise.

Be careful with stop orders. You may be picked off if the stock price rises to the precise point of the stop order and then declines.

DON'T short several stocks at once until you are experienced and have ample funds and time enough to check daily. Start with one failing stock; if you make money, you will be ready for further speculations.

DO rely on the odd-lot selling indicator. This is available from several technical advisory services or can be set up on your own. It is calculated by dividing the total odd-lot sales into

SELLING AGAINST THE BOX

This is a favorite year-end tactic that can freeze your paper profits and postpone taxes. You sell short against shares you own. The short sale brings in immediate cash and the profit (loss) is deferred until the short position is covered—next year. Here's how it works:

On March 1, Mary buys 100 shares of XYZ Corp. at 40. By July the stock is at 60, but the market is weakening and Mary gets nervous. She sells short 100 shares of XYZ with her own shares as collateral.

Her long position (the 100 shares bought at 40) remains in a margin account, where it represents collateral.

Her short position is made in a different "short account."

What are Mary's choices?

1   If the stock stays around 60, she may elect to deliver her stock against her short sale, which was made at 60, after January 1. This will postpone taxes until the new year and will also give her a 20-point profit (60 − 40 = 20).

2   If the stock drops from 60 to 50, she can deliver her stock and take a 20-point profit (60 − 40 = 20) as in choice 1, or she can take a 10-point profit by buying back her short sale. In this case she remains an investor in the company with the original stock at a cost of 40.

Commissions should be considered in selling against the box; they become a factor.

Under the wash sale rule (see page 291), there will be no tax loss if the short sale is covered by buying the same or identical securities within 30 days before or after the date of the original short sale. In other words, if Mary sells short at 60 and then her stock moves up in price within a short period of time and she covers the short sale by purchase within 30 days, the loss is *not* a tax loss; it is simply added to her original cost (40 per share). If she covers the short sale by purchase after 31 days, the loss is valid for tax purposes.

SOURCE: Joel Fein, Silberberg, Rosenthal & Co., New York.

the odd-lot short sales and charting a 10-day moving average. When the indicator stays below 1.0 for several months, it's time to consider selling short. When it's down to 0.5, start selling.

Conversely, when the indicator rises above 1.0, do not sell short and cover your positions. And if you hesitate, cover all shorts when a 1-day reading bounces above 3.0.

DO set target prices but be ready to cover when there's a probability of an upswing. There will usually be a resistance level. If this is maintained with stronger volume, take your profit. You can't afford to try to outguess the professionals.

BREAKING EVEN

Before you hang on to a stock in hopes that its price will rise so that you can break even, check the table. A stock must rise 100% to correct a 50% decline! If your stock declines from 100 to 50, it has dropped 50%. But it will take a

IF A STOCK DROPS THE FOLLOWING PERCENTAGE	IT NEEDS TO RISE THIS PERCENTAGE FOR YOU TO BREAK EVEN
5% (100 to 95)	5% (95 to 100)
10% (100 to 90)	11% (90 to 100)
15% (100 to 85)	17% (85 to 100)
20% (100 to 80)	25% (80 to 100)
25% (100 to 75)	33% (75 to 100)
30% (100 to 70)	42% (70 to 100)
40% (100 to 60)	66% (60 to 100)
50% (100 to 50)	100% (50 to 100)
60% (100 to 40)	150% (40 to 100)
75% (100 to 25)	300% (25 to 100)

doubling in price (a 100% increase) to rise from 50 back to 100. *Moral:* Take losses early; set stop orders to protect profits; stop dreaming.

PROGRAM TRADING

The latest situation individual stock investors should be aware of is "program trading," a complicated strategy used by institutions whereby computers trigger buy and sell orders. During the past 3 years it has added to market volatility and was blamed for much of the market's drop in October 1987.

Program trading is the result of the introduction of index options, index futures, and computers to Wall Street. It takes advantage of the price gap between index futures and option prices and the market value of the stocks making up the indexes.

The trader uses computers to follow the price differentials and then to sell automatically at a specified point. When a number of big institutions follow the same strategy, the market swings can be large. Here are two typical trading situations:

- If the value of the S&P 500 futures contract drops below the market price of the stocks that make up the index and the

spread (or price gap) becomes wide enough, computers send out automatic signals to sell stocks. This huge sell order can lead to a drop in the price of the stocks.
- If the prices of the S&P 500 stocks fall behind the futures on the index, the computers will signal to buy these stocks and sell the futures when the spread reaches a certain amount. This can lead to a rise in stock prices.

SPACE YOUR TRADES

If you are making a large investment (500 shares or more) in any one stock, consider spacing out your purchases over a period of several days or even weeks. The commissions will be higher, but you'll gain a time span in which to review your investment decisions without committing all your funds. And if you decide that your choice was wrong, you can cancel the rest of the order.

EX-DIVIDEND DATE

Always check the ex-dividend dates before you sell. This will ensure extra income benefits.

Ex-dividend means without dividend. On the stock tables, this is shown by the symbol "x" after the name of the company in the "sales" column.

The buyer of a stock selling ex-dividend does not receive the most recently declared dividend. That dividend goes to the seller. With Consolidated Edison, the date is shown in Standard & Poor's *Stock Guide* as below.

Once a dividend is paid, it is no longer ex-dividend. Shareholders then look to the next dividend.

Going ex-dividend is actually a two-step process. The new dividend is payable to those who are "holders of record" as of a certain date. To be a holder of record, one must buy the stock at least 5 business days before the record date. On the 4th business day prior to

NAME OF ISSUE	DECLARED	EX-DIV.	RECORD	PAYMENT
Consolidated Edison	1/24	2/9	2/15	3/15/1989

AVOID ODD-LOT TRANSACTIONS

When you deal with odd lots of stocks—fewer than 100 shares—you may have to pay a premium, typically ⅛ point. This goes to the specialist handling the transaction. However, you may not be penalized if the issue is handled directly by the broker and it involves shares of a company for which the firm makes a market

SOME CORPORATIONS OFFERING A 5% DISCOUNT WITH DIVIDEND REINVESTMENT PLANS

Ball Corp.	Hexcel Corp.
Bank of Boston	Hospital Corp. of
Bowater Inc.	America
California REIT	Hydraulic Co.
Century Tel.	Illinois Power
Chase Manhattan	Inco Ltd.
Chemical New York	Kroger Co.
Commonwealth	Mellon Bank
Edison	MONY Real Estate
CP National	NCNB Corp.
Empire District	Oneida Ltd.
Electric	Piedmont Nat. Gas
Federal Realty	Santa Anita Cos.
Investment Trust	Texas Utilities
First Fidelity	Timken
Bancorp	Travelers Corp.
Green Mountain	United Water Resources
Power	Universal Foods
Hawaiian Electric	Valley Resources
Ind.	Xerox Corp.

SOURCE: Standard & Poor's, *The Outlook*, March 23, 1988.

the record date, the stock trades ex-dividend; that is, without dividend. Step two involves payment of the dividend by the corporation to the holders of record. This payment occurs 2 or 3 weeks after the official record date.

Once you have decided to sell a stable stock, you may want to delay the sale until a few days after the ex-dividend date, so you can earn the dividend. On the ex-dividend date, the stock will usually drop by the amount of the dividend but will tend to make it up in the following few days.

Ex-rights means without rights. As outlined earlier, rights offer stockholders the opportunity to buy new or additional stock at a discount. The buyer of a stock selling ex-rights is not entitled to this bargain after the announced date.

BUILDING YOUR PORTFOLIO

The simplest, easiest way to buy shares of a stock—once you own it, that is—is through a *dividend reinvestment plan,* so we'll discuss that approach first. *Dollar cost averaging* is another automatic way to add to your portfolio holdings. Neither dividend reinvestment nor dollar cost averaging requires a great deal of work or thought on your part once you've actually purchased the stock or mutual fund for your portfolio.

DIVIDEND RE-INVESTMENT

In this plan, offered by most blue chip companies, dividends are automatically reinvested in shares of a company's stock without a brokerage fee. A number also offer a 5% price discount on new stock purchases. This service is offered by corporations to strengthen stockholder relations and raise additional capital at low cost; for investors, it is a handy, inexpensive means for regular saving. It avoids the nuisance of small dividend checks and forces regular investments. It's good for growth but not for current income, because you never see the dividend check. Many corporations permit extra cash deposits, ranging from $10 to $3,000 each dividend reinvestment time. There is usually an annual cap ranging anywhere from $10,000 to $100,000 per year.

Under such a plan, all dividends are automatically reinvested in the company's stock. The company then credits the full or fractional shares and pays dividends on the new total holdings.

Because these cash dividends are reinvested automatically at regular quarterly intervals, they resemble dollar cost averaging and turn out to be a way to buy more shares of a stock when its price is low. Full as well as fractional shares are credited to your account.

☐CAUTION: You must pay income taxes on the dividends reinvested just as though you had received cash. If you buy the stock at a discount from its current market price, the difference is regarded as taxable income.

DOLLAR COST AVERAGING (DCA)

This, the most widely used direct-investment formula plan, eliminates the difficult problem of timing when to buy and sell. You purchase a fixed dollar amount of stocks at specific time intervals: 1 month, 3 months, or whatever time span meets your savings schedule. Consequently, your average cost will always be lower than the average market price. This is because lower prices always result in the purchase of more shares.

For example, if you invest $100 per month regardless of the price of the shares, the lower the market value, the more shares you buy. The stocks you buy fluctuate in price between 10 and 5 over 4 months. The first month you buy 10 shares at $10 each for a total of $100. The second month you buy 20 shares at $5 each, and so on. At the end of 4 months you have acquired 60 shares for your $400 at an average cost of $6.67 per share (400 ÷ 60). *Note:* During this same period, the average price was $7.50.

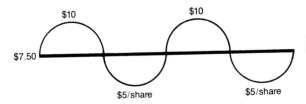

Total invested: $400
40 shares @ $5 = $200
20 shares @ $10 = 200
$400

With DCA, the type of stock acquired is important. You want quality stocks that have these general characteristics:

- **Volatility** . . . but not too much.
  Preferably, the 10-year-high price should be 2½ times the low. These swings are more common with cyclical stocks such as motors, machinery, and natural resources, but they can also be found with industries whose popularity shifts: drugs, electronics, and food processors.

In bear markets, your dollars buy more shares, but your paper losses on stock already held will be high, so you will have to have a stout heart and confidence enough to maintain your commitment. That's where quality counts.

- **Long-term growth.** These are stocks of companies that can be expected to continue to boost revenues and earnings and outperform the overall stock market. If your stock fails to keep pace with the market comeback, you will lose the main advantage of DCA. Look for stocks that are more volatile on the up side than on the down side.

- **Steady, ample dividends.** It is true that dividends, as such, have little to do with formula plans, but they can help to provide regular sums needed for periodic investments, especially when you find it difficult to scrape up spare cash.

With the right stocks and modest commitments, you may find that in a few years, the dividends will be enough to meet those periodic payments.

When you use margin, you can buy more shares with the same savings, but you will have to pay interest on your margin account. However, the interest charged will be partially offset by the dividends you receive.

$ HINT: Start your program a week or two before the date you expect to receive a dividend check from the company whose stock you plan to buy.

- **Better than average profitability.** The average profit rate of the company over a decade should be at least 10%. It's fine to be able to buy more stock when the price is low, but there's little benefit if its value does not move up steadily over the years. Corporations able to show consistent profitable growth will always be worth more in the future. With DCA, you are striving to accumulate greater wealth. This can always be done best by buying stocks of companies that make better than average profits.

- **Good quality.** This means stocks of

companies rated A− or higher by Standard & Poor's. With such criteria, you will avoid companies with high debt ratios and, usually, those whose prices swing sharply.

$ HINT: Shares of mutual funds are excellent vehicles for DCA. They provide diversification, generally stay in step with the stock market as a whole, and usually continue to pay dividends (see Chapter 6).

REVERSE DCA

This is a technique that is best used after retirement when you begin to liquidate shares of a mutual fund. Instead of drawing a fixed dollar amount (as most retirees do), you sell a fixed number of shares. The average selling price will come out higher that way.

For illustration only, the table below shows the values of fund shares that fluctuate widely over a 6-month period. To get $100 income, you must sell 10 shares in the first month, 20 in the second, etc. Over the half-year, you liquidate 75 shares at an average price of $8.

But if you sell a fixed number (10) of shares each month, your income will vary: $100 in

REVERSE DOLLAR COST AVERAGING

SHARE PRICE	$100 PER MONTH: NO. SHARES SOLD	10 SHARES PER MONTH: INCOME
10	10	$100
5	20	50
10	10	100
20	5	200
10	10	100
5	20	50
	75	$600
Average redemption price per share	$8	$10

month 1, $50 in month 2, $200 in month 4. Overall, you will cash in only 60 shares at an average redemption price of $10.

This can be dangerous for two reasons: (1) You won't get the same dollars every month, but over the same period of time you will receive as much and have more shares still invested. Yet when the price of the shares drops, you will have to unload more shares and will have fewer assets invested in the fund. (2) You cannot know in advance the correct number of shares to sell; if you have to change the formula, you may be in trouble.

$ HINT: This system is arithmetically correct but may be difficult for people who do not have additional income to live on in months when fund per-share price is low.

▶ ADVANTAGES Over the years, the average cost of all shares will be less than the average price at which you bought them. But you lose the fun and pride of judgment-based investing.

☐ CAUTION: When stock prices are falling, consistent purchases are a form of averaging down—generally a poor policy unless you are convinced that there will be a turnaround soon.

▶ DISADVANTAGES Formula plans sound simple, but they can be difficult to maintain. Most investors cannot convince themselves to sell when things are going well and to buy when the market action is unfavorable. These plans will seldom let you achieve a big killing, but they can stop you from being killed.

STOCKS FOR DOLLAR COST AVERAGING: 1990

Archer-Daniels-Midland	Pfizer, Inc.
Becton Dickinson	Pitney-Bowes
CBS, Inc.	Procter & Gamble
Clorox Co.	Quaker State Corp.
Coca-Cola	Rockwell Int'l.
Dow Jones	Rollins, Inc.
Eaton Corp.	Rubbermaid, Inc.
General Electric	Scott Paper
Goodyear Tire	Sears, Roebuck
Illinois Tool Works	Sherwin Williams
Iowa Gas & Electric	Sonat, Inc.
Kimberly-Clark	Times Mirror
Lilly (Eli)	Upjohn Co.
Long's Drug Stores	Winn Dixie Stores
Melville Corp.	Wrigley (Wm.)
Merck & Co.	Xerox Corp.
PepsiCo, Inc.	

ONE-STOP INVESTING

If you have a brokerage account, a money market fund, and a major credit card, as well as some type of checking account, you may find it useful and economical to wrap it all together and put it into a combo, or central assets, account. In this way, all your financial transactions will be handled under one roof—at a bank or brokerage firm—which saves you time, red tape, and sometimes money, too.

A typical central assets account consists of one versatile package that can include stocks, bonds, your IRA, a money market fund, and credit or debit card transactions. But you must be able to meet the minimum amount set by the brokerage firm or bank, which ranges from $5,000 to $20,000.

For a yearly fee ($25 to $100) the sponsoring bank or brokerage firm will provide unlimited checkwriting privileges on a money market account; an American Express, Visa, or MasterCard account; a line of credit; a securities brokerage account; and an all-inclusive monthly statement. An important additional benefit, known as the "sweep" feature, automatically transfers or sweeps any idle cash (from the sale of a security, from a CD that matured, or from dividends) into a high-paying money market fund. This system not only relieves you of keeping track of the money but, more important, prevents any loss of interest between transactions.

Combo plans were pioneered by Merrill Lynch in 1977 when it launched its Cash Management Account (CMA). Others soon followed Merrill's lead, and today most large brokerage firms, many of the smaller houses, and even a few discount brokerage firms offer some form of umbrella plan.

Although each firm advertises "unique features," all comprise seven basic ingredients:
- A brokerage account in which securities can be bought and sold at regular commissions
- Automatic investment of idle cash into money market funds
- A checking account, usually with free checks; minimum amounts vary
- A debit or credit card that can be used for purchases, loans, or cash
- A line of credit, that is, the privilege of

DIRECTORY OF CENTRAL ASSETS ACCOUNTS

Advest: Cash Reserve Account
   (1-212-747-4700 collect)
Citibank: Focus Account (1-800-752-0800)
Dean Witter: Active Assets Account
   (1-800-722-3030)
A. G. Edwards: Total Asset Account
   (1-212-952-7200 collect)
Fidelity: Ultra Service Account
   (1-800-343-8721)
Kidder Peabody: Premium Account
   (1-800-221-1808; 1-212-510-3000)
Merrill Lynch: Cash Management Account
   (1-800-262-4636)
Paine Webber: Resource Management
   Account (1-800-762-1000)
Prudential-Bache: Prudential Command
   Account (1-800-222-4321)
Charles Schwab: One Account
   (1-800-227-4444)
Shearson Lehman Hutton: Financial
   Management Account (1-800-522-5429)
Smith Barney: Vantage Account
   (1-800-522-9300)

---

borrowing against your credit or debit card
- Quick loans secured by the margin value of the securities held in the account, with interest charged at slightly above the broker call rate
- Composite monthly statements showing all transactions and balances

Here's how a central assets account works. Let's say you have 300 shares of Eastman Kodak that you want to sell. You call your broker with directions to make the transaction. Money from the sale is immediately invested in a money market fund, where it earns around 7.5%. The transfer of money from your securities account to the money market fund is done automatically by computer.

Then a few weeks later you write a check for $800. You do so against your money market fund, leaving a balance of several thousand dollars. You felt this was an adequate balance—

and it was, until you had a sudden emergency and needed to use that amount plus $1,500. So your broker arranged for a loan using your remaining securities as collateral. This was done in your margin account. By having an umbrella account, you avoided hours of time and miles of red tape that are customarily involved in obtaining a bank loan.

Many of the larger brokerage firms offer customers one of several funds in which to park their idle cash: a regular money market fund; a U.S. government fund, which is slightly safer but also has lower yields; and a tax-free money fund for those in high-tax brackets.

The traditional monthly statement includes:

- A list of securities held in the account
- Securities bought or sold with an indication of profit or loss
- Amount of commission paid to the broker
- Dividends received
- Interest received from the money market fund
- Number of money market fund shares
- Amount of margin loans either advanced or paid off
- Credit and debit card transactions
- Data required in preparing your income tax returns

Before you leap into a central assets account, check out the following:

- Minimum required to open the account
- Annual fee
- Commission charged
- Margin loan rate
- Method for handling debit and credit card transactions
- Frequency of sweeps into money market funds
- Number of money market funds to choose from
- Minimum amount for writing checks
- Clarity of monthly statements
- Any extras offered

You should also keep in mind some of the disadvantages of this type of account. First of all, most components of a combo account are available elsewhere. Credit card holders already have credit lines and cash advances. Debit cards can be a disadvantage, because they provide a shorter "float period"—that is, less free credit time than for a standard credit card. With the latter, you can stretch your credit or payment time up to at least 30 days, sometimes 60 or 90.

Interest rates on margin loans are sometimes higher than rates on other types of loans. Margin loan rates are determined by what banks charge the brokers for borrowed money. This is called the "broker loan rate," which is usually the same as the bank's prime rate. (Check to make certain that your margin account rate is not more than 2% higher than the broker loan rate.)

Your stocks in a margin account are held "in street name," which means in the broker's firm. Therefore, you cannot put your stock certificates in your vault. You may also be subject to "margin call" if you use the assets in your account to the point where you have no more credit, or if the value of your portfolio falls below a minimum amount. Then your broker will ask you to reduce some of the loan. If you cannot come up with the cash or additional securities, your broker may have to sell some of your remaining stock.

Some investors find that such easy access to money and loans makes it possible for them to spend more than they should. If you fall into this category, steer clear of the central assets account.

The Better Business Bureau in many areas has free material on central asset accounts, banks, and brokerage services. Contact your local office. If you live in New York, write for a free copy of the brochure *Choosing a Central Assets Account* to:

Better Business Bureau of New York
257 Park Avenue South
New York, NY 10010
1-212-533-6200
$2.00

31 MARGIN ACCOUNTS: Using Leverage

Leverage—using borrowed funds to supplement your own commitments—is a key factor in making money make money. With *real estate,* it's making a small down payment and having a large mortgage; with *securities,* it's buying on margin: using cash, stocks, convertibles, bonds, etc. as collateral for a loan from your broker. When the borrowing is kept at a reasonable level and the interest costs are modest, buying on margin can enhance profits, because your money is working twice as hard since you put up only part of the cost. Margin, then, is trading on credit and a way of using borrowing power to take a larger position in the stock market.

Leverage in the stock market is not as simple as it sounds. Successful use of margin requires sophistication, sufficient resources to absorb substantial losses when the prices of the securities decline, and the temperament to handle debt.

THE RULES

When you open a margin account and sign a margin agreement and loan consent, you are giving your broker permission to lend the securities in your account.

Margin accounts are governed by the Federal Reserve Board's Regulation T, by the New York Stock Exchange, the National Association of Securities Dealers, and by individual brokerage house rules.

1   Under the rules set forth by the Federal Reserve Board, the initial requirement for margin on stocks is 50%. So to buy $10,000 worth of securities you must put up at least $5,000. Greater leverage is allowed on government bonds, where you can borrow up to 95%.

2   The New York Stock Exchange, however, has stricter requirements. It asks members to demand that investors deposit a minimum of $2,000 in cash or its equivalent in securities in order to open a margin account. That means that if you want to buy $3,000 in stock, your initial margin requirement is actually 66⅔%, or $2,000, rather than the $1,500, or 50%, that the Federal Reserve Board requires.

3   Some brokers set even higher requirements.

All brokers hold securities purchased on margin in "street name."

The New York Stock Exchange also requires that the equity in the account be maintained at 25% to 30% at all times. This is called a "minimum maintenance margin." When the value of your portfolio drops below this level, your broker will issue a margin call, and you will have to come up with more cash or the broker will sell enough securities in your account to bring it up to the required level.

Example: Let's say you want to buy 200 shares of a $50 stock. In a regular cash account, you would put up $10,000 ($50 × 200 = $10,000). But in a margin account, you only have to put up 50% of the purchase price, or $5,000 plus commission. Your broker lends you the other $5,000 and charges you interest on it.

▶ LOAN RATE Mounting interest charges can take a big hunk out of profits in a margin account, especially if you hold your stocks a long time. You are charged interest daily based on the *broker call rate,* the rate the banks charge brokers for money. The interest the broker then charges you may run from 0.5% to 2.5% above the broker loan rate, which is currently around 8.5%. The more active and the larger your account, the lower the rate is likely to be. Dividends, of course, can help offset some of the interest.

EXCHANGE AND FEDERAL MARGIN REQUIREMENTS

Assuming you put up cash in the amount of $10,000 in each case, you could buy on margin:

- $20,000 worth of *marginable stocks*
- $20,000 worth of *listed corporate convertible bonds*

You can invest on margin in nearly every issue on the New York and American stock exchanges and in nearly 2,000 over-the-counter securities. To open an account, you must sign a margin agreement that includes a consent to loan securities. The margin account agreement states that all securities will be held "in street name"; that is, by the broker. The consent to loan means that the broker can lend your securities to others who may want them for the purpose of selling short.

$ HINT: The interest you pay on your margin account is tax-deductible to the extent that it is offset by investment income—dividends and capital gains. So to deduct

DO NOT HAVE A MARGIN ACCOUNT IF:

- You lack the temperament.
- You are dealing in small amounts of money.
- You cannot absorb a loss.
- Your portfolio consists primarily of income equities.
- You tend to buy and hold stocks.

TO MINIMIZE RISKS:

- Set stop orders above the 30% loss point.
- Borrow less than the maximum.
- Buy on margin only in a bull market.
- Watch for increases in the broker loan rate.
- Check the prices of your margined stock at least once a week to avoid a surprise margin call.

CALCULATING YOUR YIELD WHEN BUYING ON MARGIN

To determine exactly what yield you get by buying on margin, you must ascertain the return on your actual investment: the *margin equivalent yield*. You can calculate this from the accompanying formula.

The *cash yield percent* (CY%) is the return on securities bought outright. The same formulas can be used for both pre-tax and after-tax yields.

$$\text{MEY} = \left(\frac{100}{\%M} \times \text{CY\%}\right) - \left[\left(\frac{100}{\%M} - 1\right) \times \text{DI\%}\right]$$

where MEY = margin equivalent yield
%M = % margin
CY% = cash yield %
DI% = debit interest %

Example: You are on a 50% margin base, receive 12% cash yield from dividends, and pay 20% in your debit balance.

$$\text{MEY} = \left(\frac{100}{50} \times 12\right) - \left[\left(\frac{100}{50} - 1\right) \times 20\right]$$

$$\text{MEY} = (2 \times 12 = 24)$$

$$- [(2 - 1 = 1) \times 20 = 20]$$

$$\text{MEY} = 24 - 20 = 4\%$$

Thus the 12% return, with margin, dwindles to 4%.

$2,000 in interest, you must report at least $2,000 in investment income.

☐ CAUTION: The New York Stock Exchange may set special margin requirements

MARGIN CALL

If your firm requires a 30% minimum maintenance rather than 25%, to find out if you're approaching a call, multiply the price of the stock at the time you purchased it by 0.71. If it's reached that price, your phone will ring.

calling for more cash or securities or require full cash payments in very volatile stocks.

➤ SPECIAL MISCELLANEOUS ACCOUNT If you have excess cash or equity in your margin account, this is known as a special miscellaneous account (SMA). It is created by the deposit of more than 50% of the purchase price of stocks or securities bought on margin, by the accumulation of dividends, or by a rise in the value of the margined portfolio. As long as the value of your margined portfolio is at or above the minimum maintenance margin, you may use your SMA to buy additional securities, but if your account is below the minimum margin maintenance requirement your broker will use your SMA to meet the margin call.

§HINT: If you use margin, don't let your equity fall below 50%. In a volatile market, you can get in trouble very fast.

ADDITIONAL REGULATIONS

- Margin rules have been extended to some mutual funds.

- Individuals are allowed to have more than one margin account at the same brokerage house under certain circumstances, which vary from firm to firm. Check with your broker.

- Not all securities traded over the counter are marginable. Stocks under $5 usually cannot be margined.

- The NYSE sets special loan limits for individual issues that show unusual volume, price fluctuations, or rapid turnover, to discourage undue speculation.

- Customers whose accounts show a pattern of "day trading" (purchasing and selling the same marginable issues on the same day) are required to maintain appropriate margin before the transactions are made.

- Each brokerage firm sets its own margin requirements for nonconvertible bonds, municipal bonds, and U.S. government bonds.

§HINT: You may use your margin account to borrow from your broker for purposes other than to buy stocks and bonds. The rates are almost always lower than a consumer bank loan, and there are no monthly repayment of the loan payments.

PART EIGHT

TAXES AND YOUR INVESTMENTS

In 1986 the U.S. Congress passed the most massive tax overhaul in decades. Unless you master its basic points, you could unwittingly lose hundreds of dollars to the IRS. It is particularly crucial that every financial decision you make be made only after reading the following two chapters and consulting with your tax adviser.

These discussions not only explain the pertinent changes in the law but also show investors how to take advantage of these changes. Among the topics covered are:

- Margin loans
- AMT
- Your investments
- Tax shelters

TAX ALERT

As we go to press, the House has backed a capital gains tax relief proposal. The Senate has not yet acted. However, although the House proposal is not yet law, it seems likely that 1990 will see a reduction in capital gains tax rates. With any change to the tax law it is *imperative* to consult your tax adviser about how revisions to any portion of the tax law affect your individual circumstances. As of early October 1989 it is impossible to predict the final result of this latest scrambling of the tax laws. The salient points of the House-backed proposal are summarized here:

- For assets held at least one year and sold between September 14, 1989, and December 31, 1991, a decrease in the capital gains tax rate to 19.6% for those in the 28% or 33% bracket, and to 10.5% for those in the 15% tax bracket.
- The new lower rate covers stocks, bonds, real estate, timber, livestock, and some other raw materials. It does not apply to works of art, coins, and other collectibles.

- In 1992 the capital gains tax rate returns to the present ordinary income tax rates of 28% and 15%, but the proposal would exclude from tax all gains due solely to inflation after 1991.

32

DEALING WITH YOUR TAXES

By now we have all experienced filing several tax returns under the revisions wrought by the 1986 Tax Reform Act, and it's left many of us reeling from the so-called simplification. Indeed it did slash personal tax rates, but to pay for these rate reductions, the legislators either cut or eliminated a huge lineup of previously popular tax breaks, including a host of deductions, tax credits, and shelters.

The most radical change, of course, was the drop in the top tax rate for individuals from 50% to 28%, the lowest maximum rate the country has seen since 1931. In addition, cherished deductions, long used by middle- and upper-income taxpayers, were wiped away or are being phased out, including deductions for interest on consumer loans (credit cards and auto loans) and state sales tax. Eligibility for IRA deductions is reduced, home equity loans restricted, and the advantages of charitable giving diminished. Capital gains from the sale of stocks and other assets, whether long- or short-term, is now taxed at the same rate as dividends, wages, and interest income, but this may change.

This chapter is designed to show you *as an investor* ways to save on taxes, and, at the same time, invest profitably. Tax considerations are clearly important when it comes to investing, but they should never be allowed to eclipse the basics. Further ramifications of tax reform are analyzed in Chapter 10, on tax-exempt bonds; Chapter 34, on tax shelters; and Chapters 26–28, on retirement.

MARGIN LOANS

If you open a margin account you should know that the interest you pay on money borrowed from your broker for investment purposes is deductible only to the extent that it is offset by investment income (from dividends, capital gains, interest income, and royalties). For example, if you want to deduct $1,500 worth of interest on your margin loan, you must report at least $1,500 of investment income to the IRS.

Another new rule is that you must use the money borrowed to make an investment in order to deduct the interest. (Previously, you could borrow for any purpose.) Keep careful records to document the fact that you used the money for an investment.

☐ CAUTION: Money borrowed from your brokerage account for personal purposes is subject to personal interest limitations (10% deductible in 1990).

§ HINT: Determine your monthly and year-to-date margin interest expense versus income from your investments. If your investment interest expense is larger than your income, talk to your broker about converting low-yielding stocks to convertible bonds or switching tax-free munis into taxable investments. And remember, if you have excess investment interest expense, it can be carried over into the next year.

☐ CAUTION: If you borrow to hold municipal bonds or any other tax-exempt investment, interest (or margin) expense is *not* deductible.

In your annual review of your investment portfolio, keep in mind that (1) all capital gains are taxed at the same rate as dividend and regular income, but this may change; (2) there is no tax advantage to holding a stock for 1 year or longer since the favorable long-term capital gains rate has been eliminated; and (3) most tax shelters were given the kiss of death. Long-term gains will receive no special treatment and will be taxed as much as 33%.

Consequently, financial assets have gained appeal, and tax considerations are less important in buying and selling securities. High-yielding investments in particular make more sense than ever, since lower rates allow investors to keep more of this income and since the distinction between short- and long-term capital gains has been eliminated. (Of course, any stock that increases in value should not be overlooked. Appreciation remains as solid a way to make money as before tax reform.)

Lower tax rates are not the only reason to consider dividend-yielding stocks. Capital gains are now taxed like ordinary income, but this is under review.

You can still use capital losses to offset your regular income. For example, $1,500 worth of long-term losses can offset the same amount of wages. However, the amount of ordinary income that can be offset by capital losses each year is limited to $3,000.

THE ALTERNATIVE MINIMUM TAX

This tax was designed to make certain that Americans with high incomes and high deductions would still have to pay at a rate of 20% on their alternative minimum taxable income (AMTI). The 1986 Tax Reform Act increased the alternative minimum tax (AMT) to 21%. So no matter how rich you are, no matter how many loopholes or tax shelters your accountant finds for you, if you have a high income, you may still have to pay some federal income tax.

You can easily determine if you are subject to the alternative minimum tax by following these steps:

1 Add all your preference items and adjustments (see following list) to your taxable income.
2 From this amount, subtract $40,000 if you are married and filing jointly, $30,000 if you are single, or $20,000 if you are married and filing separately. If AMTI exceeds $150,000 (married filing jointly), $112,500 (single), or $75,000 (married filing separately), the $40,000, $30,000, or $20,000 must be reduced by 25% of the excess over the $150,000, $112,500, or $75,000.
3 Multiply this amount by a flat 21%. The result is your minimum tax.

If your standard tax is less than this figure, you must pay the alternative minimum tax. The AMT is imposed only when it is greater than the regular tax, reduced by certain credits.

Certain preference items and adjustments (line items that get favorable treatment on your regular income) increase your chances of being vulnerable to the AMT. Among the key items are:

- Accelerated depreciation on real property you own that was placed in service before 1987
- Certain costs often associated with tax shelters, such as research and development costs and intangible drilling costs
- State and local income tax, real estate and personal property tax, and deductible personal interest
- Tax-exempt interest on newly issued private activity bonds
- Untaxed appreciation on charitable contributions of appreciated property
- Excess of fair market value of stock acquired by exercising an incentive stock option over the amount paid, unless you sell the stock in the same year.
- Deductible portion of passive activity losses

Deductions that reduce your AMT are:

- Depletion
- Medical expenses that exceed 10% of your gross income
- Charitable contributions, generally up to 50% of your adjusted gross income
- Casualty losses in excess of 10% of adjusted gross income and the $100 floor
- Interest costs on your home
- Certain estate taxes
- Interest costs to the extent that they do not exceed your net investment income, refigured for AMT

With the new alternative minimum tax, there is a danger that certain tax shelters may reduce your regular taxable income to such an extent that you will wind up paying the larger alternative minimum tax. Monitor any sheltering you do with your accountant on a continual basis.

$ HINT: Since 1985 the IRS has required taxpayers to make estimated tax payments to cover taxes due under the AMT category. If you have substantial tax shelter write-offs, figure your AMT liability using IRS Form 6251 and then make certain this amount is covered through withholding or quarterly estimated tax payments, if appropriate.

BORROWED MONEY AND BONDS

In the past, the IRS allowed you to borrow money to buy bonds, and to the extent that the interest rate on your loan exceeded the interest income from the bond, you had a deduction. This deduction could then be used to offset other current income. Excess interest expense that is equal to the discount and interest accruing, but not includable in income, is *not* deductible. The excess interest is deductible when includable interest exceeds interest expense or when disposition occurs.

This ruling killed one of the most popular year-end tax-saving strategies of all time. In the past, you could borrow money to buy a Treasury bond or note that matured after the end of the year. The interest on the borrowed money was deductible in the current year, yet you were not taxed on it until you sold the T-bill in the next year.

Now, however, to the extent that you have unrealized income on the T-bill, you are not allowed to deduct the interest expense. Your deduction is deferred until you sell or redeem the T-bill. This also applies to other debt instruments.

DIVIDEND INCOME

In the eyes of the IRS, not every bit of your dividend and interest income is the same, and the way in which you report it can make a big difference—not only to how much income tax you must pay but also to whether or not you will be audited.

If you received more than $400 in dividend income during the year, you must fill out Schedule B, Part II, in order to report it.

➤ CASH DIVIDENDS If you received dividends from IBM, Ford Motor, General Electric, or any other corporation, the amount is reported by the company directly to the IRS. You, in turn, receive Form 1099 information slips from each corporation telling precisely how much you received for the year.

➤ STOCK DIVIDENDS There are times, of course, when you receive a stock dividend rather than cash. If nontaxable, your original cost is now allocated over a greater number of shares. If it is a taxable dividend, the basis would increase.

➤ DIVIDEND REINVESTMENT PLANS As described earlier, you may sign up for automatic reinvestment of your dividends if you own stock in certain companies. In such cases, the corporation pays your regular dividend with stock, *not* cash. The IRS maintains that since you could have had cash but elected not to, you will be taxed the same year you receive the dividend.

DIVIDENDS DON'T LIE

Geraldine Weiss, author of the book *Dividends Don't Lie,* has selected these stocks to buy and hold in 1990.

	CURRENT PRICE	DIVIDEND	YIELD	P/E
Baxter International	$20	$0.56	2.9%	15
Bristol Myers	47	2.00	4.3	16
Florida Progress	34	2.56	7.6	10
IBM	110	4.40	4.0	11
Pacificorp	35	2.64	7.6	10
Pfizer	56	2.20	4.0	12
Security Pacific	40	1.96	5.0	7
Syntex	40	1.30	3.3	15
Texas Utilities	28	2.92	10.5	7
Xerox	60	3.00	5.0	17

SOURCE: Geraldine Weiss, *Investment Quality Trends,* La Jolla, Calif., April 13, 1989.

➤ RETURN OF CAPITAL Corporations sometimes give a return of capital distribution. If this is the case it will be so designated on your 1099 slip. Most return of capital is not taxed; however, your basis of stock must be reduced by whatever the amount is. If a return of capital exceeds basis, the excess is taxable and the basis is reduced to zero.

➤ INSURANCE DIVIDENDS Any dividends you may receive on veterans' insurance are *not* taxed, and dividends received from regular life insurance are generally not taxed. However, if you are in doubt, check with your accountant or insurance company.

➤ OTHER TYPES OF DIVIDENDS Money market mutual funds pay what is called a dividend, and you should list it as such on your tax return.

If you have an interest-bearing checking account with a savings and loan or a credit union, you may collect interest, although it is sometimes referred to as dividend income. Be aware: if this interest is reported on the 1099 slip as dividends, you too should report it as dividend income.

DEDUCTIONS FOR THE INVESTOR

You can deduct the amount over 2% of adjusted gross income for certain expenses incurred to produce and collect income and to manage or maintain property held to make income. Among the deductible-as-itemized deductions are:

- Subscriptions to investment publications
- Cost of books on investing and taxes
- Clerical expenses
- Insurance on investment property
- Safety deposit box rent
- Fees for accounting or investment advice and for legal advice if related to tax or investment matters
- Related taxes, excluding federal income tax
- Expenses directly related to tax (but not investment) seminars, including transportation
- Travel expenses to visit your broker, your safe deposit box, and your tax accountant or lawyer for investment or income-tax purposes
- Computers: the cost of a computer used in managing your investments is sometimes deductible. (If you use your computer for business over 50% of the time, you can depreciate it over 5 years.)
- Losses: if you sell assets at a loss, you can deduct up to $3,000 of net losses annually.
- IRA or Keogh account custodial fees
- Securities that become completely worthless
- Penalties paid on early savings withdrawals
- Mortgage prepayment penalties
- Points paid on loan financing for primary residences, subject to limitations

TIMELY MOVES: WISE YEAR-END INVESTMENT STRATEGIES

TAX STRATEGIES

- If you have been buying or selling commodities, a different set of tax rules applies. Check with your accountant, as this ruling is extremely complicated.
- If you own stock in a corporation whose long-term outlook is favorable but whose stock has dropped in price, you may want to take a loss for tax purposes but not give up your position entirely. You can buy more stock now at the lower price and sell your original holdings 31 days later. (You must wait the 31 days in order to avoid the "wash sale rule," which prevents loss deductions on sale and repurchase transactions made within 31 days. You can buy it back after 31 days.) The risk involved is of course that the stock could continue to fall in price.
- If you own stock that has gone way up in price since you purchased it and you feel it is near its peak and you want to lock in your profit but not pay taxes this year, you can "sell short against the box" (see page 276). In other words, you can keep

your stock until the covering date next year, when you will be taxed. This is known as "closing the transaction." The gain is always taxed in the year the transaction is closed.

BOND SWAPS

Another year-end strategy that can help save on taxes is a bond swap. You'll find that under certain circumstances it pays to sell bonds worth less than their initial cost in order to set up a tax loss and then reinvest that same money in a similar bond. By converting a paper loss to an actual loss, you can offset any taxable gains earned in more profitable investments. In the process of swapping, you may also be able to increase your yield.

If you're thinking of a bond swap, don't wait until the last days of the year. It may take your broker several weeks to locate an appropriate bond.

Bond swaps involve two steps:

1   Selling bonds that have declined in price
2   Replacing these assets with similar (but not substantially identical) bonds

By immediately purchasing similar bonds for approximately the same price as the ones you sold, you restore your market position and your income.

➤ TAX BREAKS Even if you didn't make a killing in the market this year, if you took some investment profits, a bond swap can help reduce your tax bite. Here's how it works.

If you own bonds purchased when interest rates were lower, they are probably worth less in the secondary market today. If you sell them, you can take a loss that can be used, dollar for dollar, to offset any capital gains. If you have no long- or short-term capital gains, the loss can be used to offset up to $3,000 of taxable income, on a dollar-for-dollar basis. If your loss is greater than that, it can be carried over into the next year.

A bond swap enables you to keep your position by buying comparable bonds selling for approximately the same price.

In order for the IRS to recognize a loss for tax purposes, you must buy bonds of a different issuer or with a substantially different maturity date or coupon.

➤ STATE INCOME TAX A bond swap is also useful if you move from a state with no income tax to one that has an income tax. Buy municipal bonds issued by the new state that are not subject to state taxes.

➤ SWAPPING COSTS Unlike stocks and most other securities, where commissions are noted separately from the purchase or sale price, municipal bonds have their commission included in the price of the bond. Commissions range from $5 to $20 per $1,000-face-value bond, which means that a swap involving $50,000 worth of bonds could entail a commission somewhere between $500 and $2,000.

SHIFTING INCOME TO CHILDREN

According to the new tax law, unearned income of a child aged 14 or less, regardless of the source, is taxed at the parent's rate when this income exceeds $1,000 per year. But the first $500 is not taxed, and the next $500 is taxed at the child's rate. If the child is over 14, all income is taxed at the child's rate, presumably lower than the parent's.

The new law has in effect put an end to the value of the Clifford trust, which was one of the most popular ways to reduce taxes by transferring assets to children.

If you wish to give money to your children but you don't want it to be taxed at your rate, you are limited to a handful of choices. One, of course, is tax-free municipal bonds. Another is U.S. EE savings bonds. In the latter case, interest is not taxed until the bonds are cashed in. Then, when your child turns 14, you can change the portfolio mix and periodically cash in the bonds, since the income will then be taxed at the child's rate.

$ HINT: Earnings in Clifford trusts set up after March 1, 1986, will be taxed to the donor regardless of the beneficiary's age.

If you have already transferred investments to a child under age 14, you may want to put these investments into municipals or zero coupon bonds.

$ HINT: You can still make a tax-free loan up to $10,000 ($20,000 for a couple) to each member of your family per year. It is also possible to loan up to $100,000 if tax avoidance is not one of the principal purposes. Imputed interest is then limited to the borrower's investment income. This is a popular way for parents to help children buy property.

If you are involved in income shifting, keep careful records indicating that you have separate accounts for your children.

OTHER RULES TO KEEP IN MIND

➤ STATE AND LOCAL TAXES Except for sales tax, these taxes continue to be fully deductible.

➤ INVESTMENT EXPENSES These, including tax planning, the cost of this book, tax-return preparation, investment publications, and other miscellaneous items are deductible only for amounts in excess of 2% of your adjusted gross income.

➤ PENSION PLANS Employees must now be vested (or guaranteed participation) in pension plans after 5 years of employment, not 10 as was the case.

➤ CHARITABLE DEDUCTIONS Unless you itemize, you cannot deduct your charitable contributions.

➤ MEDICAL EXPENSES You can deduct medical expenses only to the extent that they exceed 7½% of your adjusted gross income.

FOR FURTHER INFORMATION

These publications are available free of charge at your local IRS office or by calling 1-800-424-FORM (3676). For a complete list of all IRS brochures, ask for publication 910, "Guide to Free Tax Services."

523 Tax Information on Selling Your Home
527 Rental Property
530 Tax Information for Owners of Homes, Condominiums, and Cooperative Apartments
550 Investment Income and Expenses
554 Tax Information for Older Americans
560 Self-employed Retirement Plans
564 Mutual Fund Distributions
575 Pension and Annuity Income
590 Individual Retirement Arrangements (IRAs)
915 Social Security Benefits
932 New Rules for Home Mortgage Interest Deduction

33

ALPHABETICAL DIRECTORY OF YOUR INVESTMENTS AND THEIR TAX STATUS

The information that follows is general in scope and intended as an introductory explanation of how taxes affect your investments. You should always consult your accountant about specific problems.

ANNUITIES

- Interest earned can accumulate tax-free until withdrawn. When it is withdrawn, only the interest earned is taxed, not your initial investment.
- If you withdraw money prior to age 59½, there is a 10% tax penalty. With qualified employer-sponsored annuities, there is no 10% penalty if you immediately transfer the money to a qualified annuity with another company.
- For other rulings, check your policy.

ANTIQUES, ART, COINS, GEMS, STAMPS, AND OTHER COLLECTIBLES

- Profits made upon sale are subject to federal income tax at the regular rate of 15%, 28%, or 33%. The purchase price is subject to state and local sales tax.

BONDS (AGENCY ISSUES)

- Interest income is subject to federal tax.
- Interest income on some agency issues is exempt from state and local taxes. Ask your broker or accountant.

BONDS (CORPORATE)

- Interest income is subject to federal, state, and local taxes.
- Gains made when bonds are sold are taxed at regular rates, but this is under review.
- Losses can be used to offset other net gains you may have, plus up to $3,000 of wages, salary, and other "ordinary" income.

BONDS (MUNICIPAL)

- Interest earned on most munis is exempt from federal income tax and from state and local taxes for residents of the state where the bonds are issued.
- Most states tax out-of-state bonds.
- Bonds issued by the Commonwealth of Puerto Rico and the District of Columbia are exempt from taxes in all states.
- Interest earned on certain "private-activity" bonds that were issued after August 7, 1986, is a tax preference item to be included in the calculation of the alternative minimum tax (see page 289). If you are not subject to the AMT, you will not pay taxes on these particular bonds.
- Some bonds are now subject to federal tax but remain exempt at the state and local levels—these include bonds to help finance convention centers.
- Illinois, Iowa, Kansas, Oklahoma, and Wisconsin tax any municipal bonds issued in their state.
- Interest earned on fully tax-exempt bonds can have a tax cost when held by retired people receiving Social Security. If you are retired and if your adjusted gross income plus half your Social Security plus tax-

exempt interest income is over $25,000 for a single return or $32,000 for a joint return, interest earned on the tax-exempt bonds *is* effectively taxable.

BONDS (PREMIUM)

- If you purchase a bond at a premium, you can only use any amortizable premium to offset your interest income. In other words, you can no longer use the premium as a deduction against other types of income. The amortized premium is subtracted directly from the interest you earn on the bond, rather than deducted as a separate expense subject to the investment interest expense limitations.

BONDS (ZERO)

- Taxes must be paid on the so-called imputed interest that accrues annually, even though, of course, no interest is actually paid to the bondholder.
- Because you must pay tax as though you had received interest, zeros are well suited for IRAs and Keoghs where interest income is deferred from taxes until withdrawn.
- Zero coupon municipals are usually exempt from federal taxes and from state and local taxes when bonds are issued in the investor's state.
- Zero coupon Treasuries are exempt from state and local taxes.

CERTIFICATES OF DEPOSIT (CDs)

- Any interest earned is subject to federal, state, and local taxes.
- Interest is taxed the year earned, not when the CD matures.

COMMERCIAL PAPER

- Any interest earned is subject to federal, state, and local taxes.

- *Exception:* commercial paper issued by state and local governments is usually, but not always, exempt from federal as well as state and local taxes.

COMMOD-ITIES AND FUTURES CONTRACTS

- Profits are taxed at 60/40 rates: 60% long-term and 40% short-term. However, this currently makes no difference.
- Profits become taxable at the end of the year, even if you have not closed out your position. The IRS, in effect, will tax you on your paper profits.
- In some cases, you can deduct paper losses, even of positions still open. These rules may apply to contracts subject to the mark-to-the-market rule. Check with your accountant.

CREDIT UNION ACCOUNTS

- Even though depositors are actually shareholders of the credit union and the money earned is known as a dividend, your earnings are regarded as interest and subject to federal, state, and local taxes.

EQUIPMENT-LEASING PARTNER-SHIPS

- Income is subject to federal, state, and local taxes.
- Deductions generated by the partnership will help shelter some of the income derived from lease payments. The key deduction is depreciation for the cost of the equipment. If the partnership borrows to pay for the equipment, interest may also be deductible.
- When deductions are greater than income, resulting losses cannot be used to shelter your salary, wages, interest, and dividend income or profits made in the stock market. The partnership losses can only be used to shelter income from other passive activities.

- If you do not have passive income (i.e., interest in a partnership or S corporation where you do not actively participate in the business), you can carry these losses forward and use them when the equipment-leasing deal has excess income.
- If the partnership is publicly traded, income and loss require special treatment, check with your accountant.

GINNIE MAE, FREDDIE MAC, AND FANNIE MAE CERTIFICATES

- The interest portion of the monthly payments you receive is subject to federal, state, and local taxes.
- Profits from the sale of any mortgage-backed security are taxed as well.

GOLD AND SILVER

- If you buy gold or silver coins or bullion, most states impose state and local sales tax. In many cases you can sidestep this tax if you do not take delivery but leave the metal with the dealer and buy certificates instead (see Chapter 22).
- Profits from the sale of gold and silver are taxed at regular rates, generally as capital gains, but this is under review.
- Dividends from precious metals stocks and mutual funds are taxed at regular rates, in the same manner as other dividends.
- Profits from futures and options: see "Commodities."

IRAS AND KEOGHS

See Chapter 26.

LAND

- Any profits made when land is sold are taxable.
- Rental income is subject to regular income tax, although it may be partially offset by deductible expenses, property costs, and mortgage interest payments.
- Land does not qualify for depreciation deductions.

- Check with your accountant regarding the status of income-producing land vis-à-vis the new passive loss rules. As we go to press, the IRS has issued proposed regulations.

LIFE INSURANCE

- When you purchase whole life insurance, part of your premium goes toward the purchase of insurance; the rest is an investment. The earned income on the investment portion builds up tax-deferred until you cash in the policy. If you die before you cash in, and the benefits are paid to your children or spouse, this buildup becomes completely income tax–free, not just tax-deferred.
- ☐ CAUTION: Single-premium annuities or life insurance policies, where you pay only one premium, no longer qualify for this tax-deferred treatment.
- If you purchase a single-premium contract after June 30, 1988, and you borrow from the contract, the loan is treated as a distribution of income on which you must pay regular income tax and, in most cases, a 10% penalty on the taxable portion. (There's no 10% penalty if distributions are made after you reach 59½ or if you are disabled or if the distribution is part of a life annuity.) The same rules apply to a partial surrender of the contract, a cash withdrawal, or the distribution of dividends that are not retained by the insurance company as a premium if received on or after the annuity starting date. If received before the annuity starting date, special rules apply. Check with your accountant.
- These rules generally apply also to any life insurance plans ("modified endowment contract") that you fund with fewer than seven annual payments of equal size.
- You must also pay income tax on distributions from single-premium contracts purchased on or after June 21, 1988, to the extent that the distributions exceed your contract investment. Distributions of less than $25,000 made after your death to cover your burial are not taxed.

MONEY MARKET DEPOSIT ACCOUNTS

- Interest earned is subject to federal, state, and local income taxes.

MONEY MARKET MUTUAL FUNDS

- Interest is subject to federal, state, and local taxes.
- With tax-exempt money market funds, interest is exempt from federal tax and possibly from state and local tax if the fund buys securities in the investor's state.

MUTUAL FUNDS

- Dividend income and capital gains distributions are usually taxed at federal, state, and local levels, except for tax-free or municipal bond funds.
- Income from municipal bond funds is exempt from federal tax and is also exempt from state and local taxes if the securities in the portfolio are issued in the taxpayer's state.
- Mutual fund companies must send investors a year-end statement documenting all distributions and their tax status (Form 1099 and/or Form 1099-B).
- When you sell your fund shares at a profit, this gain is taxed at the applicable income rate of either 15%, 28%, or 33%.
- Losses can be used to offset gains and up to $3,000 in salary, wages, and ordinary income.
- You must also pay taxes on your share of the fund's investment advisory fees. (Prior to tax reform, this was merely deducted from earnings.) The amount is indicated on Form 1099. You may be able to claim a deduction for this as an investment expense—provided that you itemize and your investment expenses and other miscellaneous itemized expenses exceed 2% of your adjusted gross income. Check with

your accountant. The rules regarding these deductions have changed several times.

OIL AND GAS PARTNER- SHIPS

- In year 1 of a drilling program, investors may receive a write-off for 60% to 90% of their investment. This deduction is derived from "intangible drilling costs"—labor, fuel, chemicals, nonsalvageable items.
- If oil is found, deductions are also derived from capital expenditures for materials and equipment (pumps, tanks, etc.). These deductions must be written off over the lifetime of the assets.
- When oil is found, income earned from the partnership is subject to regular tax rates. However "depletion" deductions may shelter 15% of the gross income of the property, subject to certain limitations.
- In an oil and gas limited partnership, you cannot use losses or write-offs in excess of income to shelter your salary or portfolio income. You can, however, use write-offs against income from this or another tax-sheltered partnership. You can also carry the write-offs forward to a year when the partnership has excess income.
- However, when the partnership interest is ended or when you dispose of your investment, any tax losses can be used to offset other income.
- *Exception:* investors with "working interests" in oil and gas partnerships (as opposed to a limited partnership investment) can use tax losses to shelter wages, salary, and ordinary income. The risk, of course, is that your entire net worth is exposed. In a limited partnership, your risk is limited to the amount you invest.
- Deductions for intangible drilling costs and depletion are preference items and used in calculating the AMT. Check with your accountant.

OPTIONS

- Profits are taxed at regular rates.
- If your option expires and is therefore worthless, this loss can be used to offset

gains and up to $3,000 of salary, wages, and ordinary income.

- If you do not exercise your option, the premium income you receive is taxed.
- If you do exercise the option, the premium is added on to the sales proceeds of the stock. It is then taxed, based on the sale of the stock.

PREFERRED STOCKS

See "Stocks."

PUBLIC LIMITED PARTNER-SHIPS

- If a limited partnership trades publicly, income earned is not passive but is considered portfolio income and current losses cannot be used to offset income from other public partnerships.
- Most funds make their largest distributions at the end of the year; call the 800 number to verify. Avoid buying fund shares just before major distributions. The fund's NAV or share price immediately drops by the amount of the distribution. By waiting for a fund to go ex-dividend, you can buy in at a lower share price and avoid paying tax. Consult IRS publication 564, "Mutual Fund Distributions."

REAL ESTATE

- Until tax reform the absolute deductibility of mortgage interest was viewed as an inalienable benefit of home ownership. But the 1986 Act and rules passed since then have changed all that. There are now two kinds of mortgage debt: acquisition indebtedness and home equity indebtedness.
- *Acquisition debt.* This is money used to purchase or substantially improve a residence. You may deduct all mortgage interest costs on up to a total of $1 million in acquisition debt for primary and secondary residences purchased or refinanced after October 13, 1987.
- *Home equity debt.* This is money you borrow using your home as collateral. You

may claim interest costs on home equity loans up to the lesser of (1) $100,000 or (2) the difference between the fair market value of your residence and the total acquisition indebtedness. The proceeds of this debt can be used for any purpose.

- *The $125,000 capital gains exclusion.* This has been expanded, so that if you are age 55 or older and you sold your home after September 30, 1988, you may be able to exclude up to $125,000 of the capital gain from your income even if you did not use the house as a principal residence for 3 of the 5 previous years. New rules offer an exception for a homeowner who, because of physical or mental handicaps, lived in residential care facilities, provided he or she lived in the principal residence for 1 of the 5 years before it was sold.

REAL ESTATE INVESTMENT TRUSTS (REITs)

- Although REITs generally do not pay taxes themselves, you as an investor do. Most dividends are taxable, even those that represent capital gains distributions from the sale of property.
- There is an exception: dividends paid out of the shareholders' equity and treated as a return of your original investment are not taxed.
- When you sell your REIT stock, any gains realized are taxed at regular rates, but this is under review.
- Losses from a REIT stock can be used to offset gains, plus up to $3,000 of salary, wages, and ordinary income.

REAL ESTATE LIMITED PARTNER-SHIPS (RELPs)

- Partnerships generate deductions based on depreciation, operating expenses, and interest, but they can be used by investors only to shelter income from this partnership or from another passive activity, not ordinary income.
- Excess deductions cannot be used to offset taxes you owe on your salary, wages,

interest and dividend income, or stock market profits.

- Income from a partnership that is greater than the deductions allowed is taxed at regular rates.
- Profits made from the sale of property are taxed at regular rates.
- Low-income housing and historic rehabilitation partnerships are exceptions to the rules. If your adjusted gross income is $200,000 or less, you can use the special tax credits offered by two types of deals to offset tax of up to $25,000 of other income. The $25,000 amount is reduced for those with higher incomes; if your income is $250,000 or above, the credit is phased out entirely.

RENTAL REAL ESTATE

- Rental income and profits when property is sold are taxed at regular rates.
- Much rental income can be sheltered by deductions and expenses, such as mortgage interest, property taxes, depreciation, maintenance, repairs, and travel to and from the property. You can write off the cost of residential properties over a period of 27½ years, or 31½ years for commercial property.
- Up to $25,000 per year in tax losses can be used to offset your wages, salary, and other income, provided that your adjusted gross income is under $100,000. This $25,000 cap is reduced 50¢ for each dollar by which your adjusted gross income exceeds $100,000. By the time your income hits $150,000, the cap is at zero. You must, however, pass the material participation test to receive this benefit.
- If your adjusted gross income is over $150,000, you can use tax deductions only up to the amount of rental income received that year. If there are any excess losses, they can be carried over until such time as you have excess income. These losses, however, can be used to offset income from other passive activities.
- If you meet the $150,000 maximum guideline, you must also actively participate in managing the property in order to take the write-offs. You must

make the management decisions, although you need not physically do the work.
- To claim losses, you cannot have less than a 10% ownership in rental property.

SAVINGS BONDS

- Interest is exempt from state and local taxes.
- Federal income tax can be deferred on Series EE bonds until the bond is redeemed or matures.
- If you roll over your Series EEs into Series HHs, federal tax on the accrued interest can again be deferred until the HH bonds either mature or are redeemed.
- Interest earned on Series HH bonds is taxed each year.
- If you elect to pay the federal tax due each year on Series EE bonds, you pay on the annual increase in redemption value of the bond. However, once you begin paying, you must continue doing so for the bonds you presently own plus any new ones you buy.
- *Children's accounts.* If a child is under age 14 the first $500 of investment income is not taxed. The next $500 is taxed at the child's rate. Any investment income over $1,000 per year is taxed at the parent's tax rate, which is presumably higher. Starting at age 14, the income is taxed at the child's lower rate. By timing bonds to come due after the child turns 14, you can save on taxes.
- EE savings bonds purchased after January 1, 1990, by a bondholder at least twenty-four years old, and used to pay college tuition for yourself, your spouse, or dependent children, are free from federal income tax provided you fall within newly established income guidelines. Since the guidelines are inflation-indexed, check with your tax adviser to see if you can take advantage of this tax break.

STOCK INDEX OPTIONS AND FUTURES

- Profits are generally taxed at regular rates.
- Profits on futures and options become taxable at the end of the year, even if you

have not closed out your position. In effect, the IRS will tax you on paper profits.

■ In some cases you can deduct paper losses, even of positions still open. Check with your accountant.

STOCK RIGHTS

■ If you sell your rights, the profit is taxed.

■ If you exercise the rights, you will eventually pay tax, but not until you sell the new stock.

■ If you receive stock rights (as opposed to purchasing them in the market) and then let them expire, you cannot claim a deduction for the loss.

■ If you purchase rights in the market and let them expire as worthless, you can deduct the loss.

STOCKS

■ Profits from the sale of stocks and dividends earned are taxed at regular rates, but this is under review.

■ Losses from sales may be used to offset any gains you have plus up to $3,000 of salary, wages, and other ordinary income.

■ Interest on margin loans may be claimed as an itemized deduction. Check with your accountant.

STOCKS (FOREIGN)

■ If you have foreign tax withheld from dividends of a foreign stock, you are entitled to a credit. To determine how much, divide your taxable foreign income by your total income, then multiply by the amount of U.S. tax. *Example:* You receive taxable foreign income of $5,000 and your total taxable income is $100,000. Divide $5,000 by $100,000 and multiply that by $28,000 (the estimated U.S. tax on $100,000). The maximum tax credit you could claim would by $1,400. Your credit would be the lesser of the amount withheld and the maximum credit calculated.

$HINT: You can also list foreign taxes as an itemized deduction on line 7 of Schedule A. But you must choose one method or the other.

TREASURY BILLS

■ Interest income is subject to federal tax but not state and local taxes.

■ The income earned is subject to taxation the year in which it matures or in which you sell it.

■ With T-bills, the dollar difference between the original price and the amount you receive when you redeem the bill is regarded as the interest income.

■ You can defer income from one year to the next by purchasing a T-bill that matures in the new calendar year.

TREASURY BONDS

■ Interest is subject to federal tax but free from state and local tax.

■ Losses from sales can be used to offset any capital gains you have plus up to $3,000 of salary, wages, and other ordinary income.

TREASURY NOTES

■ Interest income is subject to federal income tax but exempt from state and local tax.

■ Any profit made when T-notes are sold is taxed.

■ Any losses from sales can be used to offset any gains you have plus up to $3,000 of salary, wages, and ordinary income.

VACATION HOMES

■ *If a home is solely for personal use,* you can deduct mortgage interest and real estate taxes, as you can with your principal residence. Mortgage interest is not 100% deductible on third or fourth homes.

■ You can deduct mortgage interest on loans up to the amount of your original purchase price plus improvements. Special rules apply to refinancing.

■ *If a home is used for pleasure and rental,* your tax liability varies, depending on how long you rent it out and how long you use it. If you rent it out for no more than 14 days per year, there is no tax on the rental income. You do not even have to report it.

- If you use your home more than 14 days a year or 10% of the number of days rented, whichever is greater, your property qualifies as a second home. Mortgage interest and property taxes become deductible. Rental expenses can be deducted, but only up to the amount of rental income. If you have excess expenses, they can be carried forward.
- If your personal use of your house is 14 days or less a year or 10% of the number of days the house is rented out, whichever is greater, the house is a rental property (see "Rental Real Estate"). Remember, you cannot deduct more than the rental income received, nor can you deduct mortgage interest in excess of rental income, because that is allowed only if the home falls under the second home category. (This is a simplification of a fairly complicated rule. Consult an accountant.)
- When you sell a vacation home, profits are taxed at regular rates. But they do not qualify for the preferential treatment that your primary residence does. With a primary residence, taxes on the profits of a sale can be deferred as long as the profits are reinvested in a principal residence that costs at least as much as the sale price of the previous home. The special one-time $125,000 exemption of gains from the sale of a primary residence available to those age 55 or older is not extended to the sale of vacation homes. Losses from sales of vacation homes are not deductible.

WARRANTS

- Profits made when warrants are sold are taxed at regular rates.
- If your warrant expires worthless, the cost of the warrant can be used to offset capital gains plus up to $3,000 of salary, wages, and other ordinary income.
- If the warrant is converted to stock shares, no taxes are due on the transaction.

34 | TAX SHELTERS AND LIMITED PARTNERSHIPS

The simplest and usually the best tax shelter for most people is tax-exempt bonds, as explained in Chapter 10. These are *investments* whose interest is free of federal and often state taxes. But most other tax shelters are complex. They rely on tax laws to provide deductions or deferrals of income and realized appreciation. *Before you make any investment in a tax shelter, consult your tax adviser.*

Tax shelters initially were approved by Congress to encourage investment in areas that otherwise might not attract sufficient capital. With real estate, the deductions for interest, taxes, and depreciation made it possible to encourage building and owning apartment houses, office buildings, and other structures. These benefits proved to be so attractive that Congress has sharply slimmed down the tax advantages. Due to tax reform, the emphasis has shifted now to limited partnerships that generate income and defer some payment of taxes.

THE 1986 TAX REFORM ACT

The toughest provision in the tax reform law centered around tax shelters. Although shelters are not totally extinct, the deals that were set up primarily to generate large paper losses are a thing of the past. The new rulings put a crimp in using paper losses generated by shelters to reduce tax liability. Losses from most so-called passive investments—ones in which the taxpayer does not "materially" participate—can no longer be used to offset income from salary, dividends, capital gains, royalties, or interest. In other words, passive losses can be used only to offset income from other passive investments—most often, limited partnerships. Unusable passive losses, however, are not totally without merit: they can be carried forward to

offset passive income in the future or be deducted when the investment is finally sold.

Tax-sheltered investments and limited partnerships you already own get a break, since the new rulings are being phased in. In 1990, 10% of your losses from passive activities are allowed against other income.

The following shelters escaped total reform.

LIMITED PARTNERSHIPS

The most common tax shelter is built around a limited partnership. This involves a *general partner* who has expertise in the operations of the business and *limited partners* who are investors seeking specific profit opportunities and tax benefits.

The general partner assumes management responsibilities and makes all decisions. The general partner is usually a knowledgeable individual who puts up some money, receives a sizable share of the profits, is assured of income while the project operates, and accepts liability for losses in excess of partnership capital.

Private offerings, involving about 35 partners, start with an investment of $25,000 or often much more. Public offerings, with a larger number of participants, must file a prospectus with the SEC and meet certain financial standards established to protect the public. Many states set minimum requirements for investors in public offerings in order to prevent those who are unable to sustain the possible loss involved from participating. Increasingly, investors are getting greater protection. Members of the National Association of Security Dealers (NASD) must exercise "due diligence": discovering whether the general partner is competent and honest, comparing the proposal with similar deals, evaluating the likelihood of the proposed tax benefits, and determining the fairness of the proposed method of sharing profits and expenses.

In all tax shelters, be extremely wary, use common sense, and get your accountant's opinion.

SECONDARY MARKET FOR LIMITED PARTNER- SHIPS

Unlike stocks, bonds, and mutual funds, limited partnership are not as easy to get out of. However, a fledgling secondary market is growing, consisting of small investment firms that buy partnerships from investors for resale or for their own accounts. (The lifetime of a partnership is long—10 years and more.)

The industry "green sheet," published by the National Partnership Exchange of Tampa, Fla., lists partnerships for sale, including prices. The price in the secondary market is influenced by the value of the assets, economic conditions of the region, financial status of the general partner, and eagerness of the seller to sell.

☐ CAUTION: Prices for used partnerships vary widely, making it important to investigate carefully before buying or selling.

Although research about secondary partnerships is still scanty, it is increasing: Standard & Poor's new department now rates them.

💲 HINT: Even if you pay the full asset value for a used partnership, you avoid the 20%+ in commissions and fees charged by new offerings. Commissions in the secondary market range from about 8% to 12%.

FIRMS SELLING USED LIMITED PARTNERSHIPS

Chicago Partnership Board Inc.	1-800-272-6273
Equity Line Properties Inc.	1-800-327-9990 (1-305-662-4088 in Fla.)
Equity Resources Group	1-617-876-4800
Florida Income Centers	1-407-740-8141
Investors Advantage Corp.	1-800-331-9199 (1-800-282-5865 in Fla.)
Liquidity Fund Investment Corp.	1-800-227-4688
MacKenzie Securities	1-800-854-8357 (1-800-821-4252 in Calif.)
National Partnership Exchange Inc.	1-800-356-2739 (1-800-336-2739 in Fla.)
Nationwide Partnership Marketplace	1-415-456-8825
Oppenheimer & Bigelow Management Inc.	1-800-431-7811 (1-212-599-0697 in N.Y.)
Partnership Securities Exchange Inc.	1-415-763-5555
Raymond James & Associates Inc.	1-800-237-7591
Realty Repurchase Inc.	1-800-233-7357 (1-800-444-7357 in Calif.)
Springhill Financial Services Inc.	1-800-255-3264 (1-818-507-0975 in Calif.)

OIL AND GAS PROGRAMS

Senators and various interested groups from the big oil states lobbied hard in 1986 and were able to get a special exemption for "working interest" investments in oil and gas drilling. Investors here are still able to use their losses to shelter ordinary earned or investment income even if they are not active participants in these oil and gas operations. However, the tax break does not apply to limited partnerships. You must hold a working interest in a joint venture or in a general partnership to deduct losses. In other words, your liability is unlimited, which means that your total net worth is fully available to the business's creditors. Should there be an uninsured casualty or a liability, your assets could be attached.

➤ OIL AND GAS DRILLING Investors can probably write off 80% of their total investment on personal tax returns in the first year. Income in later years from successful wells may be partially offset by depletion and depreciation. Stay away from programs that spin off no income until the wells come in. If the well turns out to be dry, you'll never see a dollar.

➤ OIL AND GAS INCOME PROGRAMS Although taxes must be paid when the program ends, it is possible for investors to earn income annually equal to 8% to 10% of their investment. Most specialists regard income programs as safer than oil and gas drilling, where one merely hopes to see oil.

PUBLICLY TRADED PARTNERSHIPS (PTPs)

Some PTPs, which are set up instead of a corporation to run a business, are taxed as a partnership and are thus able to sidestep the high corporate tax rate. These include oil, gas, and real estate partnerships. In theory this means that a PTP has more cash to distribute to investors, the limited partners. In addition, various non-cash deductions, such as startup costs, depreciation, depletion, and accrued interest, are passed through to investors.

For example, a $5,000 investor may receive a $500 (10%) cash distribution, but the taxable income may be only $250 because of the legitimate pass-through deductions.

PTPs trade on the major exchanges or OTC and therefore offer far greater liquidity than straight tax shelters. However, they are also extremely volatile: any news about possible tighter tax regulations sends their prices into the basement. And most took a big beating in the October crash. The Boston Celtics, for instance, issued at $18.50, was trading around $11.00 by the end of 1987; as of May 1989 it was at $13.50. Burger King Investors fell to $13.25 from $20.00, but by the spring of 1989 it had moved up to $14.00.

$ HINT: PTPs that are active businesses and subject to corporate income tax have 10-year "grandfather" protection—if they were established before mid-December 1987, they do not pay corporate taxes until 1998.

Remember that taxes in any PTPs are merely deferred. When you sell your shares, you will owe the deferred taxes plus taxes on any profits you make. Nor is cash flow guaranteed or fixed.

➤ OIL AND GAS PTPs Oil and gas PTPs, which became popular in the early 1980s, unlike regular limited partnerships, trade on the New York and American exchanges as well as OTC.

Because they are partnerships, not corporations, they offer some tax benefits, primarily that some of their cash distributions are tax-sheltered.

OIL AND GAS PTPs

	EXCHANGE	PRICE	YIELD
Mesa Limited Partnership (A)	NYSE	$11	13.5%
Mesa Limited Partnership (common)	NYSE	10¾	18.8
Sun Energy Partners	NYSE	12⅞	7.2
Kelley Oil & Gas Partners	ASE	14⅞	8.1
Union Exploration Partners	NYSE	15⅝	16.0
Enserch Exploration	NYSE	11⅜	2.6
Dorchester Hugoton	OTC	16⅞	2.4
Snyder Oil Partners	NYSE	3⅞	16.2

SOURCE: Silberberg Rosenthal & Co., May 13, 1989.

□ CAUTION: Although these PTPs offer income, a degree of tax shelter, and potential price appreciation, they are risky. There is no guarantee that the price of oil will rise or won't drop.

➤ SELECTING PTPs   Although yields are high on most PTPs, the investment group as a whole continues to face some serious drawbacks, which you should be aware of before adding these stocks to your portfolio.

- *Little information.* Wall Street analysts do not routinely follow PTPs.
- *Cash flow problems.* Find out if the operating cash flow will cover current distributions to investors. Daniel Lee of Drexel Burnham Lambert, Inc., fears that a number of deals will have to slash distributions if the economy slows down.
- *Debatable guarantees.* Sweeteners may disguise overvalued offerings and/or expire before the deal is completed.
- *Limited liquidity.* PTPs do not trade like IBM or Xerox. Many, says Lee, "trade by appointment."

□ CAUTION: Avoid "roll-up" PTPs, in which the old-fashioned, nontraded, limited partnership tax shelters are lumped together. These often hide problems and uncertainties.

GOLD MINES

Several gold mining companies that trade OTC offer investors direct interest in the gold produced. Earnings can be paid in bullion, coins, or gold certificates, all of which the IRS deems a "return of capital assets" and thus not taxable. However, when you convert them into cash, you must pay taxes.

CATTLE

You can buy cattle on December 31 and at the same time prepay the cost of keeping the animals for the next year. You can then deduct half of these prepaid costs in

---

HOW TO READ A PROSPECTUS FAST

By law, every major tax shelter or limited partnership must submit a prospectus to shareholders. The prospectus may appear to be formidable and dull, but it will pay you to spend a few minutes reviewing the facts, figures, and statements. For those who are in a hurry:

- Read the opening summary word for word.
- Check the accounting projections and footnotes.
- Check the use of proceeds: how much will go for fees; how much will go to work for your interests?
- Check the compensation to the general partner.
- Review line by line the track record of the sponsors, participants, and employees.
- Read, with help from your tax adviser, the discussion of tax consequences. This can be tough going, but never invest in anything that you do not fully understand.
- *Do business only with reputable, established firms* that exercise "due diligence" when reviewing the general partner's financial statement, track record, experience, and technical expertise as well as the fairness of the deal itself. To double-check, get information from special services such as:

The Stanger Report, 1129 Broad Street, Shrewsbury, NJ 07702-4314

The Partnership Record, Southport Advisors, Inc., 1300 Post Road, Fairfield, CT 06430

HIGH-YIELDING PARTNERSHIPS

MLP	AREA	YIELD
Kelley Oil & Gas Partners	oil & gas	7.7%
Mesa Limited Partnership	oil & gas	13.6
Allstar Inns	hotels	18.8
Motel 6	hotels	8.9
Red Lion Inns	hotels	11.5
Burger King Investors	restaurants	11.9
Furrs'/Bishop Cafeterias	restaurants	17.8
Perkins Family Restaurants	restaurants	10.5
USA Cafes	restaurants	11.1

Yields are as of July 6, 1989.

the first year, provided certain conditions are met. (Check with your accountant first regarding the status of this shelter, as it is expected to change.)

EQUIPMENT LEASING

The main appeal of equipment leasing income funds is their cash flow. For many, the first-year distributions are 10% to 12%. Structured as limited partnerships, these funds are sold by brokers and financial planners, with the minimum investment usually $2,500 or $5,000. Your pooled money goes to buy computers, planes, trucks, railroad cars, etc., and the limited partnership then leases these to a user or lessee, generally a large corporation.

$ HINT: Reduce your potential risk by investing only in deals where solid corporations, such as General Electric, sign noncancelable leases. This type of lease protects your cash flow.

At the end of 5 to 10 years, leases generally expire, the partnership sells its equipment, and proceeds are distributed to the limited partners and the sponsor.

☐ CAUTION: Unlike real estate, equipment generally does not increase in value; in fact, it depreciates. Look for deals in which a portion of the cash flow is reinvested in new equipment.

AIRLINE LEASING

These limited partnerships, available for $2,500 and $5,000 minimums, offer high cash flow, provided they are well run. The partnership purchases used jetliners for cash to avoid the risk of extensive leveraging. The planes are then leased to airlines for 3 to 6 years. The lease payments are passed on to the investors, who typically receive 10% to 12%. Because the aircraft can be depreciated, that income is reduced during the first 3 to 4 years. Distributions thereafter will be partially taxed, but as passive income, which means it can be used to offset any passive activity loss. When the lease expires, the planes can be re-leased or sold. Often the planes retain their value, although there is no guarantee that they will.

Among the sponsors are Integrated Resources, Polaris Aircraft Leasing, and Equitec Financial.

TAX BREAK

All rental income is now subject to passive activity loss limitation rules, whether or not the taxpayer participates in managing the property.

There is one small break, however: under a special exemption, as much as $25,000 of losses from rental real estate can be used annually by those who actively participate in the rental activity *and* whose adjusted gross income is less than $100,000. For every dollar that your adjusted gross income is over $100,000, this $25,000 loss allowance is reduced by 50¢. So if you have $150,000 of income, you cannot claim a rental loss against your other income unless it's against passive income. For example, if your income is $125,000, you can take up to $12,500 in losses on rental real estate.

☐ CAUTION: Have your accountant review the prospectus carefully before investing. Possible FAA rulings on plane age limits could hurt these partnerships. In addition this high-risk investment area continually faces problems, as in the recent filing for Chapter 11 protection by Integrated Resources.

LOW-INCOME HOUSING

Under the new law, tax credits are available to those who buy, build, or rehabilitate low-income housing. The credits, which are based on a percentage of costs, excluding the cost of the land, could work out to be equal to 90% of your investment over 10 years. The credits can offset regular income tax, subject to certain limits, but are phased out if your adjusted gross income is over $200,000. If your income exceeds $250,000, there are no credits.

For newly constructed properties not federally subsidized, the annual credit is 9%. For acquisition of existing buildings and/or where federal subsidies are used, it is 4%.

☐ CAUTION: This is a high-risk investment and should be examined carefully by an accountant. Avoid projects of inexperienced developers.

$ HINT: Low-income and rehab participation also entitles you to a $25,000 exemption (see box). This benefit is phased out for those with adjusted gross incomes between $100,000 and $150,000. It's available whether or not you actively participate.

These new rules have hurt the real estate industry, which traditionally financed development via limited partnerships that provided tax losses to those who invested during the first years of a project. But the new rules affect others as well—no one who invests in a business without participating in its operations "on a regular, continuous, and substantial basis" can take losses to offset other income. (See also Chapter 32 on real estate.)

HISTORIC REHABIL- ITATION

One of the few tax shelters left after the 1986 Act promotes the concept of preservation—the Historic Rehabilitation Tax Credit. It was originally enacted by Congress back in the late 1970s to encourage investments in the nation's neglected older buildings. In 1981 Congress raised the credit to 25% from 10% and then in 1986 dropped it back to 20% or 10%, depending on the building (10% for nonresidential buildings put into service prior to 1936 and 20% for all certified historic structures).

$ HINT: A tax credit is not a deduction: it provides a dollar-for-dollar reduction in the actual amount of income tax you owe.

The tax credit is only applicable to depreciable buildings—those used in a trade or business or held for the production of income, such as a commercial or residential rental property. A nondepreciable building may qualify as a certified historic structure *if* it is the subject of charitable contributions for conservation purposes.

Individual investors can participate most easily by buying units in a qualified limited partnership. They are especially suitable for those who earn less than $200,000 annually.

An important outcome of the new rulings is that partnership units are priced lower. Syndicators have been forced, in fact, to reduce their units from $100,000 (before 1986 tax reform) to $5,000 or $10,000. The lower per-unit cost enables investors to stay below the

---

> ## CERTIFIED HISTORIC STRUCTURES
>
> - A *certified historic structure* is any structure that is listed individually in the National Register of Historic Places, maintained by the Department of the Interior, *or* located in a registered historic district and certified by the Secretary of the Interior.
> - A *registered historic district* is any district that is listed in the National Register of Historic Places *or* designated under a state or local statute that has been certified by the Secretary of the Interior as "containing criteria which will substantially achieve the purpose of preserving and rehabilitating buildings of significance to the district."

$25,000 passive loss limitation. Syndicators typically project that within 4 to 10 years, substantial cash flow from rental income will be passed on to investors, in addition to the tax credit.

There are some potential pitfalls:

- In most cases you must hold your units for a minimum of 5 years to get full tax benefits.
- Very few partnerships are old enough to have posted a track record.
- The maximum credit is limited to the amount of tax you would pay on $25,000 of income. For instance, if you're in the 28% tax bracket, your maximum credit would be $7,000 (28% of $25,000).

> ## LEADING SYNDICATORS OF HISTORIC PROPERTY
>
> Dover Historic Properties, Philadelphia (1-800-468-4017)
> Greater Boston Development, Inc., Boston (1-617-439-0072)
> The Lockwood Group, St. Louis (1-314-968-2205)

- Inexperienced developers can run into a bevy of problems. If they don't adhere closely to the National Park Service guidelines, they will be denied the tax credit.

In selecting a partnership:

- Check the developer's past projects.
- Select a syndicator or developer who knows the historic rehab field.
- Check out the location.
- Find out what the projected rents are.
- Front-end fees should not exceed 15%.

- Choose a partnership with a 10% annual return.

FOR ADDITIONAL INFORMATION

Department of the Interior
Parks Service
P.O. Box 37127
Washington, DC 20013-7127
1-202-343-1100; 1-202-343-9623 (recording)

The following sample portfolios contain investment ideas that are geared toward the various stages of your life. Many of them, particularly the stocks, should be held at least a year or more. The portfolios are divided into five life-style categories: investors who are just out of school, those who are newly married, those having a family, the empty nesters, and finally, those approaching or in retirement. Even though all the suggestions are above average in quality, market conditions and interest rates shift rapidly, so actively monitor your portfolio year-round.

Discuss your stock and bond selections with a reliable pro. And try to buy when securities are undervalued and have bright prospects and when you can get full price and a profit. If you make a mistake, sell quickly so you'll minimize your losses.

Don't be foolish and listen to siren calls of hope; *do* be wise and base your decisions on the facts.

IF YOU'RE JUST OUT OF SCHOOL

This is a time for new beginnings—you're on your own, perhaps for the first time in your life, and although your income is modest, it's likely to increase quite quickly. Your responsibilities are limited—perhaps only to you and your cat—so you can focus your financial attention on building up a solid cash base. Follow these 9 steps to achieve financial independence:

Step 1. Set goals (see suggestions in the box).

Step 2. Open a bank account. If you're new in the area, try the same institution your company uses.

Step 3. Get a credit card and pay all bills on time to establish a good credit rating.

Step 4. Open a money market mutual fund. A list of high-yielding funds appears on page 31.

Step 5. Sign up for the automatic payroll savings plan where you work and have 3% to 5% of your paycheck transferred into your money market fund.

Step 6. After you've accumulated three months' worth of living expenses you're ready to invest. (Try to keep housing costs to 30% or less of take-home pay.) Begin by purchasing several short-term CDs with different maturities, either at a local bank for convenience or with an out-of-the-area bank that has higher rates. Check *Barron's* (a weekly) or Friday's *Wall Street Journal* for a list of the nation's top-yielding CDs.

Step 7. Purchase 100 shares of stock in the company you work for, if you have faith in its future, using the company's stock purchase plan, if one exists. You'll avoid a broker's commission and you may be able to buy shares at a discount.

Alternative: Buy 100 shares of a company whose product you use or like, or one that is within the industry where you work. *Suggestions:* IBM, Compacq Computer, Reebok, Nike, Liz Claiborne, and L. A. Gear. Use this as a learning experience, as your introduction to the stock market.

Step 8. Study the financial condition of your local electric or gas utility company. Read the annual report and check the rating in *Value Line.* If the utility is rated #1 or #2 in safety, add 100 shares to your portfolio. If your particular utility is not a smart investment, select one of those listed in Chapter 14 on utilities.

Step 9. After a year or two you can afford to take greater risks with your money. Consider the sample portfolios that follow and incorporate those choices that you find appealing, keeping in mind that it is essential to diversify—between

PORTFOLIO FOR THE RECENT GRAD

INVESTMENT	AMOUNT	DETAILS
Money market account	3-months' living expenses	Add cash gifts, bonuses, freelance income
Cetificates of deposit	Due in 3, 6, and 12 months	Roll over if rates go up
Company you work for	100 shares	Use employee stock purchase plan
or		
IBM, Compacq Computer, Reebok, Nike, Liz Claiborne, L.A. Gear	100 shares	Monitor carefully
Electric utility	100 shares	Reinvest dividends
IRA	$2,000	Stock or CD

types of investments as well as types of industries.

IF YOU'RE NEWLY MARRIED OR LIVING WITH A SIGNIFICANT OTHER

Now that you've added someone else to your life, review and revise your financial goals. Draw up a new set of your own as well as some joint goals. Just because you are part of a team doesn't mean that all your goals must match. Some can be his or hers, and some should be united. Decide whether to invest jointly or separately or do a little of both, keeping in mind that your dual incomes give you doubled investing and saving power.

Step 1. Review the portfolio for the recent grad. All suggestions there should be part of your financial life, too.

Step 2. Focus on the housing issue. You've probably been renting, but now together, by putting aside 3% to 5% of both your salaries, you can save a sizable amount for a down payment on a house or co-op. Begin by purchas-

---

GOALS FOR THE RECENT GRAD

- Pay off college loans
- Build up nest egg
- Buy a car
- Save for a vacation

---

ing Treasury notes with two- to four-year maturities. Put the semiannual monthly interest payments in your money fund. This cash plus your CDs can be combined with your Treasuries when the latter come due.

Alternative: Treasury zeros require less cash to purchase. For example, those with a 7.9% coupon due May 1994 are priced at just 68¾. You'll receive $1,000 per note in 1994 (but no interim interest payments).

Step 3. Because you have a lot of time to build assets, securities should be primarily for growth, not income, at this point in your life. Check the list of suggested stocks in the box. Regard them as long-term holdings, yet monitor earnings trends regularly and be prepared to sell.

Step 4. If you are in the 28% tax bracket, put 10% to 15% of your investments in municipal bonds or a unit investment trust.

Step 5. If you and your spouse spend weekends going to flea markets, auctions, or garage sales, consider becoming a knowledgeable collector. Every year the "Investor's Almanac" section of this book contains ideas for building a savvy collection. Check your library for previous editions.

➤ MEAD CORP. (MEA) This diversified paper and forest products company reports steadily increasing business from schools, corporations, and retail sellers. Rising earnings are expected to offset purchase price of Michi, the electronic publisher, made in early 1989. A long-term holding.

➤ SYSCO CORP. (SYY) This company distributes food to restaurants, hospitals, hotel/motel chains, and educational institutions. A leader in its field,

PORTFOLIO FOR THE NEWLY COUPLED

INVESTMENT	AMOUNT	DETAILS
Company you work for	100 shares	Use employee purchase plan, when available
Electric utility company	100 shares	Reinvest dividends
U.S. Treasury notes or zeros	$5,000 minimum	Hold until maturity
Municipal bonds or UIT	$1,000 minimum	Hold until maturity
Neuberger & Berman Partners Fund	$1,000 minimum	Call 1-800-367-0770
or		
Mead Corp.	100 shares	Price: $39
		Yield: 2.2%
Sysco Corp.	100 shares	Price: $47
		Yield: 0.8%
Montgomery Street Income Securities, Inc.	200 shares	Price: $19½
		Yield: 9.6%
Community Psychiatric	100 shares	Price: $32½
		Yield: 0.5%
Disney (Walt)	100 shares	Price: $97½
		Yield: 0.5%

Prices are as of July 7, 1989.

Sysco is also in a recession-resistant industry and expected to weather any economic downturn.

➤ MONTGOMERY STREET INCOME SECURITIES, INC. (MTS) A closed-end diversified investment company with 70% of assets in high-quality debt instruments. These shares, with their impressive 9.6% yield, are suitable for the most conservative investors, regardless of age.

➤ COMMUNITY PSYCHIATRIC (CMY) This company owns 40 psychiatric hospitals and 67 kidney dialysis centers. Overlooked by the investment world for a number of years, its shares are just beginning to be noticed by the institutions. Hold for near-term price appreciation.

➤ DISNEY (WALT) (DIS) This newly revamped corporation makes movies, videotapes, and records and also owns and operates the Disney theme parks. Successful 1989 films, such as *Dead Poets Society* starring Robin Williams, are giving Disney a place in the movie world once again. Attendance is up at the entertainment parks, where the occupancy rate for the 4,500+ rooms is nearly 100%.

IF YOU HAVE A FAMILY

Nothing is ever quite as exciting or expensive as raising a family. Depending upon where you live and how extravagant you are, raising a child from birth to 18 can set you back anywhere from $47,412 to $112,017, according to the 1988 estimates by the U.S. Department of Agriculture. Then add college expenses, currently running $4,000 to $18,000 per year, and the total bill ranges from $63,400 to nearly $200,000—and that's just for one child!

Step 1. As soon as you know you're going to have a family, check your firm's maternity leave and possible benefits for the father and your health coverage.

Step 2. Put all or part of the mother-to-be's salary in a money market fund or other liquid investment and practice living on one salary, which may be the case when the baby arrives, at least at the beginning.

Step 3. Then put half of your money market fund into a series of CDs, staggered to come due at various dates, for example, one every two months after the baby is born. This will provide an influx of much-needed cash.

Step 4. Start a college education fund before the baby leaves the hospital's nursery. Begin by putting all gifts of cash or securities the baby receives in a custodial account under the Uniform Gifts to Minor Act in the baby's name. You'll need to get your child a Social Security number. When he or she reaches adulthood (18 or 21, depending upon the state), this money must be turned over to the child. (See Chapter 32 for tax implications.)

Step 5. For suggestions on saving for college, see the special section below.

Step 6. At this stage your portfolio should be both income- and growth-oriented—income, to cover extra costs of the family, and growth, to make it possible to move into a larger home, add on to your present one, save for college tuition, and finance any expansion of your family. See the suggested stocks and bonds in the table.

➤ AMERICAN CAPITAL BOND FUND (ABC) This diversified closed-end management fund states its investment objective to be income and conservation of capital. ABC invests solely in non-convertible debt securities. Approximately 80% of its assets are in high-quality instruments. These shares, with their 10.7% yield, should be held for income.

➤ CLOROX (CLX) The nation's largest producer of bleach is a debt-free, cash-rich company. Its basic business remains healthy, reflected in the continually rising price. Management plans on moving further into the competitive detergent business, using the well-known Clorox name to capture market share.

➤ CPC INTERNATIONAL (CPC) This leading food manufacturer and corn refining company is in a recession-resistant industry. Its well-known brand names include Knorr soups, Hellmann's mayonnaise, Skippy peanut butter, Mazola corn oil, Karo syrup, and Thomas' baked goods.

➤ PACIFIC TELESIS (PAC) This company has strong telephone operations in California, as well as a foothold in the cellular business that is growing at a rate of over 50% annually. Expect dividend increases, which can easily be covered by strong cash flow. Its yield of 4.5% is high for a common stock.

➤ DOW JONES (DJ) The publisher of the *Wall Street Journal* and *Barron's* suffered after the market crash of 1987. However, with the market picking up and the public moving back in, this sleeping giant is expected to wake up. View as a solid blue chip company with earnings recovery likely during the next 12 months.

IF YOU'RE AN EMPTY NESTER

These are the peak payout years of your life, whether you are married or single, with or without adult children. You can now afford to focus on maintaining a comfortable life-style,

PORTFOLIO FOR THOSE WITH A FAMILY

INVESTMENT	AMOUNT	DETAILS
Company you work for	100 shares	Use employee purchase plan
Electric utility company	100 shares	Reinvest dividends
Municipal bonds or UIT	$1,000 minimum	Hold until maturity
Neuberger & Berman Partners Fund	$1,000 minimum	Sell when you've reached your profit point
U.S. Treasury notes	$5,000 minimum	Use if needed to purchase house or pay child expenses
American Capital Bond Fund	200 shares	Price: $20⅝ Yield: 10.7%
Clorox	100 shares	Price: $40 Yield: 3.1%
CPC International	100 shares	Price: $63 Yield: 2.9%
Pacific Telesis	150 shares	Price: $41⅜ Yield: 4.5%
Dow Jones	100 shares	Price: $35 Yield: 2.0%

Prices are as of July 7, 1989.

ALTERNATIVE PORTFOLIO SUGGESTIONS FOR ALL AGES

- *Buy Occidental Petroleum bonds, 11¾s, due 2011, selling at 107.* Five bonds at 107 each will cost $5,350. Annual income from these junk bonds will be approximately $587.50.
- *Buy Puerto Rico general obligation public improvement municipal bonds, 7.75s, due 2017, priced at $104.* Total cost for ten bonds is $10,400. Annual income will be approximately $775. Puerto Rican municipals are exempt from local, state, and federal taxes in all 50 states.
- *Buy government zeros, due May 2005, with a yield of 8.17%.* Cost per bond is $280. Total cost for $10,000 worth of bonds is $2,800. In the year 2005 you will receive the full $10,000.
- *Consider tax-exempt bonds.* When you are in the 28% or 33% tax bracket, buy municipal bonds or tax-free bond funds to reduce your tax bite. If you live in a high-income-tax state, seek out double- and triple-exempt issues. And consider using a tax-free money market fund if you keep considerable amounts in a regular bond.

caring for your own aging parents, fueling an expanding business or career. During this period your income is probably the highest it will ever be, which enables you to make more aggressive investments than when you were footing the bill for college education or just getting started. Look at a second home or rental property, additional growth-oriented stocks, precious metals, and even some junk bonds. Fund your 401(k) or Keogh plan to the fullest and set up a tax-deferred annuity, keeping in mind that tax-free issues are all-important at this stage.

➤ STUDENT LOAN MARKETING (SLM) Sallie Mae is a federally chartered corporation that purchases and services student loans. Its business is protected by the government guarantee of its loans and low exposure to interest-rate movement.

➤ K MART (KM) The second-largest retailer in the world, K mart owns Kresge, Walden Books, and K mart stores. This company is continually the subject of takeover rumors.

➤ MCA, INC. (MCA) This entertainment company, which makes movies and shows for TV, is rich in real estate holdings. It, too, is often listed as a possible takeover candidate.

➤ MORTGAGE REALTY & TRUST (MRT) This Pennsylvania-based REIT (real estate investment trust) has an exceptionally high yield, which is accompanied by above-average risk. However, its conservative management thus far has produced a steady cash flow from its properties. The dividend is well covered at this time.

PORTFOLIO FOR AN EMPTY NESTER

INVESTMENT	AMOUNT	DETAILS
Student Loan Marketing	150 shares	Price: $40 Yield: nil
Occidental Petroleum 11 3/4s 2011, 107	5 to 10 bonds	Reinvest income or use to purchase real estate
K mart	100 shares	Price: $37½ Yield: 4.4%
Con Edison 8.4s 2003, 96	5 to 10 bonds	Reinvest income
MCA, Inc.	100 shares	Price: $60 Yield: 1.1%
Mortgage & Realty Trust	200 shares	Price: $18 Yield: 11.3%

Prices are as of July 7, 1989.

IF YOU'RE RETIRED OR ABOUT TO BE

Now the emphasis should be on income plus some growth. Safety should be paramount unless you have sufficient money from an inheritance or sale of your home. Top-rated bonds, blue chip stocks, and high-yielding securities are most appropriate during these years. In addition to the specific suggestions that appear in the table, take a look at these investments:

- *Treasury bonds.* As we go to press, U.S. Treasury bonds with the longer maturities, i.e., those due in 30 years, are yielding a little over 8%.

- *High-yield bonds.* If you are willing to assume some risk, put a small portion (5% to 10%) in a high-yield or junk bond mutual fund or select your own.

- *Zero coupon bonds* to mature at or soon after your retirement date. Put these in your tax-sheltered pension plan, where taxes are deferred. Remember, zeros do not pay annual interest, but you must pay annual taxes on the imputed income.

- *Ginnie Maes or Fannie Maes* that pay high yields through monthly checks. Most pass-throughs are fully paid out in less than 15 years, so time your certificate purchase to coincide with your retirement. If you are younger, look into CMOs, a

similar investment with more predictable payout dates, described in Chapter 11.

➤ EXXON CORP. (XON) Since the Alaskan oil spill, the tide of opinion has been against these shares, yet they have held up remarkably well in price. Hold as a speculation that these shares will appreciate substantially in one to two years. In the meantime, collect the dividends.

➤ COASTAL CORP. These bonds are issued by a large utilitylike natural-gas-pipeline company. Coastal is heavily leveraged in order to pay for recent acquisitions. The company is well managed.

➤ ALLERGAN PHARMACEUTICAL, INC. (AGN) A new stock, the result of a spin-off from SmithKline Beckman, Allergan is a global ophthalmic company and holds 16% of that market. It also manufactures and distributes skin care products. Rapid growth expected.

SPECIAL TIPS FOR PAYING COLLEGE TUITION

PAYING FOR COLLEGE: A SPECIALIZED PORTFOLIO

College, like owning a home, is part of the American dream. Both are expensive and require saving as far in advance as possible. By the year 2000, tuition and expenses for four years at a private school are expected to hit $120,000, and even more at

PORTFOLIO FOR THOSE RETIRED OR ABOUT TO BE

INVESTMENT	AMOUNT	DETAILS
American Electric Power	200 shares	Price: $28\frac{3}{8}$
		Yield: 8.2%
AT&T 8 3/4s, 2000 at 99	5 to 10 bonds	Use interest income or reinvest
Mutual of Omaha Interest Shares	200 shares	Price: $13\frac{7}{8}$
		Yield: 11%
1838 Bond Deb. Fund	150 shares	Price: $19\frac{5}{6}$
		Yield: 9.3%
Exxon Corp.	100 shares	Price: $44
		Yield: 5.1%
Coastal Corp. 11 3/4s 2006, 101	5 to 10 bonds	Monitor these junk bonds
Commonwealth Edison 9 1/8 2008, 97	5 to 10 bonds	Use interest income or reinvest
Allergan Pharmaceutical	100 shares	Price: $23½
		Yield: nil

Prices are as of July 7, 1989.

an Ivy League school. But it doesn't have to be bleak. The earlier you begin saving, the easier it will be to write those tuition checks. Whether your child is one week or one year old or a teenager, these strategies will ease the way.

➤ EE SAVINGS BONDS These bonds, which are discussed thoroughly in Chapter 8, were paying 7.35% interest in mid-1989. The rate is adjusted twice a year and has a guaranteed minimum, currently 6%, if you hold the bonds at least five years. You can defer paying federal taxes on them until they mature or are cashed in. Interest earned is exempt from state and local taxes.

The interest you earn on Series EE savings bonds bought after December 31, 1989, is exempt from federal taxes if you use the money to pay tuition for your dependent children, your spouse, or yourself. This means a current yield of 7.5% on EEs held five years is a better investment than tax-free munis yielding 6.5%. To qualify, you must buy the bonds in your name or your spouse's, not your child's. *Caution:* Only families with adjusted gross incomes of less than $60,000 ($40,000 for singles) qualify for the full exemption. As income rises, the exemption is phased out and eliminated entirely at $90,000 ($55,000 for singles).

➤ MUNICIPAL ZERO COUPON BONDS Like savings bonds, municipal zeros sell at a discount to their face value. A $250 zero, for example, will be worth $1,000 at maturity. You do not receive annual interest payments; instead your interest comes in a balloon payment at maturity. Zero munis are tax-free. Buy issues with call protection so your bonds won't be called in before maturity. Time maturities to meet college years.

➤ GROWTH STOCKS OR MUTUAL FUNDS Buy shares or stock if your child is at least five years away from college.

➤ DEFERRED ANNUITIES You can arrange an annuity to start paying out income when your child turns 18. Earnings inside annuities grow on a tax-deferred basis until paid out. Single

SAVINGS BONDS PAY FOR COLLEGE

The earlier you start saving, the more you will have when your child is ready for college.

CHILD'S AGE	VALUE AT AGE 18, BASED ON MONTHLY DEPOSITS OF:	
	$50	**$100**
1	$17,356.08	$34,712.16
6	10,328,96	20,657.92
10	6,025.72	12,051.44
12	4,226.88	8,453.76

Assumes an annual interest rate of 6%, the current minimum rate. Rate is often higher.

SOURCE: U.S. Treasury.

premiums require a one-time lump sum payment; flexible or variable premiums can be paid in a series of contributions.

FOR FINANCIAL AID

You don't have to do it all by yourself. For information on scholarships and financial aid programs, consult these sources when your child enters high school:

Oreon Keeslar, *Financial Aid for Higher Education* (Dubuque, Iowa: William C. Brown, Publisher, 1989), $36.80. Lists 3,000+ programs.

Robert and Ann Leider, *Don't Miss Out: The Ambitious Student's Guide to Financial Aid* (Alexandria, Va.: Octameron Press, 1988), $5.

Gerald Krefetz, *How to Pay for Your Children's College Education* (New York: College Board Publications, 1989), $12.95.

The Federal Student Aid Information Center: 1-800-333-INFO.

INVESTMENT ANALYSIS AND INFORMATION SOURCES

Now that you are well acquainted with the various types of investments available, the next step, of course, is deciding which ones to select for your personal portfolio. Do you want common stocks? If so, which ones? Perhaps you would benefit from bonds or convertibles. Yet selecting the best and avoiding the worst requires skill and knowledge. That's where investment analysis enters the picture.

In this section you will learn the various techniques used by the experts in selecting all types of securities. You will come to know how to recognize the potential profit in stocks, bonds, and mutual funds and how to spot the winners and avoid the losers. Among the topics covered are:

- How to find quality
- Reading a company's balance sheet and annual report
- Getting the most out of statistics
- Following technical analysis
- Studying the charts
- Using newsletters

In Part 3 we explained the various types of stocks and the analytical tools for evaluating securities. You may want to review these points as you now learn precisely how to select top-quality securities on your own.

USING AND EVALUATING
INVESTMENT NEWSLETTERS

LEARNING FROM THE GURUS

Promises of 100% annual returns on your investments, guarantees of market success, predictions of great riches—these and other flamboyant bits of advertising have tempted more than a million people to subscribe to one of the 500 investment newsletters on the market. Are they worth the price of subscription? Some are, but many are not. Yet a well-written, carefully selected newsletter, along with other sources of information, can boost your investment awareness and consequently your performance.

Today, when the need for sound financial advice is so crucial, you're apt to be bombarded by a barrage of newsletters, each one claiming to be the answer to making a killing on Wall Street. Here are guidelines to help avoid the charlatans and opportunists and cash in on the wiser, more seasoned advisers.

A key factor to keep in mind is that from year to year, the performance success of all newsletters changes. And the selection of one or two securities or funds that either take off or bomb has enormous impact on the performance of a newsletter.

Before plunking down full price for any newsletter, take out a trial subscription to several (see suggested lists), which will cost from $10 to $55. Compare them and see if any suit your investment philosophy *and* income level. Ask your stockbroker, banker, accountant, or a reliable friend for recommendations. During the trial period, keep a record of the recommendations made.

Newsletters that do not represent a brokerage firm are no longer required to register as investment advisers with the SEC.

Often newsletters will twist their material to make it appear as though they've made a winning prediction. If the editor claims to have called a market change or picked an outstanding stock, go back to the issue and make certain this really was the case.

Although last year's success does not automatically guarantee the same for the next 12 months, it's one of the few benchmarks available. Try to determine a newsletter's overall track record. (For a list of mutual fund timers, see page 70.)

Another way to study the newletter industry is to read the reports of those who rank the publications or provide summaries of their contents. These include the following:

Hulbert Financial Digest
316 Commerce Street
Alexandria, VA 22314
1-703-683-5905
$135 per year; $37.50 for 5-month trial subscription

Tracks 117 newsletters based on their stock recommendations.

Dick Davis Digest
P.O. Box 9547
Ft. Lauderdale, FL 33310-9547
1-305-531-7777
$120 per year

Summarizes tips given by other investment services.

Timer Digest (Jim Schmitt, ed.)
P.O. Box 1688
Greenwich, CT 06836
1-203-629-3503
$175 per year

Follows 40 market timers.

POINTS TO CONSIDER

DOES THE NEWSLETTER:
- Contradict itself from one issue to the next?
- Explain changes in recommendations?
- Evaluate its mistakes?
- Update its mistakes?
- Take credit for predictions it did not make?
- Present stale news, dated prices and statistics?
- Offer a hotline service?
- Include commissions and fees in its performance results?
- Leave you feeling confused—or is the advice clear, especially sell decisions?
- Provide sample portfolios with instructions, rather than just lists of equities with no advice?

A BAKER'S DOZEN

Among the newsletters that have been successful in either predicting the market or giving financial advice are:

Cabot Market Letter
P.O. Box 3044
Salem, MA 01970
1-508-745-5532
$195 per year

Dessaurer's Journal
P.O. Box 1718
Orleans, MA 02653
1-508-255-1651
$195 per year; $35 for 2 months

Dow Theory Forecasts
7412 Calumet Avenue
Hammond, IN 46324
1-219-931-6480
$198 per year

Dow Theory Letters
P.O. Box 1759
La Jolla, CA 92038
1-619-454-0481
$225 per year

Growth Stock Outlook
4405 East West Highway
Bethesda, MD 20814
1-301-986-5866
$175 per year

Investors Intelligence
30 Church Street
New Rochelle, NY 10801
1-914-632-0422
$124 per year; $24 for 3 months

Mutual Fund Specialist
P.O. Box 1025
Eau Claire, WI 54702
1-715-835-9870
$95 per year

The Option Advisor
P.O. Box 46709
Cincinnati, OH 45246
1-513-772-3535
$120 per year; $66 for 6 months

Princeton Portfolio
1-609-497-0362
$225 per year
Sent, by computer only, every Tuesday; more frequently depending upon market activity

Professional Tape Reader
P.O. Box 2407
Hollywood, FL 33022
1-305-923-3733
$275 per year

Prudent Speculator
P.O. Box 1767
Santa Monica, CA 90406
1-213-395-5275
$200 for 17 issues

Systems & Forecasts
150 Great Neck Road
Great Neck, NY 11021
1-516-829-6444
$175 per year; $55 for 3 months; nightly telephone hotline

The Zweig Forecast
P.O. Box 360
Bellmore, NY 11710
1-516-785-1300
$245 per year; $50 for 3 months

TRACKING INSIDER TRADING

The sales and purchases of any company's stock by the firm's officials can be an indication of stock price trends. It's not foolproof, but if you have time to do the research, you may unearth some interesting situations. A handful of newsletters chart this so-called insider trading.

Consensus of Insiders (Barry Unterbink, ed.)
P.O. Box 24349
Fort Lauderdale, FL 33307
1-305-776-3994
$59 per year—hotline only

The Insiders (Norman Fosback, ed.)
3471 North Federal Highway
Fort Lauderdale, FL 33306
1-305-563-9000
$49

Value Line
711 Third Avenue
New York, NY 10017
1-212-687-3965

Street Smart Investing (Kiril Sokoloff, ed.)
13-D Research
Southeast Executive Park
100 Executive Drive
Brewster, NY 10509
1-914-278-6500
$350 per year

Emerging & Special Situations
(Robert Natale, ed.)
Standard & Poor's Corp.
25 Broadway
New York, NY 10005
1-212-208-8000
$180 per year

Additional sources are listed in Chapter 24, on takeovers.

FOR FURTHER INFORMATION

The best way to check out any newsletter is to ask for a sample issue or a trial subscription. Or take advantage of a special sample offer:

Select Information Exchange
2315 Broadway, 4th floor
New York, NY 10024
1-212-874-6408
25 services for $18

FINDING QUALITY INVESTMENTS:
Your Key to Making Money

QUALITY RANKINGS

The number one criterion for successful investing is always *quality*. In the stock market, quality is determined by a corporation's investment acceptance, financial strength, profitability, and record of growth. *Standard & Poor's Stock Guide, Value Line Investment Survey*, and *Moody's Handbook of Common Stocks* each assign quality ratings to companies on the basis of past performance in earnings and dividends, corporate creditworthiness, and the growth and stability of the company.

STANDARD & POOR'S

The Standard & Poor's categories range from A+ (highest) to A (high), A− (above average), B+ (average), B (below average), B− (lower), to C (lowest). With the exception of banks and financial institutions, which are rated NR (no ranking), most publicly owned corporations are listed. *Never invest in any company rated below B+*, and always check recent earnings to make certain that the quality rating is still deserved.

VALUE LINE

The Value Line Investment Survey is a weekly service that reports on 1,700 stocks classified into 92 industry groups. A report on each industry precedes the individual stock reports. Each stock is given two rankings: one for "timeliness" (the probable relative price performance of the stock within the next 12 months) and one for "safety" (the stock's future price stability and its company's current financial strength). Within these two categories each stock is assigned a rank from 1 (the highest) to 5 (the lowest). Here's what the rankings mean:

➤ **VALUE LINE TIMELINESS**

RANK 1 (highest) Expect the stock to be one of the best price performers relative to the 1,700 other stocks during the next 12 months.

RANK 2 (above average) Expect better than average price performance.

RANK 3 (average) Expect price performance in line with the market.

RANK 4 (below average) Expect less than average price performance.

RANK 5 (lowest) Expect the poorest price performance relative to other stocks.

➤ **VALUE LINE SAFETY**

RANK 1 (highest) This stock is probably one of the safest, most stable, and least risky relative to the 1,700 other stocks.

RANK 2 (above average) This stock is probably safer and less risky than most.

RANK 3 (average) This stock is probably of average safety and risk.

RANK 4 (below average) This stock is probably riskier and less safe than most.

RANK 5 (lowest) This stock is probably one of the riskiest and least safe.

PICKING GROWTH STOCKS

It sounds as though it is easy to pick growth stocks, but true growth equities are relatively rare, because their companies must combine growth with profitability.

Example: In base year 1, on a per-share basis, the stock's book value is $10.00; earnings $1.50; dividends 50¢; leaving $1.00 for reinvestment. This boosts the book value, in year 2, to $11.50 per share. At the same 15% return on equity, the per-share earnings will be $1.75 and dividends will be 60¢, leaving $1.15 for reinvestment. And so on.

At the end of only 4 years, on a per-share basis, the book value will be $15.25; earnings, $2.30; dividends, 90¢; with $1.40 put back into

HOW A QUALITY INVESTMENT GROWS

	PER SHARE			
YEAR	BOOK VALUE	EARNINGS	DIVIDENDS	REINVESTED
1	$10.00	$1.50	$.50	$1.00
2	11.50	1.75	.60	1.15
3	13.25	2.00	.76	1.25
4	15.25	2.30	.90	1.40

the business. Thus the underlying worth of this quality company is up 52.5%, and in normal markets, such profitable growth will bring a much higher valuation for the stock.

Compare these projections with the past records of several of your most successful holdings and you'll see why quality stocks are always worth more in the long run. The truest, most valuable growth companies are those that continue to report ever-higher revenues and earnings and, as a result, greater book values.

So, in choosing growth stocks, weigh carefully the record, over at least 5 years, and then project a realistic future.

GUIDELINES FOR SELECTING GROWTH FIRMS

Throughout this book, you'll find checkpoints to help you make money with your investments. With small, unseasoned companies, you are always taking extra risks, but the reward can often be worthwhile. To keep the odds in your favor, use these guidelines:

- **Read the annual report backward.** Look at the footnotes to discover whether there are significant problems, unfavorable long-term commitments, law suits, etc.
- **Analyze the management's record** in terms of growth of revenue and earnings and, especially, return on stockholders' equity.
- **Find a current ratio of assets to liabilities of 2:1 or higher.** This indicates that the company can withstand difficulties and will probably be able to obtain money to expand.
- **Look for a low debt ratio with long-term debt no more than 35% of total capital.**

This means that the company has staying power and the ability to resist cyclical downturns.

- **Compare a stock's price-earnings ratio** to those of other companies in the same industry. If their ratios are higher, this may be a sleeper. If the PE multiple is above 20, be wary. Such stocks tend to be volatile.
- **Look for stocks with strong management,** little debt, and a return on investment high enough to generate internal growth.
- **Concentrate on companies whose earnings growth rate has been at least 15%** annually for the past 5 years and can be projected to be not much less for the next 2 years.

Keep in mind that (1) you are buying the future of the company, (2) increasing revenues are not enough (the real test is increasing profits), and (3) the stock market is built on hype, and that's easy with new companies that do not have a long, successful record.

ESTABLISHED COMPANIES

The corporation does not have to be young to have growth potential. There are opportunities with old companies where there's new management, a turnaround situation, or R&D-based developments. Analyst James Wolpert lists these ever-important developments:

- **Strong position in an evolutionary market.** Find an industry or market that is bound to move ahead and check the top half dozen corporations. The leaders are probably the best bets, but do not overlook the secondary companies. They may provide a greater percentage gain on your investment.
- **Ability to set prices at profitable levels.** This is important in service industries where greater volume can bring proportionately higher profits as overhead remains relatively stable. The same approach applies to companies making or distributing branded merchandise.
- **Adequate funds for R&D.** With few exceptions, future growth of any corporation is dependent on finding new and better products, more efficient methods of doing business, etc. Look for a

CALCULATING GROWTH RATES

ANNUAL RATE OF EARNINGS INCREASE PER SHARE	JUSTIFIED P/E RATIOS			
	5 YEARS	7 YEARS	10 YEARS	15 YEARS
2%	15	15	13	12
4	17	17	16	16
5	18	18	18	18
6	19	19	20	21
8	21	22	24	28
10	23	25	28	35
12	25	28	33	48

Note that there should be only a small premium when a low growth rate remains static over the years. A 5% annual gain in EPS justifies the same P/E no matter how many years it has been attained. But when a company can maintain a high rate of earnings growth, 10% or more, the value of the stock is enhanced substantially.

SOURCE: Graham and Dodd, *Security Analysis,* 4th ed. (New York: McGraw-Hill, 1962).

company that is building for that sort of future.

- **Control of a market.** IBM is in a dominant position, not because of price but because of its ability to engineer new computers and office equipment and to provide good, continuing service at reasonable cost to the customer.

- **Strong technology base.** This is a valuable, but not essential, asset. Growth companies usually start with expertise in specific areas and then move out into other products and markets.

- **Growing customer demand.** This means a total market that is growing faster than the GNP. In the early years of new items, almost any company can prosper, because the demand is greater than the supply. Later, when production has caught up, the strong, better managed firms will survive and expand their positions.

- **Safety is always important,** but with common stocks, the foremost consideration should be profitable growth: in assets, revenues, and earnings.

RISING EARNINGS AND DIVIDENDS

Despite some temporary setbacks, American business continues to make more money and to pay out higher dividends.

In selecting stocks, check the growth of earnings and dividends. Select companies that have posted rising earnings and dividends not for just a year or two but fairly consistently over a 5-year period.

- **Look for a high compound growth rate:** at least 15% to 20% annually. Compounding means that every year earnings are 20% higher than in the prior year. The table shows a theoretical example of earnings growth of 20% compounded annually.

Example: To find earnings growth for any one year, subtract the earnings per share of the prior year from the earnings per share of the year in question. Then divide the difference by the base year (i.e., the prior year) earnings.

In 1986, Eckveldt Technology earned $1.20 per share. In the prior year, it earned $1.00 per share.

$$\begin{array}{r} \$1.20 \\ -\ 1.00 \\ \hline 0.20 \end{array} \div \$1.00 = 20\% \text{ growth rate}$$

In the next year, in order to maintain a 20% growth rate, Eckveldt would have to report an increase of 20% of $1.20, or $1.20 × 0.20% = 24¢. Therefore, earnings expectations are $1.44 per share in the third year ($1.20 + 24¢ = $1.44). Tables for compound growth rates are available from your stockbroker.

- **Look for the earnings trend as reported for two consecutive quarters:** if profits fall, find out why. The decline may be temporary and reflect heavy investments in new products or markets. But if the

EARNINGS GROWTH RATE

Year 1	$1.00 × 20% = 0.20 = $1.20
Year 2	$1.20 × 20% = 0.24 = $1.44
Year 3	$1.44 × 20% = 0.29 = $1.73
Year 4	$1.73 × 20% = 0.35 = $2.08

WHAT ARE EARNINGS WORTH?

ANNUAL GROWTH RATE	WHAT $1.00 EARNINGS WILL BECOME IN 3 YEARS AT GIVEN GROWTH RATE	THE P/E RATIO YOU CAN PAY TODAY TO MAKE 10% ANNUAL CAPITAL GAIN AND EXPECT P/E RATIO IN 3 YEARS TO BE	
		15×	30×
4%	$1.12	12.6	25.3
5	1.16	13.1	26.2
6	1.19	13.4	26.8
7	1.23	13.9	27.7
8	1.26	14.2	28.4
9	1.30	14.7	29.3
10	1.33	15.0	30.0
12	1.40	15.8	31.6
15	1.52	17.1	34.3
20	1.73	19.5	39.0
25	1.95	22.0	44.0

SOURCE: Knowlton and Furth, *Shaking the Money Tree* (New York: Harper & Row, 1979).

drop indicates real trouble, consider selling.

Similarly, if profits rise, be just as curious. If they are the result of higher sales and lower costs, this could be the start of something big. But if the improvements come from accounting changes, it's far less impressive and probably temporary.

HINT: *Never fall in love with any stock.* If the corporate prospects are dim, why hang on? If you are convinced that it is still a quality company, you can buy back at a lower price.

HOW TO DETERMINE REAL GROWTH AND PROFITABILITY

In selecting stocks for its clients, Wright Investors' Service relies heavily on two fundamental measure of corporate growth and profitability: *earned growth rate* (EGR) and *profit rate* (PR). These reveal the ability of management

PROFITS: PHANTOM OR REAL?

It sounds great when a company reports debt reduction, but the wise investor should check to see how this is accomplished. One of the newest methods is to swap bonds for stock. This is like buying back the mortgage on your home. You save current dollars but lose the benefit of the old low interest rate.

Example: A wily investment banker accumulates large amounts of old low-coupon bonds that have been selling at deep discounts, say, 70¢ on the dollar. The banker then swaps this debt for shares of common stock, which are then sold to the public . . . at a modest profit. On its books, the corporation shows a "profit" because the price of the bond was far below the face value that would have to be paid at the future redemption date.

Similarly, watch out when a company keeps reducing its debt by new stock offerings. Since the interest is a business expense, the net cost is about half that of the same dollars paid out in dividends. When debt is repaid from the proceeds of new common stock, the same dividend rate requires greater after-tax profits.

to make the money entrusted to them by stockholders grow over the years. You can use the same technique.

➤ EARNED GROWTH RATE   The EGR is the annual rate at which the company's equity capital per common share is increased by net earnings after payment of the dividend—if any. *It is a reliable measure of investment growth because it shows the growth of the capital invested in the business.*

$$EGR = \frac{E - D}{BV}$$

E = earnings
D = dividend
BV = book value

The book value is the net value of total corporate assets, that is, what is left over when all liabilities, including bonds and preferred stock, are subtracted from the total assets (plant,

STANDARD & POOR'S A+-RATED STOCKS LISTED ON THE NEW YORK STOCK EXCHANGE WITH DIVIDEND AND EARNINGS-PER-SHARE INCREASES FOR 1980–1987

Aerospace Industry
Rockwell International

Apparel

Automotive

Beverages and Bottlers
Anheuser-Busch
Coca-Cola

Business
Jostens Inc.
Wallace Computers

Chemicals
Clorox Co.
Morton Thiokol

Drugs, Cosmetics
Abbott Laboratories
American Home Products
Bristol-Myers
Kimberly-Clark
Lilly (Eli)
Pfizer, Inc.

Electrical
Emerson Electric
General Electric

Financial and Bank Industry
Barnett Banks
BayBanks Inc.
Central Fidelity Banks
First Virginia Banks

Foods
Borden, Inc.
ConAgra Inc.
Dean Foods
Flowers Industries
Heinz (H.J.)
Hershey Foods
Kellogg Co.
Planters Corp.
Quaker Oats
Ralston Purina

Health Care

Paper, Printing, Publishing
De Luxe Corp.
Donnelley (R.R.) & Sons
Dow Jones
Dun & Bradstreet
Gannett Company
Knight-Ridder

Restaurants
McDonald's Corp.

Retailers
Albertson's, Inc.
Dayton Hudson
May Department Stores
Mercantile Stores
Super Valu Stores
Walgreen Co.

Transportation

Utilities
American Water Works
Citizens Utility "B"
Consolidated Edison
Potomac Electric
Tucson Electric
Wisconsin Energy Corp.

Miscellaneous
Bandag, Inc.
Philip Morris Cos.
Rockwell Int'l
Rubbermaid
Sysco Corp.
U.S. Tobacco
Universal Corp.

SOURCE: Standard & Poor's, July 1989.

equipment, cash, inventories, accounts receivable, etc.). It is sometimes called stockholders' equity and can be found in every annual report. Many corporations show the book value over a period of years in their summary tables. A good growth company will increase its equity capital at a rate of at least 6% per year. The table at right shows why American Home Products (AHP) qualifies as a top growth company.

To determine the EGR for AHP in 1987, take the per-share earnings of $5.73 and subtract the $3.34 dividend to get $2.39. Then divide this by the book value at the *beginning of the*

year: $17.42. Thus, the EGR for that year was 13.7%:

$$\text{EGR} = \frac{5.73 - 3.34}{17.42} = \frac{2.39}{17.42} = 13.7\%$$

➤ PROFIT RATE   The PR is equally important in assessing real growth, because it measures the ability of the corporate management to make money with your money; it shows the rate of return produced on shareholders' equity at corporate book value. It is calculated by dividing the earnings per common share by the per-share

THE GROWTH STOCK PRICE EVALUATOR
How to Weigh Prices of Growth Stocks in Terms of Their Future Gains in Earnings or Cash Flow

IF— A STOCK NOW SELLS AT THIS MANY TIMES ITS CURRENT EARNINGS OR CASH FLOW:	—AND YOU BELIEVE ITS AVERAGE ANNUAL GROWTH IN EARNINGS OR CASH FLOW PER SHARE (COMPOUNDED) WILL BE: THEN—HERE IS HOW MANY TIMES ITS PROJECTED EARNINGS OR CASH FLOW PER SHARE 5 YEARS HENCE THE STOCK IS CURRENTLY SELLING AT:						
	10%	15%	20%	25%	30%	40%	50%
12	7.5	6.0	4.8	3.9	3.2	2.2	1.6
14	8.7	7.0	5.6	4.6	3.8	2.6	1.8
16	9.9	8.0	6.5	5.2	4.3	3.0	2.1
18	11.2	9.0	7.3	5.9	4.9	3.3	2.4
20	12.4	10.0	8.1	6.6	5.4	3.7	2.6
22	13.7	10.9	8.9	7.2	5.9	4.1	2.9
24	14.9	11.9	9.7	7.9	6.5	4.5	3.2
26	16.1	12.9	10.5	8.5	7.0	4.8	3.4
28	17.4	13.9	11.3	9.2	7.5	5.2	3.7
30	18.6	14.9	12.1	9.8	8.1	5.6	3.9
32	19.9	15.9	12.9	10.5	8.6	5.9	4.2
34	21.1	16.9	13.7	11.1	9.2	6.3	4.5
36	22.4	17.9	14.5	11.8	9.7	6.7	4.7
38	23.6	18.9	15.3	12.5	10.2	7.1	5.0
40	24.8	19.9	16.1	13.1	10.8	7.4	5.3
42	26.1	20.9	16.9	13.8	11.3	7.8	5.5
44	27.3	21.9	17.7	14.4	11.9	8.2	5.8
46	28.6	22.9	18.5	15.1	12.4	8.6	6.1
48	29.8	23.9	19.4	15.7	12.9	8.9	6.3
50	31.1	24.9	20.2	16.4	13.5	9.3	6.6

This evaluator can be used to make your own projections. It is most useful when studying fast-growing companies with above-average growth rates and cash flow, because it shows that if your growth assumptions are correct, the P/E ratio based on your cost today will be more modest.

Example: The stock of a small high-technology corporation is selling at 30 times current earnings. You estimate that over the next 5 years, earnings will grow at an average annual compound rate of 20%. The table shows that if this projection is correct, the stock will be selling at 12.1 times its anticipated 5-years-hence profits.

This evaluation technique can be reversed. Today the stock is selling at a multiple of 30, but you are not so sure about its future profits. From experience, you are willing to pay no more than 12 times future 5-year earnings for any growth stock. Checking the table, you find that the average annual growth rate must be 20% compounded annually to meet your investment standards. This stock just meets your criteria.

The Growth Stock Price Evaluator does *not* show the *future* price-to-earnings multiple or cash flow. They might be lower than, the same as, or greater than they are today.

book value of the common stock, again at the *beginning of the year.*

Using AHP as an example:

$$PR = \frac{5.73}{17.42} = 32.8\%$$

The consistently strong record of AHP has been a major reason for the rise in the stock price, from 28 in mid-1981 to 74 in July 1987.

CHECKPOINTS FOR FINDING QUALITY COMPANIES

- **Improving profit margins.** This is an excellent test, because wider PMs almost always indicate increased earnings per share within a short period of time.

    The gross profit margin (sometimes called the operating profit margin) shows a company's operating income, before taxes, as a percentage of revenues. It is listed in many annual reports and most statistical analyses. It can be calculated by dividing the operating income (total revenues less operating expenses) by the net sales. Generally, a gross PM of 12% indicates a company that deserves further study. Anything below that, especially when it is lower than the previous year, is a danger signal.

    The gross profit margin is useful in comparing companies within a given industry. However, since it varies widely among industries, avoid interindustry comparisons. For example, supermarket stores have lower gross PMs than many others.

- **Plowed-back earnings.** The fastest-growing companies will almost always be the stingiest dividend payers. By reinvesting a substantial portion of its profits, preferably 70% or more, a company can speed expansion and improve productive efficiency. Any corporation that plows back 12% of its invested capital each year will double its real worth in 6 years.

- **Strong research and development.** The aim of research is knowledge; the aim of development is new or improved products and processes. A company that uses reinvested earnings largely for new plants and equipment will improve its efficiency and the quality of its products, but it may not grow as fast in the long run as a company that spends wisely to develop new and better products.

     A prime test for aggressive growth management is whether the company is spending a higher than average percentage of its revenues for research and new process and product development. *With good management, dollars spent for R&D constitute the most creative, dynamic force for growth available for any corporation.* It is not unusual for the thousands of dollars used for research to make possible millions of dollars in additional sales and profits.

WHAT TO AVOID

To spot the nonachievers among companies in a growth industry, look for these danger signals:

- **Substantial stock dilution.** This means that a company repeatedly and exclusively raises funds through the sale of additional common stock, either directly or through convertibles. There's no harm in small dilution, especially when there are prospects that the growth of earnings will

---

DISCOVERING BARGAINS

Benjamin Graham, in his book *Security Analysis*, looks for bargains in stocks, which he defines as the time when they trade at:

- A multiple of no more than twice that of the prevailing interest rate: that is, a P/E ratio of 16 vs. an interest rate of 8%
- A discount of 20% or more from book value
- A P/E ratio of 40% less than that of the S&P index P/E
- A point where current assets exceed current liabilities and long-term debt combined

---

continue. But beware of any company with heavy future obligations. Too much dilution merely enlarges the size of the company for the benefit of management and leaves stockholders with diluted earnings.

- **Vast overvaluation as shown by price-earnings ratios of 30 or higher.** This is a steep price to pay for potential growth. Take your profits, or at least set stop-loss prices. When any stock sells at a multiple that is double that of the overall market (usually around 14.56), be cautious.

BEHIND THE SCENES:
How to Read Annual Reports

Some are flashy, some are plain; some are fat and some are thin; but all annual reports are the single most important tool in analyzing corporations to decide whether to buy, hold, sell, or pass by their securities. In a few minutes, you can check the corporation's quality and profitability and, with closer study, learn a great deal about the character and ability of management, its methods of operation, its products and services, and, most important, its future prospects. If you own securities of the corporation, you will receive a copy of the annual report about 4 months after the close of its operating year. If you are considering becoming a shareholder, get a copy from your broker or by writing the company (get the address from Standard & Poor's, Value Line, Moody's, or other reference books at your library).

First, skim the text, check the statement of income and earnings to see how much money was made and whether this was more than that of previous years, and review the list of officers and directors for familiar names. Later, if you're still interested, you can follow up the points of interest.

The statements will always be factually correct, but the interpretations, especially those in the president's message, will naturally be the most favorable within legal and accounting limits.

If you are considering a stock to buy, look at 3 years' annual reports. Here's what to be aware of:

➤ TRENDS In sales, earnings, dividends, accounts receivable. If they continue to rise, chances are that you've found a winner. *Buy* when they are moving up; *review* when they plateau; *consider selling* when they are down.

➤ INFORMATION *From the tables:* corporate financial strength and operating success or failure. *From the text:* explanations of what happened during the year and what management projects

for the future. If you don't believe management, do not hold the stock.

➤ POSITIVES New plants, products, personnel, and programs. Are the total assets greater and liabilities lower than in previous years? If so, why—tighter controls or decreases in allocations for R&D, marketing, etc.?

If the profits were up, was the gain due to fewer outstanding shares (because of repurchase of stock), to nonrecurring income from the sale of property, or to higher sales and lower costs?

➤ NEGATIVES Plant closings, sales of subsidiaries, discontinuance of products, and future needs for financing. Not all of these will always be adverse, but they can make a significant difference with respect to what happens in the next few years.

If the profits were down, was this because of the elimination of some products or services? Price wars? Poor managerial decisions?

➤ FOOTNOTES Read these carefully because they can point up problems. Be cautious if there were heavy markdowns of inventory, adverse governmental regulations, rollovers of debt, and other unusual events.

➤ BALANCE SHEET To see whether cash or liquid assets are diminishing and whether accounts receivable, inventories, or total debts are rising. Any such trend can serve as a yellow flag, if not a red one.

➤ FINANCIAL SUMMARY Not only for the past year but for the previous 5 years. This will provide an overall view of corporate performance and set the stage for an analysis of the most recent data.

In the stock market, *past is prologue.* Few companies achieve dramatic progress or fall on hard times suddenly. In most cases, the changes have been forecast. The corporation with a long, fairly consistent record of profitable growth can be expected to do as well, or better, in the years ahead and thus prove to be a worthwhile holding.

The erratic performer is likely to move from high to low profits (or losses). And the faltering company will have signs of deterioration over a 2- or 3-year period.

READING THE REPORT

When you review the text, you will get an idea of the kind of people who are managing your money, learn what they did or did not do and why, and be able to draw some conclusions about future prospects.

➤ BEGIN WITH THE SHAREHOLDERS' LETTER This message from the chairman outlines the company's past performance and its prospects. Compare last year's letter with this year's facts. Did the company meet its previously stated goals? Beware of the chairman who never mentions any problems or areas of concern. If there were failures, there should be logical explanations. Management is not always right in its decisions, but in financial matters, frankness is the base for confidence. If previous promises were unfulfilled (and that's why you should keep a file of past annual reports), find out why. If the tone is overly optimistic, be wary. If you are skeptical, do not hold the stock or buy.

➤ WATCH FOR DOUBLE-TALK Clichés are an integral part of business writing, but they should not be substitutes for proper explanations. If you find such meaningless phrases as "a year of transition" or some of the locutions listed in the box, start getting ready to unload. There are better opportunities elsewhere.

➤ STUDY THE BALANCE SHEET This presents an instant picture of the company's assets and liabilities on the very last day of the fiscal year. Divide the current assets by the current liabilities to get the current ratio. A ratio of 2:1 or better signals that there are enough assets on hand to cover immediate debts. (We return to balance sheets in the next section.)

➤ LOOK AT LONG-TERM DEBT Divide long-term debt by long-term capital (i.e., long-term debt plus shareholders' equity). If it is below 50%, the company is probably solid, but, of course, the more debt, the less cash to help weather rough times.

➤ REVIEW ACCOUNTS RECEIVABLE Listed under current assets, this figure reflects the payments for products or services that the company expects to receive in the near future. If receivables are

growing at a faster pace than sales, it may indicate that the company is not collecting its bills fast enough.

➤ LOOK AT CURRENT INVENTORIES If inventories are rising faster than sales, the company is creating or producing more than it can sell.

➤ LOOK AT NET INCOME PER SHARE Note if this figure, which reflects earnings, is trending up or down.

➤ COMPARE REVENUES AND EXPENSES If expenses are greater than revenues over time, management may be having trouble holding down overhead. Discount earnings increases that are due to a nonrecurring event, such as sale of a property or division. Nonrecurring items should be explained in the footnotes. The footnotes also reveal changes in accounting methods, lawsuits, and liabilities.

➤ STUDY THE QUALITY AND SOURCE OF EARNINGS When profits are entirely from operations, they indicate management's skill; when they are partially from bookkeeping, look again. But do not be hasty in drawing conclusions. Even the best of corporations may use "special" accounting.

Examples: In valuing inventories, LIFO (last in, first out) current sales are matched against the latest costs so that earnings can rise sharply when inventories are reduced and those latest costs get older and thus lower. When oil prices were at a peak, Texaco cut inventories by 16%. The LIFO cushion, built up over several years, was a whopping $454 million and transformed what would have been a drop in net income into a modest gain.

Such "tricks" are one reason why stocks fall or stay flat after annual profits are reported. Analysts are smart enough to discover that earnings are more paper than real.

➤ READ THE AUDITOR'S REPORT If there are hedging phrases such as "except for" or "subject to," be wary. These phrases can signal the inability to get accurate information and may forecast future write-offs.

➤ LOOK AT FOREIGN CURRENCY TRANSACTIONS These can be tricky and often difficult to understand. Under recent revisions of accounting rules, it's possible to recast them retroactively when, of course, they can be favorable. One major firm whose domestic profits had been lagging went back 4 years with its overseas reports and boosted its per share profits to $7.08 from the previously reported $6.67 per share.

HOW TO TRANSLATE THE PRESIDENT'S MESSAGE

Here are some of the techniques used in writing annual reports to phrase comments in terms that tend to divert the reader's attention away from problems.

WHAT THE PRESIDENT SAYS	WHAT THE PRESIDENT MEANS
"The year was difficult and challenging."	"Sales and profits were off, but expenses (including executive salaries) were up."
"Management has taken steps to strengthen market share."	"We're underselling our competitors to drive them out of the market."
"Integrating the year's highs and lows proved challenging."	"Sales were up; profits went nowhere."
"Management worked diligently to preserve a strong financial position."	"We barely broke even but were able to avoid new debts."
"Your company is indebted to the dedicated service of its employees."	"We don't pay 'em much, but there's not much else to cheer about."

CONSOLIDATED STATEMENT: FRED MEYER, INC.

FISCAL YEAR ENDED ($ IN THOUSANDS EXCEPT PER-SHARE AMOUNTS)

	JANUARY 31, 1987	FEBRUARY 1, 1986	FEBRUARY 2, 1985 (53 WEEKS)
Net sales	$1,688,208	$1,583,796	$1,449,108
Cost of merchandise sold	1,200,379	1,135,836	1,053,689
Gross margin	487,829	447,960	395,419
Operating and administrative expenses	430,469	397,841	354,914
Income from operations	57,360	50,119	40,505
Interest expense, net of interest income of $1,679, $2,983, and $3,090	11,945	17,652	19,565
Income before income taxes and extraordinary items	45,415	32,467	20,940
Provision for income taxes	21,350	13,000	8,000
Income before extraordinary items	24,065	19,467	12,940
Extraordinary items	(1,530)		2,649
Net income	$ 22,535	$ 19,467	$ 15,589
Earnings per Common Share			
Income before extraordinary items	$ 1.15	$ 1.06	$ .73
Extraordinary items	(.07)		.15
Net income	$ 1.08	$ 1.06	$ .88
Weighted average number of common shares outstanding	20,870	18,355	17,790

Most international corporations have elaborate systems for hedging against fluctuations in foreign currencies. These are relatively expensive, but they tend to even out sharp swings in the value of the dollar. Wall Street hates uncertainty and tends to prefer stocks of corporations that try to protect their monetary positions. That's a good example to follow.

➤ CHECK FOR FUTURE OBLIGATIONS You may have to burrow in the footnotes, but with major companies, find out about the pension obligations: the money that the firm must pay to its retirees. One way to boost profits (because this means lower annual contributions) is to raise the assumed rate of return on pension fund investments. When General Motors increased its projected rate of return to 7% from 6% a year, it added 69¢ per share to its reported earnings. This is OK as long as the higher yield is justified by investment performance.

➤ CALCULATE THE CASH FLOW Add after-tax earnings and annual depreciation on fixed assets and subtract preferred dividends, if any. Then compare the result with previous years. Cash flow is indicative of corporate earning power because it shows the dollars available for profits, new investments, etc.

➤ BEWARE OF OVERENTHUSIASM ABOUT NEW PRODUCTS, PROCESSES, OR SERVICES Usually, it takes 3 years to translate new operations into sizable sales and profits. And the majority of new projects are losers.

➤ PAY SPECIAL ATTENTION TO THE RETURN ON EQUITY (PROFIT RATE) This is the best measure of management's ability to make money with your money. Any ROE above 15% is good; when below, compare the figure with that of previous years and other firms in the same industry. Some industries seldom show a high rate of return: for example, heavy machinery because of the huge investment in plants and equipment and utilities because of the ceiling set by public commissions.

➤ WATCH OUT FOR EQUITY ACCOUNTING Where earnings from other companies, which are more than 20% owned, are included in total profits. There are no cash dividends, so the money cannot be used for expansion or payouts to shareholders. This maneuver can massage the reported earnings, but that's about all. Teledyne, a major conglomerate, reported $19.96 per share profits, but a close examination revealed that $3.49 of this was from equity accounting—phantom, not real, earnings.

BALANCE SHEETS MADE SIMPLE

DETERMINING VALUE

The idea is to buy low and sell high. This sounds easy, but it isn't. You must determine what is *low* and, to a lesser degree, what is *high*. That's where value comes in. The surest way to make money in the stock market is to buy securities when they are undervalued and sell them when they become fully priced. *Value shows the range in which a stock should be bought or sold and thus provides the base for investment profits.*

Value itself is based on financial "facts," as stated in the corporate reports. Projections, by contrast, are based on analyses of past performance, present strength, and future progress. When you select quality stocks on the basis of value (or undervaluation), you will almost always make money—perhaps quickly with speculative situations, more slowly with major corporations. You can identify value *if* you understand the basics of financial analysis, our next step.

HOW TO ANALYZE FINANCIAL REPORTS

Financial analysis is not as difficult as you may think, and once you get the swing of things, you can pick the few quality stocks from the thousands of publicly owned securities. If you are speculation-minded, you can find bargains in securities of mediocre or even poor corporations.

Several basic figures and ratios show the company's current and prospective financial condition, its past and prospective earning power and growth, and therefore its investment desirability or lack of desirability.

Publicly owned corporations issue their financial reports on an annual, semiannual, or quarterly basis. Most of the information impor-

tant to the investor can be found in (1) the balance sheet; (2) the profit and loss, or income, statement; and (3) the change in financial position or "flow of funds" data. In each of these three sections you should look for:

- *The key quantities:* net tangible assets, changes in working capital, sales costs, profits, taxes, dividends, etc.
- *The significant rates and ratios:* price-earnings multiples, profit rates, growth in net worth, earnings, dividends, etc.
- *The comparison of a corporation with a standard:* that of its industry, the stock market, the economy, or some other broader base.

The following data and explanations are digested from *Understanding Financial Statements,* prepared by the New York Stock Exchange. They do not cover every detail but will get you started. For a copy, write to the address given at the end of the chapter, or ask your broker for one.

INCOME AND RETAINED EARNINGS

Here's where you find out *how the corporation fared for the past year* in comparison with the two previous annual reporting periods: in other words, how much money the company took in, how much was spent for expenses and taxes, and the size of the resulting profits (if any), which were available either for distribution to shareholders or for reinvestment in the business. Income and retained earnings are the basis for comparisons, both between years for this company and between firms in the same or similar businesses.

SALES

How much business does the company do in a year? With public utilities, insurance firms, and service organizations, the

STATEMENT OF INCOME AND RETAINED EARNINGS ($ millions)
"Your Company"

	DECEMBER 31 YEAR-END		
	CURRENT YEAR	PREVIOUS YEAR	2 YEARS AGO
SALES	$115.8	$110.0	$104.5
Less:			
COSTS AND EXPENSES			
Cost of goods sold	$ 76.4	$ 73.2	$ 70.2
Selling, general, and administrative expenses	14.2	13.0	12.1
Depreciation	2.6	3.5	2.3
	$ 93.2	$ 89.7	$ 84.6
OPERATING PROFIT	$ 22.6	$ 20.3	$ 19.9
Interest charges	1.3	1.0	1.3
Earnings before income taxes	$ 21.3	$ 19.3	$ 18.6
Provision for taxes on income	11.4	9.8	9.5
Net income (per common share for year: current, $5.24; last, $5.03; 2 years ago, $4.97)*	$ 9.9	$ 9.5	$ 9.1
RETAINED EARNINGS, BEGINNING OF YEAR	42.2	37.6	33.1
Less dividends paid on:	$ 52.1	$ 47.1	$ 42.2
Preferred stock ($5 per share)	(.3)	(.3)	—
Common stock (per share: this year, $3.00; last year, $2.50; 2 years ago, $2.50)	(5.4)	(4.6)	(4.6)
RETAINED EARNINGS, END OF YEAR	$ 46.4	$ 42.2	$ 37.6

* After preferred share dividend requirements

term "revenues" is often used instead of sales. In the past year, corporate sales in the sample corporation shown were up $5.8 million, a gain of 5.3%, not quite as good as the 5.5% rise the year before. Net income per share (middle) was also just slightly better: $0.4 million (to $9.9 from $9.5), +4.2%. Check these figures against those of the industry and major competitors. They may be better than they appear.

COSTS AND EXPENSES

➤ COST OF GOODS SOLD The dollars spent to keep the business operating. The $3.2 million more was less than the $5.8 million increase in sales.

➤ SELLING, GENERAL, AND ADMINISTRATIVE EXPENSES The costs of getting products or services

to customers and getting paid. These will vary with the kind of business: high for consumer goods manufacturers and distributors because of advertising; lower for companies selling primarily to industry or government.

➤ DEPRECIATION A bookkeeping item to provide for wear and tear and obsolescence of machinery and equipment, presumably to set aside reserves for replacement. The maximum calculations are set by tax laws. Typically, a straight-line accounting method might charge the same amount each year for a specified number of years.

With companies in the natural resource business, the reduction in value is called depletion, and it too is calculated over a period of years.

By changing the type of depreciation, a company can increase or decrease earnings, so always be wary when this happens.

OPERATING PROFIT

Operating profit consists of the dollars generated from the company's usual operations without regard to income from other sources or financing. As a percentage of sales, it tells the profit margin: a rising 19.5% in the last year compared with 18.5% the year before.

➤ INTEREST CHARGES The interest paid to bond-holders. It is deductible before taxes. The available earnings should be many times the mandated interest charges: in this case, a welcome 17 times before provision for income taxes (i.e., $22.6 ÷ $1.3 = 17).

➤ EARNINGS BEFORE INCOME TAXES The operating profit minus interest charges. When companies have complicated reports, this can be a confusing area.

➤ PROVISION FOR TAXES ON INCOME The allocation of money for Uncle Sam—a widely variable figure because of exemptions, special credits, etc., from about 5% for some companies to 34% for industrial corporations.

➤ NET INCOME FOR THE YEAR *The bottom line.* This was 4.2% better than the year before—about the same as recorded in the previous period. This was no record breaker and works out better on a per-share basis: $5.24 vs. $5.03.

One year's change is interesting, but the true test of management's ability comes over 5 years.

Use this figure to make other comparisons (against sales: 8.5% vs. 8.6% the year before) and then relate this to returns of other companies in the same industry. The average manufacturing corporation earns about 5¢ per dollar of sales, but supermarkets are lucky to end up with 1¢ against shareowners' equity: the profit rate (PR). Here, the PR was a modest 13%.

To find the earnings per share, divide the net income (less preferred dividend requirements) by the average number of shares outstanding during the year. This is the key figure for most analysts. It is also used to determine the price-earnings (P/E) ratio: divide the market price of the stock by the per-share profits. If the stock was selling at 30, the P/E would be 10—slightly above the average of most publicly owned shares.

➤ RETAINED EARNINGS The dollars reinvested for future growth, always an important indication of future prospects. If the company continues to boost this figure, its basic value will

increase. At the same PR, earnings will increase, and eventually so will the value of the common stock.

Here the company keeps plowing back more: $4.6 million last year vs. $4.5 million the year before. (Subtract the retained earnings at the beginning of the year from retained earnings of the previous year: $37.6 − $33.1 = $4.5.)

➤ DIVIDENDS The amount paid out to shareholders for the use of their money. The $5 per share paid on the preferred stock is fixed. The payments for the common move with profits: last year up 50¢ per share to $3.00 from the flat $2.50 of the 2 prior years.

Note that this statement shows earnings retained as of the beginning and end of each year. Thus the company reinvested $46.4 million for the future.

BALANCE SHEET ITEMS

Now that you know what happened in the last year, it's time to take a look at the financial strength (or weakness) of the corporation. On page 335 is a typical balance sheet. Use it as the basis for reviewing annual reports of the companies in which you own, or plan to own, securities. The headings may vary according to the type of industry, but the basic data will be similar—and just as important.

CURRENT ASSETS

Items that can be converted into cash within 1 year. The total is $48.4 million this year, $4.2 million more than last year.

➤ CASH Mostly bank deposits, including compensating balances held under terms of a loan—like keeping a savings account to get free checking.

➤ MARKETABLE SECURITIES Corporate and government securities that can be sold quickly. In the current year, these were eliminated.

➤ RECEIVABLES Amounts due from customers for goods and services. This is a net amount after a set-aside for items that may not be collected.

➤ INVENTORIES Cost of raw materials, work in process, and finished goods. Statements and foot-notes describe the basis, generally cost or current market price, whichever is lower. To handle the

BALANCE SHEET ($ millions)
"Your Company"

ASSETS	DEC. 31 CURRENT YEAR	DEC. 31 PRIOR YEAR	LIABILITIES AND STOCKHOLDERS' EQUITY	DEC. 31 CURRENT YEAR	DEC. 31 PRIOR YEAR
Current Assets			**Current Liabilities**		
Cash	$ 9.0	$ 6.2	Accounts payable	$ 6.1	$ 5.0
Marketable securities	—	2.0	Accrued liabilities	3.6	3.3
Accounts and notes receivable	12.4	11.4	Current maturity of long-term debt	1.0	.8
Inventories	27.0	24.6	Federal income and other taxes	9.6	8.4
Total current assets	$ 48.4	$ 44.2	Dividends payable	1.3	1.1
			Total current liabilities	$ 21.6	$ 18.6
Property, Plant, and Equipment					
Buildings, machinery, and equipment, at cost	104.3	92.7	**Other Liabilities**	3.6	2.5
Less accumulated depreciation	27.6	25.0	Long-term debt 5% sinking-fund debentures, due July 31, 1990	26.0	20.0
	$ 76.7	$ 67.7			
Land, at cost	.9	.7	**Stockholders' Equity**		
Total property, plant, and equipment	$ 77.6	$ 68.4	5% cumulative preferred stock ($100 par: authorized and outstanding, 60,000)	6.0	6.0
			Common stock ($10 par: authorized, 2,000,000; outstanding, 1,830,000)	18.3	18.3
Other Assets			Capital surplus	9.6	9.6
Receivables due after 1 year	4.7	3.9	Retained earnings	46.4	42.2
Surrender value of insurance	.2	.2	Total stockholders' equity	$ 80.3	$ 76.1
Other	.6	.5			
Total other assets	$ 5.5	$ 4.6			
Total Assets	$131.5	$117.2	**Total Liabilities and Stockholders' Equity**	$131.5	$117.2

additional business, these were up over those of the previous year.

PROPERTY, PLANT, AND EQUIPMENT

The land, structures, machinery and equipment, tools, motor vehicles, etc. Except for land, these assets have a limited useful life, and a deduction is taken from cost as depreciation. With a new plant, the total outlays were $11.6 million more, with depreciation up $2.6 million.

OTHER ASSETS

Identifiable property is valued at cost. Intangibles such as patents, copyrights, franchises, trademarks, or goodwill cannot be assessed accurately, so they are omitted from the computation of tangible net worth or book value.

If an increase in sales does not follow an increased investment, management may have misjudged the ability to produce and/or sell more goods, or the industry may have reached overcapacity. If a company's plant and equipment show little change for several years during a period of expanding business, the shareholder should be cautious about the company's progressiveness. In this example, both fixed and total assets grew steadily.

LIABILITIES AND STOCKHOLDERS' EQUITY

Divided into two classes: current (payable within a year) and long-term (debt or other obligations that come due after 1 year from the balance sheet date).

➤ ACCOUNTS PAYABLE Money owed for raw materials, other supplies, and services.

➤ ACCRUED LIABILITIES Unpaid wages, salaries and commissions, interest, etc.

➤ CURRENT LONG-TERM DEBT Amount due in the next year. This usually requires annual repayments over a period of years.

➤ INCOME TAXES Accrued federal, state, and local taxes.

➤ DIVIDENDS PAYABLE Preferred or common dividends (or both) declared but not yet paid. Once declared, dividends become a corporate obligation.

➤ TOTAL CURRENT LIABILITIES An increase of $3 million needed to finance expansion of business.

➤ LONG-TERM DEBT What's due for payment in the future less the amount due in the next year. Although the total was reduced to $20 million, an additional $6 million of debentures was issued.

STOCKHOLDERS' EQUITY (or CAPITAL)

All money invested in the business by stockholders as well as reinvested earnings.

➤ PREFERRED STOCK Holders are usually entitled to dividends before common stockholders and to priority in the event of dissolution or liquidation. Dividends are fixed. If cumulative, no dividends can be paid on common stock until the preferred dividends are up to date.

Here each share of preferred was issued at $100, but its market value will move with the cost of money: up when interest rates decline, down when they rise.

➤ COMMON STOCK Shown on the books at par value, an arbitrary amount having no relation to the market value or to what would be received in liquidation.

➤ CAPITAL SURPLUS The amount of money received from the sale of stock in excess of the par value.

➤ RETAINED EARNINGS Money reinvested in the business.

➤ TOTAL STOCKHOLDERS' EQUITY The sum of the common par value, additional paid-in capital, and retained earnings less any premium attributable to the preferred stock: what the stockholders own. The increase of $4.2 million is a rise of about 5%—not bad, but not as much as should be the mark of a true growth company.

CHANGES IN FINANCIAL POSITION

This presents a different view of the financing and investing activities of the company and clarifies the disposition of the funds produced by operations. It includes both cash and other elements of working capital—the excess of current assets over current liabilities.

The balance sheet shows that the working capital has increased by $1.2 million (current assets of $48.4 million exceeded current liabilities of $21.6 million by $26.8 million at the end of the year vs. $25.6 million the year before).

Sales and net income were up; the contribution to working capital from operations decreased to $13.6 million vs. $15 million the year before. This was narrowed to $.4 million by the proceeds of the $7 million in long-term debt, $1 million more than the proceeds from the sale of preferred stock the year before.

The difference between the funds used last year and the year before was $1.1 million, reflecting a heavier investment in productive capacity against a larger repayment of long-term debt the year before.

With increased capacity, the company should be able to handle higher sales. The additional cash may be a good sign, but when too much cash accumulates, it may indicate that management is not making the best use of its assets. In financially tense times, cash is still always welcome.

SEVEN KEYS TO VALUE

1 **Operating profit margin (PM)** The ratio of profit (before interest and taxes) to

STATEMENT OF CHANGES IN FINANCIAL POSITION ($ millions)
"Your Company"

	DEC. 31 CURRENT YEAR	DEC. 31 LAST YEAR	DEC. 31 2 YEARS AGO
FUNDS PROVIDED			
Net income	$ 9.9	$ 9.5	$ 9.1
Changes not requiring working capital:			
Depreciation	2.6	3.5	2.3
Increase in other liabilities	1.1	2.0	1.4
Funds provided by operations	$13.6	$15.0	$12.8
Proceeds from long-term debt	7.0	—	—
Proceeds from sale of 5% cumulative preferred stock	—	6.0	—
Total funds provided	$20.6	$21.0	$12.8
FUNDS USED			
Additions to fixed assets	$11.8	$ .5	$ 6.2
Dividends paid on preferred stock	.3	.3	—
Dividends paid on common stock	5.4	4.6	4.6
Payments on long-term debt	1.0	15.0	—
Increase in noncurrent receivables	.8	.1	.3
Increase in other assets	.1	—	.2
Total funds used	$19.4	$20.5	$11.3
Increase in working capital	$ 1.2	$ .5	$ 1.5
CHANGES IN COMPONENTS OF WORKING CAPITAL			
Increase (decrease) in current assets:			
Cash	$ 2.8	$ 1.0	$ 1.1
Marketable securities	(2.0)	.5	.4
Accounts receivable	1.0	.5	.8
Inventories	2.4	1.0	1.3
Increase in current assets	$ 4.2	$ 3.0	$ 3.6
Increase in current liabilities:			
Accounts payable	$ 1.1	$ .9	$ .6
Accrued liabilities	.3	.5	.2
Current maturity of long-term debt	.2	.1	.5
Federal income and other taxes	1.2	1.0	.8
Dividends payable	.2	—	—
Increase in current liabilities	$ 3.0	$ 2.5	$ 2.1
Increase in working capital	$ 1.2	$ .5	$ 1.5

sales. As shown on the statement of income and retained earnings, the operating profit ($22.6) divided by sales ($115.8) equals 19.5%. This compares with 18.5% for the previous year. (Some analysts prefer to compute this margin without including depreciation and depletion as part of the cost, because these have nothing to do with the efficiency of the operation.)

When a company increases sales substantially, the PM should widen, because certain costs (rent, interest, property taxes, etc.) are pretty much fixed and do not rise in proportion to volume.

2   **Current ratio**   The ratio of current assets to current liabilities is calculated from the balance sheet: $48.4 ÷ $21.6 = 2.24:1. For most industrial corporations, this ratio should be about 2:1. It varies with the type of business. Utilities and retail stores have rapid cash inflows and high turnovers of dollars, so they can operate effectively with low ratios.

When the ratio is high, say 5:1, it may mean that the company has too much cash and is not making the best use of these funds. They should be used to expand the business. Such corporations are often targets for takeovers.

3   **Liquidity ratio**   Again referring to the balance sheet, the ratio of cash and equivalents to total current liabilities ($9 ÷ $21.6 = 41.7%). It should be used to supplement the current ratio, because the immediate ability of a company to meet current obligations or pay larger dividends may be impaired despite a high current ratio. This 41.7% liquidity ratio (down from 44.1% the year before) probably indicates a period of expansion, rising prices, heavier capital expenditures, and larger accounts payable. *If the decline persists, the company might have to raise additional capital.*

4   **Capitalization ratios**   The percentage of each type of investment as part of the total investment in the corporation. Though often used to describe only the outstanding securities, capitalization is the sum of the face value of bonds ($26.0) and other debts *plus* the par value of all preferred and common stock issues ($18.3 + 6.0 = $24.3) *plus* the balance sheet totals for capital surplus ($9.6) and retained earnings ($46.4).

Bond, preferred stock, and common stock ratios are useful indicators of the relative risk and leverage involved for the owners of the three types of securities. For most industrial corporations, the debt ratio should be no more than 66⅔% of equity,

		CURRENT YEAR	PRIOR YEAR
1	Operating profit margin	19.5%	18.5%
2	Current ratio	2.24	2.38
3	Liquidity ratio	41.7%	44.1%
4	Capitalization ratios:		
	Long-term debt	19.7%	20.8%
	Preferred stock	6.0	6.3
	Common stock and surplus	80.3	72.9
5	Sales to fixed assets	1.1	1.2
6	Sales to inventories	4.3	4.5
7	Net income to net worth	12.3%	12.5%

or 40% of total capital. Higher ratios are appropriate for utilities and transportation corporations.

In this instance, looking at the balance sheet, the long-term debt plus preferred stock ($26.0 + $6.0 = $32.0) is 87.2% of the $27.9 equity represented by the common stock ($18.3) and surplus ($9.6), and 30.1% of total capital.

5   **Sales-to-fixed-assets ratio**   Using both the statement of income and retained earnings and the balance sheet, this ratio is computed by dividing the annual sales ($115.8) by the year-end value of plant, equipment, and land before depreciation and amortization ($104.3 + $0.9 = $105.2). The ratio is therefore 1.1:1. This is down from 1.2:1 the year before.

This ratio helps to show whether funds used to enlarge productive facilities are being spent wisely. A sizable expansion in facilities should lead to larger sales volume. If it does not, there's something wrong. In this case, there were delays in getting production on stream at the new plant.

6   **Sales-to-inventories ratio**   Again referring to both statements, you can compute this ratio by dividing the annual sales by year-end inventories: $115.8 ÷ $27 = 4.3:1. The year before, the ratio was 4.5:1.

This shows inventory turnover: the

number of times the equivalent of the year-end inventory has been bought and sold during the year.

It is more important in analyzing retail corporations than in analyzing manufacturers. A high ratio denotes a good quality of merchandise and correct pricing policies. A declining ratio may be a warning signal.

7 **Net-income-to-net-worth (return on equity) ratio** One of the most significant of all financial ratios. Derived by dividing

COMPANIES WITH STRONG BALANCE SHEETS

COMPANY	S&P RANK-ING	LONG-TERM DEBT AS % OF EQUITY	CASH RATIO (CASH AND EQUIVALENTS TO CURRENT LIABILITIES)	1988 EARNINGS PER SHARE*	INDICATED DIVIDEND	YIELD	1987–1988 PRICE RANGE	CURRENT PRICE	P/E RATIO†
Int'l Flavors & Fragrances	A	0	1.39	$3.25	$1.60	3.2%	$58–37$\frac{1}{4}$	$50	15.4
Houghton Mifflin	A–	1	0.06	1.90	0.62	1.8	41$\frac{3}{8}$–20$\frac{3}{4}$	34	17.9
Block (H.R.)	A	2	1.50	1.82	0.88	2.8	34$\frac{3}{4}$–20	31	17.0
Raytheon Co.	A+	2	0.06	7.15	2.00	3.0	84$\frac{7}{8}$–57$\frac{1}{4}$	67	9.4
NCR Corp.	A	5	0.59	5.20	1.24	2.0	87$\frac{1}{4}$–44$\frac{1}{8}$	61	11.7
Melville Corp.	A+	5	0.06	5.40	2.10	3.1	84–44$\frac{1}{4}$	67	12.4
Bristol-Myers	A+	7	1.31	2.85	1.68	3.8	55$\frac{7}{8}$–28$\frac{1}{4}$	44	15.4
Merck & Co.	A+	7	0.81	8.50	3.84	2.4	223–122	158	18.6
Armstrong World	A–	7	0.14	3.65	0.90	2.5	47$\frac{3}{8}$–22$\frac{1}{2}$	36	9.9
Pfizer Inc.	A+	8	0.38	4.50	2.00	3.7	77–41$\frac{1}{4}$	54	12.0
Minnesota Mining & Mfg.	A	9	0.02	4.45	2.12	3.4	83$\frac{1}{2}$–45	62	13.9
Medtronic Inc.	A–	10	0.56	6.15	1.04	1.1	108$\frac{1}{2}$–64	96	15.6
Schlumberger Ltd.	A–	10	1.07	1.50	1.20	3.3	51–26	36	24.0
Zurn Industries	A–	11	0.53	1.75	0.68	3.0	30$\frac{3}{4}$–15	23	13.1
Community Psychiatric Centers	A	12	1.70	1.55	0.32	1.5	32$\frac{1}{4}$–17$\frac{15}{16}$	22	14.2
UST Inc.	A+	12	0.53	2.80	1.48	4.9	32$\frac{1}{4}$–19$\frac{1}{2}$	30	10.7
Abbott Laboratories	A+	13	0.34	3.25	1.20	2.4	67–40	49	15.1
Schering-Plough	A	14	0.65	3.40	1.20	2.3	57$\frac{3}{8}$–31$\frac{1}{4}$	53	15.6
Lilly (Eli)	A+	14	0.71	5.00	2.30	2.8	107$\frac{3}{4}$–57$\frac{3}{4}$	81	16.2
Exxon Corp.	A	14	0.21	3.80	2.00	4.5	50$\frac{3}{4}$–32	44	11.6
Int'l Multifoods	A–	20	0.15	2.55	1.18	3.8	39$\frac{3}{4}$–22$\frac{1}{2}$	31	12.2
Dean Foods	A+	20	0.10	2.40	0.54	1.8	38$\frac{1}{2}$–22$\frac{3}{4}$	30	12.5
Syntex Corp.	A	22	0.75	2.50	1.00	2.7	48$\frac{3}{8}$–23	37	14.8
Upjohn Co.	A+	26	0.55	2.25	0.72	2.3	53$\frac{3}{4}$–22$\frac{5}{8}$	32	14.2
Waste Management	A	26	0.08	1.90	0.36	1.0	48$\frac{1}{2}$–27$\frac{3}{4}$	36	18.9
Amoco Corp.	A	26	0.29	5.65	3.50	4.7	90$\frac{1}{4}$–57	75	13.3
Maytag Corp.	A–	27	0.04	2.20	1.00	4.3	32$\frac{5}{16}$–17	23	10.5
Johnson & Johnson	A	28	0.47	5.40	1.68	2.0	105$\frac{3}{8}$–55	84	15.6
Archer-Daniels-Midland	A–	30	0.61	2.10	0.10	0.5	27$\frac{3}{4}$–16$\frac{11}{16}$	20	9.5
Emerson Electric	A+	30	0.08	2.30	1.00	2.9	42$\frac{3}{8}$–26$\frac{3}{4}$	34	14.8
Coca-Cola	A+	30	0.42	2.70	1.20	3.1	53$\frac{1}{8}$–28$\frac{1}{2}$	39	14.4

* Estimated

† Based on estimated 1988 earnings

SOURCE: Standard & Poor's, *The Outlook,* March 23, 1988.

the net income from the statement of income and retained earnings ($9.9) by the total stockholders' equity from the balance sheet ($80.3). The result is 12.3%: the percentage of return that corporate management earned on the dollars entrusted by shareholders at the beginning of each year. Basically, it's that all-important PR (profit rate).

This 12.3% is a slight decrease from the 12.5% of the prior year. It's a fair return: not as good as that achieved by a top-quality corporation but better than that of the average publicly held company. *The higher the ratio, the more profitable the operation.* Any company that can consistently improve such a ratio is a true growth company. *But be sure that this gain is a result of operating skill, not of accounting legerdemain or extraordinary items.*

RATIOS AND TRENDS

Detailed financial analysis involves careful evaluation of income, costs, and earnings. But it is also important to study various ratios and trends, both those within the specific corporation and those of other companies in the same industry. Analysts usually prefer to use 5- or 10-year averages. These can reveal significant changes and, on occasion, point out special values in either concealed or inconspicuous assets.

➤ OPERATING RATIO   The ratio of operating costs to sales. It is the complement of *profit margin* (100% minus the PM percentage). Thus if a company's PM is 10%, its operating ratio is 90%. It's handy for comparing similar companies but not significant otherwise.

PMs vary with the type of business. They are low for companies with heavy plant investments (Ingersoll-Rand) and for retailers with fast turnovers (The Limited) and high for marketing firms (Gillette).

➤ INTEREST COVERAGE   The number of times interest charges or requirements have been earned. Divide the operating profit (or balance available for such payments before income taxes and interest charges) by the annual interest charges.

According to the statement of income and retained earnings, the interest (fixed charges)

was covered 17.4 times in the past year and 20.3 times in the previous year. This is a high, safe coverage. If earnings declined to only 6% of the past year's results, interest would still be covered. As a rule, a manufacturing company should cover interest 5 times; utilities, 3 times.

Keep in mind that when a company (except utilities or transportation firms) has a high debt, it means that investors shy away from buying its common stock. To provide the plants, equipment, etc., that the company needs, management must issue bonds or preferred shares (straight or convertible to attract investors). There are some tax advantages in following such a course, but when the debt becomes too high, there can be trouble during times of recession. All or most of the gross profits will have to be used to pay interest, and there will be nothing or little left over for the common stockholders.

By contrast, speculators like high-debt situations when business is good. With hefty profits, interest can be paid easily, and the balance comes down to the common stock. Typically, airlines with heavy debt obligations for new planes do well in boom times. An extra 10% gain in traffic can boost profits by as much as 30%.

➤ PAYOUT RATIO   The ratio of the cash dividends to per-share profits after taxes. Fast-growing corporations pay no or small dividends because they need money for expansion. Profitable companies pay out from about 25% to 50% of their profits. Utilities, which have almost assured earnings, pay out more. But be wary when those dividends represent much more than 70% of income.

It's pleasant to receive an ample dividend check, but for growth, look for companies that pay small dividends. The retained earnings will be used to improve financial strength and the operating future of the company. *And they are tax-free.*

➤ PRICE-TO-BOOK-VALUE RATIO   The market price of the stock divided by its book value per share. Since book value trends are usually more stable than earnings trends, conservative analysts use this ratio as a price comparison. They check the historical over- or undervaluation of the stock, which in turn depends primarily on the company's profitable growth (or lack of it).

Because of inflation, understatement of assets on balance sheets—and, in boom times, the enthusiasm of investors—often pushes this ratio rather high. On the average, only stocks of the most profitable companies sell at much more than twice book value. Investors believe that these corporations will continue to achieve ever-higher earnings. But if the stock prices rise too high, their decline, in a bear market, can be fast and far.

➤ PRICE-EARNINGS (P/E) RATIO   Calculated by dividing the price of the stock by the reported earnings per share for the past 12 months. Such projections can be made *only* for stocks of quality corporations with long, fairly consistent records of profitable growth. They will not work for shares of companies that are cyclical, erratic, or untested. There can be no guarantee that these goals will be attained as soon as anticipated. Wall Street is often slow to recognize value and always takes time to come to intelligent decisions.

➤ CASH FLOW   A yardstick that is increasingly popular in investment analysis. Reported net earnings after taxes do not reflect the actual cash income available to the company. Cash flow shows the earnings after taxes *plus* charges against income that do not directly involve cash outlays (sums allocated to depreciation, depletion, amortization, and other special items).

A company might show a net profit of $250,000 plus depreciation of $1 million, so cash flow is $1,250,000. Deduct provisions for preferred dividends (if any), and then divide the balance by the number of shares of common stock to get the cash flow per share.

Two types of cash flow are important:

■ *Distributable cash flow:* the amount of money that the company has on hand to pay dividends and/or invest in real growth. If this is negative, there are problems. If it's positive, fine, *unless* the company pays out more than this figure in dividends and is thus liquidating the firm.

■ *Discretionary cash flow:* distributable cash flow minus dividends, that is, how much money is left to grow with, after allocations for maintenance and dividends. Companies do not actually set aside such funds, but, they must ultimately have the money in some form—cash savings or borrowing.

HOW TO DETERMINE A PRUDENT P/E RATIO

Analysts usually justify their recommendations by adjusting the multiple of the price of the stock by estimated rate of future growth or by cash flow per share rather than by reported earnings. In both cases, these are attempts to justify a predetermined decision to buy. The projections appear plausible, especially when accompanied by tables and charts and computer printouts. But in most cases, they are useful only as background and not for the purpose of making decisions on the proper level to buy or later to sell. The calculations depend a good deal on market conditions and your own style, but here's one approach for those "supergrowth" stocks that will be suggested by your friends or broker.

Example: According to your financial adviser, the stock of a "future" company now selling at 40 times its recent earnings will be trading at "only 16 times its projected earnings 5 years hence *if* the company's average earnings

---

DIVIDENDS AS A PERCENTAGE OF EARNINGS: 1988

COMPANY	PAYOUT
Atlanta Gas Light	77%
Baltimore Gas & Electric	56
Brooklyn Union Gas	67
Citicorp	40
Consolidated Edison	71
Contel Corp.	63
Delmarva Power & Light	86
Diversified Energies	69
Dominion Resources	66
Duke Power	62
Florida Progress	70
New England Electric System	70
Oklahoma Gas & Electric	79
Rochester Telephone	66
Royal Dutch Petroleum	58
SCANA Corp.	81
Southern New England Telecom.	62
Washington Gas Light	82

SOURCE: Standard & Poor's, June 1988.

growth is 20% a year." (See price evaluator, page 326.)

If you are speculating with this type of "hot" stock, you should compare it with other opportunities and on some basis decide how reasonable this projection really is.

A handy formula is

$$\text{Prudent P/E ratio} = GRTQM$$

G = growth
R = reliability and risk
T = time
Q = quality
M = multiple of price to earnings

➤ GROWTH The company's projected growth in earnings per share over the next 5 years. The basic compound interest formula is $(1 + G)^5$, where G is the projected growth rate, as shown in the price evaluator and prudent P/E multiples table. This omits dividend yields because they are usually small in relation to the potential capital appreciation.

➤ RELIABILITY AND RISK Not all projected growth rates are equally reliable or probable. A lower projected growth rate is likely to be more reliable than a very high projected one (30% to 50% a year).

Logically, you can assign a higher reliability rating to a noncyclical company (utility, food processor, retailer) than to a corporation in a cyclical industry (aluminum, machinery, tools).

➤ TIME Another factor is the assumed length of the projected growth period. If you can realistically anticipate that the company will continue its rate of growth for the next 10 years, a 10% rate for its stock is more reliable than a 15% rate for a company whose growth visibility is only 3 to 5 years.

If you are uncertain about the corporation's consistency, you should assign it the greater risk.

➤ QUALITY As you know, this is the single most important investment consideration.

➤ MULTIPLE OF PRICE TO EARNINGS This is a comparative measurement. The first step is to determine the P/E for an average quality nongrowth stock. This is done by relating the current yield on guaranteed, fixed income investments (savings accounts, corporate bonds) to the P/E multiple that will produce the same yield on the nongrowth stock.

$$P/E = \frac{D}{IR}$$

P/E = price/earnings ratio
D = dividend as percentage payout of earnings
IR = interest rate

Thus a stock yielding 8% on a 70% payout of profits must, over a 5-year period, be bought and sold at 7 times earnings to break even on capital and to make as much income as could be obtained over the same period via the ownership of a fixed-income investment continually yielding 10%:

$$P/E = \frac{7}{10} = .7$$

Note: This is *not* a valid comparison in terms of investment alone. Since the nongrowth stock carries a certain amount of risk in comparison to the certainty of a bond or money market fund, the stock should sell at a lower multiple, probably 5 to 6 times earnings.

Other key items used in analysis are:

➤ EARNINGS GROWTH RATE A formula that gives the rate at which a company's profits have increased over the past several years. You can find the earnings growth rate in annual reports or from your broker. Then divide it by the P/E and compare this number with the Standard & Poor's 500 to decide whether to buy or sell. Keep in mind that in good years the average growth rate for the Standard & Poor's 500 stock index has been 16% and the average P/E 8, so the index for the purposes of this formula should be divided by 2.

For example, let us assume that Company XYZ has an earnings growth rate of 40% per year. Its P/E is 20; its index is therefore 2, only equal to the Standard & Poor's average—nothing to get excited about.

Another company, the LMN Corporation, has an earnings growth rate of 40% also; however, its P/E is 15, so its index comes out to be 2.6. Because this ratio is above the Standard & Poor's index of 2, it is an apparent bargain.

➤ PERCENTAGE BUYING VALUE This is a variation of the formula developed by John B. Neff of the Windsor Fund. It uses the current yield plus the rate of earnings growth divided by the current P/E ratio. If the result is 2 or more, the stock is worth buying:

PRUDENT PRICE-EARNINGS MULTIPLES FOR GROWTH STOCKS

IF YOU PROJECT EARNINGS PER SHARE (AFTER TAXES) TO GROW IN NEXT 5 YEARS AT AN AVERAGE COMPOUNDED RATE OF:	WITH THESE QUALITY RATINGS* THESE ARE APPROXIMATE PRUDENT MULTIPLES THAT REPRESENT THE MAXIMUM CURRENT PRICE TO PAY:				
	B	B+	A–	A	A+
5%	12.0	12.9	13.7	15.0	16.7
6%	12.5	13.4	14.3	15.8	17.4
7%	13.0	14.0	14.9	16.5	18.2
8%	13.6	14.5	15.6	17.1	18.9
9%	14.1	15.1	16.2	17.8	19.7
10%	14.6	15.7	16.8	18.5	20.4
15%	17.4	18.7	20.1	22.0	24.5
20%	20.2	21.8	23.4	25.7	28.6
25%	23.0	24.7	26.6	29.3	32.7
30%	25.2	27.3	29.4	32.5	36.2
35%	28.5	31.0	33.5	37.1	41.5
40%	31.9	34.8	37.7	41.7	46.7

*Standard & Poor's designations. If not rated, use B; if a new, untested firm, use a conservative rating based on comparison with similar companies, preferably in the same industry.

CY = current yield
EG = earnings growth
P/E = price-earnings ratio
PBV = percentage buying value

$$\frac{CY + EG}{P/E} = PBV$$

$$\frac{1.4 + 20}{22} = 9.7\% = buy$$

$$\frac{8.6 + 2}{7.7} = 1.32\% = sell \ or \ do \ not \ buy$$

► RETURN ON EQUITY AND P/E: TOTAL RETURN Most investors tend to think about their gains and losses in terms of price changes and not dividends, whereas those who own bonds pay attention to interest yields and seldom focus on price changes. Both approaches are mistaken. Although dividend yields are obviously more important if you are seeking income, and changes in price play a greater role in growth stocks,

knowing the *total return* on a stock makes it possible for you to compare your investment in a stock with a similar investment in a corporate bond, municipal, Treasury, mutual fund, etc.

To calculate the total return, add (or subtract) the stock's price change and the dividends received for 12 months and then divide that number by the price at the beginning of the 12-month period. *Example:* An investor bought a stock at $42 per share and received dividends for the 12-month period of $2.50. At the end of 12 months, the stock was sold at $45. The total return was 13%.

Dividend	$2.50
Stock price change	$3.00
	$5.50 ÷ $42 = 13%

► CORPORATE CASH POSITION Developed by Benjamin Graham, granddaddy of fundamentalists.

- Subtract current liabilities, long-term debt, and preferred stock (at market value) from current assets of the corporation.
- Divide the result by the number of shares of common stock outstanding to get the current asset value per share.
- If it is higher than the price per share, Graham would place the stock on his review list.

CHECKPOINTS FOR FINDING UNDERVALUED STOCKS

- A price that is well below book value, asset value, and working capital per share
- Ample cash or liquid assets for both normal business and expansion
- A current dividend of 4.5% or more
- Cash dividends paid for at least 5, and preferably 10, years without decrease in dollar payout
- Total debt less than 35% of total capitalization
- Minimum current dividend protection ratio of at least 1:4 ($1.40 earnings for each $1.00 in dividends), preferably higher
- A P/E ratio lower than that of prior years and preferably below 10 times projected 12-month earnings

LOW-P/E STOCKS

STOCK	PRICE (APRIL 1989)	P/E RATIO
ASARCO Inc.	28	4.7
Federal Paper Board	25	4.8
Alcan Aluminium	32	4.9
Georgia-Gulf	41	5.3
Great Northern Nekoosa	39	5.4
Cyprus Minerals	39	5.6
Mallard Coach	8	5.7
Aluminum Co. of America	63	5.9
Dow Chemical	92	6.1
Navistar Int'l	6	6.3
Lukens Inc.	28	6.4
Marshall Industries	17	6.5
MNC Financial	46	6.7
Potlatch Corp.	32	6.9
Penney (J.C.)	52	7.3
Georgia-Pacific	44	7.3
Home Savings Bank	17	7.6
Summagraphics	13	7.6
Fleet/Norstar Financial	27	7.8
Westvaco Co.	29	8.1
Barnett Banks	34	8.1
Gulf States Utilities	9	8.2
CoreStates Financial	43	8.5
Olin Corp.	52	8.7
Varian Associates	26	8.7
Reebok Int'l	14	8.8
Ohio Edison	20	8.9
Commonwealth Edison	33	9.0
PPG Industries	43	9.1
General Instrument	29	9.1

SOURCE: Standard & Poor's, *The Outlook,* April 19, 1989.

- A company that sells at 4 or 5 times cash flow and that generates excess cash, which can be used to expand or repurchase its stock

- Inventories that are valued lower than their initial cost or their immediate market value (check Value Line or S&P for figures)

LOW P/Es PAY OFF

Investors often get excited about stocks with high P/Es. They figure the stocks are so popular that their prices will keep on rising. But the facts prove otherwise: stocks with low P/Es (seemingly those with the worst prospects) outperform those with high multiples.

Low P/Es are often found in mature industries, in low-growth and blue chip companies. In general, low-P/E companies pay higher dividends, although there are many exceptions.

High P/Es, by contrast, tend to be found in newer, aggressive growth companies, which are far riskier than those with lower P/Es.

$ HINT: Look for companies with high sales per share in cyclical industries (auto, aluminum, rubber) that are temporarily depressed. When industry conditions change and profit margins increase, the turnaround in earnings can be dramatic.

COMPANIES REPURCHASING THEIR STOCK

When corporations set up a program to buy back their shares, it's a bullish sign. Over a 12-month period, one survey showed, 64% of such stock outpaced the market.

Repurchase of a substantial number of shares automatically benefits all shareholders: profits are spread over a smaller total, there's more money for dividends and reinvestments, and there's a temporary price increase for the stock in many cases.

USING TECHNICAL INDICATORS

Technical analysis is a way of doing securities research using indicators, charts, and computer programs to track price trends of stocks, bonds, commodities, and the market in general. Technical analysts use these indicators to predict price movements.

If you understand the basics of both technical and fundamental analysis, you'll have a great advantage as an investor.

TA is neither as complex nor as esoteric as many people think. It's a tell-it-as-it-is interpretation of stock market activity. The technician glances at the fundamental values of securities but basically concentrates on the behavior of the market, industry groups, and stocks themselves—their price movements, volume, trends, patterns; in sum, their supply and demand.

Basically, TA is concerned with what *is* and not with what *should be.* Dyed-in-the-wool technicians pay minimal attention to what the *company* does and concentrate on what its *stock* does. They recognize that over the short term, the values of stock reflect what people *think* they are worth, not what they are really worth.

Technical analysts operate on the assumption that (1) the past action of the stock market is the best indicator of its future course, (2) 80% of a stock's price movement is due to factors outside the company's control and 20% to factors unique to that stock, and (3) the stock market over a few weeks or months is rooted 85% in psychology and only 15% in economics.

THE DOW THEORY

There are a number of technical theories, but the granddaddy is the Dow theory. It is the oldest and most widely used. As with all technical approaches, it is based on the belief that stock prices cannot be forecast accurately by fundamental analysis but that trends, indicated by price movements and volume, can be used successfully. These can be recorded, tracked, and interpreted because the market itself prolongs movements: investors buy more when the market is rising and sell more when it's dropping.

This follow-the-crowd approach enables the pros to buy when the market is going up and to sell or sell short when the market turns down. For amateurs, such quick trading is costly because of the commissions involved and the need for accurate information. But when properly used, TA can be valuable in correctly timing your buy and sell positions.

The Dow theory is named after Charles H. Dow, one of the founders of Dow Jones & Company, Inc., the financial reporting and publishing organization. The original hypotheses have been changed somewhat by his followers, but broadly interpreted, the Dow theory signals both the beginning and end of bull and bear markets.

Dow believed the stock market to be a barometer of business. The purpose of his theory was not to predict movements of security prices but rather to call the turns of the market and to forecast the business cycle or longer movements of depression or prosperity. It was not concerned with ripples or day-to-day fluctuations.

The Dow theory basically states that once a trend of the Dow Jones Industrial Average (DJIA) has been established, it tends to follow the same direction until definitely canceled by *both* the Industrial and Railroad (now Transportation) averages. The market cannot be expected to produce new indications of the trend every day, and unless there is positive evidence to the contrary, the existing trend will continue.

Dow and his disciples saw the stock market as made up of two types of "waves": the *primary wave,* which is a bull or bear market cycle of

TECHNICAL VS. FUNDAMENTAL ANALYSIS

Technical analysis focuses on the changes of a company's stock as illustrated on daily, weekly, or periodic charts. Volume or number of shares traded is included, and from this "technical" information future price movements are forecast.

Fundamental analysis of industries and companies, by contrast, centers on the outlook for earnings and growth. Analysts study such factors as sales, assets, earnings, products, services, potential markets, and management.

several years' duration, and the *secondary* (or *intermediary*) *wave,* which lasts from a few weeks to a few months. Any single primary wave may contain within it 20 or more secondary waves, both up and down.

The theory relies on similar action by the two averages (Industry and Transportation), which may vary in strength but not in direction. Robert Rhea, who expanded the original concept, explained it this way: "Successive rallies, penetrating preceding high points with ensuing declines terminating above preceding low points, offer a bullish indication . . . (and vice versa for bearish indication). . . . A rally or decline is defined as one or more daily movements resulting in a net reversal of direction exceeding 3% of either average. Such movements have little authority unless confirmed by both Industrial and Transportation Averages . . . but confirmation need not occur in the same day."

Dow did not consider that his theory applied to individual stock selections or analysis. He expected that specific issues would rise or fall with the averages most of the time, but he also recognized that any particular security would be affected by special conditions or situations.

These are the key indicators of the Dow theory:

- **A bull market is signaled as a possibility** when an intermediate decline in the DJIA stops above the bottom of the previous

intermediate decline. This action *must be confirmed* by the action of the Transportation Average (DJTA). A bull market is confirmed after this has happened and when on the next intermediate rise *both* averages rise above the peaks of the last previous intermediate rise.

- **A bull market is in progress** as long as each new intermediate rise goes *higher* than the peak of the previous intermediate advance and each new intermediate decline stops *above* the bottom of the previous one.

- **A bear market is signaled as a possibility** when an intermediate rally in the DJIA fails to break through the top of the previous intermediate rise. A bear market is *confirmed* (1) after this has happened, (2) when the next intermediate decline breaks through the low of the previous one, and (3) when it is confirmed by the DJTA.

- **A bear market is in progress** as long as each new intermediate decline goes *lower* than the bottom of the previous decline and each new intermediate rally fails to rise as high as the previous rally.

A pure Dow theorist considers the averages to be quite sufficient to use in forecasting and sees no need to supplement them with statistics of commodity prices, volume of production, car loadings, bank debts, exports, imports, etc.

➤ INTERPRETING THE DOW THEORY The Dow theory leaves no room for sentiment.

A primary bear market does not terminate until stock prices have thoroughly discounted the worst that is apt to occur. This decline requires three steps: (1) "the abandonment of hopes upon which stocks were purchased at inflated prices," (2) selling due to decreases in business and earnings, and (3) distress selling of sound securities despite value.

Primary bull markets follow the opposite pattern: (1) a broad movement, interrupted by secondary reactions averaging longer than 2 years, where successive rallies penetrate high points with ensuing declines terminating above preceding low points; (2) stock prices advancing because of demand created by both investors and speculators who start buying when business conditions improve; and (3) rampant speculation as stocks advance on hopes, expectations, and dreams.

$ HINT: A new primary trend is not actually confirmed by the Dow theory until *both* the DJTA and the DJIA penetrate their previous positions.

➤ CRITICISM There are analysts who scoff at the Dow theory. They point out that the stock market today is vastly different from that in the early 1900s when Dow formulated his theory. The number and value of shares of publicly owned corporations have increased enormously: in 1900, the average number of shares traded *annually* on the NYSE was 59.5 million. Now that's the volume on a very slow *day*.

The sharpest criticism is leveled against the breadth, scope, and significance of the averages. The original Industrial index had only 12 stocks, and today's 30 large companies do not provide a true picture of the broad, technologically oriented economy. Critics point out that the Transportation average is also unrepresentative, because some of the railroads derive a major share of their revenues from natural resources, and the airlines and trucking companies are limited in their impact. Add the geographic dispersal of industry, and Transportation is no longer a reliable guide to the economy.

Finally, the purists argue that government regulations and institutional dominance of trading have so altered the original concept of individual investors that the Dow theory can no longer be considered all-powerful and always correct.

To most investors, the value of the Dow theory is that it represents a sort of think-for-yourself method that will pay worthwhile dividends for those who devote time and effort to gaining a sound understanding of the principles involved.

➤ WHAT'S AHEAD In July 1989, Richard Russell, whose *Dow Theory Letters* newsletter is the leading authority on the theory, stated, "What about the current situation? On the face of it, it would appear that corporate America is one big asset play, and if you're a public corporation you're fair game. Behind the whole takeover syndrome is the ease with which raiders and takeover specialists are able to raise money, plus the U.S. tax system which allows individuals and corporations to write off the interest on debt. Day after day, the most active list on the NYSE is dominated by takeover situations while rumors of additional new takeovers fill the air. . . . Yet this is still a bear market. Under the Dow Theory, once a bull market hits its peak (which occurred in 1987), the bear takes over. The bear market continues until stocks have discounted the worst that can be seen ahead. . . . The worst is when stocks decline to the point where they represent great values. . . . The public is totally disenchanted, Wall Street sentiment has turned black, volume is extremely low, yields on blue-chips are high. . . . Those are the conditions that prevail at a true bear market bottom. And we haven't seen anything like that—yet." (*Dow Theory Letters*, P.O. Box 1759, La Jolla, CA 92038; $225 per year)

PSYCHOLOGICAL INDICATORS

Keeping in mind that the stock market is rooted 15% in economics and 85% in psychology, some analysts predict the future by using such technical indicators as these:

➤ BARRON'S CONFIDENCE INDEX (BCI) This is published weekly in the financial news magazine *Barron's*. It shows the ratio of the yield on 10 highest-grade bonds to the yield on the broader-based Dow Jones 40-bond average. The ratio varies from the middle 80s (bearish) to the middle 90s (bullish).

The theory is that the trend of "smart money" is usually revealed in the bond market before it shows up in the stock market. Thus, *Barron's Confidence Index* will be *high* when shrewd investors are confident and buy more lower-grade bonds, thus reducing low-grade bond yields, and *low* when they are worried and stick to high-grade bonds, thus cutting high-grade yields.

If you see that the BCI simply keeps going back and forth aimlessly for many weeks, you can probably expect the same type of action from the overall stock market.

➤ OVERBOUGHT-OVERSOLD INDEX (OOI) This is a handy measure, designed by *Indicator Digest*, of a short-term trend and its anticipated duration. Minor upswings or downturns have limited lives. As they peter out, experienced traders say that the market is "overbought" or "oversold" and is presumably ready for a near-term reversal.

➤ GLAMOR AVERAGE Another *Indicator Digest* special, this shows what is happening with the institutional favorites, usually trading at high multiples because of their presumed growth potential and current popularity (in a bull market). By and large, this is a better indicator for speculators than investors.

➤ SPECULATION INDEX This is the ratio of AMEX-to-NYSE volume. When trading in AMEX stocks (generally more speculative) moves up faster than that in NYSE (quality) issues, speculation is growing. It's time for traders to move in and for investors to be cautious.

BROAD-BASED INDICATORS

➤ ODD-LOT INDEX This shows how small investors view the market, because it concentrates on trades of less than 100 shares. The small investor is presumably "uninformed" (a somewhat debatable assumption) and so tends to follow established patterns: selling as the market rises; jumping in to pick up bargains when it declines. The signal comes when the odd lotter deviates from this "normal" behavior.

When the small investor distrusts a rally after a long bear market, that investor gives a bullish signal: initial selling is normal, but when this continues, it's abnormal and a signal to the pros to start buying.

➤ MOVING AVERAGE LINES You can also watch the direction of a stock by comparing its price to a *moving average* (MA). A moving average is an average that's periodically updated by dropping the first number and adding in the last one. A 30-week moving average, for example, is determined by adding the stock's closing price for the current week to the closing prices of the previous 29 weeks and then dividing by 30. Over time, this moving average indicates the trend of prices.

A long-term moving average tends to smooth out short-term fluctuations and provides a basis against which short-term price movement can be measured.

Moving averages can be calculated for both individual stocks and all stocks in a group— say, all those listed on the NYSE or all in a particular industry. Technical analysts use a variety of time frames: 10 days, 200 days, 30

weeks, etc. In most cases they compare the moving average with a regular market average, usually the Dow Jones Industrial Average. For example:

- As long as the DJIA is *above* the MA, the outlook is bullish.
- As long as the DJIA is *below* the MA, the outlook is bearish.
- A confirmed downward penetration of the MA by the base index is a *sell* signal.
- A confirmed penetration of the MA is a *buy* signal.

Beware of false penetrations, and delay action until there is a substantial penetration (2% to 3%), upward or downward, within a few weeks. In other words, don't be in a hurry to interpret the chart action.

MAs are vulnerable to swift market declines, especially from market tops. By the time you get the signal, you may have lost a bundle, because prices tend to fall twice as fast as they rise.

If you enjoy charting, develop a ratio of the stocks selling above their 30-week MA. When the ratio is over 50% and trending upward, the outlook is bullish. When it drops below 50% and/or is trending down, there's trouble ahead.

MOST ACTIVE ISSUES, NYSE, MAY 2, 1989

NYSE	VOLUME	CLOSE	CHANGE
Union Carbide	9,010,900	31⅝	+¼
Southern Co	2,967,900	23½	
Avon Products	2,745,400	32¼	+3⅝
Illinois Power	1,867,600	13¾	
U S Shoe Corp	1,662,900	17⅛	+½
Merrill Lynch	1,641,500	28¾	−⅛
Texaco Inc	1,496,300	54¼	+¼
AT&T	1,256,600	34½	−⅜
Wis Enrg	1,246,400	x26¾	+⅛
Sealed Air Corp	1,209,100	50¾	+½
IBM	1,178,300	113⅜	−⅝
Cineplx Odeon	1,081,900	15	+⅞
Cooper Cos	1,069,500	4⅜	+⅛
Carson Pirie	1,050,900	27	+4⅜
Exxon Corp	1,030,200	42⅞	−¼

SOURCE: Wall Street Journal, May 2, 1989.

$ HINT: The longer the time span of the MA, the greater the significance of a crossover signal. An 18-month chart is more reliable than a 30-day one.

➤ BUYING POWER   Buying power basically refers to the amount of money available to buy securities. It is determined by the cash in brokerage accounts plus the dollar amount that would be available if securities were fully margined. The bottom line: the market cannot rise above the available buying power.

The principle here is that at any point investors have only so much money available for investments. If it's in money market funds and cash, their buying power is stored up and readily available, not only to move into stocks but to push up prices. By contrast, if most investor buying power is already in stocks, there's little left for purchasing more stocks. In fact, in this situation investors could actually push the price of stocks down should they begin to sell.

Buying power is shown by these indicators:

■   Rising volume in rallies. Investors are eager to buy, so the demand is greater than the supply, and prices go up.

■   Shrinking volume on market declines. Investors are reluctant to sell.

With this technical approach, volume is the key indicator: it rises on rallies when the trend is up and rises on reactions when the trend is down.

$ HINT: Volume trends are apt to reverse before price trends. Shrinking volume almost always shows up before the top of a bull market and before the bottom of a bear market.

One other measure of buying power is the percentage of cash held in mutual funds. The Investment Company Institute in Washington, D.C., publishes this figure every month. In general, the ratio of cash to total assets in mutual funds tends to be low during market peaks, because this is the time when everyone is eager to buy stocks. The ratio is high during bull markets.

$ HINT: When cash holdings, as compiled by the Investment Company Institute, are above 7%, it's considered favorable; 9% to 10% is out-and-out bullish.

➤ MOST ACTIVE STOCKS   This list is published at the top of daily or weekly reports of the NYSE, AMEX, and NASDAQ, and it gives the high, low, and last prices and change of 10 to 15 volume leaders. Here's where you can spot popular and unpopular industry groups and stocks.

Forget about the big-name companies such as Exxon, GE, and IBM. They have so many shares outstanding that trading is always heavy. Watch for repetition: of one industry or of one company. When the same names appear several times in a week or two, something is happening. Major investors are involved: buying if the price continues to rise, selling if it falls.

Watch most-actives for:

■   *Newcomers,* especially small or medium-sized corporations. When the same company pops up again and again, major

NYSE PERCENTAGE GAINERS . . .

NYSE	CLOSE	CHANGE	% CHANGE
Carson Pirie	27	+4⅜	+19.3
Cullinet Sftwr	6⅜	+1	+18.6
Avon Products	32¼	+3⅝	+12.7
WMS Indus	10⅛	+1⅛	+12.5
Fischbach	17	+1⅜	+8.8
Emerald Mtge	3⅜	+¼	+8.0
Jepson Corp	10⅞	+¾	+7.4
Milton Roy Co	13⅜	+⅞	+7.0
Stanhome Inc	27⅛	+1¾	+6.9
Service Merch	18⅜	+1⅛	+6.5
Texfi Indus	8¼	+½	+6.5
Utd Merchnts	4¼	+¼	+6.3

. . . AND LOSERS

ToddShipyrd	2⅛	−¼	−10.5
Data-Design	6⅜	−⅝	−8.9
FairchildIndus	16	−1⅜	−7.9
CycareSys	6¾	−½	−6.9
Kollmorgen	23¾	−1½	−5.9
WedgestnFn	2	−⅛	−5.9
DiamondOff	10¼	−⅝	−5.7
LTVCorp	2⅛	−⅛	−5.6
FairfieldCom	6⅜	−⅜	−5.6
WesternUnion	2⅛	−⅛	−5.6
DresherInc	4⅜	−¼	−5.4

SOURCE: Wall Street Journal, May 3, 1989.

shareholders are worried (price drop) or optimistic (price rise). Since volume requires substantial resources, the buyers must be big-money organizations. Once they have bought, you can move in, *if* the other fundamentals are sound.

- *Companies in the same industry.* Stocks tend to move as a group. Activity in retailers such as Sears and K mart *could* signal interest in this field.

➤ PERCENTAGE LEADERS This list is published weekly in several financial journals. It's primarily for those seeking to catch a few points on a continuing trend.

Although the value of the percentage leaders list has diminished recently because of the high gains scored by takeover or buyout candidates, it is still a way to spot some potential winners and to avoid losers. If you're thinking about making a move, check this list first. You may find several yet undiscovered stocks moving up in price.

➤ ADVANCES VERSUS DECLINES (A/D) This is a measure of the number of stocks that have advanced in price and the number that have declined within a given time span. Expressed as a ratio, the A/D illustrates the general direction of the market: when more stocks advance than decline on a single trading day, the market is thought to be bullish. The A/D can be an excellent guide to the trend of the overall market and, occasionally, of specific industry or stock groups. The best way to utilize A/D data is with

a chart where the lines are plotted to show the cumulative difference between the advances and the declines on the NYSE or, for speculative holdings, on the AMEX. The total can cover 1 week, 21 days, or whatever period you choose, but because you're looking for developing trends, it should not be too long.

The table below shows a week when the volume was stable but the trend was down: almost neutral on Monday, a pleasant rise on Tuesday, and then downhill for the rest of the week. A chart will show previous periods and make possible projections.

Many analysts prefer a moving average (MA) based on the net change for the week: 3,844 advances and 4,403 declines, for a net difference of 559. To make plotting easier, you can start with an arbitrary base, say 10,000, so the week's figure would be 9,441 (10,000 − 559).

The following week there's a net advance of 1,003, so the new total would be 10,440, etc. When you chart a 20-week MA, divide the cumulative figure by 20. When you add week 21, drop week 1. *Result:* a quick view of market optimism or pessimism.

To spot trouble ahead, compare the A/D chart with that of the DJIA. If the Dow is moving up for a month or so but the A/D line is flat or dropping, that's a negative signal. Watch out for new highs and lows on the A/D chart. Near market peaks, the A/D line will almost invariably top out and start declining before the overall market. At market lows, the A/D line seldom gives a far-in-advance warning.

Be cautious about using the A/D line alone. Make sure that it is confirmed by other indicators or, better yet, confirms other signals.

➤ VOLUME Trading volume, or the number of shares traded, is an important indicator in interpreting market direction and stock price changes. Changes in stock prices are the result of supply and demand, that is, the number of people who want to buy a stock and the number who want to sell. The key point here is that a rise or fall in price on a small volume of shares traded is far less important than a move supported by heavy volume. When there's heavy trading on the up side, buyers control the market, and their enthusiasm for the stock often pushes its price even higher.

$ HINT: Volume always precedes the direction of a stock's price.

LONDON'S *FINANCIAL TIMES* INDEX

The *Financial Times* Index is a British version of the Dow Jones Industrial Average. It records data on the London Stock Exchange: prices, volume, etc. Because it reflects worldwide business attitudes, it's a fairly reliable indicator of what's ahead, in 2 weeks to 2 months, for the NYSE.

There are, of course, temporary aberrations due to local situations, but over many years it has been a valuable technical tool. Since London is 5 hours ahead of New York, early risers benefit the most.

NYSE ADVANCES AND DECLINES: HIGHS AND LOWS

	MONDAY	TUESDAY	WEDNESDAY	THURSDAY	FRIDAY
Total issues	2,020	2,021	2,031	1,891	1,997
Advances	758	936	658	739	393
Declines	812	645	960	790	1,196
Unchanged	450	440	413	462	408
New highs	23	20	20	23	10
New lows	47	44	65	61	64
Sales (000 shares)	86,972	97,798	118,932	125,384	98,351

SOURCE: Barron's.

➤ MOMENTUM This indicator measures the speed with which an index (or stock) is moving rather than its direction. Index changes are seldom if ever abrupt, so when an already rising index starts to rise even faster, it is thought likely to have a longer continuing upward run.

To measure momentum effectively you need to compare current figures to an index or previous average such as a 30-week moving average or the S&P 500.

➤ NEW HIGHS OR LOWS Every day the newspaper prints a list of stocks that hit a new price high or low for the year during the previous day's trading activity. Technical analysts use the ratio between the new highs and the new lows as an indication of the market's direction. They believe that when more stocks are making new highs than new lows, it's a bullish indication. If there are more lows than highs, pessimism abounds.

$HINT: You should not use these figures as an absolute prediction of the future course of the market, because for a while a number of the same stocks will appear again and again. Also, the further into the year it is, the more difficult it is for a stock to continually post new highs.

These figures are most effective when converted to a chart and compared with a standard average. As long as the high and low indicators stay more or less in step with the Dow Jones Industrial Average or the S&P 500, they are simply a handy confirmation. But when the high-low line starts to dip while the average moves up, *watch out:* internal market conditions are deteriorating.

This index of highs and lows exposes the underlying strength or weakness of the stock market, which is too often masked by the action of the DJIA. In an aging bull market, the DJIA may continue to rise, deceptively showing strength by the upward moves of a handful of

---

ADDITIONAL ADVICE

- **Breadth.** The fewer the issues moving with the market trend, the greater the probability of imminent reversal of that trend.
- **Industry breadth.** Using the *Barron's* reports on 35 industry groups, set up an A/D line by cumulating the difference between the groups that advanced that week and those that declined. Ignore unchanged industries and gold (which moves from other pressures).
- **Tenacity.** If the technical position remains the same for the market or stock, hold to your original opinion but recheck the basic data.
- **Keep it simple.** Most things done well are also done simply. If you must resort to complex computer programming and model building, chances are that you have not mastered the basics. The long-term action of the stock market is based on common sense, so the best approaches are always simple.

major stocks; but closer examination will usually reveal that most stocks are too far below their yearly highs to make new peaks. At such periods, the small number of new highs is one of the most significant manifestations of internal market deterioration. The reverse is the telltale manner in which the total number of new lows appears in bear markets.

USING THE INDICATORS

Never rely on just one technical indicator. Only rarely can a single chart, ratio, average, MA, or index be 100% accurate. When an indicator breaks its pattern, look for confirmation from at least two other guidelines. Then wait a bit: at least 2 days in an ebullient market, a week or more in a normal one. This won't be easy, but what you are seeking is confirmation. These days a false move can be costly.

This emphasis on consensus applies also to newsletters, advisory services, and recommendations. If you select only one, look for a publication that uses—and explains—several indicators. Better yet, study two or three.

CHARTS: A VALUABLE TOOL FOR EVERYONE

Charts are a graphic ticker tape. They measure the flow of money into and out of the stock market, industry, or specific stock. They spotlight the highs and lows and point up how volume rises and falls on an advance or decline, illustrating the long-term patterns of the market and individual stocks.

Charting is simple, but interpretation can be complex. Even the strongest advocates of TA disagree about the meaning of various formations, but they all start with three premises: (1) what happened before will be repeated, (2) a trend should be assumed to continue until a reversal is definite, and (3) a chart pattern that varies from a norm indicates that something unusual is happening. More than almost any other area of TA, chart reading is an art and a skill rather than a solid body of objective scientific information. It is an aid to stock analysis but not an end.

Charts are not surefire systems for beating the market, but they are one of the quickest

and clearest ways to determine and follow trends. But all charts provide after-the-fact information.

The best combination for maximum profits and minimum losses is fundamental analysis supplemented by graphic technical analysis. Charts report that volume and price changes occur. Proper interpretation can predict the direction and intensity for change, because every purchase of every listed stock shows up on the chart.

Watch the bottom of the chart as well as the progress lines. This shows volume, and *volume precedes price.* A strong inflow of capital eventually pushes up the price of the stock; an outflow of dollars must result in a decline. To the charted results, it makes no difference who is doing the buying or selling.

Keeping in mind that charts are not infallible. Use them to:

- **Help determine when to buy and when to sell** by indicating probable levels of support and supply and by signaling trend reversals
- **Call attention, by unusual volume or price behavior,** to something happening in an individual company that can be profitable to investors
- **Help determine the current trend:** up, down, or sideways, and whether the trend is accelerating or slowing
- **Provide a quick history of a stock** and show whether buying should be considered on a rally or a decline
- **Offer a sound means for confirming or rejecting** a buy or sell decision that is based on other information

$ HINT: Charts are history. By studying past action, it is often possible to make a reasonably valid prediction of the immediate future.

WIDELY USED CHARTS

The most commonly used types of charts are point-and-figure (P&F) and bar charts. For best results, they should be constructed on a daily or weekly basis.

If you have time, charting can be fun and highly educational. All you need is a pad of graph paper: plain squares for P&F charts, logarithmic or standard paper for bar charts.

P&F CHARTS

P&F charts are one-dimensional graphics. They show only price changes in relation to previous price changes. There are no indications of time or volume. The key factor is the change in price direction.

Some professionals think that P&F charts are oversimplified and consider them useful only as short-term guides and as a quick way to choose between two or three selections.

In making a P&F chart, the stock price is posted in a square: one above or below another, depending on the upward or downward movement of the price. As long as the price continues in the same direction, the same column is used. When the price shifts direction, the chartist moves to the next column.

In the chart shown here, the stock first fell in a downward sequence from 68 to 67 to 66. Then it rose to 67, so the chartist moved to column 2. The next moves were down to 62, up to 63 (new column), and so on. Most chartists start the new column only when there is a distinct change, typically 1 point, but for longer projections, 2 or 3 points.

Note how a pattern is formed with various resistance levels where the price of the stock stayed within a narrow range (57–56 and later 48–47). The chart signals each shift from such a base: down from 56 to 51; up from 47 to 52.

POINT AND FIGURE CHART

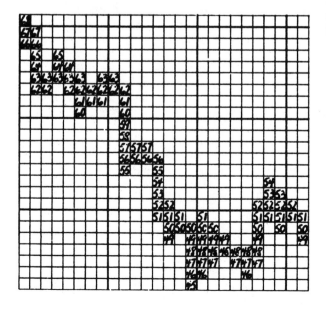

The best way for an amateur to learn about P&F charts is to copy them. Take a stock that has been plotted for many years and slowly recopy its action on a piece of graph paper. Then draw in the trend lines: the uptrend line on the high points, the downtrend line along the low points. Then draw your channels, which are broad paths created by the highs and lows of a definite trend. (Without a trend your channel will be horizontal.)

P&F charts have disadvantages: they do not portray intraday action or consider volume. The financial pages report only the high (62), low (59¼), and close (61½). This does not show that the stock might have moved up and down from 60 to 62 several times during the day.

Despite the omission of volume on P&F charts, many technical analysts feel that volume should always be checked once there is a confirmed trend on the chart. Rising volume on upward movements and dwindling sales on the down side usually indicate that the stock has ample investor support. It's always wise to be on the same side as volume.

BAR CHARTS

These graphics record changes in relation to time. The horizontal axis represents time—a day, week, or month; the vertical coordinates refer to price. To follow volume on the same chart, add a series of vertical lines along the bottom. The higher the line, the greater the volume. On printed charts, adjustments are made so that everything fits into a convenient space.

BAR CHART

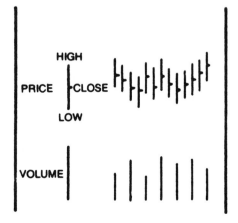

In plotting a bar chart, enter a dot to mark the highest price at which the stock was traded that day; add another dot to record the low. Draw the vertical line between the dots to depict the price range, and draw a short horizontal nub to mark the closing price. After a few entries, a pattern will begin to emerge.

HEAD-AND-SHOULDER CHARTS

Almost every chartist has favorite configurations. They include such descriptive titles as the rounding bottom, the flag, the pennant, the tombstone top, the Prussian helmet formation, the megaphone top, and the lattice formation. One of the most popular formations is *head and shoulders* (H&S).

Oversimplified, the head-and-shoulders chart portrays three successive rallies and reactions, with the second reaching a higher point than either of the others. The failure of the third rally to equal the second peak is a warning that a major uptrend may have come to an end. Conversely, a bottom H&S, formed upside down after a declining trend, suggests that an upturn lies ahead.

➤ LEFT SHOULDER This forms when an upturn of some duration, after hitting a climax, starts to fall. The volume of trading should increase with the rally and contract with the reaction. *Reason:* People who bought the stock on the up trend start to take profits. When the technical reaction takes place, people who were slow to buy on the first rally start buying on the technical reaction.

➤ HEAD This is a second rally that carries the stock to new highs and is followed by a reaction that erases just about all the gain. Volume is high on the rally, yet lower than when forming the left shoulder. *Reason:* Investors who missed both the earlier actions start buying and force new highs.

This is followed by another drop as those who hesitated earlier see the second reaction and start acquiring the stock as it is sold by early buyers.

➤ RIGHT SHOULDER The third rally fails to reach the height of the head before the reaction. This is a sign of weakness. Watch the volume. If it contracts on a rally, it's likely that the price structure has weakened. If it increases, beware of a false signal.

➤ BREAKOUT This occurs when the stock price falls below the previous lows. At this point, most of the recent buyers have sold out—many of them at a loss.

No H&S should be regarded as complete until the price breaks out below a line drawn tangent with the lows on the left and right shoulders. This is called the neckline.

INTERPRETING CHARTS

The charts from Securities Research Company (SRC) shown here are typical of those available from technical services. They can be valuable tools to improve the selection of securities and especially the timing of purchases and sales. Similar graphics are available for industry groups and stock market averages.

Do *not* buy any stock when the chart shows a confirmed downtrend. Buy *up* stocks in *up* groups in an *up* market. And unless you are holding for the long term, consider selling when there's a downtrend in the stock, the industry, and the market.

SRC offers two books of charts on stocks: blue for long-term trends over 12 years, red for short-term trends over 21 months. By using both, you get a better idea of the character, history, and probable performance of the stock.

LONG-TERM CHARTS

Ⓐ CAPITALIZATION Information on the corporation: dollars of bonds and preferred stocks (in

HEAD AND SHOULDERS CHART

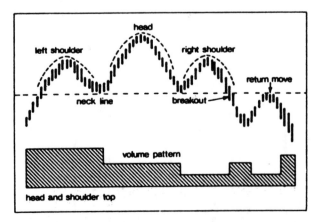

head and shoulder top

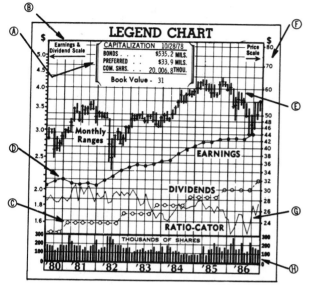

SOURCE: Securities Research Company, A Division of United Business Service Company, 208 Newbury St., Boston MA 02116.

millions); number of common shares outstanding (in thousands); and book value per common share.

Ⓑ EARNINGS AND DIVIDENDS Per-share data scaled from $1.40 to $5.50.

Ⓒ DIVIDENDS The annual rate of interim dividend payments. The circles mark the month in which the payments were made. Extra or irregular payouts (not shown) are typed in.

Ⓓ EARNINGS On a per-share 12-month-ended basis as shown by the solid black line. Dots indicate whether the company issues quarterly, semiannual, or annual earnings reports.

Ⓔ MONTHLY RANGES Shows the highest and lowest prices for the stock each month. Crossbars indicate the closing price.

Ⓕ PRICE SCALE This shows the dollar price of the stock, against which the monthly ranges are plotted.

Ⓖ RATIO-CATOR A guideline used by SRC. The plottings are obtained by dividing the closing price of the stock by the closing value of the DJIA on the same day. The resulting percentage is multiplied by a factor of 4.5 to bring the line close to the price bars and is read from the right-hand scale. The plotting indicates whether the stock has kept pace, outperformed, or lagged behind the general market.

Ⓗ VOLUME The number of shares traded, in thousands, each month on an arithmetic scale. Watch when there are extremes: high volume with rising prices (early 1981); low volume with falling values (mid-1986). Volume comes before price.

SHORT-TERM CHARTS

Here the data are similar to those of the longer-term charts but cover the action for only 21 months.

➤ EARNINGS For the last 12 months. Read from the left border to find the changes in dollar-per-share profits.

➤ DIVIDENDS On an annual basis; ✕ indicates the ex-dividend date, ○, the dividend payment date.

➤ MOVING AVERAGE FOR 39 WEEKS Each dot represents the average of the closing prices of the 39 most recent weeks. When used with the price bars, it helps you determine trends as well as buying and selling points.

➤ RATIO-CATOR Shows the relative performance of the stock. It is calculated by dividing the closing price of the stock by the closing value of the DJIA on the same day and then multiplying by 7.0.

Note: In plotting the short-term chart, the price range, earnings, and dividends are shown on a uniform ratio scale: that is, the vertical linear distance for a 100% move is the same

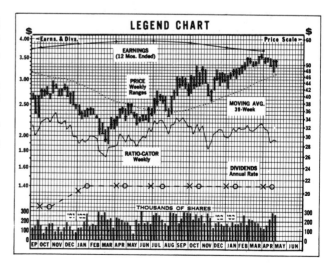

SOURCE: Securities Research Company, A Division of United Business Service Company, 208 Newbury St., Boston, MA 02116

any place on the chart regardless of whether the rise was from $5 to $10 or from $20 to $40. Thus all charts of all stocks are comparable.

USING TREND LINE CHARTS

The key to the successful use of charts, and most technical analysis, is the premise that *a trend in force will persist until a significant change in investor expectations causes it to reverse itself*—or as Martin Pring puts it, "on the assumption that people will continue to make the same mistakes they have made in the past." To discern that trend, the chartist draws lines connecting the lowest points of an upward-moving stock and the highest points of a down-ward-moving stock. This trend line is a reliable indicator about 80% of the time, because it predicts the immediate action of the stock or market.

The shrewd investor rises with the trend: buying when there's a confirmed upward move, considering selling when there's a definite down-swing. Generally, the stock will move along that line—regardless of the direction. There will be interim bounces or dips, but most stocks hold to that pattern until there is a clear change.

Trend lines establish bases. The uptrend line becomes a support level below which an upward-moving stock is not likely to fall. The downtrend line marks a resistance level above which the stock is not likely to rise.

$HINT: Before you invest—or speculate—in any stocks, check the chart and draw trend lines. Buy when the trend is up;

hold or do not buy when it is moving down. The best profits always come when you buy an up stock in an up industry in an up market—clearly evident from trend lines on charts. And, of course, when you sell short, it's the opposite.

Technical analysis, especially charts, can be a valuable aid to timing if you remember these three points:

- Unless you are extremely optimistic and can afford to tie up your money for a while, *never* buy any stock until its chart is pointing up.
- *Always* check the chart action before you sell. You may think that the high has been reached, but the chart may disagree and make possible greater gains.
- If the chart shows a downtrend, consider selling. If it's a good investment, you can buy the stock back later at a lower price. If it's not, you'll save a lot of money.

Properly employed, technical analysis can be an important adjunct to fundamental investing and, more often than not, it will keep you humble!

FOR FURTHER INFORMATION

Robert D. Edwards and John Magee, *Technical Analysis of Stock Trends* (Boston: John Magee, Inc., 1966).

Martin Pring, *Technical Analysis Explained*, 4th ed. (New York: McGraw-Hill, 1985).

Jeffrey Weiss, *Beat the Market* (New York: Viking Penguin, 1985).

In keeping with Wall Street jargon and financial reporting, initials are used frequently. Here are some of the most widely used:

EXCHANGES

➤ NYSE: NEW YORK STOCK EXCHANGE 11 Wall Street, New York, NY 10005, 1-800-656-8533. This is the oldest and largest exchange in the United States. To be listed, a corporation must:

- Demonstrate earning power of $2.5 million before federal income taxes for the most recent year and $2 million pretax for each of the preceding 2 years
- Have net tangible assets of $18 million
- Have market value of publicly held shares of $18 million
- Report a total of 1.1 million common shares publicly held
- Have 2,000 holders of 100 shares or more

➤ AMEX: AMERICAN STOCK EXCHANGE 86 Trinity Place, New York, NY 10006; 1-212-306-1000. These corporations are generally smaller and less financially strong than those on the NYSE. The firm must have:

- Pretax income of at least $750,000 in its last fiscal year or in two of the last three
- Stockholders' equity of $4 million
- 500,000 shares of common, exclusive of holdings of officers or directors
- 800 public stockholders or a minimum public distribution of 1,000,000 shares together with a minimum of 400 holders of 100 or more shares
- Market price of $3 minimum with $3 million market value

➤ OTC: OVER THE COUNTER This is the market for securities that are not listed on major exchanges. The trading is conducted by dealers who are members of NASD (National Association of Securities Dealers, 1735 K Street NW, Wash-

ington, DC 20006; 1-202-728-8000) and who may or may not be members of other exchanges. Trading is by bid and asked prices. The primary market is NASDAQ (National Association of Securities Dealers Automated Quotations), which consists of about 200 of the most actively traded issues. Some 2,500 other stocks are quoted in daily financial summaries.

➤ CBOE: CHICAGO BOARD OF OPTIONS EXCHANGE La Salle at Van Buren, Chicago, IL 60604, 1-312-786-5600. The major auction market for calls and puts, primarily on NYSE stocks, and recently for special types of options such as those on Treasury bonds.

➤ ACC: AMEX OPTIONS EXCHANGE 86 Trinity Place, New York, NY 10006; 1-212-306-1000. The division of AMEX that trades puts and calls, almost entirely on NYSE-listed stocks.

➤ CBT: CHICAGO BOARD OF TRADE La Salle at Jackson Boulevard, Chicago, IL 60604; 1-312-435-3500. A major market for futures contracts: commodities, interest rate securities, commercial paper, etc.

➤ CME: CHICAGO MERCANTILE EXCHANGE 30 South Wacker Drive, Chicago, IL 60606; 1-312-930-1000. Futures contracts for commodities, T-bills, etc., and the Standard & Poor's 500 index.

➤ COMEX: COMMODITY EXCHANGE (FORMERLY NEW YORK COMMODITY EXCHANGE) 4 World Trade Center, New York, NY 10048; 1-212-938-2900. Futures and options of a limited number of commodities and metals (gold, silver, and copper).

➤ NYCE: NEW YORK COTTON EXCHANGE 4 World Trade Center, New York, NY 10048; 1-212-938-2650. Trading in futures in cotton and orange juice.

➤ IMM: INTERNATIONAL MONETARY MARKET; 1-312-930-1000. This is located at the Chicago Mercantile Exchange and trades in futures of foreign currency and U.S. Treasury bills.

➤ KCBT: KANSAS CITY BOARD OF TRADE 4800

OTHER STOCK EXCHANGES

U.S.

Boston Stock Exchange 1 Boston Place, 38th floor Boston, MA 02108	1-617-723-9500
Cincinnati Stock Exchange 49 E. 4th Street, Suite 205 Cincinnati, OH 45202	1-513-621-1410
Midwest Stock Exchange 440 S. LaSalle Street Chicago, IL 60605	1-312-663-2222
Pacific Stock Exchange 301 Pine Street San Francisco, CA 94104 or 618 South Spring Street Los Angeles, CA 90014	1-415-393-4000
Philadelphia Stock Exchange 1900 Market Street Philadelphia, PA 19103	1-215-496-5000
Spokane Stock Exchange Seafire Financial Center Spokane, WA 99201	1-509-624-4632

CANADIAN

Alberta Stock Exchange 300 Fifth Avenue SW Calgary, Alberta T2P 3C4	1-403-262-7791
Montreal Stock Exchange 800 Victoria Square Montreal, Quebec H4Z 1A9	1-514-871-2424
Toronto Stock Exchange Exchange Tower 2 First Canadian Place Toronto, Ontario M5X 1J2	1-416-947-4700
Vancouver Stock Exchange 609 Granville Street Vancouver, British Columbia V7Y 1HY	1-604-643-6590
Winnipeg Stock Exchange 2901 One Lombard Place Winnipeg, Manitoba R3B 0Y2	1-204-942-8431

Main Street, Suite 303, Kansas City, MO 64112; 1-816-753-7500. Trades in futures of commodities and Value Line futures index.

➤ NYFE: NEW YORK FUTURES EXCHANGE 20 Broad Street, New York, NY 10005; 1-212-623-4949. A unit of the NYSE that trades in the NYSE composite futures index.

➤ NYME: NEW YORK MERCANTILE EXCHANGE 4 World Trade Center, New York, NY 10048; 1-212-938-2222. Trading in futures of petroleum and metals.

FEDERAL AGENCIES

➤ SEC: SECURITIES AND EXCHANGE COMMISSION 450 Fifth Street NW, Washington, DC 20549; 1-202-272-7440. A federal agency established to help protect investors. It is responsible for administering congressional acts regarding securities, stock exchanges, corporate reporting, investment companies, investment advisers, and public utility holding companies.

➤ FRB: FEDERAL RESERVE BOARD 20th and C Streets NW, Washington, DC 20551; 1-202-452-3000. The federal agency responsible for control of such important investment items as the discount rate, money supply, and margin requirements.

➤ FDIC: FEDERAL DEPOSIT INSURANCE CORPORATION 550 17th Street NW, Washington, DC 20429; 1-202-393-8400. An agency that insures bank deposits.

➤ FSLIC: FEDERAL SAVINGS AND LOAN INSURANCE CORPORATION 1700 G Street NW, Washington, DC 20552; 1-202-906-6600. An agency that insures deposits with savings and loan associations.

➤ CFTC: COMMODITY FUTURES TRADING COMMISSION 2033 K Street NW, Washington, DC 20581; 1-202-254-3067. This is a watchdog for the commodities futures trading industry.

STOCK MARKET AVERAGES

AVERAGES VS. INDEXES

➤ DOW JONES AVERAGES The most popular indicators of the direction of the stock market, these were devised in 1884 by Charles H. Dow, a founder and first editor of the *Wall Street Journal*. The makeup of the Dow Jones averages appears in the box. Each is simply an average price of the stocks in the group, derived by adding up the prices and dividing by the number of stocks represented. Each average measures the stocks' performance during one day. When one of the companies in the average declares a stock split or dividend, the divisor is reduced in size to accommodate the change. Initially the

STOCKS IN DOW JONES AVERAGES AS OF MAY 1988

Industrials (DJIA)

Allied Signal	International Paper
Alcoa	McDonald's Corp.
American Express	Merck & Co.
AT&T	Minnesota Mining &
Bethlehem Steel	Mfg.
Boeing	Navistar Int'l
Chevron	Philip Morris Co.
Coca-Cola	Primerica
Du Pont, E.I.	Procter & Gamble
Eastman Kodak	Sears, Roebuck
Exxon Corporation	Texaco, Inc.
General Electric	Union Carbide
General Motors	United Technologies
Goodyear Tire	USX
International Business	Westinghouse Electric
Machines	Woolworth (F.W.)

Transportation (DJTA)

Allegis Corp.	Federal Express
American President	Norfolk & Southern
Lines	NWA, Inc.
AMR Corp.	Pan American Corp.
Burlington Northern	Ryder Systems
Canadian Pacific	Santa Fe Southern
Carolina Freight	Pacific
Conrail	Southwest Air
Consolidated Freight	TWA
CSX Corp.	Union Pacific Corp.
Delta Airlines	U.S. Air Group

Utility (DJUA)

American Electric Power	Niagara Mohawk Power
Centerior Energy	Pacific Gas & Electric
Columbia Gas System	Panhandle Eastern Corp.
Commonwealth Edison	Peoples Energy
Consolidated Edison	Philadelphia Electric
Consolidated Natural Gas	Public Service
Detroit Edison	Enterprises
Houston Industries	So. California Edison

divisor was 30; today it's 1.5. For many years the Dow Jones Industrial Average hovered around 100, peaking at 386 in 1929 just prior to the crash. After the crash it climbed back up slowly, never moving much past 200 until World War II, when it hit 700. In 1966 it reached 1,000. It fell again to 570 in 1974 only to return to 1,000 two years later. In August 1987 the Dow posted an all-time high of 2722.42, but 2 months later, on October 19, it plunged a record 508 points to 1738.74. Since then there have been numerous ups and downs and slow signs of a modest recovery. In early July 1988 it reached 2158.61, the highest point since the October crash. A year later, in July 1989, it was 2,456.56.

The Dow is often criticized for the fact that a high-priced stock, such as IBM, has a greater impact on the index than lower-priced issues. In other words, the stocks are *not* equally weighted, so on any given day, a fluctuation of significance in one or two high-priced stocks can distort the average. As a result, the Dow is useful for tracking the direction of the market over the long term but is often less reliable on a daily or even weekly basis. With only 30 stocks, it is also thought to be too small.

➤ STANDARD & POOR'S 500 INDEX This index addresses some of the criticism of the Dow and has challenged its premier position. The S&P 500, devised in 1957, is weighted according to the market value of each stock in the index. Covering 500 stocks, it is computed by multiplying the price of each stock by the number of shares outstanding. This gives larger and more influential corporations more weight.

Despite their different approaches, the averages and the index move together most of the time, especially on major swings.

$ HINT: Keep in mind that the Dow figure is about 10 times larger than the S&P 500. That's because S&P tried to devise an index that was more nearly comparable to the average dollar price of all stocks traded on the NYSE.

➤ DOW JONES INDUSTRIAL AVERAGE (DJIA) The oldest and most widely used stock market average. It shows the action of 30 actively traded blue chip stocks, representing about 15% of NYSE values, on a weighted basis: for example, IBM at 110 carries more than 3 times the weight of Woolworth at 35.

MARKET INDICATORS, INDEXES, AND AVERAGES

Whether you're bullish, bearish, or uncertain, you can get a reading on the direction of the market, interest rates, and the overall economy by following some of the key statistics (or indicators) regularly churned out by Wall Street and Washington. These should be regarded not as gospel but rather as tools to help you make informed and intelligent decisions about your investments and for timing moves between stocks, bonds, and cash equivalents. Make a point of jotting down these numbers on your own chart and track the trends. You will see definite patterns between the market, interest rates, and the money supply. (The indicators are presented in alphabetical order.)

ECONOMIC INDICATOR	COMPOSITION	WHAT IT PREDICTS
Consumer price index (CPI)	The average price of consumer goods and services	The direction of inflation and changes in the purchasing power of money
Dollar index	The value of the dollar as measured against major foreign currencies	Domestic corporate profits and multinational earning power
Dow Jones Industrial Average (DJIA)	30 major companies whose stock is held by many institutions and individuals; index is price-weighted so that moves in high-priced stocks exert more influence than those of lower-priced stock	Action of the stock market, which in turn anticipates future business activity
Employment figures and payroll employment	Number of people working or on company payrolls	Potential consumer spending, which in turn affects corporate profits
Gross national product (GNP)	Total goods and services produced in United States on an annual basis; inflation can distort the accuracy of this figure, so subtract inflation from GNP to get "real" GNP	General business trends and economic activity
Index of industrial production (IIP)	Shown as a percentage of the average, which has been tracked since 1967; base is 100	Amount of business volume
Money supply: M1	Currency held by the public plus balances in checking accounts, NOW accounts, traveler's checks, and money market funds	Extent of consumer purchasing power and liquidity of public's assets, used by Federal Reserve as a gauge for predicting as well as controlling the pace of the economy; when M1 shows a big increase, the Fed usually reduces the money supply, which sends interest rates up; Fed reduces M1 by selling Treasuries; tightening of M1 serves to curb inflation; an increase in M1 fuels inflation
M2	M1 plus time deposits over $100,000 and repurchase agreements	
M3	M2 plus T-bills, U.S. savings bonds, bankers' acceptances, term Eurodollars, commercial paper	

ECONOMIC INDICATOR	COMPOSITION	WHAT IT PREDICTS
Standard & Poor's 500 stock index	Indexed value of 500 stocks from NYSE, AMEX, and OTC; more useful than the Dow Jones Industrial Average because it's broader; includes 400 industrials, 40 public utilities, 20 transportations, and 40 financials; stocks are market-value weighted; that is, price of each stock is multiplied by the number of shares outstanding	Direction of the economy and the market; good leading indicator because the market tends to anticipate future economic conditions
Three-month Treasury bill rate	Interest rate paid to purchasers of T-bills	General direction of interest rates; gives indication of the Federal Reserve system's fiscal policy; for example, during a recession, the Fed increases the amount of currency in circulation, which serves to lower the T-bill rate; during inflation, currency is reduced and the T-bill rate rises; rising interest rates tend to reduce corporate profits because of the increased costs of borrowing; therefore, a continual rise in T-bill rates presages a decline in the stock market; falling rates help stock and bond prices
Wage settlements	Percentage changes in wages that come about because of new labor contracts	Price changes for goods and services; sharply higher wage settlements result in higher inflation rates

Furthermore, cash dividends tend to reduce the average as each stock passes its ex-dividend date, and percentagewise, a stock that falls from 100 to 50 loses 50% of its value, but when it moves back, the gain is 100%.

In recent years, the composition of the average has been changed to reflect the growing scientific, consumer, and international roles of American business: IBM replaced Chrysler and Merck was substituted for Esmark, Inc.

The DJIA is determined by dividing the closing prices by a divisor that compensates for past stock splits and stock dividends. The average is quoted in points, not dollars.

➤ DOW JONES TRANSPORTATION AVERAGE (DJTA) This is made up of the stocks of 20 major transportation companies. Recent changes have substituted a trucking firm (Carolina Freight) and an airline (U.S. Air Group) for merged railroads.

➤ DOW JONES UTILITY AVERAGE (DJUA) This consists of 15 major utilities to provide geographic representation. With more firms forming holding companies to engage in oil and gas exploration and distribution, its value is greater as a point of reference than as a guide to the market's evaluation of producers of electricity and distributors of gas.

➤ DOW JONES COMPOSITE INDEX Also called the 65 Stock Average, this combines the other three indexes and consists of 30 industrials, 20 transportation, and 15 utility stocks. It is not widely followed.

➤ STANDARD & POOR'S COMPOSITE INDEX OF 500 STOCKS A market-value-weighted index showing the change in the aggregate value of 500 stocks, it consists mainly of NYSE-listed companies with some AMEX and OTC stocks. There are 400 industrials, 60 transportation and utility companies, and 40 financial issues. It represents about 80% of the market value of all issues traded on the NYSE but actually reflects the action of a comparatively few large firms. Options on this index trade on the Chicago Board Options Exchange and futures on the Chicago Mercantile Exchange.

➤ STANDARD & POOR'S 100 STOCK INDEX This consists of stocks for which options are listed on the Chicago Board Options Exchange. Options on the 100 Index are listed on the Chicago Board Options Exchange and futures on the Chicago Mercantile Exchange.

➤ WILSHIRE 5000 EQUITY INDEX This is a value-weighted index derived from the dollar value of 5,000 common stocks, including all those listed on the NYSE and AMEX and the most active OTC issues. It is the broadest index and thus is more representative of the overall market. Unfortunately, it has not received adequate publicity. The Wilshire is prepared by Wilshire Associates in Santa Monica, Calif. No futures or options are traded on the Wilshire.

➤ NYSE COMPOSITE INDEX A market-value-weighted index covering the price movements of all common stocks listed on the Big Board. It is based on the prices at the close of trading on December 31, 1965, and is weighted according to the number of shares listed for each issue. The base value is $50. Point changes are converted to dollars and cents to provide a meaningful measure of price action. Futures are traded on the NYFE and options on the NYSE itself.

➤ NASDAQ-OTC PRICE INDEX This represents all domestic OTC stocks except those trading on exchanges or having only one market maker. It covers a total of 3,500 stocks and is market-value weighted. No futures or options are traded.

➤ VALUE LINE COMPOSITE INDEX This is an equally weighted index of 1,700 NYSE, AMEX, and OTC stocks tracked by the *Value Line Investment Survey*. Designed to reflect price changes of typical industrial stocks, it is neither price- nor market-value weighted. Options trade on the Philadelphia Exchange and futures on the Kansas City Board of Trade.

➤ AMEX MAJOR MARKET INDEX Price-weighted, which means that high-priced stocks have a greater influence than low-priced ones, this is an average of 20 blue chip industrials. It was designed to mirror the Dow Jones Industrial Average and measure representative performance of these kinds of issues. Although produced by the AMEX, it includes stocks listed on the NYSE. Futures are traded on the Chicago Board of Trade.

➤ AMEX MARKET VALUE INDEX Once known as the ASE Index, this is a capitalization-weighted index that measures the collective performance of 800 issues in all industries, including ADRs, warrants, and common stocks. Cash dividends are assumed to be reinvested. Options are traded on the AMEX.

➤ DOW JONES BOND AVERAGE This consists of bonds of 10 public utilities and 10 industrial corporations.

➤ DOW JONES MUNICIPAL BOND YIELD AVERAGE This is a changing average that basically shows the yields of low-coupon bonds in 5 states and 15 major cities.

➤ BARRON'S CONFIDENCE INDEX Weekly index of corporate bond yields published by *Barron's*, the financial newspaper owned by Dow Jones. It shows the ratio of the average yield of 10 high-grade bonds to the Dow Jones average yield on 40 bonds. The premise is that when investors feel confident about the economy they buy lower-rated bonds.

➤ BOND BUYER'S INDEX Published daily, it measures municipal bonds.

amortization: Gradual reduction of a debt by a series of periodic payments. Each payment includes interest on the outstanding debt and part of the principal.

arbitrage: Profiting from price differences when a security, currency, or commodity is traded on different markets. Also, to buy shares in a company that is about to be taken over and sell short the shares of the acquiring company.

asset: A possession that has present and future financial value to its owner.

ATMs: Automated teller machines, located primarily at banks. Upon insertion of a magnetically coded bank identification card, the computer-controlled machine will dispense cash that you request or deposit money to your account and indicate the status of your account on a viewing screen. No teller is necessary, and the majority of ATMs are open 24 hours.

blue chip: The common stock of a well-known national company with a history of earnings growth and dividend increases, such as IBM or Exxon.

bond: A security that represents debt of an issuing corporation. Usually, the issuer is required to pay the bondholder a specified rate of interest for a specified time and then repay the entire debt (also known as face value) upon maturity.

bull and bear cycles: The up-and-down movements of the stock market. A bull believes that prices will rise and buys on that assumption. A bull market is a period when stock prices are advancing. A bear believes that security or commodity prices will decline. A bear market is marked by declining prices.

call: A feature of many bonds giving the issuer the right to call in or redeem the bonds before their maturity date.

capital: Also called capital assets; property or

money from which a person or business receives some monetary gain.

cash equivalents: The generic term for assorted short-term instruments such as U.S. Treasury securities, CDs, and money market fund shares, which can be readily converted into cash.

central asset or combo account: Brokerage, money market fund, and checking account combined with a credit card. Offered by both banks and brokerage houses, some central asset accounts include forms of life insurance, mortgages, traveler's checks, and other special features.

certificates of deposit: Also called CDs or "time certificates of deposit"; official receipts issued by a bank stating that a given amount of money has been deposited for a certain length of time at a specified rate of interest. CDs are insured by the U.S. government for up to $100,000.

charts: Records of price and volume trends as well as the general movement of stock and bond markets, economic cycles, industries, and individual companies, updated continually. Chartists believe that past history as expressed on a chart gives a strong clue to the next price movement. They "read" the lines to determine what a stock has done and may do.

combo account: See *central asset or combo account.*

commodities: Goods, articles, services, and interest rates in which contracts for future delivery may be traded. These range from precious metals, food, and grain to U.S. Treasury securities and foreign currencies.

common stock: See *stock, common.*

compound interest: The amount earned on the original principal plus the accumulated interest. With interest on interest plus interest

363

on principal, an investment grows more rapidly.

convertibles: Bonds, debentures, or preferred stock that may be exchanged or converted into common stock.

correction: A reverse downward in the prices of stocks, bonds, or commodities.

credit card: A plastic card issued by a bank or financial institution that gives the holder access to a line of credit to purchase goods or to receive cash. Repayment may be required in full in 30 days or in installments. Compare *debit card.*

credit union: A nonprofit financial institution formed by a labor union, company employees, or members of a cooperative. Credit unions, which offer a range of financial services, tend to pay higher interest rates than commercial banks.

debit card: A deposit access card that debits the holder's bank account or money market account immediately upon use in purchasing. There is no grace period in which to pay; payment is transferred immediately and electronically at the moment of purchase. Compare *credit card.*

discount rate: The interest rate the Federal Reserve charges member banks; it provides a floor for interest rates banks charge their customers. See also *prime rate.*

disinflation: A reduction in the rate of ongoing inflation.

DJIA (Dow Jones Industrial Average): Price-weighted average of 30 blue chip stocks, representing overall price movements of all stocks on the New York Stock Exchange.

effective annual yield: Rate of return earned on your savings if you do not incur service charges or penalties.

face value: Value of a bond or note when issued. Corporate bonds are usually issued with $1,000 face value; municipals with $5,000; T-bills with $10,000. Also called *par value.*

FDIC (Federal Deposit Insurance Corporation): An independent agency of the U.S. government whose basic purpose is to insure bank deposits. Depositors are covered up to $100,000, at an insured bank.

financial futures: Contracts to deliver a specified number of financial instruments at a given price by a certain date, such as U.S. Treasury bonds and bills, GNMA certificates, CDs, and foreign currency.

financial planner: A person who handles all aspects of your finances, including stocks, bonds, insurance, savings, and tax shelters.

front running: A trader knowing in advance of a block trade that will affect the price of a security and buying to profit from the trade.

FSLIC (Federal Savings & Loan Insurance Corporation): An independent agency of the U.S. government that insures deposits held in the savings institutions of members for up to $100,000.

futures: See *commodities.*

government or municipal bonds: Contracts of indebtedness issued by the U.S. Treasury, federal agencies, or state and local governments, which promise to pay back the principal amount plus interest at a specified date.

index: A statistical yardstick that measures a whole market by using a representative selection of stocks or bonds. Changes are compared to a base year. Futures are now sold on stock indexes, such as the S&P 500.

index arbitrage: Profiting from the difference in prices of the same security. In program trading, traders buy and sell to profit from small price discrepancies, using computers that monitor both the S&P 500 stock index and futures contracts on the index. When there is a larger than normal gap, the computers notify the traders to sell.

index future: A contract to buy or sell an index (Standard & Poor's, for example) at a future date. An index is a statistical yardstick that measures changes compared to a base period. The New York Stock Exchange Composite Index of all NYSE common stocks is based on a 1965 average of 50. *Note:* An index is not an average.

inflation: An increase in the average price level of goods and services over time.

institutions: Organizations that trade huge blocks of securities, such as banks, pension funds, mutual funds, and insurance companies.

interest: Money paid for the use of money. See also *discount rate; prime rate.*

junk bonds: High-risk, high-yielding bonds, rated BB or lower.

LBO (leveraged buyout): The purchase of a corporation by using a large amount of debt, much of it short-term bank loans secured by the assets of the company being acquired. After the buyout is completed, the acquired company issues bonds to pay off a portion of the debt taken on in the takeover.

liability: A debt; something owed by one person or business to another.

limited partnership: Investment organization in which your liability is limited to the dollar amount you invest; a general partner manages the project, which may be in real estate, farming, oil and gas, etc.

liquid: Cash or investments easily convertible into cash, such as money market funds or bank deposits.

liquidity: The ability of an asset or security to be converted quickly into cash.

"Mae" family: Various mortgage-backed securities either sponsored or partially guaranteed by a handful of government agencies or by private corporations, such as the Government National Mortgage Association (GNMA, or "Ginnie Mae") and the Federal Home Loan Mortgage Corporation ("Freddie Mac").

margin: The amount a client deposits with a broker in order to borrow from the broker to buy stocks.

mark to the market: The value of any portfolio based on the most recent closing price of the securities held.

mature: To come due; to reach the time when the face value of a bond or note must be paid.

money market fund: A mutual fund that invests only in high-yielding, short-term money market instruments such as U.S. Treasury bills, bank certificates of deposit, and commercial paper. Shareholders receive higher interest on their shares than in a bank money market account.

money market instruments: Short-term credit instruments such as Treasury bills, commercial paper, bankers' acceptances, CDs, and bank repurchase agreements.

municipal bonds: Also known as "munis"; debt obligations of state and local entities. For the most part, the interest earned is free from federal taxation and often from state and local taxes as well.

mutual fund: An investment trust in which an investor's dollars are pooled with those of thousands of others; the combined total is invested by a professional manager in a variety of securities.

net asset value (NAV): The price at which you buy or sell shares of a mutual fund. To determine NAV, mutual funds compute their assets daily by adding up the market value of all securities owned by the fund, deducting all liabilities, and dividing the balance by the number of shares outstanding. The NAV per share is the figure quoted in the papers.

net worth: Total value (of cash, property, investments) after deducting outstanding expenses or amounts owed.

option: The right to buy (call) or sell (put) a certain amount of stock at a given price (strike price) for a specified length of time.

over-the-counter (OTC) stock: A security not listed or traded on a major exchange. Transactions take place by telephone and computer network rather than on the floor of an exchange.

portfolio insurance: When the stock market falls by a certain amount, computers notify money managers, who then protect their portfolios by selling a stock index future (a contract on a basket of stocks). The cash raised from this sale helps offset the drop in the value of the portfolio.

preferred stock: See *stock, preferred.*

prime rate: Rate banks charge their largest and best customers. See also *discount rate.*

program trading: Computerized institutional buying or selling of all stocks in a program or in an index on which options and futures are traded.

prospectus: A summary of data on an issue of securities that will be sold to the public, enabling investors to evaluate the security and decide whether or not to buy it. The SEC regulations determine what basic information must be set forth in every prospectus.

put: An options contract giving the investor the right to sell a specified number of shares by a certain date at a certain price.

SEC (Securities and Exchange Commission): A federal agency with power to enforce federal laws pertaining to the sale of securities and governing exchanges, stockbrokers, and investment advisers.

sharedraft: Interest-bearing checking account at a credit union.

SIPC (Securities Investor Protection Corporation): An independent agency established by Congress to provide customers of most brokerage firms with protection similar to that provided by the FDIC for bank depositors, in the event that a firm is unable to meet its financial obligations.

stockbroker: An agent who handles the public's orders to buy and sell securities, commodities, and other properties. A broker may be a partner of a brokerage firm or a registered representative, who is an employee of a brokerage firm. Brokers charge a commission for their services.

stock, common: A security that represents ownership in a corporation.

stock, preferred: A stock that pays a fixed dividend and has first claim on profits over common stocks for the payment of that dividend. The dividend does not rise or fall with profits.

stock right: A short-term privilege issued by a corporation to its existing stockholders granting them the right to buy new stock at a stated price.

strike price: The dollar amount per share at which an option buyer can purchase the underlying stock or a put option buyer can sell the stock. Also called the *exercise price.*

takeover: When the controlling interest of a corporation is taken over by a new company. Takeovers can be friendly or hostile.

takeover candidate: A company that may be acquired by another corporation.

tax bracket: The percentage rate at which the top dollar of an income is taxed. The current tax brackets for individuals in the United States are 15%, 28%, and 33%.

tax shelter: An investment that allows an investor to realize significant tax benefits by reducing or deferring taxable income.

Treasury securities: Bonds issued by the U.S. Treasury and federal agencies that are sold at half their face value, beginning at $25 for a $50 bond. The term includes U.S. savings bonds; Treasury bills, which have a face value of $10,000, are sold at a discount, and mature in 1 year or less; Treasury notes, which have a face value of $1,000 or $5,000 and mature in 2 to 10 years; and Treasury bonds, which mature in 10 to 30 years and have a face value of $1,000. Interest on Treasuries is exempt from state and local income taxes.

triple tax-exempt bonds: Municipal bonds exempt from federal, state, and local taxes for residents of the states and localities that issue the bonds.

warrant: A security, usually issued with a bond or preferred stock, giving the owner the privilege of buying a specified number of shares of a stock at a fixed price, usually for a period of years.

vested interest: The nonforfeitable interest of a participant in a pension plan. You will not lose that portion of your benefit should you leave the job.

yield: The income paid or earned by a security divided by its current price. For example, a $20 stock with an annual dividend of $1.50 has a 7.5% yield.

zero coupon bond: A bond that pays no current interest but is sold at a deep discount from face value. At maturity, all compounded interest is paid and the bondholder collects the full face value of the bond (usually $1,000). EE savings bonds are zeros.